CRIMINOLOGY

A CANADIAN PERSPECTIVE NINTH EDITION

RICK LINDEN

University of Manitoba

NELSON

NELSON

Criminology, Ninth Edition
by Rick Linden

VP, Product Solutions, K–20:
Claudine O'Donnell

Senior Publisher, Digital and Print Content:
Leanna MacLean

Marketing Manager:
Claire Varley

Content Development Manager:
Suzanne Simpson Millar

Photo and Permissions Researcher:
Jessie Coffey

Senior Production Project Manager:
Imoinda Romain

Production Service:
SPi global

Copy Editor:
Matthew Kudelka

Proofreader:
SPi global

Indexer:
SPi global

Design Director:
Ken Phipps

Cover and Interior Designs:
Liz Harasymczuk

Cover Image:
TheaDesign/Shutterstock.com

Compositor:
SPi global

Library and Archives Canada Cataloguing in Publication

Criminology (Toronto, Ont.)
Criminology : a Canadian perspective / Rick Linden, University of Manitoba. — Ninth edition.

Includes bibliographical references and index.
Issued in print and electronic formats. ISBN 978-0-17-679606-8 (softcover).—ISBN 978-0-17-683128-8 (PDF)

1. Criminology—Canada—Textbooks. 2. Textbooks. I. Linden, Rick, editor II. Title.

HV6807.C76 2019
364.971
C2018-904671-6
C2018-904672-4

ISBN-13: 978-0-17-679606-8
ISBN-10: 0-17-679606-1

To Christopher, who gave so much and asked so little
and
Dan Koenig, a wonderful colleague and friend

BRIEF TABLE OF CONTENTS

CONTENTS

PREFACE

Since it was first published in 1987, *Criminology: A Canadian Perspective* has been used to introduce this field to more than 100,000 students across the country. At the time the first edition came out, most criminology courses in Canada were taught using American texts. It was our intention to provide a text that was written *by* Canadians, *for* Canadians. Over the last three decades, the discipline of criminology has grown from a few widely scattered faculty members to a large community of academics, researchers, practitioners, and students. The ninth edition of *Criminology: A Canadian Perspective* continues to reflect their work. That said, criminology remains an underfunded discipline in Canada relative to many other countries. That is why much of the new theoretical and empirical work in the field continues to come from the United States and Europe. This new edition represents our continued effort to provide you with the best Canadian scholarship in combination with the most relevant research from other countries.

Advantages of a Multi-authored Text

The many different theories proposed to explain criminality are continually being revived and revised. Often the popularity of a particular theory owes as much to ideological commitment and academic fashion as it does to its explanatory power. As a result of this unresolved diversity, the pages of many texts are littered with the bodies of straw men, set up only to be sacrificed to the author's favourite approach. The authors of this text are among Canada's leading criminologists. The advantage of a multi-authored text is that the diverse perspectives of criminology can be fairly represented. In this book, each chapter is written by someone who has used the perspective in his or her own research and who understands its strengths and weaknesses.

Organization of the Text

This book is intended as a text for a one-term course in introductory criminology. While the book deals extensively with theories about the causes of crime (which have largely been developed elsewhere), its purpose is to provide students with information about crime in Canada.

The chapters have been organized into three parts. ***Part 1: Crime and Society*** provides some of the basic information about crime: the sources of criminal law, the legal elements of crime, the sources of information about crime, the social correlates of criminal behaviour, a discussion of women and crime, and a look at victimization and at the role of victims in the justice system. This part provides the student with the background necessary to assess the theories of crime causation presented in ***Part 2***. In ***Part 2: Explanations of Crime***, all of the major theories are covered, including biological, psychological, and sociological explanations. In ***Part 3: Patterns of Criminal Behaviour***, three serious and frequent types of crime—organized crime, white-collar crime, and cybercrime—are discussed. Street crimes such as break and enter, robbery, and assault are discussed throughout the text. This arrangement of chapters is just one way of presenting the material; instructors are encouraged to assign these chapters in whatever order best suits their course needs.

Features of the Text

Each chapter begins with a brief *Introduction* and a list of *Learning Objectives* and concludes with a *Summary* and *Net Work* (Internet activities). *Questions for Critical Thinking* are presented at the end of feature boxes and at the end of each chapter. This text also features margin notes. In the margins, *Google Terms* refers students to interesting related websites. Also in the margins is a running glossary, which defines the key terms next to the paragraphs in which they first appear. A full *Glossary* and *Bibliography* are provided at the end of the text.

New to the Ninth Edition

This edition of *Criminology: A Canadian Perspective* provides us with the opportunity to update crime statistics, add new research material, and make revisions that have been suggested by reviewers.

Chapter 1, "Crime, Criminals, and Criminology," includes a new case study of domestic terrorist Aaron Driver and has an interesting update to the existing study of the killers of Constable Dennis Strongquill that discusses how one of Strongquill's sons has begun a healing process with one of his father's killers. The chapter also looks at the role of the media in mass killings, including school shootings, and discusses the debate about how the state determines which mass killings should be considered acts of terrorism. Chapter 3, "Criminal Law," has significant changes reflecting changes in the law. The most significant of these relates to the *Carter* case, which led to the Medical Assistance in Dying Act, which is discussed in a new box. Also significant here is the new legislation that allows NCR accused to be declared "high risk accused." Besides updating crime statistics, Chapter 4, "Counting Crime," has added a section on the impact of cybercrime on crime statistics. Chapter 5, "Correlates of Criminal Behaviour," also has updated statistics. Chapter 6, "Feminism and Criminology," has a new section critiquing the "women's liberation" theory of crime and a discussion of the high "unfounded" rates for sexual assault complaints by some police services. It also introduces the notion of "victim-criminalization" for women who are in trouble with the law.

Chapter 8, "Early Theories," now includes an exercise that allows students to look at their own beliefs about human nature and relate these to several types of criminological theories. Chapter 9, "Psychological Theories," has a new lead author and several new sections, including one on evolutionary theory, as well as an expanded discussion of psychopathy. Chapter 11 has a new box on the possible impact of Bill C-13 on cyberbullying. A new Focus box in Chapter 15, "Deterrence, Routine Activity, and Rational Choice Theories," outlines various factors such as self-checkout and self-driving cars that will have an impact on crime in the future.

Chapter 16 has an expanded discussion of the definition of organized crime and a new discussion of how organized crime groups insulate themselves against enforcement and prosecution. Chapter 17 has been updated with many examples and now includes the bread price-fixing case involving Loblaws and other large grocery chains and the Harvey Weinstein sexual abuse scandal. The chapter now also includes sections on the role of drug manufacturers in the opioid crisis, the residential school abuse addressed by the Truth and Reconciliation Commission, and the Volkswagen emissions testing fraud. Finally, Chapter 18 tracks the evolving business of cybercrime and examines the impact of regulations on cyberbullying.

Instructor Resources

About the Nelson Education Teaching Advantage

The **Nelson Education Teaching Advantage** (**NETA**) program delivers research-based instructor resources that promote student engagement and higher-order thinking to enable the success of Canadian students and educators. Visit Nelson Education's **Inspired Instruction** website at www.nelson.com/inspired/ to find out more about NETA.

The following instructor resources have been created for *Criminology: A Canadian Perspective*. Access these ultimate tools for customizing lectures and presentations at www.nelson.com/instructor.

NETA Test Bank

This resource was written by Cindy Gervais of Fleming College. It includes more than 800 multiple-choice questions written according to NETA guidelines for effective construction and development of higher-order questions. Also included are more than 350 true/false, and 250 essay questions.

The NETA Test Bank is available in a new, cloud-based platform. **Nelson Testing Powered by Cognero®** is a secure online testing system that allows instructors to author, edit, and manage test bank content from anywhere Internet access is available. No special installations or downloads are needed, and the desktop-inspired interface, with its drop-down menus and familiar, intuitive tools, allows instructors to create and manage tests with ease. Multiple test versions can be created in an instant, and content can be imported or exported into other systems. Tests can be delivered from a learning management system, the classroom, or wherever an instructor chooses. Nelson Testing Powered by Cognero for *Criminology: A Canadian Perspective* can be accessed through www.nelson.com/instructor.

NETA PowerPoint

Microsoft® PowerPoint® lecture slides for every chapter have been created by Stephen Schneider of Saint Mary's University. There is an average of 35 slides per chapter, many featuring key figures, tables, and photographs from *Criminology: A Canadian Perspective*. In addition, up to five discussion questions are interspersed throughout the chapters, with suggested talking points included in the Notes section. Each chapter also includes at least one suggested activity. NETA principles of clear design and engaging content have been incorporated through-out, making it simple for instructors to customize the deck for their courses.

Image Library

This resource consists of digital copies of figures, short tables, and photographs used in the book. Instructors may use these jpegs to customize the NETA PowerPoint or create their own PowerPoint presentations. An Image Library Key describes the images and lists the codes under which the jpegs are saved. Codes normally reflect the Chapter number (e.g., C01 for Chapter 1), the Figure or Photo number (e.g., F15 for Figure 15), and the page in the textbook. C01-F15-pg26 corresponds to Figure 1-15 on page 26.

MindTap

Offering personalized paths of dynamic assignments and applications, **MindTap** is a digital learning solution that turns cookie-cutter into cutting-edge, apathy into engagement, and memorizers into higher-level thinkers. MindTap enables students to analyze and apply chapter concepts within relevant assignments, and allows instructors to measure skills and promote better outcomes with ease. A fully online learning solution, MindTap combines all student learning tools—readings, multimedia, activities, and assessments—into a single Learning Path that guides the student through the curriculum. Instructors personalize the experience by customizing the presentation of these learning tools to their students, even seamlessly introducing their own content into the Learning Path.

Student Ancillaries

MindTap

Stay organized and efficient with **MindTap**—a single destination with all the course material and study aids you need to succeed. Built-in apps leverage social media and the latest learning technology. For example:

- ReadSpeaker will read the text to you.
- Flashcards are pre-populated to provide you with a jump start for review—or you can create your own.
- You can highlight text and make notes in your MindTap Reader. Your notes will flow into Evernote, the electronic notebook app that you can access any-where when it's time to study for the exam.
- Self-quizzing allows you to assess your understanding.

Visit www.nelson.com/student to start using **MindTap**. Enter the Online Access Code from the card included with your text. If a code card is not pro-vided, you can purchase instant access at NELSONbrain.com.

Acknowledgements

It is long-standing practice for authors to thank families for not making demands, and spouses, or close friends, both for moral support and for those unspecified but essential services that writing seems to require. Since my wife and children had already reached their tolerance limit with my work schedule, I decided that I couldn't just disappear into my office and reappear two years later with a book. Thus it is to them that I owe my wise decision to get help from the friends and colleagues who co-authored the text. For the time I did spend writing, I thank for their support Olive, Brad, Chris, Robin, Shawn, Tyler, and Amanda. By the fourth edition, all of my children were old enough that they no longer cared about my working hours. However, their place at my worktable was taken by pets, and I thank Nicholas, Morris, Annie, Edward, Timothy, Hannah, and Emily for ensuring that all of the pages in this manuscript (back in the days when manuscripts had pages) and now my computer keyboards, have been stepped on or slept on by an orange cat. Callie also added some black cat hair to the mix. Note to pet fans: we usually have three cats at a time, so the turnover rate is not as high as it seems.

Courtesy of Olive Linden

As usual, working with the people at Nelson Education has been a delightful experience. For significant improvements in this ninth edition, I thank Leanna MacLean and Suzanne Simpson Millar, as well as Matthew Kudelka for his copyediting skills. Jessie Coffey did the photo research and text permissions.

The authors would like to thank the reviewers of the current edition: Diane Crocker, Saint Mary's University; Tracey Marshall, Durham College; Diane G. Symbaluk, MacEwan University, and others.

The authors continue to benefit from the reviews of previous editions; those reviewers include Bill Avison, Joshua Barath, Jane Barker, Marilyn Belle-McQuillan, Thomas Bernard, Augustine Brannigan, David Brownfield, Tullio Caputo, Elaine DeCunha-Bath, Sange de Silva, Robert Drislaine, Karlene Faith, Tara Bruno-Fidler, Thomas Gabor, Colin Goff, Jim Hackler, Stephanie Hayman, Sheilagh Hodgins, Carl Keane, Gail Kellough, Heather A. Kitchin, John Martin, Pamela Nancarrow Snow, Robynne Neugebauer, Norman Okihiro, Gary Parkinson, Lisette Patenaude, Michael Petrunik, Karen Richter, Vincent F. Sacco, Les Samuelson, Bernard Schissel, Alfredo Schulte-Bockholt, Rashmee Singh, Phillip C. Stenning, Lee Stuesser, Diane Symbaluk, David Ryan, James Williams, and Austin T. Turk.

I would also like to thank each of the authors who contributed to the book. I appreciate your enthusiastic responses to revision suggestions and your efforts to meet deadlines. I continue to enjoy and to learn from your work.

Individual authors wished to make the following acknowledgments: J. Evans (Chapter 4)—"The author wishes to thank the Canadian Centre for Justice Statistics for providing much of the data presented in this chapter."

Rick Linden
University of Manitoba

Crime and Society

Part 1 of this book provides some basic information about crime: the origins of our criminal law, the legal elements of crime, the sources of information about crime, and the social correlates of criminal behaviour.

Chapter 1 introduces you to the discipline of *criminology*, the scientific study of crime and criminals. This chapter examines the role played by rules and shows how these rules are sometimes formalized in laws. The chapter also looks at different ways of defining crime and shows that because crime is socially defined, the definition of crime can change over time. The chapter concludes with discussions of "green" criminology, terrorism studies, and surveillance studies, three of the newest subfields of criminology, to show how the discipline continues to evolve.

In Chapter 2, we learn how our legal system has developed as we have evolved from simple hunting and gathering societies to modern industrial ones. The increased complexity of modern societies has generated the need for formal legal systems to maintain order. We also learn why some social harms are defined as illegal while others are not.

The legal elements of a crime are *actus reus* (the physical element) and *mens rea* (the mental element). These are discussed in Chapter 3, along with the defences available to an accused, a history of criminal procedure, and an outline of the social factors that affect how specific types of crime are defined.

We cannot study crime unless we can measure it. Chapter 4 describes how we count crime using government statistics, victimization surveys, and self-report surveys. None of these methods is completely adequate; you will learn the strengths and weaknesses of each.

Before we can explain a phenomenon like crime, we must know how it is distributed demographically. In Chapter 5, several correlates of crime are discussed, including age, sex, race, social class, and spatial location. Chapter 6 considers issues involving women and crime in more depth. The explanations of crime discussed in Part 2 of the book should be judged according to how well they account for these regularities.

Finally, Chapter 7 discusses issues faced by victims of crime. About one in four Canadian adults are victimized by crime each year, and the cost to these victims is estimated at $80 billion a year. Several important international protocols guide the ways in which countries treat victims, and in this regard, Canadian governments do not provide adequate victim services. Instead of investing to support victims and to prevent future victimization, governments have chosen to invest billions of dollars in the police, courts, and prisons.

1

Crime, Criminals, and Criminology

RICK LINDEN
University of Manitoba

Learning Objectives

After reading this chapter, you should be able to

- Define the term *criminology*.
- Understand the different subjects studied by criminologists.
- Explain the role played by rules in our lives and understand how these rules can become formalized in law.
- Understand the different ways of defining crime: a strict legal definition; an expanded legal definition that goes beyond just considering the criminal law; a definition based on the protection of people's human rights; and a definition that places acts of deviance and crime on a continuum ranging from minor acts of deviance to serious offences that almost everyone agrees are wrong.
- Explain how crime is socially defined and how people's ideas about crime change over time.
- Understand the two main theoretical perspectives (conflict and consensus) on how some acts get defined as criminal and others do not.
- Understand the new subfields of green criminology, terrorism studies, and surveillance studies.

Canadians are fascinated by crime. Our media are saturated with stories about crime and criminals. Movies, television shows, and video games are filled with depictions of violence and other criminal behaviour. While crime is a matter of public concern and a favourite form of entertainment, it is also the subject of serious academic study. This chapter introduces you to the discipline of criminology, the scientific study of crime and criminals.

A Violent Crime: The Sand Brothers

Robert and Danny Sand grew up in rural Alberta. Their father had served time in jail in his youth for a variety of crimes but gave up crime when he was 20 years old and supported his family through a variety of jobs. Their mother ran a business in a small town where both parents were respected community members (Staples 2002). As youngsters, Robert and Danny were constantly in trouble, along with several of their closest friends, who made up a group composed of the only mixed-race boys in their town. The boys had difficulty in school and were frequently suspended. In junior high they got into more serious trouble, and when he was 15 years old, Danny was sent to a youth centre for beating up another student. The boys began to steal cars and use drugs. Staples described the situation of the brothers and their friends:

> Their contact with adults was minimal. No teachers, because the teens had all dropped out. No parents, because most didn't live at home. They relied on each other to figure out the world, believing their friends were closer and wiser than any adult. They're all there to protect each other, and they can't see past that, says [one of the mothers] . . . They had an inkling of the difference between right and wrong. They certainly understood when someone did wrong to them, or to one of their closest friends. They just didn't see it as a problem to rob or injure someone outside of their group. It was us vs. them, with them being teachers, the RCMP, car owners, property owners, anyone with something they wanted to grab. (Staples 2002, D2)

In 1998, Robert received a seven-year jail sentence for armed robbery and Danny ended up in jail for several crimes, including attacking a police officer. After his release, Danny tried to run down a police officer with a stolen truck. After this incident, he joined Robert in Drumheller Penitentiary, where he got a tattoo that read "Fearless, Painless, Senseless."

In October 2001, Robert was released to a halfway house. He could find only menial work, and he reunited with Laurie Bell, a former girlfriend who was a heavy drug user. He violated his parole by leaving the halfway house. In December, Robert, Laurie, and Danny headed for the Maritimes, where they had vague plans for making a new life. They never made it past Manitoba.

In the midst of a crime spree that included robbing a bank, breaking into homes, and stealing several vehicles, they made it to the town of Russell, Manitoba. Shortly after midnight, Danny drove onto the highway without stopping at a stop sign. When RCMP constables Brian Auger and Dennis Strongquill tried to stop the vehicle, Robert fired several shotgun blasts at the police. When the police drove away, Danny chased the police SUV into town. He rammed the SUV after it stopped at the Russell RCMP Detachment. Robert fired at Constable Strongquill, who was trapped in the damaged police vehicle. Four shots hit Constable Strongquill, who died almost immediately.

The RCMP tracked the trio to a motel near Wolseley, Saskatchewan. A police sniper fatally wounded Danny Sand; Robert Sand and Laurie Bell were captured and charged with first-degree murder. While awaiting trial, Robert kept a diary in which he reflected on the shooting:

> I was in one of my moods so I asked to see the pictures again of my case. There are pics of trucks burnt, crashed shot up etc. Homes broken into, property of ours and others and of course pics of the dead cop, shot up cop cars and Dan. Now I've seen them before and without emotion, I've no more tears to shed. But I was looking at this man, on a table. And I started to think, he's just a man, and shouldn't be dead. He had a family and friends, and now he's a body on a table. I realized it's not the man I hated, but the uniform he wore. His flag, colours of war. But seeing

him without his uniform I felt bad for the loss of his life. But then I flipped to the pics of Dan, and my thoughts changed. Cause now I felt that the other man is right where he should be. And losses on both sides are to be expected, only Dan took my place. And when I looked upon the cop car I felt pride, and remembered the battle, I remembered how these enemy soldiers fled in fear and [sic] cowardess. . . . They should beware that the moment they fly their flag, wear their uniform. That they're at war and people die in war, everyone has their enemies.*

Robert Sand, who physically attacked his own lawyer in court at the end of his trial, is serving a life sentence after being convicted of first-degree murder; Laurie Bell was convicted of manslaughter.

One challenge facing the discipline of criminology is to make sense of cases like this one. Why did the Sand brothers live such wild and undisciplined lives? Why did they aggressively pursue Constable Strongquill and his partner? Why did Robert see the world as a war zone? What can we do to prevent tragedies like this in the future?

Criminologists have considered a wide range of theories to explain crime. Some focus on biology—could Robert and Danny have inherited traits from their parents that made their criminality more likely? Others look at an individual's psychological makeup—were the Sand brothers psychopaths, or could other mental conditions have caused their behaviour? Other theories are sociological—what role did their family and friends play in their violence? Could the schools have done a better job motivating the brothers to study and to become involved in legitimate outlets for their energy? What role did racism and the brothers' poor economic prospects play in their lives?

These questions are complex, and we may never be able to explain individual cases like this one. However, even if we could explain the factors that led Robert Sands to kill Constable Strongquill, the same explanation might not apply to other murders, because different homicides may have little in common. Some involve intoxicated people who stab friends during drinking parties; others involve a settling of accounts among organized criminals; some abusive men kill their wives and children; some corporate executives kill their customers by selling defective products in order to enhance their profits, or kill their employees by providing unsafe working conditions; and some predators kill children after having sex with them. In your criminology course, you will learn about these and many other patterns of criminal behaviour.

A Footnote to the Sands Case

While this case happened about two decades ago, it has recently been in the news again. In Chapter 2 you will read about restorative justice. As the authors of that chapter note, "advocates of restorative justice seek to return the focus of the justice system to repairing the harm that has been done to the victim and the community." The murder of Constable Strongquill would not seem to be a case in which restorative justice would be appropriate. However, several years ago Ricky Strongquill, son of the murdered constable, decided to contact the man who had killed his father (McIntyre 2017). Ricky had been living with

*Excerpt from Mike McIntyre, *Nowhere to Run: The Killing of Constable Dennis Strongquill* (Winnipeg: Great Plains Publications, 2003), 195. Reprinted with permission.

anger about the killing and with hostility towards Sand. However, he felt that the anger was taking a toll on him and was responsible for his involvement with drugs and alcohol. Believing the only way to turn his life around was to face his issues over his father's death, he reached out by sending a letter to Robert Sand through a BC restorative justice organization. Sand replied by telling him that "I also haven't spent a single day without thinking of your father, my brother and everything that happened in those dark days. I've lived a life of many regrets but the loss of our loved ones and the widespread trauma I've caused is by far my biggest"* (McIntyre 2017, 3).

The men have met, and Strongquill says they have become friends and that they have been able to help each other heal. He believes that his father would approve of this forgiveness and describes a moment shortly after he left his prison meeting with Robert Sand. Ricky had stopped beside a lake to think about what had just happened: "An eagle, perched on a rock eating a fish, was staring at him. His father's traditional name had been 'Eagle Man.' 'I got that surge of emotion. I felt like my dad's spirit was around me'" (McIntyre 2017, 4).

A White-Collar Crime: The Downfall of Conrad Black

A very different case illustrates the diversity of the behaviour studied by criminologists. In the spring of 2007, Conrad Black and several co-accused faced charges in the United States relating to the fraudulent acquisition of funds that should have gone to shareholders of Hollinger International. The funds instead had been taken by the accused, who were managers (but not owners) of the company.

Black's background was very different from that of the Sand brothers. His father was wealthy, and Conrad had a comfortable childhood. He attended Toronto's Upper Canada College, an elite private school, but was unhappy with its discipline. He broke into school offices to steal and alter school records. On one occasion, he and several accomplices stole some final exam papers. Perhaps anticipating his later business career, Black had earlier copied the academic records of all the students, so he knew who would be prepared to pay the most for the exam papers. His motivation was not entirely commercial:

> I was going to reduce the school's whole academic system . . . to utter chaos while achieving a spectacular mark for myself having done virtually no work. . . . By the last week of the school year, I had almost completely undermined the system . . . I had more power than our jailers. (Black 1993, 15)

The scheme unravelled when one of Black's customers confessed to cheating and Black was expelled from the school.

After graduating from law school, Black entered the newspaper business. He and two partners bought a small, money-losing Quebec paper, the *Sherbrooke*

*Excerpt from McIntyre, Mike. 2017. "Face to Face with his Father's Killer." *Winnipeg Free Press*, 4 July. Web. Reprinted with permission of The Winnipeg Free Press.

Record. Black and his partners discovered a formula for increasing profits. They fired 40 percent of the employees (a step that Black reportedly described as "drowning the kittens": Plotz 2001, n.p.) and modernized the production process. They cut costs relentlessly. At the same time, Black by his own account began a pattern of behaviour that later led to serious legal problems: at the same time they were cutting even the most minor expenses at the newspaper, they operated "what amounted to a modest slush fund for our preferred causes and tenuously business-connected expenses" (Black 1993, 72).

Several times throughout his business career, Black attempted to transfer money from the corporations he ran—but that were owned by public share-holders—to his own personal accounts.

Black purchased other small papers and eventually acquired several impor-tant international papers and launched Canada's *National Post*. His corporation, Hollinger International, controlled the world's third-largest newspaper chain (McNish and Stewart 2004). Black moved to England and in 2001 gave up his Canadian citizenship so that he could accept admission to the British House of Lords and the title Lord Black of Crossharbour.

Then in 2001, shortly after he took his seat in the House of Lords, his finan-cial empire began to unravel. He was challenged by investors at Hollinger's shareholders' meeting. They wanted to know why their investment in Hollinger was not profitable while Black and other senior executives were getting very wealthy. He was forced to step down from his position as CEO of Hollinger. An investigation committee established by the board of directors accused Black and other executives of running a "corporate kleptocracy" that had conspired to steal $400 million from Hollinger that should have been paid out to shareholders. The report concluded that "Black and [another executive] were motivated by a 'ravenous appetite for cash' . . . and Hollinger International . . . 'lost any sense of corporate purpose, competitive drive or internal ethical concerns' as the two executives looked for ways to 'suck cash' out of the company" (McNish and Stewart 2004, 288).

While he was under investigation, Black continued to demonstrate the impe-rious attitude that had characterized his career. In response to criticisms of his extravagance, such as his use of company jets, he responded:

> There has not been an occasion for many months when I got on our plane without wondering whether it was really affordable. But I'm not prepared to re-enact the French Revolutionary renunciation of the rights of nobility. We have to find a balance between an unfair taxation on the company and a reasonable treatment of the founder-builder-managers. We are proprietors, after all, beleaguered though we may be. (McNish and Stewart 2004, 92)

In 2005, criminal fraud charges were filed in the United States against Black and three other executives for conspiring to take funds from Hollinger Interna-tional for their own gain. This was illegal because the corporation was owned by the shareholders, not by the men who managed the company.

Black was also charged with misusing corporate money for personal expenses. Also, Black and his chauffeur were videotaped violating a court order by removing a number of boxes of documents from his Toronto office, so he also faced charges of obstruction of justice.

In July 2007, Black was convicted on four charges and acquitted on nine others. He was convicted of obstruction of justice because of the documents he had removed from his office and for several fraud offences. He was sentenced to six and a half years in prison and ordered to make restitution of $6.1 million. After Black had served two years in a Florida prison, the US Supreme Court set aside his fraud convictions and sent the case back to the lower courts for reconsideration, and Black was released from prison. An appeal court upheld his convictions for fraud and for obstruction of justice. His sentence was reduced to 42 months, and he was ordered back to prison to serve the remainder of his term. He returned to Canada in 2012.

In contrast to what happened to the Sand brothers, the law and the legal system did very little to try to deter Black. While his behaviour was predatory, most of his business practices were legal, and he was widely praised for his business acumen. Because of his wealthy background, his life was not affected by his serious misconduct at Upper Canada College—which he blamed on the school itself. While he eventually was sent to prison, it is not surprising that he was only prosecuted in the United States, given that Canada has a very poor record when it comes to holding corporate criminals to account (see Chapter 17).

Black's case too poses questions for criminologists. Black is a highly intelligent and articulate man whose family background guaranteed him a very comfortable lifestyle. What then were his motivations for ignoring the law? And why did he think his position should allow him to break the rules that applied to everyone else? How do we explain the fact that wealthy people also commit crimes?

Terrorism: The Life and Death of Aaron Driver*

Aaron Driver came from a strong Christian family. His parents served in the Canadian military. According to his father, Aaron changed dramatically after the death of his mother when he was seven years old. He had a troubled childhood, was often in serious scrapes, and broke off relations with his family on several occasions.

Aaron settled down in his late teens when his girlfriend became pregnant, but their relationship fell apart in 2012 after their baby was stillborn. After moving from Ontario to Winnipeg to join his father and stepmother, he sought comfort in religion, mostly through online reading and dialogue. Christianity did not provide the answers he wanted, so he began reading Muslim websites, which he found more satisfying. He also began attending mosques in Winnipeg, but he felt they were not conservative enough, so he focused his religious attention on the Internet. He became attracted to radical ISIS websites and became active in their networks, often using aliases.

*Sources used when writing this section were McKeon, 2017, Shephard, 2016, and Woods (2015a, 2015b, and 2016).

Aaron Driver leaving a Winnipeg court following his peace bond hearing in February 2016. Six months later the RCMP would use this photo to identify him as the person in a martyrdom video sent to them by the FBI. In the video, Driver was wearing the same hat and balaclava as he wore in this photo. This identification enabled the police to intercept him before he could carry out an attack.

THE CANADIAN PRESS/John Woods

Using one of these aliases, he gave lengthy media interviews to the *Toronto Star* and the CBC, during which he was quite open about his radical views. He publicly praised the terrorist attacks in 2014 in which two members of the Canadian military were killed, one in Ottawa, the other in Quebec. Driver said these attacks were justified because Canada had deployed CF-18 fighter jets to attack ISIS targets in Iraq.

Not surprisingly, he came to the attention of police and intelligence officials because of his online activities and his interviews. During this period, Driver's family tried to be supportive, but they were unable to get him to change his ideas. The Muslim community in Winnipeg also tried unsuccessfully to work with him. At the same time, he was in regular contact with an online network of ISIS supporters known as the "*baqiyah*' family" (Shephard 2016), who encouraged one another to take action in support of ISIS.

In 2015 he was arrested in Winnipeg. While out on bail, he was put on a peace bond that restricted his movements and his computer use on the grounds that he might participate or contribute to the activities of a terrorist group. Still under a peace bond, he moved to Strathroy, Ontario, to live with his sister's family. He had a job but continued his online involvement with ISIS.

On 10 August 2016, the FBI reported to the RCMP that they had seen a martyrdom video that indicated someone was planning an imminent suicide attack in Canada. A man in a balaclava had posted a warning video online:

"O Canada . . . you received many warnings. You were told many times what will become of those who fight against the Islamic State." Driver's eyes darted to the left. He tugged his balaclava. A little swagger. "No, no, by Allah, you still have much to pay for." His voice rose. He dragged out the word "no" and shook his head in anger. "You still have a heavy debt which has to be paid. You still have Muslim blood on your hands, and, for this, we are thirsty for your blood." He ended the video with a pledge to ISIS leader Abu Bakr al-Baghdadi and a vow to answer the call for "jihad in the lands of crusaders." (McKeon 2017, 14)

The would-be bomber was wearing a balaclava over his face, but the RCMP was able to identify Driver and immediately sent a number of officers to his residence. They arrived just as he was getting into a taxi with a bomb on his way to a shopping mall in downtown London, Ontario. When the police arrived, Driver detonated a bomb in the taxi. It did not fully detonate, and an injured Driver was able to get out of the taxi. He was subsequently shot to death by the police.

Terrorism raises some interesting issues for criminologists. Do the theories we have developed to explain other types of crime also help us understand recruitment to terrorist organizations? And why do only some of the people who are attracted to terrorist ideologies actually commit violent acts? LaFree and colleagues (2018) found that two theories of crime causation do predict who will be involved in violent terrorism. Unstable employment (a variable that is part of social control theory: Chapter 14) and ties to radical peers (a variable that is central to differential association theory: Chapter 13) are both correlated with acts of violence. Another important question is whether knowledge developed by criminologists can be used to help keep disaffected young people from becoming radicalized.

What Is Criminology?

The term **criminology** is used in several different ways. Detectives in mystery novels, forensic scientists, and crime analysts on television shows are sometimes referred to as criminologists, as are physicists and biochemists who specialize in studying the trajectories of bullets or DNA. Most commonly, the term is applied to academics who study crime and the criminal justice system. In this text, we will follow the definition given by two famous American criminologists, Edwin Sutherland and Donald Cressey: "Criminology is the body of knowledge regarding crime as a social phenomenon. It includes within its scope the processes of making laws, of breaking laws, and of reacting to the breaking of laws. . . . The objective of criminology is the development of a body of general and verified principles and of other types of knowledge regarding this process of law, crime, and treatment" (1960, 3). This definition implies that criminologists take a scientific approach to the study of crime.

criminology
The body of knowledge regarding crime as a social phenomenon. It includes the processes of making laws, breaking laws, and reacting to the breaking of laws. Its objective is the development of a body of general and verified principles and of other types of knowledge regarding this process of law, crime, and treatment.

Why Should We Study Crime?

It is important for us to know more about crime. Social scientists believe it is intrinsically worthwhile to learn more about all aspects of our social lives, including criminal behaviour and society's response to that behaviour. Learning about crime can tell us a lot about our society. For example, the United States has a much higher rate of violent crime—particularly firearms crime—than Canada. The United States also has a much harsher justice system than Canada (see Chapter 15). These differences highlight important value differences between the two countries. Also, just as an understanding of a disease helps medical scientists develop cures, we need to understand crime before we can reduce it. Finally, crime directly or indirectly affects all of us. Many of us have been victims of crime, and all of us pay for the costs of crime and the crime control system.

CRIME AND THE MEDIA

The media shapes our views about crime and criminals. Writers of television shows and movies use violence to attract viewers and to sell tickets. Editors and reporters select the crime news we hear and read and construct the way this news is presented to us in order to attract an audience.

Unfortunately, the picture of crime presented by the media is often inaccurate. For example, most crime is property crime, yet most media stories deal with violent crime. Typical of research in this area was a review of all the crime-related stories reported over two months in an Ottawa newspaper (Gabor 1994). Over half the stories focused on violent crimes, particularly murders. Yet violent crimes made up only 7 percent of reported crimes in Ottawa, and the city averaged just six murders per year. While violent crimes were over-reported, property crimes rarely received much attention. The portrayal of crime in the fictional media is even more distorted. Television series such as *Breaking Bad*, *The Sopranos*, and *Fargo* feature very graphic violence, as do many movies and novels.

The popularity of programs like *CSI* and its spinoffs has affected people's perceptions of the justice system. Some prosecutors have noted the "*CSI* effect," which they believe has caused crime victims and jury members to expect more definitive forensic evidence than is available outside the fictional laboratories of a television show (Dowler, Fleming, and Muzzatti 2006).

Why do the media misrepresent crime by focusing on violence? The primary goal of the media is to make profits by selling advertising. Stories that attract viewers or readers will boost ratings and circulation even if these stories do not represent the reality of crime. The informal news media rule "If it bleeds, it leads" reflects the public's fascination with sensationalized, bloody stories about mass murders and terrorist attacks.

The media's misrepresentation of crime has consequences. First, Canadians greatly overestimate the amount of violent crime and have a fear of crime that is higher than the actual risk of victimization. Second, the media provide a distorted stereotype of offenders. Violent crimes are most often committed by relatives, friends, and acquaintances—not by the anonymous stranger so many of us fear. The media also present distorted views of the racial dimensions of crime. Wortley found that while the crime rate is actually lower among immigrants than among those who are Canadian-born, the media perpetuate stereotypes: "One popular columnist, for example, wrote that 'our culture is not used to this type of savagery' and that 'this type of crime is the direct result of choosing too many of the wrong immigrants' . . . Another reporter maintained that 'White Canadians are understandably fed up with people they see as outsiders coming into their country and beating and killing them" (2009, 349).

Our fear of crime and our collective image of the criminal have an impact on government policy. Actual crime trends are irrelevant—when the public feels that crime is out of control, it expects the government to do something about it. Crime rates are declining, yet increasing media coverage of crime and pressure from a variety of interest groups have compelled the federal government to toughen many laws over the past two decades.

Indeed, the media may be *contributing* to crime. The linkage between media violence and violent behaviour is complex, and researchers disagree about the degree to which television influences behaviour as opposed to simply reflecting a pre-existing interest in violence. There is, though, a body of evidence concluding that children who are exposed to extensive television violence are more likely to be violent themselves (Christakis et al. 2013).

In addition, the news media may provide patterns for criminal acts such as rampage shootings. In the spring of 2014, North America saw three mass shootings within a two-week period, including the ambush deaths of three RCMP officers in Moncton, New Brunswick. While there were differences between these tragic events, there were also similarities, and some researchers believe that these similarities were a result of media reporting of previous events. That is, shooters carefully plan their actions based on their knowledge of what others have done.

This theory helps explain the similarities between rampage killings and why these events often occur in clusters. Many school shootings in the United States have been modelled after the 1999 Columbine High School shooting. To give just one example, in the 2018 school shooting that killed ten people in Santa Fe, Texas, the shooter copied the Columbine shooters in that he wore a black trench coat, used a sawed-off shotgun, carried Molotov cocktails and canisters of carbon dioxide gas, and wore a similar medallion with a hammer-and-sickle on it (Fernandez, Turkewitz, and Bidgood 2018). Concerning clustering, Towers and colleagues (2015) found that mass killings involving firearms increase for a 13-day period following an event involving four or more deaths—an increase that does not appear for events involving three or fewer victims who were hit but not necessarily killed. The latter events are less likely to be widely publicized.

Australian psychiatrist Paul Mullen has interviewed several rampage shooters and has described a number of characteristics common to many of them (Alberici 2007). Typically they are young males who have few friends and few intimate relationships. They are resentful, and they blame others for their unhappiness. They issue "manifestos," often on social media, outlining their grievances and explaining their killing sprees (Knoll 2010). Their shootings are a way of getting revenge for the injustices they feel they have suffered. Many plan to commit suicide at the end of the killing spree. They are also gun-obsessed, and firearms play a central role in their lives. Unlike many offenders, they carefully plan their killings and use what Mullen has termed "cultural scripts" learned through media reports of previous rampage killings.

There is also evidence that mass shooters seek to have their killings publicized through the media. A man who killed ten students at an Oregon college in 2015 had earlier posted a blog about a television journalist who killed two of his former colleagues in Virginia earlier that year: "I have noticed that so many people like him are all alone and unknown, yet when they spill a little blood, the whole world knows who they are. A man who was known by no one, is now known by everyone. His face splashed across every screen, his name across the lips of every person on the planet, all in the course of one day. Seems the more people you kill, the more you're in the limelight" (Frank 2018). The man alleged to have killed ten people in Toronto in 2018 had praised a California mass shooter prior to renting a van and driving down a sidewalk at high speed. Concern with publicity was also shown by the fact that the shooter who killed 49 people at the Pulse nightclub in Orlando in 2016 stopped shooting periodically during his three-hour rampage to check to see what news about the shooting had been posted on Facebook.

It is obvious that most people who see violent movies or who read news stories about mass shootings do not commit murders. That said, many researchers believe that media exposure can influence people who are predisposed to commit violence. Researchers who have studied rampage killings have recommended that the media reduce coverage of these events (Knoll 2010). However, these events draw extensive public interest and high ratings, so there is almost no chance these recommendations will ever be adopted.

What the media ignore about crime may be as important as what they report. Some have criticized the media for failing to cover the story of large numbers of missing women in Vancouver until Robert Pickton was charged with 26 murders (he likely committed many more). A missing child from a middle-class home will generate an avalanche of publicity; by contrast, it was not considered important or newsworthy that dozens of lower-class women—many of whom were sex trade workers—had gone missing in Vancouver. Pickton's trial generated international coverage, but the media focused on the gruesome crimes and did not consider broader social issues such as legal policies that were endangering sex trade workers, the fact that so many of the victims were Indigenous, or the state's role in producing socially impoverished neighbourhoods such as Vancouver's Downtown Eastside, where Pickton found most of his victims (Hugill 2010).

The media's focus on dramatic cases of violent crime also means that actions such as environmental crimes, where damage accumulates slowly but may eventually cause massive harm to people and property, are less visible and hence less likely to engage the public (Henry and Lanier 1998). Highly publicized violent crimes can mobilize the public and politicians to demand tougher penalties—California's "three strikes law" (see Chapter 15) is but one of many examples of this. The public is far less aware of the harm resulting from corporate and white-collar crime and rarely demands that governments take action against it.

While the media generally do not provide an accurate picture of crime, some journalists have done excellent work in shedding light on crime and justice issues. In Chapter 4 you will read about a series of newspaper articles examining how police departments handled sexual assault complaints (Doolittle 2017; Leeder 2017). Police services in some communities were much more likely than others to classify sexual assault complaints as "unfounded." Based on extensive research, the series has led to significant improvements in how some departments approach these complaints.

Questions for Critical Thinking

1. Because of the contagion of mass shootings, many of which are school shootings, some have suggested that the media change the way they report on these events. Can you suggest some changes in reporting practices that might reduce the frequency of mass deaths? What factors might make these changes difficult to implement?

2. Why do you think people are so drawn to stories about violence?

The Discipline of Criminology

The discipline of criminology has six main areas: the definition of crime and criminals, the origins and role of law, the social distribution of crime, the causation of crime, patterns of criminal behaviour, and societal reactions to crime.

SEARCH FOR:
Criminal Code of Canada

Defining Crime and Criminals

Not all social harms are criminal, and not all criminal acts are harmful. Thus we must consider how societies decide which acts to define as crimes. There are also questions concerning who should be defined as a criminal for criminological research purposes. Should we include someone who has been charged with a criminal offence but not convicted? What about someone who has committed a crime but not been charged? And how about the person who has been convicted of violating workplace safety laws after an employee was killed on the job, when the conviction is obtained under occupational health and safety laws rather than under the Criminal Code?

The Origins and Role of the Law

It is important to understand the social origins of our laws as well as the role that law plays in society. Why are some acts defined as criminal, while others are dealt with under other types of legislation or are not sanctioned at all?

The Social Distribution of Crime

To understand crime we must know such things as the characteristics of people who commit crimes; trends in the occurrence of crime over time; and differences among cities, provinces, and countries regarding the rates and types of crime. These and other dimensions of the social distribution of crime help criminologists understand the causes of crime.

The Causation of Crime

One of the most important questions for criminologists is why some people commit crimes while others live more law-abiding lives. In this text you will learn about a wide variety of explanations of criminal behaviour.

Patterns of Criminal Behaviour

Criminal acts are defined by law in terms of categories such as homicide, theft, and sexual assault. Criminologists have conducted extensive research analyzing the patterns of these offences. Among the questions asked by criminologists are these: Who are the offenders? Who are the victims? Under what social circumstances are offences most likely to occur? What are the consequences for crime victims? How can particular types of crime be prevented?

Societal Reactions to Crime

Historically, societies have responded to crime in many different ways. In Canada, we normally process law violators through a criminal justice system that includes the police, the courts, and the corrections system. Criminologists have studied each of these institutions very extensively.

This text does not cover the criminal justice system, because at most colleges and universities it is covered in a separate course. However, a brief overview of that system will help you understand how it deals with people who are charged with crimes.

The federal government has exclusive jurisdiction over criminal law and procedure. This means the provinces and territories cannot pass or amend the criminal law. However, the provinces are responsible for administering the justice system. Because of this division of powers, the Canadian criminal justice system is quite complex.

For example, there are many different levels of responsibility for policing. The federal police force—the RCMP—enforces some federal laws, such as the Controlled Drugs and Substances Act, for which it is responsible in all provinces and territories. It also acts as a provincial police force in all jurisdictions except Ontario, Quebec, and parts of Newfoundland and Labrador, which have their own provincial police forces. The provinces pay the RCMP for these services under provincial policing contracts. The RCMP also acts as a municipal police force in some communities. While most of these are small communities, the RCMP also does urban policing under contract in larger communities, most notably in the BC Lower Mainland. While the City of Vancouver has its own municipal force (like most of Canada's large municipalities), several adjoining cities, including Surrey and Richmond, are policed by the RCMP. In 2016 there were almost 69,000 police officers in Canada (Greenland and Alam 2017).

The courts, too, come under both federal and provincial jurisdiction. The provinces are responsible for appointing some judges and for administering the "lower" courts, which deal with most criminal cases, including those involving young offenders. Higher-level courts that try serious criminal cases are the responsibility of the federal government, as are the provincial appeal courts. Appeal courts do not try cases; rather, they hear appeals of cases decided by other courts. At the top of the hierarchy of courts is the Supreme Court of Canada, which hears appeals of decisions made by provincial and federal courts of appeal.

Responsibility for corrections is also split. Offenders who receive sentences of less than two years are dealt with by the provincial government and go to provincial jails. The provinces are also responsible for offenders who receive community dispositions, such as probation or restitution. A sentence of two years or more is served in a federal institution run by the Correctional Service of Canada. This service also supervises offenders who are released into the community prior to the expiration of their sentence. The release decision is made by a separate body, the National Parole Board.

Rules and Laws: The Regulation of Behaviour

All groups have rules. Society cannot function without them—if we are to live and to work with others, rules are necessary. We must also have a reasonable expectation that other people will obey the rules. Think of the chaos that would result if each driver decided which side of the road he or she would drive on each day, or which stop sign he or she would decide to obey. Most of the time, most of us conform to the **norms** our group prescribes. Of course, not all members of the group obey all the time. All of you have broken many rules, perhaps even some important ones. In this text we consider the topic of crime—behaviour that breaks the rules. How do rules get established? Why do people break them? How do groups respond to such violations?

We follow most rules without consciously thinking about them. Following accepted ways of walking and talking is almost automatic because these norms

norms
Established rules of behaviour or standards of conduct.

have been internalized. Often we cannot even specify all the rules that govern a particular behaviour. For example, when you learn a foreign language you become aware of many rules, such as those governing verb tenses, which you aren't consciously aware of when using your first language. However, we do think about other rules. Many of us may wish to drive above the speed limit, park illegally, or use illegal drugs but refrain from doing so because of our fear of penalties, while others may consciously break these rules.

Think of some of the informal rules (or folkways) that govern your conduct. When you were younger, your parents probably tried to persuade you to eliminate some of your favourite habits such as eating with your fingers and banging your toys on the furniture. These are very basic rules—others can be more complex. For example, how are you to address the Queen or the Lieutenant-Governor if you meet them? Whose name do you mention first when you introduce your 22-year-old spouse to your 60-year-old employer? What are we to make of these rules, which seem, on their face, to be trivial or silly? Rules help us select from the vast numbers of potential behaviours of which we are capable. Do we bow, kiss, or shake hands as a greeting? Which of two persons holds a door for the other? Who gets served first and last at dinner? How do we handle important milestones such as marriage and death? While the way each society solves these little problems may vary widely, each society has provided solutions.

These solutions avert potential chaos, and following them enhances our sense of belonging. The penalties for not following these rules are usually informal—the disapproval of family, friends, or colleagues, or perhaps a reprimand from an organization to which the violator belongs. However, we normally don't think of the penalties but continue to obey these rules because we have been taught to obey them and because they are part of belonging to the group.

Of course, not all actions are governed solely by these informal means of social control. Why do some informal rules become more formal regulations or laws? Consider the early days of the automobile. Driving was not regulated, and the rules of the road were those that applied to horse-drawn carriages. When automobiles were open and speeds were slow, drivers gave right of way to other drivers who had higher social status, just as was done when walking down the street. But as speeds increased and as drivers ranged farther from home, this became impractical and the state had to establish more formal regulations. In such cases, the law exists when order can no longer be maintained through informal rules. The law also deals with behaviour that is too serious to be left to informal mechanisms.

What Is a Crime?

The concept of "crime" has been developed relatively recently (Chapter 2). That does not mean that people didn't do harmful things to one another in earlier times, but this harmful behaviour was handled very differently. Prior to the 18th century, in most societies offences were handled privately by the wronged individual and their family. The early courts in Europe and North America dealt with religious and civil law rather than with criminal law.

The Legal Definition of Crime

The most common definition of crime is a *legalistic* one that defines a crime as an act or omission that violates the criminal law and is punishable with a jail term, a fine, and/or some other sanction. This **legal definition of crime** is satisfactory for most purposes and will fit most of the crimes discussed in this text. However, some criminologists have argued for a sociological definition of crime that encompasses a broader range of harmful behaviour than this strict legal definition provides.

Is White-Collar Crime Really Crime?

Edwin Sutherland was one of the most important figures in the development of criminology. In his presidential address to the American Sociological Association in 1939, he argued that focusing only on violations of the criminal law presented a misleading picture of crime. Limiting criminological research to offences such as burglary, assault, and theft—which were dealt with in the criminal courts—led to the conclusion that crime was primarily a lower-class phenomenon. He pointed out that many **white-collar crimes** were being committed by middle- and upper-class people in the course of their business activities. Criminologists neglected these crimes because they were not usually dealt with by the criminal courts:

> The crimes of the lower class are handled by policemen, prosecutors, and judges, with penal sanctions in the form of fines, imprisonment, and death. The crimes of the upper class either result in no official action at all, or result in suits for damages in civil courts, or are handled by inspectors, and by administrative boards or commissions, with penal sanctions in the form of warnings, orders to cease and desist, occasionally the loss of a license, and only in extreme cases by fines or prison sentences. (1940, 8)

Sutherland argued that even though they are not dealt with in criminal courts, the great harm caused by white-collar criminals made it imperative that criminologists study them. He was suggesting that the definition of crime be expanded to encompass the violation of other types of laws.

Human Rights Violations as Crime

Another attempt to expand the definition of crime was made by Herman and Julia Schwendinger (1970), who advocated a definition of crime based on **human rights** rather than on legal statutes. If an action violated the basic rights of humans to obtain the necessities of life and to be treated with respect and dignity, criminologists should consider it a crime. Thus government policies that create poverty and homelessness should be studied as crimes along with other practices that cause social harm, including imperialism, sexism, and racism. Advocates of this approach feel that the criminal law has been established by those in power so that acts committed by powerful people are not criminalized. Therefore, they feel the law is biased against the poor. The Schwendingers' proposal explicitly places criminology on the side of the poor and powerless.

legal definition of crime
A crime is an act or omission that violates the criminal law and is punishable with a jail term, a fine, and/or some other sanction.

white-collar crime
Crime that is committed by people in the course of their legitimate business activities.

human rights
The minimum conditions required for a person to live a dignified life. Among the rights set out by the Universal Declaration of Human Rights are the right to life, liberty, and security of the person; the right to be free of torture and other forms of cruel and degrading punishment; the right to equality before the law; and the right to the basic necessities of life.

Proponents of green criminology, discussed later in this chapter, take a similar view. Many corporations engage in practices that do enormous harm to the environment and to individuals but that do not violate laws or environmental regulations. For example, multinational companies have built factories in China where environmental regulations are lax (Shuqin 2010). While legal, many of these factories contribute massive amounts of pollution. Green criminologists argue that practices such as these should be studied, despite their legality, because of the harm they cause (Gibbs et al. 2010).

SEARCH FOR:
Universal Declaration of Human Rights

A Continuum of Crime and Deviance

While few criminologists would limit their work to the strict legal definition of crime, most would not make the definition as broad as the human rights approach suggests. John Hagan defined crime in a way that reflects how most criminologists view their discipline. Hagan (1985) wrote that a definition of crime must encompass not only violations of the criminal law but also

> a range of behaviors that for all practical purposes are treated as crimes (e.g., Sutherland's white-collar crimes), as well as those behaviors that across time and place vary in their location in and outside the boundaries of criminal law. In other words, we need a definition that considers behaviors that are both actually and potentially liable to criminal law. (49)

Hagan proposed that deviance and crime be considered on a continuum ranging from the least serious to the most serious acts. Seriousness can be assessed on three dimensions:

- *The degree of consensus that an act is wrong.* Most people feel that mass murder is wrong, but there is much less agreement over 17-year-olds using cannabis.
- *The severity of the society's response to the act.* Murder is punishable by death in some societies and by life imprisonment in others. On the other hand, minor drug offences may be ignored by the police.
- *The assessment of the degree of harm of the act.* Drug use and illegal gambling are often considered to be "victimless" crimes that harm only the offender, while serious crimes of violence are considered to be very harmful.

These three dimensions are usually closely related, but not always. The operators of the Westray Mine, whose unsafe practices resulted in the death of 26 Nova Scotia miners, caused great harm (Box 17.1). But even though most Canadians would probably agree that this negligence was wrong, none of those responsible for the mine were ever penalized for their actions. This approach recognizes that "the separation of crime from other kinds of deviance is a social and political phenomenon" (Hagan 1985, 49) and allows criminologists to consider a broad range of behaviours, including some types of deviance that may not be against the law. Hagan's approach is illustrated in Figure 1.1, which shows four major categories of crime and deviance: consensus crimes, conflict crimes, social deviations, and social diversions. This book will not specifically consider social deviations and social diversions; the distinction between consensus and conflict crimes is an important one that will be discussed in several chapters.

FIGURE 1.1 ■ Hagan's Varieties of Deviance

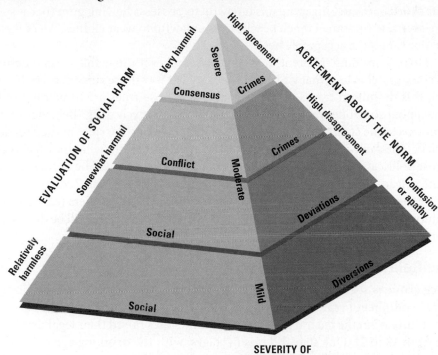

Source: John Hagan. (1991). *The Disreputable Pleasures: Crime and Deviance in Canada*, 3rd ed. Toronto: McGraw-Hill Ryerson. p. 13. Reproduced with permission of McGraw-Hill Ryerson Ltd.

Crime Is Socially Defined

Can you think of any type of behaviour that *everybody* condemns? Most people might think killing another person is always evil, but this is not the case. Soldiers are considered heroes for killing the enemy during a war. Society allows police officers to kill under some circumstances, and all of us have the right to kill a person who is threatening us with lethal force. Even those who commit what most of us would call murder are not always classified as murderers by the courts. For example, a man may kill his neighbour and be found not guilty by reason of insanity (now called "not criminally responsible on account of mental disorder"). If the same man was sane but intoxicated at the time of the offence, he might be found guilty of manslaughter rather than murder. Thus even for an act as serious as killing another person, we must understand the act's social context before we can determine whether it is deviant and how it should be classified.

Other types of crime and deviance are also socially defined. An act is deviant only in the context of a set of rules, and those rules vary widely from group to group. There are some broad similarities in acts that are defined as deviant. For example, most societies, most of the time, disapprove of members killing one another or plotting the violent overthrow of the government. However, there are also great differences between societies and within societies over time. Some societies classify as unlawful acts that are tolerated or even encouraged in Canada, while others permit practices that we condemn. For example, in Saudi Arabia women are not permitted to open a bank account without male permission or to wear short skirts, in Singapore it is unlawful to possess chewing gum (because it is messy), and on some French beaches it is unlawful to wear clothes. All of these practices are quite acceptable here.

There is nothing inherent in any act that makes it unlawful. We can define deviance as behaviour that violates the rules, whatever those rules may be. However, this definition leaves us with problems. Whose rules are to be followed? What about someone who belongs to an outlaw motorcycle gang? Behaviour that conforms to the standards of that group will often violate the rules of the broader society. The same is true of those who use terrorism to fight what they feel is an unjust political system. If the revolution is successful, they will be heroes. Many political leaders, including Fidel Castro of Cuba and China's Mao Zedong, gained power through violence. However, if the revolution fails, the leaders will be killed or imprisoned. This important question of "Who sets the rules?" will be discussed more fully later in this chapter.

The Relativity of Crime

Since crime is socially defined, the rules can change. A situation in the United States a number of years ago highlighted how changeable the law can be. Because of pressure from the federal government, many states raised their legal drinking age from 18 to 21. One state did this in stages, with the drinking age rising one year each January 1. In a television interview, a university student whose 18th birthday was in late November described what he was facing for the next three years. Each year, he would be able to legally drink alcohol from his November birthday until midnight on 31 December. Since the drinking age changed with the new year, he would have to return to soft drinks until the following November when he turned 19. This would go on every year until he was 21, which meant that he could legally drink for less than six months out of the 36 months between his 18th and 21st birthdays.

A more significant example is the fact that several decades ago, the sexual acts of LGBTQ people were prohibited by the Criminal Code and subject to maximum penalties ranging from 5 to 14 years (Rodgers 1962). When former prime minister Pierre Trudeau was the federal justice minister, he declared that the "state has no place in the bedrooms of the nation" and removed these sections from the Criminal Code. Since that time there have been dramatic changes. LGBTQ people now have the right to get married, and for most Canadians the controversy over this issue has disappeared.

These examples show that criminal and noncriminal are not two distinct categories. There is an overlap between the two, and the line between them can be ambiguous. We often speak as if the world was divided between criminals and noncriminals. However, we have all broken the law at times—does this mean we are all "criminals"? In fact, phrases like "everybody does it" are used to justify crimes that are committed by "respectable" people (Gabor 1994), including stealing from employers, not reporting tips and other income on tax forms, and downloading copyrighted material. How do people draw the line between respectable citizens who occasionally do bad things and those they consider "criminals"? What are the implications of thinking of crime as being a matter of degree?

Who Makes the Rules? Conflict versus Consensus Theories of Law

Of course, the law is not completely subjective or arbitrary. Many criminal laws reflect serious social harms that are illegal in most societies and that most people condemn. However, as you have learned, the exact form of the laws and the specific behaviours prohibited vary greatly in different places and at different times. Why are some acts subject to criminal sanctions while others are not?

One of the most important criminological questions is "Who sets the rules?" Who decided that selling heroin is illegal while selling cigarettes is respectable? Who determined that an impaired driver who causes the death of a pedestrian can be severely sanctioned, while an employer whose violation of workplace safety rules causes death may receive only a small fine? The issue of how rules are made and enforced is an important one. There have been two distinct approaches to this question—the consensus and conflict perspectives.

The Consensus Approach

Consensus theorists believe that law represents the consensus of the people. That is, the law reflects the **values** shared by most members of a society. For example, several Muslim countries have institutionalized *sharia* law, which is explicitly based on the Koran, which means the law reflects those societies' religious values. Similarly, many of the early European settlers in the United States were Puritans who left England for the colony of Massachusetts so that they could freely practise their religious beliefs. The laws of the new colony reflected those beliefs. Much of their legal code of 1648 was taken directly from the Bible, and many crimes were punishable by death. Capital crimes included "idolatry, witchcraft, blasphemy, bestiality, sodomy, adultery, rape, man stealing, treason . . . cursing or smiting of a parent, stubbornness or rebelliousness on the part of a son against his parents, and homicide committed with malice prepense, by guile or poisoning" (Haskins 1969, 37). Religious values are not the only ones enshrined in law, but these examples illustrate how values become codified into law.

The consensus view is also supported by the fact that there is broad agreement regarding many laws, particularly those dealing with murder, burglary, and street crimes such as robbery. Studies that have asked people to rate the seriousness of a broad range of criminal offences have shown considerable agreement among people from Canada and the United States concerning the rankings of these offences (Normandeau 1966; Akman, Normandeau, and Turner 1967).

The Conflict Approach
Class Conflict Theory

Conflict theorists do not believe that laws reflect a consensus of members of society. **Class conflict theorists** believe that laws are passed by members of the ruling class to maintain their privileged position by keeping the common people under control. Activities that threaten the powerful are defined as illegal, and the legal mechanism of the state is used to enforce the laws. A historical example shows how the law can be used to further the aims of the politically powerful. After the Riel Rebellion in 1885, Hayter Reed, the Assistant Commissioner of Indian Affairs,

consensus theory
Laws represent the agreement of most of the people in society that certain acts should be prohibited by the criminal law.

value
A collective idea about what is right or wrong, good or bad, and desirable or undesirable in a particular culture.

class conflict theory
Laws are passed by members of the ruling class in order to maintain their privileged position by keeping the common people under control.

used the Indian Act to control the Indigenous population. He deposed many of the chiefs he felt were disloyal and undermined the authority of other Indigenous leaders by instructing his staff to deal directly with individuals and families rather than with the bands. He also confined band members to their reserves by ordering the implementation of a pass system that had no justification in law:

> Officials of the [North-West Mounted Police] were never comfortable with the absence of any legal foundation for the pass system. The lack of a legal basis in this case undermined the validity of all NWMP operations: they were trying to demonstrate to the Indians that the police enforced a rational system of laws that operated to the benefit of all. . . . In 1893 a circular letter was issued directing all police officers to refrain from ordering Indians without passes back to their reserves.
>
> Hayter Reed would have none of these weak-kneed, legalistic concerns. He urged the police to continue enforcing the pass system on the grounds that the "moral responsibilities of the Indian Department transcended treaty obligations." Reed's views triumphed. By at least 1896 the police had reversed their position. In that year Commissioner Herchmer issued a circular letter instructing police who encountered any Indian without a pass to "use all possible pressure to persuade him to return to his reserve." (Carter 1990, 153–54)

Reed was using the legal system to restrict the movement of Indigenous people, whom he believed represented a threat to the government and to the white settlers who were moving onto the Prairies.

Group Conflict Theory

group conflict theory
A theory that attempts to explain certain types of criminal behaviour as resulting from a conflict between the interests of divergent groups.

Not all laws reflect consensus in society, nor do they necessarily involve the dominance of one class over another. **Group conflict theory** is a perspective that recognizes that all laws are the result of a political process and that this process typically involves a conflict or a debate among various interest groups. Some debates have continued for decades. For example, in 1988 the Supreme Court of Canada decided that laws restricting abortion were unconstitutional. Since then, divisions over the legality of abortion have meant that Canada has had no criminal law concerning abortion. Because the groups on different sides of this issue are so committed to their positions, it is unlikely that any such laws will be passed in the near future.

Cannabis is another issue where Canadians have very different views. In 2012 the Conservative government passed new, tougher laws that legislated mandatory prison terms for growing as few as six marijuana plants, if the marijuana was for trafficking purposes. However, only a few years later a Liberal government passed legislation that legalized cannabis use for most Canadians. This shift in policy reflects a split in attitudes towards nonmedical cannabis use. Shortly before passage of the legislation, 54 percent of Canadian respondents believed that nonmedical use was either completely or somewhat acceptable. On the other hand, 40 percent found it somewhat or completely *un*acceptable (Statistics Canada 2017). Thus there is still significant dissatisfaction with the new legislation, though this may diminish following legalization.

Abortion and cannabis use are issues that divide Canadians. For another example, see Focus Box 1.2, which looks at the split over animal cruelty legislation.

Possession of cannabis could once lead to a lengthy jail sentence, but since 2018 it has been legally available to Canadian adults.

An Evolving Discipline: Green Criminology, Terrorism Studies, and Surveillance Studies

To show how the criminological perspective can help us understand contemporary issues, this chapter concludes with a discussion of three of criminology's newest branches: green criminology, terrorism studies, and surveillance studies. Each of these new areas is challenging the discipline by presenting new ways of defining and understanding crime as criminologists engage with significant changes in the world.

Green Criminology

Criminologists are developing a "green criminology" to contribute to the debate about the causes and consequences of environmental destruction, and to use their expertise to help address this problem.

Green criminology is rooted in the environmental and animal rights movements. Environmental issues include air and water pollution and harm to natural ecosystems such as oceans and forests. Criminologists interested in animal rights study "individual acts of cruelty to animals and the institutional, socially acceptable human domination of animals in agribusiness, in slaughterhouses and abattoirs, in so-called scientific experimentation and, in less obviously direct ways, in sports, colleges and schools, zoos, aquaria and circuses" (Beirne and South 2007, xiv; see also Box 1.2). These theorists have introduced the concept of "speciesism," which refers to discrimination against nonhuman animals. Thus green criminology encompasses a broad range of behaviours ranging from acts that are clearly harmful, such as dumping toxic waste in the ocean, to acts that many people consider to be acceptable, such as eating meat or wearing leather shoes.

The range of work done by green criminologists has been broad:

- They have documented the existence of lawbreaking with respect to pollution, disposal of toxic wastes, and misuse of environmental resources.

- They have raised questions relating to the destruction of specific environments and resources in ways that are "legal" but ecologically very harmful to plants, animals, and humans.

- They have challenged corporate definitions of good environmental practice and emphasized the claims of nonhuman nature to ecological justice.

- They have emphasized the dynamic links between distribution of environmental "risk" and distinct communities, particularly how poor and minority populations experience disproportionate exposure to environmental harm.

- They have investigated the specific place of animals in relation to issues of "rights" and human–nonhuman relationships on a shared planet.

- They have criticized the inadequacies of environmental regulation in both philosophical and practical terms.

- They have exposed corporate attempts to stifle environmental critique and dissent through the use of public relations propaganda and strategic lawsuits against public participation.

- They have reconsidered the nature of victimization in relation to environmental changes and events, including social and governmental responses to this victimization.

- They have explored the ways in which law enforcement officials—particularly the police but also environmental protection authorities—have intervened with regard to regulation of fisheries, prosecution of polluters, and conservation of specific environs and species.*

*Rob White, "Green Criminology and the Pursuit of Social and Ecological Justice," in *Issues in Green Criminology: Confronting Harms Against Environments, Humanity and Other Animals*, ed. Piers Beirne and Nigel South (Portland: Willan, 2007), 33–34. Reprinted by permission of Taylor & Francis Group.

Jobs such as dismantling ships, which can cause environmental damage and harm to workers, are often contracted to countries where environmental and occupational health and safety laws are very lax and where wages are low. This photo shows workers near Mumbai, India, breaking up ships for recycling as scrap.

AP Photo/Rafiq Maqbool

FOCUS   BOX 1.2

ANIMAL CRUELTY LAWS IN CANADA

Laws do not just happen: they are the result of complex social processes. The passage of particular laws is influenced by individuals and groups whose interests would be affected by the law. Green criminologists are critical of the fact that the voices of environmentalists are often not heard by politicians, who are also being lobbied by corporate interests that can profit from environmental damage. Current efforts to improve Canada's animal cruelty legislation show how different groups try to ensure that legislation reflects their interests.

Canada has made only minor changes to its animal cruelty legislation since 1892, and many believe that stronger laws are needed to prevent animal abuse. Many critics of the current legislation cite an Edmonton case in which two men tied a dog to a tree and beat it to death with a baseball bat. The men were not convicted of animal cruelty because the evidence showed that the dog died when it was first hit with the bat so it did not suffer cruelty. It is very difficult to get convictions for people who neglect their animals, for the Crown must prove that the neglect was "willful." Thus a farmer whose animals have starved to death will be acquitted unless it can be proved that he or she acted willfully. This is why very few people in Canada have been convicted of animal abuse.

New animal cruelty laws have been before Parliament since 1999. However, the proposed legislation has been opposed by those who fear the laws would affect their livelihood—hunters, trappers, farmers, and medical researchers who experiment on animals. In 2008, Parliament was faced with two competing bills. The first, S-203, involved minimal changes beyond making the penalties tougher for existing offences. The second, C-229, would have added significant protection for animals. It would have removed the "willful neglect" provision and would have made it more difficult to kill stray animals. The second bill was supported by many groups, including the Canadian Veterinary Medical Association and virtually all of Canada's humane societies and animal support organizations. On the other side were groups such as the Canadian Sportfishing Industry Association,

which claimed that the proposed legislation would jeopardize the $10 billion-a-year sport fishing industry by making it "possible for a Grandfather to face a federal criminal prosecution for taking his grandchildren fishing" (CSIA 2007). Opponents claimed that the bill would give animals the same legal standing as humans and would encourage animal rights "terrorists" to keep attacking medical researchers (Senate Committee on Legal and Constitutional Affairs 2006). Proponents of Bill C-229 argued that the bill excluded harm done to animals for lawful reasons such as hunting and medical experimentation, but this interpretation was challenged by opponents. The Conservative government passed S-203 in 2008; the bill that would have done much more to protect animals (C-229) has never been passed.

Most recently, a private member's bill proposed by a Liberal MP proposed three new measures: a ban on importing shark fins into Canada, for 100 million sharks were dying every year as a result of that trade; a ban on the importation of cat and dog fur into Canada and a requirement for proper labelling of fur; and a tightening of Criminal Code measures concerning animal abuse (including "brutal and vicious killing"), animal fighting, negligence, and bestiality. The bill was soundly defeated in Parliament, with the most of the governing Liberals joining the Conservatives in opposing the changes. A major reason for opposing the legislation was concern about moving animals out of the property section of the Criminal Code. As in the past, the main opponents of the bill were fishing and hunting organizations and farming groups.

Questions for Critical Thinking

1. Legislation often involves compromise among groups supporting and opposing a particular course of action. Why is compromise so difficult to achieve with the issue of animal rights?

2. What impact would stronger animal cruelty legislation have on meat producers and medical researchers? Do you think that animals should have the same rights as human beings?

Green criminologists believe that criminology should study socially harmful actions as well as acts that violate the criminal law. Some environmental harms are illegal. One of Canada's worst environmental disasters was a case of water pollution in Walkerton, Ontario, that resulted in seven deaths and caused more than 2,000 people to fall seriously ill. The operators of the water treatment plant who failed to test the water and who falsified test results were successfully prosecuted, but politicians such as former Ontario premier Mike Harris, whose government's policies contributed strongly to the tragedy (O'Connor 2002), were not pros-ecuted. However, many actions that are much more serious in the long term, such as the emission of huge quantities of greenhouse gases in the production of oil from Alberta's Oil Sands (Smandych and Kueneman 2010), and the clear-cutting of tropical rain forests, are not against the law and are often supported by governments. Green criminologists argue that the damage to the planet caused by destructive environmental practices can be far more serious than the illegal acts that have traditionally been the focus of criminological study (Lynch and Stretesky 2007). Global warming could cause mass starvation, migration from countries where drought has caused the collapse of agriculture, and conflict between countries over water resources and food supplies (South 2010).

Green criminology is grounded in the philosophy of ecological citizenship. This means that notions of morality and rights should be extended to "nonhuman nature" (White 2007, 35) and that societies should adopt a notion of ecological citizenship that obliges them to recognize that the environment must be protected for future generations. This requires a global perspective because the effects of environmental crimes go far beyond the borders of any single country. This also demonstrates the relativity of crime. Wind and water can easily carry pollution from a country with weak laws and lax enforcement to neighbouring countries that may themselves have strong environmental laws and effective enforcement (White 2011). There are few mechanisms in international law to deal with these transnational issues.

Terrorism Studies

terrorism
The illegitimate use of force to achieve a political objective by targeting innocent people.

A global perspective is also important in the growing field of **terrorism** studies. Criminologists became more interested in terrorism after the al-Qaeda attacks on the United States on 11 September 2001. Criminologists have looked at several aspects of terrorism, including the recruitment and training of terrorists, the organization of terrorist organizations, links between terrorism and other types of criminality, and the social control of terrorism. Here we will consider two aspects of terrorism studies: the social definition of terrorism, and the degree to which Western nations have violated the rule of law in their "war on terror."

The Social Definition of Terrorism

There is no universal agreement on the definition of terrorism—the argument is often made that "one man's terrorist is another man's freedom fighter" (Ganor 2002). However, a simple definition that captures much of our sense of what ter-rorism involves is as follows: terrorism is "the deliberate use or the threat to use violence against civilians in order to attain political, ideological and religious goals" (Ganor 2002, 288).

One reason why an agreed-upon definition is difficult to establish is that "terrorism" is a socially constructed term. Turk has stated the issue:

> Contrary to the impression fostered by official incidence counts and media reports, terrorism is not a given in the real world but is instead an interpretation of events and their presumed causes. And these

interpretations are not unbiased attempts to depict truth but rather conscious efforts to manipulate perceptions to promote certain interests at the expense of others. When people and events come to be regularly described in public as terrorists and terrorism, some governmental or other entity is succeeding in a war of words in which the opponent is promoting alternative designations such as "martyr" and "liberation struggle." (2004, 272)

Thus the 9/11 al-Qaeda attack on the United States is generally defined as terrorism by Western countries but is seen by some in other countries as martyrdom for a just cause. The subsequent US invasion of Iraq was not considered terrorism by political authorities in Western countries because the Americans resisted this labelling even though thousands of innocent civilians were killed during the Iraq War. Actions such as the intensive firebombing of German and Japanese cities and the use of nuclear weapons on Hiroshima and Nagasaki by the Allies during the Second World War were not defined as terrorism because those who won the war were able to impose their definitions of these actions.

Section 83.01 of Canada's Criminal Code defines terrorism as an act committed "for a political, religious or ideological purpose . . . with the intention of intimidating the public." Two recent cases that did not result in terrorism charges being laid have resulted in debates about how this definition is applied. In 2017, Alexandre Bissonnette entered a Quebec City mosque with a pistol and a rifle and murdered six worshippers. Bissonnette had considered killing people in a shopping mall, but chose the mosque because he felt he would possibly be killing a religious extremist so he would be saving lives (Marin 2018). Bissonnette was convicted of six counts of first-degree murder, but his act was generally considered to be a mass shooting rather than an act of terrorism because he wasn't affiliated with any terrorist groups. However, one can ask whether opinions would have been different if a Muslim man had carried out the shooting in a Christian Church. In the United States, where right-wing groups (including white supremacists) have been responsible for more killings than Islamic jihadists, the government has been reluctant to call these actions terrorism (Fisher and Taub 2017). An example is Dylann Roof, who entered a predominantly black church in South Carolina and murdered nine members of the congregation. He told police he carried out the shooting in order to start a race war. Roof was convicted of hate crimes but was not charged with terrorism.

Another definitional complication is that while we normally view terrorism as referring to acts committed against a government, the term can also be applied to actions committed by a government against its own people. Joseph Stalin, who ruled the Soviet Union from 1924 to 1953, and Mao Zedong, who controlled China from 1949 to 1976, each killed millions of their own people in order to maintain their political control. These are but two of many similar examples.

FOCUS

BOX 1.3

TERRORISM IN CANADA

Most Canadians are probably unaware that Canada has had problems with terrorism in the past. Kellett (2004) tracked more than 400 terrorist incidents in Canada between 1960 and 1992. Most of these incidents involved Canadians attacking domestic targets, and most were committed by two groups: the FLQ and the Sons of Freedom Doukhobors. The FLQ (Front de libération du Québec) was committed to the separation of Quebec from Canada. It financed its political activities through crimes such as credit card fraud and robbery. During the 1960s the group was responsible for nearly 100 bombings, including an attack on the Montreal Stock Exchange that injured 27 people. It also kidnapped and murdered Quebec cabinet minister Pierre Laporte in 1970.

The Sons of Freedom Doukhobors were a very different group. They were a pacifist religious group who rejected government involvement in their lives and who refused to pay taxes, to send their children to school, or to register births and deaths. As a result, the BC government removed many of their children from their homes and forced them into residential schools. The group's protests against the government and against other Doukhobors culminated in more than 100 bombings and arson attacks on public facilities such as schools and power lines between 1960 and 1962.

The worst incident of Canadian-based terrorism was the 1985 bombing of Air India Flight 182. A bomb placed in a Boeing 747 in Vancouver exploded over the Atlantic Ocean, killing all 329 people on board. At almost the same time, a bomb placed on another Air India flight from Vancouver exploded at Japan's Narita Airport, killing two baggage handlers. The bombings were blamed on Canadian militant groups supporting a Sikh homeland in India. One man, Inderjit Singh Reyat, pleaded guilty to a charge of manslaughter and building the bombs; he received a 15-year prison sentence. The men accused of placing the bombs, Ajaib Singh Baghri and Ripudaman Singh Malik, were later acquitted. In 2010, Reyat was convicted of perjury in the Baghri and Malik trial and sentenced to an additional nine years in prison.

Terrorist activities have continued into this century. In 2006, 18 men were arrested in the Toronto area on charges of planning terrorist attacks in Canada. While not a well-trained or well-organized group, they made plans to detonate several truck bombs and to storm Parliament Hill and behead Prime Minister Stephen Harper. They held training camps north of Toronto (which featured the uniquely Canadian touch of visits to Tim Hortons along with lessons in using firearms and discussions of jihad), and they tried to order several tons of ammonium nitrate to use in their truck bombs. They were arrested before they got a chance to put any of their plans into action. Eleven of the men were convicted of a variety of charges; their leader received a sentence of life imprisonment. Most incidents since then have involved "lone wolf" terrorists who have acted on their own, usually with support from online forums. The most notable incident occurred in 2014 when Michael Zehaf-Bibeau killed a soldier standing guard at the National War Memorial and then was killed by authorities when he stormed inside the Parliament Buildings with a weapon.

From MURRAY/LINDEN/KENDALL. *Sociology in Our Times*, 5E. © 2011 Nelson Education Ltd. Reproduced by permission. www.cengage.com/permissions.

Terrorism and Rule of Law

Ericson has observed that Western societies have placed a priority on preventing terrorism at all costs: "Normal legal principles, standards, and procedures must be suspended because of a state of emergency, extreme uncertainty, or threat to security with catastrophic potential. The legal order must be suspended to save the social order" (2007, 26). To fight terrorism, the state has assumed greater powers. Enhanced methods of surveillance and control have been put in place, and normal restraints, such as the requirements for due process and protection of the rights of accused persons, have been ignored in the search for security. For example, the US government has held hundreds of Muslim prisoners in Guantanamo Bay, which is US-controlled territory in Cuba, so that normal American due process rights need not apply. These prisoners are not classified by the Americans as prisoners of war but rather as "unlawful enemy combatants," so the rights provided to prisoners of war by the Geneva Convention also do not apply.

The mandates of Canadian security agencies have broadened since 9/11 (Murphy 2007). Billions of dollars have been added to the budgets of security agencies, including the RCMP, the Canadian Security and Intelligence Service (CSIS), and the Canadian Border Services Agency. New anti-terrorism legislation has expanded the powers of the police and other security agencies. Also, the emphasis on prevention requires that the police use extraordinary tactics, including "the use of paid community informants, extensive community surveillance, broad intelligence-gathering, targeted ethnic and religious profiling, and a preventative security-policing tactic called 'threat disruption'" (Murphy 2007, 456).

Many governments have violated the rights of their own citizens in the War on Terror. The most notorious Canadian case involved Maher Arar, a Syrian-born Canadian citizen. Arar was returning from a holiday in Tunisia in 2002 when he was apprehended in New York by US officials. Because he was suspected of having ties to al-Qaeda, he was immediately sent to Syria (a practice known as rendition), where he was tortured in a Syrian prison, likely at the request of US intelligence agencies. He returned to Canada after a year in Syrian custody.

A government inquiry into the Arar case concluded that the RCMP had violated its own policies by providing US authorities with information about Arar that was inaccurate and unfairly negative (Commission of Inquiry into the Actions of Canadian Officials in Relation to Maher Arar, 2006). The RCMP and CSIS did not cooperate with the Department of Foreign Affairs to help secure Arar's return to Canada, and Canadian officials leaked inaccurate classified information about Arar to the media following his return to Canada. The RCMP also concealed information from senior government officials about their handling of the case.

Following the inquiry, the Canadian government formally apologized to Arar and paid him $10.5 million in compensation. US Senator Patrick Leahy's comment on the Arar case expresses the impact of anti-terrorism programs on the rule of law in many countries: "Maher Arar's case stands as a sad example of how we have been too willing to sacrifice our core principles to overarching government power in the name of security when doing so only undermines the principles we stand for—and makes us less safe" (*Ottawa Citizen,* 2007).

Surveillance Studies

Governments have always wanted to know more about what citizens are up to, especially in totalitarian countries, where surveillance is often oppressive. However, the technological capacity for surveillance has grown so quickly that massive amounts of personal information are now available. Four Canadian surveillance studies scholars have outlined the problem:

> Today, our lives are transparent to others in unprecedented ways. In Canada, as elsewhere, many kinds of organizations watch what we do, keep tabs on us, check our details, and track our movements. Almost everything we do generates an electronic record: we cannot go online, walk downtown, attend a university class, pay with a credit card, hop on an airplane, or make a phone call without data being captured. Personal

information is picked up, processed, stored, retrieved, bought, sold, exchanged. Our lives—or rather, those traces and trails of data, those fragments of reality to which our lives can be reduced—are visible as never before, to other individuals, to public and private organizations, to machines. (Bennett et al. 2014, 3)

What exactly is surveillance? Bennett and colleagues define it as "any systematic focus on personal information in order to influence, manage, entitle, or control those whose information is collected (2014, 6).

Governments are relying increasingly on information to govern us, and corporations use our information for their profit. This is not necessarily a bad thing. Government tracking of prescription drug use can help ensure that people are not taking drugs that interact with one another and that addicts are not getting opiate prescriptions from several different doctors. Police have reduced crime by targeting their efforts on crime hot spots and by monitoring high-risk offenders. Starbucks customers may appreciate receiving a discount coupon on their phones when they walk near a Starbucks location, and Amazon's suggestions for book purchases based on our buying history can help us select new books.

But surveillance can also cause harm. In 2014, Ontario's Privacy Commissioner filed a court action against the Toronto Police Service because it refused to stop releasing information about attempted suicides to other agencies. The action was precipitated by a case involving a woman who missed a Caribbean cruise after she was refused admission to the United States because she had attempted suicide several years earlier.

A youthful indiscretion captured in a photo and posted online may cost a person a job when a potential employer views it many years later. Facebook conducted experiments in which they altered the news feeds of hundreds of thousands of subscribers to see if having increased numbers of positive or negative stories altered the tone of users' subsequent posts. Today's unprecedented level of surveillance means that each of us has given up power to the governments and corporations that are collecting and analyzing information about us. Once information has been collected, individuals no longer have control over how it is used.

Bennett and colleagues point out another consequence of the collection of personal information: that information may be used for social sorting, as the data are used to make decisions about our lives. The Ontario woman who had attempted suicide was barred from the United States, and a person on welfare or sick leave may be subjected to extra scrutiny to ensure they are not earning extra money. An unintended example of social sorting is provided by Brayne (2014), who found that among people who have been involved with the justice system, the desire to avoid surveillance can limit involvement with institutions such as banks, schools, and hospitals that track and share information. This can impede their reintegration into society; it can also have impacts on their health, employment, and access to other services.

Technology can simplify the sorting process. European governments are using data in cellphones to verify the identities of immigrants claiming refugee status and using cellphone tracking data to determine whether people are lying about their countries of origin or about their routes to the country in which they are claiming refugee status.

Surveillance issues are becoming more complex. A major issue is the increasing capacity of corporations and governments to link surveillance technologies, as commercial companies aggregate data from multiple sources and as governments establish fusion centres that integrate a variety of different databases to enhance security or to monitor and deliver government services. Drones are quickly multiplying, and they have unique surveillance capabilities. They are being used globally by military and intelligence agencies; police departments are using them for surveillance and for taking overhead photos of auto accidents and crime scenes; and hydro and pipeline companies are using them to conduct safety inspections of their power lines. If your neighbour has a small drone, what privacy rights do you have if he chooses to hover it above your fenced backyard or beside your second-story window transmitting live video of your activities back to his computer screen?

Society has not yet worked out an appropriate balance between privacy rights and the need for more surveillance in order to protect the population and enable companies to provide better service to customers. This means that surveillance issues will continue to be important and that this new field of criminology will become an important source of theory and data about surveillance and privacy issues.

Facebook, Google, Amazon, DNA, and Your Privacy*

Social Media and Privacy You have just tweeted to a friend that you're going for coffee. As you pass a coffee shop, a coupon arrives on your phone offering 50 cents off a large cup of coffee. A person who is travelling to Paris uses an online site to book a hotel room. Because she is using a Mac, the hotels that come up on the booking list are more expensive than if she had used a PC. A new college graduate has submitted a resumé for a job. The potential employer looks at the applicant's Facebook site, finds photos of the applicant using drugs at parties, and decides not to hire the person. In each of these cases, information that a person might expect to be private has been used by a third party. In the first two cases, the information was sold to an advertiser.

Online sites such as Facebook, Google, and Twitter provide a useful service for hundreds of millions of users. However, many users do not understand the role of Facebook. They think they are *clients* of Facebook, but they are actually its *products*—because Facebook makes money by selling access to personal information. Because of the information people provide to the site, Facebook can charge a premium for ads that are tailored to the interests of a particular audience. The more information Facebook, and other sites such as Google, can provide to advertisers, the greater the profits—and both these companies are enormously profitable. Some Facebook apps are able to obtain data from friends of users, and Facebook is also able to harvest information from people who are not even Facebook users. Facebook even collects biometric facial data on users—information that can be used for a broad range of purposes, including law enforcement. The European Union has banned this practice, but it is still used in other parts of the world.

---

*Portions of this section have been adapted from Murray, Linden, and Kendall (2017).

Search engines such as Google make billions of dollars from tracking the key words you use. If you search for terms such as *headache* or *upset stomach*, you may receive ads or coupons for remedies for these maladies. Google also tracks your information across its different products, such as Gmail and YouTube, to develop more complete profiles of users in order to personalize the service.

Privacy concerns became an issue in 2018. Cambridge Analytica, a multinational data analytics company whose slogan is "We find your voters and move them to action" was accused of using data from 87 million users to help with several political campaigns including that of Donald Trump. These data enabled Cambridge Analytica to precisely target specific kinds of information that met the interests of each potential voter.

The US Congress required Facebook CEO Mark Zuckerberg to testify, and he promised that Facebook would do a better job of ensuring privacy. However, at the time this is being written, it is not clear if Facebook will make significant changes (which could reduce their profits) or if politicians in the United States or Canada will require any changes.

Amazon has also been criticized because of privacy issues. It has developed a facial recognition system called Rekognition which can identify faces on the street, in large crowds, or even on police body-worn camera images. It has been selling this technology to US police agencies, and civil liberties groups such as the American Civil Liberties Union (ACLU) have raised concerns that the technology violates peoples' privacy rights.

Online DNA Matching One of the most elusive serial killers in US history was the Golden State Killer, who was linked to 12 murders and more than 50 rapes between 1972 and 1986. The police had stored his DNA but were unable to find a match in their DNA database. However, some cold case detectives knew of the popularity of DNA testing services such as Ancestry DNA and found that they could upload DNA profiles on a genealogy website called GEDmatch. They uploaded the sample and, while the suspect's DNA was not on the site, they did find a match with the suspect's relatives. The DNA was traced to the great-great-great grandparents of the killer. From these people—who lived about 200 years ago—investigators painstakingly created about 25 family trees involving thousands of people (Jouvenal 2018). They eventually narrowed possible suspects down to a former California police officer. After putting him under surveillance, they recovered an item with the suspect's DNA on it and found that it matched DNA recovered at crime scenes. The 72-year-old was charged with eight counts of murder.

While this case displays rather remarkable detective work, it also raises some troublesome privacy issues. It is highly unlikely that until now, people who submitted their DNA to a genetic testing service ever envisioned that it might be used to put one of their relatives in prison. And certainly their relatives would never have imagined that they could be traced because of the actions of a relative they might not even know.

Facial Recognition

A final example of how our privacy is at risk is that in 2018, Ticketmaster began partnering with a company called Blink Identity, which has developed facial recognition systems for the US Department of Defense. Ticketmaster's goal is for concertgoers to enter its venues (concerts and sports events) by means of facial scanning rather than tickets. This will require a massive surveillance database. Also, if the system is hacked, criminals might be able to access our biometric information. A hacked credit card can be cancelled; we cannot be reissued another face.

QUESTIONS FOR CRITICAL THINKING

1. Think of a law that people are currently lobbying to change. What changes are being advocated? Why do some people want to change the law? If anyone is resisting the legal change, why are they offering this resistance? What do you think will be the outcome of this attempt at legal change?
2. Consider Figure 1.1, which shows different types of crime and deviance. Think of behaviours that fit into each of the four categories (consensus crimes, conflict crimes, social deviations, and social diversions). Can you think of examples of behaviours that have moved from one category to another?

Summary

- In this text the term *criminology* refers to the body of knowledge regarding crime as a social phenomenon. It includes within its scope the processes of making laws, breaking laws, and reacting to the breaking of laws. The objective of criminology is to develop a body of general and verified principles and of other types of knowledge regarding this process of law, crime, and treatment.

- The discipline of criminology includes six major areas: the definition of crime and criminals, the origins and role of law, the social distribution of crime, the causation of crime, patterns of criminal behaviour, and societal reactions to crime.

- Our behaviour is strongly influenced by norms, many of which we have internalized. Much of the time we don't even consciously think about the rules that govern our behaviour. Most of the time, rules are enforced through informal means such as the disapproval of family and friends; however, in some cases the rules are formalized into laws.

- Legally, crime is defined as an act that violates the criminal law and is punishable with jail terms, fines, and other sanctions. Criminologists have expanded on this definition. Discussing white-collar crime, Sutherland said that criminologists should also include violations of other types of laws in addition to criminal law. The Schwendingers proposed that crime be defined as a violation of human rights. Hagan felt that criminologists should consider deviance and crime as a continuum ranging from minor acts of deviance to serious crimes.

- Crime is socially defined. No behaviour is inherently good or evil, and we must understand the social context of an act before we can determine whether it is deviant and how it should be classified. Also, the form of laws and the specific behaviour that is prohibited vary greatly in different places and at different times.

- Consensus theorists believe that laws represent the will of most of the people in a particular society. By contrast, conflict theorists feel that law reflects power relationships in society, as those with power use the law to help maintain their position. Some laws fit each of these perspectives.

- Like other disciplines, criminology continually moves into new research areas. Three of the newest subfields in criminology are green criminology, terrorism studies, and surveillance studies.

NET WORK

Privacy is a major concern among criminologists who study surveillance. Do you know how much Facebook and Google know about you? You will likely be surprised when you find out. Because these social media sites may change, I won't provide specific instructions on how to obtain this information, but rather links to two sites that provide instructions that may still work. If they don't, just Google the instructions.

For Facebook, follow these instructions: https://www.facebook.com/help/405183566203254.

https://www.sciencealert.com/how-to-find-out-your-facebook-data-advertising-likes-download.

For Google: https://www.cnbc.com/2018/03/29/how-to-download-a-copy-of-everything-google-knows-about-you.html *OR* https://www.theguardian.com/commentisfree/2018/mar/28/all-the-data-facebook-google-has-on-you-privacy.

The Social Context of Dispute Settlement and the Rise of Law

2

RODNEY KUENEMAN
University of Manitoba

EVAN BOWNESS
University of British Columbia

Learning Objectives

After reading this chapter, you should be able to

- Understand some of the fundamental differences between small-scale societies and industrial societies.

- Trace the evolution from community-based dispute resolution processes in small-scale societies to the law as created and enforced by the state in industrial societies.

- Understand the emergence and consolidation of material resources and power in human societies and how this concentration has made it difficult to control the actions of elites.

- Discuss how law is shaped by various interests, the limitations of relying on the state to uphold social order, and some of the key threats to contemporary state legitimacy and the rule of law.

- Critically analyze the state's focus on street-level crime.

- Understand the importance of restorative dispute settlement processes in small-scale societies and relate this to their recent reappearance in modern state systems.

- Understand why knowledge of social and historical context is important in understanding the existence and operation of legal systems.

All human communities have to deal with conflict and develop ways of maintaining social order. In small-scale societies, people lived face-to-face and were known to one another, so when disputes arose, victims or their relatives were responsible for returning harmony to the relations between conflicting parties. As societies grew in size and complexity and became increasingly impersonal and unequal, the law emerged as a formal tool for managing discord. In this chapter we use sociological and historical perspectives to explore the changing social context of dispute settlement. We begin with a discussion of small-scale societies, then move to an analysis of the concentration of social power and its relationship to the formation of states and the rise of law. This sets the stage for an analysis of two current weaknesses in modern-day states: they are failing to sufficiently regulate corporate behaviour, and they are over-emphasizing street-level crime. We conclude with a discussion of what we see as a return to principles of personal dispute settlement in the form of restorative justice.

This textbook is about crime. It is important to realize that crime does not exist in all societies. In a technical sense, a crime is a violation of a law, and not all societies have had formulated laws. While each society has had to develop a moral order complete with stated expectations for acceptable behaviour, not all societies have developed laws to restrain their members. The creation of law requires the existence of a central body, such as a **state**, that develops law and enforces compliance with it. This is not merely a matter of semantics. For much of human history, social order was maintained by other means.

It is equally important to note that for most of human history, criminal law as we know it has not been part of the social fabric. In societies without a state, harms between individuals were resolved by various forms of redress. Even in societies with a state apparatus, many disputes are regulated by civil law. Under civil law, the state adjudicates between the parties to the dispute in an effort to repair the damage. Criminal law comes into existence at the point where the state declares itself to be the injured party for certain types of infractions. In its narrowest sense, criminology is concerned with this subset of laws and social infractions. But to understand the broad question of social order, it is important to see criminal law in a historical and social context that considers the full spectrum of dispute settlement practices.

The analysis in this chapter follows Lenski (1966), who emphasized the changing **mode of production** in his classification of societies, which had five categories: hunting and gathering, pastoral, horticultural, agricultural, and industrial. We will look at how the social context of dispute resolution changed as hunting and gathering societies slowly evolved into industrial societies. Particularly important to this analysis is the evolution of the **class** structure of society and how this relates to dispute settlement and the law. This chapter will show how any discussion of custom, law, and dispute settlement must be placed in its social context if we are to understand how each human society settles the troubles that arise within it. As patterns of societal and economic organization change, so do forms of dispute settlement.

Dispute Resolution in Small-Scale Society

Small-Scale Society and the Origin of Law

For most of human existence, we lived in small hunting and gathering communities. Within these communities, cooperation and **kinship** ties were the essential means of preserving harmony and restoring order. Many of these societies had no centralized structure for decision making, which meant that these communities had to rely on various mechanisms to keep the peace.

The general goal of dispute settlement processes is to restore order. However, the nature of the social order, and the groups that have gained the most advantage as a result of that order, have changed significantly throughout human social

state
As defined by Max Weber (1864–1920), the state is an institution that claims the exclusive right to the legitimate exercise of force in a given territory through the use of police to enforce laws or the army to maintain civil stability. While there have been stateless societies, most complex societies have state systems of formal government and administrative bureaucracies.

mode of production
The dominant way of organizing the creation of products and services for consumption in a society. Historically, the mode of production has evolved from subsistence-based in hunting and gathering societies to commodity-based in industrial capitalist societies.

class
A concept advanced by Karl Marx (1818–1883) to describe a social group's relationship to what is produced in a given mode of production. Examples discussed here include the merchant class during the transition to capitalism, the bourgeois class during the Industrial Revolution, and the elite class in contemporary capitalism.

kinship
Social relationships that stem from belonging to the same family, lineage, or cultural group.

history. This chapter will show how law emerged and evolved to maintain a system in which social inequality increased. We start with a description of the main attributes of hunting and gathering societies, which although not generalizable to all small-scale societies, is useful here as an "**ideal type**."

Without underestimating the often harsh realities of life in small-scale societies, there is no question that such communities were characterized by strong **collective solidarity**. Whether they lived in the High Arctic, on the plains, or in the tropical rain forests, hunters and gatherers were well aware that they were part of a natural ecosystem in which there were forces they could not control. They were aware of their individual vulnerability and realized that their collective life was an exercise in mutual survival. The cooperative, mutual-aid character of these societies was not accidental—the near certainty of death for those who lacked the assistance of the group strengthened the group's social cohesion and increased the members' chances for survival.

Another factor that increased solidarity was the relative absence of material inequality. In a **subsistence**-based society that generated little or no **surplus**, it was necessary for the group to share the fruits of the day's hunting or foraging. Typically, everyone received an equal share, regardless of the extent and nature of each one's contribution. In such a distribution system, there may have been collective scarcity if food was not found, but there was never relative poverty in the sense that some ate while others went hungry. Though a member was not expected to love everyone else, each individual was expected to care for all other members of the community. This ensured that they too would be taken care of in the nonproductive times of their life such as childhood, old age, and sickness. The mutual benefit that characterized social relationships in small-scale societies kept greed and selfishness in check.

Subsistence-based societies were unable to produce or store large amounts of food; this meant that food gathering and hunting were regular cooperative activities in which all able-bodied members took part. The division and distribution of food to all community members underscored the understanding that everyone had a right to the yield—food was a group possession. The need to move regularly limited the amount of personal belongings a person could accumulate, and since each member had access to the same raw materials, there was little difference in individuals' possessions. There was no individual "self" of the sort so familiar in our society; the collective interests of the entire group were all-powerful.

The absence of surplus suppressed the emergence of significant material inequality and any form of state-like political institution to manage disputes over surplus resources. Small-scale societies had no distinct source of authority independent of the collective will. In such societies, the only form of power available to special individuals was influence, which was based on status derived from hunting skill, sex, wisdom, or generosity, and not on differential access to or accumulation of material resources. Social status was a group property, not a personal attribute. The members of the group could give status and take it away. Hoebel (1973, 82) comments on the position of the Inuit headman: "[He] possesses no fixed authority; neither does he enter into formal office. He is not elected, nor is he chosen by any formal process. When other men accept his judgment and opinions, he is headman. When they ignore him, he is not." Thus, if an esteemed individual became arrogant or tried to force others to comply in ways that were

ideal type
A theoretical construct abstracted from experience that brings together observed characteristics in different contexts to generalize for analytic purposes. Empirical observations never entirely match the conceptual ideal, which instead can only be used as a standard for making higher-order observations.

collective solidarity
A state of social bonding or interdependency that rests on similarity of beliefs and values, shared activities, and ties of kinship and cooperation among members of a community.

subsistence
Production being only sufficient to meet immediate necessities.

surplus
Production of goods and services beyond immediate needs. In hunting and gathering societies there was often little if any surplus since the production from hunting and gathering was used up in subsistence. In modern societies, more is produced than is needed for subsistence, so there is a surplus that takes the form of private property.

deemed inappropriate, the group could remove the special status in the interests of the group.

In such close and intimate quarters, members were reluctant to harm or wrong one another because they relied on one another for their subsistence. Each member learned to cultivate personal restraint and impulse control in order to prevent the breakdown of a working order. Colson (1974) shows how these social circumstances fostered the development of forbearance, the avoidance of disputes, the sharing of resources, and the tolerance of human foibles. She relates how the Tonga of Zambia attempted to sidestep controversial issues and how they were reluctant to allow others to drag them into disputes. Their social structure, and their fear of attack by sorcerers, worked against outbreaks of violence or other forms of retaliation and contributed to the development of self-restraint.

Colson also notes that the Tonga did not lack "occasion for quarrels and hostility but they learn[ed] that they must control their hostility, their greed, and their envy if they [were] to survive" (61). Such communities could effectively punish any individual who consistently went his or her own way. The self-restraint that members exercised stemmed not only from the close, intimate, and friendly ties that are a product of common life, but also from the fear of reprisal and the desire to keep hostilities from surfacing and disturbing the business of living.

Dispute Settlement in the Absence of Surplus and Resource Inequality

Of course, disputes still arose in small-scale societies. Newman (1983) provides rich detail concerning the types of disputes that arose among hunter-gatherers. For instance, many disputes concerned women. Women were valuable producers, so adultery, failure to honour marriage agreements, and the taking of a woman by an enemy caused serious disruptions. While women were not necessarily considered the property of their fathers or husbands, there was an interest in controlling them as valuable resources within the kinship system. Other causes of conflict included improper food distribution, asymmetrical gift exchange, laziness, stinginess, theft, and murder. Theft was an infrequent offence among nomadic foragers because of the relative absence of property. Murders were relatively infrequent and almost always resulted from disputes over women.

Regardless of the cause, the major goal of dispute settlement in small-scale societies was to restore harmonious relations between the parties in conflict. It was essential that problems be settled as quickly as possible in mutually agreeable ways so as not to impede group life. The absence of an independent political institution meant that disputants typically had to resolve their differences without an adjudicator (Gulliver 1979). The community pressured the parties in a dispute to meet and bring an end to the discord. Each party had to exchange information with the other in order to learn the other party's needs and expectations. Through these exchanges, an attempt was made to move towards a mutually agreeable outcome and the restoration of harmony. While there were many specific variants to this form of dispute settlement, this approach resulted in a general airing of all the issues that had created friction between the parties, which helped keep the conflict from escalating and brought the dispute to mutually satisfying conclusion.

Potential troublemakers recognized that at some point they would have to confront those whom they had directly harmed.

The primary method of redress in small-scale societies was **self- or kin-based redress** (Newman 1983). The responses available ranged from public criticism, shaming rituals, and temporary ostracism to expulsion from the group, blood feuds, and reprisal killings. Because there was no centralized authority, the injured party had to initiate the dispute process. This does not mean that the victim was free to do whatever he or she wished to an offender. Each society had customary expectations regarding the appropriateness of various reprisals. Too harsh a response could lead to group disapproval and sanctions. When the reprisal was considered more serious than the original offence, the initial offence was expunged and the original offender became the injured party. It is important to emphasize here that self-redress is a regulated social process. Small-scale societies are not inherently violent, nor are they constantly feuding. It is true that disputes did escalate into blood feuds and cycles of revenge killings, but even these proceeded in an orderly fashion. Furthermore, each small-scale society had a body of custom that was coupled with the fear of reprisal; this acted as a brake on escalation by defining the appropriate level of redress for various offences. Formalized civil or criminal law was not necessary for these small, kin-based communities to restore order. An individual who violated a custom suffered the consequences.

Advisor Systems

A less common method of dispute resolution in small-scale societies was the **advisor system** (Newman 1983). This was really an extension of the self-redress method of dispute settlement because it was ultimately the victim or kin who enforced any retaliation. Disputants approached advisor, who were typically distinguished warriors, hunters, or speakers. They were mature, although not always the oldest men in the community, and they were regarded as public repositories of wisdom about customs and rituals.

self- or kin-based redress

Self-based redress exists where the society allows the harmed party to take matters into his or her own hands in order to seek a settlement. This could be revenge or a successful negotiation of some kind of compensation. Some societies resort to *kin-based* redress, which involves a member of a kin group seeking a settlement on the harmed party's behalf.

advisor system

An extension of the self- or kin-based redress system of dispute settlement. It involves—albeit in a relatively passive way—a third-party decision maker (or makers).

During feudal times, disputes were settled by individuals or kinship groups rather than through the involvement of the state.

FOCUS
BOX 2.1

TRADITIONAL INUIT AND OJIBWAY DISPUTE SETTLEMENT

The practice in one Inuit village was to call the entire village together and to put the actual event forward as a *hypothetical* event that might happen some time in the future. All people—including the miscreant and his victim—were required to put forward their views as to how things might be handled peacefully and properly were the situation ever to arise. There was no blaming, no pointing of fingers, and no requirement of explanation; nor was there ever any discussion, much less imposition, of either punitive or restitutionary response. At an Ojibway Reserve in my district similar dynamics governed. While the miscreant and his victim were summoned before an Elders Panel, there was never any discussion of what had happened and why, of how each party felt about the other or of what might be done by way of compensation. Nor was there any imposition of punishment. Each party was instead provided with a counselling Elder who worked privately to "cleanse his spirit." When both counselling Elders so signified by touching the peace pipe, it would be lit and passed to all. It was a signal that both had been "restored to themselves and to the community." If they privately arranged recompense of some sort, that was their affair. As far as the community was concerned, the matter was over. While I have not learned what the private counselling did consist of, I have been told that it did not involve retrieval and re-examination of the past in either its factual or emotional facets. It concentrated upon the future, and its spiritual component was central.

As a footnote, such ethics also cast the behaviour of native victims in a very different light. Refusal or reluctance to testify or, when testifying, to give anything but the barest and most emotionless recital of events, may of course have been prompted by fear of the accused, by fear of the court, by love for and forgiveness of the accused or by any other such "sensible" reason (including the possibility, of extreme rarity in my experience, that they are uncomfortable because they are lying). Another reason, culturally foreign to us, could be that giving testimony face to face with the accused is simply considered wrong. It was not part

of the traditional processes described above, where in fact every effort seems to have been made to *avoid* such direct confrontation. I recall one Indian woman who repeated her entire story of abuse to me in vivid detail before going into court and then asked me to do whatever I could to have the court send her very dangerous assailant to jail for as long as possible. Ten minutes later she took the witness stand and absolutely refused to say anything of an accusatory nature. When such witnesses regularly ask why they have to repeat their stories in court when they have already told "us" (meaning the police and the Crown), I have come to suspect that it is more than fear or embarrassment at work. I suspect instead that it is perceived as ethically wrong to say hostile, critical, implicitly angry things about someone *in their presence*, precisely what our adversarial trial rules have required. . . . In fact, we have taken this legal challenge into our daily lives, exhorting each person to open up with the other, to be honest and up front, to get things off our chests, and so on, all of which are, to traditional native eyes, offensive in the extreme. When they refuse to follow the exhortations of our rules, we judge them as deficient in rule-obedience or, worse still, rule-less. In our ignorance we have failed to admit the possibility that there might be rules other than ours to which they regularly display allegiance, an allegiance all the more striking because it is exercised in defiance of our insistent pressures to the contrary.

Questions for Critical Thinking

1. Discuss three ways in which this method of dispute resolution differs from the way cases are handled in our criminal court system.

2. Can you think of some reasons why restorative justice does not yet play a significant role in resolving disputes in Canada?

Source: Rupert Ross (1989), "Leaving Our White Eyes Behind: The Sentencing of Native Accused." 3 *Canadian Native Law Reporter* 1 at 5–6.

The dispute settlement process was activated when one or both parties sought out one of these high-status figures. They were not required to turn to this third party, but it was expected that they would do so. Each party presented its case, and after considering the facts, the advisor recommended what should be done. He interpreted the case with respect to custom, and it was his role to ensure that the social group's conception of appropriate behaviour was protected. He was a moral authority, but he could not enforce compliance. He could, however, attempt to influence the disputants with shaming rituals and compelling arguments.

An advisor gained status by being able to settle disputes before revenge was undertaken. A demonstrated ability to resolve disputes peacefully strengthened his moral authority. In the event that the advisor overstepped his bounds, the community stopped using him as an advisor; thus, the advisor system was still firmly controlled by the community.

Most hunting and gathering societies relied on self-redress; a smaller proportion developed an advisor system. In general, the dispute settlement processes used by small-scale societies were designed to restore social integration and harmony. Any discord created by disputants interfered with the positive relationships among group members, and the group could not afford long-standing rifts of this sort. As Ross (1989) points out, traditional Inuit and Ojibway dispute settlement mechanisms provide a dramatic contrast to the assumptions embedded in the Canadian criminal justice system (see Box 2.1).

The Transformation from Small-Scale Society to the State

The Slow Emergence of Social Power and Inequality

On the whole, small-scale societies succeeded in avoiding outbreaks of serious discord. Each member of the community exercised some measure of control over others, so **power** remained diffuse. The community dealt with discord in such a way that victim and offender could again enter into harmonious interactions after a mutually agreeable settlement of a dispute had been reached. Social power was generally shared and was kept under the control of the community as a whole. It was the *group* that moved against the interests of individuals or factions when their actions were viewed as a serious threat to cohesiveness. But new forms of power led to important changes. The emergence of economic surpluses gave rise to "pyramidal" power, whereby a small **elite class** was able to monopolize control of decision making. This was, in effect, the state in its most rudimentary form.

Within the last 6,000 to 8,000 years, as a result of their own development or the diffusion of an outside culture, most hunting and gathering societies have been transformed into pastoral, horticultural, agricultural, or industrial societies (Newman 1983). At some point during this transformation, the practice of face-to-face community-led redress was ruptured. The emergence of the concept of private property slowly and progressively concentrated power in the hands of a few families and individuals. The advent of privately owned land and livestock meant that the more fortunate members of the community were able to generate a surplus. This surplus enabled them to rely less on the community for their survival. In these circumstances, some ancient patriarchs began defining women as property, to secure control of not only their labour but also their reproductive capacity, "in order to ensure that there would be determinate heirs to function as the designatable future owners of individually held accumulations of private property" (Clark and Lewis 1977, 113).

In small-scale societies, individuals had been expected to discharge their obligations directly to other community members. Slowly, the social elites were

power
Max Weber saw power as the ability to realize one's goals despite resistance from others. In small-scale societies, the power to make decisions and affect group life was not institutionalized in social structures, and it was shared by the members of the group. In modern societies, power has become formally encoded in law, and authority (the legitimate use of power) is bestowed by social institutions.

elite class
The social class that controls the majority of material resources and power in a modern society.

able to redirect this exchange to enhance their position in the changing social order. The goods that had been readily available to all members in a simple economy of sharing were now distributed in patterns that reflected the stratified nature of pastoral, horticultural, agricultural, and industrial orders. These new modes of production made it increasingly possible for powerful groups and individuals to extract surplus value from those less powerful. The ability of some people to have other people generate personal wealth for them greatly accelerated the formation of structured inequality—that is, patterns of concentrated wealth, resources, and power. Less powerful segments in society found it increasingly difficult to resist those social forces that were compromising their interests.

The state emerged in agricultural society, and it represented the interests of the powerful. The growing size and complexity of social systems gave rise to the need for large bureaucracies, which were increasingly under the control of elites, whose personal interests became fused with those of the state. Human history was thus firmly established on a course that would generate hitherto unseen levels of surplus and poverty, and therefore social inequality. The interests of entire groups were devalued and subordinated to the interests of powerful factions and the state. The equality of condition in small-scale societies had been replaced by a class system rife with disparities, and the law became a tool for maintaining that class system.

Transformation in the Forms of Dispute Resolution

Changing Forms of Dispute Settlement

As societies changed, so did the types of disputes that arose in them. For example, with the emergence of private property, theft became possible. Also, increased social inequality made theft attractive to the "have-nots." Emerging concepts of rent and contracts led to disputes that required a codified body of civil law. Finally, the emergence of surplus meant that disputes could be settled by the payment of a fine to compensate the party that had been wronged. For example, under Anglo-Saxon law, if a woman was raped, a compensatory fee was paid to either her husband or her father, depending on who exercised the rights of ownership over her at the time of the offence. The fee was not paid directly to the woman herself, because she was not perceived as the person who had been wronged by the act (Clark and Lewis 1977).

As new technologies developed, the evolution from social structures such as elders' councils, to chiefdoms, to paramount chiefdoms, and eventually states, set the stage for a legal order of intensely concentrated social power. Increased productive capacity resulted in disputes concerning property, accompanied by increasingly complex legal codifications to deal with them. The creation of chiefdoms and eventually states was accompanied by the emergence of offences such as treason, slander, and libel, and, in general, the possibility for criminal law, defined as offences against the Crown.

The transformation of the hunting and gathering social form and the emergence of new dispute-settlement processes occurred gradually. Among the greatest changes was the massive concentration of social power. Once the checks on the accumulation of wealth and power that had bound small-scale societies together were undercut, the stage was set for the emergence of a state system.

A Brief History of the Modern State

The emergence of states over the past 3,000 or 4,000 years has created a rich and complex social tapestry. We will outline some of the fundamental changes in the distribution of social power and inequality that occurred during the transition from land-based **feudalism** to the modern capitalist state. These changes set the stage for modern commercial, industrial societies and for their legal systems. The case of England provides the basis for our discussion of law in Western democratic states because our goal is to understand the social context of legal systems in Canada and the United States. The analysis of law in state systems in other historical circumstances is beyond the scope of this chapter.

A Centralization of Power

Feudalism was a social system based on land tenure that in Western Europe was at its height between 1000 and 1500 CE. Serfs were required to work the central manorial farm and to provide the feudal lord with produce and/or money payments in return for their right to use the land. This relationship was quasi-familial and was based on subjection; even so, the lord had a duty to protect and feed his serfs in hard times. The lord controlled the land, but a serf could lose the right to use it only if he neglected the land or failed to meet his obligations.

As feudalism developed, the widespread collective solidarity on which small-scale societies were based was replaced with notions of individual responsibility, and money settlements and fines were used to settle serious disputes. In small-scale societies, compliance with local customs relied on interpersonal dynamics, since no centralized source of power had emerged to enforce laws. Once feudal lords were able to consolidate some power in England, they began to develop a body of law to deal with disputes. Under this system, trial by ordeal (using such methods as walking on hot coals or reaching into boiling water to pick up a pebble) was a means of establishing guilt or innocence for those who could not find some other way to settle a dispute. This set the stage for the emergence of law, in the course of which the *dispute settlement practices used in small-scale societies were replaced by feudal lords and laws.*

Following the Norman Invasion in 1066, William the Conqueror declared himself the "supreme landlord" of all England, which meant that all individuals who held land held *his* land. Over succeeding centuries, the English kings slowly expanded and consolidated their power over the feudal landscape. These kings saw themselves, or "the Crown," as the injured party when a crime was committed because the harm was against "the king's peace." Thus compensation was paid to the nobility, the kings, and the lords and bishops rather than to kinship groups. This created the foundation for the current criminal justice system. The Crown replaced the victim as the injured party, and compensation to the victim's family was replaced by punitive fines or imprisonment.

feudalism
A system of economic and social organization found historically in several areas of the world based around a feudal manor, which included a central farm owned by a landlord and small landholdings for a class of bonded farm labourers called serfs.

common law
The legal tradition found in English Canada, derived from feudal England, where it became the practice for the king to resolve disputes. Decisions made by the king and courts became the basis for future dispute settlements throughout the realm.

SEARCH FOR:
"Historical Origins of Government's Monopoly on Criminal Justice," National Center for Policy Analysis (USA)

A central authority had emerged in England to replace the authority of feudal lords. The king's system of Royal Courts created a **common law** that became available to all individuals who sought the jurisdiction of the Crown rather than that of their family or local lord. As Jeffery (1969) has stated, "The family was no longer involved in law and justice. The State was the offended unit, and the State was the proper prosecutor in every case of crime." The law and the courts played a pivotal role in this undertaking to consolidate centralized political and economic power. The growth of trade and the rise of the merchant class also contributed to the decline of the feudal system and to the rise of towns and cities at the expense of the rural manors. Cities began to arise during the reign of King John (r. 1199–1216), and though they were situated on land controlled by feudal lords, they fell under the jurisdiction of the Crown. A new system of social relationships developed based on commerce rather than on feudal obligations.

The Coalition of Merchants and Monarchs: The Rise of the Merchant Class

William the Conqueror created a state apparatus in England when he made all nobles take an oath to establish him as their feudal overlord. With this came the power to create laws to govern the kingdom, Royal officials to protect the king's interests, and Royal Courts to dispense the king's justice. However, maintaining monarchial power was not easy. A breakdown of feudal obligations and the feudal tax system meant a loss of revenue for the Crown, which needed to find new ways to finance its military so as to maintain its legitimacy. This was accomplished by going outside the feudal system to negotiate loans with merchants, using land as collateral, at a time when merchants were gaining considerable power through the expansion of trade.

The kings wanted to consolidate their power and needed resources to accomplish this; the merchants wanted a unified and safe trading area (Chambliss 1969; Hall 1969a). The state would become the vehicle for the Crown and its merchant allies to overcome resistance to the new social order, resistance driven by bandits and rebellious land barons. To gain the support of the merchants, King Henry VIII conceded that Parliament would have control over tax revenues and the legislative function. Thus the state, which was staffed by the merchant class, would define the social order. Laws would be passed by Parliament.

The rising merchant class benefited from this new arrangement, for it allowed them greater access to land. When Henry VIII expropriated church lands, more than one-sixth of the land in England was removed from its connection to feudalism and was available for purchase. Henry sold this land to friends and allies, for whom he created peerages with seats in the House of Lords. This more than doubled the king's revenues. The feudal system continued to decline during the transition to capitalism. Many lords were tied to feudal land arrangements of rent and were financially ruined by the changes. Eventually, their lands too were freed of feudal ties and became part of the commodity market, to be bought and sold as private property in the interest of profit. In 1540, Henry VIII gave his support to the Statute of Wills, which made most land in England transmittable by will. The role of the Crown had changed from that of shared owner of land under feudalism to that of land regulator via the state, which was becoming a separate and sovereign entity.

Under feudalism, serfs had been tied to the land. Now they were freed from the land, as were the lords. In addition, much of the land that had been controlled by the church was made available as commons for serfs to graze their animals. However, the new owners enclosed a great deal of this land for wool production and thoroughly disrupted the lives of the commoners. The right of commoners to hunt, fish, and gather wood on their lord's manor was extinguished under the new property relations. For instance, the Black Act of 1723 increased the number of offences for which the courts could impose the death penalty; these harsh measures were seen as necessary to compel the common people to abandon these feudal practices (Thompson 1976). The new land regulations displaced the rural workforce, which became the new urban workforce in the factories that had been made possible by technological innovation.

These fundamental changes gave increased importance to commerce and money. The close and personal ties of fealty and its reciprocal duties and obligations were eclipsed by the abstract, anonymous transactions of money in commercial enterprise. The advent of paper currency, the growth of banking institutions, and the development of credit instruments created new opportunities for theft by trusted third parties. The famous Carrier's Case of 1473 made it clear that the law of theft would need to be refined in order to prevent intermediaries from keeping goods placed in their possession for transport (Hall 1952). In addition to this, international trade, spurred by Britain's colonial empire, necessitated an expansion and refinement of the concept of theft. Hall (1969b) describes how the law governing embezzlement was enacted to make theft of paper money and commercial bonds a crime. When a business was run by members of a household, behaviour was regulated by custom and family ties; but as businesses grew, they needed to hire employees from the community who had no other ties to the owners. Transactions between unrelated parties would henceforth be regulated by law because of the absence of customary ties between them.

Law and the Transition to Capitalism

During the mid-1500s, the king sought to further consolidate power and found that he could make great inroads into the common law by throwing his support behind the merchant class. In return for taxes and loans, the Crown placed the power of the state behind the laws of commerce and enforced these laws. Tigar and Levy (1977) documented this new alliance, in which the merchant class supported the legislative and judicial power of the Crown in exchange for the development of legal mechanisms that would strengthen their class position and increase their fortunes. This guaranteed a primary role for law and lawyers in the new industrial, capitalist mode of production. The king's support of merchant law as the law of the land helped stabilize the necessary social and legal conditions for commerce. The merchant class supported the Crown's aspirations because its members needed a stable legal system in order to conduct their affairs.

The growth of commerce, spurred by the **Industrial Revolution** and the expansion of trade, required greater uniformity and enforceability of trading arrangements. Towns, cities, and even nation-states realized that a system of laws,

Industrial Revolution
A period of social transformation from the mid-1700s until the mid-1800s, marked primarily by new manufacturing technologies and the harnessing of new forms of energy, such as coal and steam.

capitalism
The mode of production based on private property and commodities owned and produced for the purpose of generating profit.

bourgeois class
The term *bourgeois class,* or *bourgeoisie,* was used by Marx to refer to the capitalist class in modern societies following the Industrial Revolution.

and a court system to apply them, would be essential if trade was to stabilize and grow. **Capitalism** now directed the mode of production. The volume of trade, its growing impersonality, the practice of joint ventures, and the long distances involved in international trade created the need for a mechanism to secure the interests of traders. Legal contracts, which had existed since Roman times, became the dominant mechanism tying social relationships together in the new social order. According to Ferdinand Tönnies (1987), modern society came to exist as a superior power to enforce the terms set out in the contracts between members of the capitalist **bourgeois class**. Lawyers grew in number and importance as new contract forms were developed to meet the increasingly complex trade arrangements of the time. The power of the nation-state was solidified around the interests of commerce, and the role of custom and kinship was eroded. The basis for the new social order was predicated on law, in both commercial and criminal realms.

The power of the bourgeois class in Parliament grew as the power of the feudal nobility and landed aristocracy waned. Peasants and workers were not represented in this early Parliament, and as a result, the modern state developed under the influence of the bourgeoisie. The rise of the labour movement would come later, but the power of organized labour has never matched that of organized business (Miliband 1969). While advances have been made in democratizing the state, it remains a political and legal structure for the protection of property and the interests the bourgeois class.

Contemporary State Power

As feudalism and the power of the monarchy declined, the state became the dominant institution for regulating social order and settling disputes. State decisions were backed by the military and police. The state was the superior force behind the contractual arrangements of business and property, and it ensured that the terms of those arrangements were observed.

Law has become the dominant means of regulating human affairs. Legislation and administrative directives are the legal apparatus on which nation-states are now based. Property, commerce, real estate, labour, and contractual agreements are all regulated by law. Municipalities and corporations are governed by law, the protection of the environment is regulated by law, and disputes over persons and property are handled through family, civil, and criminal law. In short, the law is the principal means whereby human activity is prohibited, permitted, or required.

Interest Groups and the Law

As shown in earlier sections, the merchant class has long succeeded in promoting and protecting its interests, and in doing so it has shaped both the state and its laws. But business interest groups are not the only ones that approach the state to promote their interests. A variety of cultural, ethnic, minority, class, economic, and political interest groups also lobby the state. These diverse groups are often at odds with one another, and the state cannot satisfy everyone. Choices need to be made. Given the nature of electoral politics, the state is under some pressure to promote the values and interests of the majority as well as those of powerful minorities in order to maintain legitimacy and popularity.

Drug legislation is one example of how the state responds to various forms of outside pressure. According to Becker (1963), drug legislation in the United States was the result of the efforts of a civil servant, Harry Anslinger, whom Becker described as a "moral entrepreneur" who strongly pushed an anti-drug agenda. And according to Shirley Small (1978), who researched Canadian narcotics legislation, strong anti-Asian racism was a motivating force in campaigns for harsh drug laws. Comack (1985) has shown that these anti-Asian sentiments are best understood as having been grounded in labour disputes, which were addressed in racial rather than class terms.

Graham's (1976) analysis of amphetamine legislation demonstrated the operations of special interests. Despite strong support from the American public and the president, attempts to change the Federal Drug Administration's (FDA) control of amphetamine production failed because of pressure from powerful drug companies that were profiting from drugs sold illegally into the street drug market. A legislative remedy would have done much to promote the common good with regard to this significant problem, but the power of a lobby group that gave huge donations to political campaigns stifled the attempted changes.

Analyses of the history of rape legislation (Brownmiller 1975; Clark and Lewis 1977; Kinnon 1981) show how oppressive and patriarchal laws were enacted to protect the transmission of property in the male line of descent. Fathers used rape laws to avoid transferring property to men of whom they disapproved but who had taken their daughters by bride capture. They also sought compensation for the reduction of bride price they suffered because their daughters were no longer virgins. Husbands wanted to secure control over their wives' reproductive capacity to ensure that they transferred their property to their own sons. As a consequence of all this, women and children became the property of the man of the household, and the act of rape became an offence against the husband. Over time, as the result of feminist activism, sexual assault has been redefined as a crime against the woman who has been victimized; in some jurisdictions, including Canada, a husband can now be prosecuted for raping his wife. This, of course, means that women have succeeded in having themselves redefined as persons and not merely as the property of their fathers or husbands. But there is still a great deal of dissatisfaction regarding the capacity of the law and the justice system to protect women from sexual assault.

A Failure to Regulate

The preceding section showed that the creation of law is heavily influenced by the pressure that various interest groups bring to bear on the state. **Transnational corporations** are among the most powerful of these groups. Many of these corporations have amassed so much economic power that they are hard to regulate. Some corporations are exceeding the rates of growth of national economies, and this scale gives them considerable power to resist state regulatory efforts. When a government is too restrictive in its regulatory policies, a transnational corporation can relocate operations to another country with laws more to its liking.

transnational corporation
A corporation that has sales and production in many different nations. Because of their multinational reach, these corporations are often thought to be beyond the political control of any individual nation-state.

When environmental regulations are too strict, or when occupational safety rules are too rigid, a corporation can close its production operations in that country and head somewhere else. Corporations are responsible for environmentally damaging practices that are harmful to individuals, societies, and nature itself, and these harms are not being effectively controlled by the state and the rule of law. The following accounts of victims of avoidable harms help make the point.

Reasons, Ross, and Paterson (1981) analyzed numerous instances in which Canadian workers were needlessly exposed to risks in the workplace that resulted in injury and death. Many of these dangers were known to employers and were avoidable, which led Reasons and colleagues to suggest that these casualties were "victims without crimes." In the same vein, Dowie (1977) reported that the design problems of the Ford Pinto that resulted in passenger injury and death were known by the auto manufacturer, that these problems could have been addressed by cost-effective measures, and that the corporation chose not to make the improvements. Internal Ford memos revealed that the costs of design changes had been compared to the costs of potential litigation for death, dismemberment, and injury and that the company had decided to put Pinto passengers at risk. It is hard to conceive of the deaths and injuries caused by the Pinto as accidental when those injuries and deaths were anticipated and could have been avoided. It could be argued that these deaths were homicides and that such harmful behaviour ought to have come under the purview of the Criminal Code. Ford was, in fact, charged with homicide for one of the Pinto-related deaths, in Indiana, but it was acquitted by a jury. This kind of reckless corporate behaviour persists (see Chapter 17). Clearly, today's consumer-citizen is not being protected under the rule of law from dangerous corporate misbehaviour.

The courts could move in the direction of holding corporations and their managers accountable for harms such as the one that took place in Cook County, Illinois. In 1985, three former executives of a silver-recycling plant were convicted of murder; each received a sentence of 25 years in prison and a fine of $10,000 for the death of an employee. The company had exposed workers to cyanide gas by intentionally concealing warnings of hazards from immigrant workers. It is believed that these murder convictions were the first in the United States of corporate officials in a job-related death. To date, however, governments have not pursued a vigorous policy of bringing such corporate harms under the criminal law (see Chapter 17). This case turned out to be a rarity and not a harbinger of greater corporate accountability.

Another example of the state's failure to control industrial corporate activity relates to the asbestos industry. Asbestos is a heat-resistant mineral that has been used primarily in building insulation. The substance has known carcinogenic and disease-causing properties that kill around 107,000 people annually, according to the World Health Organization (WHO 2010). According to Brodeur (1985), the industry was aware of the health hazards related to the inhalation of asbestos particles as early as the 1930s but withheld this information from workers and did not take steps to improve workplace safety. The costs of asbestos have been enormous. A Canadian study (Tompa et al. 2017) found that considering only cases of asbestos-related lung cancer and mesothelioma *newly diagnosed* in 2011 (representing only a small portion of all such cases), the costs would be nearly $2.5 billion dollars. Juries have found asbestos corporations responsible, and this has unleashed a flood of litigants. The estimated total cost of all claims in the United States is as high as $265 billion (Carroll et al. 2002). At least 73 companies have filed for bankruptcy due to asbestos litigation (Carroll et al. 2005). In an attempt to avoid bankruptcy, many companies offered to settle asbestos claims out of court in exchange for a maximum ceiling on their liability. In this situation, the state has found itself struggling to balance the rights of individuals to damages on one hand, with the needs of corporations to keep their businesses running and protect their workers from unemployment on the other.

What makes the asbestos example especially troubling is that, while people were clearly harmed with malice and intent, those responsible were not prosecuted by the criminal law. Reasons and colleagues have made a compelling case that many "accidents" in the workplace are not unforeseen and therefore are not accidental. In their view, these harms should be conceptualized as "assaults on workers" and fall under the Criminal Code rather than Occupational Health and Safety Legislation: "It has been revealed that asbestos companies continued to expose workers to that substance in spite of the fact that they had had evidence concerning its fatal effects for some thirty years. Such conscious, premeditated, and rational behaviour undoubtedly led to thousands of deaths and disabilities. Nonetheless, asbestos companies are only liable to civil lawsuits" (1981, 6).

Transnational corporations exist to make profits for investors, and those profits have often been maximized by reckless and dangerous behaviour. The serious harm to employees, customers, and the environment that has resulted suggests that powerful human actors are currently operating beyond the control of law. Marchak (1991) described some of the serious harms stemming from the creation of **free trade zones** in Third World countries. Countries create free trade zones within their borders to attract corporations. The corporations that establish branch plants within these zones have often been able to negotiate highly favourable terms, including freedom from taxation, exemptions from labour and environmental legislation, and flexible labour regulations that allow them to hire workers very cheaply. One of the more harmful practices described by Marchak involves the hiring of noncitizen, female workers from neighbouring states in microchip production and in the garment industry. For example, "Singapore has imported Malaysian, Thai, Filipina, and Indonesian women as guest workers. These women have no citizen rights and no civil rights, and are deported if their eyesight or productivity fails to please, or if markets slow down" (147). When they are sent back home, they receive no compensation or benefits and typically face severe financial, social, emotional, and health difficulties.

At present, many such harms cannot be brought to the courts for remedy because the state has not defined them as violations of existing law. One might ask whether the modern state has truly established the rule of law when actions like these are not subject to regulation and control. In some important ways, the legal power of states has been superseded by the economic power of corporations. The law cannot impose order in areas of social life where the state has not established its jurisdiction. The absence of protection from the raw economic power of corporations places citizens in harm's way.

Snider (1999, 2000) has described in detail many acts of corporate impropriety in Canada as well as the steps the Canadian government has taken to "make corporate crime disappear." She notes that "the significance of the disappearance

free trade zone
A specially designated geographical area within a nation that is exempt from the regulations and taxation normally imposed on business. These zones are intended to facilitate cross-border production and trade. Zones like these are found along the US–Mexico border, where they are referred to as *maquilladoras*.

of corporate crime speaks volumes about the potential of state law to harness capital. The corporate counter-revolution illustrates how profoundly dependent the promulgation and enforcement of nation-state law is on the balance of powers operating within a society" (1999, 204). She describes how, when unions or social movements are strong, such as in Scandinavia, corporate "downsizing and decriminalization will be resisted longer and more effectively" (204). When they are weak, as in Canada and the United States, corporate wrongdoing is increasingly decriminalized and less and less scrutinized. She adds that progressive social movements have a vital role to play in pressuring states to use law as a mechanism for controlling harmful corporate behaviour. This makes it all the more urgent that we critique the state's failure to protect us from corporate crime (see Chapter 17).

A Coming Crisis in State Legitimacy?

A core function of the law is to foster a willingness to obey the rules. The rule of law depends in large measure on the willingness of the majority of citizens to comply with legal prescriptions and prohibitions. In other words, the citizenry must perceive the state as legitimate. So it is essential that the state system be seen as providing peace, security, good government, and protection from harm. Any state that fails to live up to its end of the social contract will eventually face a **crisis of legitimacy**, which can lead to civil unrest and threaten the state's power. In situations of widespread, sustained disobedience, the social control arms of the state may be unable to cope; they may even be overwhelmed. In many quarters, dissatisfaction is growing with the nation-state system because of its evident failure to regulate seriously harmful behaviour. Some examples of potential sources of state delegitimization include the following:

crisis of legitimacy
A situation where the state no longer maintains the authority to govern. Sometimes referred to as a legitimation crisis. A number of factors can contribute to such a crisis, for which there are only two possible resolutions: (a) the state regains legitimacy, or (b) a new governing body is instated.

1. The underregulated business practices of major corporations have introduced massive amounts of toxins into the air, water, soil, and food chain, with severe and profound consequences for human health. The soaring incidence of cancers, birth defects, and other human-caused forms of misery is a clear sign that the state has not been providing basic security from harm. Its limited effectiveness in regulating corporate behaviour is of growing concern. The responsibility to curb the harm caused by irresponsible corporations properly falls within the jurisdiction of the state, given that corporations are created by charters of incorporation approved by the state. Ineffective regulation may make people critical not only of the corporations but also of the state itself.

2. Systematic and profit-driven assaults on entire ecosystems have resulted in loss of diversity, loss of habitat, species extinctions, and deformities of plant and animal life forms. The cumulative consequences are so serious that they threaten the integrity of the world's ecosystem. This has been referred to as an "ecocide" (Broswimmer 2002). The fact that such destructive behaviour is not criminalized undermines the legitimacy of the nation-state system. Citizens expect the state to protect them and future generations from human-created sources of harm.

3. Economic inequality is approaching extremes. Today, the world's eight richest individuals (including Bill Gates of Microsoft, Jeff Bezos of Amazon, and Mark Zuckerberg of Facebook) own the same amount of wealth as the combined 3.6 billion people who comprise the bottom half of the entire global

population (Oxfam International 2017), and there have been growing calls for some form of state intervention into the distribution of wealth. The state has the legal means to limit class disparities through taxation policies that would redistribute wealth to provide basic security, health, and social justice for a greater number of people. Such progressive legislation had been used in the past, and there are increasing calls for its reintroduction. True, private wealth is private property, but it is important to remember that the notion of private property is a human invention regulated by the nation-state. The failure of nation-states to control egregious disparities of wealth has denied a large part of humanity a decent standard of living. This invites contempt for an unfeeling state apparatus, which in turn brings into question the legitimacy of the status quo and those institutions that make it possible.

These are not hypothetical concerns; we have seen signs of social upheaval, both domestically and abroad. For instance, the "Arab Spring," a wave of revolutionary uprisings in northern Africa and the Middle East, began in late 2010 when a Tunisian street vendor set himself on fire to protest the crippling unemployment plaguing the nation under then-president Zine el Abidine Ben Ali. Over the next three years, hundreds of thousands of protesters took to the streets in many countries across the region; their demands ranged from changes in specific state policies to a complete dismantling of existing governments. These demonstrations have been both nonviolent and violent. Since then, hundreds of thousands of protesters have died in struggles against police and the military. These actions have had a significant impact, spurring regime changes in Tunisia, Egypt, Libya, and Yemen and rebellions in other states, including Syria. There have been victories against oppressive states; however, grassroots efforts to democratize the region have largely faltered, and many of the fundamental issues that inspired the uprisings remain unresolved.

age fotostock/Alamy Stock Photo

These marchers were part of the Idle No More protest in Ottawa. They were marching in support of some young people who had marched 1,600 kilometres from the Whapmagoostui First Nation in northern Quebec to Ottawa in support of the movement.

Canada has seen the Idle No More movement, which Attawapiskat Chief Theresa Spence galvanized during her hunger strike in January 2013. Chief Spence called for a nation-to-nation conversation with Prime Minister Stephen Harper about omnibus legislation the federal government had introduced, which included controversial changes to the Navigable Waters Protection Act, which would have reduced protections for rivers, lakes, and coastlines. At the time, controversial projects such as the Enbridge Northern Gateway pipeline were raising concerns within Indigenous communities. The Idle No More movement was born out of a rejection of complicity in the ongoing history of colonialism and natural resource exploitation. Idle No More led to protests, flash mobs, and teach-ins across the country and has heightened awareness of issues facing Indigenous peoples in Canada.

On 26 February 2012 in Sanford, Florida, Neighbourhood Watch volunteer George Zimmerman shot and killed 17-year-old Trayvon Martin. Martin was black. In July of the following year, Zimmerman was acquitted, sparking protests across the United States, with protesters calling for an end to systemic racism and violence by the police. The protesters contended that the victims of police shootings were overwhelmingly racialized men and that those shootings reflected America's history of racism as well as the use of law to maintain inequality. The hashtag #BlackLivesMatters was created by social movement organizers Patrice Cullors, Alicia Garza, and Opal Tometi, but it wasn't until 2014, after the shooting death of Michael Brown in Ferguson, Missouri, and the uprising in its wake that the slogan became ubiquitous on the Internet through social media. A national social movement had been born, and demonstrations and rallies with thousands of participants continue to rise up in the face of the all too common occurrence of police brutality against minorities. This movement has been highly visible and has included protests by National Football League players, who have drawn attention to the movement by refusing to stand for the national anthem. The movement has been active in Canada as well, especially in Toronto, where the police have long had a poor relationship with the black community.

SEARCH FOR:
"The Path of Protest"

The growing discontent with wealth inequality in the United States has moved beyond the streets. Young people were inspired by the political campaign of Bernie Sanders, which explicitly attacked the extreme and growing economic inequality in American society. The tax reform of Donald Trump and the Republican-dominated Congress in 2017 will only accelerate this concentration of wealth and perhaps galvanize more opposition to it in US electoral politics.

In small-scale societies, every member had direct access to processes of redress; today, not everyone can afford to seek remedy through the courts. Furthermore, some serious harms are not currently subsumed under the law, and without a crime, there are few means available for victims to seek redress. Ever since feudalism gave way to capitalism, the legal process has been controlled and administered by the state, which has come to play the central role in dispute settlement. In small-scale communities, the interests of *all* members formed the basis of customary practice; today, in Western industrial societies, the interests of corporations have been given a special place in law. This has placed ordinary citizens at risk and made it more and more difficult to constrain corporations from systemically harming workers, consumers, and the ecosphere.

Full Circle: Restorative Justice and a Return to Original Forms of Dispute Settlement?

Many critics of the current justice system have advocated returning to a fundamentally different approach, one whose purpose is to restore social relationships rather than simply punish "criminals." Advocates of restorative justice seek to return the focus of the justice system to repairing the harm that has been done to the victim and the community. A key element of restorative justice is the involvement of the victim and other members of the community as active participants in the process. The restorative justice approach is meant to reconcile offenders with those they have harmed and to help communities *reintegrate* victims and offenders. The source of peace and order lies in a strong, active, and caring community. Proponents of restorative justice feel that a more humane and satisfying justice system could help rebuild communities that have been weakened by crime and other social ills.

SEARCH FOR:
Restorative Justice Online

Canada and New Zealand have led the way in the field of restorative justice. This is due at least in part to the influence of Indigenous people in these two countries. Rupert Ross (1996) discusses some of the steps undertaken in Indigenous communities that have placed a renewed emphasis on healing as the community response to individual wrongdoing. Many community leaders view the restorative justice approach as a way to restore harmonious relationships and to foster the development of healthy communities.

SEARCH FOR:
"Aboriginal Corrections Publications" Public Safety Canada

The restorative approach is not limited to Indigenous communities. The Young Offenders Act and its successor, the Youth Criminal Justice Act, mandated youth courts to look for alternative measures to traditional punishment, and options such as restitution, alternative dispute resolution, victim–offender reconciliation, community group conferences, and sentencing panels are being used much more frequently for both juvenile and adult offenders. Braithwaite and Mugford (1994) have discussed some of the ways in which the traditional practices of shame, reintegration, and healing might be introduced into modern urban settings. As outlined earlier, there are important differences in the makeup of small-scale and modern communities. When an offence occurs within the intimacy of small-scale communities it typically involves a victim and an offender who have an established bond. The trouble between them has weakened or shattered the bond, and the dispute settlement process seeks to restore the bond to the satisfaction of both parties and to reintegrate the offender into the community as a member in good standing. In modern communities, no such bond exists between many victims and offenders, who may be strangers to each other until the offence creates a connection between them. The goal of the restorative approach in this context is not to re-establish a nonexistent earlier bond; rather it is to intervene in such a way that the parties to the conflict can transform the negative ties they have to each other into positive ties. In this sense, conflict can actually serve as an opportunity for the establishment of positive bonds between former strangers, whereas normal adversarial court practice would solidify their negative ties. In other respects, the similarities are worth noting. Not only are the offender and the victim touched by the offence, but so too are their immediate circles of family and friends. To the extent that the restorative justice approach can mobilize these "communities of care" (Johnstone 2002, 51) in support of the healing process and involve them in the development of a solution they also endorse, a larger community can be created where none existed previously. The restorative approach helps empower the victims of crime in any community and increases their participation in the dispute resolution process rather than requiring them to surrender their voice to lawyers. While it is too soon to know the degree to which these practices will replace more punitive methods of justice, it is clear that these traditional ideas are being actively reconsidered.

FOCUS   BOX 2.2

RESTORATIVE JUSTICE: PRESENT PROSPECTS AND FUTURE DIRECTIONS

There is a difference of opinion as to whether restorative justice can work in communities that do not have strong social ties prior to the commission of an offence. Elmar Weitekamp sees it as follows:

Looking at the newest developments of restorative justice within the context of existing justice systems, one finds that they resemble in fact very old and ancient forms of restorative justice as used in acephelous [without governing chiefs or leaders] societies and other forms of humankind: Family group conferences, family conferences, peace circles, community circles, or circle hearings as used by indigenous people such as the Aboriginals, Maori, Inuit, the Native Indians of North America and African peoples. The new concepts and models treat crime as an offence against human relationships, recognize that crime is wrong and when it happens can further alienate the community, the family of the victim and the offender and lead to damage, disrespect, disempowerment and feelings of insecurity. The chance of the restorative justice approach is to recognize the injustice, so that in some form, equity will be restored, thus leading the participants of this process to feel safer, more respected and more empowered. It is somewhat ironic that, at the beginning of the new millennium, we have to go back to methods and forms of conflict resolution which were practised some millennia ago by our ancestors. (325)

According to this view, we need to recover the restorative practice and apply it to our efforts to repair the damage done and restore peace between parties to a dispute. There is no call for a change in the overall makeup of social relationships or other social practices of modern society. This view may be overly optimistic regarding the ability of the restorative justice principle by itself to restore peace among offenders, their victims, and their communities of care. Barbara Gray and Pat Lauderdale do not think that restorative principles will be sufficient:

Restorative justice is dependent on the foundational traditional preventative structures and practices that work together to create justice and prevent injustice. Focusing on the restorative aspects of justice without incorporating the preventative mechanisms creates injustice, for it breaks the Circle of Justice and leaves individuals and the community without the necessary cultural foundational structures to heal and prevent crime. (218)

Their point is that restorative principles are but part of a much larger social fabric that has other ways to contribute to the achievement of a Circle of Justice within the community. "The preventative mechanisms are found within the traditional teachings—for example, in ceremonies, songs, dances, stories, kinship relations, and healing and warrior societies" (218). Teachings within traditional societies promote the development of the "good mind" in each member by implanting "the concepts of love, unity, peace, equity, coexistence, cooperation, power, respect, generosity, and reciprocity" (218). Each member of the community is encouraged to use these concepts, to live in accordance with their teachings, and to retain "balance by respecting and protecting each other and the rest of the natural order" (217):

> The foundational narratives of many American Indian nations contain teachings about how humans are to live with each other and the rest of the natural world. They also provide the blueprints for societal structures: The political and spiritual form of governance, kinship relations, and specific duties and responsibilities in maintaining justice within the community. One has a duty to self and to the community to prevent injustice. . . . The duties and responsibilities of each person in the society are given and reaffirmed every time the people come together for ceremonies and social activities. (219)

> The Great Law of Peace [of the Haudenosaunee], then, is a system of checks and balances that depends not only on people not wanting to commit a transgression, but on people understanding and having the will to prevent others from breaching the peace. (220)

From this perspective, attempts to use the restorative aspect without doing the work necessary to build a larger set of preventative peacekeeping practices are unlikely to be adequate to the task.

Questions for Critical Thinking

1. Proponents of restorative justice advocate that we move away from legalistic, punishment-oriented ways of dealing with social conflict. Do you think this will work in our contemporary society? Can you find examples of restorative justice programs in your own community?

2. Some people, particularly victims of domestic violence and their supporters, have been critical of restorative justice programs. Discuss some of these criticisms.

Sources: Elmar G.M. Weitekamp, "Restorative Justice," in *Restorative Justice: Theoretical Foundations*, ed. Weitekamp and Hans-Jürgen Kerner (Portland: Willan, 2002); Gray, Barbara, and Pat Lauderdale. (2007). "The Great Circle of Justice: North American Indigenous Justice and Contemporary Restoration Programs." Contemporary Justice Review 10:2 (June): 215 25. Reprinted by permission of the publisher Taylor & Francis Ltd, http://www.tandfonline.com.

It is enticing to imagine that the use of a limited set of restorative justice principles could help repair the damage caused by anonymity, excessive individualism, a heightened form of self-interest, the erosion of cohesive communities, the competitiveness and materialism of modern society, and great inequalities of power and wealth. This is the attraction: we can repair the damage between

Photo by Ann Hermes /The Christian Science Monitor via Getty Images

A training session for a restorative justice program that is being implemented to help resolve disputes within a school system.

people who are estranged from one another without repairing the social fabric that made them indifferent strangers in the first place. While this is a small contribution to building community cohesion, it should not be underrated. There is genuine value in creating justice—the foundation for apology and forgiveness—and in creating peace and goodwill in the social circles that were disrupted by the harm done.

QUESTIONS FOR CRITICAL THINKING

1. This chapter discussed the role played by special interest groups in the passage and enforcement of particular laws. What are some of the laws that reflect the interests of some groups at the expense of others? What are some examples of laws that reflect the consensus of most members of society?
2. Assume you live in a small city. A local chemical company has been found to be improperly disposing of hazardous wastes by burying them underground. The wastes have leached into local wells and contaminated the water supply. Some say the company should be prosecuted and its operations shut down; however, the company is the largest employer in the community. Describe several ways in which the community might approach this problem. What sort of outcome is most likely?

Summary

- For most of human history, we lived in small groups. Because individuals lacked the resources to live independently, order through the enforcement of codes of conduct was based on social solidarity.

- In small-scale societies, disputes were typically settled by the parties to the dispute or by their kinship groups. The individual was expected to show a considerable degree of self-restraint, because the survival of the group depended on the cooperation of all its members.

- People in small-scale societies were relatively equal to one another. Changes in the mode of production led to new social formations in which some families and individuals gained greater access to material surplus. This led to the concentration of social power, inequality in society, and the emergence of elites, which in turn gave rise to the modern state.

- The central authority of the state undermined local kinship-based methods of resolving disputes. Harms were seen as having been done to the state, which displaced the actual victim in the dispute.

- As the merchant class grew, social life became increasingly regulated by contracts, which were regulated and enforced by an increasingly strong central state. The interests of the capitalist class became central to the state, and the rule of law became the dominant means of regulating all aspects of human affairs.

- Law is created through a process whereby various interests pressure the state. Recently, many laws have been created—or have not been created—to benefit large corporations.

- The nation-state system's ineffectiveness at providing provide peace, security, and protection from harm to large portions of humanity threatens to undermine the legitimacy of the modern state and its laws. Signs of a coming crisis in state legitimacy have appeared recently, such as the Arab Spring, Idle No More, and Black Lives Matter movements.

- In recent years we have seen a return to restorative justice practices that are similar to those used in small-scale societies.

NET WORK

You have learned in this chapter that a prominent trend in criminal justice is the return to methods of restorative justice. To learn more about methods of restorative justice, go to the Correctional Service of Canada website at http://www.csc-scc.gc.ca/publications/092/005007-5500-eng.pdf. This will give you access to a report called *Satisfying Justice*, written by the Church Council on Justice and Corrections. Using this report, answer the following questions:

1. What do the authors mean by "satisfying justice"? How can you use this concept to understand the dissatisfaction most Canadians seem to have with our current criminal justice system?
2. Describe four different types of restorative justice programs, and give an example of each.

3

Criminal Law

SIMON N. VERDUN-JONES
Simon Fraser University

Learning Objectives

After reading this chapter, you should be able to

- Define a crime.
- Identify the sources of Canadian criminal law.
- Distinguish between regulatory offences and "true crimes."
- Analyze criminal offences in terms of the *actus reus* (physical) and *mens rea* (mental) elements.
- Understand the differences between subjective and objective *mens rea* requirements.
- Describe the different ways in which a person may become a party to a criminal offence.
- Identify the basic components of the inchoate crimes of counselling, attempt, and conspiracy.
- Describe the major defences that may be raised in response to a criminal charge: not criminally responsible on account of mental disorder, mistake of fact, mistake of law, intoxication, necessity, duress, provocation, and self-defence.

Criminology is concerned with crimes and the individuals who commit them. Criminologists must acquire a basic understanding of the criminal law because it is this body of legal rules and principles that designates which types of behaviour should be prohibited and punished and whether those persons who are accused of committing crimes should be convicted and officially labelled as criminals.

What Is a Crime?

crime
Conduct that is prohibited by law and that is subject to a penal sanction (such as imprisonment or a fine).

For a lawyer, the definition of a **crime** is remarkably simple: namely, the coupling of a *prohibition* against certain conduct with a *penal sanction* (such as imprisonment or a fine). In Canada, all crimes are the products of a legislative process and are contained in statutes such as the Criminal Code. Some crimes may reflect a social consensus that certain conduct is wrong and should be punished (for example, murder and sexual assault). Other crimes may not be based on such a consensus, and a significant proportion of Canadians may not consider them to be inherently wrong and deserving of punishment (for example, possession of small amounts of street drugs for private use). While legislators must wrestle with the ongoing task of trying to bring the criminal law into line with emerging community notions of crime and justice, the police and the judiciary are required to enforce the existing criminal law, regardless of their own private views as to whether particular conduct should or should not be defined as a crime. While it is important to be aware of the intensely political nature of the process of enacting legislation dealing with crime and punishment, such considerations fall outside the scope of a chapter dealing with the existing criminal law.

What Is Criminal Law?

The body of jurisprudence known as **criminal law** includes not only the definitions of the various crimes and the specification of the respective penalties but also a set of general principles concerning criminal responsibility and a series of defences to a criminal charge. The focus of this chapter will be on the general principles underlying Canadian criminal law and the major defences that have been developed both by the Parliament of Canada and by judges in the course of deciding specific cases that have come before them.

criminal law
A body of jurisprudence that includes the definition of various crimes, the specification of various penalties, a set of general principles concerning criminal responsibility, and a series of defences to a criminal charge.

The Sources of Criminal Law

A basic question about criminal law is "Where does it come from?" There are two primary sources of Canadian criminal law: (1) legislation, and (2) judicial decisions that either interpret such legislation or state the "common law."

Federal Legislation and Criminal Law

Since Canada is a federal state, legislation may be enacted both by the Parliament of Canada and by the legislatures of the various provinces and territories. However, under the terms of the Canadian Constitution, there is a distribution of specific legislative powers between the federal and provincial or territorial levels of government. Under the terms of the *Constitution Act*, 1867, the federal Parliament has the exclusive jurisdiction to enact "criminal law and the procedures relating to criminal matters." One might think that it is relatively simple to define the term *criminal law* for the purpose of interpreting the scope of the federal criminal law power under the *Constitution Act*, 1867. However, this task is not quite as straightforward as it may appear at first glance. It was noted above that a crime can normally be defined by two basic elements: (1) a *prohibition* against certain conduct, and (2) a *penalty* for violating that prohibition. However, when the courts are required to decide whether Parliament has enacted legislation that legitimately falls within the scope of its criminal law power, a third element must be added to the definition of a crime. More specifically, the Supreme Court of Canada has ruled that the prohibition and penalty must be directed against a "public evil" or some form of behaviour that is having an injurious effect on the Canadian public. If any of these three elements is missing, the legislation may not be considered to fall within the legitimate scope of the federal criminal law power; indeed, it may be ruled invalid insofar as it intrudes into areas of legislative authority that have been specifically allocated to the provincial and territorial legislatures. Consider the problem of environmental pollution. In the case of *Hydro-Québec* (1997), the Supreme Court of Canada held that the Parliament of Canada could use its criminal law power to enact legislation that imposes penalties on those individuals who engage in serious acts of pollution. The particular legislation in question in this case was the *Canadian Environmental Protection Act*, R.S.C. 1985, c. 16. In the words of Justice La Forest, "Pollution is an 'evil' that Parliament can legitimately seek to suppress." Therefore, the *Canadian Environmental Protection Act* was considered to constitute "criminal law" because the Parliament of Canada was unequivocally concerned with the need to safeguard public health from the devastating consequences of toxic pollution. If the Supreme Court had ruled that this statute was not a genuine exercise of the Parliament of Canada's criminal law power, the Court would have ruled that the Act was invalid.

In *Reference re Assisted Human Reproduction Act* (2010), the majority of the Justices of the Supreme Court of Canada upheld the constitutionality of only a relatively small minority of the provisions of the *Assisted Human Reproduction Act* (SC 2004, c. 2). The Court ruled that many of the Act's provisions exceeded the legitimate scope of the Parliament of Canada's authority to legislate criminal law because they had usurped the exclusive jurisdiction of the provinces and territories over "hospitals, property and civil rights, and matters of a merely local nature. Section 8 of the Act states that "No person shall make use of human reproductive material for the purpose of creating an embryo unless the donor of the material has given written consent, in accordance with the regulations, to its use for that purpose." This section clearly contains a prohibition and is enforced by a penalty. Chief Justice McLachlin then identified the third requirement of a "public evil" that Parliament is entitled to address through criminal legislation. She noted that the provision "is grounded in valid criminal law purposes" and elaborated on this statement by concluding:

> At the heart of s. 8 lies the fundamental importance that we ascribe to human autonomy. The combination of the embryo's moral status and the individual's interest in his or her own genetic material justify the incursion of the criminal law into the field of consent. There is a consensus in society that the consensual use of reproductive material implicates fundamental notions of morality. This confirms that s. 8 is valid criminal law.

What important pieces of legislation has the Canadian Parliament enacted in the field of criminal law? Undoubtedly, the most significant federal statute dealing with both the *substantive criminal law* and the *procedural* law relating to criminal matters is the Criminal Code, R.S.C. 1985, c. C-46 (first enacted in 1892). "Substantive criminal law" refers to legislation that defines various criminal offences (such as murder, manslaughter, and theft) and that specifies the various legal elements that must be present before a conviction can be entered against an accused person. The term also refers to the legislation that defines the nature and scope of such defences as provocation, duress, and self-defence.

The term **criminal procedure** refers to legislation that specifies the procedures to be followed in the prosecution of a criminal case and that defines the nature and scope of the powers of criminal justice officials. For example, the procedural provisions of the Criminal Code classify offences into three categories: (1) *indictable offences*, (2) offences punishable on *summary conviction*, and (3) *"mixed" or "hybrid" offences*, which may be tried either as indictable or

criminal procedure
A body of legislation that specifies the procedures to be followed in the prosecution of a criminal case and that defines the nature and scope of the powers of criminal justice officials.

as summary conviction offences. These provisions then specify the manner in which these different categories of offences may be tried within the system of criminal courts. For example, they spell out whether these offences may be tried by a judge sitting alone or by a judge and jury, and indicate whether they may be tried before a judge of the Superior Court or by a judge of the Provincial (or Territorial) Court. Indictable offences carry the most serious penalties upon conviction of the accused. The procedural provisions of the Criminal Code are also concerned with defining the nature and scope of the powers of such officials as police officers. For example, these provisions stipulate the nature and scope of the powers of the police in relation to the arrest and detention of suspects. Likewise, the Criminal Code articulates the powers of judges in relation to the important task of sentencing convicted offenders.

In addition to the Criminal Code, a number of other federal statutes unquestionably create "criminal law." These include the *Controlled Drugs and Substances Act*, S.C. 1996, c. 19, and the *Youth Criminal Justice Act*, S.C. 2002, c. 1.

Federal and Provincial or Territorial Regulatory Legislation: Quasi-criminal Law

Under the *Constitution Act*, 1867, the provincial and territorial legislatures have been granted exclusive jurisdiction to enact legislation in relation to such issues as health, education, highways, liquor control, and hunting and fishing. This legislation may be enforced through the imposition of "a fine, penalty or imprisonment." At first blush, it may seem that the use of punishments of these types would persuade the courts to treat such legislation as criminal law—an area of legislative authority that is reserved exclusively for the Parliament of Canada. However, such regulatory legislation does not constitute "real" criminal law for the purpose of the distribution of powers under the Constitution because such legislation lacks the necessary element of "public evil" that was discussed earlier. Indeed, regulatory legislation is concerned with the orderly regulation of activities that are inherently legitimate (such as driving a vehicle or operating a business). Criminal law is directed towards the control of behaviour that is considered inherently wrong (namely, "**true crimes**" such as theft, assault, sexual assault, and willful damage to property). **Regulatory offences**, therefore, are quite distinct from the "true crimes" that arise under the Criminal Code or the *Controlled Drugs and Substances Act*, and they are, therefore, classified as quasi-criminal law ("quasi" means seeming, not real, or halfway).

Regulatory offences are generally far less serious in nature than "true crimes." Indeed, the maximum penalties that may be imposed for violation of regulatory offences are generally no more than a fine or a maximum term of imprisonment of six months, or both.

Regulatory offences are also included among a broad range of federal statutes that regulate activities that fall within the jurisdiction of the Parliament of Canada—for example, the *Competition Act*, R.S.C. 1985, c. C-34; the *Fisheries Act*, R.S.C. 1985, c. F-14; the *Food and Drugs Act*, R.S.C. 1985, c. F-27; the *Genetic Non-Discrimination Act*, S.C. 2017, c. 3; the *Human Pathogens and Toxins Act*, S.C. 2009, c. 24; the *Safe Food for Canadians Act*, S.C. 2012, c. 24; and the *Species at Risk Act*, S.C. 2002, c. 29. Along with the quasi-criminal offences created under provincial and territorial legislation, these federal regulatory offences contribute to a vast pool of quasi-criminal law that is becoming increasingly complex. Most lawyers

"true crime"
A "true crime" occurs when an individual engages in conduct that is not only prohibited but also constitutes a serious breach of community values; as such, it is perceived by Canadians as inherently wrong and deserving of punishment. Only the Parliament of Canada, using its criminal law power under the *Constitution Act, 1867*, may enact a "true crime."

regulatory offences
Regulatory offences arise under legislation (either federal, provincial, or territorial) that regulates inherently legitimate activities connected with trade, commerce, and industry or with everyday living (driving, fishing, etc.). These offences are not considered to be serious and usually carry only a relatively minor penalty upon conviction. Indeed, many regulatory offences are sanctioned by means of a ticketing system, and the fines may often be paid online.

are only acquainted with a fraction of the hundreds of thousands of regulatory offences that exist under both federal and provincial or territorial legislation. However, ignorance of the law is no excuse for those who commit regulatory offences.

Judge-Made Criminal Law

common law
The body of judge-made law that has evolved in areas not covered by legislation.

The second major source of criminal law in Canada is the large body of judicial decisions that either interpret criminal legislation or expound the **common law**—a term that refers to that body of judge-made law that evolved in areas not covered by legislation. Parliament cannot provide for every possibility or provide comprehensive definitions of every term used in the legislation it enacts. Therefore, there is always great scope for judicial interpretation of the Criminal Code. For example, in section 380 of the *Code*, Parliament has created the offence of fraud. According to section 380, fraud may be committed by "deceit, falsehood, or other fraudulent means." However, the term "other fraudulent means" was left undefined, and it was left to the Supreme Court of Canada to provide a working definition in the case of *R. v. Olan, Hudson and Hartnett* (1978), namely, "all other means which can properly be stigmatized as dishonest."

In discussing the common law it is important to recognize that historically, much of the English criminal law, upon which the Criminal Code of 1892 was loosely based, was developed by judges who were required to deal with new situations that were not dealt with by the legislation of the day. In Canada, one common law offence still exists—contempt of court. With the exception of contempt of court, the Criminal Code (section 9) has, since 1954, stated that judges cannot create any new common law crimes. However, judges have developed a number of common law *defences* that were not dealt with by legislation. For example, Canadian courts have developed a defence of necessity even though it

Terri-Jean Bedford is one of the current and former sex trade workers who challenged the constitutionality of Canada's prostitution laws. In 2013, the Supreme Court of Canada upheld their challenge and gave the federal Parliament one year to change this legislation. In response, Parliament enacted Bill C-36, the *Protection of Communities and Exploited Persons Act* (S.C. 2014, c.25).

THE CANADIAN PRESS/Colin Perkel

is not mentioned in the Criminal Code; hence, necessity is known as a common law defence. Section 8(3) of the Criminal Code preserves any common law "justification," "excuse," or "defence" to a criminal charge "except in so far as they are altered by or are inconsistent with this act or any other act of the Parliament of Canada." This provision is significant because it means that common law defences, such as necessity, may still be developed by Canadian judges.

Impact of the Canadian *Charter* of Rights and Freedoms on Criminal Law

The enactment of the *Canadian Charter of Rights and Freedoms* as part of the *Constitution Act*, 1982, heralded a dramatic new era in the relationship between judges and the elected members of the Parliament of Canada and the legislative assemblies of the various provinces and territories. As an entrenched bill of rights, the **Charter** empowers judges to declare any piece of legislation to be invalid—and of no force or effect—if the latter infringes on an individual's *Charter* rights (such as the presumption of innocence [section 11(d)] or the right not to be deprived of the right to life, liberty, and security of the person except in accordance with the principles of fundamental justice [section 7]). Canadian judges have demonstrated a willingness to use this extraordinary power when they believe it is absolutely necessary to do so. For example, in *Canada (Attorney General) v. Bedford* (2013), three current or former sex trade workers (including Terri Jean Bedford) sought a declaration that a number of Criminal Code provisions relating to prostitution* were invalid under section 7 of the *Charter* because they put the physical security of sex trade workers at risk by denying them the opportunity to employ protective measures (such as hiring security guards or screening clients) that would ensure their physical safety. The Supreme Court of Canada agreed with the Ontario Superior Court of Justice that the Criminal Code provisions at issue should be declared invalid and of no effect. Chief Justice Beverley McLachlin stated, on behalf of the Supreme Court, that "the impugned laws deprive people engaged in a risky, but legal, activity of the means to protect themselves against [the] risks of disease, violence and death" at the hands of "pimps and johns." The Supreme Court suspended the implementation of the ruling for one year in order to permit the Parliament of Canada to enact new legislation that would regulate prostitution in a manner that does not place the physical security of sex trade workers at risk. In response, Parliament enacted sections 286.1 to 286.5 of the Criminal Code, which essentially criminalize the purchase of sexual services, but not their sale (Bill C-36, the *Protection of Communities and Exploited Persons Act*, which received Royal Assent on 6 November 2014 [S.C. 2014, c. 25]).

Another example of the bold use of the *Charter* to override provisions of the Criminal Code is the case of *Carter v. Canada (Attorney General)* (2015). In this decision, the Supreme Court of Canada ruled that Canadians are entitled to access medical assistance in dying (not only physician-assisted suicide but also

Charter
The Canadian *Charter* of Rights and Freedoms is part of the Canadian constitution. The *Charter* sets out those rights and freedoms that Canadians believe are necessary in a free and democratic society.

*Sections 210 (keeping or being in a bawdy-house), insofar as this provision related to prostitution; 212(1)(j) (living on the avails of prostitution); and 213(1)(c) (communicating in public for the purpose of prostitution). Sections 212(1)(j) and 213(1)(c) were repealed so are no longer in the Criminal Code.

active euthanasia, whereby a medical practitioner directly causes the death of a consenting patient by, for example, administering a lethal injection). In the *Carter* case, the Supreme Court ruled that section 241(b) of the Criminal Code, which makes it a crime to assist someone to commit suicide, and section 14, which prohibits anyone from consenting to their own death, were invalid insofar as they denied individuals living with unbearable pain the right to access a medically assisted death. The denial of such access infringed section 7 of the *Charter*, which protects the "right to life, liberty, and security of the person." Parliament responded to the *Carter* decision by enacting the *Medical Assistance in Dying Act* (S.C. 2016, c. 3), which became law on 17 June 2016.

However, the courts are bound to take into account the provisions of section 1 of the *Charter*, which permit Parliament or the provincial or territorial legislatures to impose "such reasonable limits [on *Charter* rights] as can be demonstrably justified in a free and democratic society." This provision requires Canadian courts to engage in a balancing act in which they must decide whether the infringement of an individual's *Charter* rights can be justified in the name of some "higher good." For example, in *R. v. Sharpe* (2001), the Supreme Court of Canada ruled that certain aspects of the child pornography provisions of the Criminal Code (section 163.1) infringed the accused person's right to "freedom of thought, belief, opinion and expression"—a right that is guaranteed by section 2(b) of the *Charter*. However, the Court also ruled that the child pornography provisions constituted a "reasonable limitation" on the accused's section 2(b) right and were, therefore, justified under section 1 of the *Charter*. On the other hand, in the *Canada (Attorney General) v. Bedford* case (2013), the Supreme Court held that the Criminal Code's violation of the right of sex trade workers to personal security could not be justified under section 1 as a reasonable limitation on that right, and similarly, in the *Carter* case (2015), the Court ruled that Parliament was not justified in preventing Canadians living with intolerable pain from accessing a medically assisted death.

FOCUS   BOX 3.1

MEDICALLY ASSISTED DYING

Prior to 2016, Section 241(*b*) of the Criminal Code stated that everyone who aids or abets a person in committing suicide commits an indictable offence, and section 14 prescribed that no person may consent to death being inflicted on them. Taken together, these two provisions prohibited individuals suffering unbearable pain from seeking medical assistance to die. More specifically, the Criminal Code prohibited both *physician-assisted suicide*, where a physician helps another person to commit suicide (by, for example, providing a lethal dose of drugs which the other person takes themselves) and *active euthanasia*, where a physician directly brings about the death of an individual (by, for example, administering a lethal injection).

However, in *Carter v. Canada (Attorney General)* (2015), the Supreme Court of Canada ruled that the prohibition by s. 241(b) on physician-assisted suicide is unconstitutional. The Supreme Court unanimously decided that sections 241(b) and 14 of the Criminal Code prevent a competent adult person, who is suffering intolerable pain, from gaining access to a physician-assisted death. Sections 241(b) and 14, therefore, unjustifiably infringed on the right to life, liberty, and security guaranteed by section 7 of the *Charter* and were not saved as reasonable limitations on that right by section 1 of the *Charter*: therefore, insofar as these provisions prohibited medical assistance in dying, they were invalid and of no effect.

The Supreme Court held that the circumstances under which a competent adult person may obtain a medically assisted death are (i) there is a clear consent to the ending of life and (ii) "the person has a grievous and irremediable medical condition (including an illness, disease, or disability) that causes enduring suffering that is intolerable to the individual in the circumstances of his or her condition."

The Supreme Court suspended the declaration of invalidity of s. 241(b) for 12 months (until February 2016) to allow Parliament time to amend the Criminal Code. The Court later granted the Government of Canada a further extension of four months (until June 2016). After much debate in both the House of Commons and the Senate, Parliament enacted Bill C-14, the *Medical Assistance in Dying Act*, which became law on 17 June 2016. A new section 241(2) of the Criminal Code grants an exemption from Criminal liability for those medical professionals who provide "medical assistance in dying":

> No medical practitioner or nurse practitioner commits an offence under [s. 241(b)] if they provide a person with medical assistance in dying in accordance with [the procedures specified in subsequent provisions in the Criminal Code].

The new Criminal Code provisions define "medical assistance in dying" in a manner that includes both *voluntary euthanasia* carried out by a medical professional as well as *suicide assisted by a medical professional* (s. 241.1):

> "*medical assistance in dying*" means: (a) the administering by a medical practitioner or nurse practitioner of a substance to a person, at their request, that causes their death; or
>
> (b) the prescribing or providing by a medical practitioner or nurse practitioner of a substance to a person, at their request, so that they may self-administer the substance and in doing so cause their own death.

The new Criminal Code provisions [see s. 241.2(1)] set out the requirements that must be met before an individual may receive a medically assisted death. Among the most important

requirements are: the person concerned must be 18, competent to make decisions about their health care, and "have a grievous and irremediable medical condition." The legislation also mandates that the person must be informed of the alternatives to dealing with their suffering (for example, palliative care) before he or she gives their consent to a medically assisted death.

A critical aspect of the new legislation is the definition of "grievous and irremediable medical condition." Section 241.2(2) states that an individual only has such a condition if they meet each of the following requirements:

(a) they have a serious and incurable illness, disease or disability;

(b) they are in an advanced state of irreversible decline in capability;

(c) that illness, disease or disability or that state of decline causes them enduring physical or psychological suffering that is intolerable to them and that cannot be relieved under conditions that they consider acceptable; and

(d) their natural death has become reasonably foreseeable, taking into account all of their medical circumstances, without a prognosis necessarily having been made as to the specific length of time that they have remaining.

The new Criminal Code provisions include various safeguards to ensure, for example, that the individual applying for a medically assisted death is competent to make that decision and that there is a 10-day period during which he or she may change their mind [see Section 241.2].

Questions for Critical Thinking

1. Are the amendments to the Criminal Code consistent with the ruling of the Supreme Court of Canada in the *Carter* case? If the answer is in the negative, would there be an argument in favour of declaring one or more of the amendments unconstitutional?

2. Under these amendments, can an individual living with a mental illness that is intolerable to them obtain access to medically assisted dying?

The Basic Elements of a Crime: *Actus Reus* and *Mens Rea*

In the decision of the Supreme Court of Canada in *Mabior* (2012), Chief Justice McLachlin restated one of the most basic principles of Canadian criminal law:

> A criminal conviction and imprisonment, with the attendant stigma that attaches, is the most serious sanction the law can impose on a person, and is generally reserved for conduct that is highly culpable—conduct

that is viewed as harmful to society, reprehensible and unacceptable. It requires both a culpable act—*actus reus*—and a guilty mind—*mens rea*—the parameters of which should be clearly delineated by the law.

The study of criminal law invariably begins with the statement that every criminal offence can be analyzed in terms of two major elements: namely, *actus reus* and *mens rea*. These terms are derived from the Latin maxim, *actus non facit reum nisi mens sit rea* (which, translated literally, means that an act does not render a person guilty unless his or her mind is also guilty). This principle means that an accused person may not be convicted of a criminal offence unless the prosecution can prove the following beyond a reasonable doubt:

(a) that a particular event or state of affairs was "caused" by the accused person's conduct (*actus reus*); and

(b) that this conduct was simultaneously accompanied by a certain state of mind (*mens rea*).

In essence, the concept of *mens rea* refers to the mental elements of an offence, while the term *actus reus* refers to all the other elements that must be proved by the Crown. However, an important gloss must be placed on this seemingly simple formulation—namely, the *actus reus* of a criminal offence includes an element of voluntariness. As Justice McLachlin said, in delivering the judgment of the majority of the justices of the Supreme Court of Canada in the case of *Théroux* (1993):

> The term *mens rea*, properly understood, does not encompass all of the mental elements of crime. The *actus reus* has its own mental element; the act must be the voluntary act of the accused for the *actus reus* to exist.

The *Actus Reus* Elements of a Crime

actus reus
All the elements contained in the definition of a criminal offence, other than the mental elements (*mens rea*).

In general, it is possible to divide the **actus reus** into three separate components:

(a) conduct (a voluntary act or omission constituting the central feature of the crime);

(b) the surrounding or "material" circumstances; and

(c) the consequences of the voluntary conduct.

For example, in order to prove that an accused person is guilty of the offence of assault causing bodily harm (section 267 of the Criminal Code), the Crown must establish that the accused applied force to the body of the victim (conduct); that the force was applied without the consent of the victim (circumstances); and that the application of force caused bodily harm (consequences). Bodily harm is defined in section 2 of the Criminal Code as meaning "any hurt or injury to a person that interferes with the health or comfort of the person and is more than merely transient or trifling in nature." For example, a swollen face and bleeding nose have been considered to constitute "bodily harm," and Canadian courts have also ruled that the term even includes psychological harm.

There are some significant exceptions to the division of the *actus reus* into three elements. For example, perjury (section 131 of the Criminal Code) is an offence that does not require proof of any consequences. Provided the accused person knowingly makes a false statement with intent to mislead a court, he or she will be guilty of perjury even though not a single person actually believed the false statement. However, consequences do constitute a crucial element of the *actus reus* of most criminal offences. Consider the offences of dangerous operation of a motor vehicle causing death, and dangerous operation of a motor vehicle causing bodily harm (section 249 of the Criminal Code); these carry maximum penalties of 14 and 10 years, respectively. In contrast, the "simple" offence of dangerous operation of a motor vehicle (where the Crown does not have to prove the consequences of death or bodily harm) carries a maximum penalty of only five years. Occasionally, the *actus reus* of an offence does not contain the requirement that the accused engage in conduct of any kind; instead, the Crown must prove that the accused was found in a particular "condition" or "state." For example, it is an offence, under section 253 of the Criminal Code, to be in "care or control" of a motor vehicle while one's ability to operate the vehicle is impaired by alcohol and/or another drug or when one's blood-alcohol level exceeds 80 milligrams or alcohol in 100 millilitres of blood. This offence does not require proof that the accused person was actually driving the motor vehicle: indeed, the vehicle may be stationary. However, the offence will be established if the accused person's intoxicated condition creates a *risk* that the vehicle might be set in motion and thereby pose a danger to people or property. As Justice Fish, of the Supreme Court of Canada, stated in *Boudreault* (2012):

> "care or control", within the meaning of s. 253(1) of the Criminal Code, signifies (1) an intentional course of conduct associated with a motor vehicle; (2) by a person whose ability to drive is impaired, or whose blood alcohol level exceeds the legal limit; (3) in circumstances that create a *realistic risk*, as opposed to a *remote possibility*, of danger to persons or property.

Undoubtedly, the objective of Parliament when enacting section 253 was *preventative*. It permits police officers to intervene in a potentially dangerous situation and eliminate the risk to people and property created by the presence of an intoxicated person who is in charge of a motor vehicle.

An important question to address is whether a failure to act (an omission) can qualify as the conduct element of the *actus reus* of an offence. The answer is that a failure to act can constitute a crime only if the accused was under a preexisting legal duty to act. A good illustration is the duty owed by a parent to a small child to provide the latter with the "necessaries of life"—for example, by feeding the child and providing him or her with necessary medical care (section 215 of the Criminal Code). Under Canadian criminal law, there is no duty to rescue a stranger who is in serious danger. However, there is a duty to rescue when the person in danger is a child or spouse of the accused person or is in some other relationship that imposes a duty to act (for example, a prisoner is owed such a duty by the officer in charge of the jail). Some have argued that the criminal law is seriously deficient insofar as it does not require every adult citizen to take active steps to rescue a person who is in danger provided, of course, that the rescue may be undertaken without an unreasonable degree of danger to the rescuer. However, it may be very difficult to enforce such a duty in practice. For example, suppose a radio message is broadcast reporting that volunteers are needed to help rescue children in a collapsed school. Should everyone who hears that message be legally required to forsake what they are doing and rush to the scene of the disaster?

A final point to be made about the *actus reus* component of an offence concerns the requirement that the accused's conduct be voluntary. If a driver is repeatedly stung by a swarm of bees and crashes his or her vehicle, the accident will be considered the consequence of a series of reflex actions that were beyond the driver's control; clearly, they did not flow from the free exercise of his or her will. Similarly, if an accused person's consciousness is impaired to such an extent that he or she is unable to control his or her actions, it may be concluded that there was no *actus reus* of any criminal offence because the accused acted involuntarily. When this situation occurs, the accused may raise the defence of automatism. Automatism is a rare defence and may be successfully raised only in a very limited number of situations. For example, if an individual is hit on the head and immediately thereafter enters a state of impaired consciousness and assaults another person, he or she may claim the benefit of the defence of automatism—provided it is established that the assault constituted an involuntary action. In practice, automatism is a particularly difficult defence to assert successfully because, in the *Stone* case (1999), the Supreme Court of Canada ruled that the burden of proving the defence is placed on the accused person who raises it (normally, the Crown is required to prove every element of the *actus reus* and *mens rea* components of an offence). Stone had been charged with the murder of his wife, following a series of provocative statements she had directed at him. The accused had stabbed his wife 47 times but claimed that, at the time, he was in a state of dissociation following the shock of the "psychological blow" that had been inflicted on him by his spouse's hurtful words. More specifically, he stated that a "whoosh" sensation had swept over him and that he was unaware of what he was doing. Ultimately, the jury concluded that the claim of automatism had not been proved by Stone. However, Stone was convicted of manslaughter rather than murder because the jury concluded that there had been provocation (within the meaning of section 232 of the Criminal Code). Stone's manslaughter conviction was later affirmed by the Supreme Court of Canada, where Justice Bastarache stated that the plausibility of a claim of automatism in such cases is significantly reduced if the victim is alleged to be the "trigger" of the violence directed at him or her. A successful defence of automatism presupposes that accused persons are plunged into such a state of impaired consciousness that they are barely aware of what is happening around them. In Stone's case, the accused responded directly to what he perceived to be insults, and the jury evidently believed that his actions were those of a man who knew where he was and what he was doing.

The *Mens Rea* Elements of a Crime

mens rea
The mental elements (other than voluntariness) contained in the definition of a criminal offence.

Basically, **mens rea** refers to all the mental elements (other than voluntariness) that the Crown must prove (beyond a reasonable doubt) in order to obtain a conviction for a criminal offence. *Mens rea* is rather like a chameleon insofar as it changes its nature from one offence to another. Obviously, the *mens rea* for murder is very different from that required for theft. Furthermore, *mens rea* is not one mental state but rather a combination of mental states; indeed, it is necessary to analyze the *mens rea* required in relation to each of the three elements of the *actus reus* of any particular crime—that is, conduct, circumstances, and consequences.

The requirement that the prosecution prove *mens rea* reflects basic values that Canadians hold in relation to civil liberties. In essence, the *mens rea* requirement ensures that only those defendants who are morally blameworthy are convicted of "true crimes" under the Criminal Code. As Justice McLachlin said in the Supreme Court of Canada's decision in *Théroux* (1993),

> *Mens rea* [. . .] refers to the guilty mind, the wrongful intention, of the accused. Its function in the criminal law is to prevent the conviction of the morally innocent—those who do not understand or intend the consequences of their acts.

Subjective and Objective *Mens Rea*

There are two very distinct types of *mens rea* requirements in Canadian criminal law: (1) subjective and (2) objective.

Subjective *mens rea* is based on the notion that accused persons may not be convicted of a criminal offence unless (a) they *deliberately intended* to bring about the consequences prohibited by the law, (b) *subjectively realized* that their conduct might bring about such prohibited consequences but recklessly continued with that conduct in spite of their knowledge of the risks involved, or (c) were willfully *blind* in that they deliberately closed their minds to the obvious criminality of their actions. As Justice McLachlin explained in the Supreme Court of Canada's decision in *Creighton* (1993),

> The requisite intention or knowledge may be inferred from the act and its circumstances. Even in the latter case, however, it is concerned with "what was actually going on in the mind of this particular accused at the time in question."

Subjective *mens rea*, therefore, constitutes a requirement that the accused *deliberately chose to do something wrong*.

Objective *mens rea* is predicated on the principle that accused persons should be convicted of certain offences, not because they intended to bring about the prohibited consequences or acted recklessly, but rather because *reasonable* people, in the same situation, would have appreciated that their conduct created a risk of causing harm and would have taken action to avoid doing so. Here the fault of the accused does not lie in deliberately choosing to do something wrong; instead, the culpability lies in the fact that *the accused person had the capacity to live up to the standard of care expected of a reasonable person and failed to do so.* As the Supreme Court of Canada stated in *Beatty* (2008): "objective *mens rea* is based on the premise that a reasonable person in the accused's position would have been aware of the risks arising from the conduct. The fault lies in the absence of the requisite mental state of care." Who is the "reasonable person"? The answer to this question is simply that it is up to the judge or jury (if there is one) to decide what is reasonable in all the circumstances of the case, and no doubt, they call upon their own life experience to determine what they think is reasonable. This

subjective *mens rea*
The *mens rea* elements of a criminal offence are considered to be subjective if they are based on a determination of "what actually went on in the accused person's mind." The forms of subjective *mens rea* are intention and knowledge; recklessness; and willful blindness.

objective *mens rea*
The *mens rea* elements of a criminal offence are considered to be objective if they are based on a determination of whether a reasonable person, in the same circumstances and with the same knowledge as the accused, would have appreciated the risk involved in the accused's conduct and would have taken steps to avoid the commission of the *actus reus* elements of the crime in question.

means that it is always difficult to predict whether a judge or jury will determine that a specific defendant in a criminal trial acted reasonably. It is very important that criminologists recognize the extent to which the application of criminal law is often very uncertain and lies in the hands of individual judges and jury members whenever objective liability is at stake.

In the *Creighton* case (1993), Justice McLachlin emphasized that the "moral fault of the offence must be proportionate to its gravity and penalty." In other words, the most serious crimes, carrying the most severe penalties, should generally be based on a subjective *mens rea* requirement. Significantly, in the case of *Martineau* (1990), the Supreme Court of Canada ruled that the crime of murder is so serious and carries such a high degree of stigma that criminal responsibility for this offence must be based on subjective *mens rea*; indeed, the Court stated that the *Charter* requires that the Crown prove either that the accused deliberately intended to kill or, at the very least, subjectively foresaw that his or her conduct was likely to cause death. However, in *Creighton* (1993), the Supreme Court held that responsibility for manslaughter could be based on an objective *mens rea* requirement because the degree of stigma and the penalties attached to it were considerably less severe than is the case for murder. In Creighton's case, the accused had injected a quantity of cocaine into the arm of the victim. In order to convict Creighton of manslaughter, the Crown first had to prove that he had intentionally committed an unlawful act that had resulted in death. The unlawful act was the offence of trafficking in narcotics (trafficking includes the act of administering a drug), and there was no doubt that the victim died as a direct consequence of the injection. The *mens rea* for so-called unlawful act manslaughter is objective in nature. Therefore, the second task confronting the Crown was to prove that any reasonable person would have foreseen the risk of nontrivial bodily harm as a consequence of committing the unlawful act. The Supreme Court of Canada had no doubt that Creighton was correctly convicted of manslaughter because any reasonable person who administered a dangerous drug intravenously would foresee the risk of some degree of bodily harm.

There are three forms of subjective *mens rea* that the Crown may be required to prove in a criminal prosecution: (1) intention and knowledge, (2) recklessness, and (3) wilful blindness.

Section 155(1) of the Criminal Code provides a typical example of the subjective *mens rea* requirement of intention and knowledge; indeed, it provides that an individual commits incest if, knowing that another person is "by blood relationship his or her parent, child, brother, sister, grandparent or grandchild," he or she intentionally has sexual intercourse with that person. Usually, the *Criminal Code* will require the Crown to prove a specific mental element in addition to intention and knowledge. Take, for example, the offence of first-degree murder. Section 231(2) of the Code states that this offence is committed when murder is both "planned and deliberate." In order to convict an accused person of murder, the Crown must establish that this person either intended to kill or intended to inflict bodily harm that he or she knew was likely to cause death and was reckless (did not care) whether death ensued or not (section 229(a)). However, if the offender is to be convicted of first-degree murder rather than second-degree murder, then normally the Crown must also prove that the killing was planned and deliberate in the sense that the accused did not act impulsively and was following some pre-existing plan to kill someone. Intoxicated defendants who are found to have the necessary *mens rea* for murder will often be acquitted of first-degree murder because they acted on impulse or without thinking about what they were going to do ahead of time; these accused persons will instead be convicted of second-degree murder.

Recklessness is a form of subjective *mens rea* where the accused knows that their conduct could cause certain prohibited consequences but deliberately proceeds with that conduct because they do not care one way or the other. Take the crime of arson. Section 434 of the Criminal Code states that a person who "intentionally or recklessly causes damage by fire or explosion to property that is not wholly owned by that person" is guilty of an indictable offence and may be sentenced to a maximum of 14 years in prison. If Nero throws a lighted cigarette onto a haystack, realizing that there is a good chance the haystack will catch fire, he will be convicted of arson even if he can demonstrate that he did not start the fire deliberately and that, in fact, he hoped very sincerely that there would not be any blaze as a consequence of his actions. Nero is guilty of arson because his recklessness constitutes one of the forms of *mens rea* that is necessary for conviction under the terms of section 434.

Willful blindness is the final form of subjective *mens rea*. It exists where accused persons have every reason to make some kind of inquiry as to whether there are circumstances that would render their conduct criminal but deliberately choose to shut their eyes to the obvious because they wish to avoid being convicted of an offence. As the Supreme Court of Canada stated in *Briscoe* (2010): "wilful blindness imputes knowledge to an accused whose suspicion is aroused to the point where he or she sees the need for further inquiries, but deliberately chooses not to make those inquiries." Willful blindness is treated as being the same as actual knowledge of a circumstance that incriminates the accused person.

Objective *mens rea* has been applied to a significant number of offences under the Criminal Code. For example, the following offences have all been characterized by the courts as requiring proof only of objective, rather than subjective, *mens rea*: manslaughter, dangerous operation of a motor vehicle, assault causing bodily harm, and criminal negligence causing death or bodily harm. However, it is important to bear in mind that the courts have consistently stated that accused persons may not be convicted of "true crimes" under the Criminal Code merely because they were "careless" in the sense that their conduct fell below the standard of care expected of a reasonable person acting prudently in the same circumstances as the accused. As Justice McLachlin said in the *Creighton* case (1993), "The law does not lightly brand a person as criminal." Indeed, in *Roy* (2012), the Supreme Court of Canada emphasized that the *minimum standard* for objective liability is a *marked departure* from the standard of care expected of the reasonable person acting prudently. Furthermore, the Supreme Court of Canada has repeatedly stated that the courts should apply a "modified objective test" in such cases. This means that a judge or jury (if there is one) must ask what the accused person in the case before them actually knew about the circumstances surrounding their actions. The judge or jury must then decide whether the accused's behaviour constituted a marked departure from the standard of care expected of a reasonable person who faces the identical circumstances as the accused and who is armed with exactly the same knowledge of those circumstances. Suppose, for example, an accused person suffers a brain seizure while driving a vehicle and he or she crosses over the centre of the road and causes a fatal collision with a car that is travelling in the opposite direction. On the face of it, straying over the centre line and causing a collision constitutes a marked departure from the standard of care expected of a reasonable person. However, if the accused did not know that he or she was likely to suffer from a seizure, there would be no conviction on a charge of dangerous operation of a motor vehicle causing death [section 249(4) of the Criminal Code]. A reasonable driver, with no knowledge of the likelihood that he or she might suffer a seizure, would have behaved in the same way as the accused. However, the situation would be very different if the accused person knew that he or she was liable to experience a seizure or was subject to sudden fainting spells and nevertheless continued to drive a motor vehicle without having first obtained medical clearance to do so. Clearly, a reasonable person armed with this knowledge would never attempt to take a vehicle on the road; therefore, the accused's conduct would almost certainly be considered a marked departure from the standard of care expected of the reasonable person.

FOCUS

BOX 3.2

CONVICTION OF FIRST-DEGREE MURDER ON THE BASIS OF WILLFUL BLINDNESS

The case of *Briscoe* (2010) illustrates the principle that willful blindness will be treated as being equivalent to guilty knowledge even with respect to a charge of first-degree murder, the most serious crime in the Criminal Code. Briscoe was charged with first-degree murder on the basis that he had aided and abetted (assisted or encouraged) the commission of murder by another person. Under section 21(2) of the Criminal Code, an individual who aids/abets another to commit a crime is liable to conviction for that crime.

Briscoe drove a group of youths led by a 19-year-old man, Laboucan, to a deserted golf course. Riding with Laboucan and his associates were two young women who had been lured into the vehicle by the lie that they would be taken to a party. At the golf course, one of the young women, 13-year-old Nina Courtepatte, was brutally raped and killed by Laboucan and his gang. Briscoe, who did not participate directly in the rape and murder but stood by and watched, was nevertheless charged

with kidnapping, aggravated assault, and first-degree murder on the basis that he aided and abetted Laboucan and his associates to commit these crimes.

Photo by Ian Kucerak. Material republished with the express permission of Edmonton Sun, a division of Postmedia Network Inc.

Nina Courtepatte was a young woman who was sexually assaulted and brutally murdered near Edmonton, one of over 1,000 Indigenous women who have been murdered in Canada since 1980. Michael Briscoe was convicted after a second trial of first-degree murder even though he did not participate in the murder because he provided assistance to those who actually committed the killing and did so with wilful blindness as to their intentions.

Apart from driving the victim to the scene of her death, Briscoe provided Laboucan and his associates with items from the trunk of his vehicle that were later used as the murder weapons (a hammer, a pair of pliers, a wrench and a pipe). Also, Briscoe had heard Laboucan tell the youths in his group that he "would like to find someone to kill someone," and he knew that Laboucan was violent. The trial judge acquitted Briscoe on the basis that it had not been proved that he actually knew what Laboucan had in mind when Briscoe drove Nina Courtepatte to the golf course. However, the Supreme Court of Canada agreed with the Alberta Court of Appeal that there should be a new trial because the trial judge had not considered whether Briscoe was willfully blind with respect to Laboucan's murderous plan. Justice Charron stated that "the evidence cried out for an analysis on wilful blindness" and pointed out that Briscoe's own statements to the police suggest that "he had a strong, well-founded suspicion that someone would be killed at the golf course and that he may have been wilfuly blind to the kidnapping and prospect of sexual assault." At his new trial, in April 2012, Briscoe was convicted of first-degree murder, kidnapping, and sexual assault.

Questions for Critical Thinking

1. Given the fact that first-degree murder carries the most severe penalty possible in the Criminal Code, do you think the Crown should have been able to obtain a conviction of this heinous crime, even though it could not prove that Briscoe knew for sure that Laboucan planned to kill the victim whom he (Briscoe) transported to the scene of the homicide?

2. In principle, should wilful blindness be treated as the equivalent of actual knowledge? Is there an argument for treating it as being of lesser culpability than knowledge (as is the case with recklessness, for example)?

Although it may appear somewhat harsh to convict individuals of serious crimes on the basis of objective *mens rea*, it is clear that the courts have weakened the objective test of liability by requiring that the judge or jury take into account the subjective knowledge accused people have of the relevant circumstances surrounding their actions. Furthermore, if an accused person lacks the normal capacity of the reasonable person to appreciate that his or her conduct might create a risk of harm, that person may not be convicted of a crime, even if it is based on proof of objective *mens rea*. For example, suppose a 20-year-old man has a mental age of 10 and he hits a neighbour with a metal bar. Tragically, the neighbour dies from his injuries. In the case of a person without a severe disability, it would be relatively easy for the Crown to prove a charge of manslaughter. The *mens rea* requirements are objective in nature. The accused must be proved to have intentionally applied force to the victim, and the Crown must then proceed to establish that a reasonable person would have foreseen the risk of nontrivial bodily harm. Any reasonable person would foresee the risk of fairly serious bodily harm if an attack is carried out with a metal bar; therefore, most accused persons would be routinely convicted of manslaughter.

However, if the accused is so developmentally disabled that he or she cannot foresee that their actions may cause non-trivial bodily harm, then that individual may not be convicted of manslaughter. The essence of culpability in objective *mens rea* is that the accused had the capacity to foresee—and avoid—the risk of physical harm but did not do so. If the accused lacks this basic capacity, to convict him or her of manslaughter would amount to punishing someone who lacks any blameworthiness. In *Creighton* (1993), the Supreme Court of Canada ruled that such an outcome would infringe the fundamental principles of justice that are enshrined in the *Charter* (section 7).

Mens Rea and Regulatory Offences

Earlier in this chapter, a distinction was drawn between regulatory offences ("quasi-criminal law") and "true crimes." Where "true crimes" are concerned, the Crown usually has to prove the required *mens rea* of the offence beyond a reasonable doubt. However, most regulatory offences are considered to be offences of strict liability. This means that the Crown only has to prove the *actus reus* elements of the offence; the onus is then on the accused to prove, on the balance of probabilities, that he or she was not negligent (or that he or she "acted with due diligence"). The rationale for strict liability is that it would be extremely difficult to conduct effective prosecutions of regulatory offences if the Crown were required to prove that accused persons were negligent. Usually, the accused person has the best knowledge of the steps that he or she has taken to comply with the regulations that apply to his or her field of manufacturing or business activities, and so on. Therefore, it is fair to require the accused to present this evidence and prove that he or she acted with the due diligence expected of a reasonable person in the same circumstances. Furthermore, the penalties for regulatory offences are comparatively lenient, since they rarely include imprisonment as a realistic sentencing alternative. In any event, strict liability is infinitely preferable to a regime of absolute liability, in which the accused is not permitted to claim a lack of *mens rea* as a defence.

In the *Wholesale Travel Group Inc.* case (1991), the accused had been charged with the regulatory offence of false or misleading advertising, under the federal *Competition Act*, R.S.C. 1970, c. C–23. The Act clearly imposed strict liability insofar as it permitted the accused to raise a defence of having acted "with due diligence." Essentially, the defence would be available where the accused proved that the "act or omission giving rise to the offence" was the "result of error" and that he or she "took reasonable precautions and exercised due diligence to prevent the occurrence of such error." It was contended before the Supreme Court of Canada that, because strict liability requires accused persons to prove their innocence, it infringed the presumption of innocence enshrined in section 11(d) of the *Charter*, and was, therefore, invalid. However, the Supreme Court of Canada ultimately held that strict liability was not invalid under the provisions of the *Charter*. The *Wholesale Travel Group Inc.* case is, therefore, a decision of great importance since it has affirmed the legitimacy of the basic principles of liability that are at the heart of the vast network of regulatory legislation that governs the daily lives of all Canadians.

A vast number of regulatory offences have been enacted by the federal and provincial/territorial legislatures in Canada. In addition, countless bylaws have been created by municipalities across Canada, acting on the authority delegated to them by the respective provinces and territories. Many of the provincial/territorial regulatory offences and most of the bylaw infractions are prosecuted by means of a ticketing system (for example, the dispensing of speeding and parking tickets is a practice that is well known to Canadians). Furthermore, approximately 2,000 federal regulatory offences have been designated as "contraventions" under the *Contraventions Act, S.C. 1992, c. 47*, thus enabling prosecution through provincial/territorial ticketing systems.

Becoming a Party to a Criminal Offence

Individuals can be convicted of criminal offences even if they are not the persons who actually commit them. For example, section 21(1) of the Criminal Code provides that anyone is a party to a criminal offence who (1) actually commits it, (2) aids another person to commit it, or (3) abets (encourages) any person to commit it. In a homicide case the person who actually commits the offence would be the individual who physically kills the victim. However, a person who intentionally provides assistance and/or encouragement is liable to be convicted of murder on the same basis as the actual killer. Section 21(1), therefore, provides the courts and, in particular, prosecutors with a significant degree of flexibility. Take, for example, the notorious case of *Pickton* (2010). Robert William Pickton was involved in one of the most horrific series of murders in any country in modern times. In this case, though the evidence appeared to indicate that Pickton had committed the murders himself, the defence suggested that others may have been involved in the killings. The Supreme Court of Canada held that section 21(1) places the person who aids and or abets a murder on exactly the same footing as a person who actually commits it. Therefore, it does not matter whether members of the jury believed that Pickton actually committed the murders himself or whether he aided and/or abetted others to do so: in either case, he should be convicted of murder. Section 22 of the Criminal Code provides a similar degree of flexibility to the courts insofar as it provides that a person who counsels ("procures," "solicits," or "incites") another to commit a crime becomes a **party to a crime** even if "the offence was committed in a way different from that which was counselled" (section 22 of the Criminal Code).

An individual may also become a party to a criminal offence that has been committed by other people when he or she had previously formed a common intention with them to commit a crime. Section 21(2) of the Criminal Code deals with the situation in which two or more persons have agreed to commit a crime and to assist one another in carrying out this "common purpose." Each of these individuals is considered a party to any offence committed by the other person(s) who entered the original agreement provided that (1) this other offence was committed in order to carry out the "common purpose" and (2) these individuals either knew or ought to have known that the commission of this other offence "would be a probable consequence of carrying out the common purpose." Suppose that Chuzzlewit, Dedlock, and Murdstone agree to commit a robbery and to help one another in carrying out this "common intention." Murdstone—without consulting his colleagues in crime—kills one of the robbery victims. In these circumstances, Chuzzlewit and Dedlock would be convicted of manslaughter if they either knew or ought to have known that inflicting nontrivial bodily harm on the intended victim(s) would be a probable consequence of implementing their common intention to commit robbery. Since robbery necessarily involves an element of violence or threatened violence, any reasonable person would foresee the probability that someone may be seriously hurt; therefore, Chuzzlewit and Dedlock would almost certainly be found guilty of manslaughter. The use of the phrase "or ought to have known" indicates that the *mens rea* elements are

party to a crime
The Criminal Code specifies that one is a party to—and liable to conviction of—a criminal offence if one actually commits it, aids and/or abets it, becomes a party to it by virtue of having formed a common intention with others to commit a crime, or counsels the commission of an offence that is actually committed by another person.

objective in nature; this means that the scope of potential liability under section 21(2) is remarkably broad. The only exception to this form of objective liability arises where the offence of murder is concerned. Since the Supreme Court of Canada has ruled [in *Martineau* (1990)] that an accused person may be convicted of murder only where there was an actual intention to kill or subjective foresight of the likelihood of death, Chuzzlewit and Dedlock would be convicted of murder only if they subjectively realized that death was a probable consequence of carrying out their common intention to commit robbery.

One question that immediately springs to mind when discussing section 21(2) is whether an individual who agreed with others to commit a crime and to provide the necessary assistance to achieve his goal should be entitled to change his or her mind and withdraw from the common intention. The answer is that an individual may withdraw from the common intention, but may do so effectively only when he or she gives unequivocal notice to the other party or parties of his or her wish to abandon the criminal enterprise. Once effective notice has been given, the individual is no longer liable for any subsequent crimes committed by the other party or parties in pursuit of the common intention. However, in *Gauthier* (2013), the Supreme Court of Canada added a new prerequisite for raising the defence of abandonment of the common intention: the defence will only be successful if the accused person demonstrates that a reasonable effort was made to neutralize the effects of her or his participation or to prevent the principal offender from committing the offence.

The Use of Criminal Law as a Preventative Tool: Inchoate Offences

The criminal law permits the police to intervene and arrest those who, in some way, demonstrate that they are about to embark upon the commission of a serious crime. If members of a gang of professional kidnappers agree to abduct a particular victim and to hold him or her to ransom, the police do not have to wait until the abduction is actually carried out before they intervene. Even though the kidnapping may exist only in the intentions of the members of the gang, it is undoubtedly legitimate for the state to punish them for having participated in a conspiracy to commit kidnapping. Conspiracy is an **inchoate crime** (literally, a crime "in embryo"); once their agreement to commit a crime has been reached, the accused may be convicted of the crime of conspiracy even though the offence they originally planned to commit was never brought to fruition. Other inchoate crimes are criminal attempt and counselling an offence that is not committed.

Inchoate crimes raise questions about the civil liberties of those who are charged with having committed them. It is generally accepted that the criminal law should not punish people simply for entertaining evil thoughts. However, society does have the right to prevent individuals from translating their evil thoughts into criminal acts. The problem lies in defining the point at which the state is justified in laying a charge against someone who has not yet committed the crime that he or she has in mind. Basically, accused persons must take some

inchoate crime
A criminal offence that is committed when the accused person seeks to bring about the commission of a particular crime but is not successful in doing so. The three inchoate offences in the Criminal Code are attempt, conspiracy, and counselling.

form of action that manifests their intention to commit a crime; in counselling, the accused must encourage another person to commit a crime; in attempt, the accused must take a substantial step towards completion of a crime; and, in conspiracy, the accused must enter into an agreement to commit a crime.

Counselling an Offence That Is Not Committed

According to section 22 of the Criminal Code, it is a crime to **counsel** another person to commit an offence that is not ultimately brought to fruition. Since the main focus of the offence is on the accused person's intentions, it does not matter that no one is actually influenced by the accused person's efforts to procure, solicit, or incite someone to commit a crime. Furthermore, once their counselling action is completed, accused persons cannot escape criminal conviction merely because they change their minds and renounce their criminal intent. Box 3.3 illustrates how technological change can affect the interpretation and application of the criminal law.

counselling
Procuring, soliciting, or inciting another person to commit a crime.

FOCUS   BOX 3.3

COUNSELLING CRIME OVER THE INTERNET

Courts are constantly faced with the need to adapt the criminal law to deal with the many opportunities that rapidly developing communication technologies create for novel methods of committing crimes. *R. v. Hamilton* (2005) furnishes a noteworthy example of a case in which the Supreme Court of Canada very cautiously adapted the existing principles of criminal law to deal with a situation in which it was alleged that the Internet had been used to communicate information that was likely to incite other individuals to commit criminal offences.

Hamilton had used the Internet to sell computer files and documents to a number of individuals. These files contained detailed instructions for bomb making and burglary, as well as a program that generated credit card numbers that might be used for fraudulent purposes. Hamilton was charged with counselling the commission of four offences that had not in fact been committed—namely, making explosive substances with intent, doing anything with intent to cause an explosion, break and enter with intent, and fraud. At his trial, Hamilton readily admitted that he had read a computer-generated list of the files concerned but denied that he had actually read the contents of those files. Although he had generated some credit card numbers, he had never used them and there had been no complaints from the bank concerning their misuse.

At his trial, the judge acquitted Hamilton of all the charges against him because, in her view, Hamilton never intended that the persons to whom he sent the computer files should actually commit the offences described in them. The Crown took the case to the Supreme Court of Canada, which articulated the *mens rea* that must be proved before an accused person may be convicted of counselling an offence. According to Justice Fish,

the *mens rea* consists in nothing less than an accompanying *intent* or *conscious disregard of the substantial and unjustified risk inherent in the counselling*: that is, it must be shown that the accused either intended that the offence counselled be committed, or knowingly counselled the commission of the offence while aware of the unjustified risk the offence counselled was in fact likely to be committed as a result of the accused's conduct. [at para. 29] (Emphasis in original)

Prior to the *Hamilton* case, the courts had always applied the principle that, in order to obtain a conviction for counselling, the Crown must prove that the accused person actually intended that the offence be committed. However, the Supreme Court ruled in *Hamilton* that an accused person may also be convicted if he or she was *extremely reckless* as to the likelihood that the offence would be committed. Nevertheless, even with this expanded definition of the necessary *mens rea*, the Supreme Court affirmed Hamilton's acquittal on all the counselling charges except the charge of counselling fraud. The Supreme Court ordered a new trial on the charge of counselling fraud because it took the view that the trial judge should have found that Hamilton had the necessary *mens rea* for

(continued)

this offence. The Supreme Court noted that Hamilton had sent an e-mail "teaser" to various individuals in which he advertised software that could generate "valid working credit card numbers." Justice Fish noted that Hamilton "sought to make 'a quick buck' by encouraging the intended recipients of his Internet solicitation to purchase a device that generated credit card numbers easily put to fraudulent use." Furthermore, the Supreme Court emphasized that Hamilton knew very well that "the use of false credit card numbers is illegal." Therefore, even if Hamilton had not actually wanted the purchasers of the files to commit the offences described in them, he was at the very least extremely reckless as to the risk that the files were likely to incite the purchasers to commit the offence of fraud.

Questions for Critical Thinking

1. Do you agree with the Supreme Court of Canada's decision to expand the scope of the *mens rea* for counselling an offence to include extreme recklessness?

2. Do you think Parliament should amend the Criminal Code to make it easier to obtain convictions in such cases? For example, should individuals such as Hamilton be made criminally liable for the *negligent* transfer of files that turn out to contain information as to how to commit offences even though they may not have actually read the files in question?

Criminal Attempt

criminal attempt
A criminal attempt occurs when an individual does—or omits to do—anything for the purpose of carrying out a previously formed intention to commit a crime. The conduct in question must constitute a substantial step towards the completion of the crime that is intended.

The offence of **criminal attempt** is focused on an accused person's intention to commit a crime that is never realized. Section 24(1) of the Criminal Code provides that "everyone who, having an intent to commit an offense, does or omits to do anything for the purpose of carrying out his intention is guilty of an attempt to commit the offence whether or not it was possible under the circumstances to commit the offence." Clearly, the *mens rea* of criminal attempt is nothing short of an actual intent to commit an offence. The *actus reus* of attempt is any step taken by the accused towards the completion of the offence, provided that this step goes beyond "mere preparation" and is not considered to be "too remote" from the completed offence. For example, buying a train ticket with a view to travelling to another city in order to rob a bank would be considered "mere preparation" and "too remote" from the completed robbery to justify convicting the accused of a criminal attempt. However, if the accused person actually reaches the front doors of the bank before being arrested by the police, it is clear that the *actus reus* of the offence of attempted robbery has been established. Unfortunately, it is often very difficult to predict exactly where the court will draw the line between mere preparation and an act that warrants conviction for a criminal attempt. It should also be emphasized that a criminal attempt may be committed even though it is impossible for the accused to commit the complete offence that he or she has in mind. For example, if someone tries to steal a motor vehicle that has been totally disabled by its owner, that person is guilty of attempted theft even though it was impossible for that person to take the vehicle from the spot where it had been parked. Similarly, if an accused person mistakenly shoots a wax dummy, believing it is an enemy, that person is guilty of attempted murder. What is important is that the accused person seriously intended to commit the crime and that there is a real likelihood that, having failed on this particular occasion, the accused will try again and, perhaps, be more successful on that subsequent occasion.

Conspiracy

The crime of **conspiracy** is established when two or more individuals form a common intention to commit a crime. The Crown must also prove that each individual charged with conspiracy actually intended to put the common design into effect. The *actus reus* of conspiracy is the agreement to engage in criminal conduct, while the *mens rea* component consists of the intent not only to enter into this agreement but also to implement it. Suppose two individuals apparently agree to murder a third party. However, it later turns out that one of these individuals was actually an undercover police officer who never had any intention to act on this supposed agreement. In this case, neither of the individuals may be convicted of conspiracy. The police officer lacks the necessary *mens rea* for conspiracy, and the other individual cannot be convicted of this offence because the Crown must prove that there are at least two persons who seriously intended to implement the plan to commit murder. On the other hand, if there are two or more individuals who agree to commit murder and who fully intend to carry out their homicidal plans, they will be convicted of conspiracy even if an undercover officer is also part of this group. As long as a minimum of two individuals intend to carry out an agreement to commit a crime, there is a conspiracy. Conspiracy is a crime that provides the Crown with a number of distinct advantages. For example, certain types of evidence may be accepted at the joint trial of a group of alleged co-conspirators that would never be admitted against specific members of that group if they were tried separately. In effect, there is always the danger of "guilt by association" in conspiracy trials.

conspiracy
An agreement by two or more persons to commit a criminal offence.

Defences to a Criminal Charge

Conviction for a "true crime" should not occur unless the accused person is considered blameworthy. Just because individuals engage in conduct that, from an objective point of view, is either actually or potentially harmful does not mean they should be punished under the provisions of the criminal law. Indeed, the requirement of *mens rea* ensures that the Crown must first prove a culpable mental state or the prosecution will fail. In addition to the *mens rea* requirement, several distinct defences may be raised by an accused person in a criminal trial. Some of these defences, such as mistake of fact, basically amount to a denial that the Crown has proved the necessary *mens rea*, but other defences, such as duress, may be raised successfully even though the accused possessed the necessary *mens rea* for the offence that has been charged. Essentially, a patchwork of defences has evolved as a means of ensuring that those individuals who have a justification or excuse for their conduct are either acquitted of criminal charges or are treated more leniently (for example, by conviction for a less serious offence).

Mental Disorder as a Defence to a Criminal Charge

In the Supreme Court of Canada's decision in *Winko* (1999), Justice McLachlin said:

> In every society, there are those who commit criminal acts because of mental illness. The criminal law must find a way to deal with these people fairly, while protecting the public against further harms. The task is not an easy one.

NEL

NCRMD
The special verdict of "not criminally responsible on account of mental disorder." In order to be found NCRMD, it must be proved on the balance of probabilities that, because of mental disorder, the accused lacked the capacity to appreciate the nature and quality of the act or omission in question or to know it would be considered morally wrong by the average Canadian.

In Canada, this difficult task is undertaken through the application by the courts of the special defence of not criminally responsible on account of mental disorder (**NCRMD**). The current test that must be used in deciding whether an accused should be found NCRMD is articulated in section 16(1) of the Criminal Code:

> No person is criminally responsible for an act committed or an omission made while suffering from a mental disorder that renders the person incapable of appreciating the nature and quality of the act or omission or of knowing that it was wrong.

The first requirement of the NCRMD defence is that the accused was suffering from a "mental disorder" at the time of the alleged offence(s). The Supreme Court of Canada has adopted an extremely broad definition of mental disorder, but in practice, only those accused persons who, at the time of the alleged offence, were experiencing the symptoms associated with a severe mental disorder are likely to be found NCRMD (for example, the hallucinations and or delusions that may be caused by schizophrenia or bipolar affective disorder). Indeed, the criteria specified in section 16(1) of the Criminal Code are very restrictive: namely, that the accused was rendered incapable either of appreciating the physical nature and quality of the act or omission in question or of knowing that the act or omission is considered morally wrong by the everyday standards of the ordinary Canadian. Most individuals living with serious mental disorders understand the physical nature of their conduct (for example, most would realize that stabbing someone in the heart will cause death). Similarly, the majority of these individuals are capable of knowing that their conduct would be "morally condemned by reasonable members of society" [as Justice Louise Arbour of the Supreme Court of Canada put it in the *Molodowic* case (2000)]. However, an individual who, as a result of a mental disorder, acts under the delusion that he is "God" and that the victim is the devil would certainly not have the capacity to know that killing the victim would be considered morally wrong—as was the case in *Landry* (1991). Significantly, section 16(1) does not extend the benefit of the NCRMD defence to mentally disordered persons who claim that—as a consequence of mental disorder—they succumbed to an irresistible impulse to commit a crime; provided such individuals were capable of understanding what they were doing and that it was wrong, they are not considered to be NCRMD in Canadian criminal law.

The very narrow scope of the NCRMD defence ensures that relatively few accused persons may raise it successfully at their trial. It is significant that section 16 places the burden of proving the NCRMD defence on the shoulders of the accused person if he or she raises it at trial. In this situation, the accused has to prove the defence on the balance of probabilities. Although this provision infringes the presumption of innocence, enshrined in section 11(d) of the *Charter*, the Supreme Court of Canada ruled, in the *Chaulk* case (1990), that this infringement of the accused person's right was justified as a reasonable limitation under section 1. The Court took the view that it would be impractical to require the Crown to prove beyond a reasonable doubt that the accused was not mentally disordered—particularly in light of the fact that an accused person may refuse to cooperate with a psychiatrist nominated by the Crown to report to the court on the accused's mental condition.

Accused persons who are found NCRMD are not acquitted in the technical sense of that word. Indeed, section 672.1 of the Criminal Code states that a verdict of NCRMD constitutes a finding that "the accused committed the act or omission that formed the basis of the offence with which the accused is charged but is not criminally responsible on account of mental disorder." NCR accused may be granted (1) an absolute discharge, (2) a conditional discharge, or (3) an order holding them in custody in a psychiatric facility.

Section 672.54(a) of the Criminal Code, which deals with the disposition of NCR accused, has been interpreted as requiring that, unless a court or review board determines that an NCR accused person constitutes a "significant threat to the safety of the public," then it *must* order an absolute discharge. In *Winko* (1999), the Supreme Court of Canada ruled that the threshold for justifying the imposition of restrictions on the liberty of a person who has been found NCRMD is relatively high:

> A "significant threat to the safety of the public" means a real risk of physical or psychological harm to members of the public that is serious in the sense of going beyond the merely trivial or annoying. The conduct giving rise to the harm must be criminal in nature.*

However, public concern about the eventual release into the community of individuals found NCRMD after having carried out acts of extreme violence led to some significant amendments to the Criminal Code in 2014. The *Not Criminally Responsible Reform Act* (S.C. 2014, c. 6) was designed to make it more difficult for some NCR accused persons to be given their freedom and also to give a greater voice to victims in the decision-making process that determines the release of these individuals. The pivotal amendment in this legislation empowers the trial court, following a finding of NCRMD, to designate the NCR accused person a "high-risk accused," if they committed a serious personal injury offence and:

(a) the court is satisfied that there is a substantial likelihood that the accused will use violence that could endanger the life or safety of another person; or

(b) the court is of the opinion that the acts that constitute the offence were of such a brutal nature as to indicate a risk of grave physical or psychological harm to another person. [Criminal Code, s. 672.64(1)].

The main consequence of this designation is that the NCR accused person must be kept in strict custody in a hospital and not allowed any temporary absences unless (1) they are escorted and (2) there is no undue risk to the public. Only a court may lift the "high-risk accused" designation.

One reason for the enactment of this reform was, undoubtedly, the force of negative public reaction to the case of Vince Li, who had gruesomely murdered a fellow passenger on a Greyhound bus travelling through Manitoba in 2008. Li was diagnosed as living with schizophrenia, and psychiatrists agreed that, at the time of the homicide, Li's psychotic state had led him to believe that the victim

---

*The *Not Criminally Responsible Reform Act, S.C. 2014, c. 6* incorporated this definition into the Criminal Code and added some clarifying words: "a significant threat to the safety of the public means a risk of serious physical or psychological harm to members of the public—including any victim of or witness to the offence, or any person under the age of 18 years—resulting from conduct that is criminal in nature but not necessarily violent" (s. 72.5401).

THE CANADIAN PRESS/John Woods

Public outcry about the possibility that Vince Li would eventually be released was one of the factors that led to more restrictive laws dealing with people found NCRMD. He was granted an absolute discharge by the Manitoba Review Board in February 2017.

was an alien. Li was found NCRMD and committed to the Selkirk Mental Health Centre. Shortly after arriving at the Centre, he was authorized to take secure walks outside the facility. Many members of the public complained about the walks and about the possibility of Li's eventual release. However, in 2016, Mr. Li, now known as Will Baker, was nevertheless released into the community on strict conditions, and in February 2017 he was granted an absolute discharge. Since he was successfully taking antipsychotic medication and had fully recovered his mental health, the Manitoba Review Board no longer considered him to pose a "significant threat to the safety of the public."

One of the very first cases in which the Crown applied to have an NCR accused person declared a "high-risk accused," under the new section 672.64 of the Criminal Code, was *Schoenborn* (2017). Allan Schoenborn had killed all three of his children by smothering them, after having attacked one of them with a cleaver. However, he was determined to have committed these homicides while in a state of psychosis and found NCRMD at his trial in 2010. In 2017 a judge of the BC Supreme Court dismissed the Crown's application to retroactively designate Schoenborn a "high-risk accused." First, Justice Devlin found that the evidence did not establish that there was "a substantial likelihood that the accused will use violence that could endanger the life or safety of another person" [section 672.64(1)(a)]. Schoenborn's psychotic condition had been treated effectively by antipsychotic medication so that the underlying cause of the offences he had committed against his children no longer existed. Second, even though the killings were undoubtedly "brutal" in nature, Justice Devlin nonetheless ruled that Schoenborn had enjoyed a "prolonged remission of his psychosis and delusional disorder through antipsychotic medication" and, therefore, did not pose "a risk of grave physical or psychological harm to another person" [s. 672.64(1)(b)]. The decision in *Schoenborn* (2017) suggests that the 2014 legislation was misguided insofar as it failed to recognize that those who commit a violent offence while in a state of psychosis should not be treated as though they were culpable for their actions and that treatments for psychosis can be so effective that NCR-accused persons no longer pose a threat to anyone. Unfortunately, many members of the public continue to experience fear of the NCR accused. This fear is fuelled by the stigma that surrounds mental illness and by a lack of knowledge of the efficacy of current treatments for the psychotic conditions that caused the types of horrific violence committed by such NCR-accused as Vincent Li and Allan Schoenborn.

General Defences to a Criminal Charge

Mistake of fact may constitute a defence to a criminal charge if it causes the accused to erroneously believe that the circumstances facing him or her did not render his or her actions criminal. For example, if a woman participates in a marriage ceremony with a man, erroneously believing that her first husband is dead, she is not guilty of the crime of bigamy. The central element of the *actus reus* of bigamy is that one of the parties to a marriage ceremony is already married. If the accused honestly believes that she is a widow, then—in the circumstances as she perceives them to be—she is not committing a prohibited act because she is no longer married to her first spouse. When the accused operates under a mistake of fact, he or she is really stating that the Crown has failed to prove the necessary *mens rea* of the offence.

One of the most controversial uses of the defence of mistake of fact used to occur when an accused person who was charged with sexual assault claimed that he honestly believed he had the complainant's consent, even though he was mistaken. However, section 273.2(b) of the Criminal Code (enacted in 1992) states that mistaken belief in consent will not be a valid defence to a charge of sexual assault unless the accused took "reasonable steps, in the circumstances known to the accused at the time, to ascertain that the complainant was consenting." By requiring the accused person to act reasonably, this amendment to the Code has considerably reduced the opportunities for abuse of the defence of honest belief in consent. For example, in *Crangle* (2010), the accused had initiated sexual intercourse with his twin brother's sleeping girlfriend. The victim initially thought that the accused was her boyfriend, but as soon as she realized his true identity, she strongly objected to his actions. The accused claimed that he had an honest—albeit mistaken—belief that the victim had consented. The trial judge rejected this defence because Crangle had done nothing to make his identity perfectly clear to the victim; undoubtedly, he had failed to take reasonable steps to ascertain whether there was consent.

While honest mistake of fact constitutes a valid defence to a criminal charge, a mistake concerning the nature or scope of the criminal law does not absolve an accused person of criminal liability. Section 19 of the Criminal Code makes it clear that ignorance of the law is no excuse. This is a harsh rule but an inevitable one, since it would be impossible for the Crown to prove actual knowledge of the relevant legal principles. There are some exceptions to this rule. One of the more important exceptions arises when an official who is charged with the administration of certain

mistake of fact
Mistake of fact may be a defence where the accused person acts under the influence of an honest mistake in relation to any of the elements of the *actus reus* of the offence charged.

types of regulatory legislation gives erroneous legal advice. If the accused person reasonably relies on this advice, he or she may take advantage of the defence of "officially induced error." For example, if a factory inspector tells a manufacturer that it is acceptable to modify a certain safety device, it would clearly be unfair to convict that manufacturer of a violation of the relevant occupational safety legislation. If the manufacturer reasonably relied on the advice of the factory inspector and committed what a court later concludes is a regulatory offence, then the defence of officially induced error will come to the rescue of the manufacturer.

intoxication defence
Intoxication caused by alcohol and/or other drugs may be a defence if it prevents the accused from forming the intent required for a specific intent offence, such as murder or robbery.

Intoxication is a complex and highly problematic defence. A high proportion of violent crimes are committed by individuals who have abused alcohol and/or other drugs, and the great majority of the inmates in Canada's prisons have been diagnosed with a substance abuse disorder. If the scope of a defence of intoxication were drawn too broadly, many violent offenders would escape criminal liability even though they were considered to have ingested alcohol and/or other drugs voluntarily. One of the main effects of alcohol (and some other drugs) is to cause disinhibition—a condition in which the accused may be rendered less able to control his or her conduct. However, the courts have consistently ruled that intoxication may not be raised as a valid defence by accused persons who simply claim that alcohol and/or other drugs impaired their ability to control their conduct. Instead, the intoxication defence focuses on whether the accused's state of intoxication (from alcohol and/or other drugs) prevented him or her from forming the necessary *mens rea* for the crime in question.

FOCUS   BOX 3.4

THE CRIMINALIZATION OF THE FAILURE TO DISCLOSE ONE'S HIV POSITIVE STATUS

Section 265(3)(c) of the Criminal Code states that consent to the application of force or the threat of force is rendered invalid if it was obtained by fraud. The Supreme Court of Canada ruled in *Cuerrier* (1998) that an individual who has tested positive for HIV (the human immunodeficiency virus that causes AIDS, acquired immune deficiency syndrome) and who engages in unprotected sexual intercourse with another person without disclosing his or her HIV positive status is guilty of fraud. Therefore, any consent given to sexual activity on the part of that other person is invalid if that consent would not have been given had the other person been made aware of the individual's HIV positive status. Since transmission of HIV threatens the life of the other person, the Supreme Court of Canada has ruled that a charge of aggravated sexual assault may be laid under section 273 of the Criminal Code.

There is considerable debate as to the wisdom of criminalizing individuals who live with HIV positive status and who engage in sexual intercourse without disclosure of that status. Changes in the treatment of HIV have greatly reduced the likelihood that the virus can be transmitted. ART (antiretroviral therapy, consisting

of a "cocktail" of drugs) effectively suppresses HIV and reduces the risk of transmission of the virus to minimal levels. A person who is receiving ART will have a low viral load (a minimal level of HIV in the blood) so that the risk of transmission of HIV is very small. Some maintain that an individual who is HIV positive, but who owing to ART has a low viral load, should not be convicted of aggravated sexual assault if he or she engages in unprotected intercourse without disclosure of his or her HIV positive status. In the case of *Mabior* (2012), the Supreme Court of Canada had the opportunity to reconsider its ruling in *Cuerrier* in light of the evidence relating to the impact of ART and its ability to reduce viral load.

Mabior was charged with nine counts of aggravated sexual assault because he had failed to disclose his HIV-positive status to nine women with whom he had sexual intercourse. Mabior had been receiving ART and his viral loads were low, thereby reducing the risk of transmission of the virus. The Supreme Court of Canada set out the requirements for conviction of an accused person in Mabior's situation. Chief Justice McLachlin summarized the Court's ruling as follows:

. . . to obtain a conviction under ss. 265(3)(*c*) and 273, the Crown must show that the complainant's consent to sexual intercourse was vitiated by the accused's fraud as to his HIV status. Failure to disclose (*the dishonest act*) amounts to fraud where the complainant would not have consented had he or she known the accused was HIV-positive, and where sexual contact poses a significant risk of or causes actual serious bodily harm (*deprivation*). A significant risk of serious bodily harm is established by a realistic possibility of transmission of HIV. On the evidence before us, a realistic possibility of transmission is negated by evidence that the accused's viral load was low at the time of intercourse and that condom protection was used. However, the general proposition that a low viral load combined with condom use negates a realistic possibility of transmission of HIV does not preclude the common law from adapting to future advances in treatment and to circumstances where risk factors other than those considered in the present case are at play.

Ultimately, Mabior was convicted only of the three charges that concerned acts of sexual intercourse that had taken place *without the use of a condom*. Having low viral loads was not considered sufficient *per se* to eliminate "a realistic possibility of transmission" of the virus: in order to achieve that objective, the accused must also use a condom.

The *Mabior* case raises many questions. Is it an appropriate use of the criminal law to punish individuals who live with HIV for engaging in unprotected sexual relations and failing to disclose their HIV-positive status? Chief Justice McLachlin, on behalf of the Supreme Court, clearly took the view that this conduct is an appropriate target of the criminal law. The Supreme Court concluded that engaging in fraud and subjecting the other party in a sexual encounter to a serious risk to their life is blameworthy.

The Supreme Court also stated that failure to disclose infringes basic values enshrined in the Canadian *Charter* of Rights and Freedoms. It has been asserted by some that criminalization of the failure to disclose HIV-positive status will discourage individuals living with this condition from seeking testing and treatment. However, Chief Justice McLachlin stated that the Court had not been presented with evidence that would prove this assertion to be true.

Critics of the *Mabior* decision have focused on the lack of certainty as to the precise meaning of "a realistic possibility of transmission" of HIV. The risk of transmission depends on the nature of the sexual act in question. In *Mabior*, the Supreme Court considered only the risk associated with vaginal intercourse. The very complexity of assessing the risk for different types of sexual acts renders it most likely that expert witnesses will disagree in the courtroom. Critics have also questioned whether the Supreme Court had understood the scientific evidence concerning the risks of transmission when the individual has low viral loads. Why, if there is a low viral load and a very small risk of transmission, did the Court also impose the requirement that an individual living with HIV must use a condom?

In *Hutchinson* (2014), the Supreme Court affirmed the conviction of aggravated sexual assault, where the accused, knowing that his partner (the victim) did not want to become pregnant, deliberately sabotaged the condom by poking holes in it. The victim became pregnant. The Supreme Court ruled that the victim's consent to sexual intercourse had been vitiated by Hutchinson's fraud.

Questions for Critical Thinking

1. Do you agree that the criminal law should be used to punish individuals who do not disclose their HIV-positive status?

2. Given the efficacy of medications that reduce viral loads to a very low level, why should accused persons have to demonstrate that they also used a condom?

The defence of intoxication is primarily a "common law" defence in that it was developed by the courts in the absence of any legislation that defined its nature and scope. Traditionally, the defence has applied only to those offences that required proof of a complex form of *mens rea* known as "specific intent." Therefore, the defence of intoxication may reduce the severity of a charge (for example, from murder to manslaughter or from robbery to assault). On the other hand, it has been a long-standing principle that intoxication is not a valid defence to a charge of such "basic intent" offences as assault, sexual assault, or damage to property (mischief).* The legal rationale for maintaining the distinction

*Even if the accused person is so intoxicated that he or she is in a state that is similar to extreme mental disorder or automatism, section 33.1 of the Criminal Code denies the accused person any defence to a charge of a basic intent offence (such as sexual assault) that involves violence or a threat of violence.

between crimes of specific and basic intent is that intoxication does not normally impair people to the extent that they do not even have the minimal degree of *mens rea* required to assault someone or to damage property. Even extremely intoxicated people have some degree of awareness of what they are doing, and the acts of committing an assault or damaging property require only a very minimal degree of intent. On the other hand, assaulting someone with the specific intent to kill (murder) or forcefully taking something from another individual with the specific intent to steal (robbery) are acts that require a considerably more complex pattern of thought, and intoxication may well prevent the accused from forming the necessary specific intent that is required for conviction of these serious crimes.

If the ingestion of alcohol and/or other drugs precipitates a psychosis (a condition in which an individual loses contact with reality), should the accused person be able to assert the defence of NCRMD, under section 16 of the Criminal Code? In the case of *Bouchard-Lebrun* (2011), the Supreme Court of Canada ruled that, if the substance-induced psychosis is only short-lived and the accused person quickly recovers when the substance leaves his or her body, then he or she may not raise the NCRMD defence. However, if the accused person has a pre-existing mental disorder that is exacerbated by the ingestion of alcohol and/or other drugs or if there has been a long-standing pattern of substance abuse that has caused significant changes to the brain, then the substance-induced psychosis may provide the basis for a successful defence of NCRMD.

The defences of **necessity** and **duress** are based on the notion that it would be unfair to convict individuals of a criminal offence if they did not have a genuine choice at the time they committed it. As the Supreme Court of Canada put it in *Ruzic* (2001), "it is a principle of fundamental justice that only voluntary conduct—behaviour that is the product of a free will and controlled body, unhindered by external constraints—should attract the penalty and stigma of criminal liability." In a moral sense, individuals who act under the constraints of duress or necessity do not so voluntarily, and hence, the defences of duress and necessity are said to be based on "moral involuntariness." Both defences are conceptualized by the courts as "excuses" rather than "justifications"; as Justice Dickson said, in the Supreme Court of Canada's decision in *Perka* (1984), "An 'excuse' concedes the wrongfulness of the action but asserts that the circumstances under which it was done are such that it ought not to be attributed to the actor." Self-defence, by way of contrast, is considered to be an action that is justified. In *Ryan* (2013), the Supreme Court of Canada compared the rationale for self-defence with that for duress and necessity:

> Despite its close links to necessity and duress, self-defence, on the other hand, is a justification. . . . It "challenges the wrongfulness of an action which technically constitutes a crime". . . . In determining whether the defence is available, less emphasis is placed on the particular circumstances and concessions to human frailty and more importance is attached to the action itself and the reason why the accused was justified in meeting force with force.

necessity
Necessity may be a defence to a criminal charge when the accused person commits the lesser evil of a crime in order to avoid the occurrence of a greater evil.

duress
Duress may be a defence to a criminal charge when the accused was forced to commit a crime as a consequence of threats of death or serious bodily harm made by another person.

Necessity is a common law defence that arises when the accused person can avoid some disaster or calamity only by breaking the law. In *Perka* (1984), Justice Dickson provided an example of such a situation:

> The lost Alpinist who, on the point of freezing to death, breaks open an isolated mountain cabin is not literally behaving in an involuntary fashion. He has control over his actions to the extent of being physically capable of abstaining from the act. Realistically, however, his act is not a "voluntary" one. His "choice" to break the law is not true choice at all; it is remorselessly compelled by normal human instincts.

The "evil" that the accused person seeks to avoid must be greater than the "evil" involved in the breaking of the law, and the accused must have no reasonable legal alternative but to break the law. Take the case of a surgeon who is contemplating the surgical separation of conjoined twins who share vital organs, such as the heart or the lungs. Without an operation to separate the babies, both of them will ultimately die. However, the operation will save one of the twins, while inevitably killing the other. Is the surgeon justified in killing one twin in order to save the other? In these particular circumstances, one can assume that the defence of necessity would be available to the surgeon should he or she ever be charged with murder.

When claiming the defence of necessity, defendants may point to any circumstances that constitute a threat to life or limb. Where the defence of duress is raised, defendants are asserting that their power of choice is being overborne by another human being. In the *Hibbert* case (1995), the Supreme Court of Canada ruled that duress, like necessity, was a defence based on the concept of "normative involuntariness." Section 17 of the Criminal Code sets out the requirements for the defence of duress; however, in the case of *Ruzic* (2001), the Supreme Court of Canada ruled that some of these requirements were so restrictive that they could result in the denial of the defence to an individual who was not blameworthy. As a result, the court struck down these requirements as invalid under the *Charter*.* The Supreme Court then held that the courts should apply the "common law" defence of duress. The main elements of this defence are that the accused had been subjected to a threat of death or serious bodily harm directed either towards the accused or towards another person (such as a child or spouse). The threat must be so serious that the accused believes it will be carried out, and the court must be satisfied that it would have caused a reasonable person, placed in exactly the same position as the accused, to act as he or she did. Finally, it should be established that the accused had no obvious "safe avenue of escape." After all, if the accused had the option to escape from the person who was making threats, he or she cannot now claim that he or she was acting involuntarily.

In the *Ruzic* case, for example, the accused was charged with importing a narcotic and use of a false passport. Two kilograms of heroin had been found strapped to her body when she arrived at Pearson Airport in Toronto. Ruzic admitted the offences but asserted that she had acted under duress. Her story was that she lived with her mother in Belgrade (in the former Yugoslavia) and that she had been

---

*The Supreme Court did not declare invalid the requirement that the accused person not be a member of a gang or conspiracy that brought about the alleged situation of duress, nor did it address the list of 22 offences (ranging from murder to robbery and arson) that Parliament has excluded from the benefit of the defence. However, section 17 only applies to those who actually commit the offence (as opposed to those who are parties to offence by way of aiding/abetting, etc.).

persistently threatened by a "paramilitary" man who physically assaulted and sexually harassed her. The man had a reputation for extreme violence, and he informed Ruzic that she must take a consignment of heroin to Toronto. When the accused protested, the man threatened to harm her mother. At the time of these threats, law and order had largely broken down in Belgrade, and Ruzic said she did not inform the Belgrade police of the threats against her mother because they were "corrupt and would do nothing to assist her." The jury acquitted Ruzic on both charges, and the Supreme Court of Canada ultimately upheld the acquittal. Ruzic had met all the requirements contained in the common law defence of duress. She clearly believed that she had absolutely no alternative to bringing the heroin into Canada. If she had not done so, her mother might have been seriously harmed or killed, and seeking the assistance of the local police would have been a futile gesture given the particular circumstances in Belgrade at that time.

In *Ryan* (2013), the Supreme Court of Canada ruled that the threat that is at the core of the defence of duress must be one that is specifically made in order to coerce the accused person into committing a crime. Duress cannot be raised as a defence in situations where the real issue is self-defence. In *Ryan*, the accused was the "victim of a violent, abusive and controlling husband" and had counselled an undercover RCMP officer to kill her husband. The Supreme Court ruled that duress was not available to her.*

provocation

Provocation may be a partial defence to a charge of murder (if successful, it reduces the offence from murder to manslaughter). The required elements of provocation are (1) that the accused responded to the commission of a serious crime by the victim against the accused in circumstances that were of such a nature that an ordinary person would have been likely to lose the power of self-control, and (2) that the accused acted "on the sudden and before there was time for his (or her) passion to cool."

Other important defences are provocation and self-defence. **Provocation** is just a *partial* defence and may be raised only when the accused is charged with murder. If provocation is raised successfully by the accused, they will be convicted of manslaughter rather than murder. In *Tran* (2010), Justice Charron of the Supreme Court of Canada noted that "the accused's conduct is partially *excused* out of a compassion to human frailty." The defence is available even though the accused undoubtedly possessed the necessary intent for murder. In 2015, Parliament amended section 232 of the Criminal Code so that the only conduct that will be permitted to trigger the defence of provocation is "conduct of the the victim that would constitute an indictable offence under this Act (the Criminal Code) that is punishable by five or more years of imprisonment" [s. 232(2)]. This significant change signals Parliament's intention to severely restrict the availability of the defence to those individuals who deliberately kill another person. For example, the defence will no longer be available to those accused who commit a "crime of passion" after discovering their partner or spouse engaged in a sexual act with another person. Undoubtedly, Parliament was seeking to withdraw the defence of provocation from those individuals (nearly always men) who commit intimate partner homicide solely in angry revenge for perceived sexual infidelity or the break-up of a relationship. The most common circumstance in which provocation may now be raised is where the deceased victim was assaulting the accused, but other eligible crimes carrying a sentence of five or more years of imprisonment include sexual assault, robbery, extortion, criminal harassment, and uttering threats. However, in order to meet the Criminal Code requirements for provocation, the accused person will generally have to demonstrate that there were *aggravating circumstances* surrounding the assault or other serious crime being committed by the deceased victim. The victim may have uttered provocative words or made insulting gestures

*However, the Supreme Court entered a stay of proceedings that prevented her retrial on a charge of counselling murder.

while assaulting the accused (for example, mocking the accused person's physical or mental challenges). Even if the victim was committing one of these serious offences in aggravating circumstances, there are other onerous requirements for a successful defence of provocation. First, the alleged provocative criminal behaviour of the victim must have been "of such a nature as to be sufficient to deprive an ordinary person of the power of self-control." In *Pappas* (2013), Chief Justice McLachlin stated that "the ordinary person standard seeks to ensure that only 'behaviour which comports with contemporary society's norms and values will attract the law's compassion.'" The ordinary person would be someone with the same objective characteristics as the accused (for example, race, gender, and age), and the alleged provocation must be viewed in the specific context of the interaction between the accused person and the victim (for example, whether there has been any past history between them, such as a long history of the victim having ridiculed the accused person's alleged sexual inadequacies in front of the accused's friends or neighbours). Second, the Criminal Code requires the accused person raising the defence to establish that they acted on the alleged provocation "on the sudden and before there was time for their passion to cool." This prerequisite excludes individuals who coldly plan to take their revenge outside the immediate time frame in which the alleged provocation occurred. In *Pappas* (2013), the victim had allegedly been blackmailing (extorting money from) Pappas for 18 months and threatened to harm Pappas's mother if he ceased payment. This situation would meet the new requirement subsequently introduced in 2015, but the Supreme Court of Canada upheld Pappas's conviction of murder because he did not act "on the sudden before there was time for (his) passion to cool."

Self-defence is frequently raised as a defence to charges of assault or homicide. Recent amendments to the Criminal Code have simplified the law that defines the circumstances in which self-defence and defence of property will be accepted as complete defences to criminal charges.

Section 34 of the Criminal Code states that a person may use a reasonable amount of force in self-defence if she or he reasonably believes that they or another individual are the target of actual force or that a threat of force is being made against them. The section also sets out the factors that the courts must take into account in considering whether an accused person's use of force in self-defence was reasonable in all of the circumstances of the case. The factors listed in section 34, which are not exclusive, are: the nature of the force or threat; the extent to which the use of force was imminent and whether there were other means available to respond to the potential use of force; the person's role in the incident; whether any party to the incident used or threatened to use a weapon; the size, age, gender, and physical capabilities of the parties to the incident; the nature, duration, and history of any relationship between the parties to the incident, including any prior use or threat of force and the nature of that force or threat; any history of interaction or communication between the parties to the incident; the nature and proportionality of the person's response to the use or threat of force; and whether the act committed was in response to a use or threat of force that the person knew was lawful.

Although the self-defence provisions of the Criminal Code have been dramatically overhauled, the large body of case law concerning the "old" provisions is still relevant, particularly with respect to the issue of whether the accused person's conduct was reasonable. The Supreme Court of Canada has consistently

self-defence
Section 34 of the Criminal Code states that a person may use a reasonable amount of force in self-defence if she or he reasonably believes that they or another individual are the target of actual force or that a threat of force is being made against them.

emphasized that the basic issue is whether the particular accused person acted reasonably in light of the specific circumstances that faced him or her at the time of the assault upon him or her and in light of her or his perception of those circumstances. For example, the Supreme Court of Canada has emphasized the need to ensure that women who are the victims of domestic violence are judged by the standards of "reasonable women" who face the same circumstances of ongoing abuse and not by the standards of "reasonable men" brawling in a bar. In the *Lavallee* case (1990), the accused had shot her abusive male partner (Rust) in the back of the head. Rust was leaving Lavallee's room just after he had physically assaulted her and threatened her with death.

At Lavallee's trial for murder, a psychiatrist gave expert testimony concerning the so-called battered wife syndrome in order to help the members of the jury determine whether the accused woman's beliefs and actions were reasonable in light of her experience of chronic abuse at the hands of her partner. The psychiatrist asserted that Lavallee "had been terrorized by Rust to the point of feeling trapped, vulnerable, worthless and unable to escape the relationship despite the violence." This witness concluded that Lavallee's shooting of Rust should be viewed as "a final desperate act by a woman who sincerely believed that she would be killed that night." The jury acquitted Lavallee. The Supreme Court of Canada later upheld the acquittal and ruled that the trial judge had acted appropriately in permitting an expert witness to testify about the "battered woman syndrome" as a means of assisting the members of the jury to assess the reasonableness of Lavallee's beliefs and actions.

In a later case, *Malott* (1998), the Supreme Court of Canada suggested that this type of evidence should be presented to the jury in order to assist them in understanding at least four separate issues: (1) why an abused woman might remain in an abusive relationship, (2) the nature and extent of the violence that may exist in an abusive relationship, (3) the woman's ability to perceive when her partner was dangerous, and (4) whether she believed on reasonable grounds that she could not otherwise preserve herself from death or serious bodily harm. Section 35 also permits an individual to use force in defence of his or her real property (house, apartment, land) and/or personal property, provided the force used is reasonable in the particular circumstances.

QUESTIONS FOR CRITICAL THINKING

1. Why does Canadian criminal law place so much importance on the requirement that the Crown prove the relevant *mens rea* elements of a criminal offence? Would it not make more sense for the state to intervene and deal with offenders solely on the basis of the fact that they have committed the *actus reus* of an offence (a harmful or potentially harmful act or omission)?

2. Daphne has lived with Apollo for ten years, during which he has, on various occasions, subjected her to physical assaults, some of which have inflicted serious injuries (such as extensive bruising to the body, a broken nose, and concussion). One night, Daphne returns home late from an evening meeting and Apollo becomes furious with her. He yells that he is "going to fix her once

and for all." However, Apollo is so drunk that he passes out on the couch. Daphne goes to the kitchen and picks up a sharp knife. She then returns to the room where Apollo is sleeping and stabs him to death. Would Daphne be able to raise a successful plea of self-defence if she were charged with murder or manslaughter?

Summary

- A crime consists of a prohibition against certain conduct and a penal sanction (such as imprisonment or a fine).

- The sources of criminal law are (1) legislation and (2) judicial decisions.

- Under the terms of the Canadian Constitution, the Parliament of Canada has the exclusive authority to enact "criminal law and the procedures relating to criminal matters."

- There is a significant difference between "true crimes" that arise under the Criminal Code and regulatory offences that arise under regulatory legislation enacted both by the various provinces and territories and by the Parliament of Canada.

- The enactment of the Canadian *Charter* of Rights and Freedoms has given judges the power to invalidate criminal law that unjustifiably infringes on an accused person's *Charter* rights.

- Each criminal offence can be analyzed in terms of its *actus reus* and *mens rea* elements.

- The *actus reus* generally consists of three components: conduct, circumstances, and consequences.

- *Mens rea* may be subjective or objective.

- Subjective *mens rea* may consist of intention and knowledge; recklessness; or willful blindness.

- Objective *mens rea* is based on the requirement that there be a marked departure from the standard expected of the reasonable person acting prudently.

- An individual may become a party to a criminal offence in a number of different ways: by actually committing an offence, by aiding and/or abetting an offence, by becoming a party to an offence by way of common intention, and by counselling an offence that is committed.

- Three inchoate offences permit the police to intervene before a particular crime is committed: counselling an offence that is not committed, criminal attempt, and conspiracy.

- A successful defence of not criminally responsible on account of mental disorder (NCRMD) is not an acquittal. It is a finding that the accused person has committed the act or omission in question but may not be held criminally responsible on account of mental disorder.

- The most important defences to a criminal charge include mistake of fact; intoxication; necessity; duress; provocation; and self-defence.

NET WORK

Basic legal research is increasingly conducted online. The federal government and the governments of the provinces and territories operate websites that offer swift access via the Internet to the full text of legislation and the decisions of the courts. In addition, a number of commercial electronic database services, such as *Lexis Advance QuickLaw, Westlaw Next Cana*da (which includes *CriminalSource* and *LawSource*), *HeinOnline*, and *Canadian Human Rights Reporter* provide information concerning legislation, cases, and legal literature (journal articles and textbooks). You should be able to gain access to these databases through your university or college. If you have such access, a useful exercise might be to search for Canadian criminal cases in which the courts have discussed the defence of duress.

You may explore the powerful electronic tools that are available for research into Canadian criminal law by visiting the website of the Canadian Legal Information Institute [CANLII (https://www.canlii.org/en)]. This website provides easy access to federal and provincial/territorial legislation and court decisions. In addition, the website provides access to the decisions of various federal and provincial/territorial boards and tribunals (such as the Canadian Human Rights Tribunal and the Human Rights Tribunal of Ontario). It also contains links to various external websites that may be of particular value to students (for example, the debates of the House of Commons *Hansard* or the *Canada Gazette*, which provides "Canadians with their rightful access to the laws and regulations that govern their daily lives"). Using the CANLII website, find the report of the following case: *R. v. McLellan* 2018 ONCA 510 (CanLII), judgment issued by the Ontario Court of Appeal on 1 June 2018.

The website operated by the Department of Justice Canada is particularly useful. This site provides not only detailed information about the activities of the Department of Justice and federal developments concerning criminal law but also access to all federal legislation and regulations. The website address for the Department of Justice Canada is *www.canada.justice.gc.ca*. To locate legislation and regulations, click onto "The Laws Site" on the home page.

Using the Department of Justice Canada website, see what information is available concerning *An Act to amend the* Criminal Code *and to make related amendments to other Acts (medical assistance in dying)* (S.C.2016, c. 3), given Royal Assent on 17 June 2016.

Find the relevant website for the courts in your own province or territory (for example, in Ontario, log on to *www.ontariocourts.on.ca/en/sitemap.htm*, or, in British Columbia, log on to *www.courts.gov.bc.ca*). Both the Ontario and BC websites provide links to all of the other provincial and territorial court websites in Canada. As an exercise, find out if, during the period 2005 to 2018, your own provincial or territorial court of appeal decided any cases concerning the offence of theft (section 322 of the Criminal Code).

Counting Crime

JOHN EVANS*

4

Learning Objectives

After reading this chapter, you should be able to

- Describe how the administrative records collected in the criminal justice system are turned into statistics about crime and the characteristics of offenders and victims.

- Understand the problems of reliability and validity associated with measures of crime and offenders.

- Understand the system that produces Canadian crime and criminal justice statistics.

- Describe the trends in Canadian crime rates over the past five decades.

- Describe the strengths and weaknesses of victimization and self-reported criminality surveys and understand how these two methods enhance our understanding of the problem of crime in Canada.

This chapter is about statistics on crime and criminal justice. Over the past century, those who have tried to understand crime have relied heavily on statistical descriptions of criminal behaviour, criminals, and criminal justice responses. What we know about crime depends on the quality, coverage, reliability, and validity of our measures of crime.

This chapter describes how social scientists count crime. After discussing the problems of the validity and reliability of our measures of crime, we introduce the long-standing debate over whether crime statistics accurately reflect the amount of crime in Canada or whether they merely reflect the activities of the criminal justice system. To help you to understand the strengths and weaknesses of Canadian crime statistics, we describe how the administrative records of the police, courts, and prisons are turned into measures describing the amount of crime and the characteristics of offenders and victims. This process involves developing clear procedures concerning units of count, levels of data aggregation, definitions, data elements, and counting procedures. Particular attention will be paid to the most commonly used measure of crime: the Uniform Crime Report system (UCR). The UCR is based on crimes reported to the police across the country. Finally, the chapter describes victimization surveys and self-report studies. These provide data that are complementary to those produced by the UCR.

*The first edition of this chapter was written with Alexander Himelfarb.

Controversies over Counting Crime

The first concern of those who first sought to measure crime was coverage: How can we obtain data about the amount and nature of crime in a society? As the number of official sources of statistics have increased, and as creative **methodologies** for data collection have advanced, **reliability** and **validity** have become the most pressing concerns. In simple terms, are the methods and techniques involved in gathering statistics strong enough that anyone following the procedures would produce the same counts (reliability)? And do the statistics collected count what they purport to count (validity)?

Imagine a situation in which you wished to test a theory of crime causation. For example, what aspects of communities create pressures to greater criminality? Let us say that your theory predicts higher **crime rates** in big cities than in small towns. You are then going to need statistical data on the amount of crime in these two types of settings. How do you get these counts? You could consult police statistics. Police gather vast amounts of information on suspects, incidents, arrests, and charges. Criminologists often use these data to test their ideas. However, there have always been problems with police statistics. When police officers are dispatched to a call, each officer must use his or her own judgment to decide whether a crime has been committed or whether the call is unfounded. If the officer determines that there has been an offence, a report will be filled out by the officer and processed by police department staff. Most police departments then send the data from each incident to the Canadian Centre for Justice Statistics (CCJS), a division of Statistics Canada. Police are supposed to follow a uniform set of rules (the Uniform Crime Reporting Rules) in recording criminal incidents or calls for service. Yet it has been discovered that different police departments often use different rules for recording their information. In fact, individual police officers exercise a good deal of discretion in what they decide to record and how they record it. There may be doubts, then, about the reliability of the statistics derived from police records. However, there is perhaps an even more fundamental problem: Are suspects criminals? Are those arrested and charged criminals? Are all incidents that are recorded actual crimes, and are these incidents a complete count of crimes? Do the data provide a valid count of crime?

A particular difficulty arises in crime counts because as the reliability of a statistical measure increases, its validity as a count of crime often decreases. Thus, even though the police certainly never detect or become aware of all crimes, and despite enormous problems of reliability, their counts of crime are likely to be a far more valid reflection of the amount of criminal behaviour than are counts of convictions or counts of prisoners. The criminal justice system operates as a funnel: only some fraction of incidents result in a police record of a criminal incident, only a portion of recorded incidents result in suspects identified, only a portion of suspects are arrested or charged, only a portion of charges result in conviction, and only a portion of convictions result in incarceration (see Figure 4.1). The farther you go into the system, the more confident you can be that the count is accurate and reliable and that it is a decreasingly valid representation of all criminal behaviour. Also, there are built-in biases because some crimes (and some criminals) are more likely than others to be reported and to result in arrest, charge, conviction, and incarceration. For example, murderers

methodology
Refers to the study or critique of methods.

reliability
Identifies one of the standards (another being validity) against which the tools used to measure concepts are judged. Reliability refers to consistency of results over time.

validity
The extent to which a tool or instrument (questionnaire, experiment) actually measures the concept the researcher claims to be interested in and not something else.

crime rate
Criminologists calculate crime rates (or rates of incarceration, conviction, or recidivism) by dividing the amount of crime by the population size and multiplying by 100,000. This produces the standard rate per 100,000; occasionally it is useful to calculate a rate per million or some other figure when looking at less frequently occurring offences.

FIGURE 4.1 ■ The Crime Funnel: Break-and-Enter Offences Processed through the Canadian Criminal Justice System, 2014–16

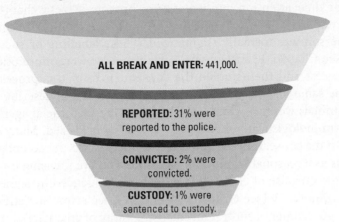

ALL BREAK AND ENTER: 441,000.

REPORTED: 31% were reported to the police.

CONVICTED: 2% were convicted.

CUSTODY: 1% were sentenced to custody.

Note: This diagram illustrates the processing of break-and-enter offences through various stages in the criminal justice system. For cautions about these data, see Box 4.3, Summary and Cautions: Using Victimization Survey Data and Data from the UCR and the Court Surveys.

Source: Adapted from Statistics Canada, special tabulation, unpublished data, Uniform Crime Reporting Survey, and the 2014 Victimization survey, Canadian Centre for Crime Statistics, 2014–2016. This does not constitute an endorsement by Statistics Canada of this product.

are more likely to be arrested and to go to jail than are corporate criminals or shoplifters. The farther you go into the system, the more obvious it becomes that you are counting something about how the system itself operates; you are counting official decisions about crime and criminals. Statistical descriptions of the prison **population** may provide valid indicators of one way that a society responds to crime. These descriptions, however, do not provide a valid measure of the amount and the nature of crime.

How have criminologists handled these problems? For a long time, they acknowledged the problems and then, when they needed data, they pretended the problems away. Kaplan's "law of the hammer" holds that when you give a small child a hammer, he or she discovers that everything needs pounding. Similarly, social scientists have often been accused of letting their methods or the most readily available statistics dictate their theories. Social scientists often find out what they are able to discover most easily and build their theories around this limited information. Many of the early theories of criminology discussed elsewhere in this text were built upon a rather uncritical acceptance of official sources of statistics. Many early criminologists used prisoners to study the differences between criminals and noncriminals. Some used police records of arrest or charge; some used court records. These criminologists rarely asked the following questions: Are all criminals equally likely to get arrested? To be charged? To be put in prison? Even when criminologists recognized the limits of the available information, they used these unreliable and often invalid measures because this was all they had.

In the 1960s and the 1970s a number of sociologists and criminologists focused their attention on the systematic biases of past theories built on official records. New theories suggested that official records showed us how the

population
Refers to all members of a given class or set. For example, adult Canadians, teenagers, Canadian inmates, and criminal offenders can each be thought of as a population.

criminal justice system operated to create crime and criminals. The statistics revealed information about the police, about the courts, and about whom they selected for their attention and worst punishments. Arrest, charge, and conviction were parts of a formal labelling process, a ceremony of degradation in which a person was formally stigmatized. These labelling or social reaction theories (see Chapter 13) asked why certain people were more often selected for this process and then studied the consequences of this process for these people. The same "crime statistics" that had been used to describe the behaviour of criminals were now being used to describe the official agents of social control. Criminologists are increasingly becoming polarized. Many seem to be returning to the conservative criminology of the past, to the acceptance of official records as a reasonable indicator of crime, and are focusing on explaining crime for the purpose of controlling it. Others, influenced by some variant of "critical" criminology (see Chapters 11 and 12), see crime statistics as simply part of the government's control mechanism, a way of characterizing the crime problem, a means of self-justification, and a reflection of more fundamental structural inequalities.

Are crime statistics whatever one makes of them? Are statistics simply a resource to tell lies or support one's own favoured position? Yes, sometimes. But they need not be. **Theories** about crime and facts about crime are built simultaneously, are mutually dependent, and shape one another. Theory without facts is indistinguishable from **ideology**; facts without theory are often implicit ideology; statistical facts without theory are numerology, often bent to ideological ends. Theorists and policymakers have often been guilty of using statistics to their own ideological ends, using crime counts to show that we are going through a crime wave, or using the same counts to show how we are living through a wave of repression. We live in an age when numerical values have a certain magic and a power to convince us, to make arguments seem true. Statistics can be dangerous if we do not know how to examine them critically.

For example, imagine that you read, in some credible source, that violence in Canadian society has risen by 100 percent over the past decade. Before you set off to explain this "fact," or before you turn your home into a fortress, you should ask just what is being counted as violence. Is it crimes? *Some* crimes? Political dissent? Violence by the state? Domestic violence? What theory or ideological assumptions have guided this choice of "fact"? And how good are the facts? How well and consistently have they been counted? Are they reliable and valid?

What have social scientists and policymakers done about the lack of good crime information? Fifty years ago the American sociologist Ned Polsky (1967) argued that our understanding of crime would never be significantly advanced if we relied on statistical data. He was concerned that sociologists and criminologists were relying too heavily on remote sources of information. They remained too distant from the criminals they wished to understand. He advocated field research in the course of which social scientists would live among, and learn from, the criminals themselves. Not surprisingly, few have followed Polsky's lead. Rather, most have worked to improve the quality of statistics based on official sources, to specify the valid uses of these statistics, and to develop innovative methodologies to complement official data and to fill gaps. Despite the problems, criminological theory and criminal justice policy remain heavily dependent on

theory
A set of concepts and their nominal definitions or assertions about the relationships between these concepts, assumptions, and knowledge claims.

ideology
A linked set of ideas and beliefs that act to uphold and justify an existing or desired situation in society.

statistics about crime and the criminal justice system. This is not to say that there are not many other ways to advance our understanding of crime. This, however, is not a research methods chapter. Qualitative techniques and other methods of studying crime should be examined elsewhere.

One can distinguish three broad types of criminal justice statistics: statistics about crime and criminals, statistics about the criminal justice system and its response to crime, and statistics about perceptions of crime and criminal justice. Theory and policy require statistics about the decisions of those who break the law, about the decisions of those who maintain it, and about what people think of all of this.

Statistics on the Criminal Justice System

The criminal justice system produces an enormous amount of raw data in the form of police reports and records, the recorded decisions of prosecutors and judges, the **administrative records** of prisons and penitentiaries, and the recorded decisions of parole boards and probation and parole services. From these administrative records the Canadian Centre for Justice Statistics (CCJS) has developed a sophisticated system of statistics on the criminal justice system.

administrative record
A collection of information about individual cases.

From Records to Statistics

Administrative records are not statistics. Records are concerned with individual cases and are intended primarily to help practitioners make decisions about these individual cases. Statistics are aggregated; they are concerned with what is common among individual cases. Statistics are meant to provide information about larger questions: planning and evaluation, policy and program development, and theory building and testing. While good records are the base, the conversion of records into statistics requires a number of conceptual decisions. The potential clients or users of the statistics must decide what it is they want to know and how they plan to use the information. Statistical systems should be built to address enduring theoretical and policy concerns.

Specifically, the following issues must be addressed before records can be converted into statistics: unit of count, **levels of aggregation**, definitions, **data elements**, and **counting procedures**.

levels of aggregation
Refers to how data are to be combined. Do we want city-level, provincial, or national data?

data element
Specification about what exactly is to be collected.

counting procedure
A consensus on how to count units and data elements.

Unit of Count: Consensus about What It Is That We Are Counting

In the course of everyday activities, police may count many different things: suspects, offences, charges, or calls for service. Typically, they work with occurrences. An occurrence may involve several offenders, several victims, and/or several offences. The unit we wish to count in a statistical system will depend on whether we are trying to learn something about police workload or productivity, or crime or victims. Recently, for example, there has been a growing awareness among policymakers and criminologists that victims have been an ignored unit of count and that we know little about their characteristics. Some units of count are specific to a particular sector. For example, the prison sector can count inmates; the court sector, convictions; and the police, suspects.

At this CompStat meeting, police officials use crime statistics to plan crime reduction initiatives.

Levels of Aggregation: Consensus about How to Combine Data

A crucial decision is the level at which we want our statistics. For example, do we want to combine police records for a city? Do we want to combine statistics for an entire province? Or region? Or nation? To the extent that we want to generalize our theories or develop or evaluate national policies, we are likely to want national statistics. But several criminologists have warned that the further you move from those who produce the data and the more you try to combine data from different sources, the more questionable is the result. They prefer the richer and more detailed information available from local police to the abstracted, less complete data available about national policing.

Definitions: Consensus about How to Define What Is Being Counted

While the Criminal Code provides a common set of definitions for counting crime, there remains a good deal of discretion regarding when an incident of crime is truly an incident, or even what, for example, constitutes an "inmate." If one wishes to count inmates, should one count those who are temporarily absent, or those on remand, or those in community correctional facilities, or those who have committed criminal acts and have been assigned to mental institutions? Common definitions are essential. Depending on how the terms are defined, you can inflate or deflate the statistics; you can make it appear that crime is higher or lower, or that there are more or fewer prisoners.

Data Elements: Consensus about What Specific Information Should Be Collected

The police will need certain kinds of information to help them in their investigative activities. This information will be far more detailed than, and sometimes quite different from, what is needed as aggregated statistics. Similarly, the police in one jurisdiction may, for their own good reasons, maintain records quite different from those of other police departments. As understandable as this is, it is extremely difficult to build aggregated statistics out of different types of records that may be incompatible.

Counting Procedures: Consensus on How to Count Units and Elements

If an offender goes on a break-and-enter spree and hits six houses in an evening, how many offences should be counted—six (one offence per house) or one (a singular spree)? And if, during a break and enter, an offender is confronted by the homeowner and assaults him or her, is this one or two offences? If one, which offence should be counted? If we agree that the most serious should be counted, how do we determine seriousness?

Canadian Criminal Justice Statistics

The questions or issues of unit of count, levels of aggregation, definitions, data elements, and counting procedures are at the base of much of the technical and critical literature on criminal justice statistics. In Canada, attempts to answer these questions have long been the responsibility of our national statistical agency, Statistics Canada. More recently, the federal and provincial governments have created a national institute—the **Canadian Centre for Justice Statistics (CCJS)**—which is a division of Statistics Canada and is governed by a board of directors of senior officials responsible for justice.

Canadian Centre for Justice Statistics
A division of Statistics Canada, formed in 1981, with a mandate to collect national data on crime and justice.

A major challenge for the CCJS is achieving agreement on priorities such as whose needs should be met. Crime statistics are used by different people and for different purposes: criminologists and researchers want to build and test theories, policymakers and analysts want to identify problems and develop and test solutions, and administrators and program managers want to plan and run their operations and to monitor and evaluate their programs. Most important, statistics serve the public interest by keeping people informed and by providing some measure of public accountability. Good statistics are important, but they are important in different ways for different users.

Canada has reasonably good national data on criminal justice inputs such as resources and expenditures. The data are now far better when it comes to outputs such as incidents, arrests, charges, convictions, and dispositions. The CCJS has developed and improved the Adult Criminal Court Survey, a census of courts in Canada. Since 2009, the survey has collected data from jurisdictions representing about 95 percent of the national criminal court caseload. Correctional statistics are the most accurate because we can count the number of prisoners in Canada and provide some information on their social characteristics. This can be quite useful for projecting future inmate populations and for planning future facilities and services. When linked to other data, these data

SEARCH FOR:
"Justice and Crime" Statistics
Canada

can also be useful for developing correctional policy. For example, how much are we using incarceration, and are we doing so in the most useful and appropriate ways?

Data on prisoners, however, do not tell us much about crime and criminal behaviours. They tell us about the criminal justice system. The confusion comes when people equate "criminal" with "prisoner." Some people are more likely to be caught; some people are more likely to be charged; some people are more likely to be convicted; and some people are more likely to be sentenced to prison or to a penitentiary. We know too much about how people get selected for incarceration to assume that prison statistics tell us very much about crime.

But what can such data show? Figure 4.2 shows the growth in the number of adults incarcerated in Canada between 1978–79 and 2015–16. In this period, the adult inmate population increased from 21,834 to 39,679. Unfortunately, there is no national count of youth in custody. Statistics Canada does not have youth custody data from Nova Scotia, Quebec, Saskatchewan, and Nunavut.

Obviously, these figures are important for administrative and planning purposes. But do these figures tell us something about growing crime in Canada? No. Do they tell us something about harsher or more punitive sentencing practices? No. In fact, if we look at the rate of incarceration (per 100,000 adult Canadians), we see that much of the growth in the penitentiary population can be accounted for by the growth of the Canadian population (Figure 4.3).

International comparisons are difficult and problematic. That said, they do tell us that Canada incarcerates people at a much higher rate than most Western European nations but at a much lower rate than the United States, where more

FIGURE 4.2 ▧ Average Daily Count of Adults in Custody

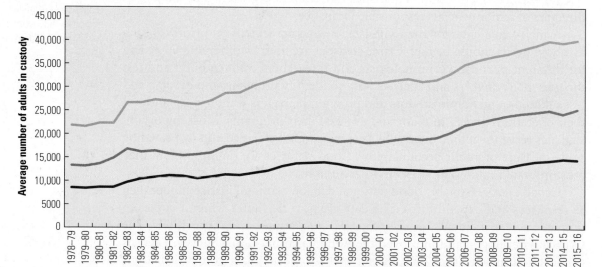

Notes: 1. Province/Territory and Canada totals exclude Prince Edward Island, the Northwest Territories, and Nunavut for comparison between years. 2. Provincial and territorial counts may include federal sentenced offenders in a provincial or territorial facility. 3. Federal counts may include provincial/territorial offenders in a federal facility and those temporarily detained in a federal facility.

Source: Statistics Canada, Canadian Centre for Justice Statistics, Correctional Services Surveys, Adult Key Indicators Report. Reproduced and distributed on an "as is" basis with the permission of Statistics Canada.

FIGURE 4.3 ■ Adult Incarceration Rates

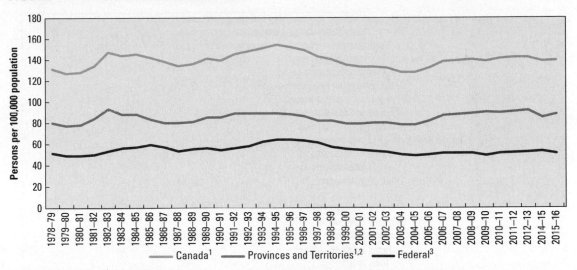

Notes: 1. Incarceration rates for provinces/territories and Canada exclude Prince Edward Island, the Northwest Territories, and Nunavut for comparisons between years. 2. Provincial and territorial counts may include federal sentenced offenders in a provincial or territorial facility. 3. Federal counts may include provincial/territorial offenders in a federal facility and those temporarily detained in a federal facility.

Source: Malakieh, Jamil. 2018. *Adult and Youth Correctional Statistics in Canada*, 2016/17. Ottawa: Statistics Canada. Reproduced and distributed on an "as is" basis with the permission of Statistics Canada.

than 2,173,800 million people were incarcerated in 2015 (US Bureau of Justice Statistics [UBJS] 2016). This is an incarceration rate of 670 per 100,000 US residents, up from 411 in 1995 (UBJS 2016) and six times the Canadian rate of 115 per 100,000 in 2015–16 (Figure 4.4). Note that this Canadian figure is a much lower rate than that shown in Figure 4.3. The difference is that the figure of 115 is based on the total population whereas the data in Figure 4.3 are based on the adult population. For international comparisons, the total population base is typically used.

Some have compared Canadian to Western European incarceration rates to argue that Canada is too punitive, that too many people are being put behind bars and stay there for too long. Others have argued that it simply means Canada has more serious crime than many other nations. The debates flourish. Statistics do not provide the answers; they indicate only where problems may exist.

How Much Crime?

It should come as no surprise that criminologists have had difficulty counting crime. Crime is typically a secretive activity. When people commit crimes, they try to avoid becoming part of the count of criminals. (They do not want to become a statistic!) The "best" crime is one that no one knows about, and no criminal justice system will ever be able to ferret out all crimes and all criminals. Some crimes are harder to detect than others, and some criminals are harder to apprehend and convict. Criminologists have long recognized that the major problem of counting crime is the so-called **dark figure of crime**—that is, crime that remains unreported, unrecorded, and largely unknown. In response to this problem, criminologists have developed a variety of ways of counting crime, or at

dark figure of crime
The amount of crime that is unreported or unknown.

FIGURE 4.4 ▪ International Incarceration Rates, G20 Countries

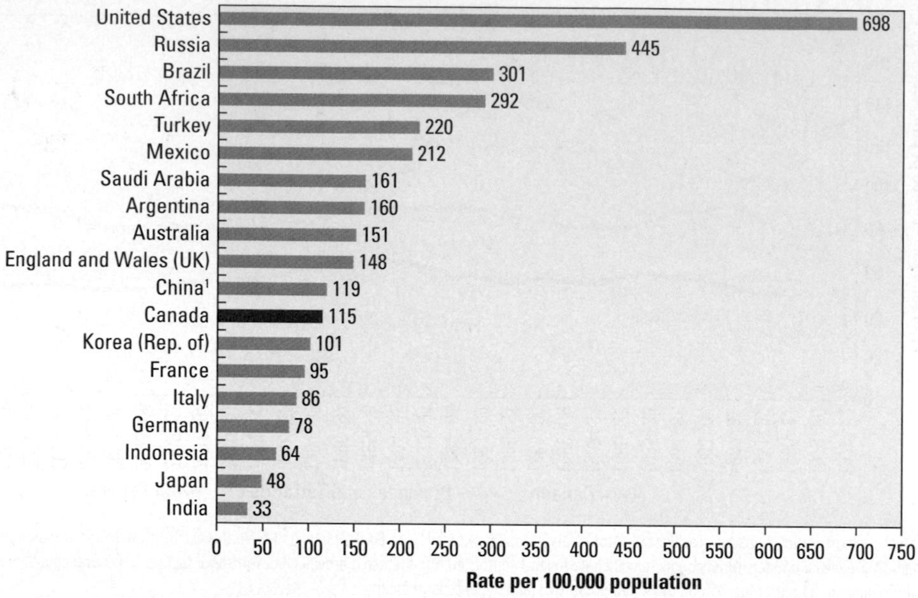

¹The figures for China include sentenced prisoners only, as figures for pre-trial and other forms of detention are not available.

Source: Walmsley, R. 2011. *World Prison Brief - World Prison Population list* (11th Edition), Institute for Criminal Policy Research; Statistics Canada, Canadian Centre for Justice Statistics, Corrections Key Indicator Report, 2015/2016. https://www.statcan.gc.ca/pub/85-002-x/2017001/article/14700-eng.htm#a14

least for describing crime patterns and trends. They have tried to rationalize and improve official statistics, but they have also developed approaches that do not depend on official counts of crime. In the next section we look at official records, victimization surveys, and self-report studies as sources of data about crime.

Official Statistics: Canadian Uniform Crime Reports

Despite their problems, we rely heavily on official counts of the amount of crime. Until 1962, we were dependent on local police records collected for police purposes, which were handled differently in each locale. Since then, Canada has had in place a system called the Canadian **Uniform Crime Reports** (UCR), which is designed to provide uniform and comparable national statistics. However, just what this system counts has been subjected to almost endless debate within criminology.

The Canadian Uniform Crime Reports have drawn heavily from a similar system in the United States, but they have also improved on the US system. First, common crime classifications and definitions are easier to arrive at in Canada than in the United States because Canada operates under a common criminal code whereas each US state has its own separate code. Second, the coverage of police departments is far more complete in Canada than in the United States. However, the two systems share some fundamental problems. Some of these are

Uniform Crime Reports (UCR)
Since 1962, Statistics Canada has published the Uniform Crime Reports based on a standardized set of procedures for collecting and reporting crime information.

being addressed by ongoing improvements to the UCR survey; others, though, are more fundamental because they are built into all official statistics.

In Canada, two versions of the UCR collection instrument operate simultaneously: the UCR Aggregate Survey (UCR1.0) and the UCR2 Incident-Based Survey, which has two versions, UCR2.0 and UCR2.1. UCR1.0, which collects summary data for nearly 100 separate criminal offences, has been in place since 1962.*

UCR2 was developed in the mid-1980s as a method of collecting more detailed information on each incident, the victims, and the accused persons. This method of data collection, in which a separate statistical record is created for each criminal incident, is known as an incident-based reporting system.

A revised version of UCR2, known as UCR2.1, was introduced in 1998. This survey introduced certain efficiencies for police services and lowered the response burden by eliminating or simplifying UCR2 variables (Statistics Canada 2010). In 2004, yet another version, UCR2.2, was introduced to add new violations and other variables.

Let us look more closely at the "seriousness rule." A number of studies (Nettler 1974; Silverman and Teevan 1975; Silverman 1980; de Silva and Silverman 1985) have documented some of the problems in the recording and scoring rules and how these rules are applied. Specifically, the studies have examined the implications of the "**seriousness rule**," which holds that only the most serious crime is to be scored in an incident involving several crimes. The concerns this rule creates are threefold: first, it deflates the total crime count, since less serious crimes are not counted separately; second, it inflates serious crimes as a proportion of the total; and third, the way in which seriousness is scored is problematic because not enough qualitative data about the crimes are recorded to use a sophisticated scale of seriousness. See Box 4.1 for a discussion of the main UCR categories and the most serious offence rule.

seriousness rule
If there are several crimes committed in one incident, only the most serious crime is counted. UCR1.0 uses the seriousness rule.

*The description of the UCR is based on the CCJS website: http://www.statcan.ca. Search for UCR.

FOCUS   BOX 4.1

UCR CATEGORIES AND THE MOST SERIOUS OFFENCE RULE

Violent incidents involve offences that deal with the application, or threat of application, of force to a person. Such incidents include homicide, attempted murder, various forms of sexual and nonsexual assault, robbery, and abduction. Traffic violations that result in death or bodily harm are included under Criminal Code traffic incidents.

Property incidents involve unlawful acts with the intent of gaining property but do not involve the use or threat of violence against an individual. Theft, breaking and entering,

fraud, and possession of stolen goods are examples of property crimes.

Other Criminal Code incidents involve the remaining Criminal Code offences that are not classified as violent or property incidents (excluding traffic). Examples are mischief, bail violations, disturbing the peace, arson, prostitution, and possession of a prohibited weapon.

Total Criminal Code incidents is the tabulation of all violent, property, and other Criminal Code incidents reported for a given year.

(continued)

Most Serious Offence

The UCR1.0 Survey classifies incidents according to the most serious offence (MSO) in the incident. In categorizing incidents, violent offences always take precedence over nonviolent offences. Within the violent and nonviolent categories, offences are then sorted according to the maximum sentence under the Criminal Code. The UCR Survey scores violent incidents differently from other types of crime. For violent crimes, a separate incident is recorded for each victim (categorized according to the most serious offence against the victim). If, for example, one person assaults three people, then three incidents are recorded. If three people assault one person, only one incident is recorded. For nonviolent crimes, one incident (categorized according to the most serious offence in the incident) is counted for every distinct or separate occurrence. Robbery is one exception to the above scoring rule. Robbery is categorized as a violent offence. Unlike all other violent offences, one occurrence of robbery is equal to one incident, regardless of the number of victims. The reason for this exception is that robbery can involve many people who could all be considered victims. In a bank robbery with five tellers and 20 customers present, 25 incidents of robbery would be counted if the normal scoring rule for violent incidents were applied. This would seriously overstate the occurrence of robbery. Thus, the total number of incidents recorded by the UCR Survey is not a census of all violations of the law that come to the attention of police. Rather, it is equal to the number of violent crimes (other than robbery) plus the number of separate occurrences of nonviolent crimes (and robberies).

Actual Incidents

When a crime is reported to the police, the incident is recorded as a "reported" incident. Police then conduct a preliminary investigation to determine the validity of the report. Occasionally, crimes reported to the police prove to be unfounded. Unfounded incidents are subtracted from the number of reported incidents to produce the number of "actual incidents." Numbers and rates of crime are calculated on the basis of "actual incidents" categorized according to the most serious offence.

Critical Thinking Questions

1. When most people think about crime rates, they are thinking of crimes reported to the police. Based on what you are learning in this chapter, how might these reported crime statistics distort the way we perceive our community's crime issues?

2. Do you agree with the way Statistics Canada applies the 'most serious offense rule' in classifying incidents?

Source: Adapted from Statistics Canada, special tabulation, unpublished data, Uniform Crime Reporting (UCR1) Survey, Canadian Centre for Crime Statistics, 1998 to 2009. This does not constitute an endorsement by Statistics Canada of this product.

gross counts of crime
A count of the total amount of crime in a given community, making no distinction between crime categories.

Concerns have also been expressed that the crime categories used are too general, allowing too many different kinds of acts to be recorded in the same way. For example, thefts and attempted thefts are recorded under the same category.

Furthermore, as previously indicated, it is not always entirely clear just what it is we want to count. In Canada, the count of crimes includes violations of the Criminal Code, violations of other federal and provincial statutes, and violations of some municipal bylaws. Many of these criminal and quasi-criminal laws are not what most Canadians think of as crime. Most people, when they think about crime, are thinking about particular offences. They are not thinking about the Criminal Code and the full range of behaviours legally defined as criminal. When we seek to count crime, we are invariably struck with a complex mix of these two sets of definitions. For this reason, **gross counts of crime** may be very misleading. For example, in 1969 the Ouimet Report pointed out that total convictions for all criminal offences in Canada increased by an alarming 2500 percent between 1901 and 1965. The report added, however, that 98 percent of the increase was accounted for by summary convictions—less serious crimes—particularly traffic offences. Thus, much of the apparent increase in crime actually reflected the increased use of automobiles in Canada during this period. With the report of the gross crime counts alone, most people would no doubt have had horrific visions of violent predators preying on innocent victims, rather than the more accurate vision of careless motorists abusing one another and pedestrians. This is why UCR programs count offences within particular offence categories—it is so that each offence can be examined separately.

Another often-cited problem is that the Canadian UCR treats property crimes and personal crimes differently. Several property crimes, even if they involve different victims, may be recorded as a single offence if they are considered part of the same incident. This is not the case for personal offences. However, even for personal offences, the UCR1 survey collects very little information about victims and offenders. The CCJS has sought to rectify this by developing the UCR2, which as we saw above collects data on characteristics of the victim and the accused as well as characteristics of the incident itself. As a result of the most serious offence scoring rule, less serious offences are undercounted by the aggregate survey. However, the incident-based survey allows up to four violations per incident, permitting the identification of lesser offences.

By 2009 the response rate from police respondents to the UCR surveys was virtually 100 percent. UCR2 data provide a rich source of information for Canadians. Continuity with the UCR aggregate survey data is maintained by converting the incident-based data to aggregate counts at year end.

The question remains, however, whether the new and improved Canadian UCR will provide us with an accurate count of crime or even a reasonable indicator of crime and crime trends. Can official statistics ever tell us about total crime? Are official statistics useful only for understanding the criminal justice system?

We have discussed the Canadian UCR under the heading of criminal justice statistics because these official data may tell us more about police activities than about crime. "Official violations" statistics are, in part, a product of policy decisions within the criminal justice system—that is, decisions about which criminal infractions deserve the most police attention and resources. Furthermore, crime statistics are the product of individual police decisions made in the exercise of police discretion regarding what crimes are serious enough to attend to, record, and pursue. In fact, the ways in which police and police departments apply crime recording and scoring procedures reflect, to some extent, the policing style and policy of the particular police department. Because combining or comparing statistics from different departments is highly problematic, the CCJS has developed elaborate rules and procedures for collecting and verifying data.

Police statistics are also shaped by public perceptions, concerns, and fears. The police depend on the accounts of victims and witnesses. In other words, victims and witnesses must recognize an act as a criminal justice matter, must believe it to be of sufficient seriousness to warrant a report to the police, and must believe that reporting the act is worthwhile—all this before the police make their decisions about how to respond to and record an act (see, for example, Shearing 1984).

Official crime statistics, then, are shaped by both commonsense and legal definitions of what constitutes crime. These statistics reflect the decisions of many people, not simply the behaviours of criminals. Official counts of crime will change as legal definitions change, as commonsense definitions change, and as the priorities of agents of law enforcement change. For example, if Parliament made premarital sex illegal, we could well expect a rather sharp increase in crime. Would this be reflected in official crime counts? To the extent that there are no direct victims to bring these offences to police attention, the answer is probably no. Much would depend on the priority attached to enforcement of this offence.

Consider two less hypothetical examples. As official statistics reveal to us increasing rates of family violence, theoretical explanations of the crisis in the nuclear family abound. But has the incidence truly increased, or have Canadians become less tolerant of such behaviour and more willing to bring such incidents to police attention? Have police become more sensitive to the seriousness of the problem and more likely to record the incidents as crimes? In other words, has the incidence of family violence increased, or have the definitions and reporting and recording behaviours changed? For those students wanting more statistical and substantive information on this topic, the CCJS website provides a wealth of excellent studies on family violence and victimization of women.

Drug offences fall under the Controlled Drugs and Substances Act. In 2017 there were about 96,515 drug offences reported by police, of which 47,992 were cannabis offenses. Total drug offences were 7 percent lower than in 2016 and 20 percent lower than a decade earlier. Cannabis offenses in 2017 declined by 14 percent from 2016. As well, the number of persons charged with cannabis-related offences declined by 21 percent from 2016 to 2017 (Allen 2018). This, no doubt, reflects a certain amount of police discretion. Legalization of marijuana was in the Liberals' platform for the last election, and since taking power they have introduced legislation to legalize marijuana with an effective date of 17 October 2018, so many police agencies are no longer as concerned about enforcing cannabis laws.

It is worth noting as well that while police-reported cannabis offences have been going down, use has not. In 2015, 12 percent of Canadians aged 15 years and older, or 3.6 million people, had used cannabis in the past year compared with 11 percent in 2013, according to the Canadian Tobacco, Alcohol and Drug Survey conducted every two years.

Because statistics for victimless crimes such as drug use are as much a result of police priorities and budgets as they are of the amount of criminal behaviour, official statistics may not tell us much about the actual prevalence of these behaviours.

What, then, *can* the UCR tell us? The total Criminal Code offence rate nearly doubled, from 2,771 offences per 100,000 Canadians at the inception of the UCR in 1962 to 5,334 in 2017. Figure 4.5 shows the trend line during this period. Both violent and property crime rates increased steadily until 1992 and then declined or stabilized through 2013. Violent crimes (748 per 100,000 in 2016) were consistently much lower than property crimes (2,466 per 100,000).

Those who work with crime statistics generally refer to *crime rates* when they wish to take into account the size of the population. The crime rate is simply the number of incidents for every 100,000 Canadians. References to rate rather than incidence ensure that comparisons from jurisdiction to jurisdiction, or over time, do not reflect changes in population size rather than differences in criminal behaviour.

In 2017, Canada had 660 homicides (first- and second-degree murder, manslaughter, and infanticide). There have been year-to-year fluctuations in Canada's homicide rate; however, it has generally been declining over the past few decades. The rate of homicides in 2017 was over 40 percent lower than the peak rate recorded in 1975. In the shorter term, the rate in 2017 was slightly higher than the previous 10-year average, at 1.8 homicides per 100,000 population (see Figure 4.6).

Crime has been declining in recent years. The crime rate rose from 1962 to 1991 but has generally declined since then (see Figure 4.5, which shows the levels of all recorded offences for the period 1962–2017). The police-reported crime rate

FIGURE 4.5 ■ **Police-Reported Crime Rates, 1962–2017**

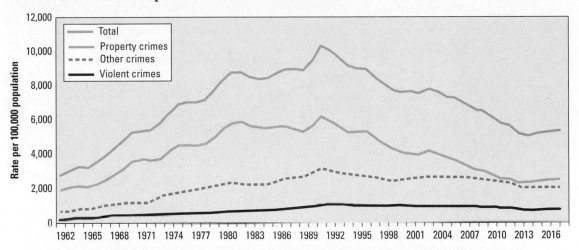

Source: For years 1962–2005: Adapted from Maire Gannon, Crime Statistics in Canada, 2005, *Juristat*, Vol. 26, no. 4, p. 16 (2006), http://www.statcan.ca/bsolc/english/bsolc?catno=85-002-X&CHROPG=1; For years 2006–201: Adapted from Kathryn Keighley, Police-reported crime statistics in Canada, 2016, *Juristat*, (85-002-X).

FIGURE 4.6 ■ **Homicide Rate per 100,000 Canadians, 1961–2017**

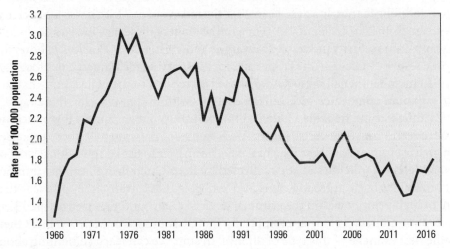

Source: Statistics Canada, *Homicide in Canada, 2016*. https://www.statcan.gc.ca/daily-quotidien/171122/cg-b001-eng.htm, and Data on homicide are available back to 1961 in CANSIM table 253-0001.

in 2013 was the lowest recorded since 1969 and was 33 percent below the police-reported crime rate in 2003. There has been a slight increase since that time.

Crime Severity Index

To address the matter of the crime rate being driven by high volumes of less serious offences, the CCJS developed crime severity indexes (CSI). CSI values are available from 1998. The crime severity index is calculated by assigning each offence a weight derived from actual sentences given by the criminal courts. The more serious the average sentence, the greater the weight. Thus, more serious offences have a greater impact on the severity index. Figure 4.7 shows the crime severity indexes from 1998 to 2017.

In 2016 and again in 2017, the Crime Severity Index (CSI), which measures both the volume and the seriousness of police-reported crime in Canada, rose slightly

FIGURE 4.7 ■ Police-Reported Crime Severity Indexes, 1998–2017

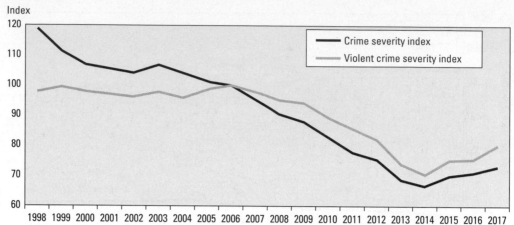

Note: Additional data are available on CANSIM (Table 252-0052). Crime Severity Indexes are based on *Criminal Code* incidents, including traffic offences, as well as other federal statute violations. The base index was set at 100 for 2006 for Canada. Populations are based upon july 1st estimates from Statistics Canada, Demography Division.

Source: Statistics Canada, Canadian Centre for Justice Statistics, Uniform Crime Reporting Survey. http://www.statcan.gc.ca/pub/85-002-x/2017001/article/54842-eng.htm. Reproduced and distributed on an "as is" basis with the permission of Statistics Canada.

after declining for nearly a decade. In 2017 the index was at 73. This was a 24 percent decrease from 2007 (Allen 2018). (For a full account of these new indexes, including a youth crime severity index, see Dauvergne and Turner 2010.) Table 4.1 shows the crime severity values and the crime rates for most of Canada's largest cities for 2017.

Remember that all these data are based on reports to the police. But what can we say about crime rates, given all the cautions with which we began this chapter? How much crime remains hidden to the police? Which crimes? How much do police recording practices shape the UCR figures? How much do these practices change over time? Are these data useless? The answer to the last question is no. For example, the homicide statistics collected by the CCJS reflect the actual number of homicides fairly accurately. It is also probable that certain other offences that are of high priority within the criminal justice system, and that victims are likely to report, are relatively well captured by the UCR program. Motor vehicle theft is the best example of this type of offence. In sum, we can learn something about the incidence of crime from these data, but we are not sure how much.

We can be more confident that if police departments across Canada are recording and reporting crimes relatively consistently, then the UCR data give us a picture of what crimes the police are processing. For example, in the 1980s, changes in policy limited police discretion in laying charges when handling domestic violence incidents. This policy has produced more official incidents of such assaults, reflecting changes in police practice if not changes in criminal behaviour (see Chapter 6).

The Impact of Cybercrime on Crime Statistics

The Internet has created huge new opportunities for people to commit crimes such as computer hacking, infecting computers with viruses, committing computer-related fraud, and producing and transmitting child pornography. Some of these online offences are substitutes for traditional crimes. For example, the offline crime of shoplifting music CDs has been replaced by the online offense of illegally downloading music. Drugs such as fentanyl are being sold online rather

TABLE 4.1 ▪ **Police-Reported Crime Severity Index and Crime Rate, by Census Metropolitan Area, 2016**

	2016—Crime Severity Index	2015 to 2016—Crime Severity Index	2016—Crime rate	2015 to 2016—Crime rate
	Index	% change	Rate	% change
Census metropolitan area				
Canada	**71.0**	**1**	**5,224**	**0ˢ**
St. John's	79.2	7	5,721	−3
Halifax	61.0	−4	4,663	−4
Moncton	75.7	−4	6,196	−9
Saint John	52.7	−6	4,305	−8
Saguenay	56.9	6	3,319	4
Quebec City	45.2	8	3,000	1
Sherbrooke	50.3	1	3,297	2
Trois-Rivières	48.7	14	2,940	−13
Montreal	57.8	−5	3,389	−5
Gatineau	56.7	6	3,688	−1
Ottawa	51.3	10	3,492	5
Kingston	55.2	−2	4,743	−1
Peterborough	55.1	0ˢ	4,280	0ˢ
Toronto	47.5	4	2,954	2
Hamilton	53.6	6	3,502	0ˢ
St. Catharines–Niagara	50.3	−4	3,519	−1
Kitchener–Cambridge–Waterloo	61.2	1	4,697	2
Brantford	86.8	13	6,138	7
Guelph	54.6	9	4,496	13
London	68.4	5	5,503	4
Windsor	65.1	4	4,425	−1
Barrie	45.4	5	3,567	−1
Greater Sudbury	63.5	7	4,532	5
Thunder Bay	85.9	6	6,259	2
Winnipeg	103.9	16	6,653	13
Regina	125.8	15	9,253	11
Saskatoon	117.8	5	8,942	6
Calgary	74.6	−6	5,260	−1
Edmonton	105.7	3	8,131	6
Kelowna	100.3	0ˢ	8,445	2
Abbotsford–Mission	91.4	−5	7,009	−6
Vancouver	94.3	−1	7,282	−1
Victoria	63.8	−12	5,689	−6

0 true zero or a value rounded to zero

0ˢ value rounded to 0 (zero) where there is a meaningful distinction between true zero and the value that was rounded

CANSIM tables 252-0051 and 252-0052. Reproduced and distributed on an "as is" basis with the permission of Statistics Canada.

FOCUS

BOX 4.2

THE USES AND ABUSES OF POLICE CRIME FIGURES

The government [is] extremely fond of amassing great quantities of statistics. These are raised to the nth degree, the cube roots are extracted, and the results are arranged into elaborate and impressive displays. What must be kept ever in mind, however, is that in every case, the figures are first put down by a village watchman, and he puts down anything he damn well pleases.—Attributed to Sir Josiah Stamp, H.M. collector of Inland Revenue, 1840–41.

Perhaps. But most reports come from citizens and not from the "watchman," and now there are elaborate rules for recording crime figures.

In cooperation with police departments, Statistics Canada has established rules governing the collection of data, complete with coding manuals, and has assigned individuals the task of verifying the reports from which the data are extracted. Local quality control measures are in effect for respondents of crime surveys to minimize the underreporting of crime. In addition, Statistics Canada runs a number of automated checks to ensure data completeness and accuracy.

However, elaborate and sound procedures developed and refined over decades can be subverted by managers determined to show their police forces in a more favourable light. Recently, the United Kingdom's Statistical Authority has withdrawn its "gold standard" status from police figures. Police crime figures can no longer be used as national statistics until the forces can demonstrate that the quality of the data meets national standards. Allegations include claims that the Metropolitan Police have understated sexual offences by as much as 25 percent. Other "fiddling" techniques have included downgrading offences to less serious ones or persuading victims not to make a complaint. In some cases, crimes were only recorded if they were solved. Other offences were kept off the books if the offender could not be traced (UK Statistical Authority 2014).

Similar dubious practices have recently been documented for Chicago, Illinois, and Los Angeles, California. In Chicago, it is alleged that new police managers, under political pressure from the mayor to show that their policing practices were working, downgraded many homicides to death investigations or caused them to disappear altogether. Other crimes were similarly downgraded, all to show that crime figures were better than in the previous year (*Chicago Magazine*, May 2014).

Other difficulties stem not so much from attempts to distort the data, but from the difficulty of investigations. In 2015 the *Globe and Mail* newspaper began an impressive investigative series on "unfounded" sexual assault complaints. Robyn Doolittle (2017), the journalist who conducted the research, found great variability across jurisdictions. The national "unfounded" rate for sexual assault was just under 20 percent, but rates for municipal police services ranged from 2 percent in Winnipeg to 51 percent for Saint John. In 115 communities, the police dismissed more than one-third of all sexual assault complaints, thus dramatically reducing their sexual assault rates. Following the *Globe and Mail* series, some police services dismissed the findings but many others opened reviews of sexual assault cases. Nearly 40,000 cases are being reviewed. New Brunswick, which had the highest unfounded rate, reported that 800 cases had been improperly classified. The most common reason for this was that the police were classifying cases as unfounded (which essentially means the police did not believe they had actually occurred) when actually, the cases simply lacked sufficient information to justify a charge (Leeder 2017). At least partly because of Doolittle's work, in 2017 the percentage of sexual assault cases classified as unfounded was 14 percent, down from 19 percent in 2016. The rate of unfounded cases for all types of crimes is 7 percent (Greenland and Cotter 2018).

Investigating sexual assault cases requires special skills and specialized training, and many forces are making improvements in these areas. The 2017 cases of sexual harassment and assault lodged against men in power in the media, politics, and elsewhere (exemplified by the #MeToo movement) may help create a climate in which victims are more likely to be believed.

Inaccurate counts do a disservice to everyone, not least police departments. Crime data are a powerful resource that can be used to target police patrols and develop partnerships with other sectors in the community—partnerships that can and should assist with prevention and enforcement. Even calls for service can be a powerful resource.

A very simple example of using crime data to direct resources involved one community in which two nearly identical apartment complexes generated vastly different numbers of calls for service (10 versus 150). The situation was closely examined, and the only significant difference between the two complexes was the quality of the management. The police chief met with management, and eventually the situation improved: calls for service were reduced so that each complex generated around 10 calls for service per month (Engstad and Evans 1980).

More recently, many police department websites have made crime data available in map form so that citizens can see which crimes are reported in which neighbourhoods throughout the city. In some cases, citizens can file an incident report online.

And, going much further, some police forces are turning to "predictive policing." A computer program analyzes crime data and predicts where certain types of crime are likely to occur. Officers use these data and their own knowledge to deploy to particular places. The program, PredPol, is being aggressively marketed and is being used by a number of forces, including the Los Angeles and Seattle police. No comprehensive evaluation of the program is yet available.

As data storage and analysis continue to get easier and cheaper, many other data analysis techniques will be developed to mine the wealth of data that incident reports contain. Some of these techniques are discussed in more detail in Chapter 15 of this text.

Critical Thinking Questions

1. What impact do you think there will be on the accuracy of crime statistics if police boards and city councils decide to hold police chiefs accountable for their city's crime rate?

2. Many police departments make their crime statistics available online. Are these statistics available in your community? If they are, what do they tell you about the distribution of crimes known to the police?

Source: Perreault, Samuel and Shannon Brennan. Summer 2010. *Criminal Victimization in Canada 2009*. Adapted from Statistics Canada Catalogue no. 85-002-X, Vol. 30, no. 2, 5. Reproduced and distributed on an "as is" basis with the permission of Statistics Canada.

than on street corners. Other cybercrimes such as computer hacking are new offences that can only be committed online. Dramatic increases in cybercrime have led criminologists to question the police-reported crime statistics showing that crime rates have been dropping over the past two decades.

Online crimes can be very difficult to detect, and the vast majority are not reflected in our official crime statistics because they are not reported. Cybercrimes may be known only to the victims or to private organizations such as credit card companies and cybersecurity companies, which often do not report them to the police. International victimization surveys suggest that far more people have had their email accounts hacked or have been victimized by identity theft than have been victims of burglary, robbery, or car theft (Bass 2015).

While data on cybercrime are very limited, Cannepele and Aebi have concluded that the available statistics show that "quantitatively, the growth of cybercrimes seems to have outweighed the drop in offline crimes (10). That is, crime rates have actually not declined if we include cybercrimes.

One of the most comprehensive sources of information about the extent of cybercrime is the Crime Survey for England and Wales (Office for National Statistics 2017). In this national survey, respondents were asked if they had been victimized online. About 10 percent of the population of England and Wales reported having been victimized by various types of online fraud, making it the most common type of crime reported. When all types of cybercrime were considered, the total was over 5 million offences representing nearly half of all the crime reported in the survey. The vast majority of victims of these offences did not report them to the police, so they don't show up in official statistics. This means that official statistics seriously underreport the actual numbers of crimes and that the trend of declining crime rates shown by police-reported crime statistics does not present an accurate picture of the degree to which citizens are being victimized.

Canadian data on this are limited. However, Bass (2015) obtained data on credit card and debit card fraud from the Canadian Bankers Association which showed that in 2013, nearly 900,000 of these offences were reported to the banks. The average loss was $550, and less than 1 percent of these crimes were reported to the police. Since there were about 2.1 million crimes reported to Canadian police departments in 2013, the total crime rate in Canada would have gone up by 42 percent if the banks had reported these offences. Rather than relying on the police, the banks have built the costs of these frauds into their business model and have focused their efforts on limiting their losses by carefully monitoring spending patterns and checking with card holders if there are unusual transactions, and by quickly cancelling cards that are being misused. This effort has been largely successful, and the banks have been able to easily absorb the losses because of the high interest rates charged by credit cards.

Governments in several countries are now trying to modify their data reporting and recording policies to ensure that crime statistics reflect crime victimization as accurately as possible.

Some optimists would argue that the UCR indicates trends in crime. The less optimistic say no, there is too much we do not know about victim reporting behaviour, about the exercise of police discretion in deciding what is criminal and what is not, about police recording and reporting practices, and about the nature and seriousness of the offences captured by the UCR. Out of these concerns have emerged attempts to develop other ways of counting crime. The most important of these is the victimization survey.

Victimization Surveys

victimization survey
A survey of a random sample of the population in which people are asked to recall and describe their own experience of being a victim of crime.

Victimization surveys ask people whether they have been victims of acts that the Criminal Code defines as criminal. They are asked to describe the nature and consequences of their victimization experiences; to describe the criminal justice response; to indicate whether victims or others brought the incidents to official attention, and if not, why not; and to indicate their perceptions of and attitudes toward crime and criminal justice in Canada. The first large-scale victimization survey in Canada was carried out in 1982 by the Solicitor General of Canada and Statistics Canada. Those interested in the methodological developments for the first large-scale victimization surveys can read Catlin and Murray (1979), Evans and Leger (1978), and Skogan (1981).

Surveys asking Canadians about their crime victimization provide valuable knowledge about crime in Canada.

wdstock/E+/Getty Images

Since 1988, Statistics Canada has conducted a victimization survey about every five years (1988, 1993, 1999, 2004, 2009, and 2014) as part of the General Social Survey. For the 2014 survey, telephone interviews were conducted with a random **sample** of around 33,127 people, aged 15 and older, living in the 10 provinces. The three territories were also covered, using a different sampling design.

Respondents were asked for their opinions concerning the level of crime in their neighbourhood, their fear of crime, and their views concerning the performance of the justice system. They were also asked about their experiences with criminal victimization. Respondents who had been victims of a crime in the previous 12 months were asked for detailed information on each incident, including when and where it occurred, whether the incident was reported to the police, and how they were affected by the experience.

Not all crimes can be captured through this survey method. One need not be a methodologist to recognize that murder cannot be included in such a survey. Nor can consensual crimes for which there are no direct victims—drug use, gambling, and the like. These consensual crimes are not captured very well through official data or through victimization surveys. Similarly, those crimes designed to keep victims unaware that they have been victimized cannot be captured accurately in victimization surveys (or official data sources). Fraud, embezzlement, employee pilferage, price fixing, and the wide range of consumer, corporate, and white-collar crimes were not included in the survey. The eight categories of crime included were sexual assault, robbery, assault, break and enter, motor vehicle theft, theft of household property, theft of personal property, and vandalism. The major findings of the 2014 survey are outlined in Box 4.3.

sample
A group of elements (people, offenders, inmates) selected in a systematic manner from the population of interest.

FOCUS BOX 4.3

CRIMINAL VICTIMIZATION IN CANADA, 2014: HIGHLIGHTS

- Just under one fifth of Canadians aged 15 years and older reported being the victim of one of the eight offences measured by the 2014 General Social Survey (GSS) on Victimization, down from just over one quarter in 2004.

- Victimization rates for all crimes measured by the 2014 GSS were lower than those reported 10 years earlier, with the exception of sexual assault, which remained stable. From 2004, the violent victimization rate fell by 28 percent, while the household victimization rate decreased by 42 percent and the rate of theft of personal property declined by 21 percent.

- Newfoundland and Labrador and Quebec recorded the lowest rates of violent victimization among the provinces, while Manitoba posted the highest rate in 2014.

- All of the Atlantic provinces and Ontario reported household victimization rates below the average for the 10 provinces, while the opposite was observed in each of the Prairie provinces and British Columbia.

- Among the census metropolitan areas (CMAs) with releasable estimates, the Calgary CMA recorded the lowest violent victimization rate while the Halifax and Winnipeg CMAs posted the highest.

- Household victimization rates were lowest in the Quebec City CMA, while most western CMAs recorded rates that were higher than the national average.

- Unlike previous GSS cycles on victimization that found similar violent victimization rates among males and females, women posted a higher rate than men in 2014. This was mainly due to the relative stability of the sexual assault victimization rate—of which the majority of victims are women—while the victimization rate of other violent crimes declined.

- Being young was the main contributing factor to the risk of violent victimization. The rate of violent victimization was highest among persons aged 20 to 24 years and then decreased gradually with age.

(continued)

- Mental health was the second most influential factor associated with the risk of violent victimization in 2014. About 1 in 10 Canadians reported a mental health–related disability, a developmental or learning disability, or self-assessed their mental health as poor or fair. These individuals combined reported a rate of violent victimization more than four times that of people who self-assessed their mental health as excellent or very good.
- Just under one-third of Canadians reported experiencing some form of abuse at the hands of an adult before the age of 15. People who experienced child maltreatment recorded violent victimization rates that were more than double those of people who did not experience child maltreatment.
- According to the GSS, in 2014 just over one-quarter of violent incidents involved a weapon and just under one in five violent incidents resulted in injury to the victim. In about half of violent incidents (excluding spousal violence), the victim knew the offender.
- About one out of seven victims of violent crime reported having suffered symptoms similar to post-traumatic stress as a result of their victimization.
- Some of the main risk factors for experiencing household victimization are living in a CMA, living in a single (detached) house, living in a dwelling for only a short time, living in a neighbourhood with low social cohesion, and renting the place that you live in.
- According to the GSS, just under one-third (31%) of criminal incidents were brought to the attention of the police in 2014, a proportion slightly lower than 10 years earlier, when 34 percent of incidents were reported. The proportions of incidents reported to the police ranged from 50 percent for break-ins to as little as 5 percent for sexual assaults.

Critical Thinking Questions

1. Victimization surveys reveal that many crimes, including serious violent crimes, are not reported to the police. Why not? What is the significance of this for society?
2. What categories of people are most likely to report having been victimized by crime in the GSS? What does this tell us about the nature of victimization?

Source: Adapted from Perreault, S. 2015. "Criminal victimization in Canada, 2014." *Juristat*. Statistics Canada Catalogue no. 85-002-X. Reproduced and distributed on an "as is" basis with the permission of Statistics Canada.

Note that of the incidents identified, just under one-third (31 percent) had been reported to the police or had otherwise come to police attention. Allowing that the victimization survey cannot capture the entire "dark" figure missed by the UCR, the survey data do reveal that many more Canadians are victimized by crime than is revealed by official statistics.

As most would guess, a large proportion of unreported crime is relatively trivial—the kinds of incidents that most of us would not expect the police to devote time or resources to investigating. For example, a few dollars stolen by somebody within the household or a toy stolen from the porch are the kinds of common incidents that are rarely reported. Nonetheless, as Table 4.2 shows, more serious incidents may often go unreported. For example, in the 2014 Victimization Survey, 95 percent of those who had been sexually assaulted did not report the incident to the police. Women assaulted by people they knew indicated that fear of revenge was one of the reasons they failed to report.

Where incidents produced great financial loss to the victim, reporting was far more likely, even more likely than for those incidents that resulted in pain or injury but no loss. Reporting property crimes, particularly when the loss was over $1,000, is less an act of justice (or even revenge) than a far more utilitarian act—seeking redress, recompense, or recovery. Thirty-one percent of criminal incidents were reported to the police in 2014. This proportion was slightly lower than that recorded ten years earlier (34%). Among all measured offences, sexual assault was the least likely to be reported to police, with just one in 20 being brought to the attention of the police.

The survey data confirm many of the concerns about official sources of crime data. Some crimes are more likely to come to police attention than others. Some

TABLE 4.2 ■ **Incidents Reported to Police, 1993, 1999, 2004, 2009, and 2014**

Incidents	1993	1999	2004	2009	2014
Theft—personal property	42	35	31	28	25
Robbery	46	46	46	43	45
Physical assault	33	37	39	34	38
Break and enter	68	62	54	54	50
Motor vehicle/parts theft	50	60	49	50	44
Theft—household property	43	32	29	23	25
Vandalism	46	34	31	33	37

Sources: For 1993–2004 data: Adapted from Gannon, Maire, and Karen Mihorean. Criminal Victimization in Canada, 2004, *Juristat*, Vol. 25, no. 7 (2006), Figure 11, p. 17 (2006), http://www.statcan.gc.ca/bsolc/olc-cel/olc-cel?catno=85-002-X20050078803&lang=eng; For 2009 data: Adapted from Perreault, Samuel, and Shannon Brennan. Criminal Victimization in Canada 2009, *Juristat*, Vol. 30, no. 2, p. 15 (2010), http://www.statcan.gc.ca/pub/85-002-x/2010002/article/11340-eng.htm. For 2014 data Perreault, S. 2015. "Criminal victimization in Canada, 2014." *Juristat*. Statistics Canada Catalogue no. 85-002-X.

categories of victims are more likely to report their victimization, and some categories of offenders (e.g., family members) are less likely to be reported. In general, it is only through such knowledge that we can begin to understand the UCR data and the dark figure of crime. Because victimization surveys are based on victims' perceptions and experiences, and because they collect information about the victims of crime, they are useful in identifying those categories of people most at risk of criminal victimization. For example, victimization surveys show that, contrary to conventional wisdom, the risk of victimization is lowest for older Canadians, especially those 65 years of age or older (see Figure 4.8). In fact, the victimization data provide a profile of crime victims that explodes many popular myths. The typical victim of crime is young, single, male, not employed full-time, and living an active social life. The number of evenings spent outside the home is

FIGURE 4.8 ■ **Violent Victimization Incidents Reported by Canadians, by Age Group of the Victim, 2014**

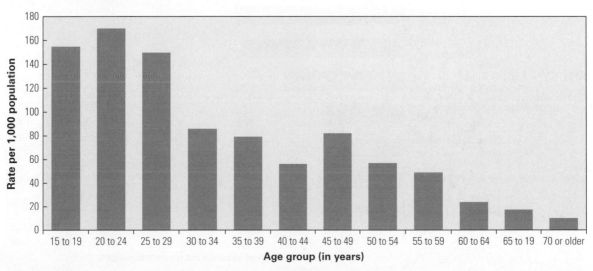

Source: Statistics Canada, *General Social Survey, 2014.* https://www.statcan.gc.ca/pub/85-002-x/2015001/article/14241-eng.htm. Reproduced and distributed on an "as is" basis with the permission of Statistics Canada

one of the best predictors of whether a person has been victimized. Some of the reasons for these patterns of victimization are discussed in Chapter 15.

Perhaps most important, victimization surveys allow us to go beyond merely counting crime. They provide data on the costs of victimization (including financial losses and physical injuries) and on the concern and fear that victimization may produce. These data also allow us to explore various dimensions of seriousness. Clearly, victimization hits some harder than others. In 2014, women experienced violent victimization at a rate 20 percent higher than men. Seniors have very low rates of victimization; in fact, age was the key factor associated with violent victimization. Reasons for not reporting and reporting crimes are shown in Figures 4.9 and 4.10, respectively.

Victimization surveys cannot measure all crimes. They are dependent on the vagaries of human memory and are subject to the kinds of criticisms levelled against any survey, including the fact that some people may not tell interviewers the truth.

FIGURE 4.9 ■ Top 15 Reasons for Not Reporting Crime Victimization, 2014

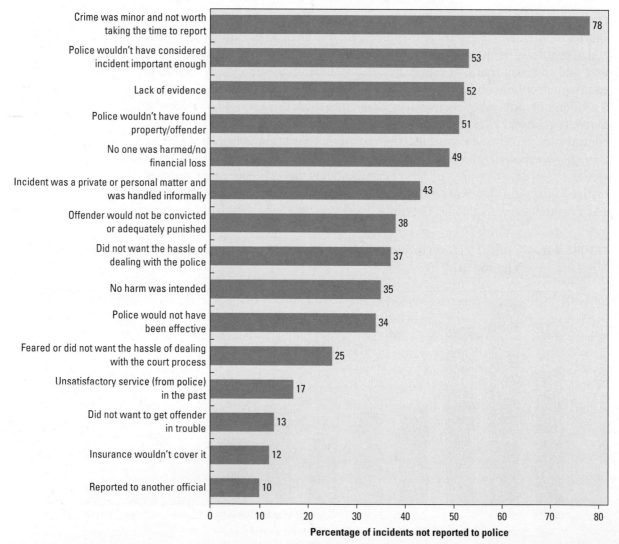

Source: Statistics Canada, *General Social Survey, 2014.* https://www.statcan.gc.ca/pub/85-002-x/2015001/article/14241/tbl/tbl10-eng.htm. Reproduced and distributed on an "as is" basis with the permission of Statistics Canada.

FIGURE 4.10 ■ **Reasons for Reporting Crime Victimization, 2014**

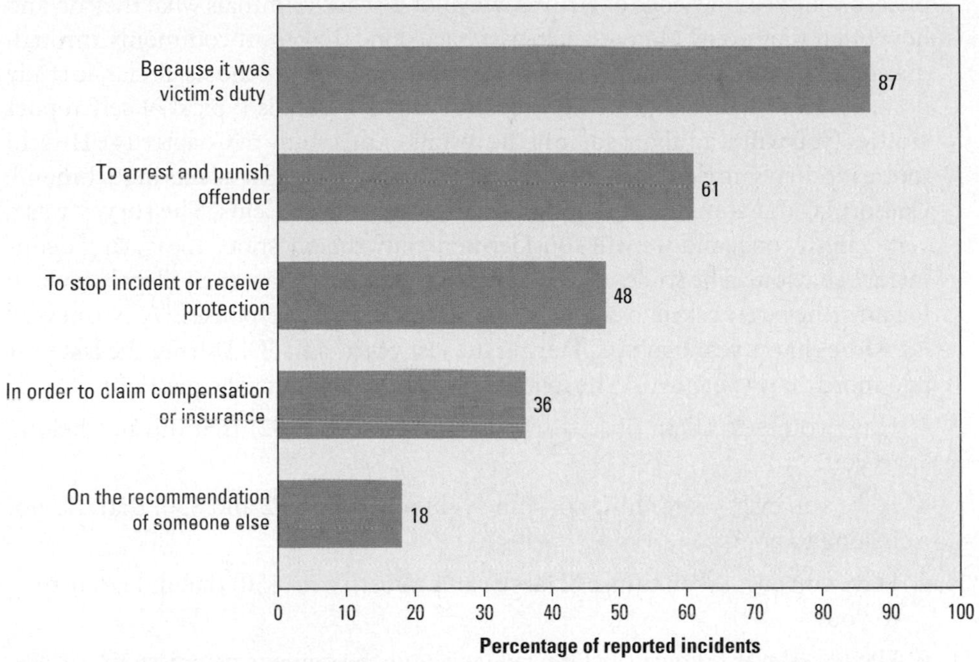

Source: Statistics Canada, *General Social Survey, 2014.* https://www.statcan.gc.ca/pub/85-002-x/2015001/article/14241/tbl/tbl10-eng.htm. Reproduced and distributed on an "as is" basis with the permission of Statistics Canada.

Victimization surveys are dependent on respondents' ability not only to recall incidents and their details, but also to place the incidents correctly in time. We know that respondents are fallible. And, as Skogan (1978) suggests, well-educated, articulate respondents are more likely than others to talk to interviewers and to give rich and full accounts of their victimization experiences, thus perhaps biasing the data. There is reason as well to be cautious about interpreting data on domestic and sexual assaults that have been collected through surveys. Respondents may well be reluctant to discuss such experiences with an interviewer. Also, the methodology is still relatively young. Special methods will be needed to get data about rural victimization and victimization of Indigenous Canadians. Also, special methodologies are required to measure white-collar crime, consensual crime, and what has come to be called enterprise crime—organized crime and the crimes of organizations and the state. More information is also required on the psychological and emotional impact of victimization. The 2014 survey made a good start on this by adding questions to better measure the consequences of victimization, including questions based on the Primary Care Post-Traumatic Stress Disorder Screen (PC-PTSD) tool. These questions revealed that one in seven violent crime victims suffered symptoms consistent with a suspected PTSD.

Despite the limitations, these data provide us with the opportunity to go beyond counting incidents and to gain some understanding of what it is we are counting. The data are an essential complement to other sources of crime statistics.

Self-Report Studies

Yet another approach to generating data on the nature and distribution of crime is the self-report study. The people who know the most about crime are those who break the law. Rather than relying on police data, which will inevitably be incomplete, or on the knowledge of victims, why not just ask criminals what they do and how often they do it? Many sociologists have done this, most commonly through questionnaires given to students in junior and senior high schools. A classic study done by Travis Hirschi (1969) in the San Francisco area is typical of **self-report studies** (you will read about some of the results of this study in Chapter 14). Hirschi took a random sample of all the junior and senior high school students in Richmond, California, and administered questionnaires to 5,545 students. The survey was a very lengthy one, and we will consider here only the questions measuring delinquent behaviour. The students were asked six questions about their illegal conduct; for each, they were asked to check off one of the following responses: "A. No, never"; "B. More than a year ago"; "C. During the last year;" and "D. During the last year and more than a year ago." The following were the delinquency questions:

self-report study
A method for measuring crime involving the distribution of a detailed questionnaire to a sample of people, asking them whether they have committed a crime in a particular period of time. This has been a good method for criminologists to determine the social characteristics of offenders.

- Have you ever taken little things (worth less than $2) that did not belong to you?

- Have you ever taken things of some value (between $2 and $50) that did not belong to you?

- Have you ever taken things of large value (worth over $50) that did not belong to you?

- Have you ever taken a car for a ride without the owner's permission?

- Have you ever banged up something that did not belong to you on purpose?

- Not counting fights that you may have had with a brother or sister, have you ever beaten up on anyone or hurt someone on purpose?

Hirschi looked at responses to these delinquency questions and compared them with other measures, including such things as students' reports of their

FOCUS   BOX 4.4

SUMMARY AND CAUTIONS: USING VICTIMIZATION SURVEY DATA AND DATA FROM THE UCR AND THE COURT SURVEYS

Victimization Surveys

These surveys provide rich data, but remember that they collect information on a limited set of crimes—eight in the Statistics Canada surveys. Uniform Crime Report (UCR) surveys cover more than 100 offence types. When considering these data, use caution. Refer back to Figure 4.1, "The Crime Funnel." The 2014 victimization survey estimated that there were 441,000 break and enters in Canada. Note that these are break-and-enters of households. Break-and-enter offences against businesses are not included. Thousands of break and enters are therefore excluded from the victimization survey but are included in police and court data. This affects each subsequent item in the funnel. The figure is an illustration only.

Defining Courts-Based Data and Police Incident-Based Data

Police
The procedures used to collect UCR data have been discussed earlier in this chapter.

Courts
The purpose of the Adult Criminal Court Survey (ACCS) and the Youth Court Survey is to provide a national database of statistical information on the processing of cases through the adult and youth criminal court systems. The surveys consist of a census of Criminal Code and other federal statute charges dealt with in adult criminal courts and youth courts.

Counting Procedures

The basic unit of count for the Court Surveys is the case. A case is one or more charges against an accused person or corporation, where the charges receive a final disposition on the same date. Charges are linked to a case on the basis of the accused identifier and the date of the last court appearance.

Most Serious Offence and Decision Rules

When a case has more than one charge, it is necessary to decide which charge will be used to represent the case (since a case is identified by a single charge). In multiple-charge cases, the "most serious decision" rule is applied. Decisions are ranked from the most to the least serious as follows: (1) guilty, (2) guilty of a lesser offence, (3) acquitted, (4) stay of proceeding, (5) withdrawn, dismissed, and discharged, (6) not criminally responsible, (7) other, and (8) transfer of court jurisdiction.

In cases where two or more offences have resulted in the same decision (e.g., guilty), the "most serious offence" rule is applied. All charges are ranked according to an offence seriousness scale, which is based on the average length of prison sentence and rate of incarceration. If two charges are tied according to this criterion, information about the sentence type (e.g., prison, probation, and fine) is considered. If a tie still exists, the magnitude of the sentence is considered.

Comparisons between Courts and Police UCR Survey Data

Counts from the UCR survey for offences cleared by charge are not comparable to the Adult Criminal Court Survey (ACCS) figures for charges disposed of. There are many reasons for this. In part, it is the result of the scoring rules used by the UCR survey.

The UCR survey counts violent offences by the number of victims in the incident; nonviolent offences are counted by the number of separate incidents.

For example, two persons break into a house and subsequently commit vandalism and theft. This would be considered as one police incident. Assuming the charges were laid and the matter proceeded to court, there would be a minimum of six charges—three charges for each accused.

In addition, the differences in the "most serious offence" rule between the courts and police surveys can result in court cases and police incidents being represented by different offences even though they may have been part of the same crime.

Furthermore, the published UCR figures include offences involving youths, while the ACCS case counts include only the very few youth offences that have been transferred to adult court (less than 100 per year).

Moreover, information is captured in the UCR with the laying of a charge, while in the ACCS information is captured upon the court rendering a decision. This time lag in data collection between the two surveys further affects comparability.

Critical Thinking Questions

1. To what extent do official statistics measure the amount of crime in society? What are the major biases in official statistics?

2. In 2010, former Conservative public safety minister Stockwell Day tried to explain why his government was increasing spending on prison construction even though crime rates were declining. His response was that the prisons were needed because of increases in unreported crime. Can you figure out why this response was nonsensical?

friends' behaviour, and their family and school relationships, in order to shed some light on what caused some students but not others to become delinquent. He was using self-report studies to try to overcome some of the weaknesses of police data. In most cases, the results of self-reporting have supported the view that there are systematic biases.

Because self-report studies supposedly avoid these biases, they have been particularly important in research and theory on the causes of crime and delinquency, especially the relationship between social class and crime. For a long time, these studies were not very carefully scrutinized. A major project to determine the reliability of self-report studies was carried out by Hindelang, Hirschi, and Weis (1981). They concluded that the self-report method does demonstrate that people are willing to report crimes, both those known and those not known to officials, and that respondents' reports are internally consistent. A difficulty arises in that it appears that different populations answer self-report questions in different ways. Lower-class males and black males in the US study are more likely to underreport their own criminal behaviour than are middle-class white males. Similarly, in Canada, Fréchette and LeBlanc (1979, 1980) confirm that while self-report studies do uncover much hidden delinquency and raise questions about the biases in official statistics that show the preponderance of lower-class crime, previous self-report studies have also masked the fact that lower-class crime is typically more serious and persistent.

In 2006, Canada participated in the International Self-Reported Delinquency Study, which was conducted in more than 30 countries. Canada's study was conducted in Toronto schools, sampling youth in grades seven to nine. According to the International Youth Survey, over one-third (37%) of students in grades seven to nine in Toronto reported having engaged in one or more delinquent behaviours in their lifetime, through acts of violence, acts against property, or the sale of drugs. The lifetime prevalence was higher among boys (41%) than among girls (32%) (Savoie 2007).

There are two related problems with self-report studies. First, it would appear that those who are typically law-abiding are more likely to report completely their occasional infractions than are the more committed delinquents to report their more serious and frequent infractions. Second, differences between official statistics of delinquent behaviour and self-report data may reflect not simply biases in official data, but biases in the self-report method as well. The official data are likely to include more serious offences, and self-report data are more likely to include more minor infractions, as you can see from the items used in Hirschi's studies. (Note that the dollar amounts in Hirschi's questions reflect the value of the dollar in the 1960s.)

There are a number of other, more technical problems with self-report studies. For example, there are sampling problems—it is difficult to get "hard-core criminals" in a sample for several reasons, including the fact that they are less likely than other youth to be in school, where most of these surveys are administered. A recent study, however, did show moderate agreement between self-reports and official data for a group of serious delinquents (Piquero, Schubert, and Brame 2014). There are also disagreements regarding which offences to select, which produce the most reliable and valid data, and which scoring procedures best suit the uses of the data (see Hindelang, Hirschi, and Weis 1981; Thornberry and Krohn 2000). Although self-report studies are never likely to be an instrument for counting crimes, recent methodological refinements have enhanced their potential to address fundamental questions about crime and the correlates of crime.

Self-report studies are also useful for examining trends. In Ontario, the Centre for Addiction and Mental Health has conducted surveys every two years since 1977. Large samples of students in grades nine through twelve fill out anonymous surveys on their use of alcohol and drugs. The data show that both drug and alcohol use have been declining over time (Boak et al. 2013).

Self-report data can be used for other purposes as well. By using formal self-report surveys such as Hirschi's or by interviewing criminals in prison or in other, less restrictive situations, we can learn a great deal about their motivations for committing crimes and the techniques they use to commit crimes. This information can help us understand the causes of crime and how to prevent it. In later chapters of this book you will read about many of the lessons that criminologists have learned from talking to criminals.

The Future of Crime and Criminal Justice Statistics

The importance of good statistics for planning, policymaking, and administration has long been recognized within the criminal justice system. The founding of the CCJS is a recognition—in a country with shared jurisdiction for criminal justice—of the importance of developing national commitment and national strategies for producing and sharing criminal statistics.

New information technology holds great promise for improving the official records that form the basis of most criminal justice statistics on prisons, courts, and police. Only through a nationally coordinated effort can we avoid the danger of developing incompatible systems in each province (or worse, each municipality) and develop a coordinated national system of justice.

The methods for counting crimes are still in their formative stages. Some of these methods, like the UCR, rely on official records (designed in accordance with UCR rules) and therefore suffer the limitations of all such official statistics. Nevertheless, recent advances in police management information systems and crime classification systems hold great promise in terms of providing us with a measure of calls for police service, police caseloads, and police activity. The richer information from the UCR2 will help here. Other methods, like victimization surveys, draw on people's experiences and therefore suffer from the limitations of all such surveys. Significant progress has been achieved in Canada in developing and refining victimization surveys and self-report studies.

How much crime is there in Canada, and what are the trends? Is it bad and getting worse? Do we have cause for alarm? Are things good and getting better? Do we have cause for complacency? Depending on your bias and prejudices, the state of the art allows you to find some evidence and numbers to justify either extreme. But with the improvements in our knowledge about crime and the development of new methods, we are coming to recognize the complexity of the questions. When taken together, the UCR and the victimization surveys encourage neither alarm nor complacency. Overall, there is certainly less serious crime than most Canadians assume based on media accounts and the high visibility of sensational incidents. At the same time, we are starting to uncover some particular kinds of serious incidents that have remained hidden for too long. Sexual assault and family violence are two important examples. New crimes such as cybercrime are badly underreported. Much more work is needed. Only through an integrated program of criminal justice statistics that recognizes the limits of any one source of information will we be able to build powerful theories of crime and sound policies and programs for crime prevention and control.

QUESTIONS FOR CRITICAL THINKING

1. The media do not accurately portray the nature and extent of crime in Canada. Can you find examples in your own community of media distortions of crime? Why do the media behave in this way? What are the consequences of these distortions?
2. How are self-report studies used in criminology? Can you find examples of the use of self-report data in later chapters of this book?

Summary

- Statistics can help us better understand the nature and extent of crime in Canada. But to interpret these crime statistics properly, we must understand their strengths and weaknesses.

- The quality of official statistics varies depending on their sources. Corrections data are the most reliable and valid because the task of counting prisoners can be done accurately. By contrast, crimes known to the police, the most commonly used statistics, will always be biased by inconsistencies in reporting and recording, although the CCJS is very stringent about verifying data.

- Administrative records can be the basis of statistics if clear procedures are developed about units of count, levels of data aggregation, definitions, data elements, and counting procedures.

- The Canadian Uniform Crime Report (UCR) system is designed to provide uniform and compatible national statistics. There is much debate about just what is counted. Some hold that the UCR provides a reasonable estimate of crime rates. Others hold that what is being measured is criminal justice processing.

- The crime rates provided by the UCR, based on crimes reported to the police, have declined since the peak year of 1991. Both violent and property crimes have declined. The police-reported crime rate in 2013 was the lowest recorded since 1969, 33 percent below the police-reported crime rate in 2003. In 2016, the national CSI increased 1 percent from 70.1 in 2015 to 71.0, but remained 29 percent lower than a decade earlier in 2006.

- Victimization surveys provide an alternative and complementary method of measuring crime. These surveys ask random samples of the population about their victimization experiences. They also provide data on important issues such as reasons for reporting and not reporting crimes to the police.

- Self-report studies are not serious rivals of either the UCR or victimization surveys as a method of measuring crime. However, they do have a useful place in answering specific questions related to understanding the causes and correlates of crime.

- Developing Canada's national statistics will take continued effort and commitment from all the actors in the system. The CCJS has made great progress, and the statistics now available are much better than they were 10 or 20 years ago.

NET WORK

Canadian crime statistics are compiled by the Canadian Centre for Justice Statistics, which reports the annual number of crimes reported to the police. Go to the Statistics Canada website and find the report "Police-Reported Hate Crime in Canada, 2016." What are hate crimes? Have they been increasing in recent years?

Correlates of Criminal Behaviour

TEMITOPE ORIOLA
University of Alberta

Learning Objectives

After reading this chapter, you should be able to

- Describe the major correlates of criminal behaviour.
- Explain the trends and patterns of age and gender distribution of criminal behaviour.
- Demonstrate an understanding of the relationship between race and crime.
- Explain the reasons for the overrepresentation of Indigenous people in the criminal justice system through the colonial model, the trauma transmission model, and critical race theory.
- Critique cultural theories of Indigenous overrepresentation in crime.
- Analyze the relationship between drug and alcohol use and crime.
- Demonstrate an understanding of the complex interplay of socioeconomic status and crime.
- Explain how crime rates vary by spatial location or geographic region in Canada.

This chapter focuses on **correlates** of criminal behaviour. Correlates of crime are variables that are connected with crime. A correlate is "a phenomenon that accompanies another phenomenon and is related in some way to it" (Hartnagel 2012). Generations of researchers have examined socio-demographic variables that are correlated with crime. These include offenders' age, gender, ethno-racial background, and socioeconomic status, as well as the spatial location of offences. This chapter explores how these variables or correlates are associated with crime. The aim is to answer questions such as these: Who is likely to be involved in crime? How is crime gendered? What does age have to do with criminality? Does race have any relationship with crime?

It is important to understand that correlation is not the same as causation. Thus, while the correlates we will be examining are in some ways connected with criminal behaviour, they do not necessarily *cause* crime. No single factor explains any particular crime. Each correlate should be viewed as one of a much more complex assortment of factors that contribute to criminal acts. Thus, a change in a correlate of crime may not necessarily lead to a change in crime. Six major correlates of crime are examined in this chapter: age, gender, race, drug and alcohol use, socioeconomic status, and spatial location.

correlate
A phenomenon that accompanies another phenomenon and is related in some way to it.

Age as a Correlate of Criminal Behaviour

Young people are disproportionately represented in crime generally and in violent crime in particular. Figure 5.1 shows the age distribution of persons accused of crime in 2011. It illustrates an established pattern: criminal activity intensifies in adolescence and young adulthood and declines thereafter (Hartnagel 2012). The exceptions are political crimes, corruption, and other white-collar crimes; all of these require structural opportunities and employment opportunities that are not yet available to young people. Figure 5.2 shows that persons aged 35 to 89 were responsible for 42 percent of all cases completed in adult criminal court in 2014–15; persons aged 18 to 34 were involved in 58 percent of all cases (Maxwell 2017).

Most crimes committed by Canadian youth are nonviolent (Perreault, 2013). Theft under $5,000 is the most common offence committed by youth (Allen and Superle, 2016). The most common violent crime among Canadian youth is level 1 assault. Level 1 assaults are assaultive acts that do not cause any physical harm to victims. Other violent crimes frequently committed by youth in 2012 were uttering threats, assault level 2, and robbery (Allen and Superle, 2016). Assault level 2 is the category of assaults that involve carrying, using, or threatening to use an imitation or real weapon (Dauvergne, 2009). The 2014 data also show that Canadian youth were heavily involved in crimes such as cannabis possession, administration-of-justice violations, and mischief. Administration-of-justice violations include failure to report to court, while mischief is the crime of vandalism. It involves unlawful interference with somebody else's property, thereby causing damage. Most serious youth crimes were down in 2014: there was a 38 percent decrease in youth-perpetrated homicides in 2014, and mischief (−13%) and theft

FIGURE 5.1 ■ **Persons Accused of Crime, Aged 12 to 65 Years, 2011, Canada**

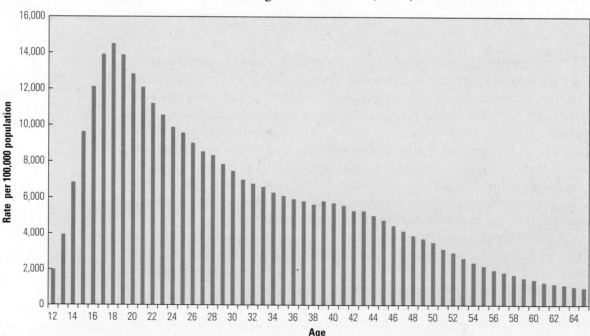

Source: Brennan, Shannon. *Police-reported crime statistics in Canada, 2011*, chart 15, Statistics Canada. Reproduced and distributed on an "as is" basis with the permission of Statistics Canada.

FIGURE 5.2 ■ **Cases Completed in Adult Criminal Court, by Age Group of the Accused, 2014–15, Canada**

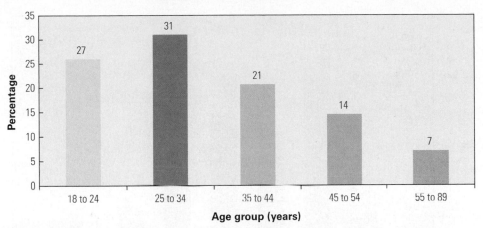

Note: Includes information on accused persons aged 18 years or over at the time of the offence. Excludes cases in which the age and/or the sex of the accused was unknown. A case is one or more charges against an accused person or company that were processed by the courts at the same time and received a final decision. Data excludes information from superior courts in Prince Edward Island, Ontario, and Saskatchewan as well as municipal courts in Quebec due to the unavailability of data.

Source: Maxwell, Ashley. *Adult Criminal Court Statistics in Canada, 2014/2015*, chart 9, Juristat (2017). Available at www.statcan.gc.ca/pub/85-002-x/2017001/article/14699-eng.htm. Reproduced and distributed on an "as is" basis with the permission of Statistics Canada.

under $5,000 (–4%) also declined (Boyce, 2015). Only 45 percent of youth accused were formally charged in 2014, a continuation of a trend towards diversion that began in 2003, when the Youth Criminal Justice Act was introduced (Boyce, 2015).

Homicide generally represents less than 1 percent of violent crimes committed by Canadian youth (Taylor-Butts and Bressan 2006), but is worth discussing because of its seriousness. Figure 5.3 shows the percentage of persons of various age categories accused of homicide in 1991 and 2016. Persons aged 12 to 24 committed 32 percent of all homicides in Canada in 2016 and 36 percent of homicides in 1991. In contrast, only 13 percent (2016) and 8 percent (1991) were committed by people aged 50 and above. Persons aged 12 to 24 made up only 16 percent of the Canadian population in 2016 and 14 percent in 1991, while persons aged 50 and above constituted 38 percent of the population in 2016 and 30 percent in 1991 (Statistics Canada, Table 051-0001). Of the 480 persons accused of homicide in 2016, only 22 (4.58%) were youth (aged 12–17) (David 2017). This was nearly 40 percent lower than the number of youth (36 persons) accused of homicide in 2015 (David 2017).

Woodworth, Agar, and Coupland (2013) found that youth homicide offenders were more likely than adults to victimize strangers. They also found that youth are more likely than adults to commit homicides as a group rather than as lone individuals. This suggests that peer influence is a critical factor in youth violence. The rate of violent youth crime in Canada is two to three times lower than the rate among American youth (Li 2008).

Why Do Young People Commit More Crimes than Adults?

Matza (1964) first drew attention to the notion of **maturational reform**—that there is a reduction in criminal offending as individuals get older. The basic explanation for maturational reform is that adolescence is a period of transition marked by ambiguity. Young people at this stage are neither children nor adults

maturational reform
The fact that people are less likely to commit crime as they grow older.

FIGURE 5.3 ■ **Percentage of Persons Accused of Homicide by Age Group, 1991 and 2016, Canada**

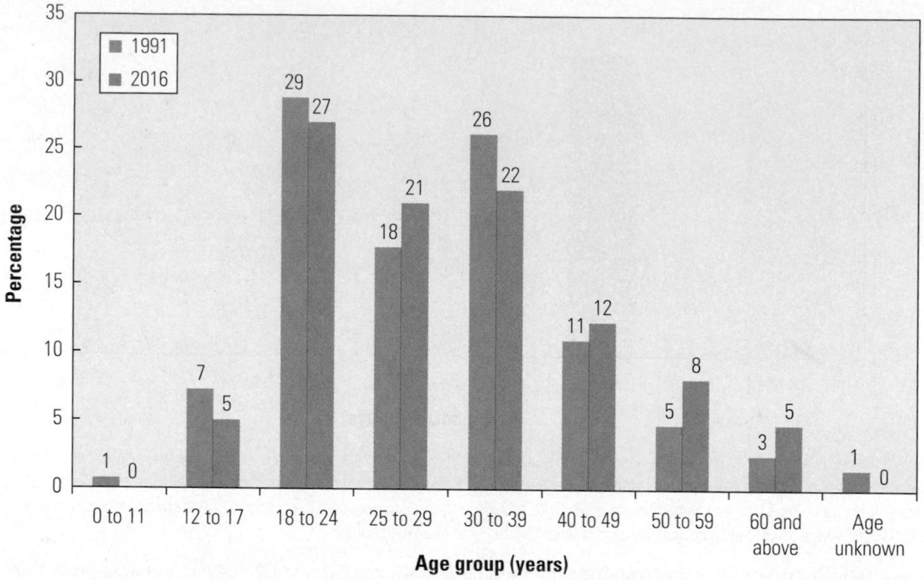

Note: Homicide includes the Criminal Code offences of murder, manslaughter, and infanticide; includes all persons who are accused (by police) as having committed a homicide. Data in this figure do not necessarily agree with data from the Uniform Crime Reporting Survey, where youth accused include a small number of persons under the age of 12.

Source: Statistics Canada. Table 253-0003 - Homicide survey, victims and persons accused of homicide, by age group and sex, Canada, annual (number), CANSIM (database). Reproduced and distributed on an "as is" basis with the permission of Statistics Canada.

and may not be fully committed to conventional values. Their infractions, Matza argues, are temporary. The confusion, marginality, and "in-between-ness" of adolescents' social position may be conducive to criminal behaviour, for these provide little incentive for noncriminal lifestyles; adults, by contrast, enjoy greater incentives to conform, such as jobs and marriage (Hartnagel 2012). For instance, money is required to participate in the consumerist youth culture of Western societies (Greenberg 1979, cited in Hartnagel 2012). Young people may shoplift or steal if their parents are unable or unwilling to pay for the latest phones and tablets. Hartnagel also suggests that older people may have become more skilled at avoiding detection, and that as they age, they may be physically unable to engage in certain kinds of criminal behaviour.

The notion of maturational reform encompasses three factors that may cause crime to decline. First, aging brings physiological limitations. Second, the formation of various types of social bonds, such as work, marriage, and children, means that individuals have other people who depend on them to make the "right" choices. Third, maturational reform involves a more socially responsible trajectory of human agency. A relatively simple example of this is that beyond a certain age, "getting wasted" on weekends may no longer sound as attractive a course of individual or group action as it is for younger people.

The notion of maturational reform is intertwined with life course theory. Life course theory is concerned with the "role of age-graded transitions and social controls" (Salvatore and Markowitz 2014, 629). Life course theorists articulate how social bonds (Chapter 14) such as attachment to a spouse, pursuit of education, and the onset of major life events or turning points such as having children or stable employment help reduce the likelihood of involvement in crime (Salvatore and Markowitz 2014; Laub and Sampson 2001). Laub and Sampson offer a life course theoretical framework for understanding desistance from criminal behaviour. They argue that desistance is an underlying causal process whose end product is reducing or ending involvement in criminal activity. Some of the major factors over the life course that contribute to desistance from crime are "aging; a good marriage; securing legal, stable work; and deciding to 'go straight,' including a reorientation of the costs and benefits of crime" (2001, 4). For most individuals, many of these watershed moments take place in adulthood, and they are believed to contribute to reduced criminal offending (Salvatore and Markowitz 2014; Laub and Sampson 2001).

Life course theorists have begun to study the "romance–crime nexus" (Larson and Sweeten 2012, 606). Larson and Sweeten examined the effect of breakup of nonmarital romantic relationships on the offending patterns of 10,438 young people aged 17 to 21 in the United States. They found that male offending increases after the breakup of a nonmarital romantic relationship, but that breakup is not associated with female offending. Also, young people who enter into a new relationship after a breakup avoid engaging in criminal activities but increase their alcohol consumption and illicit drug use.

Gender as a Correlate of Crime

Have you ever wondered why most criminals are males? This section focuses on four key questions in the gender distribution of police-reported crime. First, what is the proportion of females accused of crime compared to males? Second, what are the percentages of females and males under the supervision of correctional services at the provincial and federal levels? Third, what is the gender distribution of convicted persons who have been designated "dangerous offenders" in Canada? And fourth, is there evidence supporting the notion of role convergence between males and females as regards crime? The answers to these questions provide a gendered picture of criminality.

SEARCH FOR:
Women and the Criminal Justice System: Juristat

Females are less likely to be charged with criminal offences. That said, the past three decades have seen an increase in the number of females charged with criminal involvement—21 percent of adults charged with a Criminal Code offence in 2009 versus 15 percent in 1979 (Mahony 2011b). Despite the increase, males are still greatly overrepresented in crime. The level of involvement of males and females varies by type of crime. In 2014–15, for instance, males made up 80 percent of all accused persons in adult criminal courts (Maxwell 2017). Males were generally more likely than females to be involved in violent and serious offenses (Figure 5.4). Males made up 98 percent of the accused in sexual assault cases, 89 percent of robbery cases, 86 percent of homicide cases, and 77 percent of major assault cases. Females were most commonly accused of theft (35%) and fraud (33%) (Maxwell 2017). Female youth had higher rates of police-reported crimes than did their older counterparts (Mahony, Jacob, and Hobson 2017).

Gartner, Webster, and Doob (2009, 182) found that women's imprisonment has not increased in the past few decades in Canada despite significant media attention to female crime and a perceived increase in incarceration rates of women. Figure 5.5 shows that females made up 25 percent of all admissions

FIGURE 5.4 ■ **Percentage of Charges in Adult Criminal Courts, by Gender, 2014–15 (Selected Criminal Offences)**

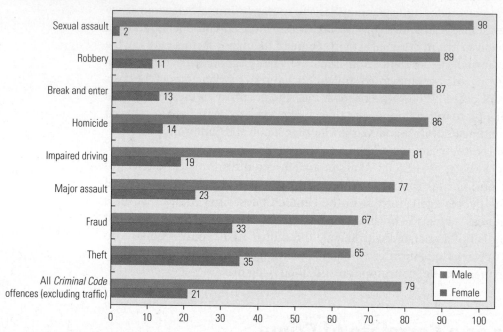

Source: Statistics Canada, *Adult Criminal Court Statistics in Canada, 2014–15*. Reproduced and distributed on an "as is" basis with the permission of Statistics Canada.

FIGURE 5.5 ■ **Youth Custody and Community Services (YCCS), Admissions to Correctional Services, by Age Group and Gender, 2015–16, Canada**

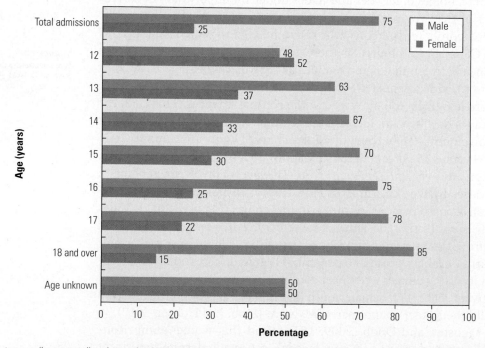

Note: The total does not necessarily represent all provinces and territories, as there are variations in the availability of data for certain jurisdictions and years.

Source: Statistics Canada. Table 251-0011 - *Youth Custody and Community Services (YCCS), Admissions to Correctional Services, by Sex and Age at Time of Admission*, annual (number), CANSIM (database). Available at www5.statcan.gc.ca/cansim/a26?lang=eng&id= 2510011 (accessed: January 31, 2018). Reproduced and distributed on an "as is" basis with the permission of Statistics Canada.

to youth correctional services in 2015–16. The pattern is similar among adults. Females made up 8 percent of inmates in sentenced custody at the federal level (which indicates sentences of at least two years), and 7 percent of those admitted to community supervision (Reitano 2017). Male inmates also dominate provincial and territorial prisons. Women constituted only 16 percent of adults admitted to provincial and territorial prisons in 2015–16 (Reitano 2017). Adult female sentences were generally shorter those given to male counterparts.

Why do women receive more lenient treatment in the courts? The main reason is that males commit more serious crimes, especially more violent offences. A second factor that influences court decisions is female offenders' responsibility for young children (Kruttschnitt 2013).

Women and Violent Crime

As shown in Figure 5.6, 86 percent of persons accused of homicide in 2016 were male (Statistics Canada 2017a). This is down slightly from 89 percent in 2012 (Boyce and Cotter 2013). Most homicide victims are male (75%) (Figure 5.7).

FIGURE 5.6 ■ Distribution of Persons Accused of Homicide, by Gender, 2016, Canada

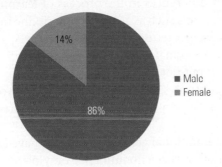

Note: Homicide includes Criminal Code offences of murder, manslaughter, and infanticide; includes all persons who are accused (by police) of having committed a homicide. Data in this figure do not necessarily agree with data from the Uniform Crime Reporting Survey, where youth accused include a small number of persons under the age of 12.

Source: Statistics Canada. Table 253-0003 - Homicide survey, victims and persons accused of homicide, by age group and sex, Canada, annual (number). Reproduced and distributed on an "as is" basis with the permission of Statistics Canada.

FIGURE 5.7 ■ Distribution of Victims of Homicide, by Gender, 2016, Canada

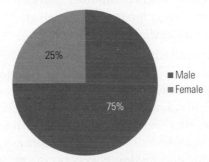

Note: Homicide includes Criminal Code offences of murder, manslaughter, and infanticide.

Source: Statistics Canada. Table 253-0003 - Homicide survey, victims and persons accused of homicide, by age group and sex, Canada, annual (number). Reproduced and distributed on an "as is" basis with the permission of Statistics Canada.

The category "dangerous offender" sheds light on those considered most violent among the population convicted of serious crime. Canada's dangerous offender law (section 753 of the Criminal Code) separates out the most aggressive criminal recidivists among those who have been convicted of a violent and/or sexual criminal offence. A person who has been classified as a dangerous offender can be held in prison for an indeterminate period. Of nearly 500 persons held in 2013 under the "dangerous offender" law, only one was a woman.

Both males and females are more likely to be killed by males. Females are more than twice as likely as males to be killed by their spouse (Mahony 2011a; Ansara and Hindin 2010). When a woman commits a violent crime, it is often against someone closely related to her. Victims of female acts of violence in 2015 were the spouse or some other intimate partner (36%), an acquaintance (35%), a stranger (12%), or a family member (17%) (Mahony, Jacob, and Hobson 2017). Males are more likely to direct their violence at acquaintances, especially when the crime is homicide.

Heimer and De Coster (1999) have made an important contribution to our understanding of the gender gap in violent crime by examining structural positions and cultural processes, including social learning. They conclude that:

1. Violent delinquency is a function of the social learning of violent definitions of appropriate behaviour by both males and females.
2. There are gender differences in the process of learning violent definitions. Direct parental controls such as aggressive discipline influence violent definitions for males to a greater degree than for females, while indirect parental controls, such as emotional attachment to family, influence girls' learning of violent definitions but not boys'.
3. Direct parental controls such as supervision of the youth's friendships help reduce violent delinquency in boys but have no importance for violence committed by girls.
4. Girls who accept traditional gender definitions have lower rates of violence; such ideational notions have no influence on violence by boys.
5. Violence by boys *and* girls is shaped by position in the social structure, but the influence of position in the social structure over criminal behaviour in boys and girls differs.
6. Boys have higher rates of violent delinquency partly because they tend to learn more violent definitions and gender definitions and have greater experience with violent crime than girls.
7. Boys tend to learn more violent definitions than girls because of their experience with violence and lower levels of emotional attachment to their families. (Heimer and De Coster 1999, 302–3)

Studies of structural disadvantage factors, such as poverty, on male violent crime have produced fairly consistent results. The most violent males are those who are the most disadvantaged. Steffensmeier and Haynie (2000, 428) found that structural disadvantage variables (poverty, income inequality, a female-headed home, etc.) were also associated with female violent crimes. More specifically, they found that structural disadvantage had "significant effects" on robbery and homicide and modest effects on the rates of larceny, burglary, and aggravated assault committed by women. Even so, structural disadvantage has a greater impact on male than on female criminal behaviour. Marriage has been found to attenuate criminal behaviour in men (Laub and Sampson 2001). For disadvantaged women, motherhood is the primary factor reducing drug use and delinquent behaviour (Kreager, Matsueda, and Erosheva 2010).

The pathway to criminality is fundamentally gendered (Chapter 6). Daly (1992) described five pathways for women's involvement in crime:

1. "Harmed and harming women": These women have endured abuse and have had a difficult family life. The abuse was likely perpetrated by an adult male, and they may have been abandoned or abused by their mother. They suffered the loss of loved ones when they were young, and they are regarded as "out of control" by family members. They resorted to substance abuse, particularly in their early teens. Daly argues that such women commit crimes when intoxicated or because they are unable to control their anger.

2. "Battered women": These women's criminal activities are precipitated by an abusive partner. Relationships with violent men are the defining factor in the criminal activity of such women.

3. "Street women": These women suffered serious levels of abuse in childhood or in present relationships. What distinguishes "street women" from "harmed and harming women" is street involvement. Street women are street-involved and engage in various survival mechanisms, such as prostitution, drug selling, and theft. Such women tend to have longer criminal histories and are more likely to have spent time behind bars.

4. "Drug-connected women": These women have engaged in illicit drug use and sale in part because of their relationships with people, usually family and partners, who were involved in drugs. Such women are not necessarily drug-addicted, nor do they have long criminal histories (see also Kruttschnitt, 2013).

5. "Other women": This category refers to persons with no history of unfavourable family life, who have not suffered abuse, and who are not street-entrenched, but who are engaged in crime for economic gain.

Is There Evidence for the Role Convergence Hypothesis?

The study of gender differences in criminal behaviour has a long history (Walklate 2012). Lombroso and Ferrero (1895, 27) provided some the earliest explanations for gender differences in crime. These focused on supposed "pathological anomalies" and the sexualization of female offenders. These issues persisted in the literature for many decades   for example, in the work of theorists such as Freud (1933) and Pollak (1950) (see Chapter 6).

These biological theories have been challenged. Criminologists have shown that explanations for gender differences in criminal behaviour are embedded in social structure, particularly in patriarchal traditions and the attendant gender roles. Those roles are well-defined so that males and females are held to widely divergent standards and expectations with regard to what constitutes appropriate behaviour (Hartnagel 2012; Hagan, Gillis, and Simpson 1985).

The home in particular is a site of acculturation and gender contestation. It is in the home that boys and girls learn appropriate behaviours. While the power control theory developed by Hagan, Gillis, and Simpson (1985, 1987) is discussed more fully in the next chapter, we can note here that they concluded that girls are subjected to greater control than their male siblings in the same household. Daughters are objects of control, and the main instrument of control is the mother, who is assigned that role by her husband. This cuts across social classes, albeit with varying intensity (1987). Male children from the employer class are more delinquent than their female counterparts in part because they are not as tightly controlled by the mother and are not deterred by the risk of punishment (1985). It follows that gender equality has begun to bridge sex differences in crime, for it is freeing females from excessive control: "When daughters are freed from patriarchal family relations, they too become delinquent" (1987, 814).

Gender roles are produced by and reflect the structures and ideologies of society (Cotter, Hermsen, and Vaneman 2011). Societal expectations and the widely acknowledged double standards for women have implications for how women and men live their lives, navigate social settings, and behave in general. The influence of societal standards and gender roles can be expected to extend to delinquent or criminal behaviour (Hartnagel 2012). In theory, then, when there is a convergence of the roles and duties of the sexes, a decline in gender differences in crime should also occur. This **role convergence hypothesis** posits that as women leave the domestic sphere for the world of wage labour, there should be an increase in female crime. Some have suggested that the expansion of employment opportunities for women should lead to an increase in female property crime (Simon 1975).

The gender gap in crime has declined, but much depends on the time period we are considering and on the offences being considered (Kruttschnitt 2013). Crime statistics indicate a growing involvement of women in some types of violent crime; however, this is not supported by self-report studies. Stevens, Morash, and Chesney-Lind (2011) found that young girls in 2000 were twice as likely to be charged as their 1980 counterparts, while the pattern for boys remained constant. Policing and other bureaucratic practices may play a major role in the increasing numbers of women charged with both property (Steffensmeier and Streifel, 1992) and violent offenses. Some have argued that the gender gap is shrinking because of a *reduction* in *male* criminal behaviour (Rennison 2009). Lauritsen, Heimer, and Lynch examined data from 1973 to 2005 and concluded that police practices were not solely responsible for the narrowing gender gap. They argued that the gender gap had narrowed in recent times because of a decrease in male offending rates and an increase in violent offending among females, especially in crimes such as aggravated assault, robbery, and simple assault (Lauritsen, Heimer, and Lynch 2009, 386). According to their study, the greatest increase in female involvement was in minor property offences such as shoplifting, credit card fraud, and passing bad cheques. This perhaps reflected the feminization of poverty more than any changes in gender roles (see Chapter 6).

Given the increased numbers of women in the labour force, one area in which role convergence might be expected is corporate crime. But despite the increase in the number of women in nontraditional corporate positions, women are not as engaged in corporate crime as men. A study of criminal convictions for corporate crime in seven federal districts in the United States found that 14 percent of men's cases involved indictments against organizations while only 1 percent of women's cases involved the same (Daly 1989). In terms of occupational crime, however, Daly found that the female share of bank embezzlement was nearly 50 percent. Daly also

role convergence hypothesis
The hypothesis that as the work roles of women become similar to those of men, so will their involvement in crime.

found that 60 percent of the female bank embezzlers worked as tellers and that 90 percent were involved in some form of clerical duties. This suggests that women occupied positions that presented few opportunities for serious financial crime. This has implications for the scale of the embezzlement committed by women; men were better positioned in their organizations to steal more. Most of the male criminals but almost all of the female criminals were "little fish" (1989, 789). This is generally consistent with female involvement in theft and related property offences at the street level. Also, Daly found that men were more likely to commit occupational crime in concert with others, whereas women often acted on their own. Acting in a group may increase the magnitude and seriousness of (white-collar) crime. Additionally, women (36%) were twice as likely as men (18%) to cite financial need for their families as the main motivation for their white-collar crime.

More recent research has supported Daly's findings on gender patterns in corporate crime. Women's pathways to corporate criminality were found to be "relational." For instance, a study by Steffensmeier, Schwartz, and Roche (2013) found that one third of women defendants had a personal relationship—typically spousal—with a male mastermind. The second pathway for women's corporate crime was "utility"—that is, these women were occupying positions that made them the "conduit or instrument of manipulation" of financial data rather than the persons behind the criminal behaviour. In this study, 68 percent of the women had been charged as co-conspirators. Steffensmeier and colleagues found that three-quarters of women participated in the white-collar crime because of pressure or directives from male bosses. In some cases, they were co-signers of fraudulent tax returns filed by a male spouse.

Most female participants in criminal conspiracies received lower rewards from their crimes than their male counterparts. The women who received high compensation for their criminal activities were the spouses of male masterminds. Steffensmeier and colleagues also found that there were no all-female conspiracies, fewer than 10 percent of corporate offenders were women, and women earned far less than men in corporate crime even when they had a high rank in the organization and played a prominent role in the fraudulent scheme. Overall, women were only involved in petty corporate crime; men were involved in both petty and major corporate crime.

QUESTIONS FOR CRITICAL THINKING

1. Why are youth overrepresented in police-reported crime statistics?
2. Discuss how the notion of maturational reform is used to explain why older people are less involved in crime than are youth.

Race and Crime

Race is not as strongly related to crime as age and sex (Hartnagel 2012). Research on the interplay of race and crime in Canada (Pederson, Malcoe, and Pulkingham 2013; Wortley and Owusu-Bempah 2011; Fitzgerald and Carrington 2010; Henry and Tator 2005) is not nearly as extensive as in the United States

(Peterson, 2012; Peterson and Krivo, 2010; Shedd and Hagan 2006). This is partly because police in Canada rarely report information on race (Owusu-Benpah and Millar 2010, 97). The exception is information about Indigenous offenders.

An attempt in 1990 by Statistics Canada to collect data on the race of offenders was rejected because of lack of cooperation from most police organizations and because of broad criticism of the policy (Hartnagel 2012). The idea of collecting race and crime statistics has been controversial in Canada (Wortley and Tanner, 2003; Wortley, 1999; Johnston, 1994; Roberts, 1994). Wortley (1999) has summarized this debate. Opponents of race-based crime statistics believe that the idea should be abandoned because of the poor quality of police-reported crime statistics, the difficulties inherent in measuring race, and the possibility that such statistics might be used to justify racist theories of crime and, consequently, discriminatory treatment of minorities (1999, 263). On the other hand, supporters of these statistics argue that race-based data are required to verify the accuracy of claims that certain groups are receiving differential treatment in the criminal justice system; that such statistics may provide tools to challenge biological theories and other ideas about the race–crime relationship; and that banning the collection of race-based, police-reported data will not prevent the spread of racist ideology (1999, 265). Support for the collection of race-based crime statistics has continued in more recent times on similar premises (Millar and Owusu-Benpah 2011; Owusu-Benpah and Millar 2010).

The evidence that does exist suggests that some minority groups are overrepresented in police-reported crime statistics. This overrepresentation is believed to be present in all Western societies (Tonry 1997), though the specific groups that are overrepresented vary by jurisdiction. In Canada and Australia, for instance, Indigenous people are overrepresented. In the United States, New Zealand, Germany, and Turkey, African Americans, Maoris, and Turks and Kurds, respectively, are overrepresented. In Canada, the minority groups that are overrepresented vary by location. In Greater Toronto, for example, blacks are overrepresented, while Indigenous people are overrepresented on the Prairies.

Evidence from surveys and self-report studies (Wortley and McCalla 2007) points to differential outcomes for various ethno-racial groups in Canada's criminal justice system. Wortley and Owusu-Bempah (2011) found that blacks are 6.5 times more likely than whites to state that they know a friend or family member who has been racially profiled by the police (2011, 401). They conclude that "black racial background appears to be a master status that attracts police attention and significantly contributes to police decisions to conduct street interrogations" (2011, 402). Also, blacks are more likely to perceive police stops as unfair, and this may have an impact on their demeanour in encounters with the police. A Toronto survey conducted by Wortley and Tanner (2005) found that black high school students who were not involved in any criminal or deviant activity were four times more likely to report being stopped and six times more likely to be searched by police than their white colleagues who were also not involved in crime. Fitzgerald and Carrington's (2011) analysis of the National Longitudinal Survey of Children and Youth (NLSCY) found that Indigenous, black, and West Asian youth were three times more likely to report contact with the police. The same study found that the least delinquent minority youth had the greatest contact with police, so delinquency involvement does not explain why they were stopped and/or searched by police. Fitzgerald and Carrington (2011, 473) also found that though youth who were involved in violent delinquency had a higher probability of contact with the police, this variable did not reduce the effect of race on contact with police.

Mascoll and Rankin (2005) reported that a majority of black Toronto police officers who participated in a focus group discussion stated that they had been stopped and searched by their colleagues when they were off duty "for no other reason than the colour of their skin" (cited in Tanovich 2006, 1–2). The Commission on Systemic Racism in the Ontario Criminal Justice System (1995) found a differential pattern in how citizens are stopped by police. Nineteen percent of Chinese male residents, 25 percent of white male residents, and 43 percent of black male residents reported having been stopped in the previous two years. The study also reported that "there was widespread perception among Black, Chinese and White Torontonians that judges discriminate on the basis of race" (1995).

Similar data have been put forward by the Office of the Correctional Investigator, the government-appointed oversight agency for Correctional Service Canada. In a 2012–13 report, the agency stated that in 2013, 40 percent of inmates in federal prisons were non-Caucasians. A case study by the (former) correctional investigator, Howard Sapers, indicated that black inmates were concerned about "prejudicial attitudes by some corrections staff" who assumed they were gang members. According to Barrett (2013), this assumption may be contributing to the disproportionate number of black prisoners in maximum security facilities, as well as to segregation placements, use of force by prison staff, more charges while in prison, and a lower likelihood of being paroled despite lower rates of recidivism.

The 2016–17 report of the Office of the Correctional Investigator (2017, 55) concluded that "four years later very little appears to have changed for Black people in federal custody." Today, Canadians of African descent comprise 8.6 percent of the federal inmate population although they are less than 3 percent of the general Canadian population. However, this represents a 9 percent *decrease* in the federal black inmate population since 2013 (2017). This contrasts with the 6.3 percent decrease in the overall inmate population.

Evidence from the United States shows a similar pattern of differential arrests and sentencing disparities. Blacks are arrested for drug offences at 2 to 11 times higher rates than whites, and black offenders receive sentences that are 10 to 20 percent longer than those given to white offenders for the same crimes (Peterson 2012, 307). According to The Sentencing Project (2014), there are 2.2 million persons in US prisons or jails, and more than three-fifths of them are minorities. Current estimates are that one out of 17 white men, one out of 6 Latino men, and one out of 3 black men will go to prison at some point in their lives. Similar statistics for women show that one in 111 white women, one out of 45 Latino women, and one out of 18 black women will be incarcerated at some point in their lives.

It is widely contended that in the United States, the death penalty is discriminatory. Cohen and Smith (2010) analyzed the social and geographic distribution of candidates for the death penalty. They found that accused persons of minority background in urban centres surrounded by majority white suburban counties were more likely to receive the death penalty. Missouri has handed down more death sentences than the three larger states of New York, California, and Florida. Yet a death sentence is rarely handed down in three districts dominated by minorities: the District of Columbia, Puerto Rico, and the Southern District of New York. "These three federal districts account for 55 of the 460 death-authorized cases but are not responsible for a single death sentence" (2010, 465). This analysis suggests that when offences that are punishable by death are held constant, whether the death penalty is applied depends on the race of the accused and the community where the offence was committed.

There are two competing explanations for the overrepresentation of minorities in the criminal justice system: the **differential offending hypothesis** and the **differential treatment hypothesis**. The differential offending hypothesis states that there are actual differences between racial groups in terms of the incidence, level of seriousness, and persistence of offending patterns (Fitzgerald and Carrington 2011; Owusu-Benpah and Millar 2010). The differential treatment hypothesis (Fitzgerald and Carrington 2011) states that structural inequality in the administration of justice, from police patrols to courtrooms to correctional services, is responsible for the overrepresentation of minority groups in the criminal justice process. Fitzgerald and Carrington (2011, 453) divide the differential treatment hypothesis into three parts:

1. The police often give closer attention to people who meet certain social criteria (young lower-class males), and minority group members may disproportionately be included in these groups.
2. Certain social spaces tend to experience greater police surveillance than others—for example, areas with concentrated social disadvantage marked by relatively high levels of unemployment, poverty, and social disorder—and these areas are often inhabited by newer immigrant groups and poor minorities (see also Sampson, Raudenbush, and Earls 1997).
3. The police may be influenced by race or ethnicity in the exercise of their discretion and authority. This includes decisions about whether or not to stop, search, or arrest a suspect. Contact with police is typically the first step in the criminal justice process.

Indigenous Peoples and the Canadian Criminal Justice System

Indigenous people are overrepresented in the criminal justice process. They are 4.9 percent of the Canadian population (2016 Census) and 7 percent of the Canadian youth population, but they make up a much higher proportion of the prison population. Figure 5.8 shows that the share of Indigenous youth in custody has increased since 1997–98. Indigenous female youth are more highly overrepresented in youth custody. In 2015–16, 31 percent of the male youth population in custody and community services were Indigenous males; Indigenous females represented 44 percent of female youth admitted to custody and community services. Indigenous adults are also greatly overrepresented in the prison population. Although Indigenous adults made up 3 percent of the Canadian adult population, they comprised 26 percent of those admitted to provincial and territorial services and 28 percent in federal custody in 2015–16 (Reitano 2017). Indigenous persons constituted 38 percent of female admissions to provincial and territorial sentenced custody and 31 percent of admissions to

differential offending hypothesis
There are actual differences between racial groups in terms of the incidence, level of seriousness, and persistence of offending patterns.

differential treatment hypothesis
Structural inequality in the administration of justice (from police patrols to courtrooms to correctional services) is responsible for the overrepresentation of minority groups in the criminal justice process.

FIGURE 5.8 ■ **Representation of Aboriginals (Male and Female) in Total Admissions to Youth Custody and Community Services (YCCS), 1997–98 to 2015–16, Canada**

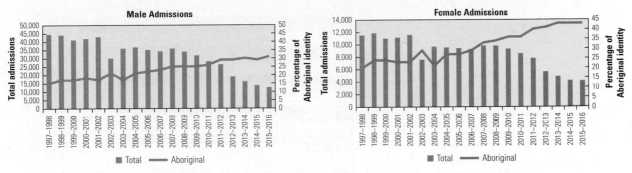

Note: Admissions are collected each time a person begins any type of custodial or community supervision, and describe and measure the case flow in correctional agencies over time. The same person can be included several times in the admission counts where the individual moves from one type of legal status to another (e.g., from open to secure custody) or re-enters the system in the same year. As such, admissions represent the number of entries within a fiscal year to sentenced custody, to remand, and to community supervision regardless of the individual's preceding or following legal status.

Source: Statistics Canada. Table 251-0012 - Youth custody and community services (YCCS), admissions to correctional services, by sex and aboriginal identity, annual (number). Reproduced and distributed on an "as is" basis with the permission of Statistics Canada.

federal sentenced custody. The figures for Indigenous males were 26 percent and 23 percent, respectively. In 2015–16, 87 percent of persons in custody in the Northwest Territories were Indigenous, compared to 52 percent of the general population (Figure 5.9). The situation is similar in other provinces and territories—for example, in Saskatchewan (77% versus 16%), Yukon (72% versus 23%), Manitoba (76% versus 17%), and Ontario (12% versus 2%).

The Canadian Criminal Justice Association (2000; cited in Greenberg, Grekul, and Nelson 2012, 237) has provided a summary of the problems confronting Indigenous peoples in the Canadian criminal justice process:

1. Indigenous accused are more likely to be denied bail.
2. More time is spent in pretrial detention by Indigenous people.
3. Indigenous accused are more likely to be charged with multiple offences and often for crimes against the system (failing to appear).
4. Indigenous people are more likely not to have representation at court proceedings.
5. Indigenous clients, especially in northern communities where the court party flies in on the day of the hearing, spend less time with their lawyers.
6. Indigenous offenders are more than twice as likely to be incarcerated than non-Indigenous offenders.
7. Indigenous Elders, who are spiritual leaders, are not given the same status as prison priests and chaplains in all institutions.
8. Indigenous people often plead guilty because they are intimidated by the court and simply want to get the proceedings over with.

A recent report by the Office of the Correctional Investigator (2017, 50) noted that Indigenous inmates were:

1. Released later in their sentence.
2. Disproportionately overrepresented in segregation placements, use-of-force interventions, maximum security institutions, and self-injurious incidents.
3. More likely to be returned to prison due to suspension or revocation of parole.

FIGURE 5.9 ■ **Aboriginal Adult Admissions to Custody, by Province and Territory, 2015–16, Canada**

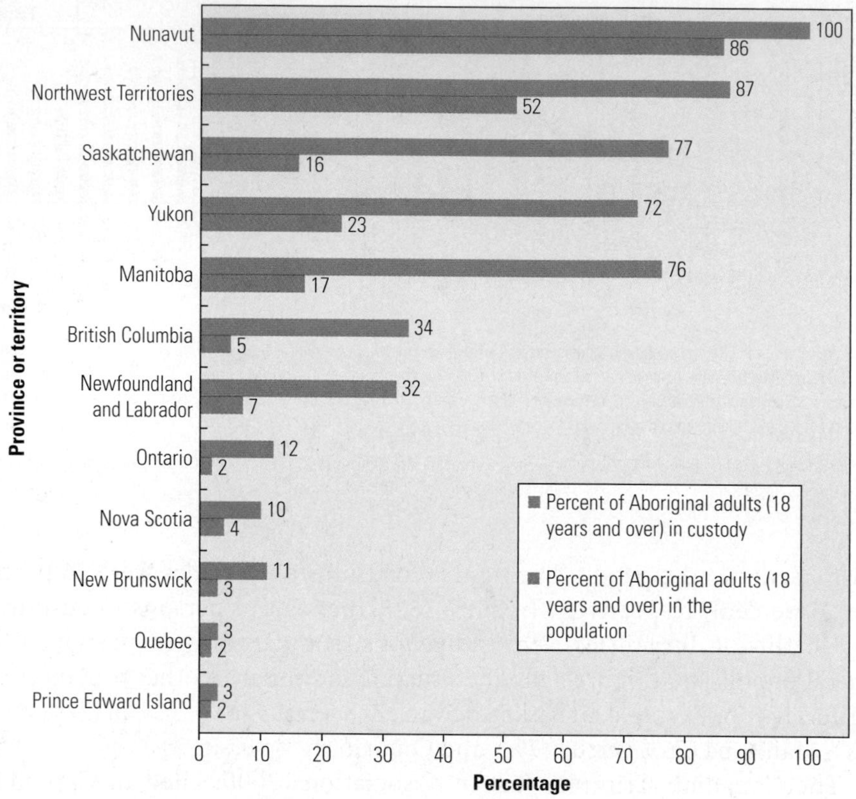

Note: Excludes Alberta due to unavailability of data. Population estimates based on 2011 National Household Survey.

Source: Statistics Canada, Canadian Centre for Justice Statistics, *Adult Correctional Services Survey and Integrated Correctional Services Survey*, Table 3. Available at: https://www.statcan.gc.ca/pub/85-002-x/2017001/article/14691/tbl/tbl03-eng.htm (accessed: January 31, 2018). Reproduced and distributed on an "as is" basis with the permission of Statistics Canada.

The Office of the Correctional Investigator (2017) estimates that between 2007 and 2016, the federal inmate population grew by less than 5 percent while the number of Indigenous persons in federal prisons increased by 39 percent. The number of Indigenous persons in federal prisons has grown "every single year" over the last 30 years (2017, 48). The result is that 26.4 percent of all federal inmates are Indigenous (2017). These statistics are alarming, given the proportion of Indigenous persons in the general population.

Why Are Indigenous People Overrepresented in the Criminal Justice System?

Several explanations have been offered for the overrepresentation of Indigenous people in the criminal justice system. They include cultural theories, the colonial model, the trauma transmission model, and critical race theory.

SEARCH FOR:
The Aboriginal Justice Inquiry of Manitoba: Volume 1

Cultural Theories

Cultural theories of crime examine the traits, characteristics, or way of life of an identifiable group to explain the involvement of members of that group in the criminal justice process. Such theories analyze the development of a subculture (or counterculture) that runs contrary to the dominant culture. Research on the prevalence of violence in poorer segments of society has a long history (Wolfgang and Ferracuti, 1967). For instance, Anderson's *Code of the Street* (1999) captures the subculture of the inner city, the quest for respect, and the potential for interpersonal violence (see Chapter 10).

Cultural theories of Indigenous overrepresentation in the criminal justice process come close to cultural conflict theory (see Chapter 11). Indigenous cultures are viewed as different from the dominant Euro-Canadian culture in content and/or manner of expression (Hartnagel 2012). Indigenous cultures' emphasis on sharing, and their traditional approaches to dispute resolution—which emphasize mediation and healing—are viewed as unsuited to the adversarial system imported from Europe. The common law system's norms, values, and procedures are alien to Indigenous people and predispose them to conflict with the law (Dumont 1993).

Cultural explanations for the overrepresentation of Indigenous people in the criminal justice system are problematic for several reasons. First, they presuppose a monolithic Indigenous culture when in fact, Indigenous peoples and their cultures are diverse. Second, a static Indigenous culture is assumed; Indigenous culture is presented as a calcified relic of the past and hence as uninfluenced by the dominant culture in which it in embedded. Third, there seems to be an assumption that there is a particular kind of behaviour that constitutes *Indigenous behaviour*. Fourth, cultural explanations inadvertently pathologize Indigenous peoples' cultures. Underlying that is a presumption that there is an objective standard that makes Indigenous cultures delinquent. Such explanations are simplistic and do not fully engage with a bidimensional phenomenon: the process of incorporating Indigenous cultures without allowing them access to legitimate opportunity structures in Canadian society. Indigenous people, like all Canadians, are inundated with the prevailing ideas and ideals about socially desirable material goods in our consumerist culture. Indigenous unemployment numbers are higher than for other Canadians. This suggests several factors are involved: deculturalization from Indigenous ways of life; acculturation or assimilation into Euro-Canadian ways of life; and structural exclusion. As Young argues in *The Exclusive Society* (1999, 81), there can be "*cultural inclusion and structural exclusion*" (italics original) as two sides of a coin in a group's relationship with the wider society. Consequently, scholars are increasingly giving attention to *structural explanations* of Indigenous overrepresentation in crime statistics.

Structural Theories

Structural theories situate the locus of criminality in the historical context and prevailing structures of society rather than in individual or group pathology. The key argument is that institutional arrangements—particularly the distribution of socially valuable resources such as education and jobs—and the routine functioning of the criminal justice system are major explanatory factors

These North-West Mounted Police members from Fort Macleod are shown visiting Calgary in 1886. The NWMP was established to keep order during the European settlement of western Canada.

Glenbow Archives NA-5656-3

for ethno-racial profile of crime statistics. The judgment of the Supreme Court of Canada in *R v Gladue* (1999) provides a backdrop to structural explanations of the overrepresentation of Indigenous peoples in the criminal justice system:

> The background factors which figure prominently in the causation of crime by aboriginal offenders are by now well known. Years of dislocation and economic development have translated, for many aboriginal peoples, into low incomes, high unemployment, lack of opportunities and options, lack or irrelevance of education, substance abuse, loneliness, and community fragmentation. These and other factors contribute to a higher incidence of crime and incarceration.

This statement is sociological rather than legalistic. The Supreme Court notes the "unique systemic or background factors which may have played a part in bringing the particular aboriginal offender before the courts."

Three structural explanations are examined here: the colonial model, historic trauma transmission model, and critical race theory.

The Colonial Model

The colonial model was made popular by Frantz Fanon (1963; 1967). More recent works by Tatum (1994), Agozino (2003), and Gabbidon (2010) have shed more light on the links between colonialism and crime. The colonial model takes a socio-psychological perspective. It focuses on the intersection of "structural oppression, alienation and three adaptive forms of behaviour—assimilation, crime or deviance, and protest" (Tatum 1994, 34). Tatum's typology includes four stages of colonization. In the first, the territory of one racial group is invaded by another. The goal in this phase is to acquire valuable resources such as gold or furs. In the second stage, a colonial society is formed. At this stage, processes of cultural imposition, cultural disintegration, and cultural re-creation occur. Cultural imposition means that the Native populations are forced to adopt the values and ways of life of the colonial power. This leads to the collapse or decentring of the norms and values of the colonized group. As a consequence, a society develops in which the old norms and values have given way to different values that inferiorize the Native population. In Canada, this stage of Indigenous colonization was carried out by residential schools, which were established in the 1870s and eventually numbered more than 130 (Truth and Reconciliation Commission 2014). The residential schools made systematic efforts "to assimilate Aboriginal children into mainstream society by removing the 'Indian within them'" (Charles and DeGagné 2013) through a process of "aggressive civilization" (Rand 2011, 56). The physical and sexual abuse suffered by Indigenous children was an arguably unintended consequence of implementing the schools' main objective.

In the third stage, Native peoples find themselves governed by representatives of the colonizer's power, such as the police and the military. In Canada, the North-West Mounted Police (later renamed the RCMP) set out to pacify the Indigenous population so that the West could be settled (Kelly and Kelly 1973). That forceful effort has strongly shaped the relationship between law enforcement agencies and Native populations. During this third stage, minor infractions by the dominated group are likely to come to the attention of law enforcement, given that the latter's mission is to pacify the group. This reduces the likelihood that colonized populations will cooperate with the police and perceive them as fair, which has implications for whether or not people obey the law (Jackson and Bradford 2010; Tyler 1990). Fourth, the colonial society develops a caste system based on race. As a result, access to socially valuable resources such as land, jobs, and education is shaped by racial considerations. This provides opportunities for settler populations as well as an economy of disadvantage for natives. Concentrated disadvantage increases the likelihood of criminal behaviour (Thompson and Gartner 2014; Peterson 2012; Sampson, Raudenbush, and Earls 1997).

These four processes have psychological and social consequences for the colonized population. One consequence is what Wright (1994, 20) calls mentacide—the "deliberate and systematic destruction of a group's minds with the ultimate objective being the extirpation of the group." Each member of the colonized group bears the burden of proving that he or she is not inferior to the dominant group and is a well-adapted member of the colonial society (Gabbidon 2010). Another consequence is "cultural limbo," or double alienation. A colonized population is routinely and forcefully expected to shed its Native identity, language, and customs. The Native people are thus neither fully themselves nor part of the colonizer's racial group. They occupy an in-between state that is both confused and confusing.

The resulting alienation and ambiguity may manifest itself in crime, particularly through self-hate (Gabbidon 2010). Self-hate may be evident in the desire of the colonized not to identify with their traditional customs, which have been discursively rendered primitive. The self-hate may also be projected onto the group: "The alienation can result in attacks against the people that the colonized now hate the most: *themselves*" (2010, 6; italics in original). When people are alienated from their group, the consequence may be horizontal violence in the dominated community. Horizontal violence refers to violent acts by a person within his or her social class. Overtly violent crimes are rarely between classes. Scholars have only recently begun to focus on the physical and sexual abuse *between* students (in addition to abuse by staff against students, which had been the subject of earlier studies) in the residential school system (Charles and DeGagné 2013).

Most of the violent acts reported to police, including homicides, are intra-class—usually, committed by people of lower socioeconomic status on members of their own social category. This is partly a result of internalized anger caused by blocked opportunity and of self-destructive coping mechanisms such as alcoholism and drug abuse (Gabbidon 2010; Tatum 1994; Brownridge 2010). High rates of psychiatric disorders, hypertension, and various serious crimes, particularly homicide, are common in oppressed communities (Tatum 1994). The colonial model of crime focuses on how the conditions fostered by colonialist expansion generate particular institutional arrangements that produce a kind of subject who is susceptible to committing (violent) crimes. While the colonial model seems rather deterministic, it does not necessarily negate human agency. Rather, it demonstrates that colonialism has consequences for human psyche and actions, such as criminal behaviour. It also indicates that historical context matters when we examine criminal statistics.

Historic Trauma Transmission Model

This model is closely related to the colonial model in that it emphasizes the social and psychological consequences of colonialism. Cynthia Wesley-Esquimaux and Magdalena Smolewski (2004) are leading proponents of the historic trauma transmission model as it relates to Indigenous communities in Canada. The model explicates the "aetiology of social and cultural diffusion that devastated Aboriginal communities for so many years" (65). The focus is on how historic trauma manifests itself socially and psychologically. In particular, this model demonstrates how "acculturation (and a loss of the social self) is often associated with alcoholism, drug addiction, family disintegration and suicide" (66). As is shown in this chapter, many of these variables, such as drug misuse (see page 143), are correlated with crime.

This model argues that when a group of people experience physical extermination, cultural genocide, and colonial subjugation, members of the group develop "learned helplessness" (66). This is a shared form of fatalism in which members of a group believe that no action on their part can alter the course of their lives. "Such a person or group becomes passive, inactive and hostile, ascribing social failures to personal, internal causes and blaming themselves for their helplessness (internal attribution). This internal attribution of failure results in decreased sense of self and social esteem" (66).

Traumatic memories are passed from one generation to the next down four main avenues (76). First, through biological channels, which include inherited predispositions to post-traumatic stress disorder (PTSD) and fetal alcohol spectrum disorder (FASD). These conditions have been linked to some Indigenous youths' inability to articulate thoughts, and also to their confusion with adjudication processes (Greenberg, Grekul, and Nelson 2012). Second, traumatic memories are passed on through storytelling and other culturally sanctioned behaviours. Third, historic trauma is passed on as a direct result of violence, deficient parenting, the acting out of abuse, and other social ills. Fourth, there are psychological avenues involving memory and individual recollections of pain, suffering, and debilitating social conditions (66).

Qualitative studies have consistently linked the residential school system to abuse and suicidal thoughts in Indigenous communities (Charles and DeGagné 2013; Rand 2011). This supports the notion of trauma transmission. A recent quantitative study (Elias et al. 2012) lends support to the historic trauma transmission model. That study used a First Nations sample of 2,953 Manitoba adults. About one-third of the sample had attended residential school; the rest had not. Attendance at residential schools was associated with a history of abuse. Abuse was also more common among respondents who had not attended a residential school but whose parents or grandparents had done so. Overall, the historic trauma transmission model provides a context for understanding the socio-genesis of the conditions in Indigenous communities that face severe social problems, including crime.

Critical Race Theory

The earliest strands of this theory are found in the works of Derrick Bell (Delgado and Stefancic 2012). Critical race theory emerged in the 1980s as a counter-hegemonic strategy. It challenges the policies and dynamics and taken-for-granted assumptions of institutional power. It adopts a **social constructionist approach** to race, the law, and justice. A social constructionist approach questions the idea that there is a social reality that is observable or measurable, positing instead that multiple realities pervade the social world. In other words, crime is what a society defines it to be and is not an objective fact.

The notion of "legal indeterminacy" is central to critical race theory. This concept means that "not every legal case has one correct outcome" (5). In other words, court decisions are not always predictable: an accused person may be given a long term in prison for the same criminal behaviour for which another accused person was acquitted. Critical race theory focuses on racial subordination, racism, and discrimination. It also examines the intersection of race, gender, and class in the criminal justice process.

Critical race theory makes several assumptions. These include the idea that the law reflects the dominant group's norms and values and favours that group. It also presupposes that the enforcement and interpretation of the law is subjective. That is, the law is not colour-blind. The theory also holds that racism in the justice process is not an aberration; rather, it is "normal." The theory also assumes that though the average member of society views the law as something tangible, like the weather, the law is in fact not an objective entity. Its enactment, enforcement, and interpretation are subjective processes; as a result, groups that are not well situated to make, enforce, and interpret laws often bear the brunt of the criminal justice system. So from this perspective, Indigenous people are over-represented in the criminal justice system because of their systematic exclusion from the conventional opportunity structures of society and because of overpolicing and harsh sentences.

Mirchandani and Chan (2002, 9) have emphasized the need for a shift in analysis from "race" to "racialization." **Racialization** is a process whereby "categories of the population are constructed, differentiated, inferiorized and excluded" (Anthias 1998, 7). It comprises the processes by which meanings are attributed to particular objects, features, and processes of individuals and/or

social constructionist approach to crime
This approach questions the idea that there is an observable or measurable social reality, and instead proposes that a crime is whatever a particular society defines it to be.

racialization
A process in which categories of the population are constructed, differentiated, inferiorized, and excluded.

THE CANADIAN PRESS/Adrian Wyld

Senator (formerly Honourable Justice) Murray Sinclair was the chair of the Truth and Reconciliation Commission, which was established to help deal with the consequences of the residential school system. Senator Sinclair also made an important contribution to Canada by co-chairing Manitoba's Aboriginal Justice Inquiry several decades ago.

groups, in such a way that those features are given special significance and carry a set of additional meanings (Miles 1989, 70). Essentially, this process leads to the construction of "races as real, different and unequal in ways that matter to economic, political and social life" (Commission on Systemic Racism, 1995). For Tanovich (2006, 14), racialization involves the following:

- Selecting some human characteristics as meaningful signs of racial differences.
- Sorting people into races on the basis of variations in these characteristics.
- Attributing personality traits, behaviours, and social characteristics (e.g., criminality) to people classified as members of particular races.
- Acting as if race indicates socially significant differences among people.

Race or racialization remains a critical variable in the criminal justice system. For instance, "race structures citizen views of the police" (Cao 2011, 14). This is supported by research conducted by Wortley and Owusu-Bempah (2011), Shedd and Hagan (2006), and Henry and colleagues (2000), among others. Indigenous people and visible minorities in particular are more likely to hold negative views of the police and other criminal justice agencies, though perceptions and experiences vary among groups (Sprott and Doob 2014). There are consequences for criminal justice when suspects believe—rightly or wrongly—that their race or racialization played a role in their arrest, sentence, or treatment in custody. First, it may attenuate the legitimacy of the criminal justice process (Wortley and Owusu-Bempah 2011; Cao 2011). Second, those who feel discriminated against are less likely to trust the agents and agencies of criminal justice (Cao 2011). This is a question of public confidence. People who have no confidence in the police are less likely to cooperate with them, to report criminal activity, to serve as witnesses, to engage in jury duty, and so on. Confidence in the police is important because only a small fraction of crime is discovered by police officers; most crimes that come to the attention of the police are reported by the public.

Drug and Alcohol Misuse as a Correlate of Crime

The use of illicit drugs is strongly correlated with street crimes including murder, robbery, auto theft, and mischief (Buxton, Tu, and Stockwell 2009). Drugs such as cocaine, crack, and heroin are often involved in debates about the drug–crime nexus (Bennett and Holloway 2005, cited in Hartnagel 2012). Seventy percent of offender release suspensions involve alcohol and other substances (Weeks et al. 1994). More recently, Public Safety Canada (2014) has estimated that three out of four inmates enter custody with substance abuse issues and that for around 50 percent of federal inmates, "there is a direct link between their substance use and criminal behaviour."

Three factors link drug and alcohol use and crime. First, efforts to support an addiction can lead to involvement in crimes; second, individuals may commit crimes because they are under the influence of drugs or alcohol (Pernanen et al., 2002; Buxton et al. 2009); third, the mere possession of illegal drugs in and of itself is a crime. Drug possession accounts for 4.8 percent of police-reported crime in BC (Buxton et al. 2009).

This analysis is closely related to Goldstein's (1985) model, which suggests that drugs cause crime in three ways: psychopharmacological, economic compulsive, and systemic. First, the psychopharmacological dimension means that drugs have the capacity to change behaviour and make people break laws. People under the influence of substances such as alcohol, stimulants, or barbiturates become "excitable" and "irrational" (494). Examples of psychopharmacological violence include spouse or child abuse and barroom brawls. Moreover, a substance user's state of intoxication may lead to contact with the police, although a large volume of such incidents go unreported. Second, the economically compulsive dimension implies that crime may be committed in order to secure drugs to feed a habit. Thus, a chronic drug user may resort to robbery, prostitution, shoplifting, or drug dealing to support her addiction, especially for relatively expensive drugs such as cocaine and heroin, which are noted for their addictiveness. Third, the systemic dimension indicates that "violence is intrinsic to involvement with any illicit substance" (497). In other words, being involved in the sale and use of banned commodities like cocaine or heroin invariably connects individuals with a complex web of interactions with criminal actors and networks. Goldstein (497) lists some of the ways in which engagement in illicit drug distribution or sale may enmesh people in criminal interactions and activities:

1. Disputes over territory between rival drug dealers.
2. Assaults and homicides committed within dealing hierarchies as a means of enforcing normative codes.
3. Robberies of drug dealers and the usually violent retaliation by the dealer or his/or bosses.
4. Elimination of informers (as a routine business activity).
5. Punishment for selling adulterated or phony drugs.

6. Punishment for failing to pay one's debt.
7. Disputes over drugs or drug paraphernalia.
8. Robbery violence related to the social ecology of copping areas (i.e., neighbourhoods where drug distribution or sale takes place)*.

More recent evidence lends support to Goldstein's drug-violence model. For instance, the annual expenditure by Canadians on cannabis prior to legalization in 2018 was estimated at between $5 billion and $6.2 billion, compared to $9.2 billion on beer and $7 billion on wine (Macdonald and Rotermann 2017). Attempts by criminal syndicates to exploit the illegal drug trade often generate violence. For example, the Quebec biker wars between 1994 and 2002 led to violent clashes between Hells Angels and the Rock Machine over who would have access to the lucrative wholesale drug distribution trade in Quebec, particularly in Montreal (Schneider 2013). By the end of 1997, there had been 313 violent incidents, including 81 bombings and 71 attempted murders (Criminal Intelligence Service, Canada 1998, cited in Schneider 2013). Clearly, homicides and other violent criminal activities associated with the drug trade are major issues confronting law enforcement agencies in Canada, where increases in organized crime-related homicides have been recorded (Schneider 2013) despite the overall decline in Canada's murder rate since 1966 (Perreault 2013; Mahony 2011a).

While individual illicit drug users may not appreciate the level of violence involved in getting their fix, the multifaceted connection between crime and the demand for illegal drugs is well-established. A self-report study of 667 illegal drug users in Edmonton, Montreal, Quebec City, Toronto, and Vancouver found that participants were involved in drug dealing (27%) and property crimes (16%), particularly theft (Manzoni, Fischer, and Rehm 2007). The study also found that crack use was associated with property crime in Toronto and that cocaine use and sex work were closely related in Montreal and Quebec City (Manzoni, Fischer, and Rehm 2007).

The Canadian Tobacco, Alcohol and Drugs Survey [CTADS]) measures the use of alcohol and illegal drugs by Canadians aged 15 and over (see Health Canada 2014; CTADS 2015). The results of the 2015 survey show that 77 percent (or 22.7 million) of Canadians reported drinking alcohol the previous year. More males (81%) than females (73%) indicated past-year alcohol use. Young adults aged 20 to 24 exhibited "riskier patterns in their consumption of alcohol than youth (15–19 years) and persons aged 25 and over" (CTADS 2015).

Alcohol consumption is directly correlated with multiple social harms, including crime (Rehm and Room 2009). Participants in the 2012 Canadian Alcohol and Drug Use Monitoring Survey (CADUMS) survey were asked whether they had experienced any of four harms—being verbally abused, feeling threatened, being emotionally hurt or neglected, and being physically hurt—due to somebody else's drinking habits. One in seven respondents (14%) reported suffering one harm because of somebody else's drinking. About 2.2 percent of respondents reported that they had been physically hurt; 6.3 percent felt threatened; 7.1 percent felt emotionally hurt or neglected; 8.9 percent suffered verbal abuse.

---

*Republished with permission of SAGE Publications, Inc. Journals, from *Journal of Drug Issues*, P.J. Goldstein, "The Drugs-Violence Nexus: A Tripartite Conceptual Framework," Vol. 15 (1985); permission conveyed through Copyright Clearance Center, Inc.

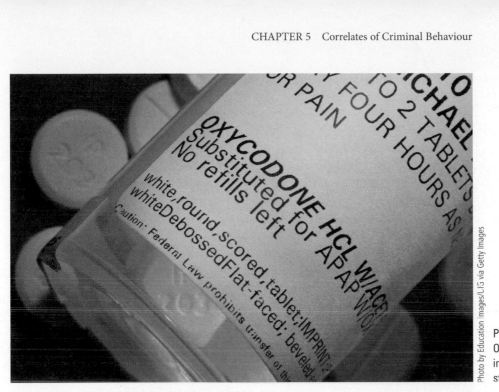

Prescription drugs such as OxyContin and oxycodone are increasingly being sold on the street and used by addicts.

Figure 5.10 shows the past-year prevalence of use of illicit substances in Canada. The 2015 Canadian Tobacco, Alcohol and Drugs Survey (CTADS) found that 12.3 percent of Canadians used cannabis; 1.2 percent, crack cocaine; 1.2 percent, hallucinogens (excluding salvia); and 0.7 percent, ecstasy. The use of cannabis may change by the time you read this because of the legalization of cannabis. Three percent of males reported using illicit substances (excluding cannabis) compared with only 1 percent of females. Young adults aged 20 to 24 used illicit drugs at a higher rate (9%) than 15- to 19-year-olds (5%) and adults aged 25 and older (1%) (CTADS 2015).

FIGURE 5.10 ■ Percentage of the Population Using Drugs in the Past Year, 2012 and 2015

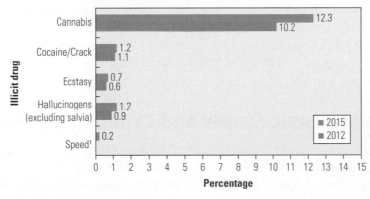

[1]2012 estimate suppressed due to high sampling variability.

Sources: *Canadian Tobacco, Alcohol and Drugs Survey (CTADS), 2015.* Table 14. Available at www.canada.ca/en/health-canada/services/canadian-tobacco-alcohol.html (accessed: January 31, 2018). *Canadian Alcohol and Drug Use Monitoring Survey (CADUMS), 2012.* Available at www.canada.ca/en/health-canada/services/health-concerns/drug-prevention-treatment/drug-alcohol-use-statistics/canadian-alcohol-drug-use-monitoring-survey-summary-results-2012.html (accessed: January 31, 2018). Reproduced and distributed on an "as is" basis with the permission of Statistics Canada.

Students rarely use substances other than cannabis, alcohol, and tobacco (Clark 2009). Street youth, however, often report rates of illicit drug use (cocaine, ecstasy, etc.) and associated risks that are higher than the national average for both their peers and the general population. In a study conducted with youth from Vancouver and Victoria, Duff and colleagues (2009, 519) identified three "high risk" categories: the club and "party drug" scenes, street-entrenched users aged 19 and over, and street-involved youth aged 15 to 19. The use of illicit substances has implications for contact with the law. These drugs have a negative impact on lives (68%). That impact is felt on relationships (48%), finances (26%), and school-related activities (20%). Eight percent of club drug users reported having "legal problems" (534).

In their At-Risk Youth Study of 991 street-involved young people in Vancouver, Lianping and colleagues (2013) reported that police contacts were associated with daily cannabis use, daily heroin use, crack pipe/syringe sharing, public drug use, and drug dealing. These findings suggest that the possession and/or use of illegal substances increases the likelihood of encounters with police. These encounters may result in the young person being processed in the criminal justice system, particularly when governments have intensified efforts to reduce the supply and use of illegal drugs. Illicit drug use is also associated with higher rates of mortality. According to BC Vital Statistics (2005), for instance, the Downtown Eastside, where drug use is high, has a mortality rate seven times higher than for Vancouver as a whole (cited in Buxton et al. 2009, 450). Life expectancy in this neighbourhood is nine years lower for men and three years lower for women (BC Vital Statistics 2005). The use of fentanyl has dramatically increased the health risks of using drugs. In BC there were 1,156 fentanyl-related deaths in 2017, compared to 670 in 2016 (BC Coroners Service, 2018).

The misuse of prescription medication has become an increasing concern. The United States and Canada have been ranked first and third vis-à-vis consumption of prescription opioids per capita (Fischer et al., 2009, 57). The same study indicates the level of abuse of medical prescription drugs. The sale of drugs for money and the exchange of prescription drugs for nonprescription drugs is especially prevalent in Toronto and Victoria. Such exchanges include prescription opioids and other drugs such as cannabis and crack. Fischer and colleagues also found found that 77 percent of study participants in Toronto and 80 percent in Victoria were involved in this illicit trading. They concluded (63) that prescription opioids are often used concurrently with illegal substances like crack and cannabis. Also, the delineation of drug dealers from users was a false one: drug users in the Toronto–Victoria study were often dealers, and vice versa (65).

Socioeconomic Status and Criminal Behaviour

Historically, the lower classes have been seen as responsible for crime. In eighteenth-century Paris and London, there were concerns about the proliferation of "dangerous" or "criminal classes" in society (Silver 1967). These concerns were expressed in Canada and the United States in the nineteenth and twentieth centuries (Boritch and Hagan 1987; Myrdal 1962). The early dangerous classes were unemployed single people involved in crime (Silver 1967). The term "underclass" (Myrdal 1962, 1963) has become more prominent in common and scholarly discourse to explain criminal activity; it refers to the cultural underpinnings of people at the margins of society.

The underclass is defined by "poverty, crime, poor education, dependency, and teenage out-of-wedlock childbearing" (Lenmann 1986, 41, cited in Hagan 1992, 2). This category often has political and racial connotations (Hagan 1992).

Police-reported statistics primarily identify lower-class offenders, and social disorganization theories (Chapter 14) identify crime with lower-class communities. This view was challenged when Edwin Sutherland (1940) brought attention to white-collar crime; this was followed two decades later by the pioneering self-report delinquency studies conducted by Nye and Short (1957; Nye, Short, and Olson 1958). Nye and colleagues concluded that class had no statistically significant relationship with delinquency. This generated a major debate that was influenced by a research review by Tittle, Villemez, and Smith (1978), who concluded that the negative association between socioeconomic status (SES) and crime was small and had declined over the previous four decades.

The relationship between SES or class and crime is complex (Wright et al. 1999; Clelland and Carter 1980; Tittle and Meier, 1990). Official statistics and self-report studies often provide divergent results about SES–crime relationship (Tittle, Villemez, and Smith 1978).

The term "socioeconomic status" is increasingly being used as a substitute for the Marxian term "class" in social science research generally and criminology in particular (see Tittle and Meier, 1990), albeit not without some objections (see Hagan, Gillis, and Simpson 1985). SES is typically measured as a composite of three key variables—education, income, and occupation (APA, 2014).

Criminologists now recognize that people with low SES are overrepresented in police-reported statistics partly because the criminal behaviour of the "middle and upper crime class systematically escaped official notice" (Gaylord and Galliher 1988, 68). John Hagan made an important statement about the class–crime debate in his 1991 American Society of Criminology (ASC) presidential address. He argued (1992, 9) that the "relationship between class and crime is class and crime specific." That is, various classes are involved in different kinds of criminal behaviour because they have differential access to opportunity structures for committing crime. Male children of employer-class parents were found to be more likely to commit copyright violations (Hagan and Kay 1990), while theft was common among young people from poorer families (Sabates 2008).

Wright and colleagues (1999) made three fundamental findings concerning the link between SES and crime or delinquency. First, the link between SES and crime is an indirect one that operates through mediating variables, which include people's attitudes, behaviours, neighbourhood, peer networks, family conditions, cultures, economic opportunities, and so on. Second, low SES promotes delinquency—that is, it serves as a catalyst for delinquency because it causes alienation, financial strain, and aggression even while reducing individuals' educational and occupational aspirations. Third, and rather counter-intuitively, high SES promotes delinquency by reducing adherence to conventional values while increasing social power and risk-taking behaviours. Wright and colleagues concluded (190) that there are causal links between SES and delinquency (i.e., through the mediating factors above) but "little overall correlation." The three analytic distinctions they made are crucial for us to understand the findings of the studies discussed below.

Recent work supports the idea that the SES–crime relationship depends on the type of crime being studied. Recall that the three SES measures are education, income, and occupation. For instance, Aaltonen and colleagues (2012) examined police-reported data about violence committed by men in Finland between 2005 and 2007. They found that having no secondary education, earning low income, and being unemployed increased the risk of committing violent acts.

Property crimes in the United States are committed mostly by uneducated males (Lochner 2004). Increased educational attainment has been found to reduce theft, burglary, drug offences, and vandalism (Sabates 2007). Partner abuse in New Zealand has been linked to poverty and poor educational achievement in adolescence (Moffitt and Caspi 1999). Sabates (2008) used data from the United Kingdom to investigate the conviction rate for three cohorts of people born between 1981 and 1983. According to that study (404), an increase in educational attainment led to "3.7, 56.1 and 6.7 fewer convictions per 1000 students for burglary, theft and vandalism and drug-related offences, respectively." The same study found that theft convictions were reduced by 1,233; convictions for vandalism and drug offences by 148; and convictions for burglary by 85. This translated into £3.2 million savings on victim services and healthcare in each of the three local education authorities that were studied.

In the United States, high school completion reduces the likelihood of incarceration by 3 percent for blacks and by 1 percent for whites (Lochner and Moretti, 2004). Over the life course, people with higher levels of education are less involved in crime than those with lower levels of education (Hansen 2003). The association between education and crime is not one-dimensional: older and better-educated people generally commit more sophisticated crimes, while younger and uneducated people commit crimes that require few or no skills (Lochner 2004; Levitt and Lochner 2000).

Aaltonen and colleagues (2012, 1206) contend that education is the "most robust predictor of both male-to-male and male-to-female violence," with the least educated males committing higher levels of violence against females and other males. Sabates (2008), however, cautions that education does not necessarily reduce violent crime, as violent crime is more closely related to poverty (Ludwig, Duncan, and Hirschfield 2001). Aaltonen and colleagues (2012, 1207) conclude that the most violent men are overwhelmingly from low SES.

Employment is another crucial SES variable. Sampson and Laub (2005) argue that finding a stable job is a watershed event that reduces recidivism. Conversely, high unemployment rates lead to intensification of criminal acts (Arvanites and Defina 2006). Evidence from the United States (Lin 2008) and Belgium (Hooghe et al. 2011) indicates that areas with high unemployment rates experience higher levels of violent and property crime. There is a gender dynamic in terms of employment and intimate partner violence (IPV). IPV is higher in homes where husbands are unemployed and wives are employed (MacMillan and Gartner 1999). Women with low household incomes and low levels of education face a higher risk of intimate partner violence (IPV) (MacMillan and Kruttschnitt 2005). This implies that IPV generally declines with high SES (Abramsky et al. 2011). However, IPV and general crime often have distinct risk factors. Aaltonen and colleagues (2013) found that unemployment is correlated with property crime but not with violent crime and drunk driving. Other studies caution that for those involved in criminal activities, transitioning to stable employment is a *result* of desisting from crime, rather than a *cause* of desisting from crime (Skardhamar and Savolainen 2014).

Spatial Location as a Correlate of Crime

Studies of crime and place show that different streets, neighbourhoods, cities, states/provinces, and countries have different patterns of crime.

It can be difficult to compare police-reported statistics from various countries. These difficulties relate to criminal code differences, policing practices and capabilities, the relationship between the police and the public, and the latter's willingness to report criminal behaviour, among other factors (Hartnagel 2012). Homicide statistics are often used to compare different jurisdictions, because those data are fairly comparable across different jurisdictions. Homicides, after all, are more likely than other crimes to be reported and to be investigated by authorities (UN Office on Drugs and Crime, 2011). Also, there are similarities in how homicide is defined and counted across different countries—at least relative to many other types of offences (Nivett 2011).

Figure 5.11 presents data on homicide rates in selected countries. The United States has the highest rate of homicide among its peer countries—4.9 per 100,000. The United States recorded 17,250 murders in 2016. Canada's homicide rate—1.7 per 100,000—is nearly three times lower than that of its neighbour. Police in Canada reported 611 homicides in 2016 (David 2017). Homicide makes up less than 1 percent of all violent crimes in Canada and is near its lowest level since 1966 (Perreault 2013; Boyce and Cotter 2013). Most other peer countries shown in Figure 5.11 have even lower homicide rates than Canada. Developing countries tend to have higher homicide rates (de Souza and Miller 2012; Pridemore 2011).

FIGURE 5.11 ■ **Homicide in Selected Countries, 2015**

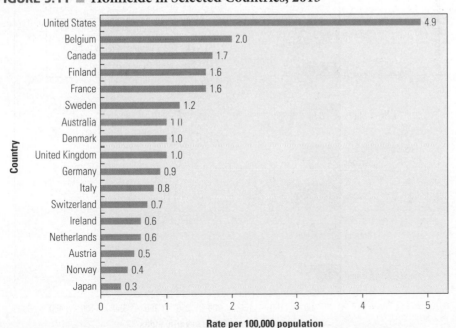

Rate per 100,000 population

Source: United Nations Office on Drugs and Crime. *Statistics.* Available at www.unodc.org/unodc/en/data-and-analysis/statistics.html (accessed: 16 February 16, 2018).

Different regions in Canada have very different patterns of crime. Figure 5.12 shows how the provinces and territories rank on the 2017 Crime Severity Index (CSI). The territories have the highest rates of crime, followed by Saskatchewan and the other western provinces. Ontario, Quebec, and the Atlantic provinces reported relatively similar crime rates.

Figure 5.13 shows the violent crime severity index (CSI) in census metropolitan areas. In 2017, Winnipeg (154) had the highest violent CSI; Thunder Bay (141) and Saskatoon (108) were second and third respectively (Allen, 2018).

FIGURE 5.12 ■ **Police-Reported Crime Severity Index, by Province and Territory, 2017, Canada**

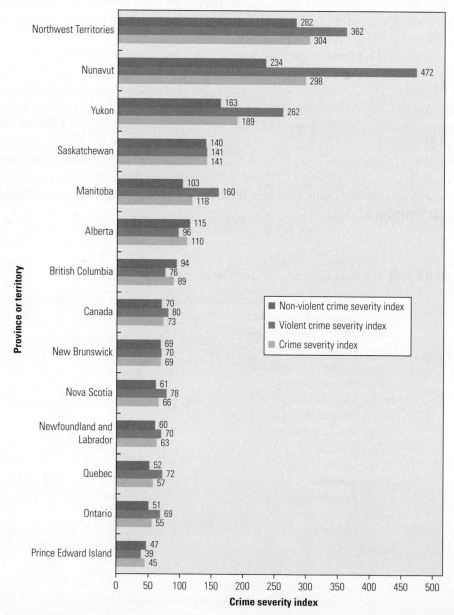

Source: Allen, Mary. 2018. *Police-Reported Crime Statistics in Canada, 2017*. Ottawa: Statistics Canada. Reproduced and distributed on an "as is" basis with the permission of Statistics Canada.

FIGURE 5.13 ■ **Police-Reported Violent Crime Severity Index, by Census Metropolitan Area, 2017, Canada**

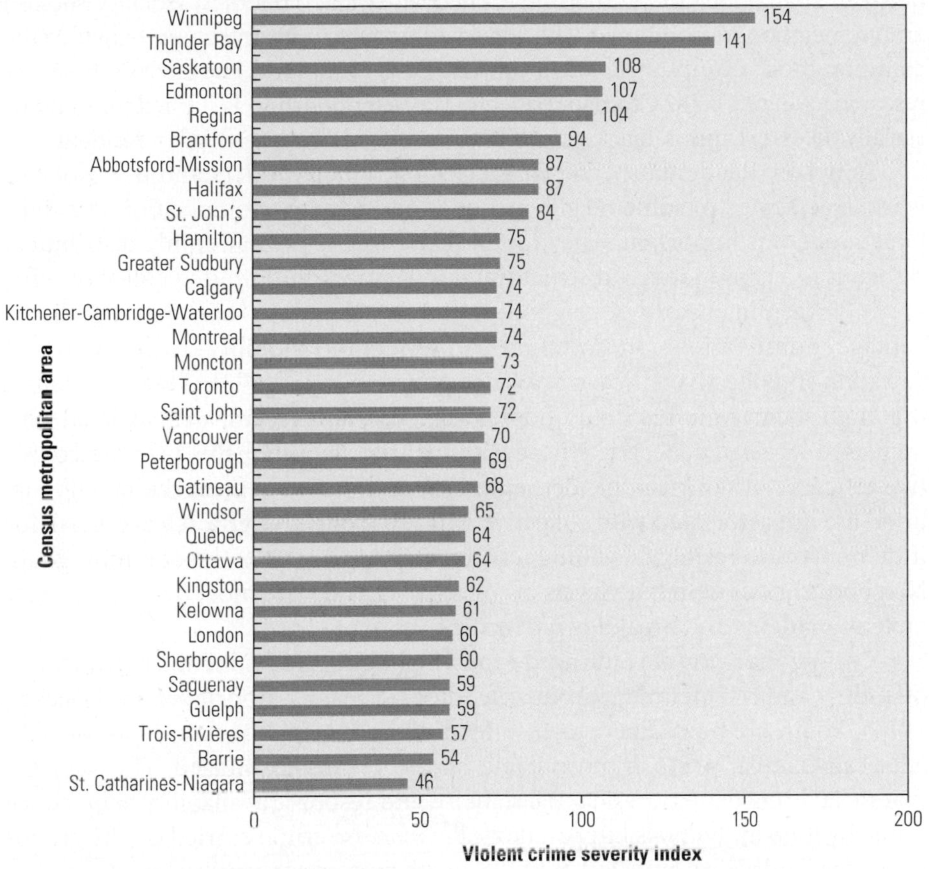

Source: Allen, Mary. 2018. *Police-Reported Crime Statistics in Canada, 2017.* Ottawa: Statistics Canada. Reproduced and distributed on an "as is" basis with the permission of Statistics Canada.

Among the Census Metropolitan Areas, Thunder Bay had the highest homicide rate in 2017; Abbotsford ranked second while Edmonton was third (Allen, 2018). There is also an interesting rural–urban differential: rural areas have higher violent crime rates than larger urban centres but lower property and total crime rates (Francisco and Chenier, 2007).

The relationship between neighbourhood characteristics and crime is a hot topic among criminologists today (Peterson 2012; Sampson, Raudenbush, and Earls 1997; Weinrath, Young, and Kohn 2012). Current evidence from the United States indicates that neighbourhood matters. There is evidence, for example, that violent juvenile criminal behaviour declines when families move to wealthier neighbourhoods (Ludwig, Duncan, and Hirschfield 2001). Peterson (2012) argues that residential segregation—the occupation of distinct built spaces by specific ethno-racial groups—which leads to "ecological dissimilarity" in terms of available resources and opportunities in these various ethnic enclaves, is responsible for the racial gap in police reported crime in the United States. "A large part of the racial difference in neighbourhood crime is because Whites and Blacks often live in ecologically dissimilar areas" (311).

The development of collective efficacy theory by Sampson and colleagues (Sampson 2012; Sampson, Raudenbush, and Earls 1997) has shed light on the link between spatial location and crime. Collective efficacy refers to "social cohesion among neighbours combined with their willingness to intervene on behalf of the common good" (Sampson, Raudenbush, and Earls 1997, 918). The theory is based on research involving 8,782 Chicago residents. The neighbourhoods studied were ethno-racially diverse. Latinos, blacks, and whites each made up one-third of residents.

Sampson, Raudenbush, and Earls (1997) sought to understand why violence was concentrated in some neighbourhoods and why the composition of neighbourhoods was important. They found that crime is not randomly distributed; rather, it is a consequence of structural disadvantage and limited collective efficacy. "Three dimensions of neighbourhood stratification—concentrated disadvantage, immigration concentration and residential mobility—explain 70% of variation in collective efficacy across neighbourhoods" (923). They also found that high socioeconomic status, homeownership, and age are all associated with increased levels of collective efficacy. Residential stability helps increase collective efficacy; by contrast, gender, ethnicity, and years spent in the neighbourhood are not associated with collective efficacy. Collective efficacy is crucial, for it demonstrates residents' willingness to work together for the common good. Neighbourhoods with high levels of collective efficacy are more likely to prevent violent incidents and breakdown of order.

An Arizona study of youth aged 8 to 17 highlights the distinction between solo offending and co-offending (group offending) (Schaefer, Rodriguez, and Decker, 2014). Youth are more likely to co-offend when a neighbourhood has racially/ethnically similar peers, is more stable, and is less disadvantaged. This suggests that racial homogeneity, residential stability, and resource availability help reduce crime by lone individuals but paradoxically *increase* crime carried out by groups (Schaefer, Rodriguez, and Decker 2014). In other words, the mutual trust and solidarity generated by residential stability, availability of resources, and ethno-racial similarity also provide an incentive for criminality by individuals acting in groups.

Neighbourhood context and characteristics have been used to explain criminal behaviour in some Canadian cities. Thompson and Gartner (2014), for example, examined the social ecology of homicide in Toronto. They found that economic disadvantage and the proportion of residents in the age cohort 15 to 24 were positively correlated with homicide in that city. In other words, neighbourhoods with higher numbers of young people, higher levels of unemployment and poverty, and lower educational attainment had higher rates of homicide.

As noted earlier, Indigenous people are overrepresented at every stage of the criminal justice process. This phenomenon has been linked to the characteristics and social contexts of the urban neighbourhoods in which Indigenous people live. Fitzgerald and Carrington (2008) found that Indigenous people are more likely to live in higher-crime neighbourhoods, which increases the likelihood that their behaviour—criminal and noncriminal—will attract the attention of the authorities. The consequence is that Indigenous people are seven times more likely than non-Indigenous people to be identified as offenders (545). Also, socioeconomic disadvantage and residential mobility (structural features) play a significant role in Indigenous crime rates. The overrepresentation of Indigenous people in police-reported crime statistics in Winnipeg, Saskatoon, and Regina is a function of their living conditions in those cities (La Prairie 2002).

Ex-offenders tend to live in resource-poor parts of cities and to return to the same neighbourhoods after their release (Kirk 2012). A US study found that offenders have higher chances of recidivism when they return to neighbourhoods with low socio-economic status (Kubrin and Stewart 2006). Generally, changing neighbourhoods and routines after incarceration reduces the chances of reoffending (Kirk 2012). Kirk (2009) found that the likelihood of reincarceration declined by 1 percent for every 10 miles parolees moved from their previous neighbourhood. Sharkey and Sampson (2010) found that although the likelihood of engaging in violent crime increased among adolescents who changed neighbourhoods within Chicago, those who moved outside the city experienced a reduction in their violent behaviour.

Policing practices in neighbourhoods are fundamental to crime detection and police-reported crime. Sacks (1972) used the concept of "incongruity procedure" to describe the conduct of police work: "the police are occupational specialists on inferring the probability of criminality from the appearances persons present in public spaces" (282–83). This is a matter of socially sorting who is "in place" and who is "out of place" (Sacks 1972). In other words, police match spaces with faces or appearances. This is particularly relevant in cities that have racially segregated neighbourhoods (Peterson 2012). Incongruity procedure involves "appearential ordering," or drawing inferences about people's behaviour from the appearances they present in public spaces (Lofland 1973, 48–49; Sacks 1972). Decisions about who looks suspicious, who possesses drugs, or who is in the wrong neighbourhood are sometimes made on the basis of appearential ordering. This micro-sociological process entails considering a potential suspect's manner of dress, hair arrangement, facial cues, gait, speech, and overall demeanour.

However, appearential ordering may be cumbersome in urban settings because in the "modern city, appearances are chaotic, [while] space is ordered" (Lofland 1973, 82). Appearential ordering has declined and spatial ordering has become predominant in modern cities as a result of socioeconomic, political, demographic, and technological changes (56–66). This has contributed to the designation of some spatial locations as "high-risk" neighbourhoods and thus warranting greater scrutiny, which in turn may contribute to the crimes that are discovered in such areas.

Conclusion

This chapter has examined six correlates of crime: age, gender, race, drug misuse, socio-economic status, and spatial location. None of these correlates in and of itself explains criminal behaviour. Overall, crime rates arise from a complex interplay of macro-sociological, community, family, and individual factors. At the structural level, criminologists recognize the importance of factors such as socioeconomic conditions, housing, and access to employment, education, and other valuable resources in the social production of crime and criminals. These structural factors reflect the broader political economy of societies (Sampson, Raudenbush, and Earls 1997) and transcend individual characteristics, neighbourhoods, regions, and other units of analysis.

QUESTIONS FOR CRITICAL THINKING

1. Discuss the four explanations for Indigenous overrepresentation in the criminal justice process.
2. What is the relationship between drug misuse and crime?
3. Using the collective efficacy theory, analyze the relationship between spatial location and crime.

Summary

- This chapter examines six correlates of crime: age, gender, race, drug and alcohol misuse, socio-economic status, and spatial location.

- In all societies, younger people commit more crime than older people. Most types of crime peak during the teen years and decline steadily thereafter. However, the peak is later for some types of violent offences and for white-collar and corporate crimes.

- Women commit less crime than men, particularly for serious and violent offences. While females have increased their level of involvement in crime since the 1960s, most of this increase has been for minor offences such a shoplifting and low-level fraud, which many researchers believe reflects the feminization of poverty over that period of time.

- In most countries, there are racial and ethnic differences in crime. These differences are due to some combination of differential offending and differential treatment by the justice system. Criminologists have developed a number of theories to explain differential offending by minority groups, including these: cultural theories, the colonial model, trauma transmission model, and critical race theory.

- Drugs and alcohol are major contributors to crime. There are three factors linking drug and alcohol use and crime: efforts to support addictions can lead to involvement in crimes; an individual may commit crimes because they are under the influence of drugs or alcohol; and the possession of illegal drugs in and of itself is a crime.

- The linkage between socioeconomic status and crime is complex and varies by type of crime. The best evidence suggests that violent crimes and many other types of street crime are disproportionately committed by people from the lower classes, while upper-class people are disproportionately involved in serious forms of white-collar and corporate crimes.

- Different countries, provinces, cities, and neighbourhoods have very different rates of crime. There are a variety of different explanations for these differences.

NET WORK

Statistics Canada provides a great deal of information about crime and its correlates over the Internet. To learn more about correlates of crime, first go to the
Statistics Canada home page at http://www.statcan.ca/start.html. Under "Browse
by Subject," click on "Crime and Justice," then "Crimes and Offences," then
"Summary Tables."

1. Click on the table "Crimes by Type of Violation, by Province and Territory."
   Using the data in that table, answer the following questions: How do the
   provincial and territorial crime incidents and rates vary across the country
   when you compare all Criminal Code violations, violent Criminal Code violations, and property crime violations? How do drug violations vary across
   the country?

2. Then click on the table "Homicide Offences, Number and Rate, by Province
   and Territories." Using the data in that table, answer this question: How do
   the provinces rank in terms of the number of homicide offences in 2013?
   Does their rank vary depending on the year?

3. Then click on the table "Victims and Persons Accused of Homicide, by
   Age and Sex." Using the data in that table, answer the following questions:
   Regarding homicide victims, what is the five-year trend for male and female
   victimization? Is the trend the same for male and female victims under the
   age of 12? What about for male and female victims ages 18 to 24? Other age
   categories?

6

Feminism and Criminology

ELIZABETH COMACK
University of Manitoba

Learning Objectives

After reading this chapter, you should be able to

- Explain the various theories that have been developed to understand women's involvement in crime.

- Understand the social, cultural, and legal factors that pertain to the issue of male violence against women.

- Appreciate some of the connections between a woman's law violations and her experiences of victimization.

- Appreciate the gains to be made in making gender a more central focus of criminological inquiry.

Like other academic disciplines, criminology has been a male-centred enterprise. Despite the use of generic terms such as "criminals," "defendants," and "delinquents," most of criminology has really been about what men do. As a consequence, women have been rendered invisible in much criminological inquiry. When women are looked at as offenders, their small numbers relative to men have typically been used to justify or rationalize this neglect. In 2015, for instance, less than one-quarter of those (youth and adults) accused by Canadian police of a Criminal Code offence were female (Mahony, Jacob, and Hobson 2017). When women were looked at as victims, violence against them was not a major area of concern. Official statistics on crime indicated that offences such as rape were relatively infrequent, and victim surveys reported young males to be the group most at risk from crime. Perhaps even more significant is that even though the subject matter of criminology has been men, criminologists have done very little work on men *as* men. In short, they have neglected to consider the "maleness" of their subjects. Over the past four decades, there has been a growing awareness of the implications these omissions hold for the discipline. This has come about largely through feminists' engagement with criminology. Feminist criminologists are striving to move women—and analyses of gender—from the periphery to the centre of criminological inquiry. This chapter describes these efforts with a view to clarifying the kinds of issues and questions that are now commanding criminologists' attention.

The Invisibility of Women

The feminist engagement with criminology began more than 40 years ago when pioneers in the discipline, such as Marie-Andrée Bertrand (1967) and Frances Heidensohn (1968), first called attention to criminology's amnesia when it came to women. Heidensohn (1968, 171), for instance, described analyses of women and crime as "lonely uncharted seas" and stated the need for a "crash programme of research which telescopes decades of comparable studies of males." In its initial phases, however, the feminist engagement with criminology consisted of a critique of existing approaches to explaining crime. This critique took two paths. Initially, writers like Dorie Klein (1973) and Carol Smart (1976, 1977) focused attention on the **sexism** of the small body of theories that had been developed to explain women's crime. Other writers soon broadened the focus to include the invisibility of women in the mainstream theories within the discipline.

sexism
Attributing to women socially undesirable characteristics that are assumed to be intrinsic characteristics of that sex.

Theories of Women's Crime

The Conservative Approach

A particular pathway can be followed when tracing the initial attempts to explain women's criminality. It begins with the publication of Lombroso and Ferrero's *The Female Offender* in 1895 and is followed by Thomas's *The Unadjusted Girl* in 1923, Glueck and Glueck's *Five Hundred Delinquent Women* in 1934, and Pollak's *The Criminality of Women* in 1950. Each of these works reflected a **conservative approach** to understanding differences in criminality between men and women. Specifically, "difference" was rooted in biology. Women were viewed as "naturally" inferior to men, and that inferiority was used to explain women's criminality.

conservative approach
An approach that understands "difference" between men and women as biologically based sex differences. Women are viewed as "naturally" inferior or unequal to men.

For example, in applying the concepts of atavism and social Darwinism (see Chapter 8), Lombroso and Ferrero suggested that women possessed limited intelligence. They were also less sensitive to pain than men, full of revenge and jealousy, and naturally passive and conservative. Women's natural passivity, for instance, was caused by the "immobility of the ovule compared to the zoosperm" (Lombroso and Ferrero 1895, 109). Atavistically, women were seen as displaying fewer signs of degeneration than men. The reason, according to Lombroso and Ferrero, was that women (and nonwhite males) had not advanced as far along the evolutionary continuum as (white) males and so could not degenerate as far. Given that women were relatively "primitive," the criminals among them would not be highly visible. However, those women who were criminal were cast as excessively vile and cruel in their crimes. They combined the qualities of the criminal male with the worst characteristics of the female: cunning, spite, and deceitfulness. Criminal women were seen as lacking the "maternal instinct" and "ladylike qualities" and thus as genetically more male than female.

First published in 1923, Thomas's (1967) work on female delinquency was premised on a similar kind of biological determinism. Thomas suggested that human behaviour was based on four "wishes": for adventure, security, response, and recognition. These wishes corresponded to features in the nervous system, which were expressed as biological instincts of anger, fear, love, and the will to gain status and power, respectively. However, Thomas asserted that men's and women's instincts differed both in quantity and quality. Since women had more varieties of love in their nervous systems, their desire for response was greater than men's. According to Thomas, it was the need to feel loved that accounted for women's criminality, and especially for prostitution.

Glueck and Glueck (1934) continued in this same tradition with *500 Delinquent Women*. The Gluecks described the women in their study as a "sorry lot. Burdened with feeblemindedness, psychopathic personality, and marked emotional instability, a large proportion of them found it difficult to survive by legitimate means" (299). The view of criminal women as "Other" is clearly evident in the Gluecks' work: "This swarm of defective, diseased, antisocial misfits . . . comprises the human material which a reformatory and a parole system are required by society to transform into wholesome, decent, law-abiding citizens! Is it not a miracle that a proportion of them were actually rehabilitated?" (303).

Pollak's (1961) work attempted to account for what he described as the "masked" nature of women's crime. Skeptical of the official data on sex differences in crime, Pollak suggested that women's crime was vastly undercounted. He put forward the view that female criminality was more likely to be hidden and undetected. Women were more often the instigators than the perpetrators of crime. Like Eve in the Garden of Eden, they manipulated men into committing offences. Women were also inherently deceptive and vengeful: they engaged in prostitution, they blackmailed their lovers, as domestics they stole from their employers, and as homemakers they carried out horrendous acts on their families (for example, poisoning the sick and abusing children). According to Pollak, woman's devious nature was rooted in her physiology. While a man must achieve erection in order to perform the sex act, and hence will not be able to conceal orgasm, a woman can fake orgasm. This ability to conceal orgasm gave women practice at deception. Pollak also suggested that female crime was caused by the vengefulness, irritability, and depression women encountered as a result of their generative phases. For example, menstruation drove women to acts of revenge by reminding women of their inferior status (and their ultimate failure to become men) (see Box 6.1). The concealed nature of their crimes, the vulnerability of their victims, and their chivalrous treatment by men who could not bear to prosecute or punish them, all combined to "mask" women's offences. When these factors were taken into account, according to Pollak, women's crimes were equal in severity and number to those of men.

As Heidensohn (1985, 122) notes, these early approaches to explaining women's crime lent an aura of intellectual respectability to many of the old folktales about women and their behaviours. They reflected widely held assumptions about "women's nature," including the good girl/bad girl duality and a double standard that viewed sexual promiscuity as a sign of "amorality" in women but "normality" in men. Relying on "commonsense" anecdotal evidence and circular reasoning—that is, "things are as they are because they are natural, and they are

| FOCUS | BOX 6.1 |

THE "WOMAN PROBLEM"

In the following passage, Otto Pollak offers us an illustration of a male-centred view of what has been traditionally referred to as the "woman problem" and its relationship to female criminality:

The student of female criminality cannot afford to overlook the generally known and recognized fact that [women's] generative phases are frequently accompanied by psychological disturbances which may upset the need satisfaction balance of the individual or weaken her internal inhibitions, and thus become causative factors in female crime. Particularly because of the social meaning attached to them in our culture, the generative phases of women are bound to present many stumbling blocks for the law-abiding behaviour of women. Menstruation with its appearance of injury must confirm feelings of guilt which individuals may have about sex activities which they have learned to consider as forbidden. As a symbol of womanhood, it must also, because of its recurrent nature, aggravate any feeling of irritation and protest which women may have regarding their sex in a society in which women have had, and still have, to submit to social inequality with men. In both instances, it must lead to a disturbance of the emotional balance of the individual and this becomes potentially crime-promoting. Pregnancy in a culture which frowns upon illegitimacy and fosters in large sectors of society limitation in the number of children or even childlessness must become a source of irritation, anxiety, and emotional upheaval in many instances. The menopause in a society which makes romance and emotional gratification the supreme value in a monogamous marriage system must be experienced, at least by married women, frequently as a threat to the basis of their emotional security if not to their general marital existence. In view of these cultural implications of the generative phases and their psychological consequences, it is difficult to understand why the existing literature contains so little discussion of their possible crime-promoting influence.

Questions for Critical Thinking

1. Pollak's views about women were not uncommon in the field of crime and criminology. Look at some of the material presented in Chapter 8 (Early Theories of Criminology) and discuss how theorists and the justice system treated women.

2. Discuss the issues involved in using PMS as a legal defence. (You may want to refer to the sections on criminal defences in Chapter 3.)

Source: Otto Pollak, *The Criminality of Women* (New York: A.S. Barnes, 1961), 157–58. Originally published by University of Pennsylvania Press (Philadelphia) in 1950.

natural because that is the way things are" (Smart 1976, 36)—the early theorists failed to call into question the structural features of their society and the gendered nature of the roles of men and women. Instead, sex (a biological difference) and gender (a cultural prescription) were treated as one and the same, with the "lady-like qualities" of the middle- and upper-class white woman used as the measuring rod for what was inherently female. The theories thereby constructed were not only sexist but classist and racist as well.

While we can look back on these early theories of women's crime with some amusement, it bears noting that the kinds of assumptions and beliefs reflected in them have not disappeared. As Klein (1973, 7) comments, "The road from Lombroso to the present is surprisingly straight." Throughout the 1960s, researchers continued to rely on the assumptions and premises of the earlier approaches (see, for example, Cowie, Cowie, and Slater 1968; Konopka 1966). Following in the footsteps of Pollak, a more contemporary version of this conservative approach to understanding the difference between men and women links hormonal changes associated with women's menstrual cycles to their involvement in crime.

Premenstrual syndrome (PMS) has been described as a condition of "irritability, indescribable tension, [and a] desire to find relief by foolish and ill-considered actions" that is thought to occur during the week or two prior to the onset of menstruation (Frank, cited in Osborne 1989, 168). Some 150 different symptoms (behavioural, psychological, and physiological) have been associated with PMS, and estimates of its incidence vary from 20 to 95 percent of the female population. There are no biomedical tests for determining the existence of PMS; it is the only "disease" not dependent on a specific type of symptom for its diagnosis. Nevertheless, PMS has been argued to be a cause of violent behaviour in women who suffer from it. It gained popularity as a cause of women's criminality in the 1980s, when PMS was introduced in two British court cases as a mitigating factor in homicide, enabling the women to receive more lenient sentences (Luckhaus 1985). Sandie Smith was convicted on a reduced charge of manslaughter and given three years' probation plus mandatory progesterone treatments. Christine English pleaded guilty to manslaughter with diminished responsibility and received a one-year conditional discharge. She was also banned from driving for a year (she had run her boyfriend over with a car).

Research linking PMS to women's criminality has been criticized for its methodological deficiencies (Morris 1987); meanwhile, feminist criminologists have questioned the validity of framing explanations for women's criminality that isolate the source of the problem in women's bodies, thereby ignoring the cultural meanings (especially with regard to menstruation) and social contexts that are at play (Kendall 1991, 1992). So long as women are pathologized as "sick" or "diseased," the broader structural factors that impinge on women's lives—and are thereby implicated in their offending behaviours—will be ignored.

The Liberal Approach

In the 1970s, theories of women's crime began to shift towards a more sociological orientation. Rather than focusing on biology, attention turned to culture. In this **liberal approach**, differences between men and women are not necessarily innate or inborn, but are learned by individuals through the process of socialization. It is the culture that marks off the differences between men and women by proscribing certain roles and behaviours as "male appropriate" and "female appropriate." In this way, "gender" has been separated from "sex" and made the key focus of inquiry.

liberal approach
Distinguishes sex (biological) from gender (cultural) and sees differences between men and women as resulting from gender roles and socialization patterns.

This liberal approach to understanding difference took the form of role theory as an explanation for female criminality. Hoffman-Bustamante (1973), for example, suggested that the lower rate of delinquency of girls can be accounted for by differential socialization and child-rearing practices. Whereas boys are encouraged to be aggressive, outgoing, and ambitious and are allowed greater freedom, girls are taught to be passive and domesticated and are more closely supervised. Since girls are taught to be nonviolent, they do not acquire the skills, technical ability, or physical strength to engage in violent acts such as gang fighting. When women do engage in violent behaviour, their actions reflect their greater domesticity. For example, women who murder are more likely to use kitchen knives than guns. The finding that women are more likely to be charged with shoplifting offences was similarly explained with reference to their gender roles and socialization. Women are traditionally the consumers in society, and when they steal, girls are more likely to take small items like makeup. Role theory, then, offered differential gender socialization as an explanation for the types and nature of offences that females commit.

Another version of role theory was put forward by Hagan and his colleagues (Hagan et al. 1979, 1985, 1987) in the form of a power-control theory of sex and delinquency. Power-control theory is intended to explain the sex differences in delinquency by drawing linkages between variations in parental control and the delinquent behaviour of boys and girls. More specifically, Hagan and his colleagues suggest that parental control and adolescents' subsequent attitudes towards risk-taking behaviour are affected by family class relations. They distinguish two ideal types of family: the patriarchal family, in which the husband is employed in an authority position in the workforce and the wife is not employed outside the home, and the egalitarian family, in which both husband and wife are employed in authority positions outside the home. Hagan and his colleagues suggest that in the former, a traditional gender division exists whereby fathers and especially mothers are expected to control their daughters more than their sons. Given the presence of a "cult of domesticity," girls are socialized to focus their futures on domestic labour and consumption activities while boys are prepared for their participation in production activities. In the latter form, parents redistribute their control efforts so that girls are subject to controls more like those imposed on boys. "In other words, in egalitarian families, as mothers gain power relative to husbands, daughters gain freedom relative to sons" (1987, 792). The authors predict that these different family forms will produce differing levels of delinquency in girls: "Patriarchal families will be characterized by large gender differences in common delinquent behaviours, while egalitarian families will be characterized by smaller gender differences in delinquency" (1987, 793).

Smart (1976) has commented that role theory can offer only a partial explanation of women's crime. Because of a failure to situate the discussion of gender roles in broader structural terms, little attention is devoted to why socialization patterns are gender differentiated and how they have come to be that way. In the absence of a structural analysis, it is too easy to fall back on explanations that view such differences as biological, not social, in their origins: "role is destiny" can therefore act as a ready substitute for "biology is destiny" (Morris 1987, 64). In endeavouring to place role theory in a broader structural context (by attending to the labour force participation of parents), Hagan and his colleagues make an important assumption: if a woman is working for wages, there will be "equality" within the household. Their formulation does not pay enough attention to the nature of women's paid work and to other variables that might be in operation (such as how power and control may be exercised between males and females within the household).

In addition to engaging in critical evaluations of the specific theories that had been developed to explain women's involvement in crime, feminist criminologists drew attention to the invisibility of women in mainstream approaches within the discipline.

The Mainstream Theories of Crime

Since the 1970s, mainstream approaches to explain crime have come under increasing scrutiny. Writers such as Leonard (1982), Heidensohn (1985), Morris (1987), and Naffine (1987) have highlighted the general failure of mainstream theories in criminology to adequately explain or account for women's involvement in crime; "mainstream" is, in effect, "malestream."

For example, in explaining crime in relation to the strain that results from the disjunction between culture goals (such as monetary success) and institutionalized means (education, jobs), Merton's anomie theory (see Chapter 10, "Strain Theories") reflected a sensitivity to the class inequalities that exist in society. The same could not be said, however, with regard to an awareness of gender inequalities. If lower-class individuals are more likely to engage in crime because of a lack of access to the institutionalized means for achieving monetary success, then women—who as a group experience a similar lack of access—should also be found to commit crime as a consequence of this strain. This is not the case.

Like strain theory, Sutherland's differential association theory is presented as a general theory of crime (see Chapter 13). In focusing on the processes by which individuals learn definitions of the legal codes as either favourable or unfavourable, Sutherland posited the existence of a "cultural heterogeneity" in society with regard to pro- and anti-criminal associations. This cultural heterogeneity accounted for men's involvement in crime; women were the anomaly or exception in that they displayed a "cultural homogeneity." In Sutherland's view, women were more altruistic and compliant than men. As Naffine (1987) has noted, Sutherland missed a great opportunity when he neglected to explore this apparent cultural homogeneity in females. Given his critical outlook vis-à-vis the individualism and competition that he felt characterized American society, an examination of women's conformity could have provided Sutherland with clues to better understand crime and its causes.

Hirschi's work on social control theory is also characterized by a neglect of the female (see Chapter 14). While other criminologists focused their attention on explaining deviance, Hirschi set out to explain conformity. In this regard, since women appear to be more conformist than men, it would have made sense to treat women as central to his analysis. Nevertheless, though he collected data on female subjects, Hirschi set these data aside and—like his colleagues— concentrated on males.

With the advent of the labelling and conflict theories during the 1960s and 1970s, the potential for a more inclusive approach to crime increased. Yet while Becker's labelling perspective raised the question of "Whose side are we on?" and advocated an approach to deviance that gave a voice to those who were subject to the labelling process, it was never fully realized in the case of women. Similarly, Taylor, Walton, and Young's *The New Criminology* (1973), which offered a devastating critique of the traditional criminological theories, failed to give any mention to women.

In general, when sex differentials in crime are considered by the mainstream theorists, the tendency has been to rely on stereotypical constructions of masculinity and femininity: men are aggressive, independent, daring, and adventurous; women are submissive, dependent, and compliant. In the process, female law violators are classed as a rather "dull lot." Even in their deviance, they are less interesting than men. Moreover, such stereotypical depictions of women have been considered "so obvious" that they require no further discussion (see, for example, Cohen 1955, 142)—let alone theoretical or empirical concern.

We saw in Chapter 5 that females commit less serious offences, in smaller numbers, and with less frequency than males. Criminologists have typically responded to these findings by formulating their theories to account for only male crime and delinquency. The ramifications of this tendency have been spelled out by Gelsthorpe and Morris:

> Theories are weak if they do not apply to half of the potential criminal population; women, after all, experience the same deprivations, family structures and so on that men do. Theories of crime should be able to take account of both men's and women's behaviour and to highlight those factors which operate differently on men and women. Whether or not a particular theory helps us to understand women's crime is of *fundamental*, not marginal importance for criminology. (1988, 103, emphasis added)

The Generalizability Problem

One issue raised by this problem with the mainstream theories of crime is referred to by Daly and Chesney-Lind (1988) as the **generalizability problem**: Can theories generated to explain male offending be modified to apply to women? Several criminologists responded to this problem by attempting to make the mainstream theories of crime "fit" women. For example, Leonard (1982) reformulated Merton's strain theory, suggesting that females may be socialized to aspire to different culture goals than males—in particular, relational ones concerning marriage and having children. If this is the case, then women's low rate of criminality would be explained by the relatively easy manner in which females can realize their goals. Nevertheless, as Morris (1987) notes, such a formulation relies on an idealized and romanticized version of women's lives. It displays an insensitivity to the strains and frustrations associated with women's familial role; furthermore, it fails to acknowledge the economic concerns that women confront. Such efforts to revise mainstream theories of crime to include women have been referred to as the "add women and stir" approach. Part of the difficulty with this endeavour is that women are presented as afterthoughts, not as integral to the arguments being developed (Gelsthorpe and Morris 1988). A more significant problem with this effort is captured by Naffine (1997, 32): "The point of these exercises has been to adapt to the female case, theories of crime which purported to be gender-neutral but were in fact always highly gender specific. Not surprisingly, the results have been varied and generally inconclusive."

generalizability problem
Raises the issue of whether mainstream theories of crime—which have largely been developed with men in mind—can be made to "fit" women.

The Gender-Ratio Problem

A second issue raised by the feminist critique of mainstream criminology is one that Daly and Chesney-Lind (1988, 119) refer to as the **gender-ratio problem**. Why are women less likely than men to be involved in crime? What explains the sex difference in rates of arrest and in the variable types of criminal activity between men and women? Attention to the gender-ratio problem sparked a plethora of studies in the 1970s and 1980s on the processing of men and women by the criminal justice system (see, for example, Scutt 1979; Kruttschnitt 1980–81, 1982; Steffensmeier and Kramer 1982; Zingraff and Thomson 1984; Daly 1987, 1989). The main question that guided much of this research stemmed from Pollak's assertion that criminal justice officials exercised "chivalry": Are women treated more leniently than men? As with the generalizability problem, the answers to this question have been mixed. For instance, research that supports the chivalry hypothesis

gender-ratio problem
Poses the question of why there are sex differences in rates of arrest and types of criminal activity between men and women.

indicates that where it does exist, chivalry benefits some women more than others—in particular, the few white middle- or upper-class women who come into conflict with the law. Also, chivalry appears to apply only to those female suspects who behave in a stereotypical fashion, that is, "crying, pleading for release for the sake of their children, claiming men have led them astray" (Rafter and Natalizia 1981, 92). In this regard, Rafter and Natalizia have argued that chivalrous behaviour should be seen as a means of preserving women's subordinate position in society, not as a benign effort to treat women with some special kindness. Naffine (1997, 36), however, points to a larger problem with this research. By turning on the question of whether women were treated the same as or differently from men, the chivalry thesis (and its rebuttal) took men to be the norm: "Men were thus granted the status of universal subjects, the population of people with whom the rest of the world (women) were compared."

The Women's Liberation Thesis

While research on the chivalry thesis was drawing the attention of criminologists in the 1970s and 1980s, another thesis began to attract considerable attention. The women's liberation thesis posits that women's involvement in crime will come to more closely resemble men's as differences between men and women are diminished by women's greater participation and equality in society. As reflected in the work of Simon (1975) and Adler (1975), this thesis suggests that changes in women's gender roles will be reflected in their rates of criminal involvement. Simon suggested that the increased employment opportunities that accompanied the women's movement would lead to an increase in opportunities to commit crime (such as embezzlement from employers). Adler linked the apparent statistical increase in women's crime to the influence of the women's movement and suggested that a "new female criminal" was emerging: women were becoming more violent and aggressive, just like their male counterparts.

While the women's liberation thesis was widely promoted by the media and law enforcement alike (see Gavigan 1993), representations of emancipated women running amok in the streets and workplaces did not hold up under closer scrutiny. For one, the thesis was premised on a particular reading of the official crime statistics: that women's crimes had in fact increased—indeed, to the point where a female crime wave was occurring. Smart (1976) suggested that this claim was supported by a "statistical illusion" in that the supposed increases in women's crime were being reported as percentages. Given the small base number of women charged with criminal offences, it did not take much of a change to show a large percentage increase. Johnson and Rodgers (1993, 104) provided an example of this problem using Canadian data. Between 1970 and 1991, charges against women for homicide increased 45 percent, but that figure reflected a real increase of only 15 women charged.

Simon (1975) based her argument on statistics for fraud, embezzlement, and forgery, suggesting that women had greater opportunities to commit white-collar offences as a result of their liberation. Despite women's increased labour force participation, however, they continue to confront vertical and horizontal segregation in the job market; that is, women are generally not in positions of trust that would enable them to commit white-collar offences. An added problem is that the crime statistics do not distinguish between different forms of fraud, so that what often appear to be white-collar offences are really more petty offences related to welfare fraud. Women, in other words, are more likely to commit "frayed-collar crime" than "white-collar crime."

Writing in the mid-1970s, Adler considered the women's movement to be a *fait accompli*; women had already fought and won their battle for equality. Four decades later, though, women still encounter inequalities in society. For instance, Canadian women continue to be overrepresented in the lower ranks of the job market and concentrated in "female occupations": teaching, nursing, clerical, sales, and service occupations. Women working full-time, full-year, earn on average $0.74 for every dollar earned by men (Moyser 2017). Adler also equated women's liberation with freedom to be male. Women's liberation, however, could be interpreted as quite the opposite: a resistance to and rejection of traditional gender stereotypes.

Naffine (1997, 32) refers to the thesis that "women's liberation" causes crime by women as "perhaps the most time-consuming and fruitless exercise" in criminology. For feminist criminologists, the main difficulty with the women's liberation thesis—as with the chivalry thesis—was that it posed a question that took males to be the norm: Were women becoming more "liberated" and thus more like men, even in their offending?

Given the difficulties encountered in efforts to respond to the generalizability and gender-ratio problems, many feminist criminologists saw the need to "bracket" these issues for the time being in order to understand better the social worlds of women and girls (Daly and Chesney-Lind 1988, 121). Cain (1990) took this suggestion further. She noted that while feminist criminologists needed to understand women's experiences, there were no tools in existing criminological theory with which to do this. Cain therefore advocated a "transgressive" approach, one that started from outside the boundaries of criminological discourse.

Criminalized Women

For many feminist criminologists, starting from outside criminology has meant resisting the temptation to fashion theories of women's involvement in crime that take crime categories (such as crimes against the person or crimes against property) as their starting point. As writers such as Smart (1989), Laberge (1991), and Faith (1993) have pointed out, "crime" is not a homogenous category. There are notable differences between women regarding the nature and extent of both their criminal involvement and their contacts with the criminal justice system. As well, crime categories are legal constructions, the end result of a lengthy process of detection, apprehension, accusation, judgment, and conviction. They represent one way of ordering or making sense of social life. Crime categories are also premised on a dualism between "the criminal" and "the law-abiding," which reinforces the view of criminal women as "Other" and thereby misses the similarities that exist between women. In this respect, criminal women are in very many ways no different from the rest of us. They are mothers, daughters, sisters, girlfriends, and wives, and they share many of the experiences of women collectively in society. Since crime is the outcome of interactions between individuals and the criminal justice system, writers like Laberge (1991) have proposed that we think in terms of "criminalized women" rather than "criminal women."

In these terms, women may commit a variety of crimes for a variety of reasons; there is no single or special theory for their criminality. As Carlen (1985, 10) has emphasized, "the essential criminal woman does not exist." In contrast to the conservative and liberal approaches that have dominated criminologists' thinking about the "difference" between men and women, a **feminist approach** understands "difference" as rooted in the structure of society. More specifically, the lives of criminalized women are located in a broader social context characterized by intersecting inequalities of class, race, and gender.

feminist approach
Understands "difference" between men and women as structurally produced by inequalities of class, race, and gender that condition and constrain women's lives.

With regard to class location, criminalized women tend to be young, poor, undereducated, and unskilled. They are most likely to be involved in property crimes (Chapter 5). Johnson and Rodgers (1993, 98) suggest that "women's participation in property offences is consistent with their traditional roles as consumers and, increasingly, as low income, semi-skilled, sole support providers for their families. In keeping with the rapid increase in female-headed households and the stresses associated with poverty, greater numbers of women are being charged with shoplifting, cheque forging and welfare fraud."

In contrast to the women's liberation thesis, feminist criminologists have suggested that increases in women's involvement in crime are connected more directly with the "feminization of poverty" than with women's emancipation. Indeed, several writers have called attention to how government cutbacks to social assistance have left increasing numbers of women and children at risk (Chunn and Gavigan 2014; Mosher 2014; Crocker and Johnson 2010). In the Province of Ontario, for example, social assistance payments were cut by 21.6 percent in 1995, "workfare" programs were implemented, and a zero tolerance policy on welfare fraud was put in place. The feminization of poverty has been accompanied by the "criminalization of poverty." Next to murderers, individuals convicted of welfare fraud have the greatest likelihood of receiving a sentence of incarceration. A 1997 study of 50 welfare fraud convictions found that 80 percent of those found guilty were sentenced to time in prison (Martin 1999).

Locating women's involvement in crime in its broader social context also involves attending to racial inequality. Indigenous people in Canada are disproportionately represented in crime statistics, but the overrepresentation of Indigenous women in Canadian prisons and jails is even greater than that of Indigenous men (Mahony, Jacob, and Hobson 2017; Reitano 2017). Drugs and alcohol have played a key role in their offences—but so too has trauma. The processes and practices of settler colonialism—including the economic marginalization of Indigenous communities, colonial state policies such as the Indian Act, the intergenerational effects of the residential schools, and the removal of Indigenous children from their homes through child welfare practices—have generated considerable trauma in the lives of Indigenous people (Hamilton and Sinclair 1991; RCAP 1996; Truth and Reconciliation Commission of Canada 2015). Drugging and drinking have become ready coping strategies for dealing with that trauma, and this draws women into the criminal justice net (Comack 2018).

Gender inequality and its links to race and class help explain prostitution and sex trade work. According to Johnson and Rodgers, women's involvement in prostitution is a reflection of their subordinate social and economic position in society: "Prostitution thrives in a society which values women more for their sexuality than for their skilled labour, and which puts women in a class of commodity to be bought and sold. Research has shown one of the major causes of prostitution to be the economic plight of women, particularly young, poorly educated women who have limited *legitimate* employment records" (Johnson and Rodgers 1993, 101, emphasis in original). Seshia's (2005) research on street sexual exploitation in Winnipeg revealed that poverty and homelessness, colonialism and the legacy of the residential schools, and gender discrimination and generational sexual exploitation all combined to lead cis and transgender women to become involved in the sex trade.

Bruckert and Parent's (2014) interviews with in-call sex workers—women who provide sexual services to clients in establishments such as massage parlours, brothels, and dungeons—reveal the parallels with the work of working-class women in other consumer services as well as how the social, moral, and criminal justice regulation of sex work creates particular challenges and problems for the women. Those challenges and problems were brought to the fore in the case of *Canada (Attorney General) v Bedford* (2013), in which three women challenged the constitutionality of three sections of the Criminal Code relating to prostitution: keeping or being found in a bawdy house (s. 210); living off the avails of prostitution (s. 212(1)(j)); and communicating for the purposes of prostitution (s. 213(1)(c)). On hearing the case in 2013, the Supreme Court ruled that these provisions were inconsistent with the *Charter* and thus invalid. Parliament was given one year in which to devise a new approach. A new law came into effect in December 2014 that criminalized the purchase of sexual services, making prostitution between adults illegal for the first time in Canadian history. While this legislation places the focus on the buyers of sexual services, it also makes it illegal to operate a business that sells sexual services (escort agencies and massage parlours). Critics, therefore, argue that women engaged in the sex trade will be forced onto the street, where the risk of encountering violence is greater.

The intersecting gender, race, and class inequalities in society that shape and constrain the lives of criminalized women provide an important backdrop for understanding their involvement in crime. As Carlen (1988, 14) notes, women make their lives in conditions that are not of their own choosing. In their efforts to transgress criminology, feminist criminologists have become increasingly aware that to understand women's lives we must bring into view women's experiences of violence at the hands of men. This violence needs to be understood as a manifestation of **patriarchy**—that is, the systemic and individual power that men exercise over women (Brownmiller 1975; Kelly 1988).

patriarchy
A system of male domination that includes both a structure and an ideology that privileges men over women.

Violence against Women

At the same time that feminist criminologists were criticizing criminology for its neglect of women, feminists in the women's movement were raising the issue of male violence against women. This issue had historically not been a matter of societal, legal, or academic concern.

The Cultural Construction of Rape

With regard to the lack of societal concern about male violence against women, feminists questioned assumptions and beliefs that dominated the public's understanding of sexual violence. The **cultural construction** of rape, for example, was

cultural construction
A perspective on a subject that is shaped by cultural assumptions rather than having a natural or objective basis.

riddled with myths and misconceptions about the nature of the act itself, as well as with stereotypical images of "true" rape victims and offenders. These myths and stereotypes—and their limitations—included the following:

- *Women "ask for it" by their dress or their behaviour.* The absurdity of this claim is revealed when we apply the same logic to victims of robbery (see Box 6.2).

- *Rape is a sexual act brought on by a man's uncontrollable sexual urges, which cannot be halted once a woman has "turned him on."* Such a view not only depicts male sexuality in a distorted way but also ignores the element of physical coercion and the effects of fear and threats on the woman.

- *When women say no they really mean yes.* This belief suggests that women are expected to be coy and flirtatious and that men are encouraged not to take no for an answer. In these terms, it legitimates the act of rape.

- *If a woman has had sexual relations in the past, she will be less credible when she says she didn't consent to sex.* This myth suggests that "bad girls" or "loose women" deserve to be raped.

- *Women cannot be trusted.* For instance, they will make false accusations against innocent men. Casting all women as inherently untrustworthy acts to silence survivors and exonerate rapists.

- *The act of rape really has little long-term impact on the woman.* So long as the harm of rape is denied, society can continue to ignore the issue and its effects on women's lives.

- *Men who commit "real" rape are an "abnormal" group in society.* Attributing rape to the actions of a small, disturbed minority in society effectively lets men as a group off the hook. Rape is thus cast as an isolated problem for psychologists and psychiatrists to deal with or is narrowly defined as a "women's issue"—not an issue that all of us need to confront.

FOCUS   BOX 6.2

WAS HE ASKING FOR IT?

In 1975, *Harper's Weekly* carried the following response to an American Bar Association finding that few rapists are punished for their crime. The article asks us to imagine a male complainant in a robbery case undergoing the same sort of cross-examination that a female complainant in a rape case does.

"Mr. Smith, you were held up at gunpoint on the corner of First and Main?"

"Yes."

"Did you struggle with the robber?"

"No."

"Why not?"

"He was armed."

"Then you made a conscious decision to comply with his demands rather than resist?"

"Yes."

"Did you scream? Cry out?"

"No. I was afraid."

"I see. Have you ever been held up before?"

"No."

"Have you ever given money away?"

"Yes, of course."

"And you did so willingly?"

"What are you getting at?"

"Well, let's put it like this, Mr. Smith. You've given money away in the past. In fact, you have quite the reputation for philanthropy. How can we be sure you weren't contriving to have your money taken by force?"

"Listen, if I wanted—"

"Never mind. What time did this holdup take place?"

"About 11 p.m."

"You were out in the street at 11 p.m.? Doing what?"

"Just walking."

"Just walking? You know it's dangerous being out on the street that late at night. Weren't you aware that you could have been held up?"

"I hadn't thought about it."

"What were you wearing?"

"Let's see—a suit. Yes, a suit."

"An expensive suit?"

"Well—yes, I'm a successful lawyer, you know."

"In other words, Mr. Smith, you were walking around the streets late at night in a suit that practically advertised the fact that you might be a good target for some easy money, isn't that so? I mean, if we didn't know better, Mr. Smith, we might even think that you were asking for this to happen, mightn't we?"

Questions for Critical Thinking

1. In what ways have rape myths and stereotypes been evident in law and legal practice?

2. To what extent is the 'cultural construction of rape' evident in films, music videos, advertising, and other aspects of Canadian culture?

Smart (1989, 28) has described this cultural construction of rape as "phallocentric," by which she is referring to "the prevailing dominance of the masculine experience of, and meaning of, sexuality. Sexuality is comprehended as the pleasure of the Phallus, and by extension the pleasures of penetration and intercourse—for men." Clearly, the more prevalent such phallocentric myths and stereotypes about sexual violence are in society, the more far-reaching will be their consequences.

For perpetrators of sexual violence, these myths and stereotypes can translate into less chance of detection, higher acquittal rates, and lighter sentences. In 2009, for instance, only 3 percent of sexual assaults were reported to police in Canada, and of those 3 percent, less than 20 percent were brought to trial (Statistics Canada 2010, 2011a, 2011b). Once failure to complain and to charge are taken into account, the likelihood that someone who commits a sexual assault will be convicted of an offence is less than 1 percent (Busby 2014).

Some of the attrition between reporting sexual assaults and convictions is explained by a study undertaken by the *Globe and Mail*. In February 2017 the newspaper began a series of reports on the issue of "unfounded" sexual assaults—those cases where women report to the police but no charges are laid because the police do not believe a crime has occurred. Data collected from police departments across the country showed that police dismiss one out of every five sexual assault reports as unfounded. Sexual assaults were nearly twice as likely as physical assaults to be designated as unfounded (20% versus 11%). Unfounded rates varied widely between jurisdictions. The study looked at 178 police services; the police in 115 (65%) of them dismissed at least one-third of sexual assault complaints as unfounded, and in some urban centres the rates were as high as 60 percent. As the *Globe* report noted, "when complaints of sexual assault are dismissed with such frequency, it is a sign of deeper flaws in the investigative process: inadequate training for police; dated interviewing techniques that do not take into account the effect that trauma can have on memory; and the persistence of rape myths among law-enforcement officials" (Doolittle 2017). In response to the report, more than 50 police services indicated that they would conduct a review of their sexual assault cases to ensure no errors have been made.

Studies also show that many rapists do not even believe they have done anything wrong. Scully and Marolla's (1984) interviews with men convicted of rape found that a large proportion of the men either denied having sexual contact with the victim or admitted to sexual acts but did not define their behaviour as rape. The men tried to demonstrate that their victims were willing and, in some cases, enthusiastic participants. One man convicted of attempting to rape a prison hospital nurse claimed: "She semi-struggled but deep down inside I think she felt it was a fantasy come true" (535). Another man who had hid in his victim's closet and later attacked her while she slept maintained that while the victim was scared at first, "once we got into it she was ok." He believed he had not committed rape because "she enjoyed it and it was like she consented" (536). A third man who beat his victim admitted that "I did something stupid. I pulled a knife on her and I hit her as hard as I would hit a man," yet he still maintained: "But I shouldn't be in prison for what I did. I shouldn't have all this time [sentence] for going to bed with a broad" (537).

For survivors of sexual violence, rape myths can mean a "double victimization." Survivors endure the humiliation and degradation inherent in the act itself, and may experience further humiliation if they report the crime to the authorities. Also, since phallocentric cultural beliefs suggest that rape is the woman's fault, survivors may feel responsible for their own victimization. As Smart (1989, 35) has argued, "the whole rape trial is a process of disqualification (of women) and celebration [of phallocentrism]." For women generally, the cultural construction of rape can produce feelings of fear and vulnerability that impose restrictions on their daily activities. One study, for example, reported that 38 percent of women (compared with 64% of men) who walk alone in their neighbourhood after dark said they felt very safe; women were three times more likely than men to say they felt somewhat or very unsafe when walking alone in their neighbourhood after dark (12% versus 4%) (Perreault 2017, 14).

The Law's Role in Condoning Male Violence against Women

Recognition of the pervasiveness of these phallocentric myths and stereotypes led to a questioning of the role that the law has played in condoning male violence against women. Feminists noted, for example, that women have historically been viewed as the "property" of men. The law upheld this view by granting husbands certain legal rights, in particular, the "right to consortium" and the "right to chastise" their wives.

Consortium generally refers to the companionship, affection, and assistance that one spouse in a marriage is entitled to receive from the other. According only husbands the right to consortium meant that wives had a legal obligation with respect to the "consummation of marriage, cohabitation, maintenance of conjugal rights, sexual fidelity, and general obedience and respect for his wishes" (Dobash and Dobash 1979, 60). This right was reflected in Canadian law until

1983. Under the old rape law, a rape was defined as having occurred when "[a] male person has sexual intercourse with a female person *who is not his wife*, (a) without her consent, or (b) with her consent if the consent (i) is extorted by threats or fear of bodily harm, (ii) is obtained by impersonating her husband, or (iii) is obtained by false and fraudulent representations as to the nature and quality of the act" (s. 143, emphasis added). It made no sense, under the law's logic, to prevent men from "consorting" with their own property; wives did not have the legal right to say no.

Besides granting a husband immunity from rape charges, the rape law reinforced the cultural construction of rape. For instance, reflecting the belief that "women cannot be trusted" when they claim they have been raped, the legislation included a corroboration requirement, whereby the accused could not be found guilty in the absence of corroborating evidence (such as cuts and bruises) supporting the testimony of the complainant. As well, under the doctrine of recent complaint, it was assumed that a woman who complained at the first reasonable opportunity was more credible or believable than one who complained some time after the rape had taken place. Because the key element in establishing the guilt of the accused in rape cases was consent, the focus of the trial rested on the woman's credibility. Her moral character came under the scrutiny of the court in the attempt to determine whether she could be believed when she said she did not consent. Defence lawyers were permitted to ask questions about the past sexual history of the complainant, reinforcing the belief that women who have had sexual relations in the past are "less credible" when they say they didn't consent to sex.

With regard to the right to chastise, the law once gave a husband the authority to use force in order to ensure that his wife fulfilled her obligations. The only restraint the law placed on a husband was that he had to apply that force in a moderate manner. When husbands went too far, and their wives died as a result, the British courts were inclined to leniency. Yet if a wife killed her husband, it was considered a "species of treason" akin to killing the king, for she was going against his authority (Edwards 1985). The law, in essence, reflected and reinforced patriarchal relations between men and women. This view continued to inform legal practice into the latter part of the 20th century. Because police officers were inclined to view violence in the home between intimate partners as a "private trouble" that was not the law's business, they were reluctant to intervene or to define the situation as a criminal matter.

Criminology's Complicity

Within criminology, male violence against women was similarly not seen as a social problem. Official statistics suggested that crimes like rape were relatively infrequent. Victim surveys—which asked respondents whether they had been victimized by crime—indicated that the group most at risk of crime victimization was young men, not women. When criminologists' attention did turn to crimes like rape, the focus was on the small group of men who had been convicted and incarcerated for the offence, and these men were typically understood as an abnormal and pathological group. Much of traditional criminology, then, tended to mirror the cultural construction of rape. In his "classic" study of forcible rape, for example, Amir (1967, 1971) introduced the notion of "victim precipitation." The concept suggests that some women are "rape prone" (because of their "bad" reputation) and that others invite rape through their "negligent and reckless" behaviour (by going to bars or hitchhiking) or through their failure to react strongly enough to sexual overtures. Amir's work essentially blamed the woman for the violence she encountered.

SEARCH FOR:
Canadian Association of Sexual Assault Centres

Breaking the Silence

In combination, the absence of societal, legal, and academic concern about the issue of male violence against women had the effect of silencing women. One of the main goals of the women's movement as it gained momentum in the 1970s was to break this silence. As women came together to share their stories, and as a result of increasing efforts to provide support and services to women (such as rape crisis centres, crisis lines, and shelters for abused women), it soon became evident that the incidence of sexual violence far exceeded what was being reported in crime statistics. In 1980, for example, the Canadian Advisory Council on the Status of Women (CACSW) estimated that one in every five Canadian women would be sexually assaulted at some point in her life and that one in every 17 would be subjected to forced sexual intercourse. Yet only one in 10 sexual assaults was ever reported to the police (Kinnon 1981). That same year, the CACSW released its report, *Wife Battering in Canada: The Vicious Circle*. MacLeod (1980), the report's author, estimated that every year, one in 10 Canadian women who is married or in a relationship with a live-in partner is battered. Yet when this finding was reported in the House of Commons (on 12 May 1982), it was met with laughter from members of Parliament. Public outrage ensued, and over the next decade, wife abuse was gradually transformed from a "private trouble" into a "public issue."

The growing awareness of male violence against women led to pressures for legislative reform. Two major changes occurred in 1983. First, the old rape law was repealed and three new categories were added to the offence of assault: sexual assault (s. 246.1); sexual assault with a weapon, threats to a third party, and bodily harm (s. 246.2); and aggravated sexual assault (s. 246.3). Under this new legislation, husbands could now be charged with sexually assaulting their wives, limitations were placed on the ability of the defence to ask questions about the past sexual history of the complainant, the corroboration requirement was dropped, the doctrine of recent complaint was formally removed, and provision was made for a publication ban on the complainant's identity. These changes were designed to redress the apparent gender inequities in the law and to reduce the trauma experienced by the complainant during the trial in an attempt to encourage the reporting of cases. Second, a national directive was issued to encourage police to lay charges in wife assault cases (previously, the decision was left to the wishes of the complainant), and police training was upgraded to emphasize sensitive interventions in cases of wife assault. These reforms led to increases in the number of charges for domestic assault. In Winnipeg, for instance, there were 629 domestic assault charges laid in 1983; by 1989, the number had increased to 1,137 charges laid (Ursel 1994).

The Montreal Massacre

The reality of violence against women was exposed most strongly on 6 December 1989, when a gunman entered a classroom at the École Polytechnique in Montreal, separated the men from the women students, declared, "You're all a bunch of feminists," and proceeded to gun them down. Fourteen women were killed that day and 13 others were wounded. The gunman's suicide letter explicitly identified his action as politically motivated: he blamed "feminists" for the major disappointments in his life. Police also found a "hit list" containing the names of prominent women (see Box 6.3). The Montreal Massacre served to reinforce what women's groups across the country had been arguing for decades: that violence against women is a widespread and pervasive feature of our society. It takes many forms, including sexual harassment in the workplace, date rape, violent sexual assaults, incest, and wife abuse.

While the murder of 14 women in Montreal has understandably received the attention it deserves, it is also noteworthy that the violence women encounter at the hands of men has become "routine." In 1993, Statistics Canada released the findings of the Violence Against Women Survey (VAWS). The first national survey of its kind anywhere in the world, the VAWS included responses from 12,300 women (see Johnson 1996). Using definitions of physical and sexual assault consistent with the Canadian Criminal Code, the survey found that half (51%) of Canadian women had experienced at least one incident of physical or sexual violence since the age of 16. The survey also confirmed the results of other research in finding that women face the greatest risk of violence from men they know. "Almost one-half (45%) of all women experienced violence by men known to them (dates, boyfriends, marital partners, friends, family, neighbours, etc.), while 23% of women experienced violence by a stranger (17% reported violence by both strangers and known men)" (Statistics Canada 1993, 2). The VAWS also found that 29 percent (or 3 in 10) of ever-married women had been assaulted by a spouse.

Missing and Murdered Indigenous Women

The gendered *and* racialized nature of violence has become more of a public issue now that attention has begun to focus on the numbers of missing and murdered Indigenous women in Canada. In 2004, Amnesty International published a report, *Stolen Sisters*, that called attention to the violence encountered by Indigenous women and pointed to the role that cultural and systemic discrimination played in perpetuating this violence, thereby impeding their basic human right to be safe from violence. The report noted that Indigenous women are five times more likely to die as a result of violence (23). It also documented many of the cases of missing and murdered women—including the disappearance of women from the streets of Vancouver's Downtown Eastside. In 2005 the Native Women's Association of Canada (NWAC) launched the Sisters in Spirit initiative, which was aimed at addressing the root causes, circumstances, and trends that led to missing and murdered Indigenous women and girls. By March 2010, NWAC had gathered information about the disappearance or death of more than 580 Indigenous women and girls across Canada (NWAC 2010). A more recent database compiled by the RCMP increased that figure to 1,181 missing or murdered Indigenous women and girls (RCMP 2014).

SEARCH FOR:
Native Women's Association of Canada

FOCUS

BOX 6.3

A TIME FOR GRIEF AND PAIN

Montreal

Fourteen women are dead for one reason: they are women. Their male classmates are still alive for one reason: they are men. While gender divides us in thousands of ways every day, rarely are the consequences of misogyny so tragic.

I found out about the murders early yesterday morning. I came home from dinner with friends about 1 a.m., and listened as usual to my answering machine. It was the last message that gave me a jolt. It was a good friend telling me that there would be a vigil last night for the 14 women who had been killed at the University of Montreal.

Not believing my ears and desperate for news, I turned on the radio. I ended up listening to an open-line show. The talk was about relationships between young men and women these days.

Most of the callers were men. They blamed the murders on everything from drugs and condom distributors in high schools to women who have made men feel insecure. Many callers said they did not understand what had happened. It's all very well and fine to be misogynous, said one caller, but you can't lose your head.

I realized, as I was listening to this show, that I was trembling. So were the voices of the female callers. I felt something I had not experienced in a long time: fear of being alone in my apartment. There were sounds at the window I would normally ignore. Now I could not. Immobilized, I was afraid to stay alone and afraid to go out.

It does not matter that the man who decided to kill 14 women—and he clearly did decide to do that—killed himself afterward; it is not of him I am afraid. I am afraid of what he represents, of all the unspoken hatred, the pent-up anger that he expressed. Hatred and anger that is shared by every husband who beats his wife, every man who rapes his date, every father who abuses his child, and by many more who would not dare.

It happened at the École Polytechnique in Montreal but it could have been anywhere.

It would be a great mistake, I think, to see this incident as some kind of freak accident, the act of a madman that has nothing to do with the society in which we live. The killer was angry at women, at feminism, at his own loss of power. He yelled: "You're all a bunch of feminists" on his way to killing 14 women.

Now there is little that is comforting to say to women. It is a time for grief for all of us; grief for those who have died, and pain at being reminded of how deep misogyny still runs in our society.

Questions for Critical Thinking

1. How do you make sense of the violence that women and girls so often encounter in their lives?

2. Is the use of the criminal justice system the most effective strategy for responding to the problem of violence against women?

Source: Diana Bronson, "A Time for Grief and Pain," *Globe and Mail*, 8 December 1989, A7. Reprinted with permission of the author.

Between 1978 and 1992, some 60 women, many of them Indigenous and involved in the street sex trade, were reported to have vanished from Vancouver's Downtown Eastside, known as Canada's "poorest postal code." As Hugill (2010) notes, however, Vancouver's crisis of missing and murdered women generated very little interest on the part of the media and the criminal justice system prior to 1998, and it was not until 2001 that police formed a Missing Women Joint Task Force to investigate these cases. In February 2002 this new unit raided the Port Coquitlam pig farm of Robert Pickton, who was eventually charged with the murder of 26 women. In December 2007 Pickton was convicted of the second-degree murder of six women and sentenced to life imprisonment.

In response to calls for action from Indigenous families, communities, and organizations, as well as nongovernmental and international organizations, the Government of Canada launched an independent National Inquiry into Missing

Many protesters across the country demanded a government inquiry into hundreds of murdered and missing Indigenous women.

and Murdered Indigenous Women and Girls in September 2016. The commission's mandate is "to examine and report on the systemic causes of all forms of violence against Indigenous women and girls in Canada by looking at patterns and underlying factors" (National Inquiry into Missing and Murdered Indigenous Women and Girls 2018).

Events such as these confirm that male violence against women continues to be a serious social problem in Canadian society. They also raise concerns about the effectiveness of the criminal justice system in responding to this pressing problem.

Recent History of Law's Response to Violence against Women

As the 1990s unfolded, many feminists became uncertain as to whether engaging with the criminal justice system to combat male violence against women was having the desired outcome. With respect to sexual assault, it appeared that the phallocentric myths and stereotypes surrounding rape were continuing to pervade the practice of law. Some judges, for instance, were making statements in court that suggested their decisions were being influenced by these myths. In a BC case heard in 1991, the judge made the following statement in his written decision: "The mating practice, if I may call it that, is less than a precise relationship. At times no may mean maybe, or wait awhile" (*R v Letendre*, cited in Boyle 1994, 141). In June 1998, an Alberta Court of Appeal judge upheld a lower court's acquittal of a man charged with sexually assaulting a 17-year-old girl. In his decision, the judge commented on the clothing worn by the young woman (a T-shirt and shorts), noting, "It must be pointed out that the complainant did not present herself to [the accused] in a bonnet and crinolines" (*R v Ewanchuk* 1999). Several decisions by the Supreme Court of Canada also raised concerns over the law's treatment of sexual assault cases.

In a 1991 ruling on the cases of *Seaboyer* and *Gayme (R v Seaboyer*, 1991), the Supreme Court struck down section 276 of the Criminal Code. Known as the "rape shield" provision, section 276 was included in the 1983 sexual assault law with the aim of preventing a woman's sexual conduct from being used to discredit her testimony. The Supreme Court ruled that, while laudable in its intent, the provision went too far and could deny the accused the right to a fair trial. Critics took exception to this decision because it left the question of whether evidence of the complainant's past sexual history would be admissible in court to the discretion of the trial judge. In response, Parliament introduced Bill C-49 in 1992, which was designed to amend the 1983 sexual assault legislation.

Under this new legislation, the rules of evidence now state that evidence that the complainant had previously engaged in sexual activity, whether with the accused or with any other person, is not admissible to support an inference that the complainant was either more likely to have consented to the sexual activity in question or was less worthy of belief. Also, a new test for judges has been provided for determining whether a complainant's sexual history may be admitted at trial. Bill C-49 also provided a definition of "consent" as it applies to sexual assault cases—"the voluntary agreement of the complainant to engage in the sexual activity in question" (s. 243.1 (1))—and specified the conditions under which there is "no consent" (for instance, where the complainant is incapable of consenting to the activity by reason of intoxication or where the complainant expresses, by words or conduct, a lack of agreement to engage in the activity). The bill also placed restrictions on the defences available to those accused of sexual assault: the onus was now on the accused to show that he or she took "reasonable steps" in the circumstances to ascertain that the complainant was consenting (s. 273.2 (b)).

The Supreme Court's ruling in *R v O'Connor* (1995) had even more profound implications for survivors of sexual assault. Bishop O'Connor was a priest and principal at a residential school near Williams Lake, BC, where four Indigenous women attended and worked. In 1991, the women laid charges of rape and indecent assault against O'Connor for incidents that occurred at the school between 1961 and 1967. The charges were stayed by the trial judge in 1992 when the Crown failed to release to the defence counsel the women's residential school records and all therapy and medical records since the time they had left the school (none of these records were in the Crown's possession). When the case reached the Supreme Court, the Court overturned the stay and ordered a new trial for O'Connor, but gave exceptionally large scope to defence access to complainants' records held by third parties. After the Court's decision, women's shelters and rape crisis centres found themselves being subpoenaed to turn over all files and counselling records relating to cases before the courts, and criminal defence lawyers were being advised by their association that they would be "negligent" if they did not subpoena complainants' files (Busby 1997, 2014).

The Supreme Court's ruling in *O'Connor* meant that confidential records, as well as personal diaries, letters, and the like, could now all be accessed. The ruling had special implications for the work of therapists and rape crisis counsellors, who could now be required to hand over any and all records or notes relating to a complainant in a sexual assault case. Critics noted that such materials are not designed to be a written record of allegations; they are maintained for therapeutic, not evidentiary, purposes. For example, one of the issues regularly dealt with in therapy sessions is the need to explore feelings of guilt or shame that a woman may experience after a rape. In the hands of the court, this could be taken as evidence of "consent" or "complicity" on the part of the woman. To this extent, the *O'Connor* decision supports the old rape myths: that women lie or make false allegations, and that they cannot be trusted. One of the main effects of the ruling was that it silenced women. Women who were sexually assaulted now had to decide whether they would seek counselling or initiate criminal prosecution of their assailant (Busby 1997, 2014).

In May 1997, in response to concerns raised over the *O'Connor* decision, Parliament passed Bill C-46 to limit the access of defendants to confidential records of complainants in sexual assault cases. The bill established more restrictive grounds for access, required the defence to establish that the records were relevant to the case at hand, and restricted the disclosure to those parts that were important to the case. Only a few months after its passage, the legislation was constitutionally challenged as a violation of the fair trial guarantees of the *Charter* and struck down by two lower courts. In 1999 the Supreme Court rendered its decision on this question in *R v Mills* (1999). While the Court held that the legislation governing the disclosure of records did not violate an accused's constitutional rights, some commentators, such as Gotell (2001, 340), argued that the decision did tame the meaning of the legislation: "To the extent that this decision eases the statutory test for disclosure put in place by Bill C-46, Canada remains a jurisdiction where women's claims of sexual violation can be discounted through records production."

More recently, an Alberta judge came under heavy criticism for his decision to acquit a man charged with the sexual assault of a 19-year-old woman in a bathroom during a house party in 2011. In hearing the case in 2014, Justice Robin Camp repeatedly referred to the complainant as "the accused." He also made several comments, such as asking the complainant: "Why didn't you just sink your bottom down into the basin so he couldn't penetrate you?" And "Why couldn't you just keep your knees together?" As well, Justice Camp indicated that the young woman had not explained "why she had allowed the sex to happen if she didn't want it." When the complainant testified that the assault hurt, the judge commented, "Sex and pain sometimes go together . . . that's not necessarily a bad thing." He also said that because the complainant was intoxicated, there was "an onus on her to be more careful." Meanwhile, the judge referred to the accused's testimony as reflecting "consensual, indeed even tender, sex" (Fine 2016). The Crown appealed the decision. The appeal court overturned the acquittal and ordered a new trial.

In November 2015 four feminist law professors launched a complaint with the Canadian Judicial Council regarding the conduct of Justice Camp, who had been promoted to the federal court in June 2015, ten months after hearing the sexual assault case. Justice Camp then volunteered to take a gender-sensitivity program and issued a formal apology to the complainant and to other women who were negatively affected by his comments. In March, 2017 the Council recommended that the judge be removed from the bench. He resigned the same day.

The accused, who had spent two years in remand custody, was found not guilty at the second trial. The judge said that the Crown did not meet the burden of proof to show guilty beyond a reasonable doubt, and that the complainant was inconsistent and lacked credibility.

This recent history of the law's treatment of sexual assault highlights a number of tensions. For one, there appears to be tension between the courts, whose decisions become binding as case law, and Parliament, which in passing statute law has endeavoured to be sensitive to the concerns raised by women's constituencies across the country. For another, there is a tension within the law with regard to competing rights, in particular, the right of a defendant to a fair trial compared to the right of a complainant to privacy. Clearly, the extent to which the legal system will be able to resolve these tensions and thereby offer women and men equal protection and treatment under the law is a matter of ongoing debate.

Although the national directive to police forces in 1983 resulted in increasing numbers of domestic assault charges entering the criminal justice system, several provinces took further steps to respond to the problem of wife assault. In Winnipeg, for example, a specialized Family Violence Court was established in 1990. The number of spousal assault cases dealt with by this court rose from 1,302 in 1990–91 to 3,543 in 1993–94, a 172 percent increase (Ursel 1998). A large part of this increase was attributable to the implementation of a zero tolerance policy on domestic violence by the Winnipeg Police Service in 1993. Under this policy, police were instructed to lay a charge when there were reasonable grounds to believe that a domestic assault had occurred, whether or not the victim wished to proceed with the matter and even in circumstances where there were no visible injuries or independent witnesses. The zero tolerance policy resulted in increasing numbers of men—and women—being charged. However, a high proportion of charges resulted in a dismissal or stay of proceedings. One Winnipeg study, for instance, found that 80 percent of charges against women and 51 percent of those against men were subsequently stayed by the Crown (Comack, Chopyk, and Wood 2000). While the intent of this more rigorous charging protocol was to assist victims of domestic violence (who are predominantly women), zero tolerance opened the way for "double charging" to occur—that is, both partners ended up being charged with an offence when police were called to the scene. Comack and colleagues found that double charging occurred in 55 percent of the cases they studied involving women accused and in 10 percent of those cases involving men. Stays of proceedings were even higher in these cases (88% and 70%, respectively). Wood (2001) found that the zero tolerance charging appeared to have a racialized impact. Prior to 1993, white men had been more likely than Indigenous men to be charged with domestic violence, but after the implementation of the police protocol in 1993, Indigenous men were more likely to be charged with domestic violence. In a similar vein, other researchers have showcased the differential impacts of mandatory charging and no-drop prosecutorial policies on immigrant and refugee women, particularly those with precarious legal status (Martin and Mosher 1995). In sum, while the changes that have occurred within the criminal justice system have a symbolic value—they carry a strong message that society is unwilling to tolerate wife abuse—feminists have questioned whether the criminal justice system, which is punitive and adversarial by nature, is the most effective means for combating the problem (see, for example, Snider 1991, 1994).

Blurred Boundaries: Women as Victims and Offenders

Breaking the silence around male violence against women has had an impact on how feminist criminologists understand the lives of criminalized women. Clearly, violence against women both reflects and reinforces women's inequality in society in relation to men. As *The War Against Women* (1991, 9) report noted, "The vulnerability of women to violence is integrally linked to the social, economic and political inequalities women experience as part of their daily lives." How, then, does this gender-based violence figure in the lives of criminalized women?

Several studies carried out in the 1990s revealed the extent of abuse experienced by criminalized women. Research conducted for the Task Force on Federally Sentenced Women, for instance, found that 68 percent of women serving a federal term of imprisonment in Canada had been physically abused as children or adults and that 53 percent had been sexually abused at some point in their lives. Among Indigenous women, the figures were considerably higher: 90 percent said they had been physically abused and 61 percent reported sexual abuse (Shaw et al. 1991, vii and 31). Another study of women in a provincial jail found that 78 percent of the women admitted over a six-year period reported a history of physical and sexual abuse (Comack 1993).

Qualitative research conducted by feminist criminologists explored women's accounts of their lawbreaking and its connections to abuse (see, for example, Gilfus 1992; Adelberg and Currie 1993; Sommers 1995; Ritchie 1996). *Women in Trouble* (Comack 1996) was built around the stories of 24 women who were incarcerated in a provincial jail. The women's stories revealed the connections between a woman's law violations and her history of abuse to be complex. Sometimes the connections are direct, as in the case of women who are criminalized for resisting their abusers. Janice, for instance, was serving a sentence for manslaughter. The offence occurred at a party:

> I was at a party, and this guy, older guy, came, came on to me. He tried telling me, "Why don't you go to bed with me. I'm getting some money, you know." And I said, "No." And then he started hitting me. And then he raped me. And then [pause] I lost it. Like, I just, I went, I got very angry and I snapped. And I started hitting him. I threw a coffee table on top of his head and then I stabbed him. (Janice, cited in Comack, 1996, 96)

Sometimes the connections become discernable only once a woman's law violations are located in the context of her struggle to cope with the abuse and its effects. Merideth, for example, had a long history of abuse that began with her father sexually assaulting her as a young child and that extended to several violent relationships with the men in her life. She was imprisoned for writing cheques on her bank account when she didn't have the money to cover them. The cheques were used to purchase "new things to keep my mind off the abuse":

> I've never had any kind of conflict with the law. [long pause] When I started dealing with all these different things, then I started having problems. And then I took it out in the form of fraud. (Merideth, cited in Comack, 1996, 86)

SEARCH FOR:
Canadian Association of Elizabeth Fry Societies

Sometimes the connections are even more entangled, as in the case of women who end up on the street, where abuse and law violation become enmeshed in their ongoing struggle to survive. Brenda had this to say about street life:

> Street life is a, it's a power game, you know? Street life? You have to show you're tough. You have to beat up this broad or you have to shank this person, or, you know, you're always carrying guns, you always have blow on you, you always have drugs on you, and you're always working the streets with the pimps and the bikers, you know? That, that alone, you know, it has so much fucking abuse, it has more abuse than what you were brought up with! . . . I find living on the street I went through more abuse than I did at home. (Brenda, cited in Comack, 1996, 105–6)

This kind of work subsequently became known as pathways research—a term that has been applied to a variety of studies, all of them sharing the effort to better understand the lives of women and girls and the particular features that led to their criminal activity (see, for example, Chesney-Lind and Rodriguez 1983; Miller 1986; Arnold 1995; Heimer 1995; Chesney-Lind and Shelden 1998). In drawing the connections between women's law violations and their histories of abuse, pathways research led to a blurring of boundaries between "offender" and "victim" and raised questions about the legal logic of individual culpability and law's strict adherence to victim/offender dualism in the processing of cases (not only for women but also for poor, racialized men; see Comack and Balfour 2004). It also had a decided influence on advocacy work conducted on behalf of imprisoned women. For instance, *Creating Choices*, the 1990 report of the Canadian Task Force on Federally Sentenced Women, proposed a new prison regime for women that would incorporate feminist principles and attend to women's needs (see Shaw 1993; Hannah-Moffat and Shaw 2000; Hannah-Moffat 2001; Hayman 2006). The near-complete absence of counselling services and other resources designed to help women overcome victimization experiences (see Kendall 1993) figured prominently in the Task Force's recommendations.

THE CANADIAN PRESS/The Waterloo Region Record—David Bebee

Grand Valley Institution for Women in Kitchener, Ontario, is one of the federal prisons for women that opened in 1997.

As Snider (2003, 364) notes, feminist criminologists succeeded in reconstituting the criminalized woman as the "woman in trouble." Less violent and less dangerous than her male counterpart, she was more deserving of help than punishment. When women did engage in violence, it was understood as a self-defensive reaction typically committed in a domestic context (Browne 1987; Dobash and Dobash 1992; Jones 1994). Nevertheless, while the concept of blurred boundaries and the construct of the woman in trouble were important feminist contributions to criminology, they had particular ramifications for the ability of feminist criminologists to counter competing knowledge claims—ones founded on representations of women not as victims but as violent and dangerous.

The Violent Woman

One decisive event that challenged the blurred boundaries between victim and offender was the Karla Homolka case. In July 1993, Homolka was sentenced to 12 years in prison for her part in the deaths of two teenage girls, Kristen French and Leslie Mahaffy. Homolka's sentence was part of a plea bargain reached with the Crown in exchange for her testimony against her husband, Paul Bernardo. The Crown had entered into this plea bargain prior to the discovery of six homemade videotapes that documented the sexual abuse and torture of the pair's victims—including Homolka's younger sister, Tammy. Bernardo was subsequently convicted of first-degree murder, kidnapping, aggravated sexual assault, forcible confinement, and offering an indignity to a dead body. He was sentenced to life imprisonment in September 1995 (McGillivray 1998, 257).

During Bernardo's trial, the real challenge came in trying to explain the role of Homolka, the prosecution's key witness. As Boritch (1997, 2) notes, "Among the various professionals who commented on the case, there was a general agreement that, as far as serial murderers go, there was little that was unusual or mysterious about Bernardo. We have grown used to hearing about male serial murderers." As it turned out, Homolka was the central enigma of the drama that unfolded; it was she who transformed the trial into an international media event.

The legal documents and media accounts of the case offered two primary readings of Homolka. The first reading constructed her as a battered wife, one of Bernardo's many victims (he had also been exposed as "the Scarborough rapist"). A girlish 17-year-old when she met the 23-year-old Bernardo, Homolka had entered into a relationship that progressed to a fairytale wedding (complete with horse-drawn carriage) and ended with a severe battering (complete with darkened and bruised raccoon eyes). According to this first reading, Homolka was under her husband's control and had no agency of her own. Like other women who find themselves in an abusive relationship, she was cast as a victim and diagnosed as suffering from the battered woman syndrome, a psychological condition of "learned helplessness" that ostensibly prevents abused women from leaving the relationship (Walker 1979, 1987). The representation of Homolka as a battered wife and "compliant victim" of her sexually sadistic husband (Hazelwood, Warren, and Dietz 1993) was meant to bolster her credibility as a prosecution witness and validate her plea bargain. This first reading met strong resistance in the media and public discourse, leading to the second reading. Journalist

Patricia Pearson (1995), for one, vigorously countered the picture of "Homolka as victim" and instead demonized her as a "competitive narcissist" willing to offer up innocent victims (including her own sister) to appease the sexual desires of her sociopathic husband. Notwithstanding their divergent viewpoints, both of these readings relied on the discourse of the "psy-professions" (psychology, psychotherapy, and psychiatry) to make sense of Homolka.

Feminist criminologists countered both of these readings. For instance, they pointed out that women are seldom charged with murder and that when they do kill, they are most likely to kill their male partner. Also, while Homolka's middle-class background and lifestyle set her apart from the vast majority of women charged with criminal offences, her efforts to conform to the standard feminine script (dyed blonde hair, fairy-tale wedding) put her in company with a host of other women.

Kilty and Frigon (2006, 2016) offer a more nuanced account in their analysis of the Homolka case. Reinterpreting the two readings of Homolka—battered wife versus competitive narcissist—as depictions of her as either "in danger" or "dangerous," they argue that these constructions are related rather than mutually exclusive. While emphasizing that the abuse Homolka endured at the hands of Bernardo does not excuse her criminality, they maintain that it did constrain her choices. As such, she was *both* a "woman in danger" *and* a "dangerous woman." Kilty and Frigon (2006, 58) argue, therefore, that "rather than constructing these two concepts as dialectically opposed one must understand them as being interdependent, or more accurately, as along a continuum." Other feminist criminologists intent on understanding the links between women's experiences of violence and their own use of violence have adopted this shift away from dualistic (victim/offender) thinking and towards the use of a continuum metaphor.

The Victimization–Criminalization Continuum

The "victimization–criminalization continuum" is used to signify the myriad ways in which women's experiences of victimization—including not only violence but also social and economic marginalization—constrain or narrow their social supports and available options and leave them susceptible to criminalization (Faith 1993). The continuum draws on insights from intersectionality theory (Crenshaw 1989) to showcase how systemic factors (relating to patriarchy, poverty, and colonialism) intersect or interconnect to contribute to women's vulnerability to victimization, thereby restricting their agency or capacity to make choices. Kaiser-Derrick (2012, 63) suggests that in contrast to the more linear pathways approach, the continuum can be envisioned as a web, "with many incursions and redirections from external forces (broad, structural issues like poverty and discrimination, as well as events within women's lives often stemming from those structural issues such as relationship dissolution or the removal of children by the state)."

Balfour (2008), for instance, adopts the victimization–criminalization continuum to explore the relationship between the inordinate amounts of violence experienced by Indigenous women and their punishment by the criminal justice system. She argues that even though sentencing reforms have been introduced to encourage alternatives to incarceration, women's narratives of violence and social isolation continue to be excluded in sentencing practices, leading to spiralling rates of imprisonment for Indigenous women. Similarly, Kaiser-Derrick (2012) shows how judges translate discourses about victimization and criminalization into a judicial approach that frames sentences for Indigenous women as "healing oriented"; in essence, Indigenous women's victimization experiences are interpreted by the courts as precipitating the need for treatment in prison.

Gendering Crime

The feminist critique of criminology and the effort to draw attention to the gendered nature of women's lives led to calls to "gender" crime more broadly. Women, it was argued, were not the only ones with a gender; men's lives too needed to be understood in gendered terms. In this regard, critics pointed out that while criminology had long been characterized by its neglect of the female, the discipline's lack of capacity to explain *male* patterns of criminal activity was just as troublesome. Since the 1990s, various criminologists have responded by initiating studies of men, masculinity, and crime.

One criminologist who has taken up this project is Messerschmidt (1993, 2004, 2012, 2013, 2015). In his endeavour to contribute to a "feminist theory of gendered crime" (1993, 62), Messerschmidt designed a theory that situates men's involvement in crime in the context of "doing" masculinity. Following on the work of West and Zimmerman (1987), gender is viewed as a "situated accomplishment." While sex is the social identification of individuals as man or woman, gender is the accomplishment of that identification in social interaction: "we coordinate our activities to 'do' gender in situational ways" (1993, 79). In the process, individuals realize that their behaviour is accountable to others and so construct their actions "in relation to how they might be interpreted by others in the particular social context in which they occur" (1993, 79). In a culture that believes there are but two sexes—male and female—this accountability will

TABLE 6.1 ■ Theories of Women's Crime

Theory	Theorists	Key Elements
Early theorists	Lombroso/Ferrero, Thomas, Glueck/Glueck, Pollak	Women's "inherent nature" and their natural inferiority to men account for the nature and extent of their criminality.
Sex role socialization	Hoffman-Bustamante	Differential socialization of females is reflected in the types of offences they commit and the nature of their participation in crime.
Power-control theory	Hagan/Simpson/Gillis	Gender differences in delinquency can be explained by variations in parental control. Girls in patriarchal families will be less free to deviate than those in egalitarian families.
Women's liberation thesis	Adler, Simon	Women's changing gender roles are reflected in the nature and extent of their criminal involvement. Women are becoming "more like men"—more aggressive and violent—and have greater opportunities to commit crime
Intersectionality theories	Carlen, Chesney-Lind, Balfour, Comack, Daly, Gilfus, Kaiser-Derrick, Morris, Naffine	Intersecting, structured inequalities of class, race, and gender (including experiences of male violence) condition and constrain the lives of criminalized women.

involve living up to the gender ideals that have been tied to each sex—that is, behaving "as a man" or "as a woman" would in a given social situation. Because we accomplish masculinity and femininity in specific situations (though not necessarily in circumstances of our own choosing), these are never static or finished products.

Messerschmidt borrows the concept of "hegemonic masculinity" from the work of Connell (1987, 1995, 2000). Connell was interested in how a particular gender order—a "historically constructed pattern of power relations between men and women and definitions of femininity and masculinity" (1987, 98–99)—comes to be reproduced in society. Connell suggested that male dominance in the gender order is achieved through the ascendancy of a particular idealized form of masculinity that is culturally glorified, honoured, and exalted. **Hegemonic masculinity** therefore references not just a set of role expectations or identity; it is a "pattern of practice" (Connell and Messerschmidt 2005, 832). Different from a male sex role, this cultural ideal may not correspond with the actual personalities of the majority of men, and it may well not be "normal" in a statistical sense, for only a minority of men may enact it. In these terms, exemplars such as sports heroes, movie stars, and even fantasy figures (such as Rambo and The Terminator) offer representations of masculinity that come to be normative in the sense that they embody "the currently most honored way of being a man." This requires all other men (including gay men and transgender men) to position themselves in relation to these representations (Connell and Messerschmidt 2005, 832).

Messerschmidt argues that it is in the process of "doing" masculinity that men simultaneously construct forms of criminality. He explains: "Because types of criminality are possible only when particular social conditions present themselves, when other masculine resources are unavailable, particular types of crime can provide an alternative resource for accomplishing gender and, therefore, affirming a particular type of masculinity" (1993, 84). Messerschmidt subsequently put his theory to work to understand varieties of youth crime, street crime, corporate crime, sexual harassment in the workplace, wife beating, and rape (Messerschmidt 1993). Key to his analysis is the thesis that gendered power is central to understanding why men commit more crimes and more serious crimes than women: crime is one practice in which and through which men's power over women can be established, and the different types of crime men may commit are determined by the power relations among them (1993, 84).

In his later writing, Messerschmidt (2004) went on to revise his theorizing on masculinity and crime in relation to the issue of "sexed bodies." Focusing on bodies as "sexed" represents an effort to transcend the sex/gender distinction found in earlier criminological theories to showcase how our bodies are more than just markers of difference (as male or female). In these terms, *embodiment* is considered central to our sense of self; it is our way of being in the world and therefore an essential part of our subjectivity or identity. How we experience our bodies as male or female is not direct or unmediated; it is a reflection of both our personal histories and the culturally shared notions of certain bodily forms. In this sense, femininity and masculinity are ways of living in differently shaped bodies and our identities as women and men are formed as ways of giving significance to different bodily forms.

hegemonic masculinity
A particular idealized form of masculinity that is culturally glorified, honoured, and exalted. For example, associating "the masculine" with physical strength, aggression, independence, ambition, lack of emotion, and heterosexuality.

Messerschmidt (2004) adopts this "sexed bodies" approach to "bring the body back in" to criminology by concentrating on embodiment as a lived aspect of gender, on the ways in which our bodies constrain and facilitate social action and therefore mediate and influence social practices. "Doing gender" is therefore both mindful and physical; "it is impossible to consider human agency—and therefore crime and violence—without taking gendered embodiment into account" (49). Utilizing case studies of two white working-class boys and two white working-class girls involved in assaultive violence, Messerschmidt explores how motivations for violence (and nonviolence) emerge in three different sites—the home, the school, and the street—in the life histories of these youth. In the process, he is able to show "how gender difference is not simply constructed between boys and girls (as most criminologists contend), but it is also prominent among boys and among girls as well as individually *across* the three settings" (131).

QUESTIONS FOR CRITICAL THINKING

1. In what ways does the victimization–criminalization continuum disrupt our understanding of individual culpability in the commission of crime?
2. How does making gender a central focus of criminology affect the ways in which criminologists study men's involvement in crime?

Summary

- One of the primary aims of the feminist engagement with criminology has been to bring women into view. This has involved a re-evaluation of the accumulated knowledge about criminalized women, the nature of their offending, and the claims made about their "differences" from males. In the process, mainstream criminologists have been forced to consider how their traditional subject matter—men and male criminality—has influenced their theories and research.

- Feminist criminologists have argued that understanding women's involvement in crime requires an awareness of the larger social context, specifically, the intersecting, structured inequalities of class, race, and gender that condition and constrain the lives of criminalized women.

- Breaking the silence around male violence against women has meant questioning the ways in which societal and legal responses reinforce and reproduce the problem.

- Making women more visible in criminology requires not simply letting women into the mainstream of the discipline but developing alternative ways of conceptualizing and studying the social world so that the interests and concerns of both men and women are included. In the process, the criminological enterprise is itself transformed.

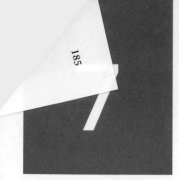

Victimology, Victim Services, and Victim Rights in Canada

IRVIN WALLER
University of Ottawa

Learning Objectives

After reading this chapter, you should be able to

- Discuss the risk of being a victim of crime and comprehend the key components of the harm suffered by victims of crime.

- Outline the way in which the traditional system of police, courts, and corrections in Canada limits the role of the victim to complainant and witness.

- Identify the key laws and international standards that provide the vision for the shift from the traditional criminal justice system to a system that embraces the needs and human rights of victims.

- Propose specific and basic ways for police to meet the needs of victims, including victims of gender-related crimes and child victims of violence.

- Specify the ways in which restitution from the offender, civil remedies, restorative justice, and compensation from the state will repair damage to victims.

- Debate ways for victims of crime to have their basic human rights respected in criminal courts.

- Understand the key components of system-wide strategies for stopping violence and repeat victimization.

- Justify actions likely to shift crime policy from the traditional system to one that embraces reducing victimization and providing services and rights for victims of crime.

For centuries, the traditional system of law enforcement, criminal justice, and corrections has focused on catching, convicting, and, in some cases fining or incarcerating offenders. The role of the victim has been limited to calling the police, collaborating with the police investigation when asked, and acting as a witness in the court case. But the conversation is shifting as federal, provincial, and municipal governments begin to focus on preventing harm to victims and providing services and rights for victims of crime.

Many criminologists blame political pressure from victims of crime for the increases in incarceration that politicians have implemented, particularly in the United States, over the past four decades. In Canada, the federal government led by Prime Minister Stephen Harper justified its actions as giving precedence to the rights of victims of crime over the rights of offenders. The Harper government focused on increasing penalties, particularly for those serving long sentences; but it has also established the Ombudsman for Crime Victims, and in 2015 it adopted the Bill of Rights for Victims.

Victimologists argue that offering empathy and expanding services and rights for victims of crime would decrease the desire of victims for punishment. They also stress that crime victims' rights would be upheld most strongly if governments invested in effective ways to *prevent* victimization; this would best be achieved by governments investing in proven prevention methods and moving away from ineffective and costly responses to crime such as reactive policing, mass incarceration, and long prison sentences.

Victims of crime are often described as the orphans of criminal justice. They are also the orphans of criminology. Many criminology students still graduate without having learned what we know about victims or about the needs and human rights of victims. This means students may be misled by many myths about victims, including the extent to which victims actually want more severe punishment.

This chapter is organized around four key areas of modern victimology: (1) prevalence, impact, and needs of victims; (2) the origins of victimology and international standards; (3) policing, victim services and compensation, courts, and restitution; and (4) how to rebalance the justice system to respect victims' human rights.

Prevalence, Impact, and Needs of Victims

As you learned in Chapter 4, weaknesses in police crime statistics have led criminologists to collect information from victimization surveys. These surveys are conducted annually in many other countries, but in Canada they are conducted only every five years, and they do not receive the attention they deserve from criminologists, the media, or politicians.

A summary of some of the data on risk of victimization provided by Statistics Canada victimization surveys is outlined in Box 7.1. The main source of data about the prevalence of victimization in Canada among adults 15 years and older is the General Social Survey (GSS). This survey shows the following:

- More than one-quarter of adult Canadians are victimized each year by one of the crimes included in the survey.

- This rate of victimization has not changed significantly over the past 20 years.

- Adult victims of violent crimes are young (the age group of 15–24 has reported being victimized more than 15 times more often than the 65 and older age group); more likely to be male, except for sexual assault; and more likely to be Indigenous (Perreault, 2015).

FOCUS   BOX 7.1

A SNAPSHOT OF VICTIMIZATION IN CANADA

On average, each year in Canadian cities of more than 1,000,000 population, interpersonal crime causes victims $1.5 billion in costs and pain and suffering. That figure includes the one in 15 adults who are victims of violence such as assault or sexual assault and the one in 7 adults who are victims of a property offence such as theft or a break-in.

Fewer than one in three victims will call the police to report the victimization, and less than one in 10 will report the offence of sexual assault.

- Fewer than three percent of victims will see "their" offender convicted.
- Local urban police services will cost $240 million out of local taxes, and other policing services will cost $160 million;.
- Correctional services will cost $180 million out of federal and provincial taxes.
- Expenditures on victim services and rights in Canada, on the other hand, are a tiny $10 million, often paid out of a tax on fines.
- With some important exceptions, police are unlikely to inform victims of the availability of services such as property repair, volunteer victim support, restitution, or compensation.

- Those working with victims are often volunteers, and those who are paid will typically be paid less than half the salary of police officers.
- Most eligible victims will not know of or receive restitution or compensation.
- Victim impact statements do not impact sentences.
- Despite a new federal Victims Bill of Rights and some provincial acts, victims do not have remedies for their rights except through the Federal Ombudsman in relation to Corrections.

Questions for Critical Thinking

1. Go back to the discussion of the development of criminal law in Chapter 2. How and why did victims lose their role in the criminal justice system?

2. What services and programs for victims of crime are available in your community?

Sources: "Statistics Canada General Social Survey 2014"; Jacob Greenland and Sarah Alam, "Police resources in Canada, 2016" (Ottawa: Statistics Canada, 2017); Julie Reitano, "Adult correctional statistics in Canada, 2015/2016" (Ottawa: Statistics Canada, 2017); Parliamentary Budget Officer, *Expenditure Analysis of Criminal Justice in Canada*, Ottawa, 2013.

Figure 7.1 shows the rates of victimization for seven of the offences included in the Statistics Canada GSS for the last six times the survey was conducted—1988, 1993, 1999, 2004, 2009, and 2014. These rates show substantial decreases in all types of crime in the 2014 survey.

repeat victimization
The phenomenon of a person being a victim of a crime more than once.

Repeat victimization of the same victim (or victim's household) has often been observed in victimization surveys. According to the 2004 Statistics Canada Survey, of those who stated that they had been victimized by a crime during the preceding 12 months, 40 percent reported that they had been victimized more than once.

As in other countries, these surveys show victimization to be concentrated in certain areas, families, and individuals. In the 2014 survey, the following categories of people were the most likely to be victims of violent crimes: women; Indigenous people; those 20 to 24 years of age; drug users and binge drinkers; those who are out frequently in the evening; those with mental health problems; people who are LGBTQ; those who had suffered maltreatment as children; and those who were homeless. Indigenous women were particularly likely to be victims of violence.

Impact of Victimization

harms to victims
The direct impact of crime on victims includes harm, such as loss, injury, pain, and emotional trauma. These can be exacerbated by the victim's experience with the police, courts, corrections, and others.

Crime causes financial loss, injury, and emotional pain and trauma to victims. These **harms to victims** can also extend to others, including the spouse, parents,

FIGURE 7.1 ■ Rates of Victimization in Canada (1988, 1993, 1999, 2004, 2009, 2014)

(a) Rates of Victimization (per 1,000 Population Age 15 Years and Older)

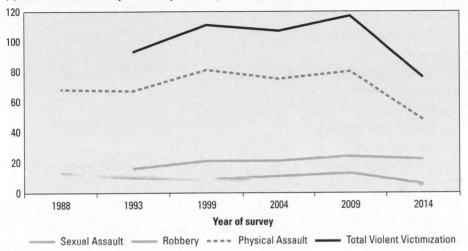

Sexual Assault ——— Robbery ----- Physical Assault ——— Total Violent Victimization

(b) Rates of Victimization (per 1,000 Households)

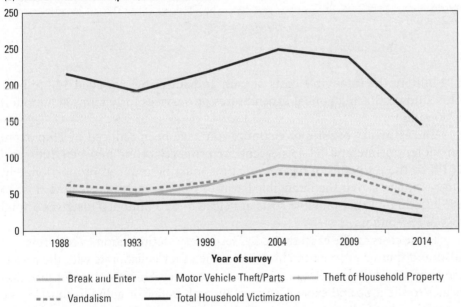

Break and Enter ——— Motor Vehicle Theft/Parts ——— Theft of Household Property
----- Vandalism ——— Total Household Victimization

Sources: Statistics Canada General Social Survey 1999; 2004; 2009; 2014.

and friends of the victims. Some of the consequences of victimization include injuries such as cuts and broken bones, diseases (STDs, HIV/AIDS, etc.), and pain; emotional trauma, which can manifest itself as anger, fear, shock, depression, or post-traumatic stress disorder and can lead to physical symptoms; and financial loss due to stolen or damaged property, medical care costs, or loss of wages.

In 2011, Justice Canada released a report showing the tangible costs and pain and suffering to victims of crime, using the victimization survey from 2004 (Zhang 2011). This report concluded that the total annual cost of harm to victims in 2008 was $83 billion (Table 7.1). The tangible costs exceeded

TABLE 7.1 ■ Estimates of Costs of Crime for Victims, 2008

Victim Costs—Tangible Costs	$ (millions)
Health care	1,443
Productivity losses	6,734
Stolen/damaged property	6,143
Total tangible victim costs	14,320
Selected Services—Tangible Costs	**$ (millions)**
Victim services and compensation programs	451
Shelters for victims	254
Other expenditures related to crime	238
Total selected services costs	943
Victim Costs—Intangible Costs	**$ (millions)**
Pain and suffering	65,100
Loss of life (homicides)	3,055
Total intangible victim costs	68,155
Grand Total	83,418

Source: Zhang Ting, "Summary Table 1: Estimated Tangible Costs of Crime in Canada, 2008," in *Costs of Crime in Canada, 2008*, Web; Department of Justice Canada, 2003. Reproduced with the permission of the Minister of Public Works and Government Services Canada, 2014.

$14 billion; the intangible costs of pain and suffering exceeded $68 billion. This study estimated annual expenditures on services for victims at a modest $750 million.

The estimates of rates of victimization have been reduced by 29 percent for violent crime and by 43 percent for property crime between 2004 and 2014, so the estimates of harm to victims must be reduced proportionately. One estimate is that the intangible harm to victims each year is now close to $45 billion and that tangible costs are close to $10 billion. This gives a total loss of $55 billion.

These costs can be exacerbated by "secondary victimization," which refers to costs and trauma experienced by victims when they collaborate with the police, the courts, and the correctional system as witnesses. Some of this victimization relates to the time and expense of meeting with police or going to court. Some is emotional as feelings and fears are stirred by revisiting what happened. Some reflects dissatisfaction with the way victims are treated by the system.

Expenditures on police, courts, and corrections are rising. By 2016 they had reached $22 billion (Table 7.2). It is estimated that between 50 and 60 percent of police costs are used to respond to 911 calls made by or on behalf of crime victims (Waller 2008; Skogan and Frydl 2004). Additional police costs—probably close to 20 percent—are incurred by the detectives investigating crimes. Some politicians assign these policing expenditures, in addition to the costs of criminal courts and corrections, as costs incurred by victims, but in fact these are costs incurred by taxpayers generally, and not always for harms to victims. However, police costs have doubled since 2000 and are expected to continue rising faster than other government expenditures.

TABLE 7.2 ■ Costs of Criminal Justice in Canada, 2016

Criminal Justice System Costs	$ (millions)
Police	14,200
Court	3,300
Corrections	4,600
Total	22,100

Source: Jacob Greenland and Sarah Alam, "Police resources in Canada, 2016" (Ottawa: Statistics Canada, 2017); Parliamentary Budget Officer, *Expenditure Analysis of Criminal Justice in Canada*, Ottawa, 2013.

Needs of Crime Victims

International organizations such as the International Association of Chiefs of Police (IACP 2008), researchers working on victims' needs, and victim organizations largely agree on eight **core rights of victims of crime**. These are articulated under three broader categories: support, justice, and governance (see Table 7.3).

Right to Recognition

Victims need to be recognized. Crimes are committed against people—they are not just an affront to the state. Human faces are associated with every robbery, rape, and assault. These are the faces of persons suffering loss, injury, and trauma at the hands of an offender who inflicted the harm.

Right to Information

Victims need to be provided with information. They need to know which services are available to them and what rights they have to recover reparation. They also need information regarding the police investigation, as well as the prosecution in criminal court if the offender is caught.

core rights of victims of crime
Legislators in different countries and intergovernmental agencies such as the UN have recognized various fundamental principles of justice and rights for victims of crime, such as the right to be informed, to receive restitution, and to be present when decisions such as bail or sentencing are being decided in court.

TABLE 7.3 ■ Core Rights for Victims of Crime and Likely Responses

	Core Needs for Victims of Crime	Right to Legislation and Implementation to Provide Support
	Support	
1	Recognition and emotional support	Trained informal and professional crisis support and counselling
2	Information on criminal justice, their case, services, and personal developments	Timely information on law enforcement, criminal justice, and corrections; case; assistance; and expected developments
3	Assistance to access practical, medical, and social services	Advocacy and assistance with repair, practical, social, and other services
	Justice	
4	Help to pay bills caused by victimization	Emergency funds and restitution from offender, compensation from state, and paid medical and mental health care
5	Personal safety and protection from accused	Prevention of revictimization and protection from accused
6	Choice to have voice in the justice process.	Choice to participate and be represented to defend safety, reparation, truth, and justice
	Good Government	
7	Best public safety	Modern strategies that reduce crime and prevent victimization
8	Implementation	Performance measures and surveys of victims as clients

Source: Irvin Waller. 2011. *Rights for Victims of Crime: Rebalancing Justice*, pp. 28–33. New York: Rowman and Littlefield. Reprinted by permission of Rowman & Littlefield Publishing Group.

Right to Assistance

Victims need to be informed about services, to be given access to these services, and to have them adequately funded. Specific services are required for victims of specific crimes; for example, rape victims, child abuse victims, and robbery victims require different types of services. Different types of services are also needed as the victims' needs evolve over time.

Right to Reparation

Victims need help to recover financially from their crime victimization. Some of this recovery should be through **restitution from the offender**. Some may be paid in **compensation from the state**. Some may come from civil suits against the offender or a third party.

restitution from the offender
Victims of any type of crime may request that the offender pay the victim money as reparation for financial or other losses caused by the crime.

compensation from the state
In most provinces, victims of crimes who suffered physical or other injuries may apply to an agency to receive lump sum or monthly payments according to provincial legislation.

Right to Be Protected from the Accused

Victims need to be protected from the accused, and not just through incarceration of the offender. Child victims and victims of domestic abuse are vulnerable to revictimization by the offender. The state needs to intervene to ensure this does not happen.

Right to Participation and Representation

Victims need to be able to participate and to be represented in the criminal justice process, whenever their personal interests are affected. Those interests may relate to restitution, information, privacy, justice, and of course their own safety. This goes beyond a victim impact statement, which only allows the victim to discuss the impact of the crime on them.

Right to Effective Policies to Reduce Victimization

Governments need to implement programs that are known to be effective in preventing the first victimization and any repetition. It is not enough to simply punish offenders after the fact.

Right to Implementation

A victim does not have a right unless there is a remedy. Many of the principles of justice and bills of rights in Canada (and in other countries) have not been adequately implemented, and the provisions for remedy are limited or nonexistent. The 2014 federal legislation provides some rights, but with an untested complaint process.

The Origins of Victimology and International Standards

In the 1960s, pioneers of what would become victimology and victims' rights began seeking changes in the treatment of victims of crime. Their motives centred on concern for victims. Some of these pioneers, shocked by the treatment of victims of violence against women, founded rape crisis centres and refuges for battered wives. The first organizations formed by crime victims—particularly by the parents of murdered children—began to demand reforms to police practices, court procedures, and parole decision making (Amernic 1984). Other reformers had different motivations. Some started victim-witness assistance programs to support the traditional system of criminal justice by attempting to increase the proportion of crime victims going to police and cooperating with prosecutors. Some promoted victim–offender mediation and restorative justice programs in an effort to make the traditional system less harsh on offenders. Some undertook the first victimization surveys to develop better data on the extent of crime.

These disparate groups became part of an international movement that brought together advocates for victims' services and rights, many of whom worked in academe or in the trenches with victims. Initially they were fighting for changes within their own countries, but soon they discovered that the problems of victims crossed national borders.

In 1979, a nongovernmental organization, the World Society of Victimology (WSV), was formed to allow all the various researchers, policy-makers, and service providers to pursue their common interests and to exchange their knowledge and experiences. This group has organized regular symposiums and sponsored courses for graduate students.

Magna Carta for Victims

The WSV quickly began to put social science knowledge, human rights principles, and international collaboration to work by influencing the UN. In 1985 the UN General Assembly adopted a landmark resolution that recognized that crimes are not just against the state—they also do harm to victims. It called for a shift away from the traditional criminal justice approach towards one that would emphasize both prevention of victimization and respect for the human rights of victims of crime. Every government in the world is part of the UN General

Several international organizations, including the UN, have been strong advocates for adopting evidence-based crime prevention programs.

Songquan Deng/Shutterstock.com

Assembly, so every government has endorsed this resolution, whose "technical" name is the UN General Assembly Resolution 1985 A/30/44 on the Declaration of Basic Principles of Justice for Victims of Crime and Abuse of Power.

The resolution commits governments to (1) implement basic principles of justice for victims of crime and abuse of power and (2) prevent victimization through a series of comprehensive measures, which include attacking social causes and fostering individual responsibility.

The UN Declaration is organized under these rubrics:

- Information on criminal justice, their case, and services
- Assistance to access practical, medical and social services
- Guidelines and training for police, health, and other services
- Reparation through restitution and state compensation
- Right and access to justice (voice in justice)

This UN Declaration has become the benchmark for basic services and rights for victims. It is often referred to as the Magna Carta for victims of crime because through it, for the first time, the UN has endorsed their basic human rights. It has also shifted the traditional system away from its obsession with courtroom battles towards comprehensive efforts to end victimization and to provide services to crime victims.

However, this shift is happening extremely slowly. The traditional system of police, courts, and corrections is vast as well as resistant to change. In part, criminology has perpetuated this by focusing on the negative aspects of sentencing and prisons without providing alternatives.

Origins of Victims' Rights Policies in Canada

The first seeds of policies to help victims in Canada were sown in the 1960s. In 1967, Saskatchewan joined jurisdictions such as New Zealand, the UK, and California in providing compensation to victims of violent crime. In the 1970s the first criminological monographs on crime victims were published on victims of burglary (Waller and Okihiro 1978) and rape (Clarke and Lewis 1977). These studies remain models of what criminology can do to focus efforts on the prevention of crime, including violence against women, and to change the response to victims.

In 1981 the US National Organization for Victim Assistance and the Canadian Council for Social Development organized a major international conference in Toronto with significant funding from the federal and Ontario governments to discuss the topic of assistance for victims of crime. That conference led to a federal–provincial task force of public servants. In 1983 that task force made a number of recommendations, including these:

1. Gather survey data on numbers of victims.
2. Provide information for victims.
3. Provide services for victims.
4. Provide restitution, compensation, and property return.
5. Protect victims from intimidation.
6. Provide victim impact statements to assist with restitution, and hold trials within a reasonable time.
7. Pay for services using a fine surtax on offenders.
8. Monitor the implementation of recommendations.

However, this report had been produced behind closed doors by public servants working for the traditional system, and it did not reflect the growing body of social science knowledge about victims. The committee's lack of attention to participatory justice and to the emotional trauma experienced by victims meant that its report neglected the importance of victim participation in justice processes, prevention of victimization, and mental health services.

In the United States, in stark contrast, the President's Task Force (1982) followed a much more scientific and more transparent procedure and arrived at a much broader and more comprehensive set of recommendations. It recommended ways the traditional system could be used to help meet the needs of crime victims. It also included major sections on mental health, as well as a draft constitutional amendment that would provide victims with standing equivalent to that of the offender at critical stages in the criminal justice process such as bail and sentencing.

In an attempt to do better than the provincial task force, Ontario's Justice Ministry organized a transparent consultation to review its recommendations. This new consultation heard from groups representing victims of crime, including the parents of children killed by drunk drivers as well as victims of sexual assault (Ontario 1984). The recommendations arising from this exercise addressed two important needs that had been overlooked by the public servants: to prevent crime, and to provide legal standing for victims in the criminal justice system. Unfortunately, the province's Attorney General, Roy McMurtry, on the advice of his officials, chose not to implement these additional recommendations, which would have aligned government policy more with the needs of crime victims than with the needs of the traditional system.

Tensions between Traditional and Human Rights for Victims

Canada supported the efforts in 1985 to get the UN General Assembly to adopt the declaration discussed earlier by organizing a preparatory meeting. However, two issues have impeded full respect for the basic human rights for victims of crime. One is resistance to change within the traditional system. The other is the gap between social science researchers and the lawyers who manage the traditional system. Unfortunately, the groups responsible for proposing and implementing reforms are part of the legal bureaucracy, which is committed to the traditional system. In Canada, this gap is sustained and exacerbated by a lack of transparency in the development of policies to meet victims' needs. This contrasts with developments in the UK and the United States, particularly at the national level.

In 1986, Manitoba was the first province to adopt legislation to provide services and some limited rights for victims of crime. This was inspired by pioneering legislation in Massachusetts, which established a compensation program that included a statement of standards for services as well as a central office to implement those standards. These and later federal legislative initiatives led to a system of fine surcharges to fund some victim services. Some assessments of these services suggest they are a patchwork; judges often do not order the **victim fine surcharge**. Unfortunately, there has not been sufficient research to measure the gap between what was promised and what was delivered.

victim fine surcharge
A monetary penalty similar to a fine, which can be assessed at sentence or added to a fine such as in a traffic violation, but can only be used by the government to fund services for victims.

In 1988, the federal and provincial ministers agreed to a Canadian Statement of Principles of Justice in an effort to "Canadianize" the UN Declaration. Though inspired by the UN resolution, this agreement fell far short of the UN position on issues of restitution, compensation, services, and a role for the victim in criminal justice.

The principles were associated with important but limited moves by most provinces to adopt legislation to provide some services for victims of crime. But these laws were often weak, and strong responsibility centres were not established to implement them. This was particularly true of Ontario. On 11 June 1996, An Act Respecting Victims of Crime—Victims' Bill of Rights was proclaimed law in Ontario. The act was described by the Ontario Ministry of the Attorney General as "a set of principles that guide how justice system officials should treat victims at different stages of the criminal justice process." The same act created an Office for Victims of Crime, but its role was limited to advising the Attorney General on victims' issues. Unfortunately, this ministry was dominated by lawyers from the traditional system, who seemed to have little interest in meeting the needs of victims and who were not familiar with current social science research and methods. As a result, there were no rights because there were no remedies. That is, the government made promises but did not provide a way for victims to ensure those promises are kept.

Though the intentions were good, these initiatives were very weak. A Canadian parliamentary committee reviewed progress on victims' services and published 17 recommendations to improve the situation. The committee held town hall meetings in different constituencies across Canada and listened to crime victims as well as experts. Their report, *Victims: A Voice Not a Veto* (Canada 2000), made significant recommendations for reform. For example, it called for the creation of an adequately funded, high-level leadership centre and for reforms to the basic principles.

When criticized by the Parliamentary Committee, the federal, provincial, and territorial governments revised their principles in 2003 to those set out in Box 7.2. As has often been the case in Canada, this was not a transparent process with input from experts and practitioners. They included some obvious good principles, but these were not drafted to facilitate effective ways to measure their implementation, as had been requested by the Parliamentary Committee. They also overlooked such basic issues as assistance to access services (other than information); help obtaining reparation, such as restitution and compensation (other than information); providing victims with a voice in justice; effective policies to prevent victimization; and ways to ensure and monitor implementation. Once again the results were disappointing, as the process was not open to victims' groups or to experts in measuring outcomes.

Some modifications have been made to the Criminal Code and to the Youth Criminal Justice Act to protect the privacy of victims, encourage restitution orders in criminal courts, and allow victim impact statements. However, the lack of attention to social science research measuring the impact of these changes means that little is known about the extent to which these provisions are, or are ever likely to be, used extensively.

Ontario has only recently started to use the victims' justice fund—the fund into which victim surcharges are paid—to expand victim services. In 2007, Ontario's Provincial Ombudsman undertook an inquiry into compensation for victims of violent crime. His report, tabled just before an election, labelled the system as "Adding

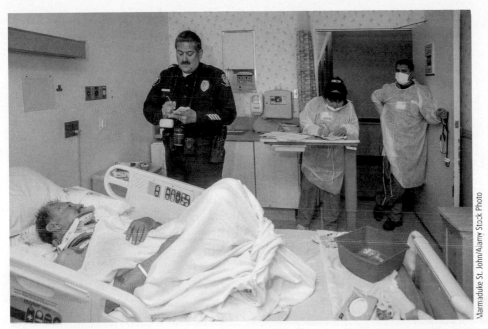

The personal costs of violent crime are very high. The costs to society include hospital costs, justice system costs, and lost productivity. Victims like this one face personal trauma, loss of income, and months of suffering. This is why many groups are advocating increased compensation and services for crime victims.

Marmaduke St. John/Alamy Stock Photo

Insult to Injury." The Ontario Attorney General responded by appointing the retiring Chief Justice of Ontario, Roy McMurtry, to investigate and make recommendations. His report measured the current services and compensation for victims of crime against the internationally agreed standards of the UN Declaration on Basic Principles of Justice. It made several practical recommendations for improvements, such as getting police to provide victims with information about victim services, using surveys of victims to measure gaps in the delivery of services, and so on. Ironically, McMurtry is the same person who more than 20 years earlier had resisted basic changes to fundamental rights for victims. His more enlightened and informed views in the recent report have still not been implemented by the Ontario government.

SEARCH FOR:
Victims Matter

Justice Canada launched an awareness campaign in 2010 called Victims Matter. It included a tool for identifying services for victims by postal code. While this is a start, these improvements fall far short of developments in comparable jurisdictions, as we will see in the next section.

SEARCH FOR:
Federal Ombudsman for Crime Victims

The Federal Ombudsman for Victims and the Bill of Rights for Victims

In 2007, the federal government established the office of the Federal Ombudsman for Victims of Crime (FOVC) to defend the rights of victims and to bring about systemic change at the federal level. The person appointed as ombudsman serves a three-year term with a staff of fewer than 10 and an equally small budget. The first appointee had to set up the office from scratch while dealing operationally with complaints (most of them concerning parole and provision of information) and identifying areas where reforms were needed.

The second appointee served two mandates. She has worked on two important reports that have helped shift the conversation in Canada towards victims. These reports have focused on restitution, the victim fine surcharge, victim impact statements, and the federal Bill of Rights. In June 2013 she organized a national meeting that brought together victims, victims' advocates, and academics to look at areas for improvement. The report of this meeting has been published on the FOVC website as *Moving the Conversation Forward*. It covers eight areas:

1. Criteria for who is a victim of crime
2. Equitable access to tangible supports for victims
3. Meaningful case information to victims
4. Awareness of and collaboration across the network of victims' services
5. Visibility of victims' voices
6. Prevention and safety
7. Equity of treatment before the law
8. Equity across all regions of the country

The same report calls for a more influential role for the FOVC and makes specific proposals for a federal Bill of Rights. In 2014, Prime Minister Stephen Harper announced legislation "to give victims of crime a more effective voice in the criminal justice system." Box 7.2 highlights the five key elements in the proposed legislation.

FOCUS   BOX 7.2

CANADIAN VICTIMS BILL OF RIGHTS

In April, 2014 the federal government introduced a bill—the Victims Bill of Rights Act—to create statutory rights at the federal level for victims of crime. This included the provision of complaint mechanisms. It became law in 2015.

Right to Information About:

- The status of the investigation and the criminal proceedings;
- The criminal justice system, the programs and services that are available to victims of crime;
- Reviews while the offender is subject to the Corrections process, or hearings after the accused is found not criminally responsible on account of mental disorder or unfit to stand trial, and the decisions made at those reviews and hearings;
- The complaint procedures that are available to them when their rights have been infringed or denied;

Right to Restitution:

- To have the courts consider making, in all cases, a restitution order against the offender;
- To have a restitution order entered as a civil court judgement that is enforceable against the offender if the amount owing under the restitution order is not paid.

Rights to Protection:

- To have their security and privacy considered by the appropriate authorities in the criminal justice system;
- To protection from intimidation and retaliation;

- To request testimonial aids (e.g., giving evidence in court by closed circuit television);

Right to Participation:

- To convey their views about decisions to be made by authorities in the criminal justice system that affect the rights of victim's rights under this Act and to have those views considered;
- To present a victim impact statement and to have it considered;

Right to Complain:

- Requirement for federal departments to create mechanisms for victims to complain if their rights have been infringed
- Separate from the bill, the federal government has proposed subsidies to facilitate complaint mechanisms by provinces in a manner that is consistent across Canada.

Questions for Critical Thinking

1. Many governments have claimed to be helping victims of crime by making sentences tougher. Why do many victim's groups not view this as a victims' rights issue?

2. While many governments have set out sound principles for ensuring greater victims' rights, the actual implementation of these principles has been very limited. Why are politicians so reluctant to keep their promises about the rights of victims?

Most experts and victims' groups are positive about this law and its provisions but are also disappointed with what it does *not* include. For example, the sections in the legislation on the right of victims to information do not state what the police should do to provide information. Also, the legislation does not extend the right to information to helping victims access services such as victim assistance or sexual assault crisis centres. Providing the right to restitution should increase its use by the courts, but the bill does not go far enough in requiring the offender to provide the court with information about his or her ability to pay. Also, the bill does not require parole boards to consider whether the offender has paid restitution. Furthermore, the onus is on the victim to bring a civil action, and this can be a complex process. In some US states, the state plays an active role in recovering the money. For example, in Vermont the state pays the restitution up to a specified amount and then sues the offender to recover the monies when necessary. The bill's section on the right to protection provides some improvements but does not specify how this protection is to be provided. The right to participation provides for limited input from the victim while continuing to allow victim impact statements. The text on complaint procedures is a start but does not identify which government department is responsible for implementing which section of the law, nor does it set any standards for these complaint procedures. If funding from the federal government is provided to provinces, then there may be some consistency in the way victims can complain across Canada.

The Federal Ombudsman for Victims of Crime has called the proposed legislation a "Cornerstone for Change" and has welcomed the proposed act, but has gone on to call for many improvements because the act addresses only four of the 30 areas of need identified by the ombudsman.

Perhaps the act's most significant weakness is that it does not specify a clear way of evaluating whether it has been properly implemented. In the United States in 2004, the federal victims' rights law included a requirement for the General Accounting Office (GAO) to monitor the implementation; as a result, the GAO has been able to recommend—on the basis of evidence—many improvements to police officers, prosecutors, and judges. Because these recommendations have been backed by evidence, the improvements have generally been made.

The rights in the bill do not refer to services, assistance, or compensation, which are the items generally considered to require the most funding. Also, funding from the federal government is very limited at this stage.

The bill's other major weakness is that it includes no reference to preventing violence. Yet current evidence suggests that a shift in funding towards proven and upstream violence prevention could achieve a 50 percent reduction in the number of victims as well as savings of billions of dollars in policing and justice system costs (see Waller 2014).

A Comparison of Canada to Other Jurisdictions

United States

In the United States, the federal Victims of Crime Act was adopted in 1984 to increase victim assistance services and criminal injuries compensation across the country. This legislation included the creation of the powerful and independently funded Office for Victims of Crime (OVC), which allocates close to $1 billion every year for victim assistance and compensation. This law has brought about dramatic improvements by ensuring that every state has a system for providing compensation to victims of violent crime and by multiplying the availability of victim assistance programs. It has also fostered research, training, and advocacy to improve rights and services for victims. In 2013, $9 billion was available in the OVC fund. Such funds come principally from fine surcharges against wealthy corporate offenders, of which the largest so far was the $1.2 billion Pfizer paid when settling allegations of fraud around Bextra and three other drugs. This shows how federal funds can be used to channel services, compensation, training, advocacy, and much more to victims of crime.

In 1994, the Violence Against Women Act was passed in the United States; it has since been reauthorized several times. This act established the Office on Violence Against Women as part of the US Department of Justice. That office is specifically mandated to improve services for female victims; its programs are tailored to issues of gender and to protecting victims from the accused.

In 2004 the United States adopted the Crime Victims' Rights Act, which provided six rights in federal courts, including the right to restitution and the right to be heard. The same act required the GAO to review how the act was operating and to recommend improvements. As a result, police, prosecutors, judges, and others have made significant improvements to services for crime victims federally. This is an important example of how social science research can improve practice.

Europe

In 2001, all member governments of the European Union (EU) adopted service standards for victims of crime. These standards cover a number of areas, including information, services, and mediation. To ensure implementation, a performance-monitoring mechanism has been established that includes independent monitoring—paid for by the EU—five years after the target dates for implementation. This independent monitoring has found many gaps. One important recommendation has been that "the role of the victim throughout the criminal justice process . . . be respected and recognised as equal to that of the accused" (Victim Support Europe, 2010).

On 4 October 2012, the 27 EU nations established minimum standards regarding the rights, support, and protection of victims of crime. This has advanced victims' rights for 500 million people and ensures that all victims of crime in Europe will have access to information and assistance and be able to get these across national borders. Certain basic rights in criminal proceedings are now guaranteed, and protections are now provided, particularly for women, children, and vulnerable victims.

The EU standards are more than political wishful thinking. They have sufficient teeth to get implemented, and they encompass training, sharing of best practices, and data to evaluate whether victims' needs are being met. If it is possible to get agreement from so many countries on both standards and ways to get them implemented, then Canada should be able to adapt this model across 10 provinces and three territories.

In Table 7.4, the Canadian Bill of Rights is compared to the US federal Victim Rights Bill and the EU directive. The table shows the general areas in which the articles will require governments to meet the minimum standards. This table is organized around the analysis in Chapters 1 and 2 of *Rights for Victims of Crime*

TABLE 7.4 ■ Comparison of the Canadian Victims Bill of Rights to the EU Directive Using the Eight Core Needs

	Core Needs of Victims	2004 US Federal Victim Rights Act	2012 EU Directive	2015 Canada Victims Bill of Rights
1	Recognition and emotional support	Recognition of victims and families; fairness; right to avoid delay	Recognition of victims and, in case of homicide, family	Recognition of victim and immediate relations
2	Information on criminal justice, case, services, and developments	Right to notice of hearings	Information	Information, including correctional
			Referral by competent authority to victim support	
3	Assistance to access practical, medical, and social services		Comprehensive support	
			Special assistance for vulnerable	
4	Help to pay bills caused by victimization	Right to full and timely restitution	Restitution (called compensation) from the offender	Restitution, including a form but victim to enforce
			Restorative justice—respecting victim rights	Information only within correctional system
			Information on State Compensation	Information only
5	Personal safety and protection from accused	Right to be reasonably protected from accused.	Protection of victims with special protection needs, including women, children, and vulnerable	Some protection, including testimonial aids
6	Choice to voice in justice	Rights to be present and get legal advice	Rights limited mainly to national law	Right limited to victim impact statement, access to parole
7	Best public safety		Information to prevent repeat victimization	
8	Implementation	Right to court enforcement of rights: complaints, training, funding; evaluation of implementation by General Accounting Office	Training, data, cooperation and 5 year reports	Only complaints

Source: Irvin Waller. *Rights for Victims of Crime: Rebalancing Justice*. (New York: Rowman & Littlefield, 2010), p. 37, Figure 2.1. Reprinted by permission of Rowman & Littlefield Publishing Group.

of the core needs of victims. Clearly, the US law focuses on both rights and their implementation by the courts. Clearly, the EU directive is impressively comprehensive; for example, it includes a commitment to evaluate every five years the extent to which its implementation achieves its goals of supporting and protecting victims.

The model law discussed below goes even further: it recommends a central office to lead implementation, standards that identify who is responsible for implementation, training for those charged with implementation, and, importantly, evaluation by social scientists to gauge whether victims are getting the services.

Policing, Victim Services, Reparation, Courts, and Prevention

Victim Services and the Police

More and more victims in Canada no longer go to the police. And even when they do, most do not get information on services, assistance, and support. Even when the police start an investigation, few victims will obtain reparation, protection, or go on to a criminal court, let alone get what they consider justice.

In Canada, the percentage of victims of crime reporting their victimization to the police has been dropping. In 2014, only 31 percent reported to the police, down from 37 percent in 1999 and more than 40 percent earlier. The details of this decline are shown in Table 7.5. The drop in reporting rates experienced in Canada has not occurred in the United States or in England. It is not clear why this decline has occurred in Canada, but one hypothesis is that fewer victims report because services and compensation are not available or well known. The UK, the United States, and the Province of Quebec, which *have* maintained their reporting rates, all have more consistent services and larger compensation payments than the rest of Canada.

In the 2004, 2009, and 2014 victimization surveys, adult Canadians who were victims of crime were asked why they did *not* report the crime to the police. The question assumed that everyone would want to report. The most frequent reasons for not reporting included that the crime did not seem important enough, that the police could not do anything about it, that the crime would be dealt with in another way, that the incident was a personal matter, or that they did not want the police involved.

TABLE 7.5 ■ Percentage of Crime Victims Reporting to Police, by Offence (1988, 1993, 1999, 2004, 2009, 2014)

Year	Sexual Assault	Robbery	Physical Assault	Total Violent Victimization	
1988	n.a.	32	35	n.a.	
1993	10	46	33	44	
1999	n.a.	46	37	31	
2004	8	46	39	33	
2009	n.a.	43	34	29	
2014	5	45	38	28	

Year	Break and Enter	Motor Vehicle Theft/Parts	Theft of Household Property	Vandalism	Total Household Victimization
1988	72	58	44	46	45
1993	68	50	43	46	48
1999	62	60	32	34	44
2004	54	49	29	31	37
2009	54	50	23	35	36
2014	50	44	25	37	36

Year	Theft of Personal Property	Total Victimization
1988	37	n.a.
1993	42	42
1999	35	37
2004	31	34
2009	28	31
2014	29	31

Sources: Statistics Canada, "Criminal Victimization in Canada, 2009," *Juristat* 30, no. 2; "Criminal Victimization in Canada, 2004," *Juristat* 25, No. 7; "Criminal Victimization in Canada, 1999," *Juristat* 20, no. 10 (Ottawa: Canadian Centre for Justice Statistics).

Surveys in other countries ask why victims *do* call the police; that is, they do *not* assume that everyone wants to report. The annual and extensive National Crime Survey in the United States shows that victims report to police because (1) victims of violence want to ensure their personal safety and ensure that others aren't victimized, and (2) property crime victims want to recover stolen property, get damages repaired, and collect insurance. Punishment of the offender is the least frequent reason why victims contact the police (Waller 2010, 60–62).

The Canadian surveys confirm a common finding in countries similar to Canada: most women who are victims of sexual assault or rape do not report their victimization to the police. Specialized surveys exist to measure violence against women and violence against children, but these are not undertaken regularly in Canada (Waller 2010, 59–60). In the United States, these surveys have found that around 800,000 adult women are victims of forcible rape each year and that only 18 percent report to the police. In a disproportionate number of these rapes, the victim is a college or university student. As many as one in five female students will graduate from university after being a victim of rape while on the university campus. Typically, the perpetrator is a male student in the same university (Fisher and Sloan 2007).

Another common finding from government surveys is that most victims who report to the police will not see their offender identified or arrested (Waller 2008, 14; 2010, 60). Overall, less than 4 percent of victims in Canada will see "their" offender convicted (Figure 7.2).

Police services in Canada are proud of their orientation towards providing service to their communities, but they have not focused on services to victims in any significant way. A major reason for the loss of confidence in the police in Canada is the lack of protocols detailing how an officer responding to a 911 call should respond. The Ontario Police Services Act sets out six principles that

FIGURE 7.2 ■ Proportion of Victimizations Reported to Police, Cleared by Charge, and Where Offender Found Guilty, Canada, 2004

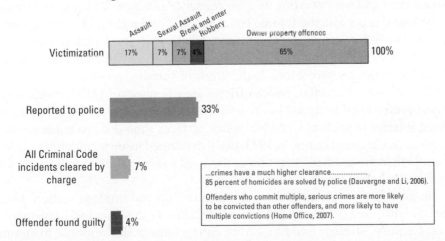

Sources: Adapted from Maire Gannon and Karen Mihorean, "Criminal Victimization in Canada, 2004," *Juristat* 25, no. 7 (2005); Mikhail Thomas, "Adult Criminal Court Statistics, 2003/2004," *Juristat* 24, no. 12 (2004); Julie Sauvé, "Crime Statistics in Canada, 2004," *Juristat* 25, no. 5 (2005).

structure 911 call responses, but only one of the principles refers specifically to respect for victims of crime. This has not yet been accompanied by the sort of procedures and assessments that IACP sees as essential to making crime victims a focus of policing. The Ontario Police Services Act (1990) requires police services to be delivered in accordance with the following principles. It is the fourth principle that is most relevant to our discussion.

1. The need to ensure the safety and security of all persons and property in Ontario.
2. The importance of safeguarding the fundamental rights guaranteed by the Canadian *Charter* of Rights and Freedoms and the Human Rights Code, 1981.
3. The need for cooperation between the police and the communities they serve.
4. The importance of respect for victims of crime and understanding of their needs.
5. The need for sensitivity to the pluralistic, multiracial, and multicultural character of Ontario society.
6. The need to ensure that police are representative of the communities they serve.*

Most Canadian police services have established crime victim services units. These units vary from municipality to municipality. Some are crisis units with mental health workers, who sometimes work in teams with police officers; others are victims' service units staffed by workers with mental health training. Still others are composed of a professional executive and trained volunteers. No systematic data are available on how many victims of what offences are served by these units or on the results of their efforts.

Another reason for the drop in confidence in the police is the failure of police to improve how they respond to female victims of sexual assault despite many high-profile failures. In Ontario, the Bill of Rights for Victims includes the right for a victim of sexual assault to get an officer of the same gender, but there is no evidence that this is ever implemented. Despite the IACP guidelines and the law in Ontario, victims of sexual assault continue to miss out on basic respect from the police.

The Jane Doe case is only one well-known example of a woman not being warned that a serial rapist was operating near her residence and then not being well treated by the investigators with the Toronto Police Service (Waller 2010, 148–49). Recently, the Toronto Police Service sent an officer to talk to students at York University; he told them they were more likely to be raped if they dressed like sluts. This caused so much outrage that people took to the streets of Toronto and Ottawa to protest.

Many senior Canadian police officers are members of IACP, which is the largest professional body for police leadership in North America. It has a sustained interest in spelling out what police services should do to enhance their response to victims of crime. In 1983, IACP developed its own guidelines, which, among other things, drew attention to the need to respond to female victims of sexual assault with female officers.

In an effort to overcome the lack of leadership and implementation, IACP worked with the US Office for Victims of Crime to develop and implement a "21st Century" strategy (see Box 7.3) to enhance the police response to victims

*This is an unofficial version of Government of Ontario legal materials. http://www.e-laws.gov.on.ca/html/statutes/english/elaws_statutes_90p15_e.htm#BK0.

of crime (IACP 2008; Waller, 2010, Ch. 3). In 2008, IACP developed a full set of tested procedures that were ready for implementation and that could be used in Canada (Waller 2010, 55–76). It proposed some simple, obvious, and practical ways to improve services to victims. For example, every officer responding to a 911 call should make the victim aware of which services are available to them with a short and simple informational brochure or wallet card (already a practice in England and Wales). Also, officers should be trained to listen to the victim with sensitivity and to provide emotional support. The guide was field-tested both in Charlotte-Mecklenburg, North Carolina (population 800,000), and in other smaller police departments.

The IACP strategy encourages police leaders to enforce implementation by all police officers and to ensure police support for victim assistance agencies outside the police service. The proposals call for simple, non-time-consuming services that responding police officers can provide to victims. In Canada, some police services ask the officer to check a form if they provided information to a victim, but it is well known that this is not enough to get victims the information they need. While there are small victim services groups in police agencies in Canada, the response by police to victims continues to fall far short of what is needed and what is possible.

A significant shift is needed in the way Canadian police respond to victims of crime. This better way of meeting the needs of victims and encouraging more reporting of crime need not be costly. Waller (2010, 75–76) proposes the

FOCUS   BOX 7.3

INTERNATIONAL ASSOCIATION OF CHIEFS OF POLICE (IACP) GUIDE TO RESPECT VICTIMS OF CRIME

The Strategy Package includes an implementation strategy, toolkit, and training so that police can enhance their response to victims of crime. It emphasizes leadership, partnering, training, and performance monitoring. Here are the seven stages:

1. *Safety*: Protection from perpetrators and assistance in avoiding revictimization.

2. *Support*: Assistance to enable participation in the criminal justice system processes and repair of harm.

3. *Information*: Concise and useful information about victims' rights, criminal justice system processes, and available victim services.

4. *Access*: Ability to participate in the justice system process and have ready availability to support services.

5. *Continuity*: Consistency in approaches and methods across agencies through all stages of the criminal justice process.

6. *Voice*: Opportunities to speak out and be heard on specific case processing issues and larger policy questions.

7. *Justice*: Receiving the support necessary to heal and seeing that perpetrators are held accountable.

Questions for Critical Thinking

1. For decades, victims' rights groups have stressed the need for the justice system to provide them with information about their specific cases. Why is this information so important to someone who has been a crime victim?

2. One of the items in the IACP package discussed in this box is access to the justice system and to support services. Why do you think that crime victims lack the ability to participate in the justice system process?

Source: Adapted from International Association of Chiefs of Police, *Enhancing Law Enforcement Response to Victims: A 21st Century Strategy* (Alexandria: International Association of Chiefs of Police, 2008).

following four steps for Canadian police to reach international standards in their response to victims of crime:

1. Improve the proportion of victims reporting to police and assess progress by holding officers accountable for providing information in a timely manner to victims.
2. Develop and follow protocols to better meet the needs of victims who are women, children, Indigenous, or a person with a disability.
3. Develop a timetable to implement the IACP strategy package to make victims a primary concern of law enforcement.
4. Ensure independent surveys of victims who report to the police to monitor the extent to which their core needs for information, referral to services, and protection among others are being met.*

Services for Victims of Crime

Canadian provinces provide health services without charge to all residents of Canada. Thus health services for physical injuries, disease, or pregnancy incurred as a result of crime are provided to all victims in Canada. While this is similar to countries such as the UK, it is markedly different from the US model, where victims can incur significant medical and hospital costs that may or may not be reimbursed by state compensation programs.

Crime victims also need emotional and psychological support following their victimization. Victims are likely to turn to their friends and family immediately following the crime to ask for advice: Where should they turn? Who should they call? What should they do?

The most universally recognized mental health issue surrounding victimization is post-traumatic stress disorder (PTSD). Following a crime, it is normal to feel shock, numbness, and disorientation. PTSD is diagnosed when these symptoms persist. Sufferers of PTSD usually have difficulty sleeping, mentally relive the experience, and feel a need to avoid normal situations that trigger memories of the original trauma. We do not know the degree to which services in Canada are adequately equipped to handle victims who suffer PTSD. If victims have private insurance through a large employer such as a corporation or government, they may be able to get a limited number of sessions with a therapist, but most victims with PTSD or other emotional trauma require much more.

Victim assistance services are expanding in Canada, but we do not know the degree to which victims are aware of these services, the adequacy of these services, or what proportion of victims access them.

Statistics Canada attempted to conduct a complete census of victims' service providers in Canada and estimated that there were 884 providers (Allen 2014). This may sound like a lot, but it reflects the reality that there is a patchwork of services with many gaps. The study found that 40 percent of the service providers were based in police agencies, 23 percent were based in the community, 8 percent were based in the courts, and 17 percent were sexual assault crisis centres. These agencies had more than 3,000 paid employees, who, along with volunteers, served

---

*Source: Waller, Irvin. 2011. *Rights for Victims of Crime: Rebalancing Justice*. New York: Rowman and Littlefield. Reprinted by permission of Rowman & Littlefield Publishing Group.

more than 400,000 victims annually. This represented about 10 percent of adults known to have been victimized, according to the Statistics Canada victimization survey. Remember, though, that we do not know how many others were not informed of these services who could also have benefited from them. Table 7.6 provides an overview of the services in Ontario.

London, Ontario, has long been at the forefront of services for victims of domestic violence, such as child abuse and wife battering. In 1972 the London Police Service began collaborating with the University of Western Ontario to establish police–social worker teams to respond to family violence—the police officer to control the situation and the social worker to help the family resolve its problems. After forming an inter-agency team to look at complementary programs, the city pioneered a battered wife advocacy clinic and world-renowned innovations in its court systems. More recently, it has launched an effective program called the 4th R to stop violence against women (Institute for the Prevention of Crime 2009; Crooks et al. 2008).

From a 2012 survey, we know that on one day there were 12,000 residents in battered wife shelters in Canada. About half were women, the other half dependent children (Mazowita and Burczycka 2014). About 380 women and 220 children were turned away on just that one day for reasons of lack of space or other problems faced by the women.

For victims of sexual assault, there are a number of sexual assault or rape crisis centres scattered across Canada, mainly in urban areas. Though there is little systematic research on these centres, they likely provide services as good as similar centres in other countries, where research has shown that they are important to victims (Waller 2010). What *is* certain is that they are typically not

TABLE 7.6 ▪ Services for Victims of Crime in Ontario

Core Need	2006 Draft Convention	Services
	Support	
1	Recognition of victims, co-victims, Good Samaritans	
2	Information	Victim Assistance and Referral Services (VCARS), Victim Quick Response Program (VQRP), SupportLink
3	Assistance—referral by police	
	Assistance—short term	Victim Support Line (VSL)
	Assistance—medium term	Sexual Assault / Rape Crisis Centres (SACs)
	Special assistance because of age, gender, disability, race	Sexual Assault /Rape Crisis Centres (SACs), Domestic Violence Court (DVC) Program, Partner Assault Response (PAR) Programs, Internet Child Exploitation (ICE) Counselling
	Justice	
4	Restitution from offender	
	Restorative Justice—respecting victim rights	
	Compensation from state	Victim Quick Response Program (VQRP), Criminal Injuries Compensation Board (CICB)
5	Protection of victims, witnesses, and experts	Victim/Witness Assistance Program (VWAP), Child Victim /Witness Program
6	Access to justice and fair treatment	
	Good Government	
7	Commitment to reduce victimization	
8	Implementation	

Sources: Ontario Ministry of the Attorney General. OVSS Programs. Web; I. Waller, *Rights for Victims of Crime: Rebalancing Justice* (Toronto: Rowman and Littlefield, 2011).

funded on a permanent basis and that despite the importance and effectiveness of their work, the salaries of staff are significantly lower than those of other justice professionals (police, lawyers, judges, etc.).

One interesting model for responding to victims of sexual assault is Nina's Place in Burlington, Ontario. Nina's Place provides specialized health care, police services, and agency referrals for women and men who have experienced sexual assault within the past 72 hours and recent domestic violence. The support is available whether the survivor has involved the police or not. It is named in memory of Nina de Villiers, the victim of a tragic assault in Burlington in 1991. Nina's Place is open 24 hours a day, seven days a week, and the services are free (Nina's Place 2011). The services offered by Nina's Place include a physical examination and treatment of any physical injuries, the collection and recording of evidence of the assault (forensic evidence within 24 hours) that can be used if the victim decides to involve the legal system, testing and counselling for possible pregnancy, risk assessment and safety planning, follow-up medical care and referral to community agencies, and counselling.

Sexual Assault Response Teams, such as that in Waterloo Region, are a recent additional response. They involve a joint commitment by various social, health, police, and violence against women groups. Unfortunately, as yet there is no research available on the outcomes of this team approach.

Basic responses to assist victims of crime in Canada lag behind those in other countries. Waller (2010, 95–96) proposes the following measures to bring Canada up to international standards:

1. Increase funding significantly and pay professional salaries for the full range of victim support services, including those for victims of sexual assault and domestic violence.
2. Develop and implement professional standards for support services along the lines of those in the UK.
3. Ensure that professional care for mental health trauma is available at no cost to the victim.
4. Schools and universities should teach citizens how to provide emotional support to victims of crime.
5. Conduct surveys to measure the gaps between the core needs of victims and the services provided to them.*

Restitution from the Offender, Compensation from the State, and Civil Remedies

Crime often involves direct financial loss, costs of services, and loss of quality of life. Victims have several potential ways to obtain reparation to recover these losses:

1. An order of restitution made in a criminal court;
2. A civil suit brought against the perpetrator of the crime;
3. A civil suit brought against a third party whose negligence may have contributed to the crime;
4. Restorative justice;
5. A payment made by a state/provincial compensation board.

*Source: Waller, Irvin. 2011. *Rights for Victims of Crime: Rebalancing Justice*. New York: Rowman and Littlefield. Reprinted by permission of Rowman & Littlefield Publishing Group.

Restitution from the Offender

Though restitution is available through criminal and juvenile courts, it is not known how often it is considered appropriately, let alone ordered or paid. We do know that programs such as a model program in Saskatchewan (Box 7.4) and various best practices in the United States have resulted in some restitution being ordered and paid.

Experts have identified key steps to get restitution paid, but these have not yet been applied in Canada. According to the US National Center for Victims of Crime (Waller 2010), restitution would be paid if jurisdictions followed seven steps:

1. Victims request restitution in writing.
2. Victims demonstrate losses.
3. The offender's assets, income, and liabilities are identified at the beginning of the justice process.
4. Restitution payments are made automatic.
5. Payments are monitored.
6. Compliance is enforced.
7. Restitution payments are made the priority over other government payments such as fines.*

Restorative Justice

There are several models for restorative justice (see Chapter 2). Most involve the victim and offender meeting with a professional coordinator or mediator. The goal is to reconcile the two parties.

*Waller, Irvin. 2011. *Rights for Victims of Crime: Rebalancing Justice*. New York: Rowman and Littlefield. Reprinted by permission of Rowman & Littlefield Publishing Group.

FOCUS   BOX 7.4

ADULT RESTITUTION AND CIVIL ENFORCEMENT PROGRAM, SASKATCHEWAN

A unique provincial program in Saskatchewan has two components—the Adult Restitution Program and the Restitution Civil Enforcement Program. The Ministry of Justice and Attorney General operates these programs to help victims receive restitution (http://www.justice.gov.sk.ca/victimsservices).

The Adult Restitution Program provides information to victims about restitution, monitors payments, works with offenders to help ensure payments are made, and works with probation officers and prosecutors to enforce restitution orders. This program ensures that the Crown is aware that the victim has suffered financial loss as a result of the crime and of the extent of the loss. A court will generally order restitution only if the amount of loss is "readily ascertainable."

The Restitution Civil Enforcement Program assists victims with the civil enforcement of restitution orders. The program pursues civil enforcement of the restitution order on the victims' behalf (when a supervised order has expired or in the case of stand-alone restitution orders). This may include, but is not limited to, the garnishment of the offender's wages and bank accounts, and seizure of personal property.

These are pilot projects being funded by the Department of Justice. Nova Scotia is currently establishing a new Restitution Program modelled on Saskatchewan's Adult Restitution Program to assist victims in obtaining restitution payments.

Questions for Critical Thinking

One of the problems with restitution and with fine surcharge programs is that some offenders are very poor and have no ability to pay. How do you think the system should handle cases like these?

Source: Adapted from Saskatchewan, *Restitution Civil Enforcement Program* (Regina: Justice and Attorney General, 2011).

Restorative justice was pioneered internationally in the region around Waterloo, Ontario, by Mennonites in the 1970s. In 1981, when the US National Organization for Victim Assistance came to Toronto for their annual conference, Ontario was a leader in restitution and supported victim–offender reconciliation programs across the province. At that time, the Church Council on Justice and Corrections took up the challenge of spreading restorative justice models across Canada. However, these are more often pioneering projects rather than comprehensive policy. By 2010, Nova Scotia had achieved one of the most extensive networks of restorative justice for juvenile offenders.

Though popular among criminologists, restorative justice models have not achieved their potential. As with many other victim innovations, the system has resisted these options. Furthermore, the victims' movement has been quick to stress that victims are not always given the same attention as the offender. Restorative justice has become an international movement in which there is more often talk in university classrooms than action in practice.

Nevertheless, research by Strang and Sherman (2007) using random control trials in Australia and the UK has demonstrated that victims prefer restorative justice to the traditional system and that, on average, offenders who go through this process are less likely to reoffend. Their data have reinforced the work by the National Association for Victim Support Schemes and Restorative Solutions to train practitioners across England and Wales.

Compensation from Government

In 1967, Saskatchewan became the first province to provide compensation to victims of violence. Since then, many provincial governments have established compensation programs to ensure that victims of violence are compensated for their losses. However, it seems that many victims are not aware of these programs. In Ontario, for example, fewer than 4,000 victims apply each year—a relatively small proportion of those estimated to be eligible. When a person is injured or killed as a result of a violent crime, the maximum (lump sum) awarded is $25,000. Also, a victim who is unable to work due to the victimization may only be awarded a maximum of $1,000 per month to cover this loss. That is equivalent to $50 a day. The Ontario program pays an average of $8,000 for pain and suffering and over $7,000 when funeral expenses are required. Quebec pays significant amounts for temporary loss of wages and for rehabilitation, using a scheme that parallels workers' injury compensation. Table 7.7 compares the main types of awards in the two programs. Overall, Quebec pays an average close to $12,000 for about 6,000 cases, whereas Ontario is more modest at about $7,000 for about 3,500 cases. Both provinces pay administrative costs to run these programs, which add several million dollars to the overall costs.

Victims of violence in the UK are informed about compensation and can use a website (www.cica.gov.uk) to make a claim. The website provides instructions on how to make a claim and indicates that the awards range from $1,000 to $800,000. Because the UK code of practice requires the police to inform victims about support services (also, they are required to inform the services that the person has been victimized), proportionately more victims get much larger awards than in most jurisdictions.

TABLE 7.7 ■ Criminal Injuries Compensation in Ontario and Quebec: Total Awards by Name of Benefit in Millions of Dollars

Ontario (2012–13)		Quebec (2012)	
Pain and suffering	$23.9		
		Rehabilitation	$9.8
Loss of wages	$0.4	Loss of work	$25.4
		Social and economic stabilization	$2.0
Funeral expenses	$0.4	Funeral expenses	$0.2
		Permanent disability	$36.5
Total	$24.7		$73.9

Note: These exclude medical expenses and legal expenses.

Source: © Queen's Printer for Ontario, 2014. Reproduced with permission. First column in table is drawn from CICB data. Second column is obtained by permission from the CIBC's Integrated Financial System (IFIS) as of 6 December 2013.

To bring restitution and compensation up to international standards, some significant investment and rethinking will be needed in Canada. After looking at what has been achieved in other jurisdictions, Waller (2010, 113–14) says that Canada should do several things to establish a similar standard, including the following: implement key steps to collect restitution from offenders; ensure that compensation paid by the state meets the costs and "pain" of victims of violent crime; provide mediation and restorative justice programs that respect the core needs of victims; and support research informing victims how to get restitution, civil suit orders, compensation, and restorative justice.

Human Rights for Victims in Criminal Courts

In Canada's criminal and youth courts, victims are still limited to the role of witness, though some are allowed to submit a victim impact statement. The impact statement is usually a written statement, but in some cases it is a brief oral statement. There are no data on the number of victims who are informed of this option or who take advantage of it.

In France, the United States, and some other countries, and in the International Criminal Court (of which Canada is an active partner), there is more scope for victim representation and participation. France has provided victims a role in the court system for more than 40 years. Victims have legal standing in the courtroom and are represented as a civil party in the criminal justice system. This combination of criminal and civil proceedings allows victims to defend their interests in the pursuit of truth, reparation, public safety, fair sentencing, and other issues simultaneously. Victims can raise concerns about personal safety and compel a more thorough investigation of the offences against them. Many cases in the French system result in restitution orders, which are paid. When this measure is "bound" to the court, the victim has a more tangible and enforceable agreement—to which the accused and the victim can agree—than is typically the case in restorative justice.

France is no longer alone in employing this civil/criminal system. Belgium, Germany, Japan, and Korea are some of the countries that in the past decade have mobilized this system by providing legal assistance to victims.

In the United States, the federal Justice for All Act, passed in 2004, provides extensive rights to protect victims and facilitate restitution. In 2008, the State of California adopted Marsy's Law, which expanded victim's rights in that state. Both these laws provide models that may be adapted to Canada over the next few years. However, some people oppose these initiatives because of concerns that they might compromise the rights of the accused.

The International Criminal Court, of which Canada is a signatory, provides even more extensive rights for victims in a system that continues to provide offenders with rights under an adversarial system (see Table 7.8).

Table 7.9 provides a schematic of the current Criminal Code and Youth Criminal Justice Act and compares it to the US Justice for All Act (Waller 2010). The Canadian Corrections and Conditional Release Act provides some additional rights to victims.

It is striking how many initiatives to support victims have been implemented in other countries but not in Canada.

Stopping Violence against Victims and Preventing Repeat Victimization

By far the best way to reduce the $55 billion harm to victims (Zhang 2011) is to prevent victimization in the first place by investing in what we know will reduce crime. In a recent book, Waller (2014) draws upon research brought together by the World Health Organization (WHO), many leading criminologists, and government agencies to show that we have the knowledge to reduce violence against women, street violence, property crime, and child abuse by 50 percent or more for a reinvestment of about 10 percent of what we are presently spending on reactive policies (Waller 2014). As we saw earlier, expenditures on policing, courts, and corrections are at $22 billion and rising. By reinvesting $2 billion smartly, we could probably reduce losses to victims by $25 billion.

Several experimental projects have allowed sophisticated random control evaluations. They have demonstrated that it is indeed possible for government to tackle the negative life experiences of persons at risk of offending to help them to live their lives without victimizing others (Waller 2014). For instance, a Canadian initiative, Stop Now and Plan (SNAP), helps children and parents regulate youth

TABLE 7.8 ■ **Participation and Representation in the International Criminal Court**

Support
Victims are protected and supported
Victims are given responses sensitive to gender, age, and other issues
Justice
Victim participation and representation (grouped) is paid by legal aid in adversarial trial and sentencing
Restitution is paid to victims through trust funds funded by offenders and others
Good Government
Trust funds contribute to awareness and prevention
Permanent infrastructure is paid for by governments with performance assessments

Source: Waller, Irvin. 2011. *Rights for Victims of Crime: Rebalancing Justice*, pp. 126–30, figure 6.4. New York: Rowman and Littlefield. Reprinted by permission of Rowman & Littlefield Publishing Group.

TABLE 7.9 ■ Comparison of Provisions for Victim Rights in the US Federal Justice for All Act with the Criminal Code and the Youth Criminal Justice Act

Justice for All Act (U.S., 2004)	Criminal Code	Youth Criminal Justice Act
1. The right to be reasonably protected from the accused.		
2. The right to reasonable, accurate, and timely notice of any public court proceeding, or any parole proceeding, involving the crime or of any release or escape of the accused.		
3. The right not to be excluded from any such public court proceeding, unless the court, after receiving clear and convincing evidence, determines that testimony by the victim would be materially altered if the victim heard other testimony at the proceeding.		
4. The right to be reasonably heard at any public proceeding in the district court involving release, plea, sentencing, or any parole proceeding.	Section 672.5 (14) Victim Impact Statements Right to have read at sentencing.	Sections 50–51 Victim Impact Statements Right to have read at sentencing.
5. The reasonable right to confer with the attorney for the government in the case		
6. The right to full and timely restitution as provided in law	Section 83.17 (2) Restitution Judge has discretion	Section 42-2-F Restitution Judge has discretion
7. The right to proceedings free from unreasonable delay.		
8. The right to be treated with fairness and with respect for the victim's dignity and privacy.		

Source: Adapted from Irvin Waller. 2011. *Rights for Victims of Crime: Rebalancing Justice*, pp. 121–24. New York: Rowman and Littlefield. Reprinted by permission of Rowman & Littlefield Publishing Group.

aggression. This program has been subjected to rigorous evaluations, many of which have demonstrated positive outcomes among children under the age of 12. Effective crime prevention programs can save a great deal of money. For example, a cost analysis of the well-known Perry Preschool Program followed participants to age 40 and found that every dollar spent on effective prevention programs saved seventeen dollars. These savings came from lower costs to victims, reduced justice system costs, lower welfare costs, higher taxes paid by program participants (who had higher incomes than non-participants), and reduced special education costs (Schweinhart et al. 2005; Waller 2014; Institute for Prevention of Crime 2009, 2.1).

Equally impressive have been programs to prevent child abuse and subsequent adolescent offending. These programs have different names, including Public Health nurse visitation programs, and Triple P's (Positive Parenting Programs). They can help parents in difficult situations raise their children in more consistent and caring ways.

In 2011 the US Justice Department announced the creation of a new website, crimesolutions.gov, to help taxpayers judge the effectiveness of state and local anti-crime programs. The cost–benefit analyses of these programs have had very impressive results, showing a huge return on investment. This is known as the "prevention dividend." The work by the Washington State Institute on Public Policy, conducted for the legislature of the State of Washington, is an important and continuing source of additional and detailed updates. We can also look to England's Youth Inclusion Projects, a series of programs developed to reach the most difficult teenagers and significantly reduce their offending. The UK did

Jim West/Alamy Stock Photo

School-based programs are among the best ways of reducing delinquency involvement.

not wait to retest the Youth Inclusion Projects. Instead, it multiplied them in 72 low-income housing estates. After great success, the number of such projects was doubled. Canada's National Crime Prevention Centre still funds only limited replications of these projects. The time is long overdue to invest in a national program that would draw from the successes achieved in other countries.

Youth are involved in many of the sexual assaults that occur in elementary and secondary schools, universities and colleges, and neighbourhoods in Canada. Fortunately, Canadian research confirms that when we change male attitudes towards violence and women, we can expect to reduce most common types of violence against women. One strategy that stands out is the "4th R," which was tested through a large-scale random control trial in Canada. It changes the attitudes of teenagers in high school regarding alcohol and drug abuse, violence, and sexual assault against women. This program was developed by a partnership of the University of Western Ontario and the City of London, Ontario, described earlier in this chapter (Crooks et al. 2008; Institute for Prevention of Crime 2009, 1.2; Waller 2014).

Some successful models for reducing crime focus on reducing the risk to victims. The first proven prevention of residential burglary occurred in Seattle in the 1970s; more than 50 percent of residential burglaries were avoided. A similar strategy in Kirkholt, England, achieved similar results: it focused on repeat burglary victims and achieved a reduction of over 80 percent (Waller 2008, 53–66).

The World Health Organization (WHO), the UN Commission on Crime Prevention and Criminal Justice, the US National Research Council, and a partnership coordinated by the Giffords Law Center have called for a three-pronged approach to reduce victimization. This approach combines enforcement with prevention as well as community treatment for persons at risk of offending. All of the involved organizations stress the importance of mobilizing key agencies such as schools, social services, housing authorities, and the police to collaboratively develop solutions to problems, implement those solutions, and follow up with careful evaluation of the results.

These strategies are at the core of a new, victim-centred vision for criminal justice. An exciting example of this has the acronym INSPIRE and is sponsored by the World Health Organization (2016). It focuses on the prevalence of violence and the consequences of violence for victims and calls for governments to harness the evidence about what stops violence. It is geared towards helping governments achieve the targets that underpin the UN General Assembly agreement for reducing violence significantly by 2030.

Another spectacular yet little-known and non-replicated Canadian example is the Winnipeg Auto-Theft Suppression strategy (see Chapter 15), which is saving Winnipeg residents about $40 million each year in auto insurance premiums.

A growing number of municipalities, including Edmonton, Montreal, Ottawa, and Waterloo Region, have established permanent leadership centres to diagnose problems and implement solutions. In 2015, these four municipalities spurred the formation of the Canadian Municipal Network for Crime Prevention (2017), which has quickly expanded to include 25 municipalities. Its main aim is to foster a community of evidence-based practice with the goal of reducing the number of victims as well as harm from victimization. This network has produced Action Briefs arguing for investment in prevention and for new resource centres (which have indeed been established in the last decade). Its strategic advocacy has helped achieve large reductions in victimization. This is very much at the cutting edge internationally of ways to stop violence instead of only punishing it.

We now know a great deal about how to stop people from becoming victims of crime. Waller (2014) has identified a number of ways in which we can do better at reducing the number of victims:

1. Shift crime policies to pre-emptive strategies orchestrated by a small secretariat to diagnose problems and to mobilize key sectors such as schools, housing, and policing.
2. Invest adequately in programs that have demonstrated their effectiveness, such as repeat victimization programs, compulsory curricula—such as the 4th R to reduce sexual assault, Triple P to stop child abuse, and the strategies used in Winnipeg to reduce car theft and now street violence.
3. Continue to tackle alcohol and drug abuse among younger adults.*

Systemic Ways to Shift, Reinvest, and Rebalance Justice for Crime Victims

In the first section of this chapter, we described the impact of crime on victims. In the second section, we saw the origins of the victimology movement in Canada and the development of international standards. In third section, we saw areas where Canada could advance towards those standards to better meet the needs of crime victims.

*Adapted from Irvin Waller. 2011. *Rights for Victims of Crime: Rebalancing Justice*. New York: Rowman and Littlefield. Reprinted by permission of Rowman & Littlefield Publishing Group.

Throughout this chapter we have seen that the traditional criminal justice system has long resisted making the changes that research shows are required to reduce victimization and to improve the lives of victims. That system has even resisted the recommendations of the Parliamentary Report—*A Voice Not a Veto*—and McMurtry's 2007 report. In 2010, Waller examined US and European innovations aimed at addressing prevention, services, and victims' rights (2010, 154–64). He focused on five key components for comprehensive implementation: an office for victims of crime; standards and training; evaluation and ombudspersons; social science surveys to foster success; and research and development.

In this section we look at four key ways to achieve the shift and reinvestment: model legislation; an independently funded institute; social science surveys and an amendment to the *Charter* of Rights and Freedoms. We then discuss the key recommendations from a national symposium in 2011, which were amplified in the federal Ombudsman's Forum in 2013 that looked at ways to help Canada achieve international standards.

Model Legislation

Fourteen international experts met in 2005 to prepare a draft report for a UN convention that would encourage governments to follow through on an 1985 resolution to reduce victimization and to implement services and rights for victims. Waller has adapted this draft into a model law that could be adopted by a Canadian province (2010, 173–83).

The model law has three major sections: support, justice, and good government. The support section includes subsections on recognition, information, and assistance. The justice section makes provisions for restitution and repayment, protection from the accused, participation, and representation. The good government section covers effective policies to reduce victimization and the all-important issues of implementation.

An Independently Funded Institute

An office for victims of crime is not enough; neither is a federal ombudsman for victims of crime. We need to create a permanently funded institute. Such an institute would require contributions from legal professionals, social researchers, and victim's rights agencies but would need to be independent of them all. This institute would likely be based at a Canadian university and would function as a central hub for education, research, and policy observation. It would work closely with service agencies in the community, the federal Victim's Ombudsman, and legal practitioners.

One such institute has already been created in Europe and could serve as a best practices model for a Canadian institute. INTERVICT—the International Victimology Institute Tilburg—was launched by Tilburg University in the Netherlands in 2005 and has continually expanded research on victimization and victim assistance in Europe. It has conducted extensive evaluations of victim legislation in the EU and has been leading the world on issues of victimization (identity theft, human trafficking, online victimization, and more).

In 2017, Benjamin Perrin published the first Canadian legal textbook on victim law. It builds on the Bill of Rights and on the positive momentum in case law that is better protecting the rights of victims. His book may be a game changer if it encourages law schools to establish courses on victim law.

Social Science Evaluations

The partnership between INTERVICT and the European Forum for Victim Support demonstrated that the landmark European Framework had not made the difference that was needed in terms of services meeting the needs of victims. As a result, the EU modified its approach to establish the 2012 directive. In the United States, the insistence that the Rights for Victims of Crime Act be evaluated by the GAO has ensured that improvements are being made in how the act is being applied.

An Amendment to the *Charter* of Rights and Freedoms

The Canadian *Charter* of Rights and Freedoms includes a number of paragraphs protecting the rights of accused and convicted persons against the powers of the state. At this time, it does not include any rights for victims of crime. So the traditional rights of defendants "trump" the basic human rights of victims, which have been recognized by the UN but not yet by Canada.

Crime victims need their rights to safety, reparation, and justice to be recognized by an amendment to the *Charter* of Rights and Freedoms. Such an amendment could include the following wording: "To have the rights of victims of crime to safety, reparation and justice respected" *and* "Balanced fairly, against rights of the accused or convicted offender" *and* "heard through participation and representation equal to that of the accused in all judicial and administrative proceedings" (Waller 2010, 168–70).

Key Actions

Every year in April, Justice Canada encourages a Crime Victim Awareness Week. In 2011 the Faculty of Social Sciences at the University of Ottawa organized a national symposium titled Crime Victim Rights: Reaching for International Standards. Delegates were invited from the federal, provincial, and municipal governments as well as from national associations.

The costs of implementing a national action plan that would include the proposals in this chapter were discussed based on estimates by Waller (2010, 164–68; 2008, 132–34). The reinvestment needed to implement all of the recommendations discussed in this chapter is approximately 10 percent of the expenditures on the traditional criminal justice system. Funding this 10 percent can be done gradually over five years.

The Canadian Resource Centre for Victims of Crime and the International Organization for Victim Assistance were the principal partners for the National Symposium. After the symposium, they called for the following:

1. A *national action plan*, including standards such as those in the UK and the model law (see above), that would apply to policing, services, restitution, compensation, prosecution, and courts; that would be sensitive to special needs such as those of women, children, and Indigenous populations; and that would have leadership offices for victims of crime;
2. A *provincial victim advocate*, supported by *surveys* to provide better data and an *institute* to focus on research and development;
3. *Provincial and municipal prevention strategies* to effectively reduce crime and promote community safety;

4. *Permanent funding* equivalent to at least 10 percent of the current expenditures on criminal justice, to be used for prevention, victim services, and rights;

5. An *amendment* to the *Charter* of Rights and Freedoms.

In this chapter, we have seen that the needs of victims have been overlooked by the traditional system. Starting with the landmark UN Declaration—the Magna Carta for victims—we have seen that an increase in the awareness of the needs of victims internationally has led to some cautious steps in Canada. These steps have included improvements in policing, victim services and compensation, and courts and restitution, but there is still a long way to go. Rebalancing the justice system to respect victims' human rights will require more than ad hoc solutions. It will also require a national action plan, serious investments in that plan, investments in effective prevention, and possibly an amendment to the *Charter* of Rights and Freedoms.

One of the most important steps for convincing legislators to make the reinvestments is to get the knowledge out to voters, taxpayers, and (potential) victims of crime, while showing how the shift towards stopping victimization and implementing victims' rights is in the interests of (potential) victims and taxpayers.

QUESTIONS FOR CRITICAL THINKING

1. What are the five most significant steps Canadian governments could take to improve the circumstances of victims of crime?

2. Given current knowledge about violence prevention, how would you shift government resources to reduce the number of victims of violence.

Summary

- About one in four adult Canadians is a victim of some type of crime every year. Though relatively few are victims of serious crime, the cumulative harm to victims was estimated at more than $80 billion for 2008.

- Canada resolved at the UN General Assembly in 1985 to invest in preventing crime and guaranteeing human rights for victims of crime (Declaration of Basic Principles of Justice for Victims), but it has not implemented these promises.

- Canadians paid more than $22 billion in 2016 for a traditional system of police, courts, and corrections that still limits the role of the victim to acting as the complainant and as a witness. Few of these funds have been invested in preventing victimization, assisting victims, and protecting the human rights of victims.

- The International Association of Chiefs of Police has developed strategic ways to enhance the police response to victims of crime, but its Canadian members have done little to implement these proven strategies.

- For more than 30 years, surveys have shown that victims of sexual violence rarely report to police, but little has been done to improve this situation.

- The personnel in victim assistance services, sexual assault crisis centres, and shelters for battered women are not paid salaries that are competitive with wages in the traditional criminal justice system. Unlike other criminal justice agencies, victims' organizations often have to reapply for funding every year.

- Compensation to victims for criminal injuries varies from province to province and in most cases is inadequate.

- Restitution and restorative justice are popular discussion points for criminologists but have been losing ground in application in Canada despite the pioneering role played by Canadian groups in the 1970s and 1980s.

- Traditional criminal courts appear to ignore or find ways to overlook sections in the Criminal Code designed to protect victims, such as the victim fine surcharge, restitution, and victim impact statements.

- Canada is at the cutting edge of programs to stop victimization, such as the Winnipeg Auto Theft Suppression Strategy, the Canadian Municipal Network for Crime Prevention, and the 4th R program, but it lacks any overall action plan and funding to shift from overreliance on the traditional criminal justice system.

- Ways to rebalance the system to meet needs and human rights for victims of crime are well known but have not yet been applied in Canada. These include social science surveys, a research and training institute, national standards, and much more.

NET WORK

1. What practical information exists on the Internet about your home town regarding the following? (a) How to report a crime to the police. (b) What services are available in your community for different types of crime victims, including a break-in, an aggravated sexual assault, and a person killed by a drunk driver. (c) How to assess harm to victims and apply for compensation from the state if you are injured in a crime, and what the key conditions are, including the maximum award that can be provided. (d) How to apply for restitution and get it paid. And (e) what your right is to a victim impact statement and how you exercise it.

2. Compare your answers to these questions to the following: (a) The information on the website of Justice Canada for crime victims (http://www.victimsmatter. gc.ca/index.html); (b) Help you can get from the Federal Ombudsman for Victims of Crime (http://www.victimsfirst.gc.ca/index.html); the British *Code of Practice for Victims of Crime* (http://www.direct.gov.uk/prod_consum_dg/ groups/dg_digitalassets/@dg/@en/documents/digitalasset/dg_073647.pdf) and the Criminal Injuries Compensation Authority (http://www.justice.gov .uk/guidance/compensation-schemes/cica/index.htm).

3. Locate the victim services act or the bill of rights for victims of crime for your province, and compare the provisions with those stated in the UN Declaration of Basic Principles of Justice for Victims of Crime and Abuse of Power (http://www.un.org/documents/ga/res/40/a40r034.htm). Then propose your best action to get them implemented.

Explanations of Crime

The field of criminology is multidisciplinary. Lawyers, sociologists, political scientists, psychologists, biologists, physicians, historians, and philosophers may all consider the study of crime as part of their discipline. Nowhere is this diversity more apparent than in the development of theories of the causes of crime.

Part 2 covers many of the most popular explanations of crime. The debate over which of these explanations is "best" is often heated, and no attempt is made to resolve this issue here. It would be premature to impose such a judgment on a field that has been described as consisting of "a number of fitful leads from one partially examined thesis to another" (Rock 1980). Instead, each theory is presented by an author who has had experience (and some sympathy) with it and who presents the theory's strengths and weaknesses. Several researchers are now trying to synthesize different approaches, and some of the authors discuss this integrative work.

Part 2 illustrates how theories of crime causation have developed over time. In Chapter 8, some of the earliest explanations of crime are discussed. The most important point made in this chapter is that explanations of crime arise from particular historical milieux and reflect the social and intellectual fashions of the day. Chapter 9 presents psychological theories, many of which focus on the traits of individuals. Chapters 10 to 15 are concerned with the sociological explanations of crime. They illustrate the diverse ways in which social structure and social processes may promote or restrain criminal behaviour.

8

Early Theories of Criminology

TULLIO CAPUTO
Carleton University

RICK LINDEN
University of Manitoba

Learning Objectives

After reading this chapter, you should be able to

- Discuss the context in which modern explanations of crime and criminality were developed.

- Identify the founders of the Classical School of criminology, the key principles of this approach, and the impact of this school on our legal system.

- Outline the criticisms of the Classical approach and the changes in the legal process that were influenced by the Positive criminologists.

- Describe the basic features of the Positive School of criminology and outline its approach and key principles.

- Show how the ideas advanced by the Positive School influenced other researchers to search for the biological causes of crime.

- Discuss how biological explanations of criminality influenced the development of this field at the beginning of the 20th century.

We begin by exploring the context in which modern criminology developed. During the Enlightenment, societal beliefs relating crime to superstition and sin were replaced by naturalistic explanations based on the idea that people are free and rational beings. This change was part of the struggle for individual rights and freedoms during the Enlightenment and reflected the view that social order was based on a social contract between the individual and the state. This in turn was based on the growing power of the rising merchant classes and the reduced influence of the feudal aristocracy, whose power rested on the ownership of the land and on the loyalty of the peasants who lived and worked on it.

This era saw the rise of the Classical School of criminology. The principle of "let the punishment fit the crime" represented the core of the philosophy of the Classical School, which maintained a belief in people's ability to reason and to act rationally. The Classical School provided the basis for our modern Criminal Code, but its principles were too rigid and inflexible in practice. The argument of later Positive School criminologists that mitigating circumstances must be considered when dealing with crime and criminals led to further reforms in how society dealt with criminals. The chapter concludes with an examination of early theories that sought the causes of crime in the biological make-up of individual offenders.

Religious Beliefs, Superstition, and Crime

Prior to the 18th century, theories about crime were inspired primarily by religious beliefs and superstition:

> From the most primitive beginnings of human history, man [*sic*] believed in the existence of spirits and magic, and . . . from the earliest days of his existence on earth, he began to ascribe various unusual phenomena of nature to the activities of evil spirits. This naturally led him to believe that any pathology in human behavior must be due to an evil spirit. (Zilborg 1969, 11)

The link between evil spirits and wrongdoing is strong in many religions. Judeo-Christian teachings offer two powerful explanations for the role evil spirits play in sinful behaviour: temptation and possession. Ideas about temptation are rooted in the belief that people exercise free will and choose to act in particular ways, even ways they know to be wrong. The Devil is thought to be at work tempting people, but righteous believers can resist the Devil's powerful allure by drawing strength from their faith. They are encouraged to do this by religious leaders, who deploy images of hell-fire and threats of eternal damnation to steel the spines of the faithful who might otherwise waver. These images and beliefs about temptation imply that people who succumb are weak and morally inferior beings. This explains how the poor, the destitute, and other unfortunate members of society have been held responsible for their lot throughout much of history. Their misfortunes are seen as the result of their own moral failures. These beliefs also provide the basis for our ideas about deterrence: most people believe that the threat of severe punishment should be enough to persuade people not to engage in misdeeds.

The second, and equally powerful, Judeo-Christian concept linking sin to evil spirits is that of possession. Wrongdoers were often suspected of being possessed by the Devil or some other malevolent spirit. These unfortunate individuals were thought to have little hope of recovering and were treated quite harshly. A host of horrifying tortures were used to drive the evil spirits from their bodies, and evidence of guilt was determined through a series of trials whose intent was to differentiate between the righteous and the sinner. These included trial by battle, trial by ordeal, trial by fire, and trial by water. In most cases, the accused had little to look forward to, whether innocent or guilty, since these trials were extremely severe and often fatal.

These practices, which reflected a belief in the power of supernatural forces, reached their peak during the Middle Ages with the notorious Inquisition and the witch craze it spawned. This period was marked by tremendous social upheaval, as Western Europe was in the midst of the transition from feudalism to capitalism. Confusion and fear followed the revolution in the material and intellectual worlds of the day. Political and religious elites sought to protect their positions and privileges and to maintain the existing order by any means possible. This included resorting to both religious and civil laws.

Medieval society was forced to change because existing social arrangements no longer met the needs of the growing European population. Poverty, misery, wars, and sickness ravaged the masses. All of this led people to question and even to challenge long-standing practices and beliefs, including those related to civil and religious authority. For example, the Protestant Reformation shook the foundations of the Christian world by challenging the power and authority of Rome. Throughout Europe, those in power were increasingly being held to account for deteriorating material conditions and social problems. It is in this context that the Inquisition and the witch craze found fertile ground. The religious and political elites began seeking ways to divert attention from themselves and to silence the rebellious members of society. Blaming existing social problems on the Devil and other evil spirits was a means to achieve both objectives. First, this diverted the public's attention from the elites and helped place blame for social problems on individuals who were identified as possessed by or in league with the Devil. Second, those in power made themselves indispensable by arguing that they alone had the knowledge and power to deal with the threat posed by the Devil (Harris 1974).

By linking morality to rebellion, the authorities effectively prevented anyone from challenging the status quo. Those who did were likely to be accused of heresy and subjected to extremely harsh punishments, including death. This is precisely what happened to those accused of witchcraft. During the 300 years in which the witch craze flourished, more than half a million people were put to death. The plight of those accused of being witches illustrates how charges of heresy were used to silence critics and quash any rebellious inclinations in the population.

Witches and others practising various forms of "magic" (often for healing purposes) had been active in Western Europe for centuries, although they were never prosecuted. This changed as a result of the growing challenge to religious and civil authorities during the 15th century. Witches served as a convenient scapegoat against whom the masses could vent their anger. Importantly, it was usually the less

Drawing and quartering was one of the many horrendous punishments given to individuals during the Middle Ages. This level of cruelty was common across Europe and was lessened only after the Enlightenment in the 18th century.

Chronicle/Alamy Stock Photo

powerful members of a community who were most in danger of being accused of witchcraft. The witch craze mainly victimized women. Indeed, throughout history, 85 percent of the people executed for witchcraft have been women (Pfohl 1985). Pfohl suggests "it is hardly surprising that during times in which the great male mastery over nature seemed least secure, times of economic hardship and political instability, the priestly finger of men often found bewitching women to blame" (39).

Economically independent women and women who lived alone and outside the protection of men were most susceptible to charges of witchcraft. Their presence in a community disrupted and threatened the male-dominated power structures. Charges of witchcraft and public executions reasserted the authority of male leaders. At the same time, however, the cruelty and sheer barbarism of the courts and their punishments fuelled cries for reform across western Europe.

Early theorizing about crime and the beginnings of our modern system of criminal justice began to emerge during this tumultuous period of European history. "It was an era of racing industrial revolution, enclosure movements, growing capitalism and growing cities" (Sylvester 1972, 2). These developments were hastened by a rapidly expanding population and by the growth of trade and manufacturing.

The feudal economy had been based on agriculture, with clearly established relations between the landowning aristocracy and the peasants who worked the land. A system of mutual rights and obligations bound these two classes together, and when this relationship was challenged, the entire system was threatened. Feudalism was unable to meet the needs of the growing population. England's population soared from 2.8 million in 1500 to 8.9 million in 1800. Similar increases were reported for the rest of Europe (Pfohl 1985). This surge fuelled a period of colonial expansion as European monarchs sought havens for their surplus populations and access to markets and raw materials, which colonies could provide. Europe's merchant classes gained considerable power during this period, for their economic activities offset mounting economic shortfalls (see Chapter 2).

Changes in the economy were mirrored by changes throughout society. Revolutionary developments were taking place in philosophy, art, music, literature, and other intellectual pursuits. Progressive thinkers of the day fought to usher Europe into a new era—"the Age of Reason" emerged during the period known as the Enlightenment. The Enlightenment thinkers argued against fanaticism and religious superstition, advocating "naturalistic" explanations of the world based on people's capacity to reason.

The Enlightenment philosophers believed that people were free and rational beings. This belief led them to call for the establishment of individual rights and freedoms. In their view, society was based on a social contract under which people chose to relinquish a small portion of their individual autonomy in order to ensure their own safety and the well-being of the entire group. These ideas were clearly contrary to the collectivist orientation of feudalism and to notions that rulers held about a privileged nobility. If realized, a system based on individual rights and freedoms could seriously undermine the bonds of fealty (duty and loyalty) that had long held feudalism together. But those same feudal bonds restricted the availability of labour and hampered the development of manufacturing and industry. Herein lies the essence of the conflict between the aristocracy and the merchants: what was useful for one was detrimental to the other. Each group fought to advance its own interests.

For all their growing economic power, the merchant classes enjoyed little political influence, for only landowners could participate in the legislatures of the day. While they were financially wealthy, the merchants owned little land and were prevented from acquiring any more. Thus, they were barred from gaining political power through landownership. The merchants turned to the legal arena to have their interests served (see Chapter 2).

The merchant classes were able to strengthen their position by financing the costly wars being fought by European monarchs over new colonies. In return for this financial assistance, the merchants gained significant legal concessions. While many of these concessions were aimed specifically at enhancing mercantile activities, they established a number of important legal principles that reflected the ideals of the Enlightenment philosophers. It was in this context that the **Classical School** of criminology made its most significant contributions to the founding of our modern criminal justice system.

The Classical School

In 1764, Cesare Beccaria published his major work, *An Essay on Crimes and Punishments*. This work did much to focus the movement for humanitarian reform that was gaining momentum throughout Europe, for Beccaria was criticizing the cruelty and inhumanity that characterized the criminal justice system of his day (see Box 8.1).

Abuses in the administration of justice were routine. Practices established in the notorious Court of Star Chamber and the institutionalized terror of the Inquisition had become commonplace. Few safeguards existed for the accused, and judicial torture had become a routine method of securing confessions and discovering the identities of accomplices (Langbein 1976).

The more popular forms of torture for these crimes included the rack, the ducking stool, thumbscrews, and other mechanical devices designed to inflict severe pain. The death penalty was administered in a number of ways, including burning at the stake, hanging, decapitation, and drawing and quartering.

In 18th-century England, as many as 350 offences were punishable by death. About 70 percent of death sentences were given for robbery and burglary (Newman 1978). Practices in the colonies were similar in the early 1800s. The first person executed in Toronto was hanged for forging a banknote worth about a dollar when he ran out of money in a tavern (Bunch 2013).

Clamour for the reform of such practices had started long before Beccaria's book was published. Humanitarian appeals were heard from jurists, writers, and philosophers of the era, including Hobbes, Locke, Montesquieu, and Voltaire. The criminal law, in particular, embodied practices that directly contradicted many of the principles advocated by the Classical theorists. It was contrary to the ideals of the social contract, for it was administered in such a way that the average citizen was denied fair and impartial treatment by the state. European society was ripe for the liberating ideas of the Classical theorists and their humanitarian reforms. Beccaria's book served as a catalyst for these sentiments. The reform of a barbaric system of justice provided an excellent focus for the ideas of the Classical theorists.

SEARCH FOR:
"Cesare Beccaria (1738–94)" Internet Encyclopedia of Philosophy

Classical School
Considered to be the first formal school of criminology, Classical criminology is associated with 18th- and early 19th-century reforms to the administration of justice and the prison system. Associated with authors such as Cesare Beccaria (1738–94), Jeremy Bentham (1748–1832), Samuel Romilly (1757–1818), and others, this school brought the emerging philosophy of liberalism and utilitarianism to the justice system, advocating principles of rights, fairness, and due process in place of retribution, arbitrariness, and brutality.

The Classical Theory of Crime

The roots of Classical criminology lie in the philosophy of the Enlightenment. Social contract theory represented a new way of looking at the relationship between people and the state. To avoid living in a state of nature that was, to use Hobbes's famous description, "solitary, poor, nasty, brutish, and short" (1958, 107), people voluntarily entered into a social contract with the state. This involved giving up some of their freedom to the state. In return, the state protected the right of citizens to live in security. In the opening chapter of his book, Beccaria wrote:

> Laws are the conditions whereby free and independent men unite to form society. Weary of living in a state of war, and of enjoying a freedom rendered useless by the uncertainty of its perpetuation, men will willingly sacrifice a part of this freedom in order to enjoy that which is left in security and tranquility. (quoted in Monachesi 1972, 73)

The reforms proposed by the Classical theorists were based on a well-developed theory of the causes of crime: people broke the law because they thought that doing so would advance their own interests. In other words, deviance was the natural result of rational self-interest. If it suits us, and if we think we can get away with it, we will break the law. Crime was understood to be a rationally calculated activity and not the result of some supernatural force or demonic possession. This was a fundamental shift from earlier explanations of criminality.

Having addressed the causes of crime, the Classical theorists turned to the problem of controlling it. The solution was to set up a system of punishment that would deter people from breaking the law. The Classical theorists believed that humans were rational beings who carefully calculated the consequences of their behaviour. Beccaria proposed that the punishment should fit the crime, that is, it should be proportional to the harm done to society. Beccaria argued this on two grounds: that this amount of punishment would be the most effective deterrent, and that this was the fairest way to punish those who were not deterred and who chose to break the law. Unfair punishment would be a violation of the social contract and would be perceived as unjust by the individual and by other members of society.

Crime would be reduced if these reforms were implemented in law because calculating criminals would see that they would not profit from their actions. The punishment would be severe enough that it cost them more than they gained from their criminal behaviour. Beccaria also proposed that punishment be swift and certain. If punishment followed too long after the act, or if it was unlikely to happen at all, then the law would not be an effective deterrent to crime. Finally, the law would be most effective in preventing crime if it was clear and simple enough that people could understand it.

Beccaria also felt that the brutality of torture and the practice of executing people for minor offences must be abolished, for they were abuses of state power. Criminal matters should be dealt with in public according to the dictates of the law. Beccaria wanted to restrict the power of judges, which had been exercised in an arbitrary manner, in private, and generally without recourse for the defendant. He sought to restrict this power by separating the lawmaking power of the

FOCUS

BOX 8.1

WITCHCRAFT AND TORTURE

It is estimated that 500,000 people were convicted of witch-craft and burned to death in Europe between the 15th and 17th centuries. Their crimes: a pact with the Devil; journeys through the air over vast distances mounted on broomsticks; unlawful assembly at sabbats; worship of the Devil; kissing the Devil under the tail; copulation with incubi, male devils equipped with ice-cold penises; copulation with succubi, female devils.

Other more mundane charges were often added: killing the neighbour's cow; causing hailstorms; ruining the crops; stealing and eating babies. But many a witch was executed for no crime other than flying through the air to attend a sabbat . . .

Torture was routinely applied until the witch confessed to having made a pact with the Devil and having flown to a sabbat. It was continued until the witch named other people who were present at the sabbat. If a witch attempted to retract a confes-sion, torture was applied even more intensely until the original confession was reconfirmed. This left the person accused of witchcraft with the choice between dying once and for all at the stake or being returned repeatedly to the torture chambers. Most people opted for the stake. As a reward for their cooperative attitude, penitent witches could look forward to being strangled before the fire was lit.

Questions for Critical Thinking

1. What are some of the reasons why people were perse-cuted for witchcraft during this period?

2. Superstitious and religious explanations of crime had devastating consequences on scapegoated and marginal-ized people. While most of us no longer believe in these explanations, can you think of ways in which some of our current explanations of crime have a negative impact on marginalized people?

Source: Marvin Harris, *Cows, Pigs, Wars, and Witches* (New York: Vintage Books, 1974).

Thousands of people were executed for witchcraft between the 15th and 17th centuries.

World History Archive/Alamy Stock Photo

legislature from the activities of the judges. His view was that the law should be determined by the legislature; it should be accessible to all; trials should be public; and the role of the judiciary should be restricted to the determination of guilt and the administration of punishment as set out in law.

These reforms represented a call for equality before the law and for due-process safeguards. The creation of graded punishments would effectively restrict the arbitrariness and inequality that characterized the existing system. By arguing that the punishment should "fit the crime," Beccaria shifted the focus away from the actor and onto the act. In this way, both noble and peasant would be judged on the basis of what they had done and not on who they were. Moreover, the judiciary would be stripped of its discretion in sentencing, since judges would be bound by punishments fixed by law. This was a powerful directive for equality, since the preferential treatment formerly accorded to those with wealth and power could no longer be granted. However, those with wealth and power had the most influence in shaping the law, so the reforms to the justice system did little to alter the fundamental inequalities based on ownership of property.

Assessing the Contributions of the Classical School

The Classical School and Legal Reform

The ideals of the social contract theorists were translated into progressive criminal justice policy through the reforms promoted by the Classical School. In the process, excesses and injustices were attacked and the foundations of our modern legal system were established. Due-process safeguards (which are taken for granted today), as well as reforms such as the guarantee of individual rights and of equality before the law, the separation of judicial and legislative functions, and the establishment of fixed penalties, remain as the legacy of the Classical School of criminology. Canada's Criminal Code and our modern criminal justice system continue to reflect the work of the Classical theorists.

Limitations of the Classical School

Despite this success, the influence of the Classical School was not all positive. A serious problem with Classical theory was Beccaria's insistence that the degree of punishment must be proportional to the degree of harm that had been done to society. At first glance this proposal seems reasonable, but in practice, it meant that the personal characteristics of the offender and the circumstances of the offence could not be considered when courts determined punishments (Roshier 1989).

Although punishments could be rationally determined on paper, their application in real life often resulted in gross injustices. The courts were bound to follow the letter of the law and could not use discretion to temper the justice being meted out. For example, the hardship that results from having to pay a $1,000 fine varies dramatically depending on whether a person is wealthy or poor. The courts, however, could not take this into account. Furthermore, they were unable to consider mitigating factors such as motive or mental competence, which would alter the responsibility of the convicted person. In this way, attempts to enforce equality resulted in a system that produced a great deal of injustice.

Changing this rigid system was one of the goals of **Neoclassical** criminologists, including the French magistrate Gabriel Tarde. Tarde rejected the notion of free will and proposed a modification of the system of punishment to recognize that there must be some individual treatment of offenders. As a result of the work of Tarde and other Neoclassical writers, courts began to take into account factors such as age (children were held less accountable), mental competence, motive, and

Neoclassical theory
Neoclassical theorists sought to allow more flexibility in the justice system—for example, by individualizing sentences to take into account offender characteristics and extenuating circumstances.

mitigating circumstances. For example, in France, the Penal Code of 1791, which reflected the views of the Classical School, was revised in 1810 and again in 1819. With each revision, the rigid nature of the code was modified to include more discretion for judges as well as consideration of extenuating circumstances.

The approach the Classical School advocated was based more on a theory of **deterrence** than on a theory of crime, and it can be assessed on these grounds. For Classical theorists, penalties did not need to be severe as long as they were swift and certain. However, for most offences, the likelihood of punishment was so small, and the time between the criminal event and any punishment was so great, that the Classical theorists' hopes of reducing crime by changing the legal codes were not as successful as they might have been. In Chapter 15 you will learn how crime reduction strategies that follow the Classical principle of certainty of punishment are much more likely to succeed than policies based on severity, but that lawmakers have often focused on "cracking down" with longer sentences rather than on improving the operations of the justice system. Thus, the failures of deterrence are due more to the failures of legislators than to Classical theory.

An additional problem with the Classical School was its overly simplified view of human nature and the theory of human behaviour that this supported (Thomas and Hepburn 1983). The Classical theorists wholly accepted the concept of the free and rational human being. This view completely ignored the objective realities faced by different individuals as they made their choices, the inequalities they experienced, the state of their knowledge at any given time, and a multitude of other factors that influenced their decisions. This problem was addressed by the Neoclassical theorists.

The ideas of the Classical School have had a strong impact on our modern criminal justice system. Legal principles such as due process and equality before the law are fundamental to our legal system. Beccaria's work had a direct influence on the drafting of the legal code of France following the French Revolution and on the US Bill of Rights, and Classical principles remain part of the legal systems of many countries. For example, in section 15 of our Charter of Rights and Freedoms, Canadians are guaranteed the right to equal treatment before and under the law. We are protected from cruel and unusual punishment by section 12. In sections 7 through 11, an array of procedural safeguards guarantee Canadians the right to due process of law. Clearly, modern criminal justice owes a great debt to the Classical theorists and the reforms they introduced. However, our legal system also incorporates many of the changes suggested by the Neoclassical reformers.

deterrence
As used in criminal justice, it refers to crime prevention achieved through the fear of punishment.

SEARCH FOR:
Canadian Charter of Rights and Freedoms, Department of Justice Canada

The Statistical School: Social Structure and Crime

The first half of the 19th century saw the emergence of an approach to criminology that differed markedly from that of the Classical School. This was evident in the work of André-Michel Guerry (1802–66) in France, Adolphe Quetelet (1796–1874) in Belgium, and Henry Mayhew (1812–87) in England. All three believed that crime, like other human behaviour, was the result of natural causes. Once discovered, these causes could be altered through the application of scientifically derived knowledge. These three men's reliance on objective empirical data, as opposed to philosophical conjecture or speculation, identified them as *Positivists*.

Members of the **Statistical School** did not share the Classical theorists' concept of the rational individual. Instead, they saw behaviour as the product of a host of factors. They systematically analyzed the statistical information available to them and tried to find a relationship between this information and crime. They analyzed such things as population density, education, and poverty (Thomas and Hepburn 1983). A great deal of their work was based on geographic or cartographic analysis, which involved plotting crime rates onto maps.

These theorists went far beyond simply describing what they learned from their maps and graphs. Many of their ideas anticipated the work of modern sociologists, in that they addressed issues related to criminal careers, delinquent subcultures, and social learning theory.

Perhaps their most significant contribution was that they uncovered the remarkable regularity of phenomena such as crime. Countries, provinces, cities, and towns all had rates of crime that were very stable from one year to the next. Even the rates of murder—a highly individualistic act—were consistent from one year to the next. They attributed this stability to elements of the social structure. Quetelet, for example, argued that "rather than being the result of our individual free wills, [our behaviour] is the product of many forces that are external to us" (Thomas and Hepburn 1983). The fact that these forces appeared in regular and recurring patterns prompted these theorists to believe that human behaviour was governed by certain laws akin to those found in the natural or physical sciences.

Anticipating much of our contemporary thinking about crime, these theorists focused on inequalities and other structural features of their society. They viewed people in unfavourable social circumstances as having few options open to them. According to Quetelet, "the crimes which are annually committed seem to be a necessary result of our social organization. . . . The society prepares the crime and the guilty are only the instruments by which it is executed" (in Beirne 1993, 88).

The influence of the Statistical School was, unfortunately, limited. This was not the result of any shortcomings of the approach; rather, it reflected the wider appeal of the biological theories of Cesare Lombroso and his colleagues. Nevertheless, these early pioneers of statistical criminology provided a uniquely sociological contribution to this emerging field of inquiry and demonstrated the value of testing theoretical formulations with empirical observations. Many contemporary theories have their roots in the work of the Statistical School.

Lombroso and the Positive School

The **Positive School** of criminology is also known as the Italian School because its most influential members were Cesare Lombroso (1836–1909) and his students Enrico Ferri (1856–1929) and Raffaelo Garofolo (1852–1934). Lombroso was influenced by the evolutionary theories of Charles Darwin, by the Positivist sociology of Auguste Comte, and by the work of the sociologist Herbert Spencer, who attempted to adapt Darwin's theory to the social world.

Like the members of the Statistical School, Lombroso brought the methods of controlled observation to the study of criminals, comparing them with non-criminals in order to isolate the factors that caused criminality. His own research was badly flawed, and his work is remembered because of his use of the scientific

Statistical School
Associated with early social scientists such as Adolphe Quetelet (1795–1874) and André-Michel Guerry (1802–66), who began to explore the structure of emerging European societies with the assistance of statistical methods. While their early use of statistics is important, they also developed a structural explanation of crime and other social problems (crime is related to the social structure, including the social conditions in which it occurs).

SEARCH FOR:
"Cesare Lombroso" Museo Criminologico

Positive School
The Italian criminologist Cesare Lombroso and his followers were among the first to study crime scientifically. They believed that crime was caused by biological factors beyond the individual's control, though social factors became more important as this school of thought changed over time.

method rather than because of the specific findings he reported, which have all been discredited. Despite their flaws, Lombroso's ideas were widely accepted at the end of the 19th century. Their popularity was partly due to the growing influence of science, in particular of Darwin's theory of evolution. It was likely also due to the comfort of the ruling classes with the view that criminals were not produced by society's flaws, as Quetelet and his colleagues had shown; rather, criminals were genetic misfits who were born to break the rules that governed the lives of civilized people (Radzinowicz 1966).

Darwin's ideas had a major influence on the Positive School:

Darwin's evolutionary thesis represents one of the most profound theories of all times. It not only offered revolutionary new knowledge for the sciences but also helped to shatter many philosophies and practices in other areas. It commanded so much attention and prestige that the entire literate community felt "obligated to bring his world outlook into harmony with their findings" (Hofstadter, 1955, 3). According to Hofstadter, (1955) Darwin's impact is comparable in its magnitude to the work of Nicolaus Copernicus (1473–1543), the European astronomer; Isaac Newton (1642–1727), the English mathematician and physicist; and Freud, the Austrian psychoanalyst. In effect, all of the Western world had to come to grips with Darwin's evolutionary scheme. (Lilly et al. 2007, 28)

The key ideas in Darwin's theory—"the struggle for survival" and "the survival of the fittest"—found fertile ground in the minds of the Positive School criminologists, who incorporated them into their thinking about criminals and how society should deal with them. Identifying criminals became a matter of searching for those physical and moral traits that differentiated more developed human beings from those who were less advanced in evolutionary terms. Incapacitation of these criminals was necessary, for little could be done to alter their genetic makeup. As you will see, some interpretations of these ideas led to a far more drastic approach called "eugenics," which promoted the sterilization and even elimination of those deemed inferior.

Lombroso worked as an army doctor and as a prison physician. He was interested in psychology and at one stage of his career was a teacher of psychiatry. These diverse interests are reflected in his theory of criminality. Lombroso's interest in physiology led him to note certain distinct physical differences between the criminals and soldiers with whom he worked. His thoughts on the subject came together during an autopsy he was performing on the notorious thief Vilella. He noted that many of the characteristics of Vilella's skull were similar to those of lower animals. In a remarkable description of the moment of discovery, Lombroso recalled:

This was not merely an idea, but a revelation. At the sight of that skull, I seemed to see all of a sudden, lighted up as a vast plain under a flaming sky, the problem of the nature of the criminal—an atavistic being who reproduces in his person the ferocious instincts of primary humanity and the inferior animals. Thus were explained anatomically the enormous jaws, high cheek-bones, prominent superciliary arches, solitary lines in the palms, extreme size of the orbits, handle-shaped or sessile ears found in criminals, savages, and apes, insensibility to pain, extremely acute sight, tattooing, excessive idleness, love of orgies, and the irresistible craving for evil for its own sake, the desire not only to extinguish life in the victim, but to mutilate the corpse, tear its flesh, and drink its blood. (Quoted in Taylor, Walton, and Young 1973, 41)

Fig. 13. Tipo comune - Assassino.

Fig. 16. Tipo comune (a fronte sfuggente) - Omicida-grassatore.

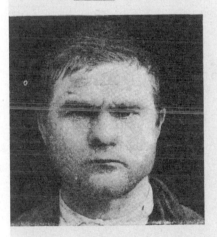

Fig. 14. Tipo comune - Omicida.

Fig. 17. Tipo comune (a fronte sfuggente) - Omicida.

Fig. 15. Tipo comune - Feritore ladro.

Fig. 18. Tipo comune (a fronte sfuggente) - Omicida-grassatore.

Chronicle/Alamy Stock Photo

The prison physician Cesare Lombroso was the founder of the Positive School of criminology. These photographs show some of those whom Lombroso felt should be classified as atavisms.

atavism
Cesare Lombroso believed that some people were born criminals. These born criminals were throwbacks to an earlier stage of evolution—atavisms—and were morally inferior to the rest of the population. Lombroso's research focused on physical differences (stigmata) that could be used to identify atavisms.

atavism
Cesare Lombroso believed that some people were born criminals. These born criminals were throwbacks to an earlier stage of evolution—atavisms—and were morally inferior to the rest of the population. Lombroso's research focused on physical differences (stigmata) that could be used to identify atavisms.

stigmata
The physical signs that a person is an atavism.

This discovery led Lombroso to believe that criminals were throwbacks to an earlier stage of evolution, or **atavisms**. His theory has been succinctly described by Gould (1981):

> These people are innately driven to act as a normal ape or savage would but such behaviour is deemed criminal in our civilized society. Fortunately, we may identify born criminals because they bear anatomical signs of their apishness. Their atavism is both physical and mental, but the physical signs, or stigmata as Lombroso called them, are decisive. Criminal behaviour can also arise in normal men, but we know the "born criminal" by his anatomy. Anatomy, indeed, is destiny, and born criminals cannot escape their inherited taint. (153)

Lombroso tested his ideas by observing imprisoned criminals. In one study, he compared the physical characteristics of a group of criminals with those of a group of soldiers and found that the criminals had many more of the atavistic **stigmata** than did the soldiers. In another piece of research, he found that stigmata were present in 30 to 40 percent of anarchists but in less than 12 percent of members of other extremist movements (Taylor, Walton, and Young 1973). He also concluded that different types of offenders were characterized by different physiological characteristics. For example, "robbers have . . . small, shifting, quick-moving eyes; bushy connecting eyebrows; twisted or snub noses, thin beards . . . and foreheads almost receding," while "habitual homicides have glassy, cold, motionless eyes, sometimes bloodshot and injected. The nose is often aquiline, or rather hawklike, and always voluminous" (1973, 70–71). He believed that women had fewer stigmata and lower crime rates than males because women were closer to their primitive origins. He concluded that women were vengeful, deceitful, and jealous, but added that their crime rates were relatively low because these negative traits were neutralized by their maternal instinct, piety, and lack of passion.

Lombroso initially postulated two types of offenders—born criminals and occasional criminals. However, in response to his critics, he later added several more categories, including the following:

1. *Epileptics.* In addition to their medical condition, epileptics also had the atavistic characteristics of criminals.
2. *Criminal insane.* This was the category of those whose mental illness had led to their involvement in crime.
3. *Criminals of passion.* These criminals contrasted completely with born criminals in that they lacked any of the criminal stigmata. They committed crimes for "noble and powerful" motives such as love or politics.
4. *Criminaloids.* This was a grab-bag category, which included anyone who committed a crime but did not fall into one of the other classifications. Lombroso felt that precipitating factors other than biological ones caused criminality among this group.

The Contribution of the Positive School

Lombroso's work attracted a large following. The stigmata were used as indicators of criminality in many trials, and Lombroso himself appeared as an expert witness several times. In one case, the court had to decide which of two brothers had killed their stepmother. Lombroso's testimony that one of the men had the features of a born criminal helped secure the man's conviction.

Lombroso's theory of criminal anthropology has not stood up to empirical test. His research was poorly conducted by today's standards. His comparison groups were chosen unsystematically, his statistical techniques were crude, his measurements were often sloppy, and he assumed that those in prison were criminals and that those not in prison were noncriminals. Some of the stigmata he mentioned in his research, such as tattoos, could not possibly have been inherited. Despite these weaknesses, his work did represent an attempt to provide a scientific explanation of the causes of criminality.

Perhaps Lombroso's most lasting contribution was his discussion of the criminal justice system. Classical theorists felt that crime could be controlled if society could design punishments to fit the crime. Positive theorists, by contrast, believed that the punishment should fit the criminal. Radzinowicz and King have nicely outlined the difference between the two perspectives: "The Classical School exhorts men to study justice, the Positivist School exhorts justice to study men" (1977, 86).

Because Lombroso believed that people became involved in criminality for different reasons, he felt they should be treated differently by the criminal justice system. If a respectable man committed murder because of passion, honour, or political belief, no punishment was needed, for that man would never repeat the crime. For other offenders, **indeterminate sentences** would best ensure rehabilitation. Born criminals should not be held responsible for their actions, though they needed to be incarcerated for the protection of society. However, this was to be done in a humane way. He recommended that prisoners serving longer sentences be treated better than those serving less time.

Some born criminals could be channelled in a socially useful direction. For example, banishment and transportation to one of the colonies might allow their tendencies to be redirected towards the difficult business of building settlements in a hostile environment. For others, more severe sanctions were required. "There exists, it is true, a group of criminals, born for evil, against whom all social cures break as against a rock—a fact which compels us to eliminate them completely, even by death" (Lombroso 1912).

Several features of our current criminal justice system stem from the concern of Lombroso and his followers with individualizing the treatment of offenders. Probation, parole, indeterminate sentences, and the consideration of mitigating circumstances by the courts have all been influenced by Lombroso's work as well as by the work of Neoclassical criminologists.

indeterminate sentence
A sentence that has no fixed release date. Release is determined by a parole authority based on the individual's behaviour.

Biological Theories in the Early 20th Century

Crime and Physical Characteristics

Lombroso's theories came under frequent attack during his lifetime. In 1889, he responded to his critics by challenging them to compare 100 born criminals, 100 people with criminal tendencies, and 100 normal people. He promised to retract his theories if the criminals did not turn out to be different from the other groups. His challenge was ultimately taken up by an English prison medical officer, Dr. G.B. Griffiths, and completed by his successor, Dr. Charles Goring, who succeeded Griffiths in 1903 shortly after the project began.

Goring carefully measured and compared the physical and mental characteristics of 3,000 English convicts with those of diverse samples of "normals," including British university students, schoolboys, university professors, Scots with mental illness, German Army recruits, and British Army soldiers (Goring 1972). After comparing these groups on 37 physical and six mental traits, Goring concluded that there was no evidence of a distinct physical type of criminal. Lombroso's "anthropological monster," he concluded, "has no existence in fact" (Goring 1913). Criminals were no more or less likely to possess stigmata than were members of the control groups. Goring did find that criminals were physically inferior to normals, but he attributed this fact to social selection processes.

Goring's most important finding was the high correlation between criminality and low intelligence. This led to his theory that crime was inherited and that the most important constitutional mechanism through which crime was genetically transmitted was mental inferiority. Unlike Lombroso, Goring did feel that hereditary predispositions could be modified by social factors such as education. However, he also supported eugenic measures, which would restrict the reproduction of the constitutional factors leading to crime.

In some respects, Goring's research was a major advance over Lombroso's. His measurement was far more precise, and he had access to statistical tools that were unavailable to Lombroso. But his work also contained a number of serious methodological flaws. Among them was the fact that he was comparing officially labelled criminals, who were not a representative sample of all criminals, with diverse groups of other people who did not represent the noncriminal population. While many of the other criticisms of Goring's research are quite technical, they are serious enough to cast doubt on his own theories as well as on his refutation of Lombroso (Driver 1972).

The search for individual differences as the cause of crime did not end with Goring. In the 1930s, anthropologist Ernest A. Hooton compared more than 13,000 criminals with a sample of noncriminals drawn from college students, firemen, hospital outpatients, militiamen, mental hospital patients, people using the change house at a public beach, and others. On the basis of this comparison, Hooton concluded that criminals were biologically and socially inferior. Among the new stigmata he attributed to criminals were such characteristics as "low foreheads, high pinched nasal roots, nasal bridges and tips varying to both extremes of breadth and narrowness," and "very small ears" (1939, 158).

While Hooton was not as concerned as some of his predecessors with the policy implications of his research, he did not hesitate to draw the obvious conclusion. Since "crime is the resultant of the impact of environment upon low grade human organisms . . . it follows that the elimination of crime can be effected only by the expiration of the physically, mentally, and morally unfit, or by their complete segregation in a socially aseptic environment" (175). These ideas formed the basis of the eugenics movement that developed in the United States at the turn of the 20th century (see Box 8.2).

Hooton's work was controversial, and his findings were challenged. He was accused of using poor scientific methods and circular reasoning. For example, he

FOCUS

BOX 8.2

CRIMINOLOGY AND EUGENICS

The term "eugenics" simply means "well born." It connotes a sense of contributing to or improving the stock of the race or the nation. The term became one of some suspicion when the goal of genetics was embraced by various political regimes and enforced through the state's coercive power as an effective instrument for social engineering. In modern times, the first extended programs in state-sponsored eugenics were developed in the United States in the late 19th and early 20th centuries. These eugenics programs grew from a constellation of ideas derived from evolutionary theory that embraced social Darwinism; from contemporaneous criminology encouraged by a scientific hypothesis supported by post-mortem studies of brains of criminals and the findings of the famous Juke Report (1875) on inheritance and criminal behaviour; from demographic concerns about dysgenics—the growth of the criminal population and the growth of the feeble-minded population because of their unrestrained breeding patterns; and from surgical advances, such as vasectomy and salpingectomy (female sterilization), in the practice of medicine. Involuntary sterilization became the instrument of this modern attempt at eugenics. The idea of genetic sterilization, the pursuit of this end as a national goal, and the procurement of means to attain their desired result were pressed by some of the most influential families, by some of the most prestigious societies and foundations, by some powerful lawyers, judges, scientists, and physicians, and by some of the most elite universities in the United States. The central notion and clearest articulation of the goals of this movement are best recorded in the words of Mr. Justice Oliver Wendell Holmes, who, writing for the majority in a 1927 United States Supreme Court decision, *Buck v. Bell*, found involuntary sterilization to be compatible with the guarantees found in the US Constitution.

Holmes concluded:

We have seen more than once that the public welfare may call upon the best citizens for their lives. It would be strange if it could not call upon those who already sap the strength of the state for lesser sacrifices, often not felt to be such by those concerned, in order to prevent our being swamped with incompetence. It is better for all the world, if instead of waiting to execute degenerate offspring for crime, or to let them starve for their imbecility, society can prevent those who are manifestly unfit from continuing their kind. The principle that sustains compulsory vaccination is broad enough to cover cutting the fallopian tubes (*Jacobson v. Massachusetts*, 197 U.S. 11). Three generations of imbeciles are enough. (*Buck v. Bell*. United States Supreme Court. Report 274, 1927)

Canada also practised involuntary sterilization, and the practice remained legal in Alberta until 1972.

Questions for Critical Thinking

1. In the next section of the textbook (Crime and Intelligence) read the discussion of the eugenics movement. What lessons do you think we can learn from the mistakes made by governments in their actions relating to this issue?

2. Have actions such as those of the eugenicists made criminologists *more* or *less* willing to accept biological theories of crime today?

Source: Margaret Monahan Hogan, "Medical Ethics: The New Eugenics: Therapy—Enhancement—Screening—Testing," International Catholic University (n.d.), http://home.comcast.net/~icuweb/c04106.htm.

used conviction for a crime as a method of separating criminals from noncriminals; he then examined the convicted groups and concluded they were inferior; finally, he used this finding of inferiority to account for their criminality (Empey 1982). Only in this way could a trait such as thin lips be turned into an indicator of criminality.

Several other criticisms of Hooton's methods are worth considering. His control group did not represent the general population. Students, firefighters, and mental patients have particular characteristics that distinguish them from the rest of the population. Furthermore, his findings show tremendous differences within the various control groups he used. In fact, the differences between his control groups drawn from Boston and Nashville were actually greater than between prisoners and controls (Pfohl 1985). As in the case of Lombroso, Hooton's attempt to link criminal behaviour to physical types was thoroughly discredited.

This kind of research has made periodic appearances in a variety of forms since the days of Lombroso and Hooton. In the 1950s, William Sheldon attempted to re-establish the link between body type and criminality in his elaboration of a "somatotype" theory. He described three basic body types, which, he argued, were related to particular personalities and temperaments. These body types were endomorphs (fat, round bodies), who had easygoing personalities; ectomorphs (tall and lean), who had introverted personalities and nervous dispositions; and mesomorphs (well-built and muscular), who had aggressive personalities and were quick to act and insensitive to pain. Sheldon related each of these types to particular kinds of criminal behaviour. He found that the muscular mesomorphs were the type most likely to become involved in delinquent or criminal behaviour.

Sheldon fared no better than his predecessors when his work was subjected to scrutiny. He had done a bad job of measuring delinquency among the young people he had studied and he had used vague and inconsistent categories that have been described as scientifically meaningless.

These criticisms could not be levelled at Sheldon and Eleanor Glueck, who followed up on Sheldon's ideas. They applied his somatotype theory to a study of 500 juvenile delinquents. They compared the bodies of 500 adjudicated delinquents with a matched sample of nondelinquents. The Gluecks concluded from their work that delinquents were more likely to be mesomorphs. However, this finding may have raised more questions than it answered. For example, it may be that mesomorphs actually look more like stereotypical delinquents than either endomorphs or ectomorphs. As a result, people may respond to mesomorphs differently and they may be more likely to be labelled delinquent than those who are nonmesomorphs. Other social selection factors may also have been involved. Youth who are athletic, muscular, and active may be better candidates for Little League baseball, hockey, or delinquency than their less-athletic peers.

Crime and Intelligence

Other biological theories have focused on a variety of factors that have been associated with individual differences. Goring suggested that instead of looking for defective body types, the focus should be on genetic weaknesses demonstrated by low intelligence.

In one famous study of family and heredity, the American psychologist Henry Goddard traced the legitimate and illegitimate offspring of an army lieutenant, Martin Kallikak. Young Martin fathered an illegitimate son with a 'feeble-minded' barmaid before he settled down and married a "respectable" woman. The study compared the descendants of Kallikak's feeble-minded mate to those of his "normal" wife. According to Goddard, the offspring of the barmaid produced a collection of deviants and 'feeble-minded' degenerates. By contrast, the family of his wife showed no such weakness (Goddard 1912).

Even if we ignore the enormous methodological weaknesses of Goddard's study (Gould [1981] has shown that the photographs of the "depraved" Kallikaks had been retouched to make them look like defectives), little is left of scientific consequence. The absence of any consideration of the social factors involved in this comparison clearly undermines Goddard's findings. It is hardly surprising that children raised in difficult and impoverished circumstances should have greater involvement in criminality than those who grew up in a better social environment.

Goddard continued his work using the Binet-Simon intelligence test, which had recently been developed in France. This IQ test was based on the notion of "mental age." Goddard studied the residents of a New Jersey mental institution and, on the basis of that work, established the mental age of 12 as the cut-off point for determining feeble-mindedness. He then applied this IQ test to the inmates of jails and prisons throughout the New Jersey area. He found that in around half the institutions, 70 percent of the inmates were at or below the mental age of 12. From these findings, he concluded that IQ was an important determinant of criminal behaviour. He also concluded that feeble-mindedness was directly inherited and could only be eliminated by denying those he called "morons" the right to reproduce (1914). Goddard also argued that "criminal imbeciles" should not be held criminally responsible for their actions. His expert testimony helped acquit at least one murderer on the grounds of criminal imbecility (Rafter 1997).

The acceptance of Goddard's position was short-lived. In 1926, Murchinson published the results of a study in which he compared IQ data from World War I army recruits with those from a group of inmates (Pfohl 1985). He found that 47 percent of the recruits, but only 30 percent of the prisoners, had IQ scores that fell below the mental age of 12. This startling finding implied that almost half of a very large sample of American men could be considered mentally feeble. The absurdity of these findings forced Goddard to lower his cut-off point for feeble-mindedness from 12 years to 9. This reduction resulted in the disappearance of any significant differences between inmates and soldiers, or anyone else for that matter (Pfohl 1985).

Despite evidence so convincing that even Goddard disavowed his earlier work, governments responded to their fear of those with low IQs by passing legislation controlling their behaviour. These laws resulted in thousands of people with intellectual disabilities in North America being forced into institutions and, in many cases, being involuntarily sterilized.

In Canada, sterilization laws were passed in Alberta in 1929 and in British Columbia in 1933. The Alberta law was not repealed until 1972. As a child growing up in Alberta, Leilani Muir was incorrectly labelled as mentally retarded. She was kept in an institution and was sterilized without her knowledge or consent. In 1995, Muir, who actually had normal intelligence, successfully sued the Alberta government and was awarded substantial damages. This case shows the problems with developing policies based on notions of individual inferiority.

The controversy over IQ tests has continued. A number of serious flaws in the assumptions behind this approach have come to light. For example, it has been suggested that high scores on these tests may have more to say about test-taking ability than they do about intelligence. Furthermore, the composition of these tests has been found to be biased in favour of the cultural locations of those who designed the tests. In a dramatic demonstration, Adrian Dove, a black sociologist, devised an IQ test based on the cultural referents and language of the black ghetto (Pfohl 1985). Black respondents who were familiar with this culture did well on the tests, but white middle-class respondents did poorly. The validity of IQ tests remains suspect, and their use has often been linked to racist ideology and propaganda.

A number of other recent formulations have sought to re-establish a link between individual characteristics and criminal behaviour. These have focused on such things as chromosomes, unusual EEG results, hypoglycemic disorders, and premenstrual tension. The results in many of these cases are similar. While it would be foolhardy to deny the biological or psychological dimensions of human behaviour, the evidence supporting a link between pathology and criminal behaviour is weak. Moreover, this approach ignores the essentially political nature of social control—what one society praises and rewards, another may condemn. Given this variability in what we define as crime, an assessment of the underlying social and political context is indispensable.

The continued search for individual differences and the erroneous identification of a normal "us" and a criminal "them" has sometimes had political overtones (see Box 8.3 for an extreme example). The emergence of a positive science coincided with the rise of a powerful capitalist class and expanded colonial activity. Both of these developments welcomed the ideological justification contained within the Darwinian notion of survival of the fittest. Social Darwinism and positive criminology flourished in this environment.

This biological–criminological approach of the Positive School offered a ready-made and "humane" way of dealing with the problems of social control.

FOCUS   BOX 8.3

BAD SCIENCE OR BAD POLITICS? CRIMINOLOGY IN NAZI GERMANY

Throughout this chapter, we have tried to link the developments in criminology to the wider social, political, and intellectual contexts from which they emerged. For example, we noted the impact of the Enlightenment and humanistic thinking on the development of the Classical School and the reforms that proponents of that school struggled to make to the criminal justice system of the day. We also noted how social Darwinism had a far-ranging influence on the type of thinking that began to gain prominence in a number of fields after Charles Darwin published his famous treatise on evolution. This included the field of criminology and the ideas promoted by the Positive School.

What happens to these ideas and theories once they become popularized depends in large part on how they are used to further particular agendas or views of the world. In the case of the eugenics movement, criminological–biological research was used to justify forced sterilizations, executions of habitual criminals, and even genocide as was the case in Nazi Germany. "Hitler himself, in a speech to the 1929 Nazi Party Congress in Nuremburg, called it outrageous that 'criminals are allowed to procreate' and demanded drastic eugenic measures" (Wetzell 2000, 180). This pronouncement eerily foreshadowed what was to come. As Rosenhaft (2001) notes,

from 1935 on, certain categories of criminals were officially treated as racially undesirable. Prostitutes, vagrants, and other so-called asocials, including Roma, or Gypsies, were taken off the streets and sent to prisons or camps indefinitely and without the right to appeal. Homosexuals, whose lifestyle contradicted both criminal law and

the racial duty to produce children, were hounded and arrested. . . . It was from managing these thousands of ordinary captives that the concentration camp system was set up right at the beginning of the regime in 1933.

The unconscionable horrors perpetrated by the Nazis could be attributed to the vicious and racist ideology of the Nazi regime. Their use of science and biological–criminological research to justify their actions, however, should serve as a cautionary tale to us all. The conclusions drawn by Richard Wetzell (2000) after his extensive investigation of German criminology during the Nazi era provide a sobering view on the role of "science":

A more complex picture of science under the Third Reich also diminishes the distance that we often perceive between "Nazi science" and our own science. Contemporary scientists as well as the general public often assume that science under Nazism was "bad" or "perverted" science. This view is reassuring because it suggests that our own, more "advanced" science does not have the same dangerous implications that "Nazi science" had. But if science under the Nazis was in fact more sophisticated, the distance between "Nazi science" and science in our own day is diminished, and we are forced to ask ourselves whether the role of science and medicine under the Nazi regime might point to dangers inherent in scientific research in the present. My point here is not to suggest that research on the genetic causes of crime, for instance, is intrinsically evil and dangerous and will necessarily lead to inhumane and murderous state policies. Rather, my point is that much of the scientific research conducted during the Nazi years was not as different from current scientific research as we would like to think. Like science before and after the Third Reich, scientific research in Nazi Germany was characterized by continual tension between the internal dynamics of science and the intellectual and political biases of the scientists and their society. This argument should make us uncomfortable in salutary ways. For it makes us realize that the connection between scientific research and the Nazi regime was more complicated than we might have thought, and it gives us a more critical view of science in our own time.

Source: Richard Wetzell, *Inventing the Criminal: A History of German Criminology: 1880–1945* (Chapel Hill: University of North Carolina Press, 2000).

This was extremely important at a time when the population was being transformed into a disciplined industrial labour force. The harsh and barbaric punishments of the past could be set aside; instead, a scientifically designed technology of control could be used to "treat" troublesome individuals. This focus on the pathologies of individuals serves to conveniently remove one's gaze from the social structure. If it is certain that problems like crime are the result of individual deficiencies, then one needn't concern oneself about the social structure. If, on the other hand, the structural sources of inequality, such as racism, sexism, and other social ills, are examined, the very nature of the society may be called into question.

What Do You Think?

Now that you have learned about some of the foundational ideas that have informed criminological thinking for over 200 years, it may be interesting to take a few minutes to think about what is at the core of your own beliefs about crime and its control. For example, you may have asked yourself why some people commit crimes and others are mainly law-abiding. What you believe about the nature of human beings and the role of those charged with the responsibility of keeping us safe may have a lot to do with your answers to this question. Before we begin a broader self-reflection, however, there are a few important ideas to consider about the thinking process itself. Here are some basic questions to think about before you explore the roots of your own criminological assumptions. Where you stand on these questions will help you better understand your own position regarding the nature of crime and its control.

TABLE 8.1 ■ Early Theories of Crime

Theory	Theorists	Key Elements
Classical theory	Beccaria	Humans were rational thinkers. Those who contemplated breaking the law considered the positive and negative consequences of their actions. A measured system of punishments was needed to deter crime.
Neoclassical theory	Tarde	Helped develop a more individualized system of criminal justice.
Statistical School	Guerry, Quetelet, and Mayhew	Explored the social causes of crime. Related structural factors such as inequality to crime.
Positive School	Lombroso	Criminals were born, not made. They were atavisms who were less evolved than the law-abiding.
Early-20th-century biological	Goring, Hooton, Sheldon, and Goddard	Related criminality to several types of theories of biological inferiority, including intelligence and body shape.

Binary Categories—Is the Issue "Black and White"? (Or Maybe a Shade of Grey?)

It is common for people to try to simplify what are often complex issues by using binary categories that divide their choices into opposing pairs. This is the idea behind saying the issue is "black and white." This kind of thinking implies that if you believe one side of the binary proposition, you have to reject the opposite side. Thus, if you believe something to be white, you can't also believe that it could be black at the same time. Binary thinking turns otherwise complex questions into "either/or" decisions. The problem is that while this may simplify the matter, decisions in real life are rarely this straightforward and there are usually many possible answers or "shades of grey" to consider in a complex issue.

Logical Consistency—One Idea Leads to the Next

Your thinking has to be logically consistent if you are to avoid holding ideas that contradict each other. For example, if you believe that people should be held responsible for their actions, you also have to believe that they have free will and chose to act the way they did. If, on the other hand, you believe that people sometimes have little or no control over their actions, then to be consistent, your views on personal responsibility have to accept that circumstances may mitigate the extent to which we can or should hold someone responsible for his or her actions. The point is that you have to be logically consistent in your thinking.

"Mixing and Matching"—Selectively Choosing Ideas from Different Theories

In addition to being logically consistent, you can't pick and choose among values or beliefs based on your personal preferences. Using the example of free will again, if you believe that people should be held accountable for their choices, you can't also believe that it is society's responsibility to make sure people make wise choices. That is, you can't believe a part of a theory that you agree with and then reject the parts with which you are less comfortable. Theories are typically logically consistent, and you can't simply pick parts of them that you like and "mix and match."

What Do These Ideas Have to Do with Historical and Contemporary Thinking in Criminology?

In the survey below, we outline some of the main questions that people have asked about crime and the role of the state in controlling it. Have a look at these questions and think about how you might answer them. What kind of criminological thinking is closest to your point of view? Based on your answers to these questions, you can better understand the foundations of your own theoretical beliefs.

Your Thinking about Crime and Its Control

Answer the following questions by selecting the option that best reflects your views. Once you have completed the survey, compare your answers to those in Table 8.2. What kind of "theorist" are YOU?

1. From your perspective, what is the nature of human beings?

    (a) Human beings have "free will" and should be held accountable for their actions.

    (b) Human beings have "free will" but are influenced in their decisions by extenuating circumstances.

    (c) Human beings don't really have "free will" but are born with various traits and predispositions that influence how they act.

2. Based on your point of view, why do people behave the way they do?"

    (a) People are selfish and look out for themselves.

    (b) People are complicated—sometimes they are selfish but other times they are considerate and compassionate.

    (c) People are pre-programmed to behave the way they do. They are born that way.

3. According to your beliefs, what is the moral foundation for human behaviour?"

    (a) People will act in their own self-interest and have to be forced to behave and follow society's rules.

    (b) People have both "good" and "evil" sides to their personalities.

    (c) Some people are simply born "bad" and there isn't much we can do except "lock them up".

4. Why do you think people commit crimes?

    (a) People commit crimes because they think they can benefit and that they won't get caught.

    (b) People commit crimes because of the circumstances they find themselves in—the opportunities appear too good to pass up at the time.

    (c) People commit crime because they are born "bad" and it's in their nature.

5. What do you think we should do with people that commit crimes?

    (a) People convicted of committing a crime should be punished according the level of seriousness of the offence.

    (b) People convicted of committing a crime should get what they deserve but not be subjected to any additional interventions by the criminal justice system (such as counselling or rehabilitation)

    (c) People convicted of committing a crime should be assessed and their punishment should be tailored to their individual personalities and characteristics.

TABLE 8.2 ■ A Model for Exploring the Foundations of Your Criminological Thinking

	Classical Theorists	Neoclassical Theorists	Positivist Theorists
1. Key Beliefs about Human Beings and the Way They Act			
"What is the nature of human beings?"	Free will	Free will but based on circumstances	Determined
"Why do people behave the way they do?"	They are rational and hedonistic. They typically choose to act the way they do to "maximize their pleasure and minimize their pain."	They are rational and choose to act the way they do but these choices are influenced by immediate circumstances. For example, they might not have all the information available to help them make their decisions.	People are born with certain predispositions and really don't have much choice in how they behave.
"What is the moral foundation for human behaviour?"	People are basically egoistic ("evil" or "selfish") and will usually act in their own best interest.	People are neither inherently "good" nor inherently "evil." They are just people who act "in the moment.".	Some people are born "good" but others are not. The latter have to be dealt with to ensure that they don't harm themselves or others.
2. Key beliefs about why people commit crimes?	People choose to commit crimes because they believe they will benefit from doing so.	People commit crimes based on the circumstances in which they find themselves.	People commit crimes because it is in their nature to behave the way they do.
3. Key beliefs about what the state should do when people commit crimes?	Let the punishment fit the crime.\n\nSevere punishments are unnecessary. What is necessary instead is enough punishment to deter people from choosing to commit crimes.	Just Deserts.\n\nThose who commit crime should get what they deserve—no more, no less.	Let the punishment fit the criminal.\n\nPeople can't help behaving the way they do, so punishments should be tailored to the characteristics of the individuals involved.
	If you "do the crime you have to do the time."	We should minimize the level of state intervention into people's lives.	Some people can be rehabilitated but others can't because of their nature. The latter have to be incapacitated to protect themselves and society.

QUESTIONS FOR CRITICAL THINKING

1. How did the development of the Classical School of criminology reflect the wider changes taking place in European society at the time? Consider how social, economic, and ideological forces influenced the founders of the Classical School.
2. Beccaria recommended that criminal law incorporate punishments that were severe enough to act as a deterrent, but not excessively harsh; certain; applied swiftly; and clear enough to be understood by all citizens. How does our current justice system measure up to these principles?

Summary

■ Early theories of crime were based on superstition and religious beliefs.

■ This view of crime changed when the Classical School of criminology became popular. Members of this school argued that people were free and rational actors and proposed that the key to preventing crime was to establish a Criminal Code based on the principle that the punishment should fit the crime.

- The Classical School had a major impact on legal systems in many countries. However, the resulting legal codes were rigid and inflexible. Other scholars proposed a series of Neoclassical reforms, which have since been incorporated into the legal systems of many countries.

- Lombroso and other members of the Positive School brought scientific methods to the study of crime. While Lombroso's biological theory has not stood up to scientific scrutiny, the application of science to criminology represented a major shift in the discipline.

- Lombroso was followed by a number of other researchers who sought to blame crime on the biological inferiority of criminals. As with Lombroso's theory, research has not supported these early-20th-century biological theories. However, they did have a major impact on the legal system, as measures such as involuntary sterilization and lengthy incarceration for "defectives" were passed in many jurisdictions.

- Most of the principles of our current justice system reflect the earlier influence of Classical, Neoclassical, and Positive theories of crime.

NET WORK

In this chapter, you have learned how Classical theory and Positivist theory have influenced how Western nations such as Canada and the United States address issues like sentencing. The debates over sentencing continue to influence public opinion and criminal justice policy today. Should the punishment fit the crime, or should we take other factors into account when sentencing someone and let the punishment fit the offender? The intensity of this debate is visible in the competing points of view expressed over two sentencing policies: (1) three strikes and (2) mandatory minimum sentences.

To learn more about these debates, follow the links below to some interesting articles and information about other useful sites.

Three-Strikes Policy: http://idebate.org/debatabase/debates/law/house-would-strike-out-three-strikes-laws

Sentencing in Canada: http://www.lawconnection.ca/content/sentencing-theory-backgrounder

Mandatory Minimum Sentencing in Canada: http://www.parl.gc.ca/Content/LOP/researchpublications/prb0553-e.htm http://www.justice.gc.ca/eng/rp-pr/csj-sjc/ccs-ajc/rr05_10/rr05_10.pdf

Review the discussion around sentencing in order to answer the following questions:

1. What is the three-strikes policy in sentencing?
2. Which theory of criminology is most reflected in the three-strikes policy?
3. Summarize the current debates over this criminal justice policy.
4. What is mandatory minimum sentencing?
5. Which theory of criminology is reflected in a mandatory minimum sentencing policy?
6. Summarize the current debate in Canada over this criminal justice policy.

9 Psychological Perspectives on Criminality

MARGUERITE TERNES
Saint Mary's University

PATRICIA A. ZAPF
John Jay College of Criminal Justice

DAVID N. COX
Simon Fraser University

NATHALIE C. GAGNON
Kwantlen Community College

RONALD ROESCH
Simon Fraser University

Learning Objectives

After reading this chapter, you should be able to

- Describe and critique the different psychological theories that have been used to explain criminal behaviour, including psychoanalytic theory, evolutionary theory, moral development theory, Eysenck's theory, social learning theory, and operant conditioning theory.

- Understand what is meant by the term "antisocial personality."

- Describe the difference between Antisocial Personality Disorder and psychopathy.

- Describe the most current theories linking crime and mental illness.

This chapter reviews different psychological perspectives on criminality. We begin with a discussion of the characteristics of psychological theories and then review various psychological theories that have been proposed to explain criminality. Next, antisocial personality and psychopathy are described, and the differences between the two are illustrated through the use of several case studies—Charles Manson, Will Baker (formerly known as Vince Li), Paul Bernardo and Karla Homolka, and Canada's most notorious criminal, Clifford Olson. We conclude with a discussion of crime and mental illness, including a review of research in this area and a discussion of the prevalence of mental illness in jail and prison populations.

Psychological Theories of Crime

There has been considerable debate over psychological explanations of criminal behaviour. Psychologists typically approach the problem of understanding, explaining, and predicting criminality by developing theories of personality or learning that account for an individual's behaviour in a specific situation. About 40 years ago, an extensive review of a decade of published research on offenders (Reppucci and Clingempeel 1978) found that nearly all the research could be characterized as reflecting one of two value assumptions. The first was the

assumption of offender deficit, which asserts that theories and interventions are premised on the notion that there is something psychologically wrong with offenders. The second was the **assumption of discriminating traits**, which holds that criminals differ from noncriminals, particularly in terms of such traits as impulsivity and aggression. Research based on this assumption involved studies of offender and nonoffender populations, utilizing a number of personality tests in an attempt to find traits that differentiated the two groups.

Critics have taken issue with psychology's reliance on these two assumptions. Reppucci and Clingempeel (1978) point to two major omissions in psychological research. One is that there is typically very little emphasis placed on studies of the strengths of offenders. Most of the research and interventions focus on deficits rather than on the positive characteristics of individuals. While the concerns of Reppucci and Clingempeel continue to have validity today, the field has made a considerable shift: research and theory increasingly recognize the importance of offender strengths (e.g., van Wormer 2001; Webster et al. 2006; Hoge, Guerra, and Boxer 2008; Jones et al. 2014). A second omission identified by Reppucci and Clingempeel is that psychological research tends to ignore the potential importance of situational and environmental factors for individual behaviour. Again, recent developments have stressed the importance of external factors in both explaining criminal behaviour and developing intervention programs to reduce recidivism (e.g., Haney 2002; Moretti, Jackson, and Obsuth 2010; Wheeler, Clare, and Holland 2013).

Others, such as Reid (2003), have been critical of psychological theories of crime that are based on the expectation that it is possible to classify individuals as criminals or noncriminals, arguing that this classification cannot be made reliably. Rather, evidence suggests that criminal behaviour is pervasive, as indicated by studies of self-reported delinquency, white-collar crime, and corporate crime (Thornberry and Krohn 2000).

Conversely, the work of David Farrington (2002; Loeber and Farrington, 2012) illustrates the importance of understanding individual differences. Farrington views criminal behaviour as the outcome of several different social and psychological factors (see also Loeber, Farrington, and Stouthamer-Loeber 2001; Loeber et al. 2001). According to him, the motivation to commit delinquent acts arises primarily out of a desire for material goods or a need for excitement. If these desires cannot be satisfied in a socially approved manner, an illegal act may be chosen. The motivation to commit delinquent acts will be influenced by psychological variables, including the individual's learning history and the beliefs he or she may have internalized regarding criminal behaviour. Eysenck and Gudjonsson (1989) support this position, suggesting that "psychological factors and individual differences related to the personality are of central importance in relation to both the causes of crime and its control." They contend that psychology, with its focus on individual differences, is the central discipline in the study of criminal behaviour and that "no system of criminology has any meaning that disregards this central feature of all criminology: the individual person whom we are trying to influence."

While the individual perspective is clearly the dominant one in psychology, there are other psychological perspectives, such as those of **community psychology** (Roesch 1988; Wilson 2004), that are quite closely akin to sociological perspectives. Commonly, such psychologists view social problems from what Rappaport (1977)

assumption of offender deficit
The view that offenders who break the law have some psychological deficit that distinguishes them from normal, law-abiding citizens.

assumption of discriminating traits
The view that offenders are distinguished from non-offenders by, for example, their high levels of impulsiveness and aggression.

community psychology
A perspective that analyzes social problems, including crime, as largely a product of organizational and institutional characteristics of society. It is closely related to sociology.

has termed a "levels of analysis" perspective. Briefly, the four levels are (1) the *individual level*, in which social problems are defined in terms of individual deficit; (2) the *small-group level*, which suggests that social problems are created by problems in group functioning, essentially problems in interpersonal communication and understanding; (3) the *organizational level*, in which the organizations of society have not accomplished what they have been designed to accomplish; and (4) the *institutional or community level*, in which it is suggested that social problems are created by institutions rather than by persons, groups, or organizations. At this level the emphasis is on the values and policies underlying institutional functioning.

An example that cuts across these four levels would be the ways in which "victimless" crimes, such as drug abuse and prostitution, are defined. If the problem is defined at the first level, individuals will be examined to determine what psychological problems they have. Once this has been determined, direct interventions will be employed in changing these individuals so that they fit into society better and conform to the existing laws. At the small-group level, the influence of peers, such as drug-abusing friends, can be viewed as influencing the individual's behaviour. At the next level, organizations such as law enforcement agencies are seen as having insufficient resources to prevent or deter individuals from engaging in criminal behaviour. Finally, if the problem is defined at the institutional level, it can be said that the problems individuals face are caused by the laws their society has created. Thus, the focus will be on changing the laws so that they do not affect people negatively. If the problem is defined at the institutional level, therapy for an individual will be inappropriate if the cause of the problem is, for example, related to socioeconomic factors (Seidman and Rabkin 1983). Community psychologists tend to define social problems at the organizational and institutional levels and have a theoretical perspective that has much in common with that of sociologists.

Haney (2002) builds on this perspective and makes a strong case for a situational approach to understanding criminal behaviour. He comments that

> a more situation-centered legal system would concentrate less exclusively on defective properties of the person and more on situational pathologies. A modern, psychologically informed criminal law would more carefully weigh the effects of environmental stressors that may have significantly altered a defendant's psychological state, and it would take into explicit account those situational pressures that may have undermined or precluded the "mature reflection" that in the past has been presumed to precede action. (34)

These concerns and alternative perspectives should be kept in mind as we consider various psychological theories of criminal behaviour. These theories focus, for the most part, on individual-level variables and explanations. The remainder of this chapter will review psychological theories that can be directly related to understanding criminal behaviour.

Psychoanalytic Theory

Although psychoanalytic theories as an explanation for criminal behaviour have fallen out of favour in recent decades as the field moves more and more towards a model of evidence-based practice, it is useful to examine the history of psychoanalytic theory, given its importance to the foundations of clinical psychology. Sigmund Freud is the figure most associated with psychoanalytic theory, but he did not make any significant attempts to relate his theory specifically to criminal behaviour. Other psychoanalysts have, however, attempted to explain criminal behaviour with psychoanalytic concepts (Alexander and Healey 1935; Friedlander 1947; Polansky, Lippitt, and Redl 1950; Bowlby 1953; Redl 1966; Abrahamsen 1973; Kline 1987).

A basic premise of psychoanalytic theory is that people progress through five overlapping stages of development. These are the oral, anal, phallic, latency, and genital stages. Freud believed that personality is composed of three forces: the **id** (biological drives), the **ego** (which screens, controls, and directs the impulses of the id and acts as a reality tester), and the **superego** (conscience). Psychoanalytic theory holds that the ego and superego are developed through the successful resolution of conflicts presented at each stage of development. It is believed that both biological and social factors are involved in the resolution of each stage (see Figure 9.1).

id
A psychoanalytical term that denotes the most inaccessible and primitive part of the mind. It is a reservoir of biological urges that strive continually for gratification. The ego mediates between the *id* and the *superego*.

FIGURE 9.1 ■ Freud's Theory of Personality

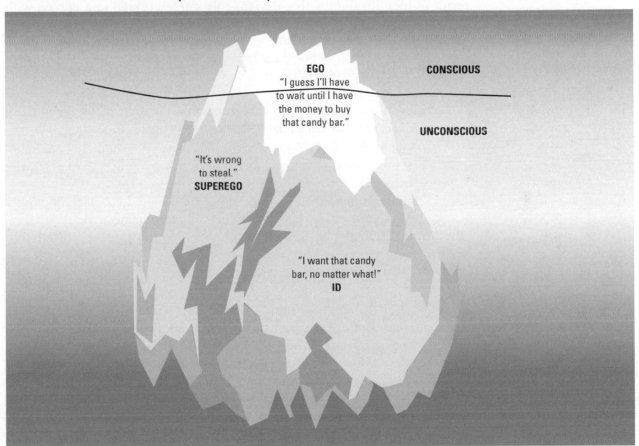

This illustration shows how Freud might picture a person's internal conflict over whether to commit an antisocial act such as stealing a candy bar. Besides dividing personality into three components, Freud theorized that our personalities are largely unconscious—hidden away outside our normal awareness. To dramatize this point, he compared conscious awareness (portions of the ego and superego) to the visible tip of an iceberg. Most of our personality—including the id, with its raw desires and impulses—lies submerged in our subconscious.

ego
A psychoanalytical term denoting the rational part of the personality. It mediates between the *id* and the *superego* and is responsible for dealing with reality and making decisions.

superego
A psychoanalytical term denoting the ethical and moral dimensions of personality; an individual's conscience. The *ego* mediates between the *superego* and the *id*.

Psychoanalytic theory presents an elaborate, comprehensive view of the psychological functioning of individuals. It deals with all aspects of human behaviour, but the discussion here will be limited to its impact on the study of criminal behaviour. Briefly, this theory suggests that criminal behaviour occurs when "internal (ego and superego) controls are unable to restrain the primitive, aggressive, antisocial instincts of the id" (Nietzel 1979). Criminal behaviour is the consequence of an individual's unsuccessful progress through the early stages of development, generally thought to be due to a failure to identify with prosocial parental figures; this leaves the superego inadequately developed or deficient (Martin, Sechrest, and Redner 1981). In line with this, psychoanalytic researchers have proposed that delinquent behaviour reflects a weak, deviant, or harsh superego that is unable to control the oral, anal, and phallic impulses that are resurrected at puberty (Schoenfeld 1971; Kline 1987). A *weak* superego, developed as a consequence of parental deprivation and lack of affection during the first few years of a child's life, results in a person with few inhibitions against antisocial behaviour, who acts in ways to satisfy his or her id, regardless of any social restraints. A *deviant* superego, developed as a result of identification with a deviant role model, results in a person with deviant values. This individual will perform criminal acts that mirror his or her parents' criminality. Finally, an individual who has developed a *harsh* superego experiences pathological levels of unconscious guilt, and performs criminal acts to subconsciously invite punishment in an attempt to assuage this guilt.

Warren and Hindelang (1979) have summarized five other interpretations of criminal behaviour that can be derived from psychoanalytic theory:

1. Criminal behaviour is a form of neurosis that does not differ in any fundamental way from other forms of neurosis (e.g., while some neurotics work too hard, others set fires).
2. The criminal often suffers from a compulsive need for punishment in order to alleviate guilt feelings and anxiety stemming from unconscious strivings.
3. Criminal activity may be a means of obtaining substitute gratification of needs and desires not met inside the family.
4. Delinquent behaviour is often due to traumatic events whose memory has been repressed.
5. Delinquent behaviour may be an expression of displaced hostility.*

SEARCH FOR:
"Freud Net," Abraham A. Brill Library of The New York Psychoanalytic Institute

socialization
The interactive process whereby individuals come to learn and internalize the culture of their society or group.

A number of studies support the view that family life is important in the process of **socialization**. Bowlby (1953) stressed that a stable attachment to a mother in the first few years of life makes it possible for the child to show affection towards others and to care about them. If this attachment does not occur, the child will be unable to show affection and, thus, may damage others without remorse through various forms of victimization. It is well-established that early childhood abuse and neglect contribute to the development of criminal and antisocial behaviour (Kerig and Becker 2014).

---

*M.Q. Warren and M. J. Hindelang, "Current Explanations of Offender Behavior," in *Psychology of Crime and Criminal Justice*, ed. H. Toch (New York: Holt, Rinehart and Winston, 1979), 166–82.

One of the difficulties in assessing psychoanalytic theory is that many aspects of it are untestable because they rely on unobservable underlying constructs. As Ewen (1988) has observed, "psychoanalytic theory presents a formidable difficulty: the most important part of the personality, the unconscious, is also the most inaccessible" (55). It is therefore the psychoanalyst who interprets the offender's behaviours and actions. Any attempt by the offender to refute the interpretation is seen as resistance and as further evidence of its truth.

As Cohen (1966) points out, "aggressive or acquisitive acts are often explained by underlying aggressive or acquisitive impulses." This explanation is a tautology in that aggressive acts are explained by aggressive impulses, but the only evidence of the aggressive impulses is the occurrence of aggressive acts. Many have suggested that psychoanalytic theory is empirically unverifiable, and verification is a necessary criterion for any scientific theory.

Another criticism of psychoanalytic theory is that studies have failed to demonstrate that criminals desire to be punished or suffer from guilt or anxiety, as one psychoanalyst (Abrahamsen 1944) suggested. In fact, as Nietzel (1979) asserts, "criminals are very successful in their efforts to prevent detection or if detected, elude official prosecution and conviction. Most offenders do not appear unduly frustrated or further guilt-ridden by the fact that their 'crime pays' at least some of the time." Despite these problems, psychoanalytic theory is regarded by some as a useful conceptual framework for understanding the importance of early development on later behaviour of all types, including criminal behaviour. Psychoanalytic theory can also be credited with highlighting important variables for researchers to explore.

Evolutionary Theory

Evolutionary psychology seeks to understand human behaviour from a Darwinian perspective of natural selection. This perspective has been used to explain a variety of psychological constructs, including altruism, group dynamics, and antisocial behaviour. According to evolutionary psychology, the human mind consists of psychological mechanisms that have evolved over hundreds of thousands of years. A psychological mechanism is "an information-processing procedure or 'decision rule' which evolution by natural and sexual selection has equipped humans to possess in order to solve an adaptive problem (problem of survival or reproduction)" (Kanazawa 2009). Evolutionary psychology seeks to understand the adaptive function of a mechanism in terms of its survival and reproductive value. Historically, adaptive problems centred on finding a mate, finding food, finding shelter, avoiding predators, and protecting children. Those who successfully adapt to their environment survive, have children, and pass their successful adaptations on to the next generation. Thus, a basic assumption of evolutionary psychology and natural selection is that a successful adaptation is housed in an individual's genetic makeup (Quinsey 2002; Tooby and Cosmides 2005; Duntley and Buss 2008).

Forensic evolutionary psychology explores the adaptive significance of antisocial behaviour. Specifically, selectionist thinking has been applied to sex differences in criminality, sexual coercion and deviance, kinship and crime, spousal assault, and persistent antisocial conduct. For example, we know that men commit more crime, particularly more violent and serious crime, than women (see Chapters 5 and 6). To account for these sex differences in criminality, evolutionary theory refers to **reproductive fitness variance**. That is, the number of offspring a woman

reproductive fitness variance
The range of possible offspring an organism can produce.

can produce is limited by pregnancy, lactation, and menopause, while men are limited mainly by the number of fertile women with whom they can mate (Quinsey 2002). The number of surviving offspring of either sex is further limited by the available resources to raise and protect offspring. Natural selection has favoured evolved psychological mechanisms that support high parental investment for women and high mating investment for men. Because women have historically been focused on raising children and keeping them safe, they are less likely to engage in risky antisocial behaviour that might jeopardize their ability to take care of their children, ensuring their survival. By contrast, since the main limitation on a man's reproductive success has historically been the number of fertile female partners, men have competed with one another for mating opportunities. To make themselves more attractive to women, men strive to make themselves appear ambitious, industrious, and wealthy. Thus, men are less risk-averse than women, especially during late adolescence and early adulthood, when competition for mates is most intense (Quinsey 2002). This theory explains not only why men commit more crimes than women but also why criminal behaviour peaks in adolescence. Further support for this theory comes from observations that violent crimes are most frequently committed by men against other men (Daly and Wilson 1988).

Evolutionary theories of criminal behaviour have faced a number of criticisms. Some have argued that by providing an adaptive explanation for criminal behaviour, evolutionary theory normalizes, legitimizes, and excuses this behaviour (e.g., Brannigan 1997). However, explaining behaviour is not equivalent to endorsing or condoning it. Also, evolutionary theory has been criticized for its deterministic nature, which suggests that behaviour is predetermined and thus there is little we can do to prevent or treat it (Bonta and Andrews 2017). However, evolutionary psychological theory is changing from a gene-based theory to a developmental biology–informed theory of evolution that accounts for environmental influences as well as genetic influences, to better explain the complexities of human behaviour (Lickliter and Honeycutt 2003). Finally, critics of evolutionary theory remind us that we do not know much about the behaviour of early humans, so much of these explanations are purely hypothetical and difficult to test (Schacter, Wegner, and Gilbert 2007). While the field of evolutionary psychology remains highly controversial, these theories contribute interesting explanations of criminal behaviour.

Theories of Moral Development

moral development theory
Refers generally to theories of individual psychology that investigate how moral reasoning emerges in the individual and develops as the individual matures.

According to **moral development** theorists, if we wish to understand criminal and delinquent behaviour we need to ask how it is that individuals develop, or fail to develop, a sense of morality and responsibility. One of the first contemporary moral development theorists was the French psychologist Jean Piaget (1932), whose research focused on the moral lives of children. To determine how children developed their ideas about right and wrong, Piaget studied how children developed the rules to the games they played. He concluded that moral reasoning develops in stages. The thinking of young children is characterized by egocentrism. That is, they project their own thoughts and wishes onto others because they are unable to take the perspective of those others. Through their interactions with others, by the ages of 11 or 12, children normally have progressed to the stage of cooperation with others. Based on this research, Piaget concluded that schools should teach moral reasoning by allowing students to work out the rules through problem-solving in the classroom.

Kohlberg, expanding on Piaget's theory, has hypothesized that there are six stages of moral development (see Table 9.1). The stages are age-related, and progression through the stages occurs as "the developing child becomes better able to understand and integrate diverse points of view on a moral-conflict situation and to take more of the relevant situational factors into account" (Jennings, Kilkenny, and Kohlberg 1983). Kohlberg believes that all individuals go through the same sequence of stages, though the pace may vary and some individuals may never progress beyond the first few stages.

Kohlberg categorizes the six stages into three levels of moral judgment development, each with two stages of moral reasoning.

The first is the *preconventional* level, characteristic of children under age 11 and of many adolescent and adult offenders. At this level, society's morals and values are understood as "do's" and "don'ts" and are associated with punishment. The preconventional person is one for whom roles and social expectations are something external to the self.

The *conventional* level reflects the average adolescent and adult in our society and others. He or she understands, accepts, and attempts to uphold the values and rules of society. For a conventional person, the self is identified with or has internalized the rules and expectations of others, especially those of authorities.

The *postconventional* level is the one at which customs are critically examined with regard to universal rights, duties, and moral principles. It is characteristic of a minority of adults after the age of 20. The postconventional person has differentiated his or her self from the rules and expectations of others and has defined his or her values by means of self-chosen principles (Jennings, Kilkenny, and Kohlberg 1983).

Carol Gilligan (1982) has criticized Kohlberg's theory of moral development, stating that it is biased in favour of males. She argues that there is variation in moral standards by gender, with females taking a more care-oriented approach to morality and males typically following a more justice-oriented approach. She believes that Kohlberg's theory does not take into account the more care-oriented approach of females and that, as a result, females rarely achieve Kohlberg's higher stages of moral development. To support her argument, she

TABLE 9.1 ■ Kohlberg's Theory of Moral Development

Level	Stage	Description	
I.	Preconventional	1. Punishment 2. Instrumental hedonism	Egocentric (What happens to me?)
II.	Conventional	3. Approval of others 4. Authority maintaining morality	Social expectations (What do others expect of me?)
III.	Postconventional	5. Democratically accepted law 6. Principles of conscience	Universality (What is best for all?)

points out that Kohlberg did not take females into account when developing his theory—instead, he based it on an empirical study of 84 males whom he followed over 20 years. Gilligan states that females typically reach only the second level (third stage) in Kohlberg's theory, a level characterized by goodness being equated with helping and pleasing others and consistent with the care-oriented approach of females to morality. She argues that Kohlberg and Kramer (1969) looked at this concept of goodness and concluded that this level of moral reasoning was adequate for women whose lives took place in the home. They contended that only when women enter the "traditional arena of male activity" do they realize that this level of moral reasoning is not sufficient, at which point they progress towards the higher stages, as men do. Gilligan (1982) points out that "herein lies a paradox, for the very traits that traditionally have defined the 'goodness' of women, their care for and sensitivity to the needs of others, are those that mark them as deficient in moral development" (18).

Other researchers have argued that moral development includes more than just moral judgment; it also has emotional aspects, such as empathy, shame, and guilt (Gibbs 2010). Empathy has both cognitive and affective components. The cognitive component considers a person's understanding of others' emotional states, while the affective component considers whether a person is able to share others' emotional states. Guilt and shame are moral emotions with differing origins. According to Tangney, Stuewig, and Mashek (2007), shame arises when a person violates society's values, while guilt occurs when a person violates his or her own moral values. An individual who feels shame will also feel embarrassment, leading to an avoidance of the situation that reflects the unpleasant experience. An individual who feels guilt will feel concern over the wrongful action and will attempt to take restorative action to make things right again. Shame, therefore, is considered to be more devastating, as it focuses on one's self-concept, rather than simply on the behaviour.

Considerable research has been done on the relationship between moral development and delinquency. Kohlberg believes that people with high moral development are more likely to make individual choices and to be less influenced by friends or by consequences of actions. Thus, there should be an inverse relationship between moral development and delinquency. A number of studies have found support for this relationship. For example, Jennings, Kilkenny, and Kohlberg (1983) reviewed a large number of studies on this relationship and concluded that "the overwhelming weight of the empirical data reviewed here supports the notion that juvenile delinquents' moral judgement is at a less advanced level than that of non-delinquent controls matched on a variety of variables." But they were careful to point out that a cause–effect relationship had not been established. Individuals at the same level of moral development may or may not become delinquent. They add that

> these studies lend support to the more modest claims that moral reasoning of increased maturity has an insulating effect against delinquency. Advanced stages of moral judgment cause one's moral orientation to be more integrated, stable and consistent. Higher reasoning makes one a more reliable moral agent and thus better able to withstand some incentives to illegal conduct postulated by a variety of sociological and psychological theories of the etiology of delinquency. (290)

This last statement suggests that moral development theory has considerable relevance for sociological explanations of criminal behaviour. Indeed, Morash (1983) has discussed at length the possible integration of moral development and sociological theories, suggesting that it may be more fruitful to study the interaction of personal and situational variables:

> Most serious delinquency would result from social conditions, primarily those that are enduring, that impinge on youths who possess the personality factors and the pre-conventional reasoning conducive to serious delinquent behavior. An advantage of this explanation is that it allows for the many pre-conventional individuals who do not break the law regularly or not at all, and it accounts for different patterns in delinquency—that is, the repeated serious delinquency and sporadic and/or less serious delinquency. (405)

More recently, Kiriakidis (2008) found that delinquents, compared to a non-delinquent sample, scored significantly higher on a moral disengagement scale. In a study examining the moral development of 72 adult male sex offenders participating in a community-based treatment program, Buttell (2002) found that sex offenders employed a level of moral reasoning that was two standard deviations lower than the national norm. Regarding the emotional components of moral development, guilt has been found to be inversely related to delinquency, while shame has a positive relationship with offending behaviour (Hosser, Windzio, and Greve 2008). In line with these findings, in a meta-analytic review of 19 studies, Van Vugt and colleagues (2011) found that moral development was inversely related to recidivism for juvenile and adult offenders.

Theories of moral development have important implications for offender rehabilitation programs (Blasi 1980). Evidence suggests that education programs that focus on moral development have positive effects on inmates' moral judgments (Power 2010). Future research will need to examine whether this increased morality leads to lower rates of criminal behaviour and recidivism.

In conclusion, there is evidence that level of moral reasoning is related to delinquent and criminal behaviour. However, the correlations reported in many studies are often quite low. Moral development may affect how an individual behaves in a given context, but it is clear that other characteristics of the individual, as well as the situation, will also be important determinants of behaviour.

SEARCH FOR:
"Hans Eysenck and Other Temperament Theorists," C. George Boeree, Shippensburg University of Pennsylvania

Eysenck's Theory of Crime and Personality

Hans Eysenck, a noted British psychologist, has developed an elaborate theory of how personality characteristics are related to criminal behaviour (Eysenck 1977). This theory has generated considerable research, in large part because it lends itself quite readily to the identification of groups of offenders and to predictions about their behaviour.

Eysenck believes that illegal, selfish, or immoral behaviour is simple to explain. These behaviours are inherently reinforcing, and hence it is more fruitful to try to explain why people do *not* commit crimes. Eysenck claims that children will naturally engage in such acts and only refrain from doing so if they are

classical conditioning
A basic form of learning whereby a neutral stimulus is paired with another stimulus that naturally elicits a certain response; the neutral stimulus comes to elicit the same response as the stimulus that automatically elicits the response.

punished. Eysenck's theory is based on **classical conditioning**. Each time a child is punished, he or she may experience pain and fear. This pain and fear may be associated with the act itself. Thus, whenever the child contemplates the act, he or she will experience fear, which will tend to inhibit the response. Eysenck equates this conditioned fear with conscience. Delinquents and criminals do not readily develop this conditioned response, either because of lack of exposure to effective conditioning practices by parents and others, or because they are less susceptible to conditioning. Eysenck (1990) states:

> Depending on the frequency of pairings between the conditioned and unconditioned stimulus in the field of social behavior, and on the precise content of the conditioning program, children will grow up to develop appropriate types of behavior. Conditionability is a crucial factor on the social or environmental side. In a permissive society where parents, teachers, and magistrates do not take seriously the task of imposing a "conscience" which would lead them to behave in a socialized manner, a large number of individuals with poor or average conditionability will acquire a "conscience" too weak to prevent them from indulging in criminal activities, although had they been subjected to a stricter regime of conditioning, they might have grown up to be perfectly respectable and law-abiding citizens.

As Eysenck points out, "strictness" is not a function of excessive strength of the conditioning process, but a result of the certainty and frequency of pairings of the conditioned and unconditioned stimuli.

extroversion
A personality characteristic associated with sociability, impulsiveness, and aggression.

There are three dimensions of personality, according to Eysenck. **Extroversion** is a personality characteristic of highly sociable, impulsive, and aggressive people. Those scoring high on extroversion have a low level of arousal and thus require more environmental stimulation. Highly introverted, introspective, and inhibited people are at the other extreme of this particular dimension. *Neuroticism* is linked to the psychiatric concept of neurosis. People who are high on this dimension are characterized by such symptoms as anxiety, restlessness, and other emotional responses. The opposite extreme of neuroticism is referred to as stability and is characterized by a relatively unreactive nervous system. The third dimension is *psychoticism*. According to Eysenck and Eysenck (1976, 47), a person who is high on this dimension is "cold, impersonal, hostile, lacking in sympathy, unfriendly, untrustful, odd, unemotional, unhelpful, antisocial, lacking in human feelings, inhumane, generally bloodyminded, lacking in insight, strange, with paranoid ideas that people are against him." Eysenck believed that levels of extroversion, neuroticism, and psychoticism are determined mainly by genetics and that most people have moderate levels of each dimension.

A number of hypotheses have been generated regarding how these dimensions relate to criminal behaviour in terms of socialization processes. Extroverts, because of their high need for excitement, their impulsivity, and their relatively weak conscience, are believed to be more prone to criminal behaviour. In addition, one can predict that persons high on both neuroticism and extroversion would be difficult to condition, making them more likely to be delinquents or criminals. Persons high on psychoticism would tend to be more serious offenders, with a propensity for violence. Hare (1982) investigated the relationship between these three dimensions and psychopathy. While neuroticism and extroversion did not correlate with measures of psychopathy, psychoticism did. This may be because each dimension taps a common element of psychopathy (criminal and antisocial tendencies) rather than those psychological features that are assumed in the diagnosis of psychopathy (e.g., lack of remorse, lack of empathy).

Eysenck and others have developed psychological measures of each of these dimensions. Research in testing predictions about offenders has produced mixed results. In their extensive and excellent review of Eysenck's theory, Farrington, Biron, and LeBlanc (1982) summarized data from 16 studies, most of which were conducted in Great Britain, and found that while offenders generally scored higher on psychoticism and neuroticism, similar results were not found for extroversion (see also Hollin 1989). This is not surprising, since some aspects of extroversion are related to criminality (e.g., impulsiveness), but others are not (e.g., sociability). More recently, Boduszek and colleagues (2012) showed that psychoticism, neuroticism, and extroversion significantly predicted criminal thinking, supporting Eysenck's theory.

Like other theories, personality theories such as Eysenck's have problems with tautology or circular reasoning. That is, in many measures of personality, the subscale that differentiates delinquents from nondelinquents includes items asking about antisocial behaviour (e.g., "Have you been in trouble with the law?")—the very thing it proposes to explain. In addition, some have criticized personality theories for failing to adequately define their terms (Einstadter and Henry 1995).

Eysenck's theory is important because it shows how psychological and social variables can be interrelated. Individuals who may have a psychological propensity to commit crime may be socialized effectively if they grow up in an environment that provides effective conditioning. Similarly, individuals with a low propensity for criminality may become criminal if their environment is too permissive. Eysenck argues strongly for the importance of individual differences, but he also recognizes the importance of societal influences: "Crime … is essentially a function of the ethos of the society in which we live; it reflects the practices of positive and negative reinforcement, of reward and punishment, of teaching and conditioning, which are prevalent, and these in turn are mirrored and reflected by the types of films we see, television programs we watch, books and newspapers we read, and teaching and examples we receive at school" (Eysenck and Gudjonsson 1989, 255). In the next section, it will be seen that social learning theory reflects this perspective more explicitly.

Social Learning Theory

Another theory that lends itself to an integration of sociology and psychology is social learning theory. Though this theory focuses on individual behaviour, it takes into account the environment's influence and the individual's social conditions. Cognitive functioning—the ability to think and make choices—is central to social learning theory.

An important element of social learning theory is **modelling**. Individuals can learn new behaviours through direct experience or by observing the behaviour of others. The latter, also referred to as vicarious learning, can be an effective and efficient way to acquire new behaviours. Albert Bandura, a Stanford University

modelling
A form of learning that occurs as a result of watching and imitating others.

professor of psychology, is a leading social learning theorist. He suggests that virtually all learning phenomena resulting from direct experiences can occur on a vicarious basis through observation of other persons' behaviour and its consequences for them (Bandura 2000).

Social learning theory has been used to explain how aggression is learned. Since this is of great concern to criminology theory, aggression will be used as an example of an application of social learning theory.

Bandura (1986) suggests that aggressive behaviour can be learned from three sources. The *family* is one source, and a number of studies have shown that children of parents who respond aggressively to problems will tend to use similar tactics. Bandura also points to research on child abuse, which shows that many children who have been abused will later become abusers themselves. Another source of aggressive behaviour can be referred to as *subcultural influences*, or the influence of social models and peers. Bandura suggests that the highest incidence of aggression is found in communities in which aggressive models abound and fighting prowess is regarded as a valued attribute. The third source of learned aggressive behaviour is *symbolic modelling*. An example of this is violence on television, which provides models of aggressive behaviour (Skoler, Bandura, and Ross 1994).

SEARCH FOR:
"Albert Bandura (1925–present)," C. George Boeree, Shippensburg University of Pennsylvania

Bandura's research on the role of film models reinforced existing concerns about the effects of television on aggressive behaviour. Geen (1983) reviewed the research on the relationship between viewing television violence and aggression. He first looked at the vast number of correlational studies, the majority of which support the conclusion that there is a positive relationship between viewing violence and aggressive behaviour. A typical study is the one by Teevan and Hartnagel (1976), which showed that high school students who described their favourite television shows as violent also reported committing more aggressive acts than students whose favourite shows were nonviolent. More recently, Anderson and his colleagues (2010) have found evidence for a relationship between playing violent video games and aggressive behaviour.

SEARCH FOR:
"What do we Know about Media Violence?," MediaSmarts

The problem with correlational research, as Geen points out, is that the direction of causation is unknown. It is possible that people who are more likely to behave aggressively simply prefer more violent television shows. Thus it cannot be concluded through correlational studies alone that viewing violence is the cause of aggressive behaviour. Cook, Kendzierski, and Thomas (1983) reanalyzed data from several large-scale studies of the effects of television violence. They concluded that an association between television viewing and aggression by children can be found regularly but that the level of association is typically quite small and often not statistically significant. Nevertheless, they conclude that the association is most probably a causal one—that watching violence on television does have an effect on children's aggressive behaviour. The same can be said for violence in music videos (Smith and Boyson 2002).

autonomic reactivity
A measurement of the extent to which an individual's physical organism reacts to external stimuli.

Besides having a direct effect on aggressive behaviour, exposure to television violence may well increase one's tolerance of violence and decrease one's sensitivity to acts of violence. Thomas and colleagues (1979) found that both adult and child subjects showed less **autonomic reactivity** to a scene of real-life interpersonal aggression if they had first watched a violent scene from a television

Psychologists have debated the degree to which violent movies and television programs contribute to violent behaviour, but the results of this research are not yet conclusive.

© iStockphoto.com/ryasick

show. Malamuth and Check (1981) reported similar results in their study of the effects of film violence on attitudes towards violence. Male and female university students were randomly assigned to view either a violent-sexual or a control feature-length film. The films were shown as part of the regular campus film program, and subjects believed they were viewing the films as a film-rating task. Several days later, unaware of any relationship between the film and the questionnaire, they were asked to respond to a number of attitude measures. Malamuth and Check found that exposure to the film portraying violent sexuality was associated with a greater acceptance of interpersonal violence against women. However, this finding was true only for male subjects. Female subjects had a nonsignificant tendency in the opposite direction: women exposed to violence tended to be less accepting of interpersonal violence than control females. It is important to realize that this study does not provide any data on whether males exposed to violence will actually behave differently towards women. However, the study does demonstrate that such exposure may have a significant effect on attitudes. Currently, exposure to violence on television is not considered a direct cause of aggressive and violent behaviour; however, it *is* considered an important risk factor that can contribute to aggressive and violent behavior (Bushman and Anderson 2015).

In his analysis of antisocial behaviour, Bandura (1986) suggests that the best deterrent to such activity is the provision of more attractive prosocial alternatives. However, he acknowledges that "when inducements to criminal acts are strong, when personal sanctions against such conduct are weak, and when people lack socially acceptable means of getting what they want, fear of punishment serves as a major deterrent to transgressive conduct." There are two forms of deterrence—direct, and vicarious. In the former, punishment is used to discourage current transgressors from such activity in the future. In the latter, punishment serves as a general deterrent to others. Bandura identifies three major sources of deterrence against criminal activity: legal sanction, social sanction, and self-sanction. Legal sanctions derive from the belief that there are legal consequences to transgressions, notwithstanding the reality that most crime goes unpunished. Citing research by Clastner (1967), Bandura states that "people who are not in the habit of breaking the law share a distorted perception of legal threats, in which they greatly overestimate the risks of getting caught and punished for unlawful acts. In contrast, offenders judge personal risks to be lower and more in line with the actual probabilities." Social sanctions reflect the negative social consequences that criminal stigmatization can have for an individual and the powerful deterrent effect this has. Self-sanctions are self-imposed moral standards; they are viewed as the most effective deterrent, for they operate even when there is no risk of detection. Bandura (1986) states: "In the absence of self-sanctions rooted in societal standards, whenever personal desires conflict with societal codes, external threats in the form of legal and social sanctions, and extensive social surveillance are needed to ensure that the rights and welfare of others are not completely disregarded."

The empirical status of social learning theory has been summarized by Akers and Jensen (2006):

> Indeed, it is reasonable to propose that the theory has been tested in relation to a wider range of forms of deviance, in a wider range of settings and samples, in more different languages, and by more different people, has survived more "crucial tests" against other theories, and is the most strongly and consistently supported by empirical data than any other social psychological explanation of crime and deviance. (37)

Operant Conditioning

Another learning theory is based on the principle of operant conditioning. This involves the use of rewards and punishments to increase the probability or frequency of a given response. B.F. Skinner is the psychologist most identified with this theory, and his research forms the basis for both the theoretical and the applied applications of **operant conditioning**.

operant conditioning
The basic process by which an individual's behaviour is shaped by reinforcement or by punishment.

One way a response can be learned is through a process referred to as shaping. This involves rewarding approximations of some target behaviour until the behaviour gradually progresses to the desired response. Behaviour can also be learned through punishment, which can involve either the withdrawal of a positive reinforcer or the introduction of a negative stimulus such as an electric shock. There have been a number of attempts to use operant conditioning theory to account for the acquisition of criminal behaviour. Notable among this work is that of Jeffery (1965) and of Burgess and Akers (1966).

Burgess and Akers (1966) and Akers (1990) conceptualize criminal behaviour in terms of operant conditioning and imitation. The main component of Akers's (1990) social learning theory is differential reinforcement. This refers to the balance of rewards and punishments that govern behaviour. In this theory, operant conditioning is the basic process by which an individual's behaviour is shaped, and this can occur through both reinforcement and punishment.

Reinforcement refers to any process that strengthens a behaviour; punishment is any process that weakens a behaviour. As applied to deviance and crime, Akers (1990) states that

> social learning is a behavioral approach to socialization which includes individuals' responses to rewards and punishments in the current situation, the learned patterns of responses they bring to that situation, and the anticipated consequences of actions taken now and in the future in the initiation, continuation, and cessation of those actions. It is a "soft behaviorism" that allows for choice and cognitive processes. It views the individual's behavior as responding to and being conditioned by environmental feedback and consequences. It does not view the individual as unreasoning and only passively conditioned. (655)

Considerable research has been conducted on the application of learning theory to the treatment of delinquents. The "teaching family" group home model launched in the late 1960s has been at the centre of group home development. The approach

> rests on the view that an adolescent's behavior patterns, behavior discriminations, and skills are functions of past behavior–environment interactions (learning history), currently ongoing behavior—environment interactions, and genetic organismic variables (Braukman, Kirigin, and Wolf 1980). In this conceptualization, inherited characteristics and environmental features in childhood, particularly parenting practices (relationship development, teaching, supervision, and discipline) affect later development. In adolescence, earlier developed antisocial patterns tend to persevere (indeed, are self-perpetuating) and can be maintained further by ongoing behavior–environment interactions associated with inappropriate parenting, deviant peers, and school failure. (Braukman and Wolf, 1987)

The group home provides a reinforcing environment designed to change existing behavioural interactions in the direction of functional and prosocial skills. The emphasis is on learning social and family life skills. The best known of these programs is Achievement Place, a program first implemented in a cottage-style treatment facility for delinquent youths in Lawrence, Kansas. (The name of the treatment facility was Achievement Place, hence the name of the program.) Youths in Achievement Place programs live in a residence with trained "houseparents." The heart of the program is a **token economy** system in which points can be earned (or lost). For example, residents can earn points for being at class on time, cleaning their bedroom, and engaging in other positive behaviours. Disruptive behaviour in the classroom, making aggressive statements or fighting, and being late for class can result in a loss of points. The points can be used to purchase privileges and material goods. Research on Achievement Place has demonstrated that "contingent token consequences could both establish behaviors basic to participation in lawful, productive intra- and extra-treatment activities, and eliminate behaviors likely to get the participants in further trouble" (Braukman and Wolf 1987). A comprehensive outcome study on the teaching

token economy
A behaviour therapy procedure based on operant learning principles. Individuals are rewarded (reinforced) for positive or appropriate behaviour and are disciplined (punished) for negative or inappropriate behaviour.

family program (Braukman, Wolf, and Ramp 1985) indicates that this approach has considerable short-term positive effects. However, the long-term implications are less positive since it is very difficult to control reinforcement following release from the institution. Because of this, increased emphasis has been placed on systematic aftercare to help maintain treatment effects.

Antisocial Personality

The study of antisocial personality provides a good example of how psychological theory can be applied to criminal populations. Some confusion has resulted from the variety of terms used to describe a similar set of behaviours: **antisocial personality disorder**, sociopathy moral insanity, antisocial personality, and psychopathy. There has been a tendency for some to use this last term very loosely as a "wastebasket" category for antisocial individuals generally. There is, however, strong empirical evidence that the traits underlying this disorder form a valid, clinically meaningful cluster (Hare and Cox 1978; Skilling et al. 2002). For many, this term is associated with images of violent and sadistic murderers as portrayed countless times on television or, all too often, demonstrated in real life. The brutal murders committed by Clifford Olson (see Box 9.3) and Charles Manson and his followers in California are frequently cited examples of psychopathy. Indeed, while there is some debate over the most appropriate diagnosis for Manson, many would argue that his behaviour best fit the clinical picture of psychopathy. As Nathan and Harris (1975, 361) point out:

> Charles Manson acted upon society in an unbelievable variety of anti-social ways. At one time or another he robbed, deceived, assaulted, exploited, seduced—and murdered. But despite the extraordinary range of antisocial acts for which he had been responsible, perhaps his most surprising characteristic was that at no time did he show guilt or remorse about anything he had done. During his trial for the Tate murders, he said, "I've considered innocence and guilt and I know the difference between them and I have no guilt" (quoted from the *New York Times*, December 25, 1969). A man who could be charming and captivating, brutal and ruthless, Manson could not be guilty, at least in his own eyes. What kind of human being feels no remorse over murder? Why would a person keep committing crimes despite repeated punishment? How can a man charm so many people and yet never relate with genuine feeling to anyone?

These questions are difficult to answer because the crimes Manson and Olson committed seem so senseless to society. However disturbing they may be, it is possible for most people to understand murders motivated by greed or passion, but the murder of Sharon Tate and others by Manson cannot be explained by either of these motivations. A Canadian case highlights the differences between psychopathy or antisocial personality disorder and more severe mental illnesses, such as schizophrenia, which might have a significant impact on one's ability to choose between right and wrong (see Box 9.1).

antisocial personality disorder
A personality disorder that involves disregard for the rights of others as well as impulsive, irresponsible, and aggressive behaviour.

FOCUS

BOX 9.1

WILL BAKER: GROTESQUE KILLING ABOARD BUS 1170

Will Baker (formerly Vince Li) was born in Dandong, China, in 1968. He graduated from university with a Bachelor of Science in 1992. Mr. Baker immigrated to Canada in 2001 and became a Canadian citizen in 2005. He was unable to find work in his field so he worked a number of menial jobs, including as a caretaker in a church, a sales assistant in a store, and a newspaper carrier. His final employer described him as a good worker albeit somewhat unusual. Despite his largely uneventful past with no criminal arrests or convictions, Mr. Baker brutally and savagely killed a fellow bus passenger in July 2008 in a fashion that is reminiscent of the gruesome movie *Silence of the Lambs*.

According to witnesses and as documented in the Agreed Statement of Facts, on 30 July 2008, in Erickson, Manitoba, at 7 p.m., Mr. Baker boarded Greyhound Bus #1170 destined for Winnipeg. He sat near the back of the bus. He was described as a tall man in his 40s, with a shaved head and sunglasses. Approximately 90 minutes later, shortly after a rest stop, Mr. Baker suddenly produced a large hunting knife and began stabbing his sleeping seatmate in the neck and chest. While most of the passengers quickly fled the bus, the driver and three other male passengers attempted to help the victim. They were chased away by Mr. Baker, who slashed wildly at them with a knife.

Mr. Baker persisted in brutalizing his victim by decapitating him and displaying his severed head to those gathered outside. Mr. Baker continued to dismember the corpse and then proceeded to perform acts of cannibalism.

The rear door was barricaded with a snipe bar to prevent Mr. Baker from escaping. In addition, the power to the bus was cut off to render the vehicle inoperable. Several minutes later, the RCMP arrived. They encouraged Mr. Baker to drop his weapon out of a small bathroom window, but he refused, while indicating, in addition to some unintelligible words, something to the effect that he had to stay on the bus forever. Two hours later the province's Emergency Response Team took over from the RCMP. Mr. Baker refused to give himself up. Instead he continued pacing the length of the bus, defiling the corpse. At approximately 1:30 a.m., five hours after the attack began, Mr. Baker was arrested when he attempted to escape through a broken back bus window. He was tasered several times, handcuffed, and placed in the back of a police cruiser. The victim's nose, tongue, and ear were found in a plastic bag in Mr. Baker's pockets. The victim's eyes and parts of his heart were never recovered and are presumed to have been eaten by Mr. Baker.

To many, this brutal crime might conjure images of Hannibal Lecter, the psychopath killer played by Anthony Hopkins in the famous movie *Silence of the Lambs*. However, there is one important difference. In *Silence of the Lambs*, Hannibal Lecter was acutely aware of his actions and knew that what he was doing was wrong. This was not the case with Mr. Baker. In fact, Mr. Baker was suffering from a mental disorder that rendered him unable to appreciate the nature and quality of his actions and to know that they were wrong.

At Mr. Baker's second-degree murder trial, which began nearly a year after the crime on 5 March 2009, the Crown and defence attorneys agreed to a number of facts. Among them was that Mr. Baker had few friends and that those he did have described him as having had mental problems. In addition, his former wife described him engaging in bizarre behaviours, including sudden and unexplained absences, bus trips to unusual locations, and rambling talk. Despite his unusual behaviour, neither his friends nor his former wife had known him to be violent. One episode of unusual behaviour resulted in the Ontario Provincial Police (OPP) picking him up on a busy highway. He was hospitalized briefly in the fall of 2005 before being released with medication. Both before and after this incident, friends and family were unable to convince him to seek medical help.

At his trial, psychiatric assessments of Mr. Baker were put into evidence. In particular, the assessments suggested that Mr. Baker was suffering from schizophrenia, a mental illness whose symptoms can include hallucinations, delusions, and paranoia. According to the psychiatrists' assessments, the voice of God had directed Mr. Baker to move from Edmonton to Winnipeg. Moreover, the voice had led Mr. Baker to believe, under a paranoid delusion, that the deceased victim was a threat to his own life, both before and after the deceased victim's death.

The judge accepted the assessments that Mr. Baker was suffering from a mental disorder. In his decision, he said:

These grotesque acts are appalling. However, the acts themselves and the context in which they were committed are strongly suggestive of a mental disorder. He did not appreciate the actions he committed were morally wrong. He believed he was acting in self-defence. (McIntyre 2009)

The judge further stated:

Persons who are profoundly ill do not have the mental capacity to intentionally commit a crime. The goal of criminal law is to punish criminals, not persons who have a

(continued)

mental illness. Moreover, a person who is driven to act by severe psychotic delusions cannot be deterred by the fear of punishment, or public denouncement. In such cases, the only way to change the behaviour of a person who is driven to act by psychotic delusions is through treatment, and where the person poses an ongoing risk to society, through treatment in a secure institution. (Pritchard, 2009)

As a result of these findings, the judge found Mr. Baker not criminally responsible on account of mental disorder (NCRMD).

Under Canadian law, no person is criminally responsible for an act committed while suffering from a mental disorder that rendered the person incapable of appreciating the nature and quality of the act or of knowing it was wrong (Criminal Code of Canada, C-46, s. 16(1)). However, not all individuals who are suffering from a mental disorder will be found NCRMD. Rather, an individual will only be found NCRMD if the mental disorder, which is defined in law as a disease of the mind, renders the person unable to differentiate between right and wrong. In *Winko v. British Columbia (Forensic Psychiatric Institute)* the Supreme Court of Canada put it this way:

> [P]eople who commit criminal acts under the influence of mental illnesses should not be held criminally responsible for their acts or omissions in the same way that sane responsible people are. No person should be convicted of a crime if he or she was legally insane at the time of the offence … Criminal responsibility is appropriate only where the actor is a discerning moral agent, capable of making choices between right and wrong.

In cases where individuals are found NCRMD, they are not admitted to jail or prison. Rather, their disposition depends on a number of considerations, including the protection of the public, the individual's mental condition, the reintegration of the individual into society, and the individual's other needs. Disposition decisions are made by specially constituted Review Boards whose duty it is to weigh these considerations. The disposition of Mr. Baker was decided by the Manitoba Review Board on 15 September 2009. His disposition order required him to be detained in a locked ward of a psychiatric hospital in Manitoba. Disposition orders are reviewed by the Review Board at least annually. When the order was reviewed on 31 May 2010, the Review Board again ordered him to be detained in a locked ward of a psychiatric hospital in Manitoba. However, this time they allowed for the possibility of escorted access to the hospital grounds (e.g., outside yard). After several years of treatment, Mr. Baker was granted conditional discharge in March 2016. On 10 February 2017, the Manitoba Review Board granted Will Baker an absolute discharge, maintaining that "the weight of evidence does not suggest that Mr. Baker poses a significant threat to the safety of the public." This means that Mr. Baker can live independently and no longer has conditions imposed by the Criminal Code Review Board, which used to include taking his medication under supervision, disclosing his address to his medical team, and having no contact with the victim's family.

Questions for Critical Thinking

1. Read the section of Chapter 3 that discusses "Mental Disorder as a Defence to a Criminal Charge." Explain why Will Baker (formerly Vince Li) was found not criminally responsible for his actions.

2. Canada's prisons are increasingly being populated by people suffering from mental disorders – according to the Correctional Service of Canada (2015), 50 percent of male and 62 percent of female federal offenders required mental health evaluation upon admission and over half of these have a confirmed mental illness. If these inmates suffer from mental illness, why are they in prison instead of in hospital?

Sources: Queen's Bench, Winnipeg Centre, (n.d.), "Between Her Majesty the Queen and Vince Weiguang Li—Agreed Statement of Facts," Winnipeg: Queen's Bench; Province of Manitoba Review Board (2009), "A Disposition Hearing held in Winnipeg, Manitoba on Monday, June 1, 2009," Winnipeg: Manitoba Review Board; Province of Manitoba Review Board (2010), "A Disposition Review Hearing held in Winnipeg, Manitoba on Monday, May 31, 2010, Winnipeg: Manitoba Review Board; Province of Manitoba Review Board (2010). "A Disposition Review Hearing held in Winnipeg, Manitoba, on February 6, 2017," Winnipeg: Manitoba Review Board.

Similarly, it is difficult to understand the motivations of "Canada's Ken and Barbie Killers"—Paul Bernardo and Karla Homolka—who were responsible for the grotesque rape and murder of three young women, including Karla Homolka's own sister. Although the prevalence of female psychopaths is lower than that of males, we are especially intrigued by these women. In parole board reports, Karla Homolka has been deemed a psychopath (see Box 9.2), though the motivation for her actions remains unclear.

This section began with a discussion of Charles Manson because it is this image that best fits the common conception of persons with an antisocial personality. It is a misleading picture, however, because many individuals with diagnoses of antisocial personality do not have a history of violence, and even among those who do, very few would exhibit the extreme forms that Manson did. The term *sociopath* was later used instead of the term *psychopath* to convey this less violent picture. More recently, the use of the term *Antisocial Personality Disorder* has become common. Although these terms are often used interchangeably, they are not synonymous.

The current edition of the American Psychiatric Association's *Diagnostic and Statistical Manual of Mental Disorder* (DSM-V; APA 2013) defines Antisocial Personality Disorder as follows: "The essential feature of Antisocial Personality Disorder is a pervasive pattern of disregard for, and violation of, the rights of others that begins in childhood or early adolescence and continues into adulthood" (701). Antisocial Personality Disorder is based mainly on behavioural evidence, in contrast to psychopathy, which is based on behavioural and affective/interpersonal criteria.

Lying, stealing, fighting, truancy, and resisting authority are typical early childhood signs. In adolescence, unusually early or aggressive sexual behaviour, excessive drinking, and use of illicit drugs are frequent. In adulthood, behaviours like these continue; also, these people are unable to sustain consistent work performance or to function as responsible parents, and they fail to accept social norms with respect to lawful behaviour. After age 30, the more flagrant aspects may diminish, particularly sexual promiscuity, fighting, criminality, and vagrancy. DSM-V estimates that the prevalence of Antisocial Personality Disorder is 3 percent for men and less than 1 percent for women. Estimates of this diagnostic classification in prison populations are, not surprisingly, considerably higher. Indeed, depending on how one interprets the diagnostic criteria, virtually all inmates could be so classified. Studies across many jurisdictions have estimated that 24 to 75 percent of the inmate population meet the criteria for Antisocial Personality Disorder (Coolidge et al. 2011; Fazel and Danesh 2002; Motiuk and Porporino 1991). A more recent study examining 1,110 male federal offenders in Canada reported that 44 percent had been diagnosed with Antisocial Personality Disorder (Beaudette, Power, and Stewart 2015). In contrast, it is estimated that between 15 and 25 percent of the inmate population in North American prisons could be considered psychopathic (Ogloff, Wong, and Greenwood 1990; Porter, Birt, and Boer 2001). Most individuals who meet the criteria for psychopathy also meet the criteria for Antisocial Personality Disorder, leading some to suggest that the former is a more severe form of the latter (Coid and Ullrich 2010). Others suggest that the interpersonal facet of psychopathy clearly distinguishes psychopathy from Antisocial Personality Disorder (Venables, Hall, and Patrick 2014).

In his book *The Mask of Sanity*, Cleckley (1976) provided a clinical description of psychopathy based on clinical observations. Cleckley described the psychopath using the following criteria: unreliability; insincerity; pathological lying and deception; egocentricity; poor judgment; impulsivity; a lack of remorse, guilt, or shame; an inability to experience empathy or concern for others and to maintain warm, affectionate attachments; an impersonal and poorly integrated sex life; and an unstable life plan with no long-term commitments.

Since the 1960s, Robert Hare and his colleagues have devoted considerable attention to developing a reliable and valid procedure for assessing psychopathy. This program has culminated in the Revised Psychopathy Checklist (PCL-R) (Hare, 1991, 2003), a 20-item checklist of traits and behaviours associated with psychopathy (see Table 9.2). Offenders with these psychopathic features commit

TABLE 9.2 ■ The 20 Items of the Psychopathy Checklist

1. Glibness / superficial charm[p]	11. Promiscuous sexual behaviour
2. Grandiose sense of self-worth[p]	12. Early behavioural problems[ab]
3. Need for stimulation / proneness to boredom[ab]	13. Lack of realistic, long-term goals[ab]
4. Pathological lying[p]	14. Impulsivity[ab]
5. Cunning / manipulative[p]	15. Irresponsibility[ab]
6. Lack of remorse or guilt[p]	16. Failure to accept responsibility for own actions[ab]
7. Shallow affect[p]	17. Many short-term marital relationships
8. Callous / lack of empathy[p]	18. Juvenile delinquency[ab]
9. Parasitic lifestyle[ab]	19. Revocation of conditional release[ab]
10. Poor behavioural controls[ab]	20. Criminal versatility

Note: The checklist is composed of two factors: [p] identifies the items that define personality traits, and [ab] identifies items descriptive of antisocial behaviour.

Source: Republished with permission of Elsevier Science and Technology Journals, from "A research scale for the assessment of psychopathy in criminal populations," *Personal and Individual Differences*, 1:2 (1980); permission conveyed through Copyright Clearance Center, Inc.

more crimes, commit a greater variety of crimes, and are more violent during the commission of their crimes (Hare 2003). Research has continued to support the use of this scale in offender populations. An excellent review of the use, and misuse, of the PCL-R has been provided by Hare. In discussing the PCL-R and its screening version, the PCL-SV (Hart, Cox, and Hare 1995), he concludes that these checklists

> provide reliable and valid assessments of the traditional construct of psychopathy. They are used widely for research purposes and for making decisions in the mental health and criminal justice systems. They are strong predictors of violence and recidivism in offenders and psychiatric patients, form a key part of current risk assessment procedures, and play an important role in many judicial decisions. (Hare, 1998c, 99)

Indeed, because of the strong relationship between psychopathy and violence, psychopathy has become one of the primary predictors used by clinicians to determine risk for future violence (Walsh and Walsh 2006). Other commentators and researchers have cautioned against overreliance on the PCL-R (or any assessment instrument) when making legal determinations and against equating the construct of psychopathy with scores on the PCL-R (see DeMatteo and Edens 2006; Skeem and Cooke 2010).

A leading theory about antisocial personality is that these individuals do not learn from negative experiences because they do not become anxious in circumstances that should elicit anxiety. Also, they do not have sufficient fear of the consequences of their behaviour (Hare 1970; Brodsky 1977). Applying Eysenck's model, reviewed earlier in this chapter, the psychopath can be viewed as an extrovert who does not easily acquire conditioned responses or, if he or she does acquire them, extinguishes them very rapidly. Given these characteristics, particularly the inability to learn from punishment or to experience fear or anxiety, it is understandable that Brodsky (1977) concludes that imprisonment is unlikely to have much effect on the post-release behaviour of such individuals.

FOCUS

BOX 9.2

PSYCHOLOGISTS SUGGEST BERNARDO AND HOMOLKA ARE PSYCHOPATHS

TORONTO—Prosecutors painted a picture of a battered woman and a controlling, abusive husband who forced her to take part in unspeakable crimes. But some experts suspect that both Karla Homolka and Paul Bernardo are psychopaths—people who aren't mentally ill but lack any conscience and single-mindedly pursue their own pleasure.

In Bernardo, they suggest, psychopathic qualities combined with sexual sadism to form an explosive mix. Some psychologists who have followed the Bernardo trial say the crimes Homolka and Bernardo admitted to committing, and their almost total lack of emotion in the witness box, suggest psychopathic tendencies.

"What bothers me about him, and her, too, is the casual way these horrific things are described on the witness stand," said psychologist Robert Hare of the University of British Columbia, one of the world's leading experts on psychopaths.

"When a psychopath commits a violent act, they're not doing it because they're malicious or malevolent or evil. They're doing it because they don't give a damn."

Bernardo was "such a good psychopath" that he found a woman who had a penchant for submissive sex that complemented his urge to dominate, said psychologist Marnie Rice of Ontario's Penetanguishene Mental Health Centre. Homolka may not have got into trouble with another man. But hooked up with Bernardo, it's possible she agreed to take part in three-way sex with kidnapped teenage girls as part of a willingly subservient role, said Rice, whose hospital houses some of the province's most dangerous offenders.

"It appears the two found each other."

Homolka testified Bernardo beat her into submission and blackmailed her over her role in the death of her sister, who was drugged and raped by the couple. Two psychologists called by the Crown suggested Homolka suffered from battered women's syndrome. Rendered helpless and hopeless by repeated beatings, someone in her shoes could feel obliged to take part in the most heinous crimes, they said. Hare is skeptical.

"We look for very simple explanations for complex behaviour," he said. "To me, battered women's syndrome does not explain what she did."

Even a psychiatrist retained by the prosecution—but not called as a witness at Bernardo's trial—said Homolka's role in the horrific crimes can't be fully explained by the abuse she suffered.

"Karla Homolka remains something of a diagnostic mystery," Dr. Angus McDonald wrote in his report, which the Bernardo jury never saw.

"Despite her ability to present herself very well, there is a moral vacuity in her which is difficult, if not impossible, to explain."

In Bernardo's case, it appears there were no ethical restraints to hold him back from sex that inflicted pain, terror and humiliation on his partner, psychologists say. Among evidence ruled inadmissible at his trial was a statement the Crown says Bernardo made to two witnesses.

"I have no conscience," prosecutors quoted him as saying. "I could kill anybody."

Experts also say his videotaping of the sexual assaults is typical of many rapists and sex killers, who keep souvenirs of their victims such as jewelry, clothing or hair. Serial killer Harvey Murray Glatman used photographs of the women he murdered in Los Angeles during the 1950s to relive his sexual fantasies.

"They're like stamp collectors," said psychologist Vern Quinsey of Queen's University in Kingston. "They look at them and think about them and try to do better next time."

Psychopaths tend to be egocentric, lack remorse or guilt and constantly seek excitement, said Hare. They're also unable to empathize with others and tend to be deceitful and emotionally shallow. Only a small percentage are physically violent, he said.

"They are predators—emotional and physical and sexual predators."

Bernardo's cool, confident and sometimes condescending demeanor in the witness box was typical, Hare said.

"A psychopath who has committed a crime and is caught is now on stage. He doesn't see himself as any sort of pariah, he sees himself as a victim of the system. . . . He's on stage, he's enjoying it, he's loving it.

"What these people do is confuse fame and infamy."

Questions for Critical Thinking

1. Why were Paul Bernardo and Karla Homolka convicted rather than being found Not Criminally Responsible on Account of Mental Disorder?

2. Babiak and Hare authored a book called *Snakes in Suits: When Psychopaths Go to Work*. The thesis of the book is that some of the qualities of a psychopath help people succeed in business. Discuss which traits might facilitate a successful corporate career.

Source: Tom Blackwell, "Psychologists Suggest Bernardo and Homolka Are Psychopaths" (n.d.). Printed with permission of *The Canadian Press*.

Newman (1998) has reviewed a position suggesting that psychopaths exhibit deficits in information processing that limit their ability to use contextual cues appropriately in the implementation of goal-directed behaviour and that interfere with effective self-regulation. Hare (1998b) suggests that while a great deal remains to be done, a convergence is developing with regard to the etiologic bases of psychopathy, one that forms "a reasonably coherent conceptual/empirical package that helps us understand how and why psychopaths differ from others in the processing and use of semantic and affective information, and in their capacity for callous, predatory behaviour" (131).

Raine and Yang (2006) indicate that there has been surprisingly little brain imaging research done on the neuroanatomical basis of psychopathy. They conclude that this is because the complexity of the clinical construct makes it "highly likely that the neuroanatomical basis to psychopathy is not simple, and that abnormalities to multiple brain mechanisms contribute to the behavioural, cognitive, and emotional characteristics that make up the psychopath" (279). They draw two conclusions from the literature. One is that the area is very much underresearched and that basic research is still required. The second is that, with regard to psychopathy, questions regarding specific brain impairments and their causes are even further removed from being answered (291). Given these limitations, several possible neuroanatomical impairments have been identified (Raine and Yang 2006; Weber et al. 2008). First, abnormalities in the prefrontal cortex would support the view that psychopaths are low-arousal, fearless, impulsive, and disinhibited individuals. Second, impairments in the hippocampus may result in dysregulation in affect and fear conditioning. Dysfunction in the amygdala has also been suggested in psychopaths (Blair 2006); this would result in a reduction in the individual's "responsiveness to the sadness and fear of potential victims" and "their ability to learn the stimulus–reinforcement associations that are necessary for moral socialization" (307). In a review of functional neuroimaging studies of psychopathic adults, Seara-Cardoso and Viding (2014) concluded that psychopaths seem to show a reduced response in brain regions associated with affective processing and increased activity in regions associated with cognitive control. A concern expressed in the identification of possible pathophysiologies in psychopathy has to do with whether they are fundamental to the disorder or are secondary consequences of it (Blair 2006).

Heilbrun (1979) conducted an interesting study of the influence of intelligence on the relationships between psychopathy, violence, and impulsiveness. His sample of 76 white male prisoners was divided into psychopathic and nonpsychopathic groups ($n = 38$). Two personality measures were used (one of which, incidentally, was validated in a study by Craddick [1962], using a Canadian prison sample). He further divided the groups into high-intelligence and low-intelligence subgroups. Heilbrun found that intelligence level does indeed have an influence on violence and impulsiveness among psychopaths. The more intelligent psychopaths were neither violent nor impulsive and were more likely to have attained educational goals. This study points to the importance of viewing persons with the label of psychopath, or antisocial personality, in multidimensional ways. Not all such individuals should be expected to be violent or impulsive.

The Heilbrun study should also serve as a reminder that studies of prison populations may present a misleading picture of antisocial personality. Most of the research on antisocial personality has used samples obtained from institutional populations. This may give a distorted view because the impressions one gains about people with antisocial personalities are, thus, based on people who committed criminal acts but were unable to avoid apprehension. Furthermore, it is certainly true that not all persons with this label are criminals (Cleckley 1976). An exception to the focus on institutionalized populations is the work of Cathy Spatz Widom (1977; Widom and Newman 1985). In one study, Widom placed an advertisement in a local newspaper asking for "charming, aggressive, carefree people who are impulsively irresponsible but are good at handling people and at looking after number one." Twenty-nine applicants were interviewed. The demographic and personality test data applied to these people revealed some interesting information about this noninstitutionalized population. Only two subjects had not finished high school, and most had some college. Nearly two-thirds had at least one arrest, but the conviction rate was quite low (18 percent), even though many of the charges were felonies. While 50 percent had been incarcerated, most had been in jail less than two weeks. The subjects scored high on the extroversion and neuroticism scale of Eysenck Personality Inventory, consistent with Eysenck's (1977) notions of psychopathy. Scores on the Minnesota Multiphasic Personality Inventory (MMPI), an objective personality test, fit the classic profile of psychopathy (high scores on the psychopathic deviate and manic scales). Subjects had low scores on the measure of socialization, and most also had low scores on the empathy scale.

Many of the results of Widom's study were similar to those drawn from institutional populations. That said, she presents a picture of somewhat more successful antisocial persons. These people are better educated and more successful at avoiding conviction and lengthy incarceration. This supports the conclusion of Widom and Newman (1985) that research on the antisocial personality must avoid a primary focus on the incarcerated criminal. Her methodology seems to have succeeded in drawing a sample of noninstitutionalized persons who meet the antisocial personality criteria. This is important, for it is vital for us to become more aware of the prevalence of psychopathy within the general population and to begin to understand better the non-criminal manifestations of this personality.

> **SEARCH FOR:**
> **Minnesota Multiphasic Personality Inventory (MMPI)**

Of direct relevance to this concern is the book by Babiak and Hare (2006) titled *Snakes in Suits: When Psychopaths Go to Work*, in which the authors examine the impact of the psychopath in the corporate working world. One might initially assume that many of the traits that psychopaths display would make it obvious to potential employers that they would not work well with others and would constitute an employment risk, but this does not appear to be the case. The authors identify four possible reasons for this contradiction. One is that some of the traits associated with psychopathy provide these individuals with skills in social manipulation. Their ability to charm others will often make them initially seem attractive and even charismatic in job interviews. It is only in retrospect that it becomes clear that the decision was not a good one. A second issue is that some of the traits associated with psychopathy may appear on the surface to indicate leadership and management skills though they actually represent a need for dominance and manipulative as well as coercive abilities that are, again, not initially obvious. A third concern reflects the evolution of today's business world, in which large, stable bureaucratic organizations have adopted a faster, more flexible, and somewhat chaotic approach to information processing. This has resulted in a change in hiring policies towards acquiring individuals who can "stir things up" and effect change quickly. As Babiak and Hare note, "the general state of confusion that change brings to a situation can make psychopathic personality traits—the appearance of confidence, strength, and calm—often look like the answer to the organization's problems. . . . Egocentricity, callousness, and insensitivity suddenly become acceptable trade-offs in order to get the talents and skills needed to survive in an accelerated, dispassionate business world" (2006, xxi). A fourth dilemma is that the decreased constraints and levels of accountability in this new fast-paced business climate create an environment that psychopaths find inviting. The personal gains available are very appealing to the psychopath, who relishes the risks and thrills involved. The relentlessness of this drive is captured in the somewhat chilling comment: "Like all predators, psychopaths go where the action is, which means to them positions, occupations, and organizations that afford them the opportunity to obtain power, control, status, and possessions, and to engage in exploitative interpersonal relationships" (2006, 97).

Clearly, the implications of corporate psychopathic behaviour for companies and their workers can be disastrous, and the authors provide numerous examples of the devastating impact that such individuals have had in history. Of course, the workplace psychopaths most often cited in the media are the investment bankers and mortgage brokers who brought down the US economy in 2008 and men, such as Bernie Madoff, who created Ponzi schemes that stole billions from investors (see Chapter 17). A concern here is that the extensive forensic research literature on psychopaths needs to be presented in such a manner that those so greatly affected by their behaviour can recognize and better understand them. However, at this time, the fascination with such individuals continues to be mostly a consequence of the overwhelmingly antisocial nature of their acts. In *Without Conscience: The Disturbing World of the Psychopaths Among Us*, Hare (1998a) captures the essence of this in his description of Clifford Olson (see Box 9.3).

As theories of crime, antisocial personality disorder and psychopathy do not completely avoid the tautology that results from failing to distinguish between the criterion (the disorder) and the outcome (crime). However, as previously noted, psychopathy not only identifies those who have committed past offences but also predicts *future* criminality—both general and violent recidivism (Hare 1998c). The construct of psychopathy has been criticized for being too simple and for disregarding the dynamic nature of human behaviour (Walter 2004). Even so, many consider psychopathy to be "the single most important clinical construct in the criminal justice system" (Hare 1998c, 99).

A final note on treatment seems appropriate. Losel (1998) reviews a position taken by Suedfeld and Landon (1978) that no effective treatments exist for this disorder. Losel writes that while our understanding of issues related to assessment, etiology, prediction, and biological, cognitive, emotional, and behavioural correlates has advanced greatly, treatment for such individuals remains an area of uncertainty. Other researchers, however, have recently noted that the treatment of psychopathic characteristics in adolescents holds some promise (Salekin, Worley, and Grimes 2010). Overall, it is suggested that treatment programs for psychopathic offenders should focus on altering and managing their behaviour rather than attempting to change their underlying personality characteristics (Quinsey et al. 2006; Wong and Hare, 2005).

FOCUS	BOX 9.3

CLIFFORD OLSON—THE PROTOTYPICAL PSYCHOPATH

Canada's most notorious and reviled criminal *was* Clifford Olson, a serial murderer sentenced in January 1982 to life imprisonment for the torture and killing of 11 boys and girls. These crimes were the latest and most despicable in a string of antisocial and criminal acts extending back to his early childhood. Although some psychopaths are not violent and few are as brutal as he, Olson is the prototypical psychopath.

Consider the following quotation from a newspaper article written around the time of his trial: "He was a braggart and a bully, a liar and thief. He was a violent man with a hairtrigger temper. But he could also be charming and smooth-tongued when trying to impress people. . . . Olson was a compulsive talker. . . . He's a real smooth talker, he has the gift of gab. . . . He was always telling whoppers. . . . The man was just an out-and-out liar. . . . He always wanted to test you to the limits. He wanted to see how far he could go before you had to step on him. . . . He was a manipulator. . . . Olson was a blabbermouth. . . . We learned after a while not to believe anything he said because he told so many lies" (Farrow 1982). A reporter who talked with Olson said, "He talked fast, staccato. . . . He jumped from topic to topic. He sounded glib, slick, like a con trying to prove he's tough and important" (Ouston 1982).

These reports by people who knew him are important, for they give us a clue to why he was able to get his young, trusting victims alone with him. They may also help explain the Crown's decision to pay him $100,000 to tell them where he hid the bodies of seven of the 11 young people he had killed.

Not surprisingly, public outrage greeted disclosure of the payment. Some typical headlines were: KILLER WAS PAID TO LOCATE BODIES; MONEY-FOR-GRAVES PAYMENT TO CHILD KILLER GREETED WITH DISGUST.

In the years after he was imprisoned, Olson continued to bring grief to the families of his victims by sending them letters with comments about the murders of their children. He never showed any guilt or remorse for his depredations; on the contrary, he continually complained about his treatment by the press, the prison system, and society During his trial he preened and postured whenever a camera was present, apparently considering himself an important celebrity rather than a man who had committed a series of atrocities. On 15 January 1983, the *Vancouver Sun* reported, "Mass killer Clifford Olson has written to the *Sun* newsroom to say he does not approve of the picture of him we have been using . . . and will shortly be sending us newer, more attractive pictures of himself" (Ouston 1982). [Quotes are from articles by R. Ouston, *Vancouver Sun*, 15 January 1982; and M. Farrow, *Vancouver Sun*, 14 January 1982.]

Olson also wrote to several criminology departments in Canada offering to help them to establish a course devoted to studying him. In 2011, he died of cancer in Archambault prison.

Source: Robert D. Hare, *Without Conscience: The Disturbing World of the Psychopaths Among Us* (New York: Guilford Press, 1998), 132–34. Reprinted with permission of the author.

Crime and Mental Illness

We begin this discussion of crime and mental illness with a most extreme statement: all crime is symptomatic of mental illness. While this may seem a preposterous statement today, many mental health professionals previously held this belief. Hakeem (1958) summarized these views:

> So powerful is the conviction of some psychiatrists that crime stems from mental disease, that they have held that the commission of crime in itself constitutes evidence of the presence of mental disease. Again, this aspect of the ideology usually draws on the medical analogy. The thesis runs as follows: just as fever is a symptom of physical disease, so crime is a symptom of mental disease.

SEARCH FOR:
"Mental Disorders and Crime: The Connection Is Real," *Crime Times*

Today, most would disagree with this position. Indeed, the current view is that while many criminals exhibit symptoms of mental illness, many do not

SEARCH FOR:
Why Canada's Prisons Can't Cope
with Flood of Mentally Ill Inmates

(Corrado et al. 2000; Markowitz 2011). In the remainder of this section, the extent to which persons charged with crimes are in need of mental health intervention will be examined.

There is widespread consensus among researchers, administrators, and front-line staff that the prevalence of mental disorder among those in the criminal justice system is greater than in the general population. So high is the prevalence of mental disorder in jails and prisons that some have referred to them as "the new mental institution[s]" (Arboleda-Florez, Crisanti, and Holley 1995, 123), the "new psychiatric emergency room[s]" (Lev 1998, 72), the "new asylum[s]" (Shenson, Dubler, and Michaels 1990), "America's new mental health hospitals" (Torrey 1995), or "alternative shelter[s]" for mentally ill individuals who find themselves homeless (Chaiklin 2001).

Notwithstanding this consensus, there is a lack of agreement with respect to the prevalence of mental disorder in jails, prisons, and other parts of the criminal justice system. This, in part, is because of a lack of consistency with regard to defining mental disorder in the literature (Hodgins 1995; Roesch, Ogloff, and Eaves 1995; Corrado et al. 2000). In a systematic review of 62 surveys of correctional samples in 12 Western countries, researchers found considerable heterogeneity among studies with regard to how mental disorder was defined (Fazel and Danesh 2002). For example, some studies examined only the most serious disorders such as schizophrenia, bipolar disorder, and major depression (e.g. Teplin, 1989, 1990a), but many others employed broader definitions that included less serious disorders such as dysthymia and anxiety disorders (e.g., Falissard et al. 2006), substance abuse disorders (e.g., Teplin 1991), and/or personality disorders (e.g., Gunn, Maden, and Swinton 1991). Other studies have not used disorder-based definitions at all, focusing instead merely on the presence of symptoms (Corrado et al. 2000).

A further consideration when examining prevalence across jurisdictions, both within and between countries, is that the true prevalence may differ markedly from one site to the next as a function of the availability of health care resources and the differing attitudes, practices, and policies of law enforcement agencies and legal institutions (Drewett and Shepperdson 1995; Harris and Rice 1997; Corrado et al. 2000). Despite arguably substantial differences in health and criminal justice policies in Canada and the United States, Corrado and his colleagues (2000) found similar rates of serious mental disorder among Canadian and US jails and prisons. Yet even within the same metropolitan centres, rates may reflect the varying characteristics of neighbourhoods. For example, researchers in the Vancouver Metropolitan Area found vastly different prevalence rates for substance misuse across two studies; this was largely attributable to the characteristics of the jails' catchment areas (Ogloff 1996; Roesch 1995).

Despite methodological and conceptual challenges, sufficient research exists to estimate the prevalence of mental disorders in various correctional settings. The studies cited most often regarding jail prevalence are those conducted by Teplin in the early 1990s (Teplin 1990a, 1990b, 1991, 1994; Teplin and Voit 1996). In her review of jail studies, she found that among jail detainees, the prevalence of *any* mental disorder ranged from 16 to 67 percent and the prevalence of *severe* mental disorder (defined largely as schizophrenia, bipolar disorder, and major depression) ranged from 5 to 12 percent (Teplin 1991). Other US surveys and reviews have reported similar estimates (e.g., Ogloff 2002; James and Glaze 2006; Scott and McDermott 2010).

There has been relatively little research in Canada examining the rates of mental disorder in Canadian jails, but the research that does exist suggests that the prevalence of mental disorder in Canadian jails is high. For example, a BC study found that the prevalence of major mental disorders was 15.6 percent (Roesch 1995). As well, the prevalence of substance use disorders was exceptionally high: over 77 percent of inmates were considered to have alcohol use or dependence disorders, and over 63 percent drug use disorders. More recently, Beaudette, Power, and Stewart (2015) examined the prevalence of mental disorders among Canadian federally sentenced men and found that 12.4 percent had been diagnosed with at least one major mental illness (i.e., bipolar disorders, major depression, and psychotic disorders). The rates of alcohol or substance use disorders among newly admitted inmates were high across the country, ranging from 37.1 percent in Quebec to 60.1 percent in the Pacific region.

Consistent with the US literature, Canadian research suggests that the prevalence of mental disorder may be lower in prisons than in jails (James and Glaze 2006; Teplin 1991). In a 2004 report profiling the health needs of federal prison inmates in Canada, researchers found that 7 percent of inmates at intake had a mental health need that required immediate attention (Canadian Public Health Association, 2004). A higher proportion of inmates reported mental health problems (31 percent of females and 15 percent of males). Moreover, a substantial proportion of incoming inmates (21 percent of females; 14 percent of males) had admitted attempting suicide in the preceding five years.

These prevalence rates should not be taken as suggesting that most inmates are healthy (Ogloff 1996). On the contrary—most inmates in Canadian jails and prisons have substantial mental health needs, particularly with respect to substance use disorders (Hodgins and Coté 1995; Roesch 1995; Lamb and Weinberger 1998; Kelly and Farrell MacDonald, 2015a, 2015b). For example, over 70 percent of the inmates in Beaudette and colleagues' (2015) study met the criteria for at least one mental disorder. Many of these individuals had co-occurring disorders (e.g., schizophrenia and substance abuse), which compounded the mental health and social problems they experienced. The Canadian findings are consistent with US studies, which have found considerable overlap between mental disorders and drug or alcohol abuse in jail populations (Abram and Teplin 1991; Abram, Teplin, and McClelland 2003).

In a unique study conducted in BC, researchers extracted data from the records of three provincial agencies to get a better understanding of healthcare and social assistance use among those who were provincially incarcerated (Somers, Cartar, and Russo 2008). This study included the records of all members of the provincial corrections population in BC from 1997–98 to 2003–4. Over 30 percent of individuals who were incarcerated during the seven-year period had been medically diagnosed with a substance use disorder. An additional 26 percent were diagnosed with a mental disorder unrelated to substance use. Among those who had a substance use disorder, more than 75 percent had a co-occurring disorder. This combination (mental disorder plus substance use disorder) was found to be particularly hazardous, resulting in significantly higher health and service costs as well as greater involvement in corrections.

The high rate of individuals with co-occurring disorders also suggests the need for treatment programs both within the jail and after release. Abram and

SEARCH FOR:
"The Prison Careers of Offenders with Mental Disorders," Correctional Service of Canada

Teplin (1991) suggested that these individuals might be particularly appropriate for alternatives to prosecution, such as pretrial diversion programs. Mental health courts are also an option for these individuals (Slinger and Roesch 2010; Honegger 2015).

The prevalence of mental disorders in jails has prompted the APA (2000) and the National Commission on Correctional Health Care (2003) to recommend, in their standards and guidelines for the delivery of mental health services in jails, that all institutions adopt a systematic program for screening individuals upon detention, a recommendation echoed by healthcare providers and researchers (Roesch 1995; Birmingham et al. 2000; Osher, Steadman, and Barr 2003; Nicholls et al. 2005). Specialized screening tools devised specifically for mental health screening in jails have started to emerge in the literature. For example, in Canada, Nicholls and her colleagues (2005) have developed the Jail Screening Assessment Tool, a semi-structured interview used to screen inmates for mental health concerns, risk of suicide and self-harm, and risk of violence and victimization. Also in 2005, researchers in the United States created the Brief Jail Mental Health Screen (Steadman et al. 2005), a screening tool for serious mental illness comprising eight yes-or-no questions.

The high prevalence of mental disorders in jails has substantial costs, not only fiscal but also humanitarian, both for inmates and for correctional staff. Jail staff perceive mentally disordered offenders as the most disruptive inmates (Kropp et al. 1989; Ruddell 2006), a perception that has found some support in the literature, but only for offenders with personality disorders (Stewart and Wilton 2017). These inmates are also at an increased risk for suicide and self-harm, victimization, and institutional maladjustments (Ogloff 2002; Nicholls et al. 2005; James and Glaze 2006; Swanson et al. 2015). These adverse events affect not only individuals entering the criminal justice system with mental health difficulties but also those who develop mental health problems during their stay (and perhaps as a result of it).

Although most people with mental illness do not commit criminal acts, there is little question that individuals with mental health problems are increasingly involved with the legal system. The first contact is usually by police officers, and there is evidence that police are increasingly encountering mentally ill individuals. A Vancouver study found that more than one-third of calls to police involved a mental health issue (Wilson-Bates 2008). As Brink et al. (2011) have suggested, there are myriad and complex reasons that people with mental illness might interact with the police, including "co-occurring substance use problems and treatment non-compliance, as well as social and systemic factors, such as improperly implemented deinstitutionalization policies, homelessness and poverty, community disorganization, poorly funded and fragmented community-based mental health and social services, hospital emergency room bed pressures, overly restrictive civil commitment criteria, intolerance of social disorder, and criminal law reforms." Police resources are further depleted because of the intense efforts involved in working with chronically mentally ill individuals and those who are suicidal. This is exacerbated when gaps in the healthcare system result in police resources being used in place of health resources to deal with mentally ill individuals (Thompson 2010).

The training provided to police officers concerning mental-health-related issues varies widely between departments; so does the use of specialized responses for calls involving people with mental illnesses. Hails and Borum (2006) found that some police agencies provided zero hours of training in handling calls involving people with mental illnesses, while others provided as many as 41 hours of training. Most of the agencies provided no post-academy in-service training hours dealing with the topic of mental illness. Hails and Borum also found that only 21 percent of agencies had a special unit or bureau within the department to assist police in handling people with mental illness. This percentage is disappointing, given findings that in some jurisdictions, specialized teams composed of a police officer and a mental health professional have helped avoid the criminalization of the mentally ill (Lamb et al. 1995). Moreover, in those rare cases where the interaction between a mentally disordered individual and the police has resulted in the need for a coroners' inquest, the recommendation most often made has been for an increase in police training so that they will be better prepared to work with individuals with mental disorder (Cotton and Coleman 2010).

There is some evidence that the discretionary powers of the police in dealing with the mentally ill have been affected by the deinstitutionalization movement. This movement resulted in the release of large numbers of patients from mental hospitals. At the same time, the civil commitment laws were changed so that commitment had to be based on findings of mental illness and dangerousness. As a consequence, police could no longer use the mental hospital as an alternative disposition to jail and were often forced to arrest a mentally ill person.

If this is true, does it suggest there is a significant relationship between crime and mental disorder? In his study of the rates of mental disorder in prisons, Gunn (1977) answered this question with a note of caution, suggesting that, since other alternatives for the placement of mentally ill persons had been blocked off, it was to be expected that a greater number of persons previously detained in mental hospitals were now ending up in prisons. As Roesch and Golding (1985) point out, the increased rate of mental disorder in prisons has been the result of "institutional and public policy practices that have nothing to do with individual deviance *per se*. In fact, the individual behavior may not have changed at all. What has changed, however, is the manner in which institutions of our society react to that individual behavior."

With these cautions in mind, it is instructive to review some studies on the extent to which persons considered to be mentally ill are arrested for criminal offences. Most of the research on arrest rates of the mentally ill has relied on police or court records. This research is limited by the availability of information in the files, which are often incomplete and inaccurate. One of the few researchers to actually observe how the police dealt with the mentally ill was Linda Teplin (1984). She was interested in examining the probability of arrest for mentally ill persons compared to persons who were not mentally ill.

Teplin's sample was 1,382 police–citizen encounters involving 2,555 citizens. Overall, the probability of arrest was low; arrest occurred in only 12 percent of 884 encounters (traffic offence and public service incidents were deleted from the total). In individual terms, 506 of the 1,798 citizens involved were considered suspect, but only 29 percent were arrested.

Does the presence of symptoms of mental illness affect the probability of arrest? Teplin's data suggest it does. Of 506 suspects, 30 were considered by observers to be mentally ill. Nearly half (14) were arrested, compared to an arrest percentage of 27.9 percent for those not mentally ill. Furthermore, this difference was not accounted for by differences in type of charge. In other words, mentally ill suspects were not arrested more often because they were suspected of committing more serious crimes. The difference held up across types of crime.

Once arrested, do mentally disordered offenders recidivate at a high level? In a meta-analysis of a large number of empirical studies, Bonta, Law, and Hanson (1998) found that mentally disordered offenders on average showed lower recidivism rates than other offenders. A diagnosis of Antisocial Personality Disorder was found to be a more potent predictor than any other clinical diagnosis. However, with respect to violence after release from custody, Borum (1996) notes that mental disorder is now considered a robust and significant risk factor for predicting violent recidivism, as mentally disordered offenders have a greater probability of committing violent offences after release. But Borum adds that most persons with a mental disorder are not violent, so it is a relative rather than an absolute risk factor. It is important to keep in mind that most mentally disordered offenders are not violent and may have a decreased risk of general recidivism. Indeed, those with mental illness are significantly more likely to be the victims than perpetrators of violence (Desmarais et al. 2014).

In conclusion, it is likely that theories of criminal behaviour that rely on models of mental illness will not account for the behaviour of most criminals. It is certainly true that some people who commit crimes can be considered mentally ill, but these individuals are only a small percentage of the total criminal population. In a legal sense, most criminals are responsible for their actions in that they are aware of their behaviour and can distinguish between right and wrong.

Each of the psychological theories reviewed in this chapter (Table 9.3) makes a contribution to our understanding of criminal behaviour. However, there is a need for greater integration of sociological and psychological perspectives so that both situational determinants and individual differences can be taken into account in attempts to explain criminal behaviour (Monahan and Splane, 1980). A study by Conger (1976) provides an excellent example of an attempt to integrate the two approaches. Conger examined the relationship between two models of delinquent behaviour: the social control model (Chapter 14) and a social learning model. Based on data collected from a sample of grade seven boys, Conger demonstrated how social learning theory, particularly the effects of differential reinforcement and punishment, can be used to explain how an individual's bonds to society can be strengthened or weakened. Conger argued that the combination of the two theories can provide a more comprehensive theory of delinquent behaviour than either theory by itself. It is likely that the same arguments can be made for any of the theories reviewed in this chapter.

In 2007, 19-year-old Ashley Smith died in Grand Valley Institution for Women of self-inflicted strangulation while guards stood by under orders not to intervene. Originally imprisoned for the minor offence of throwing crabapples at a mailman, Ms. Smith had serious mental health problems and did not receive proper treatment from the prison system. A coroner's jury headed by Dr. John Carlisle called the death a homicide. This photo shows Dr. Carlisle entering the institution.

THE CANADIAN PRESS/Colin Perkel

TABLE 9.3 ■ Psychological Theories

Theory	Theorists	Key Elements
Psychoanalytic theory	Freud	Crime results when the ego and superego cannot control the antisocial instincts of the id. This occurs because the individual has not been adequately socialized in early childhood.
Evolutionary theory	Cosmides Tooby	Through natural selection, traits that have helped humans to survive and reproduce are genetically passed on to the next generation. Criminal behaviour may have served an adaptive function for prehistoric humans.
Moral development theory	Piaget Kohlberg	Each individual must go through a sequence of moral development. Those with a high level of moral development will be more likely to make responsible choices when faced with the opportunity to get involved in criminal behaviour.
Personality theory	Eysenck	Law abiding people must develop a conditioned fear of deviance. Those who become delinquents and criminals do not develop this fear because of poor conditioning by parents or because they are less susceptible to conditioning.
Social learning theory	Bandura	Deviant behaviour such as aggression can be learned through direct experience or through modelling the behaviour of others.
Operant conditioning theory	Skinner	Individual behaviour is shaped through both reinforcement and punishment. Behaviour that is rewarded will tend to be continued; behaviour that is punished will cease.
Psychopathy	Cleckley Hare	Psychopaths seem to lack empathy for their victims and do not feel guilty about their crimes. They neither learn from their experience nor fear the consequences of their behaviour.

QUESTIONS FOR CRITICAL THINKING

1. Discuss the relationship between crime and mental illness, and describe the prevalence of mental illness in criminal populations.
2. Is prison the most appropriate place to deal with people with mental illness?

Summary

- Psychological theory is primarily concerned with explanations of behaviour at the level of the individual. Some psychological theories have been criticized for relying too much on trying to explain crime at the level of the individual and for not placing enough emphasis on environmental and situational factors.

- Certain psychological perspectives, such as community psychology, view social problems from a "level of analysis" perspective. Such levels include the individual, small-group, organizational, and institutional or community levels.

- The premise for psychoanalytic theory is a series of five stages of development (oral, anal, phallic, latency, and genital) and three components of personality (id, ego, and superego). Psychoanalytic interpretations of criminality suggest that criminal behaviour occurs when the ego and superego are unable to restrain the id.

- Evolutionary theory seeks to understand the adaptive function of criminal behaviours in terms of their survival and reproductive value. This theory has been criticized for its deterministic nature and its lack of testability.

- Kohlberg has proposed a six-stage theory of moral development, with two stages occurring at each of three levels (preconventional, conventional, and postconventional). This theory has been criticized from a feminist perspective for not adequately considering the different approaches of males (more justice-oriented) and females (more care-oriented) to morality.

- Eysenck's theory of crime and personality is based on the premise of classical conditioning. He has proposed three dimensions of personality (extroversion, neuroticism, and psychoticism), has developed measures of each of the three dimensions, and has generated a number of hypotheses about the relationship of these dimensions of personality to criminal behaviour. Eysenck's work offers a comprehensive model or theory of criminal behaviour that has yet to be validated.

- Social learning theory integrates sociology and psychology in explaining criminal behaviour. Modelling is an important aspect of social learning theory. Family, subcultural influences, and symbolic modelling are all important sources from which an individual can learn aggressive behaviour. Deterrence, by contrast, can occur through legal sanction, social sanction, and self-sanction.

- Operant conditioning is a subset of learning theory that has been proposed to explain criminal behaviour. Reinforcement and punishment are theorized as playing a large part in strengthening or weakening criminal behaviours.

A token economy is one method that has been used to change existing behavioural interactions of individuals.

- Antisocial Personality Disorder is a diagnostic label that refers to a cluster of traits that underlie a pervasive pattern of disregard for the rights of others. Such traits include lying, stealing, fighting, and truancy. Behaviours that may be characteristic of this disorder include excessive drinking or the use of illicit substances, aggressive sexual behaviour, inconsistent work performance, and a failure to accept social norms with respect to lawful behaviour.

- Psychopathy is a term that is often confused with antisocial personality. Psychopathy refers to a pattern of behavioural features that are similar to those associated with Antisocial Personality Disorder. However, in addition to these behavioural features, psychopathic individuals also display certain attitudinal features such as grandiosity, glib and superficial charm, lack of empathy, and a lack of remorse, guilt, or shame.

- Most criminals do not display any symptoms of mental illness. The prevalence of mental illness in jails and prisons is difficult to assess. However, some studies have estimated it to be between 5 and 12 percent for severe disorders and between 16 and 67 percent for any mental disorder.

NET WORK

In this chapter, you have learned about theories of moral development. You can read more about these theories at http://www.moraledk12.org.

Go to the "Moral Development and Education Overview" section of this website to read more about the work of Piaget, Kohlberg, and Gilligan. Then do the following:

1. Go to the "DBME Classroom Strategies/Guidelines for DBME Classroom Practices" section of the website and read the chapter titled "Using the Academic Curriculum for Moral Development: The Basics," found at the Domain Approach to Values Education link. Describe one of the programs that has been used to teach moral development in schools. How does this differ from the teaching program you experienced when you were in school?

2. In the same chapter, you will see a section titled "Structuring Effective Development Discussions." Can you think of a moral dilemma from fiction or from real life that would be suitable if you were doing a moral development session with first-year university students?

3. Go to the "Articles" section of the website. Using the featured articles, can you find two different contexts to which proponents feel moral development should be applied? Do you think moral development training would be useful in these contexts?

10 Strain Theories

JAMES C. HACKLER
University of Victoria

Learning Objectives

After reading this chapter, you should be able to

- Describe Durkheim's pioneering work on the relationship between crime and social structure, and understand the particular importance of his conception of anomie or normlessness.

- Discuss how Robert Merton modified Durkheim so that anomie theory became a theory of relative deprivation rather than a theory of a lack of social regulation.

- Consider that increasing the threat of punishment for misdeeds of the elite could have an impact on public morality.

- Learn that punishment tends to be used where it has little effect and is rarely used where it has a greater likelihood of changing behaviour.

- Note that strains can arise from features in the society or from situations surrounding individuals.

- Understand the strengths and weaknesses and social policy implications of strain theories.

Explaining criminality has been an age-old task. With the growth of sociology, scholars began to look at the wider relationship between crime and social structure. As you read in Chapter 1, criminological theories come from two broad theoretical perspectives—the consensus perspective and the conflict perspective

This chapter reviews some historical traditions that reflect the consensus perspective. While authors differ in their use of terms, formulations of **strain theory** fit this general orientation.

Consensus theorists assume a reasonable degree of agreement on things that matter in society. They also assume that social institutions such as the family, education, government, religion, and the economy normally all contribute to the smooth running of society. Crime occurs when something unusual happens that affects these institutions. This results in strains, stresses, and frustrations that affect behaviour.

strain theory
The proposition that people feel strain when they are exposed to cultural goals they are unable to reach because they do not have access to culturally approved means of achieving those goals.

Durkheim: The Functions of Crime and Anomie

In his book *The Division of Labor in Society* (1893), first published in France in 1893, Émile Durkheim argued that social solidarity—social groups working together towards agreed-upon goals—was an essential characteristic of human societies. These agreed-upon goals led to a set of shared norms. Without norms to guide them, societies function poorly. Such "normlessness," or anomie, occurs during periods of rapid change when social solidarity or social cohesion is reduced. The lack of a sense of community and a collective conscience leads to a breakdown in society and increases in suicide and crime.

Although some crime is normal, there must be a balance between the functional and dysfunctional aspects of deviance (see Box 10.1). Excessive crime and deviance would destroy a society, but if there were no crime at all, then society would almost be compelled to create some. According to Durkheim, even in a society of saints, someone would have to be defined as pushing the limits of proper behaviour. Behaviour may be restrained, but someone will violate the rules. Every society needs its quota of deviants.

Anomie and Normlessness

Durkheim popularized the concept of **anomie** to explain crime in more advanced and differentiated urban societies. Heterogeneity and the increased division of labour weakened traditional societal norms, loosened social controls, and encouraged individualism. When social cohesion breaks down in society and social isolation is great, society loses its traditional social control mechanisms and eventually suffers from a high rate of crime.

Anomie is often defined as a "sense of normlessness," but in *Suicide* (1897), Durkheim also refers to anomie as a condition in which individual desires, or self-interests, are no longer governed and controlled by society. In other words, self-interest, rather than norms, controls behaviour.

anomie
A concept developed by Émile Durkheim (1858–1917) to describe an absence of clear societal norms and values. Robert Merton (1910–2003) used the term more narrowly to refer to a situation in which people would adopt deviant means to achieve goals beyond their means.

Merton: The Gap between Aspirations and Means

Merton applied this idea to crime by linking **social structure** and anomie (1938). Too much emphasis on the pursuit of self-interested goals and not enough on "legitimate means" to achieve those goals leaves society "normless" or anomic. People then use illegitimate, or criminal, means to achieve their desires. For Durkheim and Merton, an anomic society places a higher priority on self-interested values such as the acquisition of wealth, status, and power, and a lower priority on collective values such as fairness, equality, and justice.

social structure
The patterned and relatively stable arrangement of roles and statuses found within societies and social institutions.

Crime is a symptom of the gap between **culturally prescribed aspirations** and the socially structured means for realizing them. The culturally prescribed aspirations are the goals held up for all members of society. Merton argues that in America, the accumulation of money and the status that results from material wealth are universal goals.

culturally prescribed aspirations
A rejection of the notion that aspirations are entirely self-created; rather, they are defined by culture and transmitted by other members of the society.

Socially structured avenues such as schooling are the accepted institutionalized means of reaching such goals. These avenues may not be a problem for some members of the society. For example, if one comes from a family in which the mother or father is a medical doctor it may be realistic for the son or daughter to aspire to the same occupation and social status. The family may live in a nice neighbourhood, the children may attend schools that encourage university education, and the home environment may encourage reading and getting good grades. Although individual characteristics, such as a certain level of intelligence, may also be required, the means to achieve culturally prescribed aspirations are available to many middle-class youths.

By contrast, the child of a poor family, especially a racialized family, could find things a bit more difficult. If the father has abandoned the family, if an older sibling has already been in trouble with the law, if the mother has been on welfare, and if the local schools are ineffective, then the means to achieve success may not be readily available. A youth coming from such an environment may not respect the school system and may have poor grades and minimal likelihood of entering university or college. However, he or she might still aspire to become a doctor and to have both the material and social rewards that accrue to that occupation.

Thus, the gap between goals and the means of attaining those goals is small for certain portions of the society but large for others. The strain resulting from the gap between goals and the means to achieve those goals may result in some sort of innovation, usually deviant in nature. In simpler terms, when society encourages people to want things but makes it difficult for certain groups to get them, members of these groups are more likely to steal to attain the things they have been encouraged to desire.

Not only is the society anomic but so is the individual. This is the condition known as *micro-anomie*—where an individual places more value on self-interest than on collective values. An individual with these values is then motivated to pursue self-interested desires and not think about or be concerned with the effect that pursuit has on the group. In a study of a sample of college students, Konty (2005) found that those students favouring "**self-enhancing**" **values** over "**self-transcending**" **values** were more likely to report having committed criminal and deviant acts. The effect of these values on self-reported behaviour was stronger than the effects of other sociological variables like race and social class. Surprisingly, Konty found that the gap between male and female offending was mostly explained by these different values. Males were more likely than females to have micro-anomic values. But simply having self-enhancing values did not produce crime and deviance if the self-transcending values were also strong. It was when self-transcending, or collective, values were weak that crime and deviance became more likely.

These arguments also fit many forms of lower-class crime, particularly among marginally employed people. Robert Crutchfield (1995) points out that lack of work influences crime. In addition, if marginally employed people reside in concentrations of similarly underemployed people, the propensity to engage in crime is greater. This description fits certain racialized groups in the United States and Canada.

self-enhancing values
Values that emphasize social status, prestige, dominance over others, and personal success.

self-transcending values
Values that emphasize appreciation, tolerance, protection, and the welfare of others.

FOCUS   BOX 10.1

DURKHEIM'S GENERAL MODEL OF DEVIANCE

In his classic work on suicide, Durkheim argues that in contrast to community-oriented or collective thinking, individualism leads to a lack of social cohesion. Suicide, crime, and general deviance are inhibited in cohesive communities.

His research showed that Protestant communities, which are more individualistic, had higher suicide rates than Catholic communities, which are more oriented towards collective thinking. From this, Durkheim concluded that individualism can cause deviant behaviour by reducing the strength of communities. One can generalize the argument from the specific act of suicide to deviance and crime in general, as illustrated in the sequence below:

An Oversimplified Model of Durkheim's Explanation of Suicide as a General Explanation of Crime

Greater individualism → Lack of social cohesion → Suicide and crime

Questions for Critical Thinking

1. Merton (and many of those who followed him) developed strain theory to explain lower-class crime and delinquency. However, some might argue that strain theory actually provides a better explanation for white-collar and corporate crime. Describe how strain theory can be used to explain the crimes of the rich and powerful.

2. Look up Durkheim's theory of suicide online. One of the types of suicide he proposes is anomic suicide, which is discussed in this box. What are the other types of suicide in his theory?

The argument also fits certain upper-class crimes in which people in business, and others, aspire to great wealth. The legitimate avenues to success may not be sufficient because of severe competition; others may be "cutting corners" in a variety of ways. Thus, one can see that no matter what the situation, if there is a gap between the desired goals and the means, innovation or illegitimate tactics are more likely.

Strain as a Feature of Society (Rather than of Individuals)

Were Merton's ideas intended to explain the behaviour of individuals or, as Thomas Bernard (1987) argued, the behaviour of aggregates or groups? Bernard argued that it was not correct to interpret strain or anomie in psychological or social psychological terms; rather, these were properties of social structures. According to Bernard, Merton's theory would predict that societies whose cultures overemphasized monetary success and underemphasized adherence to legitimate means would have high rates of instrumental crime. If legitimate opportunities to achieve those monetary goals were unevenly distributed, instrumental crime would be unevenly distributed.

One must note the distinction between *cultural* factors and *structural* factors in society. In societies in which structural features create an uneven distribution of legitimate opportunities—that is, in which there are many blocked opportunities—there will be pockets of instrumental crime, regardless of cultural values. When a culture emphasizes the ruthless pursuit of wealth, even if there is equal opportunity, crime will be widespread and such a society will have a high rate of crime. The United States and (to a slightly lesser extent) Canada fit this pattern. Other wealthy countries, like Denmark, Norway, and Sweden, seem to be less concerned with the individual pursuit of wealth. (See Table 10.1 for a summary.)

Steven Messner and Richard Rosenfeld (2007) extend this argument with their theory of institutional anomie. American culture emphasizes monetary success but places less emphasis on *legitimate* means of achieving that success. This combination of strong pressure to succeed monetarily and *weak restraints on the*

TABLE 10.1 ■ Strain Theories (Societal)

Theory	Theorists	Key Elements
Anomie: weak social regulation	Durkheim	When social cohesion breaks down, society loses its traditional mechanisms of social control and eventually suffers from a high rate of crime.
Anomie: the gap between aspirations and means	Merton	Crime occurs when there is a gap between culturally prescribed aspirations and socially structured means for realizing those aspirations.
Institutional–anomie	Messner, Rosenfeld	Strong pressures to succeed monetarily and weak restraints on the means to succeed in a society that emphasizes economics leads to crime.

means is intrinsic to the "American Dream." It contributes to crime *directly* by encouraging people to use illegal means to achieve culturally approved goals, especially monetary ones. It also exerts an *indirect* effect on crime through its links with and impact on the institutional structure, or "the institutional balance of power." One institution—the economy—dominates all others. This emphasis has created a greater potential for crime.

Modern corporations may increase this tendency towards crime by splitting production aspects from financing ones. In the past, many companies were created by individuals who were primarily concerned with producing a product or service. Of course, they hoped to make a profit. Today, one can make money trading shares while disregarding the productive activities of a company. Shareholders play no part in daily operations, nor are they committed to the product's reputation or the company's long-term success. They are simply entitled to a share of the profits. Investors who "buy low and sell high" are admired.

The prison sentence served by Conrad Black (Chapter 1) was unique in that a top corporate leader was actually punished for his criminal behaviour. It is worth noting that Black was tried, convicted, and did prison time in the United States, not Canada. Many have argued that Canadian officials would not have taken action against Black.

People in positions of power are rarely punished in the same way as those without influence. For example, Edgar Bronfman, Jr., heir to the Bronfman fortune, was convicted of insider trading in 2011 and given a 15-month suspended prison sentence, meaning he was not incarcerated (McGrath 2011). These cases illustrate a pattern among those at the top that can be described as a *subculture of power abuse*. Besides being criminogenic, such behaviour is generally antisocial and tears at the social fabric (Hackler 2006).

The robber barons of the past ruthlessly exploited others to build railways, oil companies, and steel mills; modern entrepreneurs with deviant tendencies have new strategies that offer a faster and less visible way of achieving monetary goals. Stock markets, and the variety of instruments that have been created for "investing," have created a new potential for crime. Vincent Lacroix, president of Norbourg Management, illustrates the rather complex way corporate leaders can cheat. He was convicted in 2007 of 51 fraud charges, sentenced to 12 years in prison, and fined $255,000. In 2008, Lacroix was released from prison, but as a result of further investigations, he almost immediately faced additional charges of fraud. He pleaded guilty in 2009 to 200 criminal charges of fraud, conspiracy to defraud, money laundering, and other illegal acts. His 13-year prison sentence is the longest ever received for white-collar crime in Canada. However, even though he did great social harm in embezzling the life savings of 9,000 people, he was released in January 2011 after serving only a small part of his sentence (Leblanc 2011).

Lacroix, Black, and Bronfman illustrate the weak restraints on the means to achieve wealth described by Messner and Rosenfeld (2007). Today's white-collar criminals are able to steal much more quickly than their predecessors. Enron (Chapter 17) was able to use new strategies to manipulate sales of energy in a manner not previously possible. High-speed computers offer opportunities that threaten the integrity of the stock market itself (El Akkad 2014). The corrosive aspects of this system have created unethical incentives for elites.

Occasionally, political leaders vow to crack down on corporate and white-collar crime, but such tasks are often assigned to those who have close ties with the corporate world. After a spurt of publicity, efforts to "crack down on corporate crime" tend to fade. If world leaders and lawmakers are part of a *subculture of power abuse* that condones or at least tolerates these activities, is it likely that corrective action will be taken in Canada or the United States? In this regard, Canada is the only developed country that does not have a national securities regulator. Provincial agencies, such as the Ontario Securities Commission, are handicapped in a variety of ways. For example, unlike securities investigators in the United States, Canadian investigators need wiretap approval (McFarland 2014, B4). One US prosecutor has referred to our enforcement mechanism as "quaint."

CP PHOTO/Aaron Harris

Nortel was once Canada's most valuable company. Nortel went bankrupt at least in part because its executives were more interested in increasing their bonuses than in the long-term future of the company and its thousands of employees.

Responding to Opportunistic Crimes of the Powerful

Assuming that North America wishes to reduce the crime that results from the abuse of power by corporate leaders, traditional enforcement measures could be used more successfully. Our judicial system may not be particularly effective against crimes such as family violence, but courts and watchdog agencies could deter powerful people who break the law. Long sentences for corporate criminals have become more common in the United States; by contrast, Canadian investigators have not been nearly as aggressive as their US counterparts, and Canadian sentences remain light.

Prosecution might make corporate leaders rethink certain behaviours. In 2005 the Canadian Imperial Bank of Commerce (CIBC) paid $2.4 billion to resolve a lawsuit in which the University of California alleged that CIBC "participated in an elaborate scheme to defraud investors." Both the Royal Bank of Canada and Toronto Dominion were involved with Enron, but several years after CIBC paid its $2.4 billion in the California lawsuit, the Canadian authorities decided not to proceed with charges against the other banks. This lack of enforcement sends a clear message to potential criminals. Weak restraints on the means to achieve monetary success, and the inability of watchdog agencies and our justice system to respond effectively, together increase the likelihood of white-collar and corporate crime.

So far we have focused on corporate crime, but the *subculture of power abuse* is much broader. Do the same factors that encourage corporate crime increase unethical behaviour in government? Some examples of government misconduct are discussed in Chapter 17.

Unlike in the past, *economic institutions* dominate North America today. Other important institutions—the family, education, and the political system—are now secondary. Those other institutions traditionally curbed criminal tendencies and imposed controls over the conduct of individuals; today, economic factors have overwhelmed the institutions that once socialized people into pro-social behaviour. In other nations, such as Japan and India, the family appears to rank higher on the hierarchy of institutions than in North America, and to be more influential relative to economics. Thus, the United States and Canada produce higher levels of serious crime than countries in which the institutional balance of power leans towards noneconomic institutions.

John Hagan (2010) argues that US government policy has encouraged corporate crime. During what Hagan calls the age of Roosevelt (1933–1973), the Great Depression and the Second World War led politicians to focus more on corporate crime. During the age of Reagan (1974–2008) politics reversed course, demanding harsher treatment of street criminals while reducing scrutiny and enforcement in the financial sector. Financial crimes were seen as of minor importance. Similar views characterize the administration of President Trump, whose own conduct reflects the view that financial regulation is an unnecessary barrier to business.

Government policies based on the premise that free enterprise could do no wrong created a criminogenic environment. Merton argued that the gap between aspirations and means would lead to crime by "innovation." New opportunities to "innovate" were certainly created during the Reagan era: financial inventions such as hedge funds and subprime mortgages provided even more opportunities for unethical behaviour. The economic crash of 2008–9 owed much to new, sophisticated economic inventions (see Chapter 17).

Reducing Crime by Changing the Behaviour of the Elite

Would reducing some types of crime lead to a *general* reduction in crime? It is useful to broaden the discussion to unethical, not just criminal, behaviour. I suggest that reductions in the unethical behaviour of corporate executives and other powerful people would lead to a reduction in *all* crime, including street crimes. A wide range of moral and immoral behaviour is woven into the fabric of society. In Figure 10.1, the morality curve lumps all "immoral" acts together. The skewed curve tapers off to the right; that is, minor, nasty acts are more frequent than very serious unethical acts. Shoplifters are much more common than serial killers. Many people think in terms of the broken line with its smaller bump on the right, believing there is a *unique* group of criminals who are different from the rest of us. It is common to think that corporate criminals and

FIGURE 10.1 ■ The Morality Curve

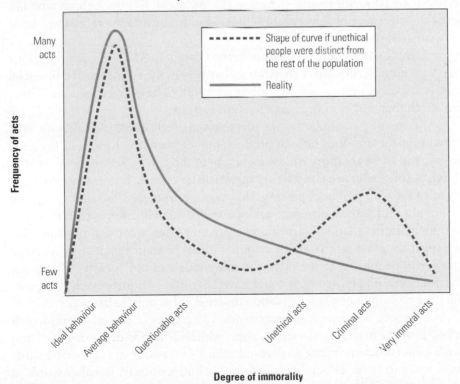

Source: James C. Hackler, *Canadian Criminology: Strategies and Perspectives*, 4th ed. (Toronto: Prentice Hall Canada, 2006), 327. Reprinted with permission by Pearson Canada Inc.

income tax evaders are somehow different from those really bad criminals who make up the bump on the right. Many apologists for corporate crime claim that there are only a few rotten apples in the barrel. Not so. Every study since Sutherland's (1949) classic work shows that crime among large corporations is *endemic*.

The dotted line with two humps leads us astray. We deceive ourselves into believing we can punish the few serious offenders, those under the smaller bump, while the rest continue as usual. Actually, the *solid* line represents reality. Furthermore, the shape stays the same. If we wish to create change, we must *move the entire curve to the left*. That is, we must target the *frequent* acts of immorality that make up the bulk of this "morality curve."

Because the social fabric of society is broad, we must think beyond criminal behaviour and consider a broad range of antisocial behaviour. Because of the magnitude of unethical behaviour in commercial activities (e.g., insider trading, unethical mortgage lending, income tax evasion), it is worth considering legislation and enforcement that would diminish these frequent and serious violations. We must also consider the structural conditions that encourage psychopathic behaviour in business.

Robert Hare of the University of British Columbia argues that individuals climbing the corporate ladder have higher levels of psychopathic traits (Babiak, Neumann, and Hare 2010). We should not be surprised, then, that graduate students entering MBA programs have more psychopathic characteristics than those in other disciplines (Heinze et al. 2010).

The 2008–9 recession was fuelled by fraudulent mortgages and irresponsible behaviour by powerful people (Chapter 17). As usual, however, those who are part of *the subculture of power abuse*—those who led us into the recession—have rarely suffered financially.

As Joanna Slater wrote at the time in the *Globe and Mail*: "Fresh revelations emerge about unscrupulous behaviour by bankers in the run-up to the financial crisis. A spasm of outrage follows, along with talk of new investigations. Then, more often than not, nothing happens" (2011, B11).

Could we use punishment more effectively to create a better-quality society? Formal punishment does little to produce higher morality. Kindness, honesty, fairness, and so on are more effectively taught in the family. Fear of being sent to jail deters some who are considering materialistic crimes, but it is not particularly effective with crimes of passion. However, a corporate CEO may give more consideration to make a product such as a motor vehicle safer, even if it costs a few dollars, rather than risk arrest and a prison sentence for willfully ignoring the danger. In other words, if our criminal justice system sent a clear message to powerful people—who are often the role models in our society—that some behaviours are simply wrong, it could have an impact. Unfortunately, the powerful have more influence on legislation that makes harmful behaviour criminal.

As a society, we pay much less attention to crimes of the powerful, which hurt citizens the most, than to street crime, which is more widely publicized and feared. Unfortunately, failing to demand ethical behaviour in corporate boardrooms leads to lower ethical standards in the entire society. In other words, a little more punishment (or threat of it) on the elite, and the clear expectation that they follow society's rules, would have an impact on many and move the morality curve to the left.

Generalizing Merton's Strain Theory to Other Cultures

Hongming Cheng (2011) argues that Chinese academics pursue the "Chinese Dream" in the same way that corporate executives and those who confront blocked opportunities pursue the "American Dream." The concept of "face" is important to the Chinese scholar, but "face" also involves wealth and power. A brilliant scholar who is poor does not receive the respect of a scholar who uses his academic base to earn money. Thus, there is pressure to cheat. Unethical professors then become role models for unethical students and contribute to deviant behaviour to achieve the "Chinese Dream." Academic fraud moves the morality curve to the right. By contrast, honest professors who are content with the real satisfactions of an academic life and who take pride in seeing their students do well as ethical individuals may move the morality curve to the left. This demonstrates that Merton's basic argument fits more than economic institutions; it also provides clues as to how the world can be changed.

Michael Hellenbach (2006) provides a good illustration of how the capitalist economic model, responding as Merton would predict, increased crime in eastern Germany. When the Berlin Wall came down in 1989, many people in the West assumed that capitalism would bring Communist East Germany a better material life. To bring modern industry to East Germany, West German companies were offered incentives; for example, a West German company could purchase a factory for one German Mark provided that it upgraded that factory. Instead, the western companies stripped the factories they had purchased for one Mark and closed them so that they would not compete with their western enterprises.

Nearly two decades ago I stayed with a fisherman in a port in eastern Germany that had been purchased by a West German firm that had agreed to revitalize it.

Martin Nangle/Alamy Stock Photo

Many residents of the former East Germany have not done well economically since the fall of the Berlin Wall in 1989.

Instead, that firm closed the port and stripped it of all usable equipment. The fishermen were all out of work. Today there are fewer jobs in eastern Germany, salaries for the same work are lower, and young people must migrate to the West to find jobs. Unemployment is high, and crime rates have risen relative to the western part of Germany. In other words, the unethical—if not downright criminal—behaviour of corporations has led directly to an increase in crime. The aspirations of young eastern Germans are high, but the means to achieve monetary goals are low. The West German corporations had monetary goals, too, but they also had access to unethical means.

The argument I am making is that just rules, respect for the law, and ethical behaviour by society's leaders all *influence the potential for crime for everyone in that society*. When the late Jim Shaw stepped down as CEO of Shaw Cable in his early fifties with a pension of $6 million per year, his behaviour was legal, but it was also an abuse of power and privilege. It had moved the morality curve to the right.

By contrast, passing and enforcing laws against white-collar crime, prosecuting income tax violations more vigorously (perhaps publishing the violators' names in the newspaper), and shaming CEOs into linking their bonuses with bonuses to all of their employees would move the morality curve to the left and reduce crime.

When two judges in Luzerne County, Pennsylvania, accepted $2.6 million in kickbacks from the owners of two private juvenile correctional facilities in return for sending children to those places (Schwartz and Levick 2010), did this reflect a capitalist system in which the profit motive leads to greed that overwhelms other values? Or does a society that tolerates and creates a subculture of power abuse increase the likelihood that those placed in positions of trust will be corrupt? Or are these two ideas connected?

Merton's theories provide us with ideas about how to reduce the harm caused by privileged predators. Figure 10.1 suggests that the successful reduction of crime and unethical behaviour among privileged predators would have far-reaching impacts on the rest of crime.

Strain as a Feature of Individuals

So far we have emphasized features of society that influence crime. Everyday life leads to strains. Some of these are simply endured. Robert Agnew (2001, 2006, 2010) has written extensively on strain on individuals and the resulting impact on delinquency. Strain can be experienced directly, but it can also be anticipated and vicarious (Agnew 2002). For example, if one anticipates being attacked on the way to school, one may skip school, which could lead to other problems.

Not all strains lead to crime or delinquency. Failing an exam may be stressful, but it may also lead to a greater commitment to study. If more study does not produce the anticipated results, it could have negative consequences and lead to a decision to engage in cheating. But strain alone does not automatically produce delinquency. Strains are more likely to lead to delinquency if they have certain characteristics:

- Are the strains high in magnitude—for example, a serious rather than a minor assault, or a large rather than a small loss of funds? A juvenile being bullied for a long time, who expects that bullying to continue, may begin to bully others.

Does the stress threaten a core identity, such as a masculine self-image? A boy from a lower-class slum may respond to any challenge to his fighting ability, but less to his skill as a good chess player.

- Are the strains unjust? Did the juvenile have a chance to tell his story? Was he or she treated with disrespect? Did his or her treatment differ from that of others? Was a racialized student treated differently than a white student for similar behaviour?

- Strains are more likely to lead to delinquency if they are linked to low social control (Agnew 2009). Social control comes in different forms. Belief systems, ties to conventional institutions (e.g., school, the family), and group membership (e.g., on a sports team) link one to society and provide restraints from delinquency (Chapter 14). A stake in the community is a stake in conformity.

- Strains are more likely to lead to crime if the crime pays off. If you need money, does stealing or selling drugs bring in enough to reduce the strain you feel? If it does not, it loses its attractiveness.

- Strains that are resolved through contact with people who are involved with crime, such as a group of boys who break into houses, are more likely to persist.

To sum up, we live in a world with many strains. These may make us work harder and spur us to do positive things. In certain circumstances, crime and deviance will be chosen to resolve those strains.

As one applies strain theory to individuals and their situations, one can see a convergence with differential association (Chapter 13) and control theory (Chapter 14). Such thinking lends itself to more universal theories of crime.

The Shift from Control to Opportunity Structures

Durkheim argued that human aspirations had to be regulated and channelled. Human aspirations being boundless, people could not always have what they wanted, so they had to be persuaded to accept what they received. When people were not persuaded, the society became anomic. The moral guidelines were now unclear. Social control broke down, and some people violated the norms established by those in power.

Durkheim emphasized the restraints that control crime, whereas Merton focused on **opportunity structures**. He posited that American society had an overriding dominant goal—material success—but that the guidelines for achieving that success were not always clear. But if this type of anomie was so widespread, why wasn't crime distributed evenly throughout society? Merton accepted the argument that crime was distributed unevenly—that it was higher in urban slums, for instance. To explain this social-class-specific crime, he redefined anomie as the disjuncture between the cultural goal of success and the opportunity structures by which this goal might be achieved. Anomie was shifted from normlessness to **relative deprivation** (as opposed to **absolute deprivation**); thus, it was not the entire community that was anomic but rather specific individuals who were committed to the goal of wealth but who found themselves barred from the means to achieve it.

opportunity structure
Opportunity is shaped by the way the society or an institution is organized or structured.

relative deprivation
Deprivation in relation to others around you, rather than judged against an absolute standard.

absolute deprivation
The inability to sustain oneself physically and materially.

Richard Cloward: Illegitimate Opportunity Structures

There are differences between legitimate and illegitimate opportunities; there are also different types of illegitimate opportunities. Cloward and Ohlin (1960) asserted that simply being subjected to socially generated strain did not enable a person to deviate in any way he or she chose. People can participate in a given adaptation only if they have access to the means to do so (Cullen 1984, 40). Even though members of the lower class may be under a great deal of strain, they are unlikely to engage in violations of financial trust, political corruption, and other white-collar crimes in order to achieve their goals because they lack access to the means of committing them. In a book he co-wrote with Lloyd Ohlin titled *Delinquency and Opportunity* (1960), Cloward extended Merton's ideas by combining them with themes found in Sutherland's "differential association" (see Chapter 13). Sutherland argued that criminal behaviour is learned through associations with others who define criminal activity favourably. While Merton emphasized legitimate means, Sutherland focused on illegitimate means (Cullen 1988). People under strain cannot become any kind of criminal they choose; they are limited by the opportunities available to them. Dealing in drugs is not automatically available to a "square" university professor as a means of supplementing her income; she probably lacks the skills and contacts to arrange a source of illegal drugs. In short, illegitimate means are not readily available to people simply because they lack legitimate means. While Durkheim and Merton developed plausible theories of structurally induced pressures, Cloward tried to explain that reasonable opportunities must exist. Advancing through the ranks of wealthy organized crime groups like the Mafia is only possible in communities where these groups reside and is only accessible to individuals who meet the group's membership criteria. Crimes like computer hacking could not be committed unless a potential criminal has some way of learning the sophisticated techniques involved in these crimes. Many less complex crimes also require the acquisition of skills and contacts.

Opportunity theory can help explain many types of deviance. Cloward and Ohlin applied their ideas to juvenile delinquency. Juveniles undergoing strain face different barriers to resolving that strain than adults do. Their responses to social barriers for achieving goals could lead to three different types of gangs or **subcultures**: *criminal, conflict,* and *retreatist* gangs.

subculture
A group of people who share a distinctive set of cultural beliefs and behaviours that differs in some significant way from that of the larger society.

There are pressures towards conventional goals, such as middle-class respectability. Juveniles who overcome the barriers they face—which most middle-class juveniles do—commit little crime. However, lower-class males may have different goals. Instead of respectability, they may prefer money, or a car or motorcycle. In certain economic conditions, they might achieve these things by working in areas in which their skills are scarce, by working in a hazardous occupation, or possibly by succeeding as a professional athlete. In other words, it is possible to be successful in a working-class style of life. These ideas differ somewhat from Merton's in that aspirations are not universal. Success can mean different things to different people.

But there are also barriers to lower-class goals (see Figure 10.2). There is an opportunity structure for those goals as well, and crime has an opportunity structure of its own. If legitimate opportunities are blocked, the next step may be to search for illegal success, but even here there are barriers. Without certain

FIGURE 10.2 ■ Barriers to Legal and Illegal Opportunities Implicit in the Work of Cloward and Ohlin (1960)

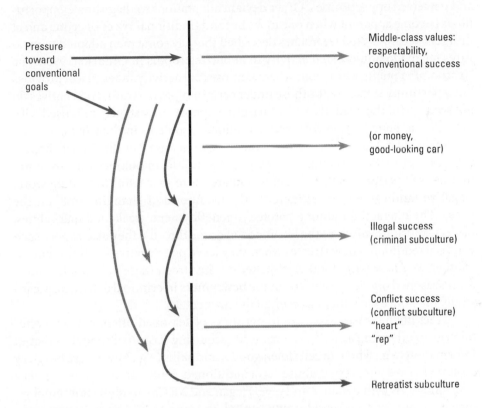

contacts, it may be difficult to get into illegal gambling or learn the skills of credit card fraud. Many juveniles will have difficulty learning the skills necessary to succeed in these areas. One may be able to steal many hubcaps, but there will be barriers to selling them in quantity. However, if there are barriers to profitable property crime, juveniles can still turn to *conflict* as a means of attaining status, at least among their peers.

Juveniles who are unskilled as thieves can show their bravery by fighting for their "turf." This will show others they have "heart"; their courageous behaviour will give them a "rep." But even conflict success has barriers. Not every juvenile is keen on wielding a bicycle chain or a knife or a gun in a gang war. Some may lack strength or courage or both. These juveniles may employ a third delinquent alternative: the use of drugs. In the *drug or retreatist* subculture there are practically no barriers.

Individual characteristics, such as race, will be related to some of these barriers. Thus, Asian youths in Vancouver may have opportunities to work with Asian gangs that extort money from restaurant owners. Blacks who have lived in Nova Scotia since the American Revolution, Jamaican youths in Toronto, and Haitian immigrants in Montreal probably have a realistic view of the barriers to legitimate and illegitimate success. Violence and drugs may be the only things left for some of them.

Marginal Opportunity Structures

Francis Cullen (1988) believes that the contributions made by Cloward are underappreciated because they focus primarily on the gap between aspirations and perceived opportunities. Other deviant adaptations to illegitimate opportunities become apparent when one looks beyond traditional types of crime and at different settings. Fred Desroches described the way some men adapted to pressures related to homosexual activity in public restrooms in Ontario (1995). The "tearoom," a public washroom where homosexual activity takes place, provides an opportunity structure for those under certain types of strain. Alternatives do not seem to fill the need; thus, this marginal opportunity structure is used with the risk that police action will create additional problems in their lives.

Street life in Vancouver offers another type of marginal or illegitimate opportunity structure (Hagan and McCarthy 1997). Youths in families that are functioning well perform better in school and are more successful in finding work. Negative family experiences increase the likelihood of "hanging out" on the street. The interactions among parental unemployment, weakened marital ties, neglect, and abuse increase the likelihood of crime directly; they also expose such youths to additional new stresses when they leave one negative environment for another. While seeking food and shelter on the street, these vulnerable youths meet seasoned offenders who coach the newcomers in criminal activities. Meanwhile, the police view them as criminally inclined.

Street life increases exposure to networks of seasoned offenders, who offer tutelage in offending as well as a means for acquiring "criminal capital"—that is, information (e.g., where to sell stolen goods) and skills (e.g., how to use burglary tools). Physical and sexual abuse has conditioned youths to respond to police confrontations with defiance and rage. Hagan and McCarthy show how employment, a source of social and **human capital**, in contrast to criminal capital, can reduce involvement in crime and street life.

Cloward's work may also help explain certain marginal activities, such as being an oil company spy. In Alberta, where many oil companies drill wells in the wilderness and try to keep their findings secret, spies from rival companies sometimes pose as hunters or wilderness trekkers to observe drilling operations without being detected. More recently, oil companies and governments have been using more modern techniques such as computer hacking and wiretapping to steal the intellectual property of oil and gas companies (US Department of Justice n.d.). These activities highlight the presence of particular opportunities and barriers to potentially profitable tasks.

Opportunity structures, including illegitimate ones, pose an interesting policy question for society. Which is more desirable: having skid row alcoholics with no opportunities, or having drug sellers and gamblers engaging in profitable activities that are seen as deviant by society? While legitimate opportunities are clearly preferable to illegitimate ones, is it possible that the integration of some borderline (or even obvious) deviance would be better than the total breakdown represented by some who have been rejected by society? In a society that must sometimes choose between levels of evils, would policymakers be wise to consider the nature of different opportunity structures and assess the impact of selected illegitimate opportunities on society? (See Table 10.2 for a summary.)

human capital
The talents and capabilities that individuals contribute to the process of production. Companies, governments, and individuals can invest in human capital, just as they can invest in technology and buildings or in finances.

TABLE 10.2 ■ Strain Theories (Individual)

Theory	Theorists	Key Elements
General strain	Agnew	Adolescents in unavoidable unpleasant environments face strain leading to anger and delinquency.
Opportunity structures	Cloward	In addition to strains that create a pressure towards criminal behaviour, there are different opportunity structures that may facilitate breaking the law. These structures are both legitimate and illegitimate.
Code of the Street	Anderson	Lack of employment opportunities leads to alternative ways of achieving respect: displaying toughness, taking another person's possessions, pulling a trigger. This helps build a reputation that prevents future challenges, but it also creates other problems.

Elijah Anderson: The Code of the Street

Elijah Anderson's *Code of the Street: Decency, Violence, and the Moral Life of the Inner City* (1999) describes the cumulative effects of structural changes on inner cities. During and after the World War II, manufacturing firms in the cities recruited many unskilled and semi-skilled workers. Many blacks, Hispanics, and other ethnic groups benefited from these opportunities. At the same time, more minorities were moving into middle-class jobs. Then, with the exporting of manufacturing to countries paying low wages, the loss of these unionized jobs that paid reasonably well had a serious impact on those at the bottom of the social scale. Barriers to participation in mainstream society persisted for young blacks as employers preferred white women and new immigrants.

AP Photo/Fier Paolo Cito

Squeegee kids are among those who have little opportunity to succeed through legitimate opportunity structures.

"The Code of the Street," according to Anderson, requires young males, and often females, to let others know how tough they are, how hard it would be for someone else to "roll on" them, how much "mess" they will take before they respond with a fist in the mouth. The most effective way of gaining respect is to manifest nerve. A man shows this by taking another person's possessions, messing with someone's woman, throwing the first punch, "getting in someone's face," or pulling a trigger. These help build a reputation that prevents future challenges (Anderson 1999, 92). Urbanik and Haggerty (2018) have recently shown that social media have expanded "the street" in a way that has created new risks for criminally involved men in a lower-class Toronto neighbourhood.

Anderson found that many of the young black men he studied lived their lives in active opposition to whites and middle-class blacks. Lacking trust in mainstream institutions, many turned to "hustling" in the underground economy (1999, 108). To be self-respecting, young men and women must exhibit contempt for a system they are sure has contempt for them.

The drug trade offers economic opportunity. However, it is organized around the code of the street, which employs violence for social control and thus contributes significantly to the violence of inner-city neighbourhoods. For those with minimal success in the legal job market, illegal activities provide alternatives: the drug trade, prostitution, welfare scams, and other rackets.

Most youths in school are "decent," but even there, the street element dominates. It victimizes those who show weakness. Thus decent kids must take on the code of the street if they are to avoid being victimized. The lack of opportunity for legitimate employment leads to strain. To achieve respect, and acquire the money that enhances respect, young people must display a willingness to use violence.

Assessing Strain Theories

When Durkheim introduced his ideas, scholars were still explaining crime primarily in terms of genetics and psychological forces. Durkheim focused attention on social forces, a radical idea at the time but now the dominant methodology for explaining crime.

Durkheim was less accurate in his description of premodern societies as stable and crime-free. In fact, many had high levels of violence. Furthermore, Western countries seem to have experienced a long-term decline in crime over the past few centuries (Pinker 2011). Setting aside present-day perceptions, during the 17th century the average citizen in most cities in Western Europe would rarely leave the security of a locked home after dark.

Merton's strain theory does not help us explain the lower crime rates of women. He takes into account the differences in opportunity that arise from social class, but he does not apply the same reasoning to blocked opportunities based on gender (Comack 2016). Women, like disadvantaged lower-class males, might be expected to be more criminal as a means to achieve universal goals. Many theorists have assumed that women experience less strain than men in the struggle to achieve through institutionalized means; however, feminist scholars reject these statements as assumptions and biases rather than fact (Morris 1987; Naffine 1987). Although the strains women experience may differ from those experienced by men, they may be at least as severe. Unless one assumes that women have more modest goals, strain theory does not explain why women are less criminal.

Despite these criticisms, strain theories do offer insights into the misbehaviour of individuals, gangs, and corporations. Recent scholars have even used anomie theory to explain deviance in dictatorship countries that are now moving in the direction of democracy (Zhao and Cao 2010; Hongming 2011). Thus, the ideas of Durkheim, Merton, and other strain theorists continue to be relevant.

The Convergence of Strain Theory and Other Perspectives

Strain theory, differential association, and control theory are increasingly being seen as complementing one another. Also, the policy implications of these different theories can be similar. For example, enabling the disenfranchised to participate more fully in what society has to offer is probably related to greater social bonding with others and a stronger belief in the rules that guide the larger society. However, when social bonds are primarily with people who condone or rationalize criminal behaviour, and with those who face similar blocked opportunities, criminal behaviour is likely. In such situations, control theory, differential association, and strain theory complement one another.

A vast oversimplification of these ideas might be as follows: (1) learning theories (Chapter 13), such as differential association, explain delinquency by *positive* relations with deviant others; (2) social control theories (Chapter 14) argue that delinquency occurs when juveniles have *little or no* attachment or social bonds to others; (3) Agnew's elaboration of strain theory emphasizes that *negative* relations and experiences in situations beyond their control lead juveniles to delinquency; and (4) all three conditions can reinforce one another and can have a reciprocal impact, increasing the likelihood of criminal behaviour. This formulation is supported by Johnson, Morris, and Menard, who conclude that "the limited existing research indicates that strains tend to decrease social bonds and increase association with delinquent peers, which in turn increases the likelihood of delinquency" (2015, 1287). However, in their own study, they concluded that the direct effects of strain were more strongly related to delinquency than the indirect effects through social control and differential association variables.

Uses of Strain Theory

Modern society has created many new illegitimate opportunities. Credit cards, computers, and the flow of information across borders have made new forms of theft possible. Even the 9/11 terrorist attacks in New York and Washington created opportunities for fraud. More than 200 people were arrested for defrauding agencies that were trying to help victims and relatives. A morgue manager, for example, was accused of stealing coffins and reselling them, and similar stories come out of natural disasters like floods and hurricanes. However, most people do not avail themselves of the vast opportunities for theft in complex societies.

Messner and Rosenfeld (2007) argue that the emphasis on material wealth in North America encourages crime. Other countries may have a different value structure. In one informal study conducted by *Reader's Digest*, 1,100 wallets were "lost" in about a dozen countries. Each wallet contained $50 in local currency and the name and phone number of the owner. About 44 percent of the wallets disappeared. However, in Norway and Denmark, every single wallet was returned (Felte 2001). Do some societies create a climate that produces more good Samaritans and where illegitimate opportunities are ignored?

John Braithwaite: Greater Class Mix and the Reduction of Crime

Braithwaite (1979) argues that one must look at the interaction between the social class of individuals and the social class of the neighbourhood in order to answer the question of whether an increase in class heterogeneity in neighbourhoods would reduce crime. He offers two propositions. The first is that crime is most likely when exposure to illegitimate opportunities is high and exposure to legitimate opportunities is low. The second states that crime is unlikely when legitimate opportunities are high or when illegitimate opportunities are low. In other words, in three out of the four possible combinations, there are factors that inhibit crime. Only when illegitimate opportunities exist *alongside* a lack of legitimate opportunities is there a marked increase in crime.

Braithwaite also argues that belonging to the lower class has more effect on delinquency for youth in lower-class areas than for youth in middle-class areas. Consequently, cities with relatively large numbers of lower-class people living in predominantly middle-class areas and relatively large numbers of middle-class people living in predominantly lower-class areas have relatively low crime rates. That is, greater class mix results in less crime.

This implies that the middle classes would be better off if they kept together; on the other hand, if the lower classes stayed together, they would be even worse off. So it may be to the advantage of those with power and influence to keep themselves segregated. The quality of life for the society as a whole, however, would be improved if residential heterogeneity characterized society.

Braithwaite's ideas seem more applicable to property crime. However, another study has shown that the roots of violent crime are also to be found in racial and economic inequality (Blau and Blau 1982). Spatial mixing in neighbourhoods would be more easily achieved with a reduction of racial and economic inequality. Some observers have suggested that Canada has a lower crime rate than the United States in part because our housing policies have been less likely to "ghettoize" the poor, though we do have some areas where there is a concentration of poverty such as Vancouver's Downtown East Side.

Reducing Upper-Class Crime

Braithwaite also argues that "too little power and wealth creates problems of living, and this produces crime of one type; too much power corrupts, and this produces crime of another type" (1979, 200). This does not mean that upper-class people are more criminal than lower-class people; rather, some powerful people abuse their occupational power. It makes little sense to ask which social class commits more crime; instead, opportunities differ by social class. If lower-class people commit crimes because of a lack of power and wealth, increasing their influence and well-being might help. Greater economic equality and a greater distribution of influence among people would modify to some extent those factors that lead to crime.

Lower-class crime may be caused by the failure to achieve success goals. By contrast, upper-class crimes arise from an unprincipled overcommitment to success goals. One study of college students found that those most dedicated to monetary success were those most likely to argue that they "can't afford to be squeamish about the means" of achieving that success. Similarly, certain occupational structures can increase commitment to illegitimate success. Quinney (1963) found that pharmacists tended to fall into two divergent categories with different role expectations: professional and business. The "professionals" were bound by guidelines for compounding and dispensing prescriptions. The "business oriented" believed that self-employment carries with it independence and freedom from control. For them, professional norms exercised less control. Prescription violations occurred more frequently among the business-oriented pharmacists. As both Quinney and Braithwaite would argue, the mutual support of like-minded individuals insulated them from the broader society, and from their professional colleagues, increasing the likelihood of crime.

Policy Implications

Five decades ago, crime prevention projects used strain theories to change opportunity structures. In hindsight, the narrow focus of these projects made it difficult for them to make significant impacts, but they illustrate attempts to apply some of the ideas reviewed in this chapter.

Opportunities for Youth (OFY) in Seattle attempted to use work opportunities to reduce delinquency, but the project met with little success (Hackler 1966). One might argue that temporary job programs do not have a meaningful impact on the larger community. However, this same project had an impact on the attitudes of the adults living in the four communities in which the project was conducted (Hackler and Linden 1970). Furthermore, parents of black children seemed particularly responsive to the idea of job opportunities for their children. Like so many programs launched during the 1960s, OFY attempted to apply strain theories. Lower-class populations did respond and became involved. Although evidence of crime reduction in the short term is lacking, the opportunity structure was altered for some lower-class families. We should not be overly cynical or skeptical. Early childhood education programs implemented in the 1960s have demonstrated that they can have a significant impact on later school achievement and, eventually, on success in the adult world (Schweinhart, Barnes, and Weikart 1993).

Unfortunately, opportunities for the lower classes may have decreased in North America over the past several decades. While there has been a dramatic increase in the wealth of the upper classes, the frequent display of luxurious lifestyles, especially on television, has created all the more strain for those who aspire to a share of that material wealth.

It may be difficult to alter the structure of society, but governments could support institutions that ease some of the strains that arise from blocked opportunities. Public policies could provide visiting nurses, training and support for disadvantaged mothers, paid family leave, and universal healthcare. The work done by Richard Tremblay and his colleagues at the Université de Montréal on early childhood development is consistent with preschool Head Start programs that help reduce the strains caused by the challenges of education (Tremblay and Craig 1995). Young people could be involved in national service programs, such as Canada's Katimavik and the US Peace Corps and Job Corps, that provide funding for higher education or training in skilled occupations. Workplaces could offer ongoing training and upgrading. In other words, some of the strains experienced in the family, school, and workplace do not have to lead to anger and attacks on society if institutions provide alternatives.

A summary of the many successful Nurse–Family Partnership programs that have been offered by David Olds and his colleagues shows how parenting can be more effective than prisons in reducing crime (Hackler 2011). Disintegrative shaming pervades our current coercive criminal justice system (Braithwaite 1989). Social support is the key ingredient in "reintegrative shaming." Andrews and Bonta (1998) have shown that individuals can control their behaviour through rehabilitation programs that make use of cognitive and behavioural therapies. Given the right setting, this can have positive outcomes and lead to legitimate ways of coping. In fact, most current crime control measures increase strain and anger. However, governments have been reluctant to move towards a noncoercive, socially supportive criminal justice system.

Scholars do not have to be in complete agreement regarding strain theory before applying many of its principles to public policy in the important pursuit of reducing the gap between rich and poor. Nor should we ignore the warning Merton voiced in his 1938 article: *"The ruthless pursuit of profit creates a criminogenic society."* Increasing opportunities for the less privileged members of society makes a great deal more sense than increasing CEO salaries and cutting taxes on the wealthiest members of society. According to strain theory, the self-serving policies advocated by many powerful people in North America in recent years will do little to help reduce crime.

QUESTIONS FOR CRITICAL THINKING

1. Researchers who have studied delinquent gangs have failed to find the three distinct criminal, conflict, and retreatist subcultures predicted by Cloward and Ohlin. Why do you think these distinct types of gangs do not exist?
2. Discuss some of the strengths and weaknesses of strain theory.

Summary

- Strain theory is part of the consensus tradition. Strain theorists assume that social institutions such as the family, education, government, religion, and the economy normally all contribute to the smooth running of society. Crime occurs when something unusual happens that affects some or all of these institutions. This results in strains, stresses, or frustrations that affect people's behaviour.

- Durkheim saw crime and other deviance as a consequence of modernity. Changes associated with modernity led to a weakening of social controls, and consequently rates of deviance increased.

- Merton modified Durkheim's theory to account for what he felt were the realities of American society. In Merton's anomie theory, crime resulted from the gap between culturally prescribed aspirations and the socially structured means for realizing those aspirations.

- Messner and Rosenfeld argued that American culture emphasizes monetary success. When combined with weak restraints on illegitimate means, this encourages economic crimes.

- To reduce crime, one must respond to a wide range of unethical behaviour, including commercial activities, safety concerns, and income tax evasion.

- Agnew suggests that adolescents located in unpleasant and stressful environments, such as school, from which they cannot escape become frustrated and angry. If legitimate coping alternatives are not available, violent outbursts and delinquency are likely.

- Cloward pointed out that illegitimate opportunities were also not equally accessible to all. As a result, he hypothesized that there are three different types of delinquent subcultures: criminal, conflict, and retreatist.

- Anderson notes that exporting manufacturing jobs overseas has made a bad situation worse in inner cities. Because traditional legitimate work is no longer available, young people have adopted a code of the street. One gains status by being tough and willing to use violence.

- Early strain theorists focused on lower-class crime, but their work also applies to white-collar and corporate crime. Upper-class crimes can arise from an unprincipled overcommitment to success. Even successful people may feel pressure to make more money and may choose to break the law in order to achieve their financial goals.

NET WORK

Go to this website: http://www.publicsafety.gc.ca/cnt/cntrng-crm/crm-prvntn/tls-rsrcs/vdnc-bsd-eng.aspx. Look at the list of programs designed to prevent crime and delinquency and select a few. Which of these programs address issues raised by strain theorists? How likely do you think it is that these programs will have an impact on crime? Why?

11 Conflict Theories

DANICA DUPONT

Learning Objectives

After reading this chapter, you should be able to

- Understand the differences between Sellin's culture group conflict theory and Vold's interest group conflict theory.
- Describe how Quinney's (1970) group conflict theory differs from both Vold's and Sellin's conflict theories.
- Know the basic elements of Marx's mode of production and what is meant by the economic base and superstructure.
- Understand the differences between instrumental Marxism and structural Marxism and the meaning of relative autonomy.
- Describe the basic elements of the left realist position.

In this chapter we will explore a number of conflict theories, including cultural conflict theory, group conflict theory, instrumental and structuralist Marxism, and left realism. The conflict perspective assumes that societies are more divided by conflict than they are integrated by consensus. Whereas consensus theorists (see Chapter 10) view the law as the codification of mutually agreed-upon societal norms and values, conflict theorists question the assumption that our laws represent the interests of society as a whole. Instead, the conflict perspective argues that the social norms and values codified into law are those endorsed by the more powerful or dominant groups in society.

Cultural Conflict Theory: Thorsten Sellin

Thorsten Sellin was one of the first criminologists to propose a conflict perspective for the analysis of crime. In *Culture Conflict and Crime* (1938), he presented a criminological theory that focused on the role of "conduct norms" in explaining crime. Sellin viewed modern society as composed of diverse cultural groups, each maintaining distinct "conduct norms" or cultural rules that govern appropriate conduct. Sellin suggested that in basic, culturally homogeneous societies the values and norms to which people subscribe will be fairly similar, so the conduct norms of the broader social group will tend to reflect a societal consensus. However, in more complex societies characterized by cultural heterogeneity, urbanization, and industrialization, an overall societal consensus is less likely, and it is more likely there will be conflict between the **conduct norms** of different cultural groups. In other words, the more complex a society becomes, the greater the probability of culture conflict.

conduct norms
Specific rules or norms of appropriate behaviour generally agreed upon by members of the social group to whom the behavioural norms apply.

According to Sellin, **cultural conflict** can arise when conduct norms clash on the border areas between distinct cultures; as a result of colonization, migration, or immigration; or when the laws of one cultural group are extended to cover the territory of another. Sellin was particularly interested in how the conduct norms of immigrant cultures could potentially come into conflict with the conduct norms of the established or dominant culture. One sphere where culture conflict appears is in the legal sphere, especially criminal law. Cultural practices in conflict with Canadian law include female genital mutilation, honour killings, marital rape, and forced marriage. While there are various ways in which social groups secure conformity of their members, the criminal law stands out because "its norms are binding upon all who live within the political boundaries of the state and are enforced through the coercive power of the state" (21).

Sellin felt that the criminal law "depends upon the character and interests of those groups in the population which influence legislation" (21). Ultimately, the social values that receive the protection of the criminal law are the ones valued by dominant interest groups. Sellin uses the term *criminal norms* to describe the "conduct norms" embodied in the criminal law that represent the values of the dominant group. The criminal law will generally reflect the social values and conduct norms of the dominant cultural group. According to Sellin, then, crime is an expression of culture conflict when individuals who act based on the conduct norms of their own cultural group find themselves in violation of the conduct norms that the dominant group has enacted into law. Box 11.1 examines the murders of Zainab Shafia, Sahar Shafia, Geeti Shafia, and Rona Amir Mohammed and briefly surveys the Canadian literature on honour killings and honour-related violence. These crimes provide an example of cultural conflict.

cultural conflict
A theory that attempts to explain certain types of criminal behaviour as resulting from a conflict between the conduct norms of divergent cultural groups.

Group Conflict Theory

George Vold

In *Theoretical Criminology* (1958), George Vold views **group conflict theory** as an explanation for certain types of criminal behaviour. Much like Sellin, Vold is interested in examining crime as it relates to conflict between groups. But where Sellin explains crime as resulting from a conflict between the conduct norms of divergent cultural groups, Vold focuses on crime that occurs as a result of conflict between diverse "interest" groups. Vold begins with the assumption that humans are "group-involved" beings whose lives are oriented towards group associations. Groups form when members have common interests that are best furthered through collective action. Groups will come into contact with one another as their interests begin to overlap and become competitive. Vold sees society as a collection of groups existing in a constantly shifting, but more or less stable, equilibrium of opposing group interests.

Vold is interested in the way the creation of law reflects the activities of antagonistic interest groups in the broader community. One interest group may seek the assistance of the state to enact a new law while an opposing interest group

group conflict theory
A theory that attempts to explain certain types of criminal behaviour as resulting from a conflict between the interests of divergent groups.

FOCUS BOX 11.1

HONOUR CRIMES IN CANADA: SITUATING HONOUR VIOLENCE

On 30 June 2009, the bodies of Zainab Shafia, 19, Sahar Shafia, 17, Geeti Shafia, 13, and Rona Amir Mohammed, 52, were found underwater, inside a submerged Nissan Sentra at the Kingston Mills Lockstation. After a three-week investigation, police arrested the father of the girls, Mohammed Shafia, 58, his second wife Tooba Yahya Shafia, 42, and their son Hamed Shafia, 21, in Montreal.

In January 2012 a jury found each of the defendants guilty of four counts of first-degree murder in the drowning deaths of the Shafias' three teenage daughters and Mohammed Shafia's first wife, Rona Amir Mohammed. The guilty verdict was the culmination of a three-month trial held in Kingston, Ontario, and was the subject of wide media coverage.

The trial opened in October 2011 with Crown attorney Laurie Lacelle's overview of the evidence gathered by police, including physical evidence, forensics, wiretaps, cellphone records, and interviews with police and youth protection workers. The Crown maintained that the three accused were guilty of the planned and premeditated murders of Zainab, Sahar, Geeti, and Rona. Over the next six weeks, the jury heard testimony from detectives, teachers, and child welfare workers that described a disturbing pattern of violence in the Shafia home, including repeated physical abuse, threats, and intimidation.

The Shafia family immigrated from Afghanistan to Canada in 2007. Mohammed Shafia, his second wife Tooba, and their seven children arrived in Montreal in June. Mohammed Shafia's first wife, Rona Amir, followed in November and was admitted to Canada on a visitor's visa as Mohammed Shafia's cousin, as polygamous relationships are not legally recognized in Canada.

As is customary in Afghanistan, Shafia had married a second wife because Rona was unable to have children.

By any measure the Shafia household was a troubled one. Zainab, 19, the eldest of the three sisters, suffered violence at the hands of her father and her brother Hamed. Just six weeks before she was killed, she ran away from home and sought refuge at a women's shelter. Sahar, 17, the middle sister, also suffered physical abuse in the home. In 2008 she confided in a teacher that she had tried to commit suicide, that her brother Hamed had assaulted her with a pair of scissors, and that her parents had threatened to pull her out of school. Geeti, 13, was the youngest of the three sisters. There were many warning signs that Geeti was troubled. She skipped class frequently and failed three out of four classes in her final semester at school. She was caught shoplifting. She told police, school staff, and a youth protection worker that she wanted to be placed in foster care and that her father and her brother Hamed had physically abused her.

On 1 June 2009, 30 days before Rona, Zainab, Sahar, and Geeti were murdered, Hamed travelled to Dubai to meet his father. While father and son were in Dubai, a Google search was entered on a laptop used by Hamed: "Can a prisoner have control over their real estate." Shafia and Hamed returned to Montreal on 13 June 2009. On 20 June, there was another Google search: "Where to commit a murder." Other searches were made in June for various bodies of water, boat rentals, bags, and metal boxes. On 22 June 2009, Mohammed Shafia bought a used black Nissan Sentra.

On 23 June the ten-member Shafia family left Montreal, travelling in two cars, the Nissan Sentra and Shafia's Lexus SUV. The children were told they were going on vacation.

Mohammed Shafia, Tooba Yahya Shafia, and Hamed Shafia were found guilty of first-degree murder for killing the Shafias' three daughters and Mohammed Shafia's first wife.

THE CANADIAN PRESS/Lars Hagberg

On 30 June 2009, at about 9 a.m., the bodies of Zainab Shafia, Sahar Shafia, Geeti Shafia, and Rona Amir Mohammed were found in the Nissan Sentra at the bottom of the lock in Kingston Mills.

Twenty days later, Mohammed Shafia was recorded on a police wiretap talking to his second wife Tooba Yahya. Shafia said: "They committed treason from beginning to end. They betrayed humankind, they betrayed Islam, they betrayed our religion and our creed, they betrayed our tradition, they betrayed everything." In a conversation recorded on 21 July between Shafia, Tooba, and Hamed, Shafia said: "Even if they hoist me up onto the gallows [unintelligible] nothing is more dear to me than my honour. Let's leave our destiny to God and may God never make me, you, or your mother honourless. . . . There is nothing more valuable than our honour" (in Friscolanti 2012).

The UN Population Fund has estimated that 5,000 women and girls are killed each year in honour-related crimes (UNPA 2000), although many women's groups in the Middle East and southwestern Asia believe the number of honour killings to be at least four times that estimate (Fisk 2010). It is almost impossible to assess the true extent of honour killings and honour-related violence because these crimes go unreported in many countries or are disguised as accidents or suicides (Warrick 2005).

What Are Honour Killings?

What, exactly, is an "honour killing"? According to Korteweg (2012, 136), "the simplest definition of honour related violence, up to and including murder, is a family-initiated, planned, violent response to the perception that a woman, as wife or daughter, has violated the honour of her family by crossing a boundary of sexual appropriateness."

While definitions of honour killings vary somewhat, certain features appear to be constant. First, honour killings almost always involve the murder of a woman or girl by her male family members. Second, the killer does not normally act alone, but with the approval or encouragement of other members of the family. Third, suspicion or rumour of an alleged impropriety is usually enough to justify an honour crime. Fourth, most experts insist an essential characteristic of an honour killing is that it is premeditated (Terman 2010, 10).

It's important to note that the term "honour killing" is controversial and that some scholars, activists, and women's organizations in Canada disagree with its use. For example, Yasmin Jiwani and Homa Hoodfar (2012) have argued for the use of "femicide" and maintain there is no material distinction between the murders of intimate partners and honour killing. In a similar vein, the Canadian Council of Muslim Women (CCMW) issued a position paper in January 2012 outlining their opposition to the term, which they argue is "divisive and dangerous," "encourages blatant racism for some," and makes others "defensive or apologetic about their religion or culture." The CCMW urges that murders of women and girls be identified as "femicide."

In contrast, Shahrzad Mojab (2012) argues that honour killing is a distinct phenomenon that cannot be equated with either domestic violence or crimes of passion. First, honour killing is premeditated, "often planned in much detail," whereas passion crimes are normally understood to be spontaneous or unplanned. Second, whereas a passion crime is normally committed by an intimate partner, honour killing is a group action, sanctioned by the family in response to "a female's violation of the codes of honour." In addition, females often participate, "usually as accomplices, in the murder." Third, honour killing is a social relationship and "aims at satisfying a demand or expectation from the community—cleansing shame and restoring honour." Domestic violence, by contrast, is typically not committed in response to pressure from family or community (129–30).

A similar point has been made by Canadian human rights activist Aruna Papp, who has been counselling South Asian immigrants and victims of violence for 30 years. Papp argues that few researchers appreciate the distinction between Western patterns of domestic violence and what Papp identifies as culturally driven abuse of girls and women in some immigrant communities. Among other differences, Western abuse is considered an aberration by kinship groups and by society in general, whereas culturally driven violence "stems from culturally approved codes around collective family honour and shame, and is condoned and even facilitated by kinship groups and the community" (2010, 7).

Ultimately, the way in which we problematize and define honour-based violence, according to Mojab (2012), has critical implications for both preventing honour crimes and protecting the lives of at-risk women and girls. She argues that the framing of honour killing as domestic violence will make it difficult to prevent, whereas seeing it as a "premeditated, collectively planned and perpetrated crime enables us to detect some early warning signs and save the lives of victims" (121). For example, her research indicates that there are often early warning indicators that a woman's or girl's life may be in danger, including physical harm, emotional troubles, and poor school performance. These indicators need to be taken seriously by teachers, social workers, school counsellors, shelter workers, and police. Mojab is convinced that we must "acknowledge honour-based violence [as] a *Canadian* problem, which requires the mobilization of educational, legal, political and social institutions in order to face it boldly and directly" (133).

Questions for Critical Thinking

1. Explain why this case is an example of a crime that can be explained by cultural conflict theory.

2. Imagine that you have been engaged by the Department of Justice to write a position paper on honour-based violence. Should honour violence be viewed as domestic violence, as some have argued? Or is it a contextually specific form of violence that is planned and premeditated, as others have maintained?

tries to resist the proposed legislation. The interest group marshalling the greater number of votes will have the most influence in determining whether the new law is enacted. Therefore Vold (1958) argues that

> the whole political process of law making, law breaking and law enforcement becomes a direct reflection of deep-seated and fundamental conflicts between interest groups and their more general struggles for the control of the police power of the state. Those who produce legislative majorities win control over the police power and dominate the policies that decide who is likely to be involved in violation of the law. (209)

For Vold, conflict between interest groups is a normal social process and one of the fundamental principles of organized political society.

Vold describes two general classes of group conflict that can result in criminal behaviour. First, some crimes arise from a conflict between the behaviour of minority groups and the legal norms, rules, and regulations of the dominant majority, which are established in law. For example, Vold argues that the delinquent gang can be understood as a minority group whose interests are in opposition to the rules of the dominant majority—the adult world of regulations established in law and enforced by the police. A further example of a minority group whose interests are in opposition to the dominant majority is that of "conscientious objectors" during wartime, who opt to serve prison sentences rather than participate in any form of compulsory wartime service.

Second, some crimes arise from a conflict between competing interest groups that are vying for power. For example, Vold argues that many crimes are the result of political revolution or protest movements whose aim is direct political reform. "A successful revolution," he contends, "makes criminals out of government officials previously in power, and an unsuccessful revolution makes its leaders into traitors subject to immediate execution" (1958, 215). Yet another example of intergroup conflict that may result in criminal behaviour is the one between management and labour unions. During strikes or lockouts, escalating tensions between management and striking workers may result in violence, property damage, and other crimes.

Vold argues that criminological theories that focus on notions of individual choice and responsibility may not be relevant in understanding criminal behaviour that occurs as a result of conflict between interest groups. This is because individual criminal behaviour that results from intergroup conflict represents, for that same individual, a type of "loyal service" to the interest group. Group conflict theory is limited to instances where criminal behaviour arises from the conflict between interest groups and does not try to explain other types of criminal acts.

Conflict theory has been criticized for its narrow scope of explanation. Critics argue that it applies to only a narrow range of crimes and that only politically or ideologically motivated crimes can be said to fit the model well. Others point out that most crime is intra-group—that is, committed by one member of a group against another member of the same group—rather than intergroup (the kind on which Vold focuses).

SEARCH FOR:
Educational Resource for Criminology

Richard Quinney

Although Richard Quinney's theoretical perspective changed significantly in his later work, his 1970 book *The Social Reality of Crime* was widely viewed as an important contribution to group conflict theory. Following Sellin and Vold, Quinney's theory of crime explains criminality as the result of conflict between groups. But whereas Sellin focuses on cultural group conflict and Vold on interest group conflict, Quinney's group conflict theory focuses on the more broadly defined notion of "segments" of society, which he defines as types of "social groupings." For Quinney, the more powerful segments or social groups are able to secure and protect their own interests by influencing the formulation, enforcement, and administration of criminal law. Sellin and Vold both view criminal law as generally reflecting the values and norms of dominant groups in society; Quinney places a much greater emphasis on the unequal distribution of power in society, especially as this relates to the formation of public policy. Vold views society as existing in a relatively stable equilibrium of opposing group interests in which all groups are able to make themselves heard in policy decision making; Quinney argues that only some interest groups are powerful enough to influence policy, because power is unequally distributed due to "the structural arrangements of the political state" (1970, 12). Quinney outlines his conflict theory of crime in six propositions:

1. *Crime is a definition of human conduct that is created by authorized agents in a politically organized society.* For Quinney, crime is not inherent in behaviour, but rather is the product of legal definitions; it is a *definition* of behaviour imposed on some persons by others.

2. *Criminal definitions describe behaviours that conflict with the interests of segments of society that have the power to shape public policy.* Quinney argues that the more powerful segments of society can incorporate their interests, values, and norms into the criminal law; thus, these powerful segments can regulate the formulation of criminal definitions. These definitions are formulated because less powerful segments of society are in conflict with other, more powerful segments.

3. *Criminal definitions are applied by the segments of society that have power to shape the enforcement and administration of criminal law.* The interests of powerful segments are represented not only in the formulation of criminal law but also in its application. The enforcement and administration of the law is delegated to legal agents (e.g., police, prosecutors, judges) who represent the interests of these powerful segments.

4. *Behavioural patterns are structured in segmentally organized society in relation to criminal definitions, and within this context persons engage in actions that have relative probabilities of being defined as criminal.* For Quinney, it is not the quality of the behaviour that makes it criminal, but rather the action taken against the behaviour. The decision as to which acts are defined as criminal is made by the more powerful segments of society, which formulate and apply criminal definitions. Thus, persons in less-powerful social segments are more likely to have their behaviours defined as criminal, because their interests are not represented in the formulation and application of criminal definitions.

5. *Conceptions of crime are constructed and diffused in the segments of society by various means of communication.* The mass media play an important role in the diffusion of criminal conceptions throughout society. A particular conception of crime is diffused throughout society and subsequently becomes "the basis for the public's view of reality" (Quinney 1970, 285). The more powerful segments of society are able to influence the mass media's portrayal of crime.
6. *The social reality of crime is constructed by the formulation and application of criminal definitions, the development of behavioural patterns related to criminal definitions, and the construction of criminal conceptions.* The sixth proposition is essentially a summation of propositions 2 to 5; thus, Quinney's model posits that the "social reality of crime" is a function of (2) the formulation of criminal definitions, (3) the application of criminal definitions, (4) the development of behaviour patterns in relation to criminal definitions, and (5) the construction of criminal conceptions. Quinney views the first proposition as a definition; thus the body of the theory comprises the middle four propositions.*

Marxist Conflict Perspectives in Criminology

In the 1970s, Marxist theories began to gain prominence in the socio-legal and criminological literature. While Marx himself had very little to say about crime, many criminologists believed that aspects of Marx's work could help analyze the relationship between crime and the broader social world. Like the conflict theories of Sellin, Vold, and Quinney, Marxist theories of crime and deviance do not look to the individual offender for explanations of crime. They do not view criminal behaviour in isolation as an individual pathology. Marxist criminology takes the position that crime "must be analyzed in the context of its relationship to the character of the society as a whole" (Greenberg 1993, 17). Marxists believe that crime is best understood in relation to the social, political, and economic structures of the society in which it occurs.

You will recall that group conflict theorists, broadly speaking, view conflict as arising from opposing group interests, and crime as resulting from the ability of more powerful or dominant groups to criminalize the behaviour of other less powerful groups, who find themselves in violation of the criminal norms and standards of the dominant majority. Marxist criminologists, by contrast, view conflict as rooted in the very structure of capitalist society, particularly capitalist economic relations. The political and economic structures under capitalism promote conflict, which in turn provides the precipitating conditions (such as unemployment) for crime to occur. Marxist criminologists focus on the relations between crime and the social arrangements of society, especially the ways in which societies organize their political, legal, and economic structures (Bohm 1982). Generally speaking, Marxist criminologists take the position that the organization of capitalist society—both its way of producing material goods and its organization of political, legal, and economic structures—has important implications for the study of the amount and types of crime present in society (Greenberg 1993).

*Copyright © 1974 From *Critique of the Legal Order* by Richard Quinney. Reproduced by permission of Taylor and Francis Group, LLC, a division of Informa plc.

Marx believed that the history of the development of human societies is best understood through the fundamental role played by production. Through production, we are able to satisfy our basic material needs, such as for food, clothing, and shelter. Marx was interested in examining the history of societies from the perspective of how production is organized, or what he referred to as the *mode of production*. The mode of production refers to the economic system whereby goods are produced, exchanged, and distributed in society. Marx identified several different modes of production throughout history, including the slave economies of ancient Greece and Rome, the agrarian economy of feudalism, and the wage-labour economy of capitalism.

The mode of production, in turn, is composed of the *forces of production* and the *social relations of production*. The forces of production refers to the tools, techniques, raw materials, and labour power used in production, while the social relations of production refers to the relations among humans with respect to the ownership of the means of production. According to Marx, the social relations of production under capitalism—that is, under the capitalist mode of production— gave rise to two major groups or classes. The bourgeoisie are the economically dominant class, who own the means of production (the land, machinery, and factories), and the proletariat are the economically subordinate class, who own no property. Because they neither own nor control the means of production, the proletariat have only their labour power to sell in exchange for their livelihood in the form of wages. It is important to note that class is *not* an attribute or characteristic of an individual or group in Marxist thought; rather, it refers to a position in a relationship (Greenberg 1993). For Marxists, capitalist society, like earlier societies, is based on class exploitation. The relationship between the capitalist class and the working class is inherently exploitative because the capitalist is able to extract the surplus labour of the worker in the form of profits. This surplus is based on the difference between the value the workers produce and what is received by the worker in wages.

Marx argued that because societies are always organized around the dominant mode of production, "the mode of production of material life conditions the social, political, and intellectual life process in general" (Marx, in Cain and Hunt, 1979, 54). Marx made use of the metaphor of a building to describe the relationship between the mode of production and other aspects of society: "The sum total of these relations of production constitutes the economic structure of society, the real foundation, on which rises a legal and political superstructure and to which correspond definite forms of social consciousness" (54).

According to Marx, in Western societies the economic base of capitalism is the foundation on which the various superstructural institutions of society are built, including political and legal institutions. Another way Marxists put this is that the economic base of capitalism has a *determining influence* on the superstructural institutions of society. Where one class is in a position of dominance over the other class (based on its ownership of the means of production) in the economic sphere, the other social institutions in society will be organized according to the interests of the dominant class (Comack 1999). The implication for Marxist approaches to law, crime, and criminology is that both the law and crime should not be studied in isolation, but rather in relation to the whole of society and particularly the economic sphere (Greenberg 1993).

The Marxist approach provides criminologists and legal scholars with a theoretical framework that allows them to study the interrelationships between the capitalist mode of production, the state, law, crime control, and crime (Bohm 1982). In addition, Marxist analysis typically involves a critical element (see also Chapter 12). It is a critique of the logic of the existing capitalist social order. In critiquing the existing society or social order, Marxian thought often begins with an analysis of the state. While Marx himself did not develop a systematic theory of the state, Marxist theorists have made use of aspects of Marx's writings to attempt to theorize the relationships between the state in capitalist society and class relations, law, crime, and crime control. It has become conventional in the criminological and socio-legal literature to distinguish between *instrumental* and *structural* Marxist theories of the state, law, and crime.

Instrumental Marxism

Instrumental Marxists generally begin with the assumption that the state in capitalist societies broadly serves the interests of the ruling or capitalist class. A well-known passage from Marx and Engels's *The Communist Manifesto* is often cited in support of **instrumental Marxism**: "The executive of the modern State is but a committee for managing the common affairs of the whole bourgeoisie" (1848, 5). For Marx, the economic structure of society determines the nature of that society's political and legal superstructure. Instrumentalist Marxists interpret Marx's statement quite literally and argue that both the state and the legal and political institutions within the state are a direct reflection of the interests of the capitalist class. Law, then, is equated with class rule—the ruling class controls the formation of law, and the focus is on the coercive nature of the law. As Tierney (1996) points out, this approach is based on an instrumentalist school of thought in political theory (Miliband 1969; Domhoff 1970), which argues that those who occupy powerful positions in the state apparatus are either capitalists themselves or strongly identified with the interests of the capitalist class.

Instrumental Marxists therefore view the state and the legal system as instruments that can be directly manipulated by the capitalist class. For example, Miliband (1969, 22) argues that because the ruling class of capitalist society owns and controls the means of production, it is able to "use the state as its instrument for the domination of society." Early Marxist studies tended to focus on how the economic power of the capitalist class provided the opportunity to influence law and law formation. An example of an instrumental Marxist position is found in Richard Quinney's book *Critique of the Legal Order* (1974). Recall that in Quinney's earlier work, he endorsed a conflict perspective on crime. However, his views changed over time. In the *Critique of the Legal Order*, Quinney (1974, 16) offers six propositions that summarize his critical Marxist theory of crime control:

1. American society is based on an advanced capitalist economy.
2. The State is organized to serve the interests of the dominant economic class.
3. Criminal law is an instrument of the state and ruling class to maintain and perpetuate the existing social and economic order.
4. Crime control in capitalist society is accomplished through a variety of institutions and agencies established and administered by a government elite, representing ruling class interests.

instrumental Marxism
The state is viewed as the direct instrument of the ruling or capitalist class. Instrumentalism is based on the notion that the processes of the superstructure are determined by the economic base.

5. The contradictions of advanced capitalism . . . require that the subordinate classes remain oppressed by whatever means necessary, especially through the coercion and violence of the legal system.

6. Only with the collapse of capitalist society and the creation of a new society, based on socialist principles, will there be a solution to the crime problem.*

The instrumentalist Marxist position may be said to offer useful insights into the sociology of the capitalist class, the relationship between class power and state power, and the place of law in capitalist society. Critics, however, point out a number of flaws in the theory. First, instrumental Marxism has been criticized for portraying the ruling class as a unified and homogeneous group, thus ignoring competing factions that may exist within the capitalist class itself. Second, instrumentalist accounts have been criticized for ignoring how the actions of ruling-class members are influenced or constrained by structural causes. For example, are there limits to any particular ruling-class member's sphere of influence, such as shifting affiliations with the current party in power in a parliamentary democracy, the deep fluctuations of the stock market, political exigencies, and so on? Third, in its argument that the law represents only the interests of the ruling class, the instrumentalist position is unable to account for legislation that is not in the immediate interest of the ruling class, such as health and safety legislation, employment standards, and so on. Fourth, critics believe that instrumentalism draws upon an overly rigid interpretation of the base/superstructure metaphor. That is, the Marxist argument that the economic base is the foundation of the superstructure is said to be deterministic. By deterministic, we mean there is a form of causality where the superstructure is a necessary consequence of the economic base. In other words, the economic base under capitalism more or less wholly determines the political, economic, ideological, and cultural superstructure. This is why the instrumentalist position argues that the state's legal and political institutions are a direct reflection of the capitalist class.

Structural Marxism

During the 1970s and 1980s, Marxist theorists developed structuralist Marxist accounts of the state, law, and crime. **Structural Marxism** disputes the instrumentalist view that the state can be viewed as the direct servant of the capitalist or ruling class. Whereas the instrumentalist position argues that the institutions of the state are under the direct control of those members of the capitalist class in positions of state power, the structuralist perspective takes the position that the institutions of the state ensure the ongoing viability of capitalism more generally. Another way that Marxists put this is that the institutions of the state must function so as to reproduce capitalist society as a whole (Gold, Lo, and Wright 1975). Structuralists view the state in a capitalist mode of production as taking a specifically capitalist form, not because particular individuals are in powerful positions, but because the state reproduces the logic of capitalist structure in its economic, legal, and political institutions. We might say that a structuralist perspective would argue that the institutions of the state (including its legal institutions) function in the

structural Marxism
The state is viewed as acting in the long-term interests of capitalism as a whole rather than in the short-term interests of the capitalist class.

*Copyright © 1974 From *Critique of the Legal Order* by Richard Quinney. Reproduced by permission of Taylor and Francis Group, LLC, a division of Informa plc.

long-term interests of capital and capitalism, rather than in the short-term interests of members of the capitalist class. Structuralists would thus argue that the state and its institutions have a certain degree of *independence* from specific elites in the capitalist class.

The idea that the state is—to a certain degree—independent of the ruling class is known as **relative autonomy**. Structural Marxists have drawn from the work of Poulantzas (1975) and Althusser (1969) to argue that the relative autonomy of the state functions to preserve the long-term interests of capital as well as the long-run stability of the capitalist structure as a whole. To begin with, we cannot assume that the capitalist class is united in its interests and homogeneous in its beliefs. The state must therefore have the relative autonomy to mediate between divergent capitalist class factions in order to preserve the long-term interests of the capitalist class as a whole (Poulantzas 1975). The relative autonomy of the state, therefore, provides a state structure "capable of transcending the parochial, individualized interests of specific capitalists and capitalist class factions" (Gold, Lo, and Wright 1975, 38). In addition, structural Marxists point to the relative autonomy of the state and its institutions to explain why many laws are enacted that do not represent the immediate interests of the capitalist class. That is, an instrumentalist Marxist position cannot account for the existence of minimum wage laws, laws against discrimination in employment, consumer protection laws, rent control, anti-trust legislation, and welfare legislation, in that these laws are not in the immediate interests of the capitalist class.

An interesting area that Canadian researchers have explored, with respect to law creation that does not seem to represent the immediate interests of the capitalist class as a whole, has been the development of anticombines legislation in Canada (Goff and Reasons 1978; Snider 1979; Smandych 1985). The aim of this legislation was to prevent corporations from monopolizing or cornering the supply of certain commodities or markets, and fixing prices. Goff and Reasons (1978) argue that Canada's first anticombines legislation—the Combines Investigation Act of 1889—came about less from the desire to protect the general populace than from the complaints of small businessmen who "felt their firms were at the mercy of big business interests" (42). For the first decade, this legislation was unenforceable because of the weak wording of the act, which stipulated that combines had to be engaged in behaviour that *unlawfully* as well as *unduly* restricted trade. Snider (1979) examined the later revisions and amendments to the act in 1923, 1935, 1952, and 1960 and concluded that "at each stage proposals were weakened or eliminated in the face of business opposition" (110). Both Snider and Goff and Reasons concluded that while reforms do occur, the state "is susceptible to the interests of powerful economic groups" (Goff and Reasons 1978, 114), and thus reforms tend to be "resisted for as long as possible by the corporate elite" (Snider 1979, 118).

Smandych (1985) argued that anticombines legislation in Canada must also be considered in relation to the increasingly vocal trade unions of the late 19th century and the growing confrontations between capital and labour. He points out that the rise of militant trade unions in the late 1800s, such as the Knights of Labour in Toronto, "owed as much to labour's hatred of monopolistic companies as it did to labour's desire to improve working conditions" (45). In addition, the Knights of Labour and other trade unions had a great deal of influence on the

relative autonomy
A term used in the structural Marxist perspective to indicate that the state has a certain amount of independence from the capitalist class and is therefore able to enact laws that are not in the immediate interests of the capitalist class.

working man's vote. Thus Smandych argued that the emergence of Canadian anti-combines legislation could be viewed as a pragmatic attempt by the government to find a "symbolic" solution to the confrontation between capital and labour, given the political influence of the more prominent trade unions.

The solution was symbolic because the immense economic and political power of the monopolistic companies of the period influenced the state to enact what was ultimately an "ineffectual law that served only to foster the reproduction of combines activity in the late 19th century" (47). As Chambliss and Siedman (1982) point out, "a great deal of state action concerns not the enhancement of profit for a particular faction of the ruling class, but the maintenance of relations of production that make capitalism possible" (312). In this way the state ensures the reproduction of capitalism as a whole. In some instances the state enacts laws that are ostensibly meant to curb the excesses of capital, yet are ineffective in their design and implementation.

In the structuralist perspective, then, the law cannot be said to exclusively represent the instrumental interests of the dominant capitalist class. Rather, structural Marxists argue that laws that benefit the less powerful reflect an ideological need to develop a widespread *consent* for the existing social order (Einstadter and Henry 2006). On this view, consensus is generated for the established order by promoting law as an impartial system that protects the public rather than private interests, and where all are equal before the law. Structuralists argue that this notion of "equality before the law," also described as "the rule of law," masks or otherwise obscures the substantive inequalities of class, race, and gender that may exist between individuals who are nevertheless considered equal before the law. Stated differently, the formal equality of each individual in the legal sphere does not extend to the economic sphere (Brickey and Comack 1989). For example, corporations and labour are treated in collective bargaining law as being on an equal footing, despite the structural inequalities between them, including the corporation's greater material and organizational resources (Bartholomew and Boyd, 1989). Structuralists therefore argue that law functions as an ideological means of reproducing capitalist social and economic relations.

Marxists sometimes use the concept of ideology to analyze legal discourse in ways that go beyond the law's manifest role as an external mechanism of regulation. Hunt (1993) has argued that "the most pervasive ideological effect of law is to be found in the fact that legal rules and their application give effect to existing social relations" (25). Law transforms the human subject into a legal subject and in so doing influences how social relations are lived and experienced. Marxists view law as ideological in the sense that it functions to both legitimate and reproduce the existing social order. In general, the concept of ideology is taken up to explore the linkages between legal discourse and the attitudes, values, and beliefs that support it. Box 11.2 examines Bill C-13, the "Protecting Canadians from Online Crime Act," and explores the often competing sets of claims-making activities that underlie the making of law in a parliamentary democracy such as that of the Canadian State.

By the end of the 1980s, a large body of critical work had been produced by Marxist scholars examining the relationships between the capitalist state, the economy, and the legal and political institutions of the state. Canadian Marxist theorists, in particular, contributed to a rich literature that explored the

FOCUS   BOX 11.2

LAW, IDEOLOGY, AND BILL C-13

At the edge of the Milky Way, in the constellation Auriga, a star shines bright for Amanda Todd, a BC teenager who took her own life in 2012 after enduring almost two years of online harassment and sexual extortion. In November 2016, "Amanda's Snowflake Star of Hope" was dedicated to the memory of Amanda by her mother, Carol Todd, who has since become an outspoken activist against cyberbullying (Todd 2016). In September 2012, a month before her death, Amanda posted a video on YouTube describing her devastating experience of cyberbullying and sexual blackmail through a series of flashcards. Amanda's haunting video went viral and received widespread coverage in the media.

In 2013, the heart-breaking news of two further teenage suicides was widely reported in the Canadian media. Saskatchewan high school student Todd Loik was 15 when he committed suicide in 2013. His mother, Kim Loik, said her son had been cyberbullied nonstop for two years. Halifax teenager Rehtaeh Parsons died after being taken off life support following a suicide attempt in April 2013. Rehtaeh endured 18 months of bullying and harassment after a digital photo of an alleged sexual assault was widely distributed at her school and on the Internet (Canadian Press, 26 September 2013).

In the wake of these deeply tragic events, in November 2013 the federal justice minister, Peter McKay, introduced Bill C-13—the Protecting Canadians from Online Crime Act—with the goal of combatting the nonconsensual dissemination of intimate images online. MacKay described Bill C-13 as composed of two distinct but related parts. The first part addressed "cyberbullying involving the non-consensual distribution of intimate images," while the second aimed to "ensure that the Criminal code and other federal legislation is keeping pace with technological changes." The overall intent of the bill, McKay elaborated, was to propose "updates to offences and to the powers of police to investigate crimes committed using electronic networks or that use electronic evidence" (Parliament of Canada, Hansard, 27 November 2013).

Bill C-13 received Royal Assent in December 2014 and came into law in March 2015. It is now a crime in Canada, punishable by up to five years in prison, to distribute intimate images of a person without their consent. Bill C-13 also gives courts the right to seize computers, cellphones, and other devices used in the offence.

The passing of Bill C-13 into Canadian law was not without controversy. While the cyberbullying provisions in the first part of the bill were broadly supported in the media and by all sides of the House of Commons, anti-cyberbullying advocates and researchers expressed concerns about the criminalization of youth behaviour and whether the criminal justice system is an appropriate venue to address cyberbullying. Also, the second part of Bill C-13 was criticized by privacy advocates, who argued that the privacy rights of Canadians were being unduly eroded by the investigative power amendments contained in the bill.

Opponents of the bill expressed two main objections. First, that the threshold to obtain warrants for transmission data had been lowered from "reasonable grounds to believe" to "reasonable grounds to suspect" that an offence has been committed. While Mackay maintained that lowering the burden of proof to reasonable suspicion was justified because transmission data contain "information with little to no privacy impact" (Parliament of Canada *Hansard*), privacy advocates argued that non-content transmission data, commonly referred to as "metadata," can be extremely revealing

Amanda Todd committed suicide after almost two years of cyberbullying. Her mother has been a leader in the campaign to pass legislation targeting this behaviour.

THE CANADIAN PRESS/Darryl Dyck

because they identify the type, date, time, origin, destination, or termination of a communication (Schmitz, December 13 2013).

The second major objection to Bill C-13 related to its controversial provision granting immunity to ISPs (Internet Service Providers) and telecom companies from civil or criminal liability for voluntary disclosure of subscriber information to police. Critics pointed out that providing blanket immunity for voluntary disclosure to police left very little legal incentive for companies to be cautious in disseminating data (Spratt 2013). However, the legality of voluntary disclosure by telecom companies has been called into question by the Supreme Court of Canada's landmark 2014 ruling in *R. v. Spencer* that police are generally required to obtain a search warrant for subscriber information absent exigent circumstances (*R. v. Spencer* [2014] 2 S.C.R. 212). After the Spencer decision, two major telecom companies—Rogers and Telus—announced they would no longer routinely disclose subscriber information to law enforcement agencies without a warrant (Bronskill 2014).

The passage of any bill into law offers us insight into the process of "lawmaking" and the often competing sets of discourses and claims-making activities that underlie the making of law. No doubt the unanticipated consequences of rapidly changing technology have created enormous challenges for lawmakers, who must first define and then address "lawbreaking" in this burgeoning "virtual world." As we have seen, the virtual space of the Internet can have real and tragic consequences for youths such as Amanda Todd who have been caught in the web of cyberbullying and responded by taking their own lives.

Cyberbullying experts point out that research into the phenomenon of cyberbullying is still at an early stage (Deschamps and McNutt 2016). What *is* cyberbullying? How does it differ from traditional bullying? Canadian researchers have argued that while the common aspects of bullying—intentionality, power differential, and repetition—may be a useful starting point, cyberbullying is a more complex phenomenon and correspondingly more difficult to define (Coburn, Connolly, and Roesch 2015). Furthermore, definitions also vary depending on one's frame of reference: cyberbullying can be viewed as a public health problem with solutions focusing on public awareness campaigns; as an education problem with interventions focused on schools, teachers, and other adults; or as a justice problem focusing on policing, criminal law, and public awareness (Deschamps and McNutt 2016).

Researchers point out that cyberbullying differs from traditional bullying in several ways. First, cyberbullying makes use of mobile phones, computers, or other electronic devices to "embarrass, threaten, sexually harass, or socially exclude" (Vaillancourt, Faris, and Mishna 2017). Second, because there is greater potential for anonymity in online harassment (Coburn, Connolly, and Roesch 2015), perpetrators may feel detached from their actions (Faucher, Cassidy, and Jackson 2015), resulting in disinhibition, essentially the "abandonment of social

rules . . . present in face-to-face interactions" (Deschamps and McNutt 2016, 53). Third, while traditional bullying is viewed as a repeated intentional act by the bully, cyberbullying is a much more amorphous phenomenon; an act of cyberbullying may be shared multiple times by multiple others and viewed in perpetuity (Vaillancourt, Faris, and Mishna 2017).

Canadian researchers have expressed concerns about whether the criminal justice system is the most appropriate venue to address the complex issue of cyberbullying. Shariff suggests that criminalizing cyberbullying "may not really solve the problems as there is a spectrum of these types of behaviours that go from mild to extreme" (Schembri 2014, n.p.). Researchers have pointed out that while cyberbullying is a common adolescent behaviour, only a small percentage of youth report having an intimate image of themselves or someone else on their cellphone, and even fewer report sharing the image (Coburn et al. 2015). Thus, some scholars have expressed concern that the criminal sanctions of Bill C-13 will protect very few victims, insofar as only a small minority of cyberbullying involves the non-consensual distribution of intimate images (Coburn, Connolly, and Roesch 2015; Cartwright 2016).

Mishna has suggested that while a court option may be effective in some cases, use of the criminal law may not be the optimal way to address cyberbullying and may have the unintended consequence of preventing some bullying victims from coming forward (Tucker 2013). Research suggests that underreporting of cyberbullying incidents is a significant issue (Vaillancourt, Faris, and Mishna 2017). Adolescents are unwilling to disclose cyberbullying to adults for a number of reasons, including fear of retaliation, losing access to technology, and the belief that adults will not understand or be able to help (Faucher, Cassidy, and Jackson 2015). Given the reluctance of youth to disclose cyberbullying, scholars have expressed concern that the possibility of criminal sanctions in Bill C-13 will exacerbate the problem of nondisclosure (Coburn, Connolly, and Roesch 2015).

Questions for Critical Thinking

1. Imagine you are sitting on a youth committee in your former high school that has been tasked with writing a position paper on cyberbullying. How prevalent is cyberbullying within your social network? How likely would you be to disclose an incident of cyberbullying to someone in authority if you (a) witnessed an incident of cyberbullying? or (b) experienced cyberbullying yourself? If you were willing to report an incident of cyberbullying, would you be more likely to disclose to (a) a parent, (b) a teacher or guidance counselor, (c) a healthcare practitioner such as a physician, psychiatrist, or psychologist, or (d) anonymously, such as through a letter, a helpline (kidshelpphone.ca), or an App (Anonymous Alert)?

2. Do you think that the criminal courts are the best way to deal with cyberbullying? Explain why or why not.

relationship between the Canadian state, its laws, and its legal institutions, as well as the relationship between the state and the criminal justice system (West and Snider 1985; Brickey and Comack 1989; Snider 1989). In addition, Canadian Marxist criminologists have also explored the broader area of corporate crime and social harm (McMullan, 1992; Snider, 2015). We will examine two further areas of Marxist research to illustrate some of the work undertaken in Marxist criminology: first, research that focuses on the crimes of the powerless, and second, research that investigates the crimes of the powerful.

Crimes of the Powerless

Stephen Spitzer

Spitzer (1975) made use of the Marxian notion of "surplus population" to formulate his "Marxian theory of deviance." He argued that the criminalization of much behaviour is directed towards those problem populations who are surplus to the labour market. These problem populations are created in two ways. First, they are created *directly* through the contradictions in the capitalist mode of production. For example, a surplus population is generated in capitalist economies as new technologies replace workers with machines, or when work is outsourced to other countries. Second, problem populations are created *indirectly* through contradictions in the institutions that help reproduce capitalism, such as the schools. For example, Spitzer argues that while mass education provides a means of training future wage labourers, this schooling also provides youths with critical insight into the alienating and oppressive character of capitalist institutions. This, in turn, can lead to problem populations in the form of dropouts and student radicals. Problem populations become candidates for deviance processing when they disturb, hinder, or call into question any of the following:

1. Capitalist modes of appropriating the product of human labour (e.g., when the poor "steal" from the rich);
2. The social conditions under which capitalist production takes place (e.g., those who refuse or are unable to perform wage labour);
3. Patterns of distribution and consumption in capitalist society (e.g., those who use drugs for escape and transcendence rather than sociability and adjustment);
4. The process of socialization for productive and nonproductive roles (e.g., youths who refuse to be schooled or those who deny the validity of family life).
5. The ideology that supports the functioning of capitalist society (e.g., proponents of alternative forms of social organization) (1975, 642).*

David Greenberg

Another theorist who makes use of the Marxian notion of surplus population is Greenberg (1993). Greenberg explains juvenile delinquency from a Marxist perspective and argues that juveniles form a "class" of their own because they share a common relationship to the means of production. That is, young people

*Spitzer, Steven. (1975). "Toward a Marxian Theory of Analysis." *Social Problems* 22(5): 638-51. Copyright © 1975 The Society for the Study of Social Problems, Inc. Reproduced by permission of Oxford University Press on behalf of the Society for the Study of Social Problems.

are excluded from economically productive activity in a capitalist society but are required to undergo training for their future productive role in the capitalist system. Juveniles can thus be considered a part of the surplus population, because they are excluded from lawful sources of income. This creates motivation towards delinquency, because juveniles' exclusion from the labour market means they cannot finance their leisure and social activities. If their parents are unable or unwilling to finance their social life to the required level, juveniles must seek out other sources of funding. Adolescent theft then occurs because of a conflict between the desire to participate in activities valued by peer culture and the lack of legitimate sources of funding to finance these activities (Greenberg 1993).

Crimes of the Powerful

Whereas researchers who focus on the Marxian notion of "surplus population" are interested in the relationship between crime and those who are *outside* the sphere of production, Marxist research on corporate crime focuses on the socially harmful conduct of those who are *inside* the sphere of production in capitalist economies. Box 11.3 explores one instance of socially harmful conduct from a Marxist perspective by examining the tainted dog and cat food produced by Menu Foods Income Fund, a pet food manufacturing facility headquartered in southern Ontario. Canadian Marxist scholars argue that the study of corporate crime is important because the losses incurred as a result of corporate malfeasance—whether it is the total dollar amount, or the number of deaths, injuries, and illnesses—are far in excess of the losses incurred as a result of street crime (McMullan 1992; Snider 2015). In an early Marxist analysis of illegal activity of US corporations, Pearce (1976) demonstrated that the dollar amount of corporate crime was much greater than the aggregate dollar amount of conventional crime. Similarly, Snider (2015) drew upon statistical evidence to argue that the total number of workers who died each year from both work-related accidents and occupationally induced diseases was far in excess of the death rate statistics for homicide and manslaughter.

This branch of Marxist criminology attempts to situate law, the state, corporate crime, and social harm within the logic of the mode of production under capitalism. Marxist theorists argue that the structure of capitalist economies and the imperative of profit maximization together create strong motivation for corporations to engage in criminal activities and other socially harmful behaviours (Henry 1986; Snider 2015). Accordingly, Marxist studies attempt to document both the nature and extent of corporate crime and to analyze the relationship of corporate criminality to the capitalist mode of production (Goff and Reasons 1978; Glasbeek 1989). Marxist criminologists are also interested in examining the contradictory role of the state in capitalist economies. That is, the state must create laws and regulate the criminal activities of corporations, but it must also protect the overall interests of the capitalist economy by reproducing the conditions necessary for capitalism to continue (Snider 2015; Gordon and Coneybeer 1999).

Structural Marxist criminology has been criticized for its tautological character. In other words, critics feel that it presents a circular argument. The theory begins with the assumption that there is class exploitation under capitalism; this is in order to demonstrate that crime, in turn, is caused by capitalist class exploitation. Structural Marxism has also been criticized for emphasizing structure at the expense of human agency—that is, at the expense of human action and ability to shape and direct the social world. A further criticism has been that the exclusive focus on class relations has precluded other considerations from entering into analysis, such as gender oppression and race oppression. Socialist feminism represents one attempt to incorporate Marxist analysis into a framework that considers the relationship between class exploitation and gender oppression in capitalist societies.

FOCUS   BOX 11.3

IS IT A CORPORATE CRIME? THE MENU FOODS PET FOOD RECALL

On 16 March 2007, Menu Foods, a pet food manufacturer headquartered in Mississauga, Ontario, announced a massive recall of 60 million cans and pouches of tainted dog and cat food. Something in its pet food—later identified as wheat flour contaminated with melamine and cyanuric acid—was causing acute kidney failure in dogs and cats. By 3 May 2007 the US Food and Drug Administration (FDA) had received unconfirmed reports of 4,150 cat and dog deaths due to the consumption of tainted food (Schmit 2007).

The scope of the Menu Foods recall was unprecedented. By 22 May, Menu Foods had issued eight separate recall notifications involving 67 brands of cat food and 64 brands of dog food, each sold in multiple varieties, sizes, and packaging formats—over 5,300 products in total (Nestle 2008). Brands identified in the recall ran the gamut from premium pet foods such as Hill's Prescription Diet, Iams, Eukanuba, and Science Diet, to discount labels such as Walmart's Ol' Roy, Costco/Kirkland Signature dog food, and Price Chopper cat food.

The news for consumers, however, went from bad to worse. The events that followed the Menu Foods recall revealed not only how easily melamine contamination could enter the pet food supply, but also how the global sourcing of food ingredients has introduced dangerous vulnerabilities into our human food supply systems. Perhaps two of the most unsettling findings that arose from the pet food recalls were the ubiquity of the global sourcing of pet and human food ingredients and the magnitude of the outsourcing of production of branded pet food to contract manufacturers.

The Menu Foods recall revealed a little-known fact about pet food production—namely, that many pet food companies, including the most trusted premium brands, do not make their own pet food but rather "outsource" this function to third-party contractors, known as "co-packers." For example, in 2003 Menu Foods signed a five-year exclusive contract with The Iams Company (purchased by Procter & Gamble in 1999 for $2.3 billion) to manufacture all Iams and Eukanuba canned and pouch pet food in the United States and Canada (2004 Menu Foods Annual Report). At the time of the recall, Menu Foods was the largest co-packer of "wet" pet food—dog and cat food in cans and pouches—in North America (Nestle 2008).

Pet owners may have been surprised to discover that well over 100 different brands of dog and cat food were made by just one company. A Marxist analysis would point to the structure of capitalist economies and the ongoing pressure on companies to extract ever-increasing amounts of surplus value in the form of profits. Under this economic model, it makes good financial sense for pet food companies such as Iams, Hill's, Purina, and Nutro to seek lower costs of production—and hence greater profits—by outsourcing their pet food requirements to third-party contractors like Menu Foods. The manufacture of wet pet food is a complicated process, after all, and requires significant investment in plant and machinery. By outsourcing production, pet food companies are able to rationalize their asset base and reduce expenses—for example, by selling off excess manufacturing capacity and eliminating the associated labour costs.

For its part, a giant co-packer like Menu Foods is able to offer significant economies of scale to its pet food clients. More efficiencies can be exploited by a giant contract manufacturer producing 120 brands of pet food than by many individual manufacturing facilities each producing one or a few brands of dog or cat food. One such efficiency Menu Foods ostensibly could offer its clients was its bulk purchasing power and corresponding ability to purchase raw ingredients in the global marketplace for much lower cost than any single pet food company could do on its own. While the extensive global sourcing of lowest-cost raw ingredients is an industry norm for both pet and human food producers (Roth et al. 2008), the Menu Foods recall has helped to demonstrate the risks inherent in the globalization of animal and human food supply chains.

At the centre of the recall was Menu Foods's fateful decision in December 2006 to switch its wheat gluten supplier to Las Vegas importer ChemNutra, which in turn sourced the wheat gluten from an obscure Chinese manufacturer, Xuzhou Anying Biologic Technology Development Co. At the time, wheat gluten from China sold for 20 cents less per pound than that produced by US manufacturers (*Maclean's*, 30 April 2007). Wheat gluten—used in pet food as a protein source and binding agent—is a derivative of wheat flour. FDA investigators were eventually able to determine that the product sold as wheat gluten by Xuzhou Anying was ordinary wheat flour intentionally adulterated with the nitrogen-rich industrial chemicals melamine and cyanuric acid (Kuehn 2009, 473). Because nitrogen content has long been used as a surrogate for testing the amount of protein in food, the addition of melamine and cyanuric acid allowed unscrupulous suppliers to fraudulently sell the cheaper wheat flour (10 percent protein) as the more expensive wheat gluten (75 percent protein).

As disturbing as it was to discover how a toxic brew of melamine and cyanuric acid could so easily compromise the pet food supply, by the middle of May 2007 a series of announcements revealed surprising vulnerabilities in our human food supply chain. According to the FDA, between 2.7 and 3 million chickens were fed "salvaged" pet food—containing the melamine-adulterated wheat flour—and subsequently sold to consumers. In addition, some 6,000 hogs were fed the contaminated pet food—with the meat from 345 of the hogs entering the human food supply before the remaining hogs could be quarantined (*Washington Post*, 2 May 2007). On 8 May 2007 the FDA announced that the melamine/cyanuric acid contaminated wheat flour had also been purchased by a Canadian manufacturer of fish pellets and subsequently distributed to at least 60 fish farms in Canada and 200 fish farms in the United States (*Washington Post*, 9 May 2007).

It was soon to become tragically clear that melamine adulteration was not limited to pet food or to feed for farm animals destined for human consumption. In September 2008, more than 294,000 infants and young children in China were sickened with kidney and urinary tract problems after consuming melamine-contaminated infant formula. By the end of November, the Chinese Ministry of Health had reported more than 50,000 hospitalizations and six infant deaths as a result of the consumption of tainted infant formula (Ingelfinger 2008). Reported symptoms included acute renal failure, kidney and bladder stones, urinary tract infections, and other renal problems (Gossner et al. 2009; Sharma and Paradkar 2010).

By the end of 2008, the hazards of our increasingly globalized food supply became apparent when an avalanche of food products imported from China were found to contain melamine. The long list of products included yogurts, frozen desserts, cereal products, confectionaries, cakes, biscuits, and protein powders. A variety of nondairy products originating in China were also found to contain melamine—including ammonium bicarbonate, powdered eggs, fresh eggs, and nondairy creamer. In total, 47 countries, including Canada, received melamine-contaminated products (Gossner et al. 2009).

ZUMA Press, Inc. / Alamy Stock Photo

This cat required veterinary care after consuming pet food containing melamine and cyanuric acid.

(continued)

A Marxist criminologist might argue that at the same time the benefits of global food production accrue to multinationals, the risks of low-cost global sourcing of products and ingredients are offloaded to individual consumers. This unfair apportioning of surplus and risk is the crux of the Marxist critique of capitalism—that is, capitalism is inherently exploitative unless it is harnessed by the weight of government regulation and by a corresponding willingness to detect and prosecute offenders. Currently, there is a lack of scientific data on the long-term health effects of melamine toxicity in humans, which makes prediction difficult with regard to the health problems that might arise in the future (Ingelfinger 2008; Sharma and Paradkar 2010). Preliminary results from animal studies are not encouraging, however; carcinogenic effects are being reported after high exposure to melamine (Gossner et al., 2009; Puschner and Reimschuessel 2011).

Is melamine adulteration a corporate crime? Marxist theorist Michalowski (1985, 314) defines crimes of capital as "socially injurious acts that arise from the ownership or management of capital or from occupancy of positions of trust in institutions designed to facilitate the accumulation of capital." There were certainly "sins of commission" committed by Chinese manufacturers, who intentionally added melamine and cyanuric acid to pet and human food ingredients to fraudulently boost the apparent protein content. Were there also "sins of omission" committed by contract manufacturers such as Menu Foods and other human food purveyors? Did their collective lack of oversight in the global pursuit of low-cost ingredients—which created an economic vacuum, which was quickly filled by unscrupulous suppliers—constitute criminal negligence? What do you think?

Critical Thinking Questions

1. This is an example of corporate crime. In Chapter 17 you will read about a number of other cases that demonstrate that our justice system does a very poor job of holding corporate and white-collar offenders to account. How would conflict theory explain this?

2. Read Focus Box 17.1, which discusses the Westray mining disaster. What does this mine disaster have in common with the Menu Foods contamination scandal?

Left Realism

The final conflict perspective we will examine is left realism, which emerged in Britain in the late 1970s and early 1980s (Young 1979; Matthews and Young 1992) and was subsequently taken up as an area of criminological inquiry by Canadian scholars (DeKeseredy 1991; MacLean 1991). In Britain, "left realism" was initially developed by Jock Young, John Lea, and Roger Matthews, who advanced a strong critique against what they described as "left idealism." Young (1979) coined the term left idealism to encompass both instrumentalist and structuralist Marxist accounts of the state, law, and crime. Left realists also criticize what they describe as conventional or orthodox criminology and argue that both Marxist and conventional criminology are superficial accounts of crime. Specifically, left realists maintain that for conventional criminology, crime is "simply antisocial behaviour involving people who lack values," while for Marxist criminology, crime is "proto-revolutionary activity, primitive and individualistic, but praiseworthy all the same" (Lea and Young, 1984, 96).

Left realists emphasize the need to examine the "square of crime," that is, the relationship between the offender, the victim, the police, and the public (Matthews and Young 1992; Young and Matthews 1992). In Britain, left realism emerged in response to the perceived failure of other types of criminology, including Marxist criminology, to pay attention to the serious harm generated by street crime, also described as "working-class crime." Left realists like Young, Lea, and Matthews have argued that Marxist critiques of capitalist society have not paid sufficient attention to the real suffering experienced by victims of street crime, particularly the poor and disadvantaged, who are typically the main victims of street crime. Street crime refers to some form of injury committed directly by one or more specific individuals against the body or property of the victim, such as murder, rape, robbery, theft, vandalism, and burglary. Left realists argue that the victims of most crimes tend to be those from the most vulnerable segments of the community and that crime is disproportionately distributed among the working class, women, and racial minorities. In addition, the majority of working class crime is intra-class; that is, both the offender and the victim tend to be from the same socioeconomic stratum (Lea and Young 1984; Lowman and MacLean 1992).

The starting point for left realists is the observation that *crime really is a problem* for the working class and other marginalized groups in the community and that working-class crime must therefore be "taken seriously" (Lea and Young 1986). Taking crime seriously, for left realists, means developing a working-class criminology that both examines and offers practical solutions to the street crime that marginalized people experience. The strategy employed to examine the problem of crime for the working class is the victimization survey (see Chapter 4). One of the first victimization studies, the Islington Crime Survey (ICS), was conducted in inner-city London in 1985. Employing self-report data, these types of surveys attempt to measure public attitudes, perceptions, and beliefs about the extent and nature of street crime in the community and the effectiveness of police in dealing with it (Jones, MacLean, and Young 1986). Left realists argue for concrete crime control programs, with the objective of offering nonrepressive crime control policies (Lea and Young 1986; MacLean 1991). Crime control policies that have been endorsed by left realists include alternatives to prisons (community service, victim restitution, weekend prison sentences for working offenders); pre-emptive deterrence (encouraging citizens' groups to cooperate with the police); transforming the police force into a police service accountable to the public; and "harnessing the energies of the marginalized" to create a "politics of crime control" (Lea and Young 1986, 360–63; Young 1992, 41–42).

TABLE 11.1 ■ Conflict Theorists

Theory	Theorists	Key Elements
Cultural conflict	Sellin	Crime occurs when individuals acting on the conduct norms of their own group are in violation of the conduct norms the dominant group has enacted into law.
Group conflict	Vold, Quinney	Interest groups (Vold) or social groupings (Quinney) attempt to protect their own interests by influencing the creation and enforcement of the criminal law.
Instrumental Marxism	Quinney	The state and the legal system are instruments that can be directly manipulated by the capitalist class. The capitalist class can thus directly influence law and law formation.
Structural Marxism	Althusser, Poulantzas	The relative autonomy of the state functions to preserve the long-term interests of the capitalist system. This helps explain why many laws are enacted that do not represent the immediate interests of the capitalist class.
Left realism	Young, MacLean, DeKeseredy	Crime really is a problem for the working class and must be taken seriously. Most working-class crime is intra-class. A major methodological tool is the victimization survey. Argues for a concrete crime control program; endorses crime control policies that are not repressive.

Left realism has made some valuable contributions to the criminology litera-ture. For example, it has sensitized us to the amount and kinds of street crime and domestic violence experienced by the most marginalized and vulnerable mem-bers of society. In turn, left realism has been subject to a number of criticisms. For example, critics have argued that the left realist position is ahistorical; that is, left realism fails to take into account the political, economic, and cultural history of the society in which crime occurs. Can the square of crime (the relationship between victims, offenders, police, and the public) really be understood by ana-lyzing responses to local victimization surveys undertaken at a particular point in time and space? O'Reilly-Fleming (1996, 10) suggests that left realism's advocacy for greater crime control may ultimately have the effect of "widening the net of social control" and thus amount to little more than increasing state powers over the marginalized and disenfranchised groups under study. Finally, Mugford and O'Malley (1991, 23) argue that left realists make use of commonsense notions (crime really is a problem) but neglect to transform these common sense notions into a defensible theoretical account.

QUESTIONS FOR CRITICAL THINKING

1. How does structural Marxism address the critiques of instrumental Marx-ism? Describe what is meant by "relative autonomy."
2. In discussing the notion of the "rule of law" and "equality of all before the law," Marxist theorists sometimes make use of the following quote by social critic Anatole France (1897): "The law in its majestic impartiality forbids both the rich and poor alike to sleep under bridges, to beg in the streets or to steal bread." What contradiction is France pointing out? How might this quotation apply to the concept of law and ideology in Marxist thought?

Summary

- Conflict theory views societies as more divided by conflict than they are inte-grated by consensus (see Box 11.1).

- According to Sellin's cultural conflict theory, crime can be viewed as an expression of cultural conflict when individuals who act based on the con-duct norms of their own group are in violation of the conduct norms that the dominant group has enacted into law.

- According to Vold's group conflict theory, crime occurs as a result of conflict between diverse interest groups. Vold makes use of group conflict theory to explain two general classes of group conflict that can result in criminal behaviour: first, crime that arises as a result of minority group behaviour, and second, crime that results from direct contact between groups struggling for the control of power in the political and cultural organization of society.

- Richard Quinney's group conflict theory explains criminality as arising from conflict between "segments" of society, which he defines as types of social groupings. The more powerful segments or social groups in society are able to secure and to protect their own interests by influencing the formulation, enforcement, and administration of criminal law. Quinney places a greater emphasis than either Sellin or Vold on the unequal distribution of power in society.

- Instrumental Marxists view the state and the legal system as instruments that can be directly manipulated by the capitalist class. Instrumental Marxists thus maintain that laws are created and enforced in the interests of the ruling or capitalist class.

- Structural Marxists dispute the instrumentalist view that the state is the direct servant of the ruling or capitalist class and argue that the state and its institutions have a certain degree of independence from specific elites in the capitalist class. Structural Marxists point to the relative autonomy of the state to help explain why many laws are enacted that do not represent the immediate interests of the capitalist class.

- Left realists emphasize that crime really is a problem for the working class and other marginalized groups in the community and that working-class crime must be taken seriously. Left realists make use of victimization surveys to examine the problem of crime for the working class, with the objective of offering crime control policies that are not repressive.

NET WORK

Go to the website of the Canadian Encyclopedia at www.thecanadianencyclopedia.com. You can access the articles "Winnipeg General Strike," "Working-Class History," and "Nine-Hour Movement" by entering the name of the article in the search box at the top of the page.

1. As the link on "working class history" points out, "the consolidation of Canadian capitalism in the early 20th century accelerated the growth of the working class." What were some of the issues that the labour unions of the time were concerned about? What argument would structural Marxists make about the Industrial Disputes Investigation Act (1907)?
2. What was the nine-hour movement? Why was this movement considered unsuccessful? What would an instrumental Marxist argument say about the nine-hour movement?
3. When was the Winnipeg General Strike and why is it considered a pivotal event in Canadian history? What was the Citizens' Committee of One Thousand and how did it differ from the Central Strike Committee? What would an instrumental Marxist argument point out about the ensuing events?

12 Critical Criminology in Canada

BRYAN HOGEVEEN
University of Alberta

ANDREW WOOLFORD
University of Manitoba

Learning Objectives

After reading this chapter, you should be able to

- Explain what it means to be "critical" in critical criminology.
- Identify the origins of critical criminology in Canada in the New Criminology and the efforts of the Human Justice Collective.
- Understand Michel Foucault's approach to the concept of power and its importance to critical criminology.
- Describe how risk and actuarialism are prevalent in contemporary criminal justice practices and how this relates to the notion of the "risk society."
- Discuss cultural criminology and its contribution to critical criminology.
- Explain Pierre Bourdieu's "field theory" and its application to crime in the work of Loïc Wacquant.
- Define Giorgio Agamben's concept of the "state of exception" and explain its relationship to sovereignty.
- Describe Jacques Derrida's notion of "deconstruction" and how it is used in critical criminology.

The downtrodden, the marginalized, and the impoverished make up the majority of individuals who are arrested by the police; they also represent the greatest number of inmates in our jails and take up the bulk of spaces on the court docket. It seems that we inhabit an unjust world made up of enormous concentrations of wealth and power on the one hand and masses of powerless people on the other. This situation raises many questions: Is this the best Canadians can hope for? If so, does this indicate a diminishment of political dreams and the loss of hope for social justice? If it does not, how do we move to a more just state? As you read this chapter, keep in mind the *face* of suffering—whether it be that of the homeless person Canadians hurry by on their way to enjoying a $4 Starbuck's coffee or the one in a news story about a starving East African child so easily flipped past on a 60-inch LED HD television—and ask what you are willing to give up to ameliorate social, economic, and political suffering.

All of this points to the dilemmas that critical criminology forces us to face. As citizens fully socialized into the social order, we rarely critically engage with our world, instead taking it for granted. Inspired by promises of "freedom" and "justice," critical criminology draws attention to hidden and overlooked injustices scattered throughout *our* world. Critical criminology attempts to highlight inequalities, discrimination, and suffering and to relate these to the discipline of criminology. Social problems abound but are easily dismissed as someone else's responsibility. Critical criminology attends to the processes through which the social world restricts human freedom and choice. It attempts to assemble and create more "just" worlds with less misery or none at all: "the possibility daily withheld, overlooked or unbelieved" (Bauman 2000).

What Is Critical about Critical Criminology?

Critical criminology promises to offer something critical. But what does this mean? To be certain, everyone is critical—at least to a certain extent. We cast judgment on movies ("*Pirates of the Caribbean* was the greatest movie of all time!"), clothing (both our own and, especially, that which belongs to others), and music ("Nicki Minaj does not sing particularly well"). Is this the pursuit in which critical scholars are engaged? Certainly not. However, defining exactly what meets and what fails to meet the "critical" bar is far more difficult than it might seem. If everyone is critical and capable of critique, what sets critical criminology apart?

Some schools of criminology have adopted an administrative approach to the question of crime and have produced policy-oriented knowledge directed towards regulating disruptions and disorders (Young 1998). The products of this mainstream criminology/criminal justice (programs such as zero tolerance and broken windows policing) appeal to politicians, who promise an eager electorate that they will be "tough on crime and the causes of crime." Such scholarship is critical to the extent that it challenges existing criminal justice orthodoxy by suggesting that we focus on minimizing criminal opportunities rather than explaining criminal motivations. However, governments and criminal justice organizations can safely adopt this brand of "critical scholarship" within their existing infrastructure without fear that these suggestions and programs will significantly change existing mandates or practices. Government agencies are now promoting and, in some cases, soliciting this type of administrative scrutiny of policy and programming, viewing it as a path towards more efficient governance and control.

By contrast, the promise implied by "critical criminology" ensures a type of critique that prefers "to take the system to task rather than tinker with its parts" (Ratner 1971, n.p.). Hogeveen and Woolford (2006) maintain that critique should not fall into the trap of conceiving of programs that work well within the existing criminal justice system; instead, critical criminologists should extend critique and thought beyond these limits. Indeed, criminal justice institutions that receive critical criminological scholarship favourably would invite their own destruction (Pavlich 2005). Critical criminologists, then, practise a transformative brand of critique that confronts inequalities and social suffering with promises of more just outcomes.

So "critical" in critical criminology implies transformation through promises of justice. But what does it mean to be "critical"? That is, if critical criminology is transformative, does this imply that transformation and critique are identical? No. Critique is a means to a transformative (just) end. Thus, while we now know that the goal of critical criminology is justice, we are yet unaware of what "critical" means. When we attempt to understand a *thing*, etymology (the origins of words) is often a productive starting point. George Pavlich (2000, 25) notes that "criticism . . . crisis and critique relate to the Greek word *Krinein* which is associated with images of judgment (judge, judging), but also with deciding, separating out, discerning, selecting, differentiating, and so on." Interestingly, early medical officials closely associated notions of critique with *Krises*, which involved the art of diagnosing crisis stages in the development of an illness. Traces of this image have survived in common medical diagnoses of patients said to be in critical condition (Pavlich 2000).

Over many years the broad meaning of the word *critical* has been reduced to such a degree that it is now almost exclusively associated with the act of judging. Take the television program *American Idol* as an example of how Western understandings of *critical* and *critique* have become whittled down to judgment. The program masquerades as a singing competition that features three "experts" who have been tasked with cutting down the hundreds of thousands of applicants to a select few while providing feedback on individual performances. In many ways, Simon Cowell, the curmudgeon among the three judges in the earlier seasons of the show, embodied the modern vision of critique as judgment. His comments have included: "That's atrocious; that's simply not good enough," and "If your lifeguard duties were as good as your singing, a lot of people would be drowning."

Judgmental critique derives its critical ammunition from the veracity of the criterion (or critical standard). Continuing with the *American Idol* example, Cowell held the contestants up to a set of normative criteria for what counts as great singing. It was the *criterion* that allowed him to render judgment ("That was atrocious"). Mainstream criminologists engage in a similar critical enterprise. For instance, many criminologists employ criteria such as recidivism rates as the standard against which to assess programmatic and legislative success or failure. Such judgmental criteria can then be employed to evaluate policing, correctional, and court practices. However, as you learned in Chapter 4, recidivism rates (the criteria) are not as robust and self-evident as once believed. Policing practices and a host of administrative conditions, including how long following their release offenders are tracked, are apt to artificially increase or reduce the criteria—the very foundations of much criminological judgment.

Critique typically implies that we are judging some *thing* against a normative standard held out as the epitome or the ultimate. Thus, when we claimed that Nicki Minaj does not sing particularly well, how did we render this assessment? We arrived at this judgment using Andrea Bocelli as our normative frame. Clearly, we must conclude—even if we prefer pop music to the operatic version—that the latter can sing better than the former. This process and strategy fixes the critic as an expert judge who, because of a certain expertise (in music, in crime, etc.), is "deemed capable of authoritatively judging the true from the false, innocent from guilty, good from bad, progressive from regressive, and so on" (Pavlich 2000, 74). Critique, as it is currently practised in criminology and elsewhere, is typically judgmental and reactive.

Forms of critique that seek to challenge the criminal justice status quo are not always appreciated. However, Pavlich (2000) claims that there was a time when critical genres in criminology had considerable influence among politicians and policymakers, especially after the publication and subsequent dissemination of Taylor, Walton, and Young's (1973) highly touted *The New Criminology*. Disenchanted with administrative brands of social science, administrators for a time looked to more radical brands of criminology for inspiration. In the spirit of 1960s radicalism, insight derived from critical questioning of the status quo was evident in governmental discourse and practice. Pleas to abolish prisons, insights into the crime-producing tendencies of the modern criminal justice process, and prisoners' rights discourses were prominent (van Swaaningen 1997). But the heyday of radical criminology was quite brief. Today, administrative and liberal strains figure most prominently at criminological conferences and in scholarly journals.

The reason why "critical voices beyond the language of pragmatic technocracy are decidedly muted," especially when compared to critical debates from less than three decades ago, is that critics have "failed to address that which distinguishes their radical precepts from proponents of administrative criminology: critique" (Pavlich 1999, 70). In recent years, drawing on the insights of philosophers such as Michel Foucault, Pierre Bourdieu, Jacques Derrida, and Giorgio Agamben (among others), critical criminologists have called for an approach that goes beyond judgment. Instead of employing one or another yardstick by which to judge the success or failure of criminal justice policies, these scholars employ an art of critique that involves destabilizing seemingly well-anchored relations in an effort to form new patterns of being that do not pander to established social logics or rely on reactive judgments (Hogeveen and Woolford 2006). A nonjudgmental critical criminology would not render judgments about existing policies, programs, institutions, or societal structures. Rather, it would suggest "other" (just) ways of being in the world. "It would summon them, drag them from their sleep. Perhaps it would invert them sometimes—all the better" (Foucault 1997). It should be noted that there are other approaches to destabilizing critique that are not represented in this chapter. Our focus is primarily on the Continental European social theoretical tradition and its influence in Canada. Other approaches, such as feminist (see Chapter 6), critical race, and Indigenous are also prominent and share a concern for directing critique towards societal patterns of domination.

Critical criminological critique attempts to move beyond complicity in government intrusion into the lives of the least powerful. It does not seek ways to better manage the poor and dangerous classes. Rather, it promises justice to those who are marginalized and discriminated against. Not justice that seeks to punish, however; instead, it promises justice through emancipation. How willing are you to address suffering in your social world?

As we hope you will learn from the rest of this chapter, following the notion of criticism set out in this section, the critical criminologist is not "critical" because he or she is bad-tempered or unconstructive; rather, the negativity of criticism is intended to open your mind to new ways of thinking about and being in the world.

Critical Criminology in English Canada

Critical criminology in Canada was invigorated in 1973 with the publication of *The New Criminology* by British criminologists Ian Taylor, Paul Walton, and Jock Young. In this wide-ranging critique of conventional criminology, Taylor,

Walton, and Young identified starting points for a "new" criminology and criticized conventional criminology for supporting the political and economic status quo, for ignoring the structural causes of crime, and for focusing instead on biological and psychological factors. Taylor, Walton, and Young (1973, 270) recommended in contrast a "fully social" criminology that

1. *. . . understands crime within its wider socio-cultural context.* Crime is not merely an event that occurs between individuals; it takes place within broader social-structural and cultural conditions. Along these lines, a ghetto drug dealer is not just an individual seeking easy money—he may also be the product of a deindustrialized inner city that has been bled of all opportunities other than McJobs because capital investment has fled to the suburbs. He may also be immersed in patriarchal cultural conditions that associate masculinity with money, power, and violence, allowing him to obtain respect and credibility through drug dealing. These are just some of the structures that may influence his decision making.

2. *. . . examines the structural and political-economic dimensions that produce criminal behaviour.* Crime is not the result of "bad," abnormal, or poorly socialized people; rather, it stems from structural conditions that produce unequal opportunities, stigmatized populations, real and relative deprivation, and other concepts that criminologists often credit as motivations for crime. For example, stigma and labelling occur not only at the micro-level when authorities and significant others impose labels on offenders and contribute to their secondary deviance (see Chapter 13), but also as the result of structural conditions that make certain individuals more likely to choose to commit crime, more likely to be caught, more likely to be punished, and therefore more likely to be labelled. This is all part of what Taylor, Walton, and Young (1973, 274) call a "political economy of social reaction."

3. *. . . probes the relationship between crime and the prevailing mode of production.* Crime occurs within societies defined by specific systems of economic production. What is defined as a crime, and the way crime is punished, often depends on this mode of production. For example, vagrancy was criminalized in Britain during the 17th century in part because cheap labour was required for the factory system (Chambliss 1969) to feed the profits of the ruling class and sustain the capitalist mode of production.

4. *. . . questions the role of power and conflict in shaping crime and criminal justice.* Crime is not simply the reflection of a societal consensus; instead, it is defined by the powerful and punished in a manner that suits their interests. Therefore, criminologists must not simply accept state-defined crime as a given. They must also question its origins and the ways in which power is implicit in its formation and application.

5. *. . . engages in a materialist analysis of the development of law in capitalist societies.* Law is not simply a matter of societal consensus but is a function of the material conditions that define our society. Therefore, the law will contain contradictions because it is a reflection of dominant material interests. For example, gambling is illegal in a private club but not in a government-run casino. Other forms of gambling, such as betting on "futures" in the stock

market, may be *encouraged* by the government. Similarly, certain drug habits, such as alcohol and coffee, are tolerated if not encouraged. In contrast, others, such as cocaine and heroin, may be viewed as unproductive and criminalized.

6. *. . . takes a dialectical approach to analyzing how individuals both influence and are influenced by dominant social structures.* The New Criminology was not simply a shift to an objectivist standpoint holding that human action is fully determined by social structures. Instead, human agency and social structures each affect the other, meaning that though human actions are influenced by their cultural and political-economic conditions, humans can also act to change these conditions.

This approach inspired several Canadian criminologists to critically assess the liberal foundations of Canadian criminology. For example, R.S. Ratner (1984) argued that Canadian criminologists had not risen to the challenge of the New Criminology and were guilty of ignoring social structures, failing to challenge state definitions of crime, and naively believing that the institutional apparatus of the criminal justice system could easily be adjusted to address systemic inadequacies and injustices.

Critical criminology soon spread to other venues. In 1985, Thomas O'Reilly-Fleming edited *The New Criminologies in Canada*; this was followed in 1986 by a special edition of the journal *Crime and Social Justice* dedicated to Canadian critical criminology (edited by R.S. Ratner) and a conference in Vancouver on the "Administration of Justice" organized by Brian MacLean and Dawn Currie. By the late 1980s, Canadian critical criminologists had banded together to form the Human Justice Collective, a loose network of scholars assembled around their concerns about the narrow focus of mainstream criminology. These scholars desired a criminology that was more sensitive to the criminogenic impacts of capitalism, patriarchy, racism, and other social structures (Dekeseredy and MacLean 1993). Out of the Human Justice Collective was born *Journal of Human Justice*. In the first issue of this journal, R.S. Ratner (1989, 6) defined critical criminology as follows:

> Although varied conceptions abound, we are all united around those premises that underscore the central role of power and conflict in shaping "criminal" outcomes, the range of vested interests that influence "crime," the need for a dialectical analysis of crime and social control that integrates materialist and idealist factors, the crucial importance of the state and the equally important need to debunk state definitions of crime, and the necessity of devising a praxis that is not conditional on the imminent collapse of capitalist society.

This unity, however, was to be short-lived: funding challenges, personality conflicts, and scholarly differences made it difficult to sustain the Human Justice Collective and its journal. Initially, it had been intended that *Journal of Human Justice* would fund itself through members of the collective adopting it as required reading in their courses. However, classroom use diminished, which placed the journal in a difficult financial position. In addition, personality conflicts had erupted within the collective, leading to disputes among members. In 1995, under these conditions, one of the editors, Brian MacLean, transported the journal to the Division of Critical Criminology at the American Society of Criminology. This move allowed for the journal's continued survival but also marked the end of its Canadian identity.

The growing eclecticism of critical criminology has produced a group of scholars who are difficult to unify under a single label. Initially, a key rift developed between two groups defined as "left realists" and "left idealists" (Young 1979). Left idealists were said to begin their inquiry into crime from abstract premises (e.g., Marxist theory) rather than empirical work. For this reason, they were criticized by realists for minimizing the harm that crime causes to the working class and for romanticizing criminals as a potentially revolutionary force.

SEARCH FOR:
Division on Critical Criminology,
American Society of Criminology

In contrast, left realists worked through local surveys of crime and victimization to try to move beyond partial criminological understandings, which typically focused only on one aspect of crime: the offender, the state, the public, or the victim. Their objective was to take the fear of crime among the working classes seriously and to answer and oppose the work of "right realists," who under the Thatcher, Reagan, and Mulroney governments had spread the popularity of punitive sanctions and administrative approaches. However, left realism did not achieve a sustained following among critical criminologists. Some viewed the reform-based agenda of left realism as compromising the critical thrust of critical criminology by participating in and legitimating the discourses of conventional criminal justice (Pavlich 1999).

The diversity of critical criminology in Canada would later expand with the popularity of neo-Marxist and post-structuralist theories imported from Continental Europe. The perspectives discussed in the rest of this chapter all derive from these origins and represent a shift in critical criminological theorizing away from distinctly political-economic perspectives. Although the premise remains that state-defined law must be challenged rather than replicated through criminological study, a great diversity of methodology and conceptualization now defines the Canadian critical criminological scene, which has also been significantly shaped by the work of several of the feminist scholars discussed in Chapter 6.

Governmentality and Power: Foucault and Criminology

governmentality
The art of governing. It transcends and is considerably broader than the traditional understanding of government as a state-directed activity. Government, then, encompasses a wide array of techniques, within and outside of the state, intended to (re)shape and (re)direct human actions.

Michel Foucault did not regard himself as a significant contributor to the discipline of criminology. On the rare occasion when he did comment on criminology, he complained that its "garrulous discourse" and "endless repetitions" only served to relieve judges, police officers, and magistrates of their guilt for delivering pain and suffering on the guilty (Foucault 1980, 47). Despite Foucault's disdain for the discipline, many scholars have applied his work towards understanding crime and its control. His penological treatise on the "birth of the prison"—*Discipline and Punish*—continues to inspire fresh criminological theorizing. More recently, scholars have used his work on **governmentality**.

SEARCH FOR:
Foucault Resources

Foucault was born in Poitiers, France, in 1926, and died in 1984 of complications from HIV/AIDS. A philosopher and historian who wrote about the history of sexuality, prisons, governance, psychiatry, and knowledge systems, he is

Jeremy Bentham developed a design for a circular Panopticon prison in which the actions of inmates would always be visible so they would behave without the need for direct discipline. Foucault used this idea as a metaphor for the way in which order is maintained by our contemporary social institutions.

heralded for his unique work on **power**. Power, for Foucault, is evident only when it is *exercised*. He did not see it as something that states or individuals can hold, accumulate, possess, or monopolize. In other words, can you show us what power looks like? Some claim often that money or wealth *is* power. Foucault would argue otherwise. For Foucault, money becomes power only when it is used or otherwise put into effect.

A further characteristic of the Foucauldian notion of power is that it is not solely negative or repressive. He embraces a more *positive* theory of power: not in terms of good or beneficial, but rather as creative. He argues that "we must cease once and for all to describe the effects of power in negative terms: it 'excludes,' it 'represses,' it 'censures,' it 'abstracts,' it 'masks,' it 'conceals.' In fact power produces; it produces reality; it produces domains of object and rituals of truth" (1979, 194). Thus, rather than viewing power in a manner that exaggerates its negative elements, Foucault urged scholars to focus on what is created when power is exercised. What is the outcome when power is employed?

A third characteristic of the Foucauldian understanding of power is the emphasis he placed on **micro-powers** that are disseminated throughout the social world. Almost everywhere we turn, everywhere we go, power operates on our bodies and souls. It seems that power is perpetually influencing our behaviour, often without our awareness. Consider your daily trip to university or college. Assuming that you are driving a vehicle of some sort, think about all the ways your behaviour is controlled while you drive. Traffic lights, signs, painted lines, photo radar, and the presence or absence of police all affect how we go about our drive.

Foucault was convinced that to intimately understand the operation of power, we must shift our focus from the state to the dispersed spaces in which power operates. This is the essence of what Foucault called discipline. **Discipline** operates at the smallest level of detail and attends to the intricacies of human behaviour through the **surveillance** and observation of individual functioning

power
Power, for Foucault, extends beyond the state. It is not a quantity to hold or possess. It is, rather, relational, such that power is only ever evident in its exercise.

micro-powers
Small and mundane relations of governance, with an appreciable effect on human behaviour.

discipline
A meticulous manner or method of training. It intends to ensure constant subjection and obedience. It involves hierarchal observation, normalizing judgment, and examinations.

surveillance
The direct or indirect observation of conduct toward producing a desired outcome (i.e., conformity).

so as to increase the efficiency and usefulness of human actions. When thinking about discipline, it is the everyday and the mundane that are important. Fully understanding power involves examining it at its main point of application: the body. Remember back to when you were learning how to write using a pencil. Recall the teacher standing over you correcting your finger placement. S/he would watch you (surveillance) and correct your mistakes to make certain you used the implement in the most efficient manner possible (positive power). To maximize the utility of our bodies and to allow hierarchal control and correction, this meticulous exercise of power is infinitely multiplied throughout the social world. As such, discipline requires that individuals be organized in space and time. Consider the timetable from public school. It provided a general framework for activity and organized our days. The timetable structured not only our *use* of time but also the *space* we were to occupy at certain points in the day. The bell organized our behaviour. What happened when the bell sounded? Being conditioned to move according to the sounding of the bell, students would get up to leave while the teacher attempted to quell the mass exodus. Thus time, space, and signals coexisted to discipline not only our minds but also our bodies (Minaker and Hogeveen 2009).

Foucault's analysis of discipline was criticized (a) for abandoning the state in its analysis and (b) for tending (supposedly) to characterize human subjects as "docile" (inactive) bodies rather than active agents (Garland 1997). Foucault's later work on governmentality addressed many of these concerns (see Box 12.1). For Foucault (1982), governmentality "must be allowed the very broad meaning which it had in the 16th century. Government did not refer only to political structures or the management of states; rather it designated the way in which the conduct of individuals or states might be directed; the government of children, of souls, of communities, of families, of the sick" (221).

Therefore, the study of governmentality should cast its gaze widely and address such broad questions as "how to govern oneself, how to be governed, how to govern others, by whom the people will accept to be governed, and how to become the best possible governor" (Foucault 1991, 45). Government(ality) entails "any attempt to shape with some degree of deliberation aspects of our behaviour according to particular sets of norms and for a variety of ends" (Dean 1999, 10).

FOCUS   BOX 12.1

RESTORATIVE JUSTICE AS GOVERNMENTALITY

Restorative justice is a broad term used to describe a range of justice practices designed to involve victims, offenders, and community members in directly resolving the harms caused by crime. For some of its proponents, restorative justice is intended to empower communities and individuals to creatively solve their own problems, to remove justice control from the hands of the state and professionals, and to allow for a justice tailored specifically to the needs of victims, offenders, and community members. All of this is to occur within informal settings such as community centres, with victims, offenders, and their families and friends as well as community members sitting in a circle to discuss what led to the crime and how its harm might be repaired.

In contrast to this representation of restorative justice as a community-led activity separate from the formal practices of the state, George Pavlich (2005) has given two reasons why restorative justice is a form of governmentality. First, it is because the participants in restorative justice meetings are encouraged to examine and reshape their conduct in relation to their experiences of crime and justice. Offenders are asked to take responsibility for their actions, victims are asked to express how the crime has affected them and to present reasonable demands for repair, and community members are asked to participate in the reintegration of the offender and the healing of the victim. Moreover, it is hoped that participation in restorative justice will transform the way these participants deal with conflict in the future. All of these aspects of restorative justice encourage individuals to accept and internalize restorative values and practices through which they might better govern themselves and their communities, thus freeing the state of this responsibility.

Second, it is because restorative justice fashions a way of understanding the world (and crime in particular) that makes the pursuit of "restorative" justice appear more rational and understandable to those involved. If restorative justice is to govern our behaviour, it must first shift how we think about crime and criminal justice. It does this by reframing core components of criminal justice. For Pavlich, this involves providing different answers to these questions:

1. What is governed? Unlike formal criminal justice, restorative justice claims to govern "harm" rather than "crime" since it is not the violations of the state's law but rather the harms suffered by individuals and communities that are of primary concern.

2. Who is governed? Those who are to be governed are all of those who have a stake in the crime and its effects— victim, offender, and community members—rather than just the offender.

3. Who governs? Whereas judges and lawyers are the individuals empowered through the practice of criminal justice, restorative justice seeks to give greater agency to victims, offenders, and community members.

4. What is appropriate governing? Instead of focusing on the past, restorative governance should be directed towards the future. It is therefore less a question of punishing a wrongdoer and more a matter of creating a dialogue among stakeholders so that they can work out how to avoid repetition of the crime.

For Pavlich, the problem with this restorative justice governmentality is that it does not represent a true alternative to the criminal justice system. Instead, restorative justice is fundamentally dependent on the criminal justice system and criminal law. For example, though restorative justice shifts our attention to the harm suffered by victims and community members, it nonetheless relies on criminal law to define the acts that are to be considered harmful. Thus, it restricts itself from addressing harms that are not codified within criminal codes (such as suffering caused by industrial pollution), as well as structural harms (such as the gender inequalities that result from patriarchal systems of domination).

Questions for Critical Thinking

1. Restorative justice is meant to empower victims and communities when they have been harmed. But how might restorative justice as governmentality allow the state to further its control over the subjects of crime?

2. In what fashion does restorative justice as governmentality depend on criminal justice policies, practices, and ways of seeing the world?

Source: George Pavlich, *Governing Paradoxes of Restorative Justice* (London: Glasshouse Press, 2005).

Critical scholars have used Foucault's writings on governmentality to understand a wide range of state and nonstate domains of governance. They have raised important insights about legal change and the centrality of law in the regulation of populations. They have also argued that critical criminology has been limited "by its emphasis on the state, and state-centred constructions of criminality, and by its failure to come to terms with how social injustices are reproduced through private institutions and modes of expertise that operate on the margins of the state and in the shadow of the law" (Lippert and Williams 2006). For example, Lippert and Williams have looked to the margins of legal governance to explore how the rise of private security affects our social world. These authors maintain that critical scholarship should focus "less on how the machinery of the state is brought to bear on the production and control of individual subjects and offenders, and more on the myriad technologies of governance and their operation across diverse social fields" such as immigration and the policing of financial disorder (706). Governmentality, then, draws scholarly attention to mechanisms *outside* the traditional state governmental machinery that structure and contour human behaviour. Recent years have witnessed the proliferation of private security firms that police a variety of venues, including the local mall, construction sites, and, as the upsurge in alarm companies continues, private dwellings. By attending to the growth of private security, "the governmentality literature presents a unique opportunity to expand the theoretical range and conceptual reach of critical criminology, and to enhance its capacity to reveal and interrogate forms of injustice and domination crafted on the margins of the state" (714–15).

Actuarialism, Risk, and the Risk Society

risk
The calculated probability of an eventuality.

Perhaps the greatest impact of Foucault's work on critical criminological studies has been on scholars' ability to understand how offenders' lives are increasingly organized around questions of **risk**. As we have seen already, Foucault was fundamentally concerned with understanding how individuals were normalized through government and discipline—that is, how they were corrected and brought into line with the needs of the larger society (O'Malley 1996). In the field of crime control, recent years have witnessed the emergence and proliferation of actuarial or "insurance"-based strategies of governance and control. It seems that Western criminal justice systems have become somewhat preoccupied with managing risks as police, probation, prisons, and halfway houses seek to minimize the likelihood of future offending (Bosworth 2004). Towards this end, many institutions employ a variety of risk prediction tools, all of them part of "actuarial justice" (Feeley and Simon 1994).

actuarial
Refers to statistical calculations of risk across time and groups.

Foucauldian-inspired theorists distinguish the everyday usage of the term *risk* from how it is construed as an **actuarial** (or insurance-based) technology. When we as citizens refer to risk, it concerns the dangers and perils connected with an objective and often immediate threat—for instance, of being struck by lightning or having our house burglarized. However, this definition and understanding of risk has to be separated from its usage in actuarial terms, where it indicates neither an "event nor a general kind of event occurring in reality, but a specific mode of treatment of certain events capable of occurring to a group of individuals" (Ewald 1991). Risk, then, is the calculated probability of an eventuality. Think of the last time you purchased car insurance. The agent likely asked you a series of questions: What is your sex? How old are you? Where do you live? Where do you work? How far do you travel to work/school? These questions were then entered into a computer, which calculated your premium based on these factors. Agents ask these questions to derive a risk score. That is, by employing aggregated data (including accident reports and police statistics) collected over time and then comparing the aggregate to your indicators, insurance companies ascertain the probability of having to pay a claim on your behalf. If you are young, male, and unemployed, your risk and insurance premium will be considerably higher than that of a married 40-year-old female who lives in the suburbs.

Events (car accidents) and populations (males, females, the elderly) are not inherent risks but become constituted as "actuarial" risks through analyses and calculations of chance. Risk understood from a Foucauldian perspective, then, is constituted in relation to the aggregation of events over time and regulated through techniques such as higher insurance rates designed to contend with individual risk factors. Simon (1988) maintains that risk-based technologies of governance have become dominant largely because of their efficiency and their ability to intensify the effectiveness of disciplinary technologies (O'Malley 1996). Probabilistic calculation is particularly evident in the youth correctional field, where the Youth Level of Service/Case Management Inventory (YLS/CMI) is employed. Andrews and Bonta (1998, 245) maintain that this tool is premised on the four principles of risk, needs, responsivity, and professional discretion. First, the *risk* principle reflects the contention that criminal behaviour occurs in predictable patterns. Second, the *needs* principle implies that recidivism will be reduced through select targeting of criminogenic need through appropriate treatment programs. Third, given that many juvenile offenders suffer from attention deficit hyperactivity disorder, fetal alcohol spectrum disorder, or oppositional defiant disorder, responsivity is crucial to any "successful" treatment option and refers to the need for service providers to deliver treatment programs in a manner that is consistent with and appropriate to the offender's ability and learning style. Finally, *professional discretion* "strategically reasserts the importance of retaining professional judgment, provided that it is not used irresponsibly and is systematically monitored" (Hannah-Moffat and Maurutto 2003, 3).

While at first blush actuarial strategies seem efficient and just, several factors raise questions about such assessments. Hannah-Moffat and Maurutto (2003, 7) have found that correctional officials and practitioners fail to conceptualize "the problems intrinsic to this kind of needs assessment and how a failure to distinguish between risk and need can result in increased surveillance of youth." Although blending of risk and need is a problem, the problems of risk-based governance are particularly troubling when applied to female and nonwhite populations (Minaker and Hogeveen 2008). Notably, "female offenders are more often deemed higher risk because of their risk to themselves, whereas high-risk male offenders are more likely to pose a risk to others" (Hannah-Moffat and Shaw, 2001). Risk assessment tools typically do not account for gender and cultural variation in offending and recidivism. For example, the tests do not adequately capture histories of physical, mental, or sexual abuse prevalent among female youth. Moreover, risk assessment tools do not adequately address the broader socio-cultural and colonial context of Indigenous youths (Hannah-Moffat and Shaw 2001).

These Foucauldian notions of risk and actuarialism are occasionally combined with Beck's concept of the "**risk society**." Beck admits that characterizing the present as the "risk society" may seem odd in light of the daily risks and dangers faced by people in pre-industrial societies—such as plagues, famine, and natural disasters. However, there is a qualitative difference between the looming hazards of our industrial present and those of earlier times. Beck suggests that today's hazards are not forces outside of us; rather, they are internal creations, and their danger originates from our own decision making (1992, 98). Our technological

risk society
An emerging societal form characterized by the production and increased awareness of human-made "risks," such as nuclear destruction and environmental devastation. More importantly, the risk society is organized around the management of such risks.

development and scientific rationality have provided us with the tools to construct the means of our own destruction—nuclear power, environmental pollution, climate change, and an assortment of life-threatening chemicals, just to name a few dangers. Moreover, Beck does not suggest that we have necessarily witnessed a quantitative increase in risk; rather, we have come to organize our societies more around the *fact* of risk.

This theoretical perspective comes to bear on critical criminology in at least two ways. First, social problems have increasingly come to be understood as "risks" to be *managed* rather than social "problems" to be *solved*. This shift in thinking is noticeable in criminological approaches that take crime to be inevitable and that prescribe various risk reduction strategies to lessen crime's social costs. Along these lines, individuals are encouraged to become responsible for protecting themselves from opportunistic crimes through the techniques of "situational crime prevention" (O'Malley 1992)—for example, by installing alarm systems in their homes or in their cars (see Chapter 15). As well, "three strikes" laws (see Chapter 15), which impose long-term prison sentences after a third criminal violation, are justified under a risk management logic as a means for warehousing repeat offenders who are perceived to pose too great a threat to the general public. This said, risk management techniques should not be painted solely as oppressive, since they can be used to establish more fair and efficient criminal justice processes under the current system—for example, by providing a calculus for justifying the diversion of less risky offenders towards an alternative sentencing or community bail program, and thus away from the formal justice system. But even with such seemingly benign applications of risk, critical criminologists remain skeptical of the individualizing and responsibilizing tendencies of risk-based approaches to crime.

Second, risk thinking transforms criminal justice practices. Risk management strategies infiltrate judicial, correctional, and law enforcement institutions, tasking criminal justice professionals with the collection of aggregated risk data and with administering risk assessments to their charges. For example, Ericson and Haggerty (1997) note how policing practices have been affected by the demands of the risk society. They cite the case of a modern police officer investigating a traffic accident. Today's officer must gather information that is pertinent not only to the courts and police records but also to the insurance companies, the public health system, provincial vehicle registries, and the automobile industry. Ericson and Haggerty report that under these new demands, a simple traffic accident "took one hour to investigate, and three hours to write about it, to account for it, and to bureaucratically process it" (Ericson and Haggerty 1997, 24).

In alerting us to these broader social changes, the "risk society" thesis serves a critical criminological function by demonstrating the effects that broad societal shifts towards increased insecurity have on the ways we think about and react to matters of criminal justice. In this sense, crime and the response to it are not taken as givens but rather as socially constituted phenomena that can be better understood by locating them in their wider social context. And by identifying this wider social context, we are able to critically assess proposed criminal justice "solutions" through an understanding of their historical contingency.

Airport security screening is one of the ways in which our society is organized around the prevention of risk.

Cultural Criminology

The social reaction perspective (see Chapter 13) brings attention to crime as a process of social interaction involving victim, offender, bystanders, and criminal justice agencies in the construction of deviant meanings and identities. This insight has been absorbed and extended in the work of cultural criminologists, who focus on crime as a cultural rather than a legal construct. These scholars turn their attention away from crime as a "real" phenomenon reflected in police data, victimization surveys, and other quantitative measures, focusing instead on "the debris of everyday life" (Morrison 2007, 254) through an aesthetic and ethnographic engagement with their subject matter. Cultural criminologists do not accept crime simply as state-defined illegality; instead, they view it as a culturally negotiated phenomenon through which people create social meaning.

SEARCH FOR:
Cultural Criminology

Hayward and Young (2004) identify five "motifs" of cultural criminology. First, cultural criminologists alert us to the importance of "adrenaline" in the commission of crime. In contrast to rational choice theorists, who portray offenders as economic actors engaged in cost-benefit analyses of whether or not to break the law, cultural criminologists acknowledge that crime is *felt*. In other words, crime may be motivated by feelings of anger, insecurity, humiliation, or excitement. Moreover, the act of crime may produce a sensual and visceral rush that incites both panic and pleasure (Katz 1988; Ferrell 1998). Thus, though a potential car thief may make a *rational* choice not to steal your car because she or he is afraid it might be a "bait car," the *attraction* of car theft may stem more from the desire to alleviate boredom through risk taking.

Second, cultural criminologists draw our attention to the "soft city" (Raban 1974). This refers to the "underlife" of the city that hides beneath structured and rationally planned urban space. Whereas urban planning attempts to direct our everyday lives through policing strategies, the design of defensive urban space, and other modalities of social control, the "soft city" bubbles up as a realm of creativity and street-level possibility. While it may seem that we are free to go and do as we please in space, careful design contours our actions in very definite directions. Consider for example the layout of an IKEA store. The interior space has been mapped so that customers are forced to wander through all the showrooms before arriving at what they want to purchase. This is no accident. IKEA designers want us to see all their products on display, hoping this will make us want to purchase more than we intended. The "soft city," by contrast, subverts planners' intentions. It is the space used, for example, by Critical Mass to launch illegal bike rallies to confront our automobile culture and to illustrate how the daily commute is part of the depersonalized and routinized destruction of human sociability (Ferrell 2004). As Ferrell (2004, 292) notes, "Critical Mass participants define their exuberantly collective bicycle rides not as traditional political protests, but as do-it-yourself celebrations enlivened by music, decoration and play." By resisting the boredom and repetition of the normal "protest march," Critical Mass seeks to reclaim the "soft city" of urban space through theatrical rallies.

Third, cultural criminologists are interested in acts of "transgression" and rule breaking that challenge the justness of laws. In this vein, prior to the legalization of cannabis, a cultural criminologist might have understood the spectacle of pro-cannabis protesters sparking joints on Parliament Hill not simply as individuals seizing the opportunity for public criminality, but also as a collective act designed to challenge the criminalization of one leisure pursuit while others (e.g., alcohol, tobacco) go uncontested—and in this case the challenge was successful. Similarly, the Critical Mass cycle rallies expose the overregulated nature of modern urban life and the ways in which this overregulation denies freedom of movement (as well as dedicated traffic lanes) to slower and less-expensive vehicles.

Fourth, cultural criminologists propose a methodology founded on an **attentive gaze**. This requires that researchers do more than sit back in their offices and peruse quantified crime data. They must engage in "an ethnography immersed in culture and interested in lifestyle(s), the symbolic, the aesthetic, and the visual" (Hayward and Young 2004, 268). This requires that they enter into the world where crime occurs and where it is represented in order to better comprehend the experiential and interpretive dimensions of crime. For example, O'Neill (2004) employs a methodology she refers to as "ethno-mimesis" that draws on media such as photography, film, performance, theatre, and text to illustrate the complexity of the emotional lives of individuals. In one such study, O'Neill and Campbell encouraged sex workers to use art and writing to represent their "issues, concerns, experiences, and ideas for change" (O'Neill 2004, 226). The final result was not only a written report but also an art exhibit and information pamphlet, which collectively combined to allow community members to express, reflect on, and relate to pressing local issues in a variety of creative ways.

Finally, the knowledge produced by cultural criminology is argued to be **dangerous knowledge** because its purpose is to question *all* knowledge, including the status of criminology as an objective science. This might be achieved by drawing on unusual sources of knowledge. For instance, in his exploration of the crime of genocide, Morrison (2007) examines photographs snapped by Nazi police battalions, visits Belgian and Bangladeshi museums, and offers a reading of Joseph Conrad's novel *Heart of Darkness*. He uses these diverse sources to criticize criminology for its dependence on crimes defined and data

attentive gaze
A methodological requirement that researchers immerse themselves where crime occurs in the everyday world in order to better understand the ways in which crime is experienced and interpreted by individuals.

dangerous knowledge
A form of knowledge that leaves no concept, notion, or idea untouched by criticism. To achieve this relentlessly critical stance, cultural criminologists often turn to diverse sources of information (e.g., novels and street-level observation) as means to reveal alternative perspectives that might shake the foundations of our taken-for-granted assumptions about crime.

generated by the state, and thereby its tendency to overlook crimes such as genocide that are often perpetrated by or beyond the state. In this sense, cultural criminology is a critical criminological project intended to relentlessly challenge the taken-for-granted assumptions of criminology and popular understandings of crime in order to expose how they are culturally constructed and delimited by a particular world view.

Morrison's focus on visual and textual representations of crimes points to a motif not covered by Hayward and Young. Many critical scholars have turned greater attention to how crime is represented in various forms of popular media. A recent example of this approach is a collection of essays edited by Steve Kohm, Pauline Greenhill, and Sonia Bookman (2016) that examines how crime is portrayed in Canadian film. Through analysis of films such as *Bon Cop, Bad Cop*, *A History of Violence*, and *Atanarjuat*, the authors examine how Canadian identity and Canadian institutions are constructed, reinforced, or disrupted through representations of crime in film.

"Field Theory" of Criminology

The sociology of Pierre Bourdieu provides insight into the cultural and economic conditions in which crime and our understanding of crime are produced, although on a much broader scale. The grounding concept of Bourdieu's theoretical work is that of the **field** (DiMaggio 1979). Bourdieu's notion of the field can be likened to a battlefield or sports field (Bourdieu 1992). It is a space of conflict and competition wherein competitors, who possess varying levels of social and economic power, vie for control. But the field is not level, nor is it without pre-existing rules. Rather, participants encounter a field that is tilted to favour the already powerful (they will play downhill) and structured by predetermined rules that all must follow.

Within a field of social activity, such as art, politics, or law, a market defined by its own measures of value is established; and in accordance with a field, actors seek the "profit of distinction"—in other words, the awards associated with a display of competence (Bourdieu 1991, 1990a, 1984). An actor's ability to display competence within a particular field depends in part on his or her **habitus**. This is one's "feel for the game"—that is, one's set of "dispositions acquired through experience" (Bourdieu 1990b, 9) that allow one to react to situations that arise within a particular field without the need to actively plot one's moves. Keeping with our sports analogy, imagine that in a game of hockey the skilled power forward Hogeveen finds a loose puck in a scrum in front of the net. In that instance, he automatically shifts the puck to his backhand and lifts it over the sprawling goalie, Woolford. Here, Hogeveen's dedication to his sport, and his practised experience of it, provides him with the embodied knowledge necessary to succeed on the ice without needing to "overthink" his game (whereas Woolford's coach might advise him to work more on his hockey habitus).

The actor's "feel for the game" within the market relations of a specific field will vary. Those endowed with greater quantities of the forms of **capital** valuable within the field (e.g., economic, symbolic, cultural, or linguistic capital) will be more capable of transmitting an aura of competence (Brubaker, 1985). Thus, within a

field
A basic unit of social activity. The social world is divided into many fields (e.g., the "artistic" field, the "academic" field, the "economic" field). Each field of activity is defined by its own market through which certain practices or dispositions are valued more than others.

habitus
A set of durable dispositions acquired through experience that allow one to achieve a "feel for the game" within a specific field of activity. These are internalized practices that serve as a "second nature" responsive to the immediate demands of everyday life.

capital
The primary field of activity for state or government actors, as well as those who are funded by the government, and where these actors compete to define and shape government resources and responsibilities.

specific "game" or market situation, actors come pre-equipped with differing amounts of capital, depending on their position(s) in the structural arrangements of society (e.g., level of education, occupation, age), and based on these factors are predisposed towards certain behaviours or practices. The valuational rules of the market ascribe to these practices and behaviours differing levels of profitability within the field, allowing some actors to feel more at home on their appointed terrain. To put this in simpler terms, if you are currently seeking a criminology degree, this may be motivated by your desire to obtain employment in the legal or juridical field (e.g., as a police officer, lawyer, or probation worker). However, success in this field will depend on more than your possession of a criminology degree or your ability to extol Merton's strain theory. You will require possession of the forms of capital most valued within this field of activity. You will acquire some of this capital through your increased knowledge about the field of law, but you might also profit from the symbolic, linguistic, and cultural capital you have obtained through the practice of writing essays, making public presentations, and reading "classic" works of literature and philosophy. These latter forms of capital equip you with an aura of competence that communicates to your future employer that you are a "capable" person (see—essays, presentations, and readings *are* important!). However, it should be noted that due to our inequitable social structures, some people enter university already in possession of a great deal of the capital needed to get a job within the juridical field and therefore are at an advantage. For example, an individual who was raised by a father/lawyer and mother/judge, who habitually thinks of the world in terms of law and adversarial justice, and who models his parents' ways of speaking and carrying themselves, is armed with a habitus that invests him with the capital needed to more easily navigate the legal profession.

In criminological analysis, Bourdieu's field theory has been most influentially used by Wacquant, who has expanded Bourdieu's notion of the "bureaucratic field" to foster better understanding of the space in which state-sponsored crime control and welfare policy are performed and intersect (see Wacquant 2009, 2010).

The bureaucratic field is "a splintered space of forces vying over the definition and distribution of public goods" (Wacquant 2010, 200). It is thus the primary field of activity for state or government actors, as well as those who are funded by the government, and it is where these actors compete to define and shape government resources and responsibilities. Those who are better positioned in this field may, for example, be able to determine which government outlays ought to be defined as "welfare" (e.g., monetary support for the poor) and which as investments (e.g., tax relief for businesses).

According to Bourdieu (1994, 1998), the bureaucratic field is characterized by two intersecting axes. On the vertical axis, at its top, rests the higher state nobility of the political elite—those governmental actors in powerful ministries such as finance and justice, who are often committed to implementing the interest-driven policies of socially dominant groups. At the bottom of this vertical axis sits the lower state nobility of government agents, whose positions require them to deal more directly with the everyday needs of citizens in areas such as health, education, and housing. Across the horizontal axis, the "left hand" and the "right hand" of the state stand in opposition to each other. The left hand refers to government departments and government-sponsored social service agencies that offer social protection and support (e.g., welfare, housing, and employment); the right hand consists of state and state-supported institutions that represent the might or force of the state, such as state departments of finance, which possess the power to impose austerity measures on all other areas of government. The various actors (i.e., upper and lower state nobilities) and institutions (i.e., left and right hands) that occupy the bureaucratic field compete with one another for control over public goods and the ability to define the terms and values that will guide state actions. To this extent, the bureaucratic field is often a fractious setting; however, there also are periods when these actors and institutions achieve coherence around a dominant set of ideas and practices, such as those that characterize neoliberalism.

Wacquant's extension of Bourdieu's work on the bureaucratic field comes primarily through his inclusion of police, courts, and prisons as part of the right hand of the state. This move allows him to map how the neoliberal era of increased flexibility, state rollbacks, and deregulation is also characterized by increases in the punitive and disciplinary might of the state. Wacquant locates the simultaneous disappearance of traditional welfare protections and expansion of punitive and surveillant workfare policies on the left hand next to the growing network of prisons designed to warehouse the risky "fractions of postindustrial proletariat" and contend with the fallout of vicious neoliberal economic policies on the right hand (Wacquant 2010, 210). Together, these processes impose a "double regulation" or "**carceral–assistential mesh**" that is the peculiar product of the neoliberal state (Wacquant 2009, xviii), under which the left hand of the state begins to function in a manner eerily similar to that of the right hand.

It is under these conditions that Wacquant observes a "deadly symbiosis" between the prison and the ghetto (Wacquant 2001). The right hand of the state transforms prisons into spaces where the recidivist poor are warehoused rather than reformed; the ghetto becomes a space where the risky poor are contained and disciplined through the government-sponsored services of the state's left hand. Consider, for example, the amount of work involved in being poor. For those welfare recipients deemed capable of work, the attitude of the state is that they should "take a job, any job." And their continued social assistance support is often dependent on them participating in government-funded employment programs, their engagement in weekly job searches, and regular meetings with their income assistance workers. On top of this, these individuals face the challenge of finding child care for children, the search for safe and affordable housing, and access to healthcare services. In their search for all of these supports, which itself can be a full-time job, the poor find themselves unable to move from certain stigmatized neighbourhoods, and meanwhile, their behaviour is increasingly observed and regulated through a battery of forms, training courses, meetings, and other requirements attached to their ongoing access to government and not-for-profit social service agency assistance.

Wacquant's Bourdieusian approach fits the label of "critical criminology" because it does not simply accept "criminalized" identities as constructed through the criminal law and its application. Instead, it seeks to identify the symbolic, cultural, and economic factors (e.g., the conditions of the bureaucratic field) that empower dominant actors to create and apply criminal categories while simultaneously disempowering subordinate groups so that they cannot resist this criminalization because they lack the necessary "capital" to achieve "profit" within various arenas of social action (or "fields").

carceral–assistential mesh
Under neoliberalism, this is a mode of "double regulation" whereby the right (e.g., prisons) and left (e.g., social welfare) jointly function to punish and discipline the poor rather than offering rehabilitation and care.

Agamben: Sovereignty and the State of Exception

In political theory and public discourse, the West is generally viewed as an asylum of human rights enmeshed within robust democracy (Ek 2006). But this image has begun to erode in the wake of the "exceptional" and seemingly extreme measures introduced after the 9/11 attacks in New York and Washington on 11 September 2001. What are we to think about the massive numbers of suspected terrorists being detained at Guantanamo Bay without ever being charged with an offence? North American governments maintain that such practices are necessary to protect the public from similar future attacks. In 2013, US whistle blower Edward Snowden released thousands of secret documents he had obtained while working as a contractor for the National Security Agency. Many of these documents revealed programs under which the United States and other countries collected information about their own citizens as well as about friendly countries. Critics have complained that many of these surveillance programs are illegal. In the United States, the government's Privacy and Civil Liberties Oversight Board has concluded that the collection of mass telephone records is a violation of privacy law and that the program has never resulted in any successful terrorism investigations (Ackerman and Roberts 2014). Snowden's leaked information was one factor that led Canada's Interim Privacy Commissioner to recommend that the federal government tighten privacy regulations and that Community Security Establishment Canada (CSEC) be required to report its activities annually to Parliament in order to improve public oversight of that agency (Office of the Privacy Commissioner of Canada, 2014).

The Snowden leaks seem to have finally awakened some public concern. For more than a decade, citizens rarely protested these intrusions into their private lives. It seems that citizens had become stoic; that is, any measures the government implemented in the name of national security (and, perhaps more important, the prevention of future terrorist attacks) had come to be perceived as appropriate—indeed, they were welcomed. North American governments' actions since 9/11 have typically been carried out in the name of protecting the nation and have been passively accepted by the citizenry.

It seems that anything and everything (including torture?) is now permitted so long as the goal is to protect the state and the public. Such a policy has lethal implications. For example, after four terrorist attacks left 52 dead and many wounded in the heart of London, England, an innocent man (Jean Charles de Menezes) was shot dead by police officers. Sir Iain Blair, the Metropolitan police commissioner, while disturbed by this tragedy, later admitted that more guiltless Londoners could lose their lives as police scoured the city for the suspected bombers. In effect, the police chief was admitting that a mistake had been made and that it might well be made again in the future. How are we to make sense of this? Giorgio Agamben has perhaps done more to help scholars, activists, and the public come to terms with the post-9/11 world than any other academic.

Agamben's work is complex and not easily classifiable. He has been heavily influenced by Foucault, Carl Schmitt, Walter Benjamin, and Saint Paul. He tends to extract the most "useful" conclusions from prominent and influential scholars and assemble them in a meaningful way, so it might be best to read him as an eclectic scholar—that is, one who does not rigidly hold to a single philosophical tradition but instead integrates many ideas, concepts, and styles into his work.

Much of Agamben's work is grounded in his concerns about the modern conditions of sovereignty. He takes his lead from Schmitt, who defined political sovereignty in his now-classic work *Political Theology*. For both Schmitt and Agamben, the **sovereign** is the one who holds the power to declare a **state of exception**, during which civil liberties are suspended (among other precautions) in the interest of defending the nation. That is, the sovereign is the one whom the juridical order grants the power to proclaim a state of exception. Declarations of this sort are typically issued after natural disasters, during wartime, and, especially, when the state is confronted by civil unrest. According to Schmitt (1985), a state of exception or emergency (as it is sometimes referred to) is declared when the sovereign deems suspension of the existing social order necessary in order for social order to be restored. Typically, the state of exception is lifted once stability is returned.

Under Canada's National Emergencies Act (1988), which replaced the War Measures Act (1914), any national, provincial, or municipal government can declare a state of emergency. The act defines an emergency as "an urgent and critical situation" that threatens Canadian citizens and the government's capacity to preserve Canadian "sovereignty, security and territorial integrity." Declaring a state of emergency empowers the government to, among other things, prohibit travel and remove people from their homes. Perhaps the most egregious invocation of such powers was the imprisonment of German and Ukrainian Canadians during the First World War and of Japanese Canadians during the World War II. (In both cases, their property was confiscated as well.) But a world war is not a necessary condition for a state of emergency to be declared. During the October Crisis of 1970, in the hunt for terrorists from the Front de libération du Québec (FLQ), soldiers in full battle attire raided the homes of Quebecers while tanks patrolled city streets. In response to a seven-year campaign of bombings that culminated in the kidnapping of a Quebec cabinet minister and a British diplomat, Prime Minister Pierre Elliott Trudeau had invoked the War Measures Act, which effectively suspended civil rights and extended the police wide-ranging powers of arrest and detention. By the time the dust had settled, nearly 500 people had been arrested and detained; of these, only 62 were ever formally charged and only 18 were convicted.

How does this make sense? How can a government simply suspend your rights? For Agamben, the answer lies in the fact that it is only by virtue of citizenship that modern states offer protections via human rights. At the same time, the nation's citizens are subordinated to the sovereign, who can decide at any time to suspend those rights (Ek 2006). That is, human rights are afforded by specific geopolitical orders (e.g., Canada) and can be suspended only by the de facto sovereign. In this way, in the name of protection or defence of society and nation, the sovereign establishes the conditions under which he or she can abandon his or her subjects and return them to a state of **naked life**—that is, life unprotected by law and rights. When a state of emergency is declared, rights-bearing citizens can be deemed enemies of the state and subjected to exceptional and extreme measures.

We should "ask ourselves if we are today witnessing a definitive paradigmatic break in conceptions of the relationship between countries and their citizens" (Minca 2006)—that is, whether we are facing the creation of an enormous space of exception within which each and every one of us, through the temporary

sovereign
One who holds supreme power in a territory or space. Agamben, following Carl Schmitt, claims that the sovereign is the one who is empowered to declare a state of exception.

state of exception
A period of time when the sovereign declares civil liberties suspended: typically in a time of national crisis.

naked life
For Agamben, naked life is akin to *Homo Sacer*—an individual who is excluded from possessing human rights and can be killed by anyone but cannot be sacrificed during a religious ceremony.

C-046350, Library and Archives Canada

During World War II, more than 20,000 Japanese Canadians (most of whom were Canadian-born) were forcibly relocated to internment camps.

suspension of law and rights, might be whisked away to a secret prison. Do you think this cannot happen in Canada? That it is a horror tale confined to the United States or Britain? In Canada, the Department of Citizenship and Immigration can remove persons deemed threatening to the security and well-being of Canadians by issuing a Security Certificate under the Immigration and Refugee Act. Under this scheme, both foreign nationals and permanent residents may be detained indefinitely without charge and without having full access to any evidence against them. In 2004 the Federal Court of Appeal ruled that both detention and the withholding of evidence are justified in the interests of national security. Human rights are violated under this legislation, including the right to a speedy trial and the right to be presumed innocent until proven guilty.

Maher Arar's arrest as a suspected terrorist attests to the "paradigmatic break" described by Minca. Arar was born in Syria and immigrated to Canada in 1987. After earning a master's degree in computer engineering, he took a job as a telecommunications engineer in Ottawa. In 2002, during a stopover in New York while he was returning from a vacation in Tunisia, US officials detained him, accusing him of links to al-Qaeda. After intense questioning, during which he was denied legal representation and phone calls, his wrists and ankles were shackled and he was taken to a nearby building, where he was detained in a cell. The next morning he faced more intense interrogation before being put on a flight to Zurich, where he was once again grilled about his suspected terrorist ties. After three months of this, Arar was deported to Syria, where he was detained and tortured (O'Connor 2006). Arar was eventually released, but only after spending a year in custody under very difficult conditions (see Box 12.2). For much of Arar's stay in Syria, the Canadian government made few efforts to help him.

An egregious tragedy in all of this is that Arar was *not* working with al-Qaeda or any other terrorist group (O'Connor 2006). But under a state of exception, such considerations—the juridical order and human rights—are of little importance compared to national security interests. It seems that the evidence that linked him to terrorism and that resulted in an innocent man being imprisoned and tortured was provided by the RCMP—in other words, by his own country's national police force! After months of public outcry and media scrutiny, former RCMP Commissioner Giuliano Zaccardelli appeared before the House of Commons Committee on Public Safety and National Security to admit that he knew his officers had passed on false information about Arar to US authorities in 2002. Previously, he had given misleading testimony that he had only been made aware of this information in the fall of 2006. Zaccardelli subsequently resigned from the RCMP.

Maher Arar's handling by Canadian and US officials prompted a commission of inquiry headed by Justice Dennis O'Connor (O'Connor 2006). Faced with nagging allegations of corruption and dereliction of duty on the part of various government and police officials, in January 2007 Prime Minister Stephen Harper offered an official apology to Arar along with $10.5 million (plus legal fees) in compensation.

FOCUS
BOX 12.2

STATEMENTS FROM MAHER ARAR'S INTERVIEW WITH AMNESTY INTERNATIONAL

"I remember one of the immigration officers on the second day at the airport he asked me to voluntarily go to Syria—of course I refused—I explained to him why. And in one of the interviews at the embassy I explained at length that I would be tortured in Syria if I am sent back. They did not seem to care . . .

"I could not believe what I saw. I saw a cell almost the size of a grave. Three feet wide 6 feet deep and 7 feet high. And when I looked at him and said what is this he just did not say anything—he did this with his hands—so basically 'I have nothing to with that.' So I entered the cell and he locked the door. The cell had no light in it; it only had two thin mattresses [two thin blankets] on the ground. And I first thought they would keep me in that place, which I now call the grave, for a short period so that they could put pressure on me. But I was kept in that dark and filthy cell for about 10 months and 10 days. That was torture . . .

"The worst beating happened on the third day and they were trying to, you know, they were asking the same set of questions some times, some times more questions and they would beat me 3 or 4 times. They would stop, they would beat me again. They would ask questions; they would sometimes take me to another room where I could hear the other people being tortured. They would keep me there for a while. They would bring me back they would beat me again ask questions sometimes they would take me to the hallway and make me stand for a couple of hours blindfolded. That third day they wanted me, they kept telling me I had been to Afghanistan and I kept telling

them no. And at the end of the day I could not take the pain any more and I falsely confessed of having been to Afghanistan . . .

"In fighting this so-called war on terror what do we do with basic human rights? Do we throw them in the garbage and forget about our values that we pride ourselves with? Those are really the main points. And as I'm talking now, there are people, human beings being tortured . . .

"I think we have reached a point where we can confirm that these abuses, or this kind of torture is happening at different parts of the world at the behest of the CIA and the Bush Administration in general. So, there needs to be an action. Unless we do something about it, if we keep silent, if governments keep silent—in a way they are complicit."

Questions for Critical Thinking

1. In what ways "state of exception" make possible the extraordinary rendition of Maher Arar?

2. Compare what Arar suffered to similar acts of "street crime" as defined by the Criminal Code (e.g., hostage taking and abduction, assault, etc.). If these acts were carried out by a regular citizen and not by state authorities, what sort of punishment would you expect? What is an appropriate action for the Canadian government to take, if we deem them liable for the harms committed against Arar?

Source: © Amnesty International, 1 Easton Street, London WC1X 0DW, UK, http://www.amnesty.org.

Jacques Derrida: Deconstruction Is Justice

Deconstruction, if such a thing exists, should open up.

—Derrida 1987, 261

For Agamben and most others, sovereignty refers to a singular entity: to a head of state or some similar figure who can decide on the state of exception. Jacques Derrida (2005), in one of his last writings before his death in 2004, argued for a more open and wide-ranging definition. In keeping with the deconstructive ethic within which he worked throughout his life, Derrida attempted to open the concept of sovereignty to other ways of thinking and relating. For him, sovereignty was intrinsic to each and all of us, insofar as the sovereign function is "anchored in a certain ability to do something" (Balke 2005). Derrida was intent on undoing language and, in the process, peering behind discourse to reveal how it does not have a determinable meaning. He wanted to show that all language exceeds the boundaries of the taken for granted (e.g., sovereignty). **Deconstruction** attempts to reveal what is *really* going on in and through language. According to Derrida, we always say more than the surface of our language reveals.

deconstruction
An opening up of seemingly closed "things." It intends to encounter the hidden and excluded elements of language, meaning, and experience.

But what is deconstruction? Derrida often defined it in negative terms by referring to what it *is not* rather than what it *is*. For example, he argued, "deconstruction is not a method or some tool that you apply to something from the outside" (Derrida, in Caputo 1997, 9). But what is it? We might say that deconstruction has to do with opening up given linguistic arrangements to the mostly silent background suppositions that give words and phrases their meaning. Given Derrida's reticence, perhaps showing deconstruction at work would aid us here. As an example, let us consider the word "promise." What does this mean to you? When you promise your mother you will be home tonight for dinner, what are you doing? On the face of things, you are giving her an assurance that you will sit down with her to eat this evening. Unless you are truly irresponsible, there is no reason to doubt the truth of your assurance. Humans typically relate to presence, to what is uttered. Nevertheless, what is unspoken in language (the perversion of the promise) is as important to determining meaning as what we hear from another. What would happen if you did not show up? Your mother would be upset that you broke your promise, and others would certainly feel let down by your absence. Such perversions of the promise are as fundamental to its meaning as carrying through with the promised event. For a promise to be such, the statement must have the potential of falling through. If it does not, if what is assured is already guaranteed, there is no promise, only perfect conjugation of the assertion ("I will be home for supper") and the event. Again using the above example, when you promise your mum you will come to dinner while sitting at the table with fork and knife in hand, you have not promised anything.

If we had only to consider the presence of speech, we could take everyone at their word and there would be no need for contracts, warranties, or oaths. Typically, however, when we hear language we do not attempt to read its hidden meaning; instead, we relate to what is laid out before us. However, and this is the important part, when speaking and writing we say much more than what is present on the page or in conversation. Deconstruction, then, attends closely to the unspoken elements that enable the central, or privileged, structure of a given meaning formation (Pavlich, 2007).

Underlying all language is a **trace**: the silent or absent element of language that provides words with an essential part of their meaning. The trace can be likened to a footprint or a comet. That is, when we observe a comet in the sky we are struck by the *presence* of the comet and/or tail. However, what is absent here is the comet's nucleus and essence, which is composed of rock and ice. When we observe a comet we are not privy to its essence—the nucleus remains hidden. The same can be said of language. No element, no idiom, can function as a sign without at the same moment referring to another that is simply not present but that gives meaning to it (Derrida 1981). While we are at liberty to separate out presence and trace for the purposes of reducing the promise to its constituents, we (obviously) do not typically perform this operation.

Opening language up to its silent constituents (the trace) is at deconstruction's core. However, before we pass such analysis off as banal wordplay of little utility to *real* social problems, let us consider the implications of "community" under the Youth Criminal Justice Act. Community-based sanctioning and interventions occupy pride of place in the act. The preamble, for example, states:

> WHEREAS members of society share a responsibility to address the developmental challenges and the needs of young persons and to guide them into adulthood; WHEREAS communities, families, parents and others concerned with the development of young persons should, through multi-disciplinary approaches, take reasonable steps to prevent youth crime by addressing its underlying causes, to respond to the needs of young persons, and to provide guidance and support to those at risk of committing crimes. (YCJA, preamble)

Without the insights of deconstruction, we are apt to quickly read over the term *community* and be off to the next of the act's many sections. Calls for community responsibility for youth crime may be laudable. However, given that the very essence of community is exclusionary, perhaps such enthusiasm should be tempered. That is, we cannot have a community—a school, a neighbourhood, a class, a town, or whatever other configuration—without exclusion. Those who belong define themselves in opposition to the excluded. If everyone were included under this or that community rubric, the term *community* would cease to hold meaning. "Community" designates divisions between and among people. Under the YCJA it is the young offenders—their deviance and criminality—who provide impetus for the creation of community in the first instance. For example, Youth Justice Committees, which are made up of community members who hear and adjudicate relatively minor crimes committed by youths, find their meaning and definition in the wrongdoings of young people. A crime committed by a young offender brings this community together. Because of his or her contravention, the young person becomes not only the rationale for the formation of community but also, by virtue of the offence, its antithesis. Pavlich (2005) maintains that this is the very essence of community: "communities are identified—implicitly or explicitly—by exclusion." Before declaring this a meaningless play of words, let us remember the repulsive consequences that may accrue when exuberance for and devotion to community has spilled over its limits: ethnic wars of annihilation have been waged, genocide has been carried out, and prisons have become overcrowded with the residues of such intolerance (Hogeveen 2006).

Communities may derive their *raison d'être* in relation to a particularly deviant and troubling other. A string of car thefts or a proliferation of graffiti in a

trace
The mark of absence in words that is the necessary condition of thought and experience (Derrida 1976).

geographical space may inspire previously disorganized citizens to band together against this provocation. Writes Hogeveen (2005):

> Recent efforts to rid (affluent) neighbourhoods of prostitutes, the use of CCTV on busy city streets, **broken windows policing**, and gated neighbourhoods are poignant examples of community inspired attempts to exclude the 'other' while shoring up a privileged lifestyle. This regulation of the 'other' may contribute to and assist in shoring up the creation of community, but it also holds the insidious possibility of contributing to exclusionary practices which limit, rather than encourage, wider and more inclusive patterns of harmony. (295; see also Pavlich, 2005)

Through the examples of promises and community, we can see that deconstructive critique involves "opening up" things to examine what lies behind and beyond presence. However, there is one word that *cannot* be deconstructed: **justice**. In common parlance, we use the term *justice* in a variety of ways: we have a justice system; there are Justices of the Peace; Canada boasts a federal Department of Justice; "justice" is used in law and legislation to imply the impartiality of the system (e.g., the Youth Criminal *Justice* Act); and there is even a village in Manitoba called Justice (northwest of Brandon). But by far the most commonplace understanding of justice (see Box 12.3) is *vengeance*. Here, justice refers to an ethic of punishment that delivers obvious signs of unpleasantness to offenders. We live in an era during which war, prison overcrowding, and vigilantism are justified in the name of justice. For example, the US government constructed Osama bin Laden as a moral monster and a lunatic for crimes perpetrated on the United States. All the while, the civilian and military death toll from the American campaign for "justice" in Iraq continued to mount. The costs in dollars and human life are spiralling out of control, while domestic atrocities and oppressions are glossed over by a nation seeking justice.

If these are all instances of "justice," how can Derrida say it does not exist? It is because Derrida seeks a different kind of justice, one that goes beyond "right, a justice finally removed from the fatality of vengeance" (1994, 21). One of Derrida's most faithful followers, John Caputo (1997), puts the situation this way: "Justice is not a present entity or order, not an existing reality or regime; nor is it even an ideal *eidos* towards which we earthlings down below heave and sigh while contemplating its heavenly form. Justice is the absolutely unforeseeable prospect (a paralyzing paradox) in virtue in which the things that get deconstructed are deconstructed" (131). For Derrida, then, "justice appears as a promise, beyond law, and is itself incalculable, infinite and undeconstructable" (Pavlich 2007, 989). It is not a thing or a person that we can hold up as exemplary, nor is it a criterion for future generations. To maintain that Canada is a just nation or that we ourselves are just would be to conclude that our work is done. It would be the height of injustice to think that justice exists here in tolerant Canada in the midst of the unimaginable suffering of Indigenous people, the tragic abuse of female partners, and the expanding extremes of poverty and wealth . . . and we could go on (Caputo 1997). But, you may conclude, the law is just . . . right? On the contrary, there are situations in which the application of law was legal but unjust (e.g., Arar, Menezes). This is not to say that law is unnecessary or that it is wrong in its conception. Only that law can be unjust in its application and in its fundamental opposition to justice.

broken windows policing
Just as houses with broken windows indicate that nobody cares about the neighbourhood, proponents of this policing style feel that tolerating minor misbehaviour will mean that residents will be afraid to use their streets. They feel that police should quickly deal with minor incivilities such as panhandling, vandalism, and other behaviours that contribute to fear of crime. Critics feel that this policing style potentially discriminates against the poor.

justice
For Derrida, since it is perpetually deferred, justice cannot be defined adequately. It is not contained in or constrained by law. It is infinite. It is "to come."

FOCUS

BOX 12.3

CRIME PAYS OFF IN CANADA

Consider the assumptions made about "justice" in the following article: What are the sources of the reporter's dissatisfaction with the Canadian criminal justice system? What expectations does she have about justice, and in what ways are they not being met? Also, note how she speaks as though her views represent taken-for-granted values that we all share and how she compares us (the "good" law-abiding, and deserving) with youth offenders (the "bad," dangerous, and undeserving).

Maybe this holiday weekend you're putting in another shift to help pay for your child's college tuition.

Maybe you are that student, worried about how you're going to put the cash together for school and your first apartment.

Or maybe you're a victim of crime, and you can't afford the counselling you so desperately need.

Too bad you're not a teen killer, because then you'd be showered—thanks to the Canadian government—with more than $100,000 a year.

It's called the Intensive Rehabilitative Custody and Supervision program or IRCS and for 24 of this country's worst youth offenders, the little-known federal justice program is akin to hitting the jackpot.

In return for accepting treatment for their mental issues, serious violent offenders can escape adult prison and do easy time instead in a youth facility, like Ontario's Sprucedale, while taxpayers spend $100,375 per inmate for academic courses, counselling, "life skills" and reintegration.

The theory is that these heavily damaged "kids" need intensive help if they are ever to find their way back into society.

What kind of help, you may ask?

Well, there was the $700 piece of wood we purchased for a killer who brutally beat and sexually assaulted 15-year-old Elisha Mercer under the Lorne Bridge in Brantford in 2001. According to a Sprucedale insider, the young murderer was given the lumber to fashion his very own homemade guitar.

"It makes us all want to vomit," says the employee, who doesn't want to be named. "The victims should be getting this money, not them."

When told by the *Sun*, Elisha's mom was outraged to learn what constitutes therapy for the killer of her only child. "It's ridiculous, absolutely ridiculous," Wilma Martin says. "These have been very hard years. My husband and I split up because of what happened, he took off and I was left to pay the mortgage and the bills. I came close to losing my home.

"I could have used $100,000."

Instead, Ottawa last year earmarked $3.4 million for the country's worst of the worst young murderers and rapists with psychological disorders.

In 2004, one of the first accepted into the new program was the 18-year-old Hamilton youth who had killed Jonathan Romero the year before. Romero, 18, had gone to Lime Ridge Mall to buy a Christmas present for his mom. Standing on the sidelines when his friend got involved in a fight, Romero was sucker punched by the youth and after falling to the ground, was savagely punched four more times in the head and neck. He died hours later in hospital.

A judge turned down the Crown's request for a 6½-year adult sentence for manslaughter and instead agreed to just 30 months in custody at Sprucedale. The young offender was deemed eligible for IRCS because—wait for it—he was diagnosed with attention deficit and hyperactivity disorder, post traumatic stress disorder, and mood disorder.

If only every kid with ADD could get free one-on-one counselling and government-sponsored perks.

The Hamilton youth was assigned a "life coach" and various IRCS counselling programs. He was released four weeks ago to a six-month reintegration period, but according to the Sprucedale worker, none of the expensive rehabilitation seemed to have any impact at all. "He felt no remorse whatsoever for his crime and anyone who worked with him over the last three years will tell you the same thing," he says. "He was a poster child for everything that was wrong with the system."

"Do I think he still poses a danger to society? You bet I do. At that summer camp, he didn't learn a thing."

(continued)

The youth, stung by a previous article slamming easy time at Sprucedale, insists he's a changed man in a letter published in the *Sun*. "Every achievement that I completed here is to the memory of that boy."

According to his former worker, the letter is just another demonstration of how he's learned to talk the talk as well as how to use the IRCS program to his advantage.

Now 20, the Hamilton killer was boasting to everyone that the federal government will now be paying for his college tuition, laptop computer, and his living expenses. On his $16,000 IRCS wish list, he also requested a plasma screen TV and new designer clothing. The insider says he doesn't know if those goodies were granted as well.

"All of this stuff," says the angry youth worker, "an average family can't afford and these kids are getting it for murdering other kids? It's unbelievable. The public needs to know."

Oh Canada, why are we such gullible souls?

Questions for Critical Thinking

1. What are the sources of the reporter's dissatisfaction with the Canadian justice system?

2. Provide examples of how the reporter uses stereotypes and unsubstantiated assumptions to create an "us" and a "them" in her narrative.

Michele Mandel, "Crime Pays off in Canada," *Toronto Sun*, July 1, 2007, http://torontosun.com/News/Columnists/Mandel_Michele/2007/07/01/4304140.html. Material republished with the express permission of Toronto Sun, a division of Postmedia Network Inc.

Criticisms of Critical Criminology

Given the diversity of critical criminological theorization, criticisms tend to be more specific to particular critical criminological approaches, rather than general and applicable to all forms of critical criminology. That said, there are a few complaints that are often heard with respect to critical criminology. The first, and the one possibly most glaringly felt by readers of this chapter, has to do with the sometimes obscure and abstract nature of critical criminological theorizing. Does critical criminology fetishize theory and disguise meaning behind

TABLE 12.1 ■ Contemporary Critical Criminology

Theory	Theorist(s)	Key Elements
Governmentality	Michel Foucault	Understandings of power and governance should be broadly conceived. Power creates subjects in dispersed locations in accordance with preconceived and useful ends.
Actuarialism, risk, and the risk society	Foucault, Beck	Social problems are no longer considered issues requiring solutions, but risks to be managed. In the "risk society" eventualities can be calculated and thus managed. Risk of victimization can be mitigated in accordance with risk factors.
Cultural criminology	Ferrell, Hayward, Young	"Crime" is culturally negotiated. The importance of adrenaline in the commission of crime is emphasized. These theorists attend to how rule breaking challenges the justness of law. It produces dangerous knowledge through critical engagement with knowledge (including criminology).
Field theory	Bourdieu, Wacquant	Society is divided into fields, which are basic areas of social activity. In the contemporary bureaucratic field, social support is increasingly disciplinary and punitive. It is taking on characteristics of the "right hand" of the state.
Sovereignty and the state of exception	Agamben	Inspired by Schmitt, Foucault, and Benjamin, Agamben has constructed a nuanced understanding of sovereignty and its exceptions. During times of crisis, emergency, or exception, subject's rights and the rule of law are suspended in the name of the sovereign.
Deconstruction	Derrida	Language is infinitely complex. Deconstruction attempts to uncover silences in discourse. Justice is an infinite promise.

difficult language? Critical criminologists would argue that such terminology is necessary to push criminological thought in new and transgressive directions, beyond the mundane, taken-for-granted meanings of regular language. A second criticism follows from the first and is perhaps the more serious one for critical criminologists: What are the practical implications of critical criminology? If critical criminology is to be more than ivory tower navel-gazing, it must have implications for the real world of crime, crime control, and social justice. And some find it difficult to discern a call to action in the theoretical language of contemporary critical criminology. Yet all of the critical criminologists with whom we are familiar aspire towards such real-world change. Their dedication is not to theory for the sake of theory, but rather to using theory to think about the worlds of crime and victimization in new, more just terms.

QUESTIONS FOR CRITICAL THINKING

1. Based on what you already know about the criminal justice system, what are you critical of within this system?
2. What does it mean to critique the criminal justice system (as critical criminology does) as opposed to simply criticizing the way it currently operates?

Summary

- Critical criminology attempts to draw attention to hidden and overlooked injustices scattered throughout our world. It seeks to highlight and genuinely grasp inequalities, discrimination, and suffering.

- Early critical criminology in Canada, inspired by Taylor, Walton, and Young's *The New Criminology*, maintained a focus on how economic power is implicated in the operations of criminal justice. Efforts to create a unified collective among Canadian critical criminologists were, however, cut short by several factors, including the growing diversity of critical criminology.

- Today's critical criminology does not maintain this dedication to a political economic approach to crime. Critique is less and less understood as a form of judgment gauged upon a fixed standard of evaluation and more and more as a means for disrupting and destabilizing taken-for-granted assumptions about and approaches to crime. The goal is not to prescribe a new social order but rather to create opportunities for unencumbered ideas and practices to arise and take form.

- Foucault contributed to critical criminology through his work on power. For Foucault, power is not solely repressive—it is also productive. Through the tactics of discipline, surveillance, and governmentality, power shapes individuals so that they are transformed (or transform themselves) into more governable subjects.

- Actuarialism, risk, and the risk society are all terms used to understand the growing fixation on insurance-like evaluations of risk and harm in contemporary criminal justice practices. Through an understanding of the broader social context producing the "risk society," critical criminologists are able to challenge the logic of various risk management approaches to criminal justice.

- Cultural criminology revives the ethnographic tradition in criminology and directs it towards discovering crime as a lived experience. Cultural criminologists investigate the cultural production and representation of crime and our understandings of crime and thereby question popular notions about crime and criminal justice.

- Bourdieu's "field theory" alerts critical criminologists to the many forms of power that are amassed and the role they play in the domination over and definition of excluded and criminalized classes. Crime, therefore, is understood as a consequence not only of economic domination but also of symbolic, cultural, and social domination.

- Giorgio Agamben points us to the power of the sovereign to define individuals as being outside of law. Thus, built into law is the state of exception—that is, the sovereign's ability to suspend rights and protections. And through this concept criminal law is vividly revealed as a source of exclusion.

- Jacques Derrida's concept of deconstruction provides critical criminologists with a tool for evaluating what is hidden or unspoken within social life and, in particular, criminal justice practices. It is a particularly powerful tool for unpacking the meanings hidden in fashionable criminal justice jargon, such as "community," "safety," and "security."

NET WORK

Visit the American Society of Criminology Divisions page at http://www.asc41.com/divisions.htm. Compare and contrast the description of the Critical Criminology Division with other divisions of the ASC. What makes it "critical" in contrast to the other divisions?

Interactionist Theories

13

ROBERT A. STEBBINS
University of Calgary

Learning Objectives

After reading this chapter, you should be able to

- Describe primary and secondary deviation and explain how primary deviation leads to secondary deviation.
- Understand the process of drift among juvenile delinquents.
- Explain how moral entrepreneurs create and enforce the law.
- Discuss the various contingencies that criminals encounter in their deviant careers.
- Understand how people are socialized into a life of crime.
- Outline the strengths and limitations of interactionist theories of deviance.

S train and conflict theories deal with causes of crime at the level of social structure. *Strain theorists* relate crime to variables such as cultural goals and the access to opportunities provided by society. For *conflict theorists*, cleavages between different groups in society and the power relations among these groups are critical in explaining criminality. *Interactionist theories*, for their part, turn our attention to the smaller details of social life. They view crime as a consequence of interpersonal relationships and of what those relationships mean.

A central concept in interactionist theories of crime is the *deviant career*, or the passage of an individual through the stages of one or more related deviant identities. This idea is at the heart of labelling theory, which explains how the social response to initial, tentative acts of deviance can move a person (not always willingly) towards a deviant identity and a deviant career. The other important interactionist theory discussed in this chapter—differential association—sets out how people learn to be criminals through interaction with other criminals and how they acquire a criminal identity.

Interactionist theory in criminology focuses on the interchanges people have with one another and on the meanings of these interchanges in the past, present, and future. Blumer (1986) notes that **symbolic interactionism**, the broader theory from which the interactionist theories of crime are derived, rests on three premises. First, people act towards the human and nonhuman objects in their lives according to the meanings those objects have for them. Second, these meanings emerge from interactions among people. Third, the meanings of objects

symbolic interactionism
A sociological perspective that focuses on the dynamics of how people interpret social situations and negotiate the meanings of these situations with others. It differs from more structurally focused perspectives in seeing individuals as actively creating the social world rather than just acting within the constraints of culture and social structure.

learned in this manner are applied and occasionally modified as individuals interpret how objects and their meanings fit particular social situations, the people in them, and their reasons for being there.

Much of this chapter is about criminal interactions, meanings, interpretations, and situations. Before turning to these processes, however, let us set the stage for discussion with a brief illustration of the three premises operating on the scene of a crime. The following interview with Allen, about 20 years old, shows how the meaning of a situation changed through social interaction with other people present in an all-night drugstore:

> From what I understand from them, they didn't go in there with the intent to rob or beat anybody up or anything. I think they only really wanted to buy some gum and cigarettes, but by being drunk, they was talking pretty tough, and so the lady behind the counter automatically got scared. . . . The druggist . . . got a little pushy or ordered them out of the store, and by them being all fired up, naturally the next thing they did was jump on him.
>
> So now what do you have? You've got a drugstore. You've got a scared lady in the corner somewhere with her hands over her face. You've got a beat-up druggist laying on the floor. You've got three dudes that came in for chewing gum and cigarettes, but now they got two cash registers. So what do they do? They take the cash. Wasn't nothing to stop them, and it was there. Why would they leave it? They're thieves anyway and supposed to be hustlers. . . . There wasn't nothing to stop them, so they just took the money. (Katz, 1990)

THE CANADIAN PRESS/Adrian Wyld

Labelling theorists believe that being found guilty in a criminal court can force a person to drastically change his or her lifestyle.

The Deviant Career

Interactionism centres chiefly on what happens to criminals once their deviant activities commence. Interactionists have observed, for example, that some groups or individuals have enough power to force the label of deviant on less-powerful groups or individuals. The **labelling** process, however, is not always accurate. It is not even always fair. Some deviants escape public detection of their behaviour. Some who have not deviated are nonetheless labelled as having done so, despite their protests to the contrary. The application of the deviant label is sometimes subject to considerable negotiation between possibly deviant people and those in a position to label them as deviant.

Thus, interactionist theory in criminology helps explain the establishment of moral rules, their application through labelling, and the long-term consequences of these two processes for deviants and for society. In interactionist theory, labelling and its consequences are viewed as unfolding within the deviant career.

A **career**, be it in deviance or in a legitimate occupation, is the passage of an individual through recognized stages in one or more related identities. Careers are further composed of adjustments to, and interpretations of, the contingencies and turning points encountered at each stage. For example, Sampson and Laub (2003) found that crime declined with age sooner or later for all the offender groups they studied. Within that pattern, however, Short (1990) noted that careers in youth crime are likely to be prolonged after certain turning points have been reached. One of these turning points is an early interest in delinquent activities; another is an interest in drugs. The inability to find legitimate employment, a career contingency, also contributes to continued criminality. Type of offence, however, has been found to be unrelated to length of career in youth crime and even to the rate at which it is perpetrated. During the careers of young offenders and other deviants, there is a sense of continuity. This sense is fostered by perceptions of increasing opportunities, by growing sophistication, and perhaps by recognition among one's associates for skill in, or at least commitment to, the special endeavour.

Primary Deviation

Lemert (1972) contributed two important concepts to the study of deviant careers: **primary deviation** and **secondary deviation**. Primary deviation produces little change in one's everyday routine or lifestyle. The individual engages in deviance infrequently, has few compunctions about it, and encounters few practical problems when performing it. A person who out of curiosity occasionally takes an opioid drug supplied by someone else exemplifies primary deviation.

Primary deviation occurs in the early stages of the deviant career, between the first deviant act and some indefinite point at which deviance becomes a way of life. Subsequently, at a still more advanced stage, secondary deviation (discussed later) sets in. According to Matza (2010), one precondition of deviance is a willingness to engage in it. That is, the individual must have an affinity—innate or acquired—for the intended act (e.g., theft, homicide, drug use). This affinity helps him or her choose among existing options. By way of illustration, imagine

labelling
According to labelling theory, deviance is a quality not of the act but of the label that others attach to it. This raises the question of who applies the label and who is labelled. The application of a label and the response of others to the label may result in a person becoming committed to a deviant identity.

career
In common use, this refers to the sequence of stages through which people in a particular occupational sector move during the course of their employment. It has also been applied to the various stages of personal involvement with criminal activity.

primary deviation
Occurs when an individual commits deviant acts but fails to adopt a primary self-identity as a deviant.

secondary deviation
Occurs when an individual accepts the label of deviant. The result is adoption of a deviant self-identity that confirms and stabilizes the deviant lifestyle.

someone who believes the rich cheat others to get their money. This person has an affinity for stealing from the rich. That affinity could lead the individual into crimes against the rich when faced with such unpleasant alternatives as poverty, unemployment, or tedious manual labour.

Underlying the willingness to engage in deviance lies a weak commitment to conventional norms and identities. Few young people have a strong value commitment to deviant norms and identities; instead, they **drift** between the world of respectability and that of deviance. They are "neither compelled to deeds nor freely choosing them; neither different in any simple or fundamental sense from the law abiding, nor the same; conforming to certain traditions in . . . life while partially unreceptive to other more conventional traditions" (Matza 1990, 28).

Matza was writing about American males who were young offenders. He found these youths firmly attached to certain marginal, masculine, *subterranean traditions* or ways of life. They found satisfaction in drinking, smoking, renouncing work, being tough, and enjoying the hedonic pleasures of "real" men. Matza's subjects saw themselves as grown and mature, but their behaviour was hardly a true picture of adult life in general in the United States.

Lemert (1972) explains how this peculiar orientation can set one adrift towards deviance:

> While some fortunate individuals by insightful endowment or by virtue of the stabilizing nature of their situation can foresee more distant social consequences of their actions and behave accordingly, not so for most people. Much human behaviour is situationally oriented and geared to meeting the many and shifting claims which others make upon them. The loose structuring and swiftly changing facade and content of modern social situations frequently make it difficult to decide which means will insure the ends sought. Often choice is a compromise between what is sought and what can be sought. . . . All this makes me believe that most people drift into deviance by specific actions rather than by informed choices of social roles and statuses. (79–80)

For young offenders (adolescent and adult), social control has failed. This failure occurs because it is important for deviant individuals to enjoy good standing with their friends in the group. Good standing is attained by honouring and practising the marginal, or subterranean, traditions that Matza describes. The quest for honour among peers helps explain how entire groups of youth can drift towards deviance (Hirschi 2001).

It appears that much, if not all, of this is applicable to Canada. For instance, a comparative study conducted in California and Alberta found that ties to peers were important in the sample of delinquent youth; being in touch with home and school were valued much less (Linden and Fillmore 1981).

The young offender subculture (see Chapter 11) is composed of many elements, one of the most important being the **moral rhetorics** (Schwendinger and Schwendinger 1985) used to justify deviant behaviour. Each rhetoric consists of a set of largely taken-for-granted guiding principles, sometimes logically inconsistent and always selectively applied according to the social situations in which youths find themselves. The rhetoric of *egoism* is most often used by those who still feel guilty about their deviant acts. Typically, these are early offenders,

drift
A psychological state of weak normative attachment to either deviant or conventional ways.

moral rhetorics
In the study of crime, this is the set of claims and assertions deviants make to justify their deviant behaviour. The moral rhetoric of a group is an important component of socialization into a deviant identity.

who have learned various ways to neutralize the **stigma** that comes with their behaviour—for example, by claiming that they steal in response to the greed and immorality of shopkeepers whose prices are unfair. Later, young offenders are more likely to use *instrumental* rhetoric when justifying their acts. Here they stress the cunning and power they bring to bear against people who are otherwise more powerful and uncontrollable. Fraud, deceit, and violence are used to pursue deviant aims whenever they appear to pay off, whenever these youths can benefit from a weak moment in the lives of such people. The main point here is that young offenders, like people in many other walks of life, justify what they do. Though the law-abiding world sees them otherwise, offenders have their ways of defending their deviant acts as morally right.

During the primary deviation stages of a deviant career, young offenders and young adults drift, in part because they lack *value commitment* to either conventional or deviant values. Value commitment is an attitude towards an identity, one that develops when a person gains exceptional rewards from assuming that identity (Stebbins 1970). Young men and women drifting between criminal and respectable pursuits have found few, if any, enduring benefits in either type of activity. This pattern, however, begins to change as their contacts with agents of social control increase.

Agents of Social Control

Those members of society who help check deviant behaviour are known as agents of social control. They include the police, judges, lawmakers, prison personnel, probation and parole officers, and ordinary citizens with an active interest in maintaining law and order as they define it. Groups of ordinary citizens and lawmakers sometimes join hands as **moral entrepreneurs**: "Rules are the products of someone's initiative, and we can think of the people who exhibit such enterprise as *moral entrepreneurs*. Two related species—rule creators and rule enforcers—will occupy our attention" (Becker 1963, 147).

The prototype of the rule creator, Becker observes, is the crusading reformer, whose dissatisfaction with existing rules is acute and who, therefore, campaigns for legal change (i.e., for adding new laws or procedures and rescinding old ones) and sometimes for attitudinal change intended to lead to "proper" behaviour. Canadian society is replete with crusades, both past and present, such as those which seek to eliminate drug abuse, discourage use of alcohol, reduce the availability of pornography, and stop the exploitation of women in the workplace. Moral entrepreneurs are currently working to curb Internet crime (for a further example involving cannabis legalization, see Box 13.1).

To conduct an effective crusade, moral entrepreneurs must construct an argument capable of convincing the community that a deep and genuine internal threat exists. This process of collective definition (Hewitt and Hall 1973; Spector and Kitsuse 2000) centres largely on the "claims-making activities" of entrepreneurs, which include these:

1. They assert the existence of a particular condition, situation, or state of affairs in which human action is implicated as a cause.
2. They define the asserted condition as offensive, harmful, undesirable, or otherwise problematic to the society but as nonetheless amenable to correction by humans.
3. They stimulate public scrutiny of the condition as the claims makers see it.

stigma
As used by Erving Goffman (1922–82), a personal characteristic that is negatively evaluated by others and thus distorts and discredits the public identity of the individual. For example, a prison record may become a stigmatized attribute. The stigma may lead to the adoption of a self-identity that incorporates the negative social evaluation.

moral entrepreneurs
Someone who defines new rules and laws or who advocates stricter enforcement of existing laws. Often such entrepreneurs have a financial or organizational interest in particular definitions or applications of law.

empirical evidence
Evidence as observed through the senses; it can be seen, touched, heard, smelled, tasted, and, to some extent, measured. This is the only form of scientifically acceptable evidence.

The claims are explained by quasi-theories. Unlike scientific theories, quasi-theories are selectively constructed to square with the claims makers' views, are seldom responsive to **empirical evidence**, and contain simple explanations for complex, ill-defined problems. The modern "conspiracy theory" is quasi-theory bearing on politics and politicians. Uscinski and Parent (2014) define conspiracy theory as a belief that a secret conspiracy has been decisive in producing a political event or evil outcome that the theorists strongly disapprove of. A conspiracy theorist is someone who either believes an existing conspiracy theory or has created it. Sometimes the same person is both creator and believer. Conspiracy theory is a label placed by moral entrepreneurs on such creators and believers. Some crimes can be the result of conspiracies; in politics, by contrast, conspiracies are usually not criminal, but rather externalized pipe dreams about how a particular event or situation has come to pass (Stebbins 2017, 85). In this regard the typical modern politician tends to parade at least four different versions of knowledge: known facts, bogus facts (intentional lies), erroneous claims to factuality (unwitting lies), and vague claims the truth of which is difficult to establish with certainty. The latter consist of, for example, platitudes, conspiracy theories, and nearly countless hyperbolic statements.

Moral entrepreneurs also enforce legislated rules, applying them to people who misbehave. Such rules provide enforcers (police, security personnel) with jobs as well as with justifications for them. Since the enforcers want to keep their jobs, they are eager to demonstrate that enforcement is effective. Yet they also realize there are more infractions than they can possibly prevent or respond to. Therefore, they must establish priorities. Thus,

> whether a person who commits a deviant act is in fact labelled a deviant depends on many things extraneous to his actual behaviour: whether the enforcement official feels that at this time he must make some show of doing his job in order to justify his position, whether the misbehaver shows proper deference to the enforcer, whether the "fix" has been put in, and where the kind of act he has committed stands on the enforcer's list of priorities. (Becker 1963)

FOCUS   BOX 13.1

MORAL ENTREPRENEURSHIP FOR LEGALIZING CANNABIS IN CANADA

Canadians have been regularly consuming marijuana and other cannabis products for nearly a century, despite their prohibition. This has been a costly practice, for the measures taken to enforce this prohibition have squandered billions of dollars on ineffective or incomplete law enforcement. These efforts have also clogged our judicial system. Various policies calling for decriminalization or legalization of the drug were recommended by the 1969–72 Commission of Enquiry into the Non-Medical Use of Drugs, the 2002 Canadian Senate Special Committee on Illegal Drugs, and the 2002 House of Commons Special Committee on the Non-Medical Use of Drugs. This prohibition will end when the Cannabis Act becomes law in 2018. Criminalization of the drug endangered Canadians because it spawned gang-related crime and the smuggling of weapons—this is one of the government's reasons for legalization.

At the 2012 Liberal Party of Canada Convention, the Young Liberals put forward a resolution calling for a new

Liberal government to legalize cannabis. This would entail the regulation and taxation of the drug's production, distribution, and use. The resolution proposed strict penalties for illegal trafficking, importation, and exportation of cannabis as well as for driving while impaired by its consumption. According to the resolution, a new Liberal government would "invest significant resources" in programs designed to prevent, and educate about, the health risks and consequences of using marijuana and the dependency it can create. Youth will be especially targeted by these programs. The Young Liberals also called for a new Liberal government to extend amnesty to all Canadians previously convicted of simple and minimal possession of the drug. Also, all criminal records related to such possession would be eliminated. Lastly, the resolution called for a new Liberal government to work with Canada's provinces and local governments to fashion a "coordinated regulatory approach" to marijuana. However, the new government would maintain "significant federal responsibility" for controlling the drug, always doing so in consideration of provincial health jurisdictions and regional concerns and practices.

Several groups, including MADD (Mothers Against Drunk Driving) became counter moral entrepreneurs to the legalization of cannabis in Canada. MADD reprinted this newspaper story on their website:

As Mothers Against Drunk Driving and police departments continue to discourage drinking driving, the likelihood of legalized marijuana becoming a reality is creating a new challenge.*

MADD Canada president Patricia Hynes-Coates says the new marijuana laws will likely increase the number of

drug-impaired drivers, and wants measures to be taken to ensure police are prepared.

"Have the saliva test available so we can actually prove impairment," said Hynes-Coates. "If we do this and we're not ready, we know that deaths will skyrocket."

Chief John Bates of the Saint John Police Department says Ottawa needs to understand a predicament faced by police departments from coast-to-coast.

"I think that those who are going to change the legislation in this country to permit people to smoke marijuana, had better be prepared to step up to help us fight impaired driving," said Chief Bates.

The chief says training drug recognition experts can be costly.

"We have to send them to the United States for training for weeks at a time," said Chief Bates. "This all comes at a cost."

Hynes-Coates was in the Maritimes on Tuesday to launch the annual Red Ribbon Campaign to combat impaired driving over the holidays.

The efforts by MADD Canada and other groups that objected to the legalization of cannabis have not succeeded, and many of the proposals of the Young Liberals have become part of the implementation framework adopted by the federal government.

Questions for Critical Thinking

1. Why was the federal government willing to legalize cannabis? What arguments did opponents use to criticize the proposed legislation?

2. Do you think other recreational drugs will eventually be legalized? Why or why not?

*From "MADD Canada concerned about marijuana legalization," CTV News, https://atlantic.ctvnews.ca/madd-canada-concerned-about-marijuana-legalization-1.3182563. Reprinted by permission of Bell Media.

Source: From Nadia Moharib, 2012. "Wheel and Weed Don't Mix, Says Study," Calgary Sun, May 17. Material republished with the express permission of Calgary Sun, a division of Postmedia Network Inc.

It is no accident, then, that the least influential members of society (e.g., the poor or certain **ethnic groups**) are often caught in the web of social control and labelled deviant out of proportion to their numbers. In other words, deviance is created in part by people in society. Moral entrepreneurs make certain laws, the infraction of which constitutes deviance. Moral entrepreneurs also apply these laws to particular people, labelling them as some kind of deviant. As Becker (1963) points out, "deviance is not a quality of the act. . . . The deviant is one to whom that label has successfully been applied; deviant behaviour is behaviour that people so label."

But rules are applied to some people and not to others; application is sometimes biased. Hence, some people remain at large as secret but potentially identifiable deviants. Others go through life falsely accused of antisocial acts. To discover why only certain people are labelled deviant, labelling theorists also study those who make the laws that deviants violate and how those laws are applied.

ethnic groups
A group of individuals having a common, distinctive subculture. Ethnic groups differ from races; the term implies that values, norms, behaviour, and language, not necessarily physical appearance, are important distinguishing characteristics.

Those publicly labelled "deviant" generally face some sort of community or societal reaction to their misdeeds (Lemert 1951). Depending on the nature of the deviance, the deviant may experience one or more of the following: imprisonment, ostracism, fines, torture, surveillance, and ridicule. All labelled deviants soon learn they must cope with stigma.

A *stigma* is a black mark, or disgrace, associated with a deviant identity. It is part of the societal reaction—that is, a collective construction by agents of social control, and by ordinary members of the community, of the supposed nature of the unlawful act and the person perpetrating it. As Goffman (1986) and Link and Phelan (2001) note, the collective image of stigma is constructed from social, physical, or psychological attributes the deviant is believed to possess. Here *imputed* possession of the attributes is far more important than *actual* possession.

After years of participant observation of outlaw motorcycle gangs, Watson (1984) and Wolf (1991) concluded that their members had a mentality and background noticeably different from what was imputed to them by the general public. They were not especially hostile to most social institutions, including government, education, and the family. Most members had finished high school and had occasionally held jobs. Some had gone to college; some were military veterans. Nearly every member had been married at least once. They were, to be sure, not particularly successful in these areas of life, which helped to account for their tendency to live for the moment. And though they were basically not violent men, they thought it important to be seen as "manly" in the most traditional sense of the term.

Secondary Deviation

The existence of moral rules and the stigma that arises when society believes those rules have been violated together set the stage for secondary deviation. Deviation becomes secondary when deviants see that their behaviour has substantially modified their ways of living. A strong desire to deviate can foster this redefinition of one's deviant activities; so can extreme feelings of guilt. But accusations of deviance are typically the most influential factor behind the redefinition. Being labelled by the authorities as a murderer, rapist, prostitute, or cheque forger and being sanctioned for such behaviour forces the deviant to change his or her lifestyle drastically. As Lemert (1972) puts it, "this secondary deviant . . . is a person whose life and identity are organized around the facts of deviance."

What does a lifestyle of secondary deviation actually consist of? Stebbins (1997) defines lifestyle as

> a distinctive set of shared patterns of tangible behaviour that is organized around a set of coherent interests or social conditions or both, that is explained and justified by a set of related values, attitudes, and orientations and that, under certain conditions, becomes the basis for a separate, common social identity for its participants. (350)

For example, drug addicts regularly buy or produce their drugs, habitually follow certain practices designed to prevent discovery by the authorities, and routinely consume the illicit substances thereby acquired. Some addicts, prostitutes among them, justify this lifestyle as an escape from intolerable working conditions. The identity of addict is pejorative, however, as the label

FIGURE 13.1 ■ **Links between Primary Deviance, Societal Reaction, and Secondary Deviance**

"junkie" clearly indicates. The links between primary deviance, societal reaction, and secondary deviance are illustrated in Figure 13.1.

Among the factors leading to secondary deviation is society's tendency to treat someone's criminality as a **master status** (Becker 1963). This status overrides all other statuses in perceived importance. Whatever laudable achievements the deviant might claim, such as a good job or a successful marriage, this person is judged in the community primarily by the fact of deviance (see Box 13.2). Liberman, Kirk, and Kideuk (2014) found that first arrests increased the likelihood of both subsequent offending and subsequent arrest. Offending and being arrested were discovered to be separate processes, however, suggesting that deviant labels trigger what the authors call "secondary sanctioning."

Lack of success in attaining respectability among nondeviants, or a perceived low probability of achieving it, may lead to interaction with other deviants. Here we consider a unique aspect of the interaction between the labelled deviant and the organized deviant group. There are several characteristics of this type of group life that stimulate or maintain such behaviour. These characteristics are effective partly because the wider community has rejected the deviant.

As Becker (1963) observed, individuals who gain entrance to a deviant group often learn from that group how to cope with the problems associated with their deviance. This makes being a deviant easier. Furthermore, the deviant acquires rationalizations for his or her values, attitudes, and behaviours, which come to full bloom in the organized group. While these rationalizations vary greatly, note that the very existence of rationalizations seems to point to the fact that some deviants feel a need to deal with certain conventional attitudes and values they have also internalized.

Prus and Sharper (1991) quote one of their respondents, who was explaining how he developed the callous attitude prized by professional card hustlers:

> When I first got involved in hustling, my attitudes were less calloused [*sic*]. I might be at a stag of some sort and say some fellow is losing a little money. Through the course of the evening, talking back and forth, you find out that maybe he just got married, or that he has some kids and here he's writing cheques and I would slow down. If you pull something like this with a crew [of hustlers], the other guys will want to know what the hell you are doing! They're waiting for you to take him, and you're saying, "Well gee, the guy doesn't have much money." You would get the worst tongue lashing! The position they take is that "You can't have feelings on the road." And it's true, if you start saying to yourself, "Well, maybe I better not beat this guy or that guy," you would soon be out of business or at least you would really cut down on your profits.

master status

A status overriding all others in perceived importance. Whatever other personal or social qualities individuals possess, they are judged primarily by this one attribute. *Criminal* exemplifies a master status that influences the community's identification of an individual.

FOCUS

BOX 13.2

THE PRISON-MADE TATTOO AS MASTER STATUS

Prison-made tattoos serve as master statuses both inside and outside the walls. For anyone who knows their meaning, particular tattoos communicate particular attitudes and memberships. These identifiers tend to override all others. (Peter Wollheim and Christine Brady, "Marked Men")

Prison-made tattoos are a form of communication for inmates who live in a situation that bans most other means of self-expression. These messages, which are easily "read" by other inmates, tell a lot about the wearer, including gang membership, status in prison, family relationships, special life events, spiritual beliefs, and personal values.

Reciprocal influences exist between prison and professional tattooing. For many years, prison tattoos emulated the techniques of professional tattoo artists. While the professional shops had access to tattoo machines as early as the 1890s, prison tattoo artists relied on a similar hand-held method that used a bundle of sewing needles affixed to a handle. Using this crude setup, a strong line could be worked that was very similar to that created by the electric machine, which also used several needles.

Tattoos made in this style have a heavy outline with little or no interior shading.

In the 1970s, prison tattoo artists began to use a single needle (often affixed to simple electric motor); this method spawned a distinct style of tattooing labelled "fineline" for the characteristic subtle details of shading that result in an almost photo-realistic product. This new look was noted by "outside" professional tattoo artists, who adopted and popularized the all-black fineline style in the mid- to late 1970s. It remains an important prison and mainstream tattoo style today.

Chris Leschinsky/Photolibrary/Getty Images

Questions for Critical Thinking

1. What do you think are some of the reasons why prison inmates get visible tattoos?

2. How can the presence of prison tattoos make it more difficult for former inmates to reintegrate into society? Use labelling theory to explain your answer.

Source: Adapted from Peter Wollheim and Christine Brady, "Marked Men: The Art and Meaning of Prison Tattoos," *The Blue Review*, 7 March 2013, http://www.thebluereview. org/prison-tattos. Reprinted with permission.

Just because group forces operate to maintain and even promote deviance, we should not assume—as Goffman (1986) apparently does—that full-fledged deviants are always members of groups. There are those who reject the label of deviant during certain phases of their career, though they may be forced into that status. Some of these individuals spend part of their career trying to re-enter conventional life, often without success. Yet the fact that they refuse to identify themselves as deviant leads them to avoid others labelled as such (e.g., shoplifters and embezzlers). There are, moreover, some forms of deviant behaviour that for whatever reason are enacted alone (e.g., rape, some cheque forging). Nevertheless, it is probably true that deviance has collective support in most instances.

The amount of interaction between individuals suspected of deviant behaviour and agents of social control, and the forms these interactions take, are extremely important for the future course of a deviant career. In fact, such interactions constitute a major set of deviant career contingencies. A **career contingency** is an unintended event, process, or situation that occurs by chance; that is, it lies beyond the control of the individual pursuing the career. Career contingencies emanate from changes in the deviant's environment or personal circumstances, or both. Movement through the career is affected by the contingencies the deviant meets along the way.

career contingency
An unintended event, process, or situation that occurs by chance, beyond the control of the person pursuing the career.

Cohen (1965) has presented this process most clearly: Alter (the agents of social control) responds to the action of ego (the deviant). Ego, in turn, responds to alter's reaction. Alter then responds to his perception of ego's reaction to him; and so forth. As a result, ego's opportunity structure is in some way modified, permitting either more or fewer legitimate or illegitimate opportunities.

As opportunities for a deviant career expand, the steady growing apart of the deviant and the control agents spawns open conflict. Some proportion of these encounters lead in the opposite direction, however, resulting in some kind of accommodation and a decrease in opportunities for a deviant career (West 1980).

This process of agent–deviant interaction is illustrated in the following circumstances associated with a shooting in downtown Toronto:

> CTV News had managed to obtain in late September 2013 an amateur video showing a Toronto police officer repeatedly striking a suspect. The suspect was at the time on the ground in a backyard of a residence near Yonge St. and St. Clair Ave. He was apparently wanted for his alleged role in a shooting in the city's center. "A witness told CTV Toronto that the suspect appeared to have been resisting arrest." The witness said that "the police warned the suspect several times not to resist. The suspect continued to resist, the police then suppressed the suspect and in the process the suspect was injured." The president of the Toronto Police Association said he had "no issue" with what the video contained. He pointed out that a gunman had attempted to murder somebody in downtown Toronto, and that the police had to take action. From what he saw in the video, he believed that the officers had acted professionally. (CTV News, 2013)

Another prominent contingency in secondary deviation is **continuance commitment**. Continuance commitment is "the awareness of the impossibility of choosing a different social identity . . . because of the imminence of penalties involved in making the switch" (Stebbins 1976). Like value commitment (mentioned earlier in this chapter), continuance commitment helps explain a person's involvement in a deviant identity. Unlike value commitment, which explains this involvement by stressing the rewards of the identity, continuance commitment explains it by describing the penalties accrued from renouncing the deviant identity and trying to adopt a conventional identity.

continuance commitment
Adherence to a criminal or other identity arising from the unattractiveness or unavailability of alternative lifestyles.

As Ulmer (1994) notes, such penalties may be structural (i.e., they flow from the social structure of the community) or personal (i.e., they flow from the person's attitudes and sense of self). Stebbins's (1976) study of male, nonprofessional property offenders in Newfoundland revealed a number of commitment-related penalties of both types. Being ex-offenders with prison records, the men in the study had difficulty finding jobs within their range of personally acceptable alternatives. The work they found was onerous, low in pay, and low in prestige. Many of the men had amassed sizable debts before going to prison, which upon release tended to discourage return to a conventional livelihood. Also penalizing were questions from casual acquaintances about the nature of criminal life and the insulting remarks these people occasionally made about those who had done jail time. Even where their records were unknown, these nonprofessional offenders often heard people express unflattering opinions about men like them.

For these reasons and others, the man with a criminal record was often inclined to seek the company of those who understood him best—namely, other criminals—and to seek the way of life that afforded him at least some money and excitement—namely, crime. The police knew all this, and they would question local ex-offenders to determine whether they were possibly guilty of certain crimes. The ex-offenders, who were trying to "go straight," saw this as an additional penalty.

What the ex-offender experiences as a string of penalties is, from another perspective, a set of expressions of the societal reaction. These expressions, when ex-offenders define them as penalizing, affect their deviant careers. Such expressions force many of them into the company of other deviants. Here they find greater understanding for their situation. Here, too, is at least the possibility of a better living than they believe exists in the conventional world.

What is the significance of all this to the process of drift? Teenagers and young adults who fail to drift *out of* crime into a more or less conventional way of life drift *into* a more or less solid commitment to crime. Once a prison record has been acquired, after several years of secondary deviation, continuance commitment develops. Most deviants in this stage of their moral careers appear to be trapped in a self-degrading form of continuance commitment. The image they have of themselves is unflattering. They would gladly abandon the world of crime if only they could find a palatable way to do so (see also Schwendinger and Schwendinger 1985).

But some criminals, including professional offenders, are quite attached to their deviant activities. Because they find leaving crime for a conventional way of life no easier than it is for the nonprofessional offender, they are also committed to deviance. Theirs, however, is a self-enhancing commitment. For these professional criminals, continuance commitment is of little consequence; they enjoy what they do and are disinclined to abandon it.

Reactions to Commitment

self-enhancing commitment
Commitment leading to a better opinion of oneself.

Generally speaking, **self-enhancing commitment** presents no problem for deviants, setting aside that they are more or less compelled to retain their nonconformist role. There is little motivation for them to leave that role for reasons of self-conception. Self-degrading commitment, however, presents a dramatically different situation. An individual committed to an identity in this manner has numerous alternatives.

self-degrading commitment
Commitment leading to a poorer opinion of oneself.

People motivated by **self-degrading commitment** have the objective alternative of redefining the values and penalties associated with their committed identity, such that they become attached to them. Basically, this alters their perception of the balance of penalties. This psychological leap from self-degrading to self-enhancing commitment in the same deviant identity is exemplified by some of the repeat offenders in Shover's (1983) study. They wrestled with the frustrating gap between their legitimate aspirations and what they could actually achieve in life. Since conventional work offered little, they turned to living from day to day, with crime being one of their more enjoyable activities.

Without really switching to a form of self-enhancing commitment, it is possible for some deviants to adjust psychologically to self-degrading commitment. This depends, of course, on how strong a motivating force the current state of self-degrading commitment actually is for them. Certain types of mildly rejected deviants seem to manage this form of adaptation. Lemert (1972) refers to them as "adjusted pathological deviants." The subsequent development of character disorders is another possibility under these circumstances (Griffiths and Verdun-Jones, 1994). Successful adjustment apparently depends in part on the availability of a role for them to play in the community.

Lemert also considers "self-defeating and self-perpetuating deviance." He cites alcoholism, drug addiction, and systematic cheque forgery as examples of this sort of vicious circle of cause and effect, characterized by an almost complete absence of durable pleasure for those involved. Finally, if the desire to escape self-degrading commitment is exceptionally strong, and if none of the alternatives mentioned so far appeals to the committed individual, suicide becomes a prominent alternative.

Undoubtedly, there are many other alternatives to self-degrading commitment besides those discussed here. Much, it seems, depends on the nature of the identity to which the deviant is committed. There are different ways in which commitment can manifest itself. Extensive research is still needed in order to isolate the kinds and circumstances of commitment and the diverse reactions to it.

For many deviants, however, commitment is not a lasting contingency in their careers once they are aware of being trapped in their identity. In fact, this is one reason for stating the case for commitment in subjective terms. That the deviant feels a certain way does not always correspond to the objective state of affairs. Criminological theory and research support this observation. For instance, Matza (1990) holds that delinquents generally end their deviant careers at maturation, with few continuing on to adult crime (see Shannon, 1988). West (1980) and Wolfgang, Thornberry, and Figlio (1987) found that many adult criminals mature out of their antisocial ways: they take up a serious romantic relationship, find a legitimate job they like better than crime, or simply decide "to settle down" (see Chapter 14). Even deviants who are attached to their way of life often experience disillusionment and shifts of interest (Sommers 2001), which is what "maturation" means in everyday terms in the world of crime (Jankowski 1991). There is always the possibility of therapy for alcoholics, gamblers, and drug addicts. And, of course, some deviance requires youthful vigour, a quality lost with increasing years (Inciardi 1974).

It is possible that self-enhancing commitment lasts longer than the self-degrading variety. Underlying this suggestion is the assumption that self-degrading commitment, while preferable to certain alternatives in the conventional world, is still undesirable in itself. A mortifying self-conception is a special penalty. It furnishes a significant part of the pressure to deal with an unpleasant state of affairs. Commitment to an identity or expectation leading to a negative self-image is a lesser-evil choice when initially compared with certain alternatives, and a greater-evil choice when subsequently compared with certain others. The strength of the individual's desire to abandon an unpleasant status is an important consideration in determining whether the transition will be made.

Socialization into Crime

Most of the theories of criminality discussed elsewhere in this book help explain why people start a life of crime. By contrast, interactionism has been interested chiefly in what happens to criminals once their deviant activities commence. Still, two areas of interactionist theory, though not causal, can be properly seen as contributions to the study of socialization into crime. They are the processes of differential association and acquisition of a **criminal identity**.

Differential Association

Sutherland set out his theory of differential association in 1939 in *Principles of Criminology*. The statement there differs little from the most recent edition written by Sutherland and Cressey (1978). The theory consists of nine propositions describing the complicated pattern of interaction that Sutherland called **differential association**:

1. People learn how to engage in crime.
2. This learning comes about through interaction with others who have already learned criminal ways.
3. The learning occurs in small, face-to-face groups.
4. What is learned is criminal technique (e.g., how to open a safe), motives, attitudes, and rationalizations.
5. Among criminals, one important learned attitude is disregard for the community's legal code.
6. One acquires this attitude by differentially associating with those who hold it and failing to associate with those who do not.
7. Differential associations with criminals and noncriminals vary in frequency, duration, priority, and intensity.
8. Learning criminal behaviour through differential association rests on the same principles as learning any other kind of behaviour.
9. Criminal behaviour is a response to the same cultural needs and values as noncriminal behaviour. For instance, one individual steals to acquire money for a new suit of clothes, while another works as a carpenter to reach the same goal. Consequently, tying societal needs and values to crime fails to explain it. (Sutherland and Cressy, 1978, 80–82)

Based on what is known about the antecedents of crime, Sutherland's theory offers a valuable albeit partial explanation of theft, burglary, prostitution, and cannabis use. Also, differential association is often a major antecedent in the use of addictive drugs and dependence on alcohol. It may even play an explanatory role in some mental disorders.

criminal identity
This social category, imposed by the community, correctly or incorrectly defines an individual as a particular type of criminal. The identity pervasively shapes his or her social interactions with others. This concept is similar to master status.

differential association
Developed by Edwin Sutherland in the 1930s, this theory argues that crime, like any social behaviour, is learned in association with others. If individuals regularly associate with criminals in relative isolation from law-abiding citizens, they are more likely to engage in crime. They learn relevant skills for committing crime and ideas for justifying and normalizing it.

However, many other factors, which dilute the importance of differential association, must be considered when explaining such behaviour. For example, two processes discussed earlier in this chapter—drift, and primary deviance—indicate that deviant motives and meanings are often gradually learned and tentatively applied and modified over time in interactions with both deviants and nondeviants (see Figure 13.2). The motives and meanings are not mere causal antecedents of criminal acts and memberships in criminal groups (Davis 1980).

Birkbeck and LaFree (1993) reviewed another set of factors. Symbolic interactionism, they note, further aids our understanding of crime by directing attention to the motives and meanings operating in the situations in which crimes are committed. In this connection, Katz (1990) found that the expressive reasons behind many criminal acts (e.g., thrill, enjoyment) are as important as the

FIGURE 13.2 ■ Commitment

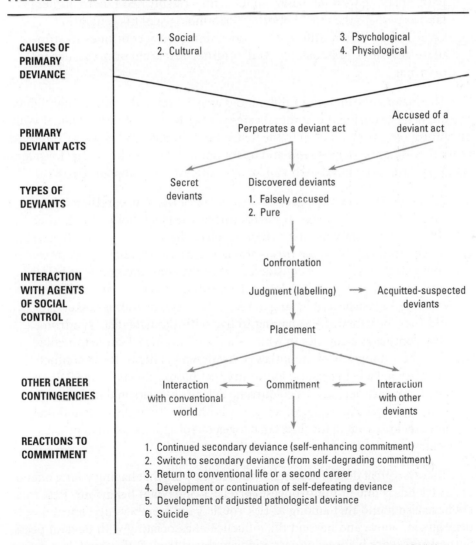

From Robert A. Stebbins, 1976. *Commitment to Deviance: The Nonprofessional Criminal in the Community.* Greenwood Publishing. Reprinted by permission of the author.

instrumental reasons (e.g., money, status). Additionally, precisely how a crime is committed and even which crimes are committed depend, in part, on decisions made on the spot by the criminal. These decisions may relate to the possibility of being apprehended, serving a longer or shorter sentence, or enduring a hostile reaction from the community to the deviance being considered.

Although the theory of differential association has been widely tested, convincing support for it has always been blocked by the difficulty of operationalizing some of Sutherland's key concepts (e.g., frequency, intensity, and duration of criminal and noncriminal associations). Nonetheless, in Matsueda's (2001) words,

> differential association theory represents one of the most important theoretical traditions in criminology. Historically, the theory brought a sociological perspective to the forefront of criminology and, with his path-breaking work on white-collar crime, established Edwin Sutherland as perhaps the most important criminologist of his generation. . . . Over 50 years later, differential association theory continues to stimulate revisions, extensions, and original research into the causes of crime.

The major contribution of differential association is that it has highlighted the importance during the criminal career of ties to deviant peers. Daniel Wolf, an anthropologist who rode with the Rebels (an Edmonton biker gang), observed that the willingness of peers to stand up for one another can be crucial for maintaining power when faced with violent opposition from competitors:

> For an outlaw biker, the greatest fear is not of the police; rather, it is of a slight variation of his own mirror image: the patch holder of another club. Under slightly different circumstances those men would call each other "brother." But when turf is at stake, inter-club rivalry and warfare completely override any considerations of the common bonds of being a biker—and brother kills brother. None of the outlaws that I rode with enjoyed the prospect of having to break the bones of another biker. Nor did they look forward to having to live with the hate–fear syndrome that dominates a conflict in which there are no rules. I came to realize that the willingness of an outlaw to lay down his life in these conflicts goes beyond a belligerent masculinity that brooks no challenge. When a patch holder defends his colours, he defends his personal identity, his community, his lifestyle. When a war is on, loyalty to the club and one another arises out of the midst of danger, out of apprehension of possible injury, mutilation, or worse. (1991, 11)

There is a great deal of research evidence showing that having young offenders as friends is one of the strongest correlates of deviant behaviour. Researchers have also found that among at-risk youth, gang membership contributes to delinquency above and beyond the influence of associating with deviant peers. Sutherland's work helps us understand why this is true. Differential association theory also points to the need to learn the skills for committing certain crimes.

These range from very simple techniques such as hitting a man over the head and stealing his watch, to taking an unlocked bicycle, to sophisticated computer crimes. According to Sutherland, people learn necessary techniques and motives, drives, rationalizations, and attitudes of deviant behaviour from others with whom they associate.

Letkemann (1973), for example, described how a former penitentiary resident learned the now-obsolete art of safecracking:

> Prior to doing his first "can" [safe] [he] bugged an older safecracker in prison "until he finally divulged how to do it." This instruction, he added was "not like a teacher–student, it was just a matter of discussion during work."
>
> When he left the prison he went back to his regular partner and described to him what he had learned about safes. His partner said this was ridiculous but [he] persuaded him to come along: "I followed the instructions to the letter. It opened—we were both overcome with it all—the ease of it all!"
>
> This first job had been a punch job [breaking into a safe without explosives]—technically the simplest. Following this [he] and his partner "opened many doors by trial and error". . . . This went on for four years; they had not yet used explosives, nor had they ever been caught punching safes. They became increasingly eager to try explosives since they found so many safes that couldn't be opened any other way.
>
> During this time, [he] was associating with other safecrackers . . . He eventually asked another safecracker whether he could borrow some grease [nitroglycerine]. "I wouldn't admit that I knew nothing about it." He obtained the grease and chose a small safe, but was unsuccessful. The next day, he discussed his problem with some more experienced safecrackers. He found he had used too long a fuse and was advised to use electric knockers [detonators]. This he did with success. (Letkemann 1973, 136)

Criminal Identities

A criminal identity is a social category into which deviants are placed by others in the community and into which, eventually, they may place themselves. That is, the process of identification of an individual as deviant has two sides. Based on a variety of criteria (e.g., appearance, actions, associates, location), members of the community come to view someone as a particular kind of criminal. The woman wearing garish, suggestive clothing who frequents a street corner in the red-light district is identified as a prostitute. The man with long, unkempt hair, dirty jeans, and a black leather jacket who rides a Harley-Davidson motorcycle is identified, as we saw earlier, as a member of a gang bent on rape, violence, and drunkenness.

Moreover—and this is the second side—community identification of people tends to be highly persuasive, even for deviants. That is, with officials, neighbours, relatives, and others asserting that these people are outlaws, it becomes increasingly difficult for them to deny the charge. At the very least, the alleged prostitute must accommodate her everyday life to such opinion, whether or not she is selling sex. The biker has the same problem.

Acquiring a community reputation, or identity, for unsavoury behaviour often furthers individual criminality. This is especially likely when the reputed criminal is forced into association with others of similar status and away from those who are "respectable." Once deviant ties are forged and nondeviant ties are sufficiently weakened, the socializing potential of differential association begins to take effect.

Limitations

Like all theories of crime and deviance, interactionist theory has its limitations. It is not itself a complete explanation for crime. It falls well short of explaining all crime under all the conditions in which it is committed. Throughout this chapter, we have discussed the strengths of the theory (summarized in Table 13.1). We now examine its limitations in terms of three critiques: neo-Marxist, empiricist, and ethno-methodological (taken from Glassner 1982). Each critique is also the nucleus of still another approach to the study of crime.

The Neo-Marxist Critique

The principal neo-Marxist objection to interactionist theory is that it fails to relate crime and other forms of deviance to the larger society. It fails to account for historical and contemporary political and economic interests. After all, deviant acts and careers do occur in such contexts.

It is further charged that in explaining deviance, labelling theorists overlook the division between the powerful and the powerless. Powerful members of society also violate laws and other norms even while establishing some of their own as moral entrepreneurs. Consider an internal investigation of the Toronto Police Service in 2004 that recommended 218 criminal charges be laid against a dozen officers for offences such as paying informants with drugs seized in other cases, stealing drugs and weapons from suspects and selling them, and extorting money from bar owners (CBC News Toronto 2007). Charges were laid against six officers. In 2012, five were convicted of obstruction of justice and three were also convicted of perjury (Small 2012). All were sentenced to 45 days of house arrest.

The concept of moral entrepreneur and the categories of secret and falsely accused deviants suggest, however, that interactionists have some understanding of power differences in society. Perhaps the fairest criticism is that they have failed to go as far as they might in linking power to concepts such as *labelling, deviant career*, and *agent of social control*. Still, the observation that labelling theory

TABLE 13.1 ■ Interactionist Theories

Theory	Theorists	Key Elements
Labelling	Lemert, Becker	Primary deviance is infrequent deviance that involves little change in routine or lifestyle. Secondary deviance occurs when deviance becomes a way of life and a part of the deviant's self-image.
Differential association	Sutherland	Crime and delinquency are primarily learned in interaction with others in small, face-to-face groups. This involves learning techniques of deviance and justifications for it.

overlooks the larger social context of deviance is a fair one. The perspective is predominantly social-psychological.

The Empiricist Critique

The empiricists have found several research weaknesses in labelling theory. Glassner (1982) discusses three of these. First, interactionists are said by empiricists to examine only, or chiefly, labelled deviants—those who have been officially identified as having deviated (charged and convicted, examined, and hospitalized). It is true that labelling theorists have often followed this narrow conception of the labelling process. Some deviants—for example, religious fanatics or occultists—are deviant and are labelled by the community as such, even though they rarely if ever gain official recognition. This exposes interactionists to the criticism that community labelling makes no practical difference to the individual.

Second, the empiricists argue that labelling as a cause of deviance is inadequately conceptualized. This is a misunderstanding. As this chapter shows, interactionists view labels as interpretations, not causes. The label of deviant is a career contingency, an event, a process, or a situation interpreted by deviants as having a significant impact on their moral careers.

Third, the empiricists claim that labelling theory lacks testable propositions. Consequently, data in this area can be explained in many different ways. They hold that quantitative statistical testing is the only definitive way to confirm propositions. Interactionists defend their approach by pointing out that qualitative methods—especially participant observation—are more appropriate for studies of interaction, labelling, career, and self-conception. These phenomena rest on definitions of the situation, images of self and others, negotiations of reality, and similar processes that are difficult to measure and are therefore largely unquantifiable. Even so, qualitative research often proceeds from the intense examination of individual groups and cases. Such studies are complicated and time-consuming, so there are relatively few of them. They tend to be exploratory rather than confirmatory; they generate hypotheses that can be tested in confirmatory research.

The Ethno-methodological Critique

The **ethno-methodologists** and conversational analysts are the modern-day inheritors of the phenomenology of Alfred Schutz. (In fact, Glassner refers to them as "phenomenologists" in his review.) Phenomenology is the study of how we perceive and understand the objects and events of reality. Reality, the phenomenologists hold, is not independent of human perception, of human consciousness. The chief concern of the ethno-methodologists with labelling theory is its tendency to neglect this question: How do people make sense of their social world?

According to Keel (2000), the perspective of ethno-methodology suggests that deviance and the deviant are not independent of the ways people socially construct the meaning of the situations in which they find themselves in daily life. The work of ethno-methodologists has led to an understanding of how deviant labels and categories are created and applied through three key processes: interpretation, typification, and negotiation. Thus, the qualities and attributes of particular individuals become lost or distorted as they are located by other people (e.g., bystanders, agents of social control) in the context of a certain category of

ethno-methodology
Ethno-methodological theory was pioneered by Harold Garfinkel. Roughly translated, the term means the study of people's practices or methods. The perspective does not see the social world as an objective reality, but as something people constantly build and rebuild through their thoughts and actions. Ethno-methodologists try to uncover the methods and practices people use to create their taken-for-granted world.

deviance. Their behaviour and identity come to represent that category of deviance, and that category in turn becomes an explanation for the behaviour or identity in question.

However, the people of interest to the ethno-methodologist are not always deviant. Rather, ethno-methodologists study how agents of social control and ordinary citizens make sense of deviants and deviant acts. Interactionists are accused of ignoring the ways in which the conventional world identifies and classifies morally offensive individuals and their behaviour. The important data for ethno-methodologists are the clues people use to identify kinds of deviants and deviant acts. People use this knowledge to reach such conclusions as "guilty" or "innocent."

To some extent, interactionists are guilty as charged. Although there are occasional hints of ethno-methodological thinking in the interactionist literature on deviance, there has been until recently a tendency to rely heavily on official definitions, or labels, of what and who is deviant. But even official definitions and their applications are informed by common sense. They, too, warrant ethno-methodological analysis.

Implications

The most profound implication of interactionist theory is that it offers a unique perspective on deviance, one that enhances understanding of this phenomenon. For instance, observations on moral enterprise underscore the arbitrariness of criminal law and call attention to patterns of local and national power (though rarely to the extent that neo-Marxists would like). Practically speaking, little can be done in a democratic society to counteract most moral enterprise. But interactionist research, at least, exposes its existence.

On a more practical level, interactionist theory stresses the damaging effects of the deviant label. These effects are of at least two types. First, the label (to the extent that the wider community is aware of it) makes re-entry into the community problematic. Nondeviants are inclined to avoid known deviants. Why? Because their own reputations could be damaged if they associated with deviants, and, possibly, because they are revolted by the deviant's lifestyle and moral behaviour. Deviants are more than rule violators. They are also outcasts.

Second, labels colour the judgments many people make of those who are labelled. Labels are names for stereotyped images. Both the images and the labels help nondeviants, including practitioners, define situations involving deviants. These two effects of the deviant label have led Empey, Stafford, and Hay (1999), among others, to argue that the juvenile courts should be used for only the most serious cases. Juvenile diversion and decriminalization programs, including Canada's Youth Criminal Justice Act, are practical responses to this implication of interactionist theory.

Interactionist theory calls attention to the deviant career as a process that helps explain deviance beyond its initial causes. One practical implication of this career is that over time, people often become committed to certain lifestyles. But to the extent that they make substantial "side bets" (Becker 1963) in one or more conventional identities, they are unlikely to deviate. Their possible deviance, if discovered and labelled, could ruin their reputation in the conventional world (e.g., the politician exposed in the press for patronizing a prostitute).

One antidote to initial or continued deviance, then, is to give people every possible opportunity to build strong side bets in "respectable" pursuits. By this reasoning, juveniles and adult ex-offenders should be encouraged to drift towards conventional interests. The interactionist concept of career is also useful here, albeit the career in mind is one of serious leisure (Stebbins 2007). This is the leisure of amateurs, hobbyists, and skilled and knowledgeable volunteers, where participants find a career in activities such as music, woodworking, or outdoor pastimes, leading to personal development realized through the acquisition of new skills, knowledge, and experiences related to a leisure activity. Two outcomes of this process are positive change in sense of self-worth and the production of a respectable social identity.

QUESTIONS FOR CRITICAL THINKING

1. Identify some legitimate "side bets" that people make that help them avoid criminal acts, and that criminals make that help them avoid further criminality.
2. Because of the influence of labelling theory, society has become more sensitive to the costs of deviant labels. List some measures taken in our youth and adult courts to reduce the number of people officially labelled by those institutions.

Summary

- Interactionist theory centres on the deviant interchanges among people and the meanings of these interchanges in the present, past, and future.

- A deviant career is the passage of an individual through the stages of one or more related deviant identities.

- Primary deviation occurs in the early stages of the deviant career. Here, deviance is enacted with little change in the person's everyday routine or lifestyle.

- The deviant drifts between two moral worlds. In youth offender subcultures, deviance is facilitated by certain moral rhetorics and by other aspects of the subterranean tradition.

- Agents of social control help check deviant behaviour. Moral entrepreneurs create and enforce rules, violation of which constitutes deviance. Thus, only some people get labelled deviant.

- When deviants see their lives as substantially modified by deviance, they have moved into secondary deviation. The rules are applied to some people and not others. Those publicly labelled deviant generally face some sort of societal reaction to their misdeeds. Labelled deviants may have to cope with stigma.

- Continuance commitment, which entails forcing a person to remain in an identity, sometimes results from these encounters. When self-degrading commitment sets in, those affected are inclined to redefine continuance penalties or otherwise adjust to this unsettling situation.

- Although the theory of criminal socialization is not central to the interactionist perspective, interactionists have contributed to the theory in two major ways. First, people learn crime through differential association with others who are already criminal. Second, they are further socialized into it by being placed in and coming to accept (often grudgingly) a criminal identity.

- Limitations to the interactionist theories have been noted by neo-Marxists, empiricists, and ethno-methodologists. At the moment, however, none of these approaches have progressed beyond finding weaknesses in the interactionist perspective.

- Interactionist theory has certain theoretical and practical implications. One is that, wherever possible, continuance commitment to deviance among juveniles should be eschewed by avoiding the official label of criminal.

NET WORK

Gun control is an issue that has seen groups of moral entrepreneurs with different viewpoints trying to influence lawmakers. Since Parliament passed Bill C-19 in 2012, gun control has been diluted through federal legislation to the point where Canada's National Firearms Association (NFA) appears chiefly concerned with maintaining the new legal status quo *vis-à-vis* ownership and use of firearms (see www.nfa.ca).

On the other side is the Coalition for Gun Control. Arguments favouring the pre-2012 version of gun control can be found at www.guncontrol.ca.

1. What claims are these two sets of moral entrepreneurs making?
2. What reasons lie behind their conflicting views?
3. What strategies do the two groups use to try to influence firearms legislation?

Social Control Theory

14

RICK LINDEN
University of Manitoba

Learning Objectives

After reading this chapter, you should be able to

- Understand the early social disorganization theories that sought to explain why crime rates were highest in neighbourhoods characterized by poverty, physical deterioration, and ethnic conflict.

- Know the importance of the social bonds of attachment, involvement, commitment, and belief in the causation of delinquency and crime.

- Explain the role of the family, the school, and the church in the causation of delinquency and crime.

- Describe the criticisms that have been made of social control theory and understand the validity of these criticisms.

- Understand the social policy implications of social control theory.

We begin by examining some of the early social disorganization theories exploring the relationship between social structure and deviance. These theories were important, because along with Merton's work (Chapter 10) they challenged the view that the sources of crime lay within the individual. Instead, they proposed that the structure and culture of the American city was responsible for deviant behaviour. Social disorganization theorists contended that disorganized communities did not provide meaningful employment to residents and did not have strong families, schools, and churches. This lack of effective social controls led to high rates of crime and other types of deviance. While the early theorists looked at the relationship between community characteristics and crime, later theorists focused more on how the social bonds of individuals help constrain crime and delinquency. The final sections of this chapter deal with some of the issues surrounding control theory and with the policy implications of the theory.

Social control theory assumes that human beings are neither good nor evil. However, we are born with the capacity to do wrong. Unlike most theories of criminality, control theory requires no special motivation for people to deviate. Given that humans naturally try to gratify themselves with no concern for right and wrong, and that the "wrong" way may be the quickest and most efficient way of achieving that gratification, it is conformity rather than deviance that must be explained. Where other theorists ask, "Why do they do it?", the control theorist is concerned with the question, "Why don't we *all* do it?" The answer given by control theory is, "We all would, if only we dared, but many of us dare not because we have loved ones we fear to hurt and physical possessions and social reputations

social control theory
The theory proposes that people refrain from committing criminal acts because they do not want to jeopardize their bonds to conventional society.

we fear to lose" (Box 1971, 140). All societies have developed ways of making people conform, and the control theorist is concerned with the processes that bind people to the social order.

Theories of Social Disorganization—Durkheim, Thrasher, and Shaw and McKay

Durkheim and Social Integration

The earliest social control theories explained how some types of social structure led to high rates of crime and deviance. Communities characterized by poverty, physical deterioration, and racial or ethnic conflict were too disorganized to exert effective control over the behaviour of residents. These early social disorganization theorists included Durkheim, Thrasher, and Shaw and McKay.

In his monograph *Suicide* (1951), Durkheim pointed out the importance of **social bonds** to our understanding of deviant behaviour. Egoistic suicide results from a situation in which a person's social ties are so weak that he or she is freed from social constraints and acts only on the basis of private interests. Anomic suicide occurs when a lack of social integration, caused by factors such as rapid economic change, leaves a society without a clear system of moral beliefs and sentiments. As a consequence, social organization is weak and the individual lacks moral guidance. If the rules are strong and if there is consensus about their validity, there will be little deviance. If the rules are weak and if there is minimal agreement about their applicability, society will be unable to regulate morality effectively, and deviance will be common. Without socially regulated goals, deviance is more likely as people pursue their aspirations without check.

We saw in Chapter 10 that in Merton's reformulation of anomie theory, he shifted from Durkheim's emphasis on a society's failure to define appropriate goals to an emphasis on the failure to define the appropriate means of reaching common culture goals, and on the unequal distribution of legitimate means of reaching these goals. The social disorganization theorists—among them Thrasher, and Shaw and McKay—were more faithful to Durkheim's view of the effects of social bonds on deviance.

Thrasher and the Gang

In his classic study *The Gang*, Thrasher located gangs both geographically and socially where there are breaks in the structure of social organization. They occur "in city slums characterized by physical deterioration, rapid succession of inhabitants, mobility, and disorganization; along economic and ecological boundaries; along political frontiers; . . . and during adolescence, an interstitial period between childhood and maturity" (Kornhauser 1978, 51). Gangs arise spontaneously in areas where social controls are weak. Gangs are not necessarily delinquent, though delinquency will often be the natural result of the activities of groups of adolescents in communities with weak social controls (Thrasher 1963). In a slum setting, delinquency was often the most exciting and interesting thing for these youths to do.

social bonds
The degree to which an individual has ties to his or her society. In Hirschi's theory, social bonds include attachment, commitment, involvement, and belief.

SEARCH FOR:
National Gang Center (USA)

Vancouver's Downtown Eastside is a very poor, high-crime neighbourhood where social controls are weak.

Shaw and McKay—Ecological Analysis

Shaw and McKay saw deviance originating not in the pathology of individuals but rather in the social disorganization of communities. Some Chicago neighbourhoods had disproportionately high rates of crime and delinquency. Rates were highest in slum areas near the city centre and generally declined as one moved outward. In many of these neighbourhoods, crime rates remained high over a long period of time, even though the racial and ethnic characteristics of the residents changed as new waves of immigrants moved into the city. Shaw and McKay attributed these high rates of crime to the failure of neighbourhood institutions and organizations such as families, schools, and churches to provide adequate social controls. Like Thrasher, they emphasized the importance of exposure to the criminal subculture that developed in these areas and that attracted young people to deviant behaviour.

Control theory was not fully developed in the work of Thrasher and Shaw and McKay. From the 1930s to the 1960s, subcultural and strain theories dominated the field of criminology and very few changes were made to the social disorganization model (Kornhauser 1978). There were several reasons why control theory all but disappeared from the scene despite this promising beginning. The most important reason was that the early research was methodologically flawed. The relationships among **independent variables** such as social class, mobility, and community diversity and crime and other forms of deviance were consistent with social control theory, but they also were consistent with other perspectives such as strain theory, and Shaw and McKay never directly measured the degree of social control that existed in a particular community. They inferred, but did not demonstrate, that higher-income communities were better organized than were lower-class slums. The research done by Shaw and McKay was also subject to the problem of the **ecological fallacy**. Consider the

independent variable
A presumed cause of a dependent variable. If unemployment is thought to cause crime to increase, unemployment is the independent variable, and crime the dependent variable.

ecological fallacy
An error made when information is gathered at a group level (the unemployment rate of a neighbourhood) and conclusions are drawn about individuals (unemployed persons). Areas with high unemployment may have high crime rates, but this does not tell us that those crimes are necessarily committed by unemployed persons.

finding that official crime rates are higher in lower-class than in middle-class areas. The conclusion usually drawn from this finding is that being a member of the lower class makes one more likely to become involved with crime. However, this inference is not necessarily true. Perhaps most crimes in lower-class areas are committed by middle-class residents of those census tracts. Perhaps the resident population is not responsible for crime at all. Engstad (1975) showed that some businesses in Edmonton, such as bars and shopping centres, attract people from other parts of the city and provide opportunities for crime. Chambliss (1973) found that middle-class adolescents migrated to other parts of the city to commit their delinquencies. Eventually, the vague and often value-laden term "social disorganization" fell into disrepute among sociologists.

Despite these problems, Thrasher and Shaw and McKay did lay the foundations for a control theory of crime and delinquency. They found that delinquents come from poorly organized communities whose institutions are not well integrated. Families are unable to adequately socialize their children, and the local schools are poor. These elements all reappear in the work of later theorists. Unfortunately, most of the later work focused on individuals rather than on neighbourhood variables. However, research from Statistics Canada focused attention again on the correlation between neighbourhood conditions and crime in several Canadian cities. This research shows that crime is heavily concentrated in economically disadvantaged neighbourhoods (Savoie 2008), just as it was in Chicago during the time of Shaw and McKay.

Early Social Control Theories—Reiss and Nye

Albert Reiss

The social disorganization theorists had been concerned with community and family controls. Reiss (1951) was the first to distinguish between *social* controls, which include ties to primary groups such as the family and community institutions, and *personal* controls, which have been internalized by an individual. If these controls are absent, if they break down, if they are in conflict, or if they cannot be enforced, delinquency will result. Using information from the files of male juvenile probationers, Reiss found that success or failure on probation was associated with the absence of social *and* personal controls.

Ivan Nye

In terms of theory, the work of Nye (1958) simply expanded on that of Reiss, but in terms of method, it was a great advance. Reiss had relied on court records of "official" delinquents; Nye developed a technique for measuring self-reported delinquency and gathered his data from a random sample of high school students in three small American cities. His work was one of the first attempts to unravel the causes of delinquency using the self-report approach.

Reiss did not elaborate on the theory underlying personal and social controls, whereas Nye explicitly stated his theoretical perspective: "Control theory assumes delinquency is not *caused* in a positive sense (motivated by the gains to be derived from it) but *prevented* (determined by the relative costs of alternative benefits) . . .

Weak controls free the person to commit delinquent acts by lowering their cost relative to available alternatives" (Kornhauser 1978, 140–41, emphasis added). Individuals are motivated to achieve certain goals as quickly as possible, but most are prevented from doing so by the laws and customs that societies have established to protect their members.

Nye believed the family was the most significant group in the development of social controls. The extent to which the family enforced controls and the degree to which family members got along determined the extent to which a child would develop internal controls. His research supported these hypotheses. Children from close families in which there was agreement on basic values were unlikely to be delinquent.

Hirschi and the Social Bond

Control theory received renewed attention in 1969 with the publication of Travis Hirschi's *Causes of Delinquency*. Hirschi developed a concise version of control theory and concluded that it explained delinquency better than did competing theories. Like earlier control theorists, Hirschi postulates that individuals are more likely to turn to illegitimate means if their bonds to society are weak or broken. For Hirschi, four linked aspects of social bonds constrain our behaviour: attachment, commitment, involvement, and belief.

Attachment

Attachment refers to the degree to which an individual has affective ties to other persons, particularly those in his or her primary group. Individuals who are sensitive to the feelings of others and close to those others will constrain their behaviour because they will not want to hurt or embarrass the people they like. Those lacking such ties will not have to consider the feelings of others and will be free to deviate. Thus, youth who do not get along with their parents will be more free to commit acts of delinquency than those who are close to their families.

attachment
The degree to which an individual has affective ties to other persons. One of the social bonds in Hirschi's theory.

Commitment

The essence of **commitment** is the pursuit of conventional goals. "The idea, then, is that the person invests time, energy, himself, in a certain line of activity—say, getting an education, building up a business, acquiring a reputation for virtue" (Hirschi 1969, 20). Engaging in deviance will put that investment at risk. The student who has worked hard in school and who aspires to a good job may reject the temptations of delinquency for fear of jeopardizing this future career. However, the youth who is failing in school and who has no career aspirations may not feel as constrained. For the second youth, the immediate rewards of delinquency may outweigh the potential long-term costs. Both commitments and attachments can change over time. For example, the phenomenon of maturational reform—as we get older, we behave better—can be at least partly explained by the fact that adults typically have a greater investment in conventional lines of activity than do adolescents, so deviance may have higher costs.

commitment
The degree to which an individual pursues conventional goals. One of the social bonds in Hirschi's theory.

Involvement

involvement
The degree to which an individual is active in conventional activities. One of the social bonds in Hirschi's theory.

Hirschi hypothesized that level of **involvement** has an impact on delinquency. If people are busy with conventional activities, they will not have time to engage in deviant behaviour. For example, a student who is busy at school and is involved in extracurricular activities will not have as much opportunity to commit delinquencies as do peers who are not as involved.

Belief

belief
The degree to which an individual believes in conventional values, morality, and the legitimacy of law. One of Hirschi's social bonds.

Our **belief** in conventional values, morality, and the legitimacy of the law will constrain our behaviour. Some conflict theorists (Chapter 11) contend that deviants are tied to value systems that are different from those of the rest of the population; Hirschi, by contrast, believes that society does have a common value system. However, individuals vary in the degree to which they believe they should obey the rules. Conflict theorists tell us that some acts that are deviant from the perspective of those who make and enforce the rules are *required* by the beliefs of members of certain subcultures. The control theorist says that deviant acts are made possible by the *absence* of beliefs forbidding them.

As you will see, research has supported Hirschi's theory, particularly for the variables of *attachment* and *commitment*. Relationships have not been found to be as strong for the other two variables. As predicted, *belief* in the law has been found to be inversely related to delinquency (Gomme 1985). A recent study in Belgium found that females had anticipated a higher threat of levels of shame/guilt (an indicator of belief in the legitimacy of the law) for getting involved in delinquency, particularly violent delinquency, than males (DeBoeck et al. 2017), though shame/guilt did reduce the willingness to engage in delinquency for both genders.

The evidence concerning *involvement* is mixed. Hirschi (1969) found that involvement in school activities is related to lower participation in delinquency, while involvement in sports, hobbies, and part-time jobs is not. More recent research has shown a stronger relationship with involvement when serious delinquency is used as the dependent variable. Booth, Farrell, and Varano (2008) found that youth who had greater involvement in a range of activities including sports, school, church, and community activities were significantly less likely to be involved in serious delinquency. However, there was less of an impact on risky behaviours such as drinking and impaired driving.

Self-Control—The General Theory of Crime

Hirschi's early work focused on external sources of social control such as family, friends, and school. In 1990, Gottfredson and Hirschi proposed that individuals with low self-control have a greater propensity to commit crimes when they have the opportunity to do so. They will also be more likely to engage in other risky behaviour such as smoking, drinking, and dangerous driving.

Individuals who lack self-control are impulsive and focus on the moment instead of planning for the future. They also have unstable personal relationships and are less likely to feel shame or remorse when their actions hurt others. When "desires conflict with long-term interests, those lacking self-control opt for the desires of the moment, whereas those with greater self-control are governed by the restraints imposed by the consequences of acts displeasing to family, friends, and the law" (Gottfredson and Hirschi 1990, xvi).

Why do some people lack self-control? For Gottfredson and Hirschi, the answer lies in early childhood socialization. Children will have low self-control if they have poor relationships with their parents or if their parents do not have good parenting skills. Those who fail to develop self-control in childhood will be more likely to be involved in crime throughout their lives; thus, the impact of poor early socialization may persist for many years.

Many researchers have studied the relationship between self-control and criminal behaviour. Using data collected during a night-time roadside survey of Ontario drivers, Keane, Maxim, and Teevan (1993) found that men and women with lower self-control had higher blood alcohol levels than other drivers. LeBlanc (1997) suggested that low self-control is just one of several psychological traits that should be a part of a comprehensive social control theory of offending. He found that Quebec youth with "egocentric personalities"—a construct similar to Gottfredson and Hirschi's notion of low self-control—had weaker social bonds and higher levels of delinquency than their peers (LeBlanc, Ouimet, and Tremblay 1988). Australian researchers found that low self-control was related to higher levels of cyberbullying (Lianos and McGrath, 2018) and that this relationship was stronger for those who spent the most time online.

While some research does support this theory, other evidence suggests it will not replace more traditional versions of control theory. In the general theory of crime, Gottfredson and Hirschi turned away from Hirschi's earlier view that ongoing social bonds make involvement in crime and delinquency less likely. Instead, they proposed that early childhood experiences can produce low levels of self-control that result in higher levels of deviance throughout the life course.

Sampson and Laub (2003) have cast doubt on this hypothesis. They obtained access to data collected by Sheldon and Eleanor Glueck (1950) involving interviews with delinquent and nondelinquent males beginning in the 1940s. Sampson and Laub were able to track these males until age 70 and even to complete interviews with many of them. Their initial analysis (1993) followed the boys from ages 17 to 25 and showed that those who developed adult social bonds, including stable jobs and cohesive marriages, were less likely to be involved in criminality than peers who did not develop these ties. Their later work (Laub and Sampson 2003, 249) looked at the men's entire lives and found that some men who had been involved in criminality encountered *turning points* that marked transitions in their lives:

> Men who desist from crime do so when they, on the one hand, experience structural turning points (for example marriage, the military) that lead to a strengthening of their social support systems and, on the other hand, make an inner resolve to change their lives. They are thus better positioned situationally to respond to the monitoring and control and the love and social support around them—turning points are not deterministic . . . Men who did not change referred to their lack of turning points and/or their own inability (often due to immaturity) to take advantage of turning points when they presented themselves. . . . Finally, in a painful and tragic way, these narratives point to the

destructive power of alcohol, brutal institutional confinement, anger, racial and ethnic division, domestic conflict, and horrific war experiences in shaping an individual's life course and in reciprocally inducing further negative turning points.

Thus, rather than remaining stable over the life course, the propensity to deviate appears to be variable. Childhood patterns of deviance are not necessarily carried into adulthood. These findings are consistent with social control theory, in that positive turning points typically involved the men developing conventional social bonds.

In the remainder of this chapter, we will look in detail at some of the research evidence bearing on control theory, discuss some issues with the theory, suggest ways in which it might be revised, and consider its social policy implications.

FOCUS   BOX 14.1

CAN MARSHMALLOWS PREDICT BEHAVIOUR?

Walter Mischel conducted a fascinating study of self-control. Mischel's daughters attended a nursery school at Stanford University, where he taught psychology. He set up a simple study to examine why some people were able to delay gratification while others were not. He asked children to sit at a small desk in a room at the nursery school. Each child chose a treat, such as a marshmallow, from a tray and then was told that they could eat the treat immediately. However, if they were willing to wait, they would get a second treat. The researcher left the room and the children were filmed while they tried to avoid eating the treat until the researcher returned. To see the children confronted by a marshmallow, go to https://www.youtube.com/watch?v=QX_oy9614HQ.

Jim West/Alamy Stock Photo

In the years following this research, Mischel's daughters occasionally discussed their friends and he noticed that the children who were able to delay eating the treat seemed to be doing better in school than those who could not wait. He followed up as many of the children as he could and found that those who had been able to delay gratification were doing better than the others in many dimensions of their lives (Shoda, Mischel, and Peake, 1990). They had fewer behavioural problems, better coping skills in adolescence, higher college entrance test scores, and less illicit drug use (Mischel et al. 2011). The ability to delay gratification is also associated with lower levels of aggression, higher self-esteem, and

less involvement in bullying (Mischel et al. 2011). Mischel concluded: "If you can deal with hot emotions, then you can study . . . instead of watching television . . . and you can save money for retirement. It's not just about marshmallows" (Lehrer, 2009, 29).

Mischel and his colleagues have found evidence that there is a neurobiological component to the ability to delay gratification and have also found that this ability can be improved through training.

This work represents an interesting dimension of self-control theory and is potentially helpful because researchers in this area have suggested strategies for improving children's abilities to control their behaviour through measures such as reframing the situation to make the stimulus (in this case, the marshmallow) less immediately appealing.

As you read more about research, you will learn that there is often disagreement about findings and the interpretation of findings. Mischel's conclusions have been criticized by Kohn (2014), who raised several concerns about the marshmallow studies. One was that rather than measuring self-control, the study was actually measuring the degree to which the children were able to come up with a distraction strategy that would keep them from thinking about the treat. Kohn claimed that this may have been a function of mental ability, so some of the subsequent outcomes may have reflected differences in mental ability rather than

self-control. A second concern was that depending on a child's previous experience, postponing gratification may have been the best choice. For children who had often faced broken promises, taking immediate gratification may have been the best option.

Questions for Critical Thinking

1. How would Kohn's view about why some children would be best to opt for immediate gratification fit with the next section of the text on family relationships and delinquency?

2. If Mischels is correct, how could self-control reduce the likelihood of delinquency involvement?

Family Relationships

Social control theory emphasizes family relationships since these provide children with the attachments that restrain their deviance. Several aspects of family relationships, including strength of family ties, parental supervision and discipline, and the role modelling provided by parents, are related to delinquency.

Strength of Family Ties

Strong family ties are important for the development of social bonds. If parents are close to their children and provide a congenial atmosphere in the home, this should deter delinquency. Children who care about what their parents think of them should be less likely to become involved in delinquency.

Many studies have shown that warm, affectionate family relationships are associated with low rates of delinquency, while mutual rejection and hostility are typical of the families of delinquents (Glueck and Glueck 1950; Nye 1958). Conflict between parents also characterizes the families of delinquents.

Parental Supervision and Discipline

Children who are adequately supervised by their parents and who are disciplined appropriately have lower delinquency rates than their peers who are not. Researchers have demonstrated the importance of parents' knowing what their children are doing and ensuring they play with friends whom the parents consider suitable (Hirschi 1969; West and Farrington 1973; Wilson 1980). Studies in Montreal and Edmonton have found that supervision was more strongly related to delinquency than any other family variable (Kupfer 1966; Caplan 1977; Biron and LeBlanc n.d.).

Closely related to supervision is parental discipline. Control theorists do not view physical punishment as the best way to control behaviour. Rather, they believe that "disapproval by people one cares about is the most powerful of sanctions. Effective punishment by the parent or major caretaker therefore usually entails nothing more than explicit disapproval of unwanted behaviour"

(Gottfredson and Hirschi 1990, 99–100). Studies have consistently found the disciplinary practices of delinquent families to be different from those of nondelinquent families. Families with inconsistent or lax discipline were much more likely to have delinquent children (West and Farrington 1973). Children learn best from discipline that is administered in a clear, consistent manner.

Strict discipline results in higher rates of delinquency, particularly if it is associated with harsh physical punishment (Fischer 1980) and if parental warmth and supportiveness is lacking (Simons et al. 2000). Very strict discipline is seen as unfair and may lead to frustration and resentment on the part of the child. Harsh punishment may gain immediate compliance, but moderate discipline is more effective in encouraging children to internalize a set of values that will ensure long-term compliance (Aronson 1984).

In his study of a poor inner-city community, Anderson described how "street-oriented" parents—his term for those who do not try to emulate the "decent-family model"—discipline their children:

> In these circumstances, a woman—or a man, although men are less consistently present in children's lives—can be quite aggressive with children, yelling at them and striking at them for the least little infraction of the rules she has set down. Often little, if any, serious explanation follows the verbal and physical punishment. This response teaches children a particular lesson. They learn that to solve any kind of interpersonal problem, one must quickly resort to hitting or other violent behaviour. (Anderson 1994, 83)

The importance of parenting style is clear from an analysis of Canada's National Longitudinal Survey of Children and Youth (NLSCY), which followed the lives of more than 23,000 children (Statistics Canada 1998). Parenting style was strongly correlated with relationship and behavioural problems in children. Children exposed to hostile or ineffective parenting were *nine* times more likely to have behavioural problems than were children who were not exposed to these parenting styles. Parenting style—particularly hostile parenting and parental harshness (Ho, Bluestein, and Jenkins 2008)—was more strongly related to behavioural problems than other factors, including income and family structure. The most aggressive children at ages 10 and 11 were much more likely than their peers to report having negative relations with their family and to feeling rejected by their parents (Sprott and Doob 2000).

In Focus Box 14.1 there is a discussion of why taking the marshmallow immediately may be the best choice for some children. Van Gelder and colleagues (2018) found that Swiss children whose parents used corporal and inconsistent punishment on them were more likely than other children to be delinquent. They found that this was partly because these disciplinary practices resulted in the children having short-term mindsets that led them to make bad decisions that got them into trouble. These youth were more likely to be impulsive and to fail to consider the long-term consequences of their actions. Van Gelder has had some success in reducing delinquency by using virtual reality technology and social media to allow youth to interact with their future selves in order to help them develop a longer-term perspective. It will be interesting to see if this use of technology continues to develop.

SEARCH FOR:
"National Longitudinal Survey of Children and Youth," Statistics Canada

Parental Role Model

Hirschi argued that strong ties to parents will act as a deterrent to delinquency regardless of the criminality of the parents. However, there does appear to be a relationship between the criminality of the parent and that of the child. West and Farrington (1973) found that boys with at least one parent convicted of a criminal offence were more than twice as likely to become delinquent as those whose parents had no convictions. "Youthful crime often seems to be part of a family tradition" (West 1982, 44). West does not feel that parents deliberately transmit criminal values to their offspring, for few of the children were involved in their parents' criminality and the parents expressed disapproval of their children's involvement in delinquency. The relationship is partly explained by the fact that parents with criminal records were lax in applying rules and did not supervise their children effectively. Consider this comment from a high-risk auto theft offender in Winnipeg who was required to wear an electronic monitoring bracelet that would notify officials if he left home after his curfew time (Pearson 2012, 104): "My friends would come over and we would party at my house, my mom didn't like that. We partied every day and she would get mad, trip out and bitch at me to turn the music down. When she was in my face I would feed her pieces [crack] until she left me alone."

In light of West's finding that criminal fathers were likely to be on social assistance and unemployment benefits and that this dependency was repeated among their sons, it would appear that families with criminal parents face a variety of problems that manifest themselves in both parental criminality and poor family relationships. Mears and Siennick (2016) conducted an extensive study of the impact of parental incarceration. They concluded that having a parent go to prison is a major turning point in the life of a child that has long-term consequences in many different domains, including criminal behaviour, mental health and drug abuse, and education and income.

Direct modelling of parental behaviour does not appear to be a major cause of delinquency, but it may be a factor in some types of offences. Rutter and Giller suggest that "criminal parents may provide a model of aggression and antisocial attitudes, if not of criminal activities as such" (1984, 183). The fact that a high proportion of abusive parents were themselves abused as children supports the view that family violence is learned in the home (Steinmetz and Straus 1980). And abusive parents contribute to delinquency in another way. In a study of homeless youths in Toronto, Hagan and McCarthy (1997) found that some of their respondents were living on the streets in order to escape abuse at home. Once on the street, their need for food, shelter, and money led them to delinquency.

Schooling

The school plays a primary role in socialization and is an important determinant of delinquency. Schools are pervasive in young people's lives. Children spend all day in classes and return to school after hours for other activities such as sports and dances. The school is an arena in which an adolescent's performance is constantly being judged. Those who are successful enjoy the prestige conferred by teachers, classmates, and parents. Those who fail may feel they have been rejected by the adult world as well as by their peers. For those who are successful and who enjoy their educational experience, school provides a stake in conformity. Those who fail do not have this stake and hence are more likely to become involved in delinquency. The correlation between school failure and delinquency is relatively strong (Hirschfield 2018). Hirschfield also reported that staying in school longer—particularly in good-quality schools—reduced delinquency involvement and that being excluded from school increased it. Rocque and colleagues (2017) tracked a cohort of British males from 8 to 50 years of age. They found very substantial differences between respondents who had records of truancy during their school days. For example, 65.1 percent of the truants had criminal records compared to 30.3 percent of nontruants.

The school affects delinquency in two interrelated ways. First, the school has taken over many of the occupational socialization functions formerly performed by the family. Formal educational qualifications have become the basis for entry into most occupations. A child's school experiences will have a profound impact on that child's future life chances. Second, the school is related to delinquency through its effects on children's daily lives. For some, the experience is interesting, pleasant, and enriching. For others, it is irrelevant, degrading, and humiliating.

Both types of impact have an effect on a student's stake in conformity. Those whose school experiences will clearly not qualify them for a meaningful occupation may not have the same degree of commitment as their peers whose expectations are higher. The daily consequences of failure and the resulting lack of attachment to the school also affect the child. In fact, research suggests that the daily problems of coping with school failure may be more strongly related to delinquency than are concerns about the future. Linden (1974) found that measures reflecting present school status (whether the child liked school, finished homework, skipped school, valued good grades, and got along with teachers) were more highly correlated with delinquency than were measures of educational aspirations and expectations. Arum and Beattie (1999) showed that students who enjoyed a school environment with small class sizes and course materials relevant to their lives had lower rates of adult incarceration than those with less positive school experiences, even when their education did not provide any labour market benefit. Using data from Canada's National Longitudinal Study, Sprott (2004) found that the classroom environment had an impact on later delinquency. Children who attended an emotionally supportive classroom between the ages of 10 and 13 had lower rates of violence two years later. Those with an academically supportive classroom environment committed fewer property crimes over the same period.

Some criminologists see a broader relationship between schools and delinquency. From a structural perspective, the school "cuts adolescents off from participating in the social and economic life of the community: it reduces their commitments and attachments" (West 1984, 169). Even within the school, the educational process involves the student in only a passive way. Polk and Schafer (1972) illustrate the irrelevance of the student role by asking what happens when a student dies. The student disappears without leaving a social ripple aside from the bereavement of family and friends. The student's role is not one that has to be filled by someone else. This marginality may contribute to delinquency by leaving the adolescent relatively free of the commitments that constrain deviance.

Religion

Conventional wisdom has long held that people with strong religious commitment are not likely to become criminals. In the early penitentiaries that were the predecessors of our current prison system, Bible study was the major rehabilitative tool (Rothman 1971). Early prison education programs were intended to provide inmates with the basic literacy skills needed to read the Bible and other religious literature; this was expected to motivate the offender to mend his ways.

This view was supported by early studies that showed a modest negative relationship between religious involvement and criminality. However, in 1969, Hirschi and Stark reported that religiosity was *not* related to delinquency. Neither church attendance, nor a belief in supernatural sanctions for rule breakers, nor the religiosity of parents, was associated with delinquency. Because the work of Hirschi and Stark was methodologically superior to that of earlier researchers (and perhaps because of a secular bias among criminologists), the results of this study were commonly accepted as definitive. Most contemporary theories of the causes of crime do not include religion as a key variable.

However, several subsequent studies have found strong negative correlations between church attendance and delinquency. How are we to reconcile these conflicting findings? Stark, Doyle, and Kent (1982) concluded that the key to resolving the contradiction was to look at differences in the communities being studied. The studies that found *no* relationship between religiosity and delinquency had been conducted in communities where religious participation was low, while the studies that *did* find a relationship had been conducted in communities that had high religious participation.

Stark, Doyle, and Kent provided evidence to support this view. They compared boys from Provo, Utah, where the church membership rate is very high, with boys from Seattle, where church membership rates are among the lowest in the United States. The relationship between attending church and not being involved in delinquency was much stronger in Provo than in Seattle. The relationship also held for adult crime. The researchers concluded that religiosity was related to reduced levels of involvement in crime and delinquency in communities where religion is important, but not in highly secular communities.

Their explanation of this finding has broader implications for social control theory. Stark and colleagues contend that an **individualistic**, psychological view of the manner in which religion constrains behaviour has led researchers astray. Rather than assuming that religion affects deviance through an individual's fear of religious sanctions, they suggest that "religion only serves to bind people to the moral order if religious influences permeate the culture and the social interactions of the individuals in question" (1982, 19). Religion has its greatest impact where it binds its adherents into a moral community in which religious teachings are salient and consistently reinforced. In these circumstances, an individual is

individualistic
A theory that focuses on explaining the behaviour of individuals and using factors or features of the individual in explaining this behaviour.

less likely to consider deviant behaviour, for the costs of violating community norms may be high and the likelihood of finding reference groups that support such violations will be relatively low. Religion has a greater impact where it is part of the community's institutional order rather than a private matter.

It seems clear that religion constrains involvement in delinquent and criminal behaviour. However, this relationship is complex: it is strongest where there is a strong religious community; it is mediated by relationships with family and friends (Elifson, Petersen, and Hadaway 1983); and it has the most impact on behaviour (such as drug use) that may not be universally condemned by other segments of society (Linden and Currie 1977; Miller and Vuolo 2018). While most of these studies were conducted several decades ago, more recent research reviews have confirmed the findings (Salas-Wright, Vaughan, and Maynard 2014).

One of the most interesting illustrations of the influence of religion on offenders comes from a study of offenders who had lengthy criminal careers despite having religious beliefs (Topalli, Brezina, and Bernhardt 2013). Some dealt with the conflict between religion and criminality by misunderstanding religious principles:

> I mean anything can be forgiven. We live in Hell now and you can do anything [transgression] in Hell. When it all end. . . . We go up there [to heaven] and the Devil comes down here. Only the Devil lives in Hell forever man all by his self. God has to forgive everyone, even if they don't believe in him. (2013, 59)

Others had a very selective view of religious doctrine:

> The way it works is this. You go out and do some bad and then you ask for forgiveness and Jesus have to give it to you, and you know wipe the slate clean. So, I always do a quick little prayer right before and then I'm cool with Jesus. Also another thing is this: if you doing some wrong to another bad person, like if I go and rob a dope dealer or a molester or something, then it don't count against me because it's like I'm giving punishment to them for Jesus. (2013, 60)

This research suggests that religious belief is a possible deterrent to crime but that some offenders are able to rationalize their behaviour so that they can continue with their chosen lifestyles.

Questions about Social Control Theory

There has been extensive research supporting social control theory. However, a number of issues have been raised about the theory, which this section will address.

How Does Control Theory Explain Upper-World Crime?

Control theory has focused on street crime and delinquency, not on occupational crime committed by high-status adults. In fact, upper-world crime would appear to contradict control theory's emphasis on the role of commitment in preventing crime because high-status people have a great stake in conformity. However, control theory can be used to understand what we need to do in order to reduce such crime.

In his analysis of the Watergate cover-up in the United States, Hagan (1985) provided a control theory of upper-world crime. The Watergate affair took place over a two-year period from 1972 to 1974. It involved efforts by highly placed US government officials to conceal their involvement in an unsuccessful plot to break into the offices of the Democratic National Committee. Ultimately, these events led to the resignation of President Richard Nixon and to the imprisonment of several of his senior advisers.

From a control perspective, these illegal events might have been prevented by the belief that such acts were wrong. However, our society has yet to clearly define upper-world morality. Politicians and business leaders rarely receive more than token punishments for illegal activities and are more likely to view their behaviour as only technically wrong rather than as criminal. Transcripts of tapes made by Nixon reveal no concern about morality or ethics. In the absence of moral constraints, "the occurrence of such behaviors will depend largely on the risk and rewards . . . associated with violating public and financial trust" (1985, 173). As you will see in Chapter 17, the rewards of upper world crime are often very great. What, then, about the risks?

The situational controls operative at the time of the initial Watergate offences were inadequate. White House aides were able to manipulate funds and personnel for criminal political reasons with little expectation of detection. One reason why there was so little expectation of detection, of course, was that the criminals here were the same people who oversaw the institutions of legal control. (Who could have been better positioned to deviate than those who controlled the FBI, the Justice Department, and so on?) Furthermore, once "caught," punishment became problematic in an atmosphere confused by discussions of pardons. The uncertainties surrounding these events emphasize the porous nature of the controls that were operating in one upper-world setting (1985, 173). You will learn in Chapter 17 that even for upper-world offenders who are not part of the political process, the likelihood of sanctions is very low.

Later in this chapter, you will learn that control theory has a message for those who wish to control deviance: monitor behaviour, recognize deviance, and punish deviant behaviour. While these principles are intended as advice for parents raising children, they are also applicable to upper-world crime. As Hagan tells us: "If there is a message to the policy-minded in the Watergate experience . . . it is that checks and balances on power are crucial. Upperworld vocations, particularly politics and business, often carry with them a freedom to deviate unparalleled in the underworld. As control theory reminds us, unchecked freedom is a criminogenic condition" (1985, 173).

Does Everyone Have the Same Motivation to Deviate?
The Role of Delinquent Peers

According to the control theorist, we would *all* be criminal or delinquent if it were not for the restraints provided by social controls, so there is no need to account for the motivation to deviate. However, this appears to be only a partial explanation. Several factors may increase the likelihood of deviance among those who lack ties to the conventional order. We will consider just one of these here—ties to deviant peers, which have been found to be strongly correlated to delinquency. Warr has summarized the research: "Criminal conduct is predominantly social behaviour. Most offenders are embedded in a network of friends who also break the law, and the single strongest predictor of criminal behaviour . . . is the number of delinquent friends an individual has. . . . Furthermore, most delinquent conduct occurs in groups" (2002, 3). Thomas (2015) has shown that there is a relationship between the *types* of delinquent behaviour of youth and that of their friends.

In the study discussed earlier that followed the lives of young boys until they turned 70, Laub and Sampson (2003) found that deviant peers had a strong influence on the lives of those men who became persistent offenders. The researchers believed this was because these peers provided the personal contacts and criminal opportunities that made ongoing criminality attractive to these offenders.

One way to address control theory's failure to account for the influence of deviant peers is to integrate the differential association (see Chapter 13) and control theories. These two theories present conflicting notions about the causes of crime and delinquency. For the differential association theorist, the crucial concept is ties to others; for the pure control theorist, it is individuals with *no* ties to others—not even to deviant others—who are the most likely to become deviant.

Control theory conceives of an individual's social bonds as having only a single dimension, weak to strong. If we blend into that theory differential association's emphasis on the importance of ties to deviant peers, however, we can see social bonds as multidimensional: conventional—weak to strong; unconventional—weak to strong. In bringing the two perspectives together, it is proposed that the first step is a weakness in the controls that bind an individual to the conventional system. An individual without these ties does not have to consider the impact his or her actions will have on institutional and personal relationships. With the person "adrift" in this way (Matza 1964), delinquency is a possible alternative. If we wish to go beyond the control theorist's reliance on natural motivation, we are then faced with the problem of accounting for the motivation to commit acts of crime and delinquency and with explaining how one learns the techniques and rationalizations that facilitate deviance.

At least part of the answer to this can be found in differential association theory. We can postulate that the adolescent's lack of ties to the conventional order will increase the likelihood of association with deviant peers, since the adolescent no longer has anything to lose by such affiliation. These ties will, in turn, increase the probability that the adolescent will be involved in deviance (see Figure 14.1).

This extension of control theory explains more of the variation in delinquency than either of the parent theories alone (Linden and Hackler 1973; Linden and Fillmore 1981). The sequential model proposed here is more consistent with control theory than with Sutherland's differential association. The control-differential association model does not necessarily entail the strong element of normative approval required by Sutherland's cultural deviance perspective. Even if this normative approval is not a factor, delinquency may be fun and profitable and is not disapproved of by delinquent peers. The internal dynamics

FIGURE 14.1 ■ Control-Differential Association Theory

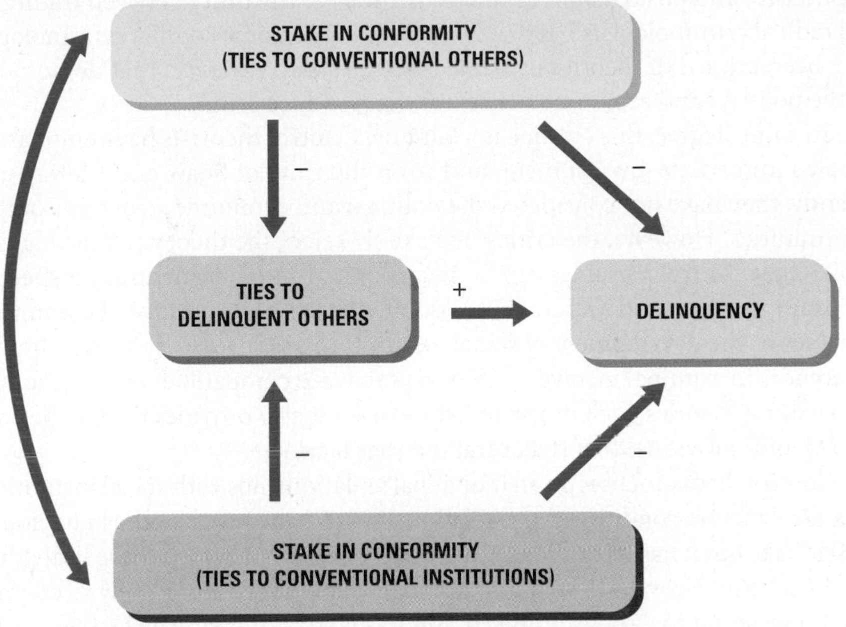

Source: Rick Linden and Cathy Fillmore, "A Comparative Study of Delinquency Involvement," *Canadian Review of Sociology and Anthropology* 18 (1981): 343–61. Copyright © 2008, John Wiley and Sons. Reprinted with permission.

of the group are such that it would be difficult for a reluctant member not to go along. Several researchers (Short and Strodtbeck 1965; Velarde 1978) have found that delinquent boys may try to look "bad" or "tough" in front of the group, even though they may express different views privately, because each believes the others are committed to such values. "An individual delinquent may wonder if or even think that his/her friends are not committed to delinquencies, but he/she can never confront the others to be sure of the degree of commitment they have" (Velarde 1978). Several of the Winnipeg high-risk auto thieves who were on electronic monitoring said that they welcomed the bracelets because they gave them an excuse to avoid going out with their friends to steal cars.

Other criminologists have integrated control theory with competing perspectives. Marc LeBlanc and several colleagues at the University of Montreal (Caplan and LeBlanc 1985; Fréchette and LeBlanc 1985; LeBlanc 1997) have folded together the variables of external social control, personality traits, and the structural conditions of sex and social status. Hardwick (2002) has shown that personality variables such as childhood temperament and self-control interact with social bonding variables and other social variables to produce delinquent and criminal behaviour. Because none of the theories you are studying in this text provide a complete explanation of crime and delinquency, this integrative work will continue.

Is Control Theory a Conservative Theory of Crime?

Many different perspectives have been used to explain crime. In the absence of consensus, some criminologists have taken an ideological approach in which theories are accepted or rejected on the basis of whether they are sufficiently conservative or radical. Robert Bohm has observed that "political and value preferences, ideology, empiricism, and positivism . . . stand in the way of any unity between traditional and radical criminologists" (1987, 327). For example, some conflict criminologists have been critical of theories of crime (such as control theory) that do not focus on the political and economic structures that produce crime.

To some degree, this critique is a fair one. Control theorists have emphasized people's immediate environment, and from the time of Shaw and McKay until recently, they have not considered the political and economic structures of their communities. However, the critics mistakenly reject the theory rather than recognize that control variables can be incorporated into a structural perspective. For example, Shaw and McKay (1942) pointed out the importance of community variables in the development of social bonds. Control theory explains individual differences in criminal involvement in ways that are compatible with any number of structural theories, including conflict theories; it also provides the link between society and individual that structural theories lack.

Control theory focuses on an individual's relationships with social institutions; structural factors condition those relationships. Crime involves the behaviour of individuals, but it has its origins in the social structure in which these individuals live. Lynch and Groves (1989) point out that "persons are more likely to conform when they stand to gain by doing so. But to make conformity attractive, society must do something for the individual; it must provide minimal satisfaction for both human and culturally defined needs. Social structures that provide for these needs are more likely to encourage conformity" (78).

When social institutions work together to support conforming behaviour, rates of deviance should be low. However, if these institutions do not work together and if individuals and groups are alienated from social institutions, rates of deviance will be high. Consider the problems faced by Canada's Indigenous people. They have far less power and fewer resources than other Canadians. They must cope with systems of education and religion imposed from outside that are not compatible with Indigenous customs and traditions. Forced attendance at residential schools and forced adoption outside the community have destroyed family ties, and crippling rates of unemployment mean no job ties. School curricula that are irrelevant to Indigenous students weaken children's attachment to their schools. Many Indigenous Canadians face daily encounters with racism. They must submit to government policies that have not allowed Indigenous communities to achieve effective institutional integration. Under these conditions, strong social bonds are very difficult to develop, and the high rates of crime described in Chapter 5 can be expected. Fitzgerald and Carrington (2008) have supported this view by showing the relationship between the structural characteristics of Winnipeg's disadvantaged neighbourhoods and Indigenous involvement in crime.

SEARCH FOR:
"Manitoba Aboriginal Justice Inquiry"

Manitoba's Aboriginal Justice Inquiry concluded: "From our review of the information available to us, including the nature of the crimes committed by aboriginal people, and after hearing the hundreds of submissions presented to us in the course of our hearings, we believe that the relatively high rates of crime among aboriginal people are a result of the despair, dependency, anger, frustration, and sense of injustice prevalent in aboriginal communities, stemming from the cultural and community breakdown that has occurred over the past century"

(Hamilton and Sinclair 1991, 91). The impact of structural conditions on social bonds and on rates of crime and other deviance is illustrated in the discussion of life in Davis Inlet, Labrador, in Box 14.2. By incorporating control elements within a structural perspective, the example demonstrates the complementarity of the control and conflict approaches.

FOCUS   BOX 14.2

THE MUSHUAU INNU OF DAVIS INLET

On several occasions over a period of several decades, Canadians were saddened by television images of young children sniffing gas in Davis Inlet in Labrador. The first incident was described by a team of researchers who studied the Mushuau Innu of Davis Inlet:

> One day in February 1992, six children in the Innu community of Davis Inlet in Labrador burned to death in a house fire. Almost a year later, six of their friends, depressed at the approaching anniversary of the tragedy and convinced that the ghost of a young Innu was telling them that they should end their own lives, barricaded themselves in an unheated shack in temperatures of −40 and tried to kill themselves by sniffing petrol. The local Innu policeman reached them in time and, with great presence of mind, videotaped their responses as they were removed to safety. Then, to show the world the horrors of life in Utshimassits (as the Innu call Davis Inlet), he passed the tape on to a television station.
>
> Over the next few days, his graphic pictures of wild-eyed children hurling themselves against the wall and screaming "Leave me alone! I want to die!" shocked Canada and made Utshimassits, after years of official neglect, the focus of national and international media attention. Journalists and television crews suddenly converged on Davis Inlet from all over North America and Europe to try to discover how a supposedly "modern" and enlightened country like Canada could produce such a vision of desolation and despair. They were scandalized by what they found.
>
> Utshimassits is a community living in almost unimaginable squalor and disarray. Rows of battered wooden shacks, looking more like a Third World refugee camp than a "western" village, line unmade roads that for most of the year are no more than sheets of dirty ice. Virtually none of the houses—except for a handful belonging to non-Innu professionals like the priest, schoolteachers and nurses—have running water or mains drainage. Sewage is simply thrown onto the ground, where it is eaten by dogs or trampled by the gangs who roam the settlement. . . .

> These conditions are reflected in the appalling health and mortality statistics for Davis Inlet, where family breakdown, sexual abuse, drunkenness and alcohol-related disease, violence, accidents and self-harm have become endemic.* (Samson, Wilson, and Mazower 1999, 6)

These problems did not exist prior to European colonization. Thus Samson and his colleagues conclude that the cultural and social disintegration of the Mushuau Innu has been caused by their past and current relationship with Canadian society. While many Indigenous communities in Canada are healthy and thriving, particularly those that own valuable land and resources, many others share at least some of the problems of the Innu.

How did colonialism cause the decline of a healthy people? The Mushuau Innu were successful nomadic hunters. However, colonial governments did not consider hunting to be an economically viable way of life and forced the Innu to give up their centuries-old way of life and settle in sedentary communities:

> After Newfoundland and Labrador joined Confederation in 1949, the federal government began to build new houses for the Innu. The houses were small (750 square feet) and built close together and had few amenities. While equipped with tubs, toilets, and sinks, the houses had no water or sewage services, few pieces of furniture, and a single power outlet. Many families used hot plates or diesel fuel to start fires to warm their homes. Gradually, the residents of Davis Inlet found themselves slipping out of touch with their traditional migratory way of life while having difficulty fully embracing a "modern" sedentary lifestyle. (Burns 2006, 68)

After their initial settlement, the entire community was moved three times. The first move, in 1948, was a forced migration from Davis Inlet to Nutak, over 300 kilometres away (Denov and Campbell 2002). The Innu were moved without their consent to a location far from their traditional hunting grounds, ostensibly to improve

---

*Samson, Colin, James Wilson, and Jonathan Mazower. (1999). *Canada's Tibet: The Killing of the Innu.* London: Survival. Reprinted by permission of the publisher.

(continued)

their economic prospects. The band did not accept the move and walked back to their former location. In 1967, they were moved to an island on Davis Inlet, again for economic reasons. However, as with the earlier move, there were no economic opportunities on the island and they were isolated during the spring thaw and fall freeze-up, during which the island was accessible only by air. Their new houses lacked running water and sewer systems and quickly degenerated to Third World standards (Denov and Campbell 2002). The move was intended to help the Innu become more economically self-sufficient, yet there were few jobs in the area.

In addition to the shift from a nomadic to a sedentary life, the horrible living conditions, and the disruption caused by the moves, other factors have contributed to the problems of the Innu. Missionaries tried to replace traditional spiritual practices with Christianity. Massive hydroelectric projects, mining, and logging have destroyed part of the traditional territory of the Innu without their approval and without compensation. The government required the traditional family-based governance structure to be replaced by a single leader. All of these changes have disrupted the cultural continuity of the people of Davis Inlet by altering their relationship with their traditional lands. The Innu have been cut off from their ties to the land, and their knowledge of how to survive on the land is not relevant to their sedentary lifestyle: "Displacement among the Innu can thus be seen as part of a painful process of dispossession and alienation of their society from the land and from the cultural and spiritual roots it nurtures, ultimately leading to a sense of powerlessness" (Denov and Campbell 2002, 24).

This discontinuity (what Durkheim would call anomie) is particularly acute among young people. The school system is a major source of their problems. Schooling interfered with learning traditional skills yet did not prepare the Innu for mainstream jobs. Because the schools did not use the Innu language, many young people could not communicate with their Innu-speaking elders. Several generations of Innu have been cast adrift between two cultures and prepared for what Samson has called "a way of life that does not exist . . . Many Innu have gradually become neither hunters nor 'modern' Canadians" (2003, 13). As a result, they face strikingly high rates of suicide, gas sniffing, alcoholism, interpersonal violence, and vandalism. In the words of one young Innu:

> We were taught in school to be doctors, nurses, store managers, teachers, that's what we were taught in school, to be one of those people. I was never taught to be a hunter or to learn about my culture, I was never taught like that, it was always the white culture that was focused in the school . . . (Samson et al. 1999, 22)*

In looking at the tragic story of the Mushuau Innu, we can see the complementarity of the control and conflict approaches. At one level, members of groups with high rates of crime and other deviance typically lack the social bonds that might tie them to the social order. However, if we ask why the strength of social bonds is less among those who, like many Indigenous people, are forced to live on the margins of society, we must turn to the work of conflict theorists and their analyses of the political and economic forces that have created the poverty, powerlessness, and inequality that shape their lives.

As a postscript to this tragedy, for many years the Innu had asked to be allowed to move from Davis Inlet back to the mainland. The federal and provincial governments spent $280 million building a new community at Natuashish (Burns 2006), about 15 kilometres from Davis Inlet, and in 2003 the move to this community

---

*Samson, Colin, James Wilson, and Jonathan Mazower. (1999). *Canada's Tibet: The Killing of the Innu.* London: Survival. Reprinted by permission of the publisher.

The Innu of David Inlet, Labrador, have been cut off from their ties to the land, and their knowledge of how to survive on the land is not relevant to their sedentary lifestyle.

Fred Lum/Globe and Mail

was completed. This led to a major improvement in housing and other physical conditions, and some social conditions also slowly improved. A report in 2015 indicated that there had only been one suicide in six years, where there had typically been four or five suicides each year in a community of 900, and according to the RCMP detachment commander crime rates had decreased by about half over a 10-year period. More young people are graduating from high school and gas sniffing is less common—a list of young sniffers that used to have as many as 60 names, is now down to 3 (Power 2015).

According to Power, community members attribute the improvement to several factors. There are now effective alcohol and drug treatment programs and people are enrolling in them. Many young people have received addictions treatment in outside communities. One reason for higher graduation rates is that the school and parents are no longer tolerating chronic absenteeism. Community leaders are trying to restore people's sense of heritage by encouraging traditional activities such as hunting and fishing. Chief Greg Rich (now Grand Chief of the Innu Nation)

had acted as a role model by being open about his own struggles and providing an example to other community members.

However, progress is slow. Substance abuse and other social problems continue—in 2017 there was another epidemic of gas sniffing (Bailey 2017). The reasons why these problems persist are complex (Burns 2006), but without question, unwinding the legacy of colonialism is a very difficult process, particularly with groups as isolated as the Innu.

Questions for Critical Thinking

1. This chapter discussed the relationship between the community and crime. Starting with the example of Natuashish, discuss some of the government policies that have led to high rates of crime and other types of deviance among Canada's Indigenous people.

2. Based on your criminology studies, what are three things that the people of Natuashish and the federal government might do to help improve the lives of the Innu people?

Policy Implications of Control Theory

Early control theorists were concerned about social policy. For example, Shaw established and worked for many years with the Chicago Area Project, trying to strengthen community ties in a slum area. To illustrate some of the possible uses to which the findings of research done from a social control perspective might be put, let us consider the role of the family and the school in delinquency prevention.

SEARCH FOR:
Oregon Social Learning Center

Policy Implications—The Family

Family relationships are an important factor in the causation of delinquency. How can society help strengthen families and make sure that parents love and care for their children?

While many of the family relationship problems of delinquents may require broad structural solutions such as a reduction in poverty rates, some small beginnings have been made in re-establishing bonds between parents and children. One of the best examples of this is the work of Gerald Patterson and his colleagues at the Oregon Social Learning Center.

Based on his experiences treating several hundred families of antisocial children and on detailed observation of interaction patterns within these families (see Box 14.3), Patterson concluded that since "antisocial acts that are not punished tend to persist" (1980, 89), the key to changing the behaviour of these troublesome children was to punish their misdeeds. Hirschi observed that "this conclusion may come as no surprise to those millions of parents who have spent years talking firmly to their children, yelling and screaming at them, spanking them, grounding them, cutting off their allowances, and in general doing whatever they could think of to get the little bastards to behave; but it is exceedingly rare among social scientists, especially those who deal with crime and delinquency" (1983, 53).

While this approach might seem disturbingly authoritarian to some, Patterson is, in fact, merely advocating techniques used by families that are successful in avoiding delinquency. You will recall that parental supervision and disciplinary practices were strongly related to delinquent behaviour. Patterson concluded that this process involves three key steps: "(1) monitor the child's behavior; (2) recognize deviant behavior when it occurs; and (3) punish such behavior" (in Hirschi 1983, 55). In a properly functioning family, the parents understand this process and the system is activated by the bonds of affection and caring between parent and child. The key is not simply punishment—many parents of problem children punished them more often and more harshly than the parents of normal children. However, the parents of problem children did not know *how* to punish their children, and punishment actually made things worse. Discipline was erratic and unpredictable and was not directed specifically at the child's misbehaviour. "The failure of parents to use reasonable reinforcements contingent on steadily monitored behaviour places the child in a situation in which he comes to understand that he cannot control by his own actions what happens to him" (Wilson 1983, 53). As a result, the children in effect train their parents (and others, such as teachers) to accept their misbehaviour.

Working with the families of pre-adolescent problem children, Patterson taught parents to shape their children's behaviour by using nonphysical punishments (such as time-outs), by rewarding good conduct, and by interacting more positively as a family. This training process was often long and difficult. Many of the parents did not like their children, did not identify with the role of parent, and refused to recognize that their children were deviant (Patterson 1980). Many were trying to cope with difficult economic and family situations as well as with the problems created by their antisocial children, and they resisted help.

Despite these problems, the program had positive results. One evaluation showed that stealing had been reduced from an average of 0.83 incidents per week to 0.07 incidents per week after the parent training program. The treatment effects persisted for six months, but within one year, stealing rates had gone back to pre-treatment levels (Moore, Chamberlain, and Mukai, 1979). This suggests that parental retraining may be necessary. Longer-term results were obtained with children diagnosed as aggressive; with them, program effects lasted longer than 12 months. The program also had a positive impact on siblings, indicating that the parenting skills of the parents had improved.

Tremblay and colleagues (1991) evaluated a similar program in which preventive treatment was provided for disruptive kindergarten boys in a low-income community in Montreal. The treatment taught social skills to the boys and trained their parents to be consistent and constructive towards their children. Two years after the treatment, the treated boys reported less fighting and less theft than comparison groups of boys who did not receive the treatment. The classroom behaviour of the treated boys also showed improvement.

More recently, the Parent–Child Interaction Therapy (PCIT) program, which is similar in many ways to the Oregon program, has shown significant impacts on parents (whose parenting skills improved and who were more satisfied with their parental roles) and children (whose behaviour improved) (Danko, Garbacz, and Budd 2016). Another approach that has been successful in improving parenting and reducing criminal and antisocial behaviour of children is home visiting

FOCUS

BOX 14.3

PARENTING DELINQUENT YOUTH

"When I met him, he was six-and-a-half years of age. There was nothing about his appearance that identified him as the boy who had set the record."

These words are those of Gerald R. Patterson, a family therapist at the Oregon Social Learning Center in Eugene. The "record" to which he referred related to the frequency—measured with painstaking care by the Learning Center's staff—with which Don, a small boy, displayed rotten behavior. Nearly four times a *minute* while in his home, Don would whine, yell, disobey, hit, or shove. When he was not at home, telephone calls from teachers and merchants would mark his progress through the neighbourhood: "He left school two hours early, stole candy from a store, and appropriated a toy from a neighborhood child."

Don had "a sleazy look about him," Patterson wrote, "like a postcard carried too long in a hip pocket." His violent outbursts were frightening; any simple request or minor provocation would trigger obscene shouts, attacks on other children, or assaults on the furniture. His mother was tired, depressed, and nearly desperate as a result of coping unaided with this monster—no baby sitter would take on the job of minding Don, whatever the pay. She nevertheless persevered, changing his wet sheets, bathing and dressing him, even feeding him, all the while talking to him in tones that vacillated between cajolery and scolding, murmurs and shouts. When her seemingly bottomless patience was at last at an end, she would threaten or hit him with a stick. That produced only temporary compliance. When the father was home, things were not much different. The shouting and fighting between Don and his younger brother continued, occasionally punctuated by the father slapping both children.

Children like Don are the youthful precursors not only of difficult teenagers, but sometimes of delinquents and adult criminals. The progression from violent, dishonest youngster to violent, dishonest teenager is not automatic, but it is common.

Questions for Critical Thinking

1. What are some of the principles involved in training people to become better parents?

2. Discuss some of the ways in which family relationships can increase or decrease the likelihood that children will become involved in delinquency.

Source: James Q. Wilson, "Raising Kids," *The Atlantic*, October 1983, 45.

programs, in which nurses make frequent visits to at-risk mothers during their pregnancies and for two years after the child is born (Olds et al. 1998).

Programs like these may be too expensive to be broadly implemented, though many communities do have nurse visiting programs. However, given the high concentration of criminality in a relatively small proportion of families, they do have some potential for reducing crime rates. The demonstration that improved parenting can have an impact on misbehaviour should encourage those who are advocating structural changes aimed at least in part at providing more family stability (e.g., better family supports, income support, and improved foster care).

The Schools and Social Policy

In assessing the role of schools in delinquency, Schafer and Polk (1967) suggest that schools fail youth in two ways: "The school not only fails to offset initial handicaps of lower-income and minority group children, but actively contributes to education failure and deterioration. If this is true, the school itself becomes an important active force in the generation of delinquency insofar as it is linked to failure" (236).

Some schools and some teachers are better than others in helping children function both academically and behaviourally. Rutter and Giller (1984) have suggested a number of factors differentiating good from bad schools. These include the standards and values set and maintained by the school, the degree to which students are allowed to participate in decision making, school and class size, staff turnover, and the degree of concentration of intellectually and socially disadvantaged pupils. Each of these factors has rather obvious policy implications.

Several studies have looked at the impact of the teacher–student relationship on students' behaviour. Some teachers provoked deviance, while others were able to get students to cooperate (Hargreaves, Hester, and Mellor 1975). Failure to get along with teachers may weaken an adolescent's commitment to school. It may also affect grades by leading teachers to make negative judgments about a youth's abilities and character. Thus, the classroom process may help weaken an adolescent's attachment and commitment to the school.

Incredible Years is a program that has succeeded in changing teachers' methods so that they are better able to teach youth with behaviour problems. It involves programs for parents, teachers, and youth, with the focus on training teachers in techniques for building positive relationships with their students. The techniques include using praise and incentives to encourage desired behaviours, giving clear instructions, using positive discipline, and helping students with problem solving. Hutchings and colleagues (2013) conducted a randomized clinical trial of the program in Wales. They found that the teachers reduced their negative behaviour towards the children and that the children engaged in less off-task behaviour and showed less negative behaviour towards the teachers. Programs such as this one hold potential for improving the educational outcomes of high-risk youth.

Schools must also ensure that their curricula are relevant to the lives of their students. This is not being achieved in Canada's North. A child who has grown up in a small settlement on the Arctic coast will be flown south to Yellowknife or another southern point for high school. Besides being cut off from family and community, the student is educated into a way of life that is very different from that which exists in their home settlement. As a result, students may no longer fit into their home communities; but at the same time, they are not completely acculturated into southern ways (Brody 1975). The consequences of this system can be increasing rates of crime and other deviance among people who lack strong community ties.

TABLE 14.1 ■ Social Control Theories

Theory	Theorists	Key Elements
Social disorganization theories	Durkheim, Thrasher, Shaw and McKay	Deviance will be highest in disorganized communities that lack social controls.
Early social control theories	Reiss, Nye	Stress the importance of personal controls, particularly those provided by the family.
Social bond theory	Hirschi	The four elements of the social bond: attachment, commitment, involvement, and belief.
General theory of crime	Gottfredson, Hirschi	Individuals with low self-control have a greater propensity to commit crimes when they have the opportunity to do so.
Control-differential association theory	Linden	Lack of ties to the conventional order will increase the likelihood of association with deviant peers. These ties will in turn increase the probability of delinquency involvement.

QUESTIONS FOR CRITICAL THINKING

1. How could you apply the principles of social control theory to reduce the amount of white-collar and corporate crime in Canada?
2. Based on your knowledge of social control theory, what changes would you make to the public school system to help reduce delinquency?

Summary

- Rather than asking, "Why do some people break the law?" social control theorists ask, "Why don't we all do it?" The answer to this question lies in the processes that bind people to conventional society.

- Early theorists, including Thrasher and Shaw and McKay, looked at community-level controls. Disorganized communities that did not provide meaningful employment to residents and did not have strong families, schools, and churches could not provide adequate social controls and would have high rates of crime and other types of deviance.

- Later social control theories focused on the social bonds of individuals. Hirschi described four interrelated aspects of the social bond that constrain our behaviour: attachment, commitment, involvement, and belief.

- Research on social control theory has pointed to the importance of the family and the school in restraining involvement in delinquency. While less research has been done with adults, this theory suggests that stable employment and a cohesive marriage are important factors.

- Among the criticisms of social control theory are these: it does not adequately explain white-collar crime; it does not account for the motivation to deviate; it is too individualistic; and it is too conservative.

- Recent theoretical work has returned to the social disorganization tradition and has once again linked societal and community factors to individual-level bonds.

NET WORK

For over two decades, the Canadian government has supported the Aboriginal Head Start program. This program is intended to help reserve communities meet the educational, emotional, social, health, and nutritional needs of children under the age of six. Some early childhood education programs have proven very successful in reducing rates of crime and delinquency. This program is based on the US Head Start program. You can find out more about Head Start at https://www.acf.hhs.gov/opre/research/topic/overview/head-start.

Using some of the evaluations you will find on this link, answer the following questions:

1. What do you think would be the impact of Head Start programs on delinquency and crime? Do you think they are a cost-effective way of reducing crime?

2. The most effective early childhood education program is the Perry Preschool program, which you can read about at http://www.highscope.org/Content.asp?ContentId=219. What lessons can those running Head Start programs learn from the Perry Preschool program?

3. How important do you think it is to involve parents in Head Start programs? Does the research show that programs involving parents are more effective than those based only in the schools?

Deterrence, Routine Activity, and Rational Choice Theories

15

RICK LINDEN
University of Manitoba

DANIEL J. KOENIG
Formerly of University of Victoria

Learning Objectives

After reading this chapter, you should be able to

- Understand the role of law as a deterrent to crime and recognize the limits of deterrence.

- Discuss how offenders make choices whether or not to commit crimes and understand the assumptions of rational choice theory.

- Discuss the routine activities approach to crime and understand the role of the motivated offender, the suitable target, and ineffective guardianship in any criminal event.

- Know the rationale behind situational crime prevention and be familiar with the research demonstrating its effectiveness.

- Understand the need for comprehensive crime prevention initiatives, including crime prevention through social development.

This chapter introduces you to several perspectives on crime with roots in the Classical theory of crime discussed in Chapter 8. Most sociological and psychological theories of crime seek to explain why people break the law and focus on the backgrounds, character, and motivations of offenders. In contrast, *deterrence theories* such as Beccaria's Classical theory focus on the factors influencing an individual's decision whether to commit an offence and assert that the legal system can be used to affect that decision.

The other theories discussed in this chapter—*rational choice theory* and *routine activities theory*—also examine the factors influencing individuals' decisions to commit specific criminal acts rather than on their backgrounds. *Rational choice theory* postulates that people break the law because they believe that crime will provide them with a reward: a burglar steals money to pay living expenses, an addict smokes crack to get high and to avoid withdrawal, a gang member shoots a rival to protect his drug business. The criminal's decision may or may not appear rational to the rest of us, but it does meet a goal for the offender. *Routine activities theory* tells us that crime will not occur unless there is a motivated offender, a suitable target, and ineffective guardianship of that target. As you will learn later in this chapter, the routine activities approach has been particularly useful for developing ways to prevent crime.

Deterrence Theory

Beccaria's Classical theory was based on rational choice—people will break the law if they think that doing so will advance their own interests. If it is to our advantage, and if we think we can get away with it, we will break the law. This implies that the best way to control crime is to set up a system of punishment that will ensure people do not find lawbreaking to be in their best interests. Beccaria believed that punishments should be severe enough to deter people from breaking the law but should also be proportionate to the nature of the crime. Also, punishment should be swift and certain. A well-crafted justice system would ensure that most people chose good over evil.

At the heart of Classical theory was the belief that humans are rational beings who carefully calculate the consequences of their behaviour. Crime would be prevented if the potential criminal realized that the costs of committing the crime were greater than the rewards. Classical theorists had great faith in the ability of a well-designed criminal code to deter criminal behaviour.

How effective is the law as a deterrent? This is a vitally important question, because our legal system is based heavily on deterrence. We know that deterrence can be effective: most people do not deliberately park where they know their car will be towed away, and do not speed when they see a police car behind them. On the rare occasions when the police have gone on strike, crime has risen dramatically. During one notable police strike in Montreal in 1969, armed robberies began to occur within minutes of the strike and huge mobs of people ran through the shopping district, breaking windows and stealing whatever they could get their hands on. Many people were injured, and a police officer was shot to death.

So the law clearly does deter. The more important policy question is whether we can make our current system more effective as a deterrent. Many people, including "law and order" politicians, believe that the best way to reduce crime is to hand down longer prison sentences. During its time in office (2006–15) Stephen Harper's Conservative government passed a number of laws intended to put more people in jail for longer periods of time. Prisons are expensive—the cost of keeping someone in a federal penitentiary is $116,000 per year (Correctional Service of Canada 2017).

It is important to know whether sending more people to jail for longer periods has an impact on crime rates and whether investing in other crime reduction strategies would keep Canadians safer. Research suggests that *certainty* of punishment is more important than *severity* of punishment—a finding that Classical theorists might have predicted. The impact of increased certainty is illustrated by the dramatic decline in obscene and harassing telephone calls after the introduction of caller ID services. Penalties did not increase, but the new technology increased the certainty that the offending caller could be identified and charged. This was much more effective than increasing penalties for the rare offenders who eventually got convicted.

Unfortunately, it has been easier for governments to pass tougher sentencing laws than to increase the certainty of punishment. Canada's federal prison population increased by nearly 20 percent between 2006 and 2015, but this increase pales when compared to the impact of harsher sentencing in the United States, where tougher laws led to a 500 percent increase in rates of imprisonment between 1972 and 2009 (Bureau of Justice Statistics, 2009). The United States now has the world's highest imprisonment rates. Much of this increase was a result of harsher penalties for drug offenders. Yet there is no evidence that mass incarceration reduces the sale and use of illegal drugs.

Does Imprisonment Deter Crime?

Steven Durlauf and Daniel Nagin (2011) reviewed the evidence on the deterrent effect of imprisonment. Most of the research they reviewed was conducted in the United States. They concluded that long prison sentences "are difficult to justify on a deterrence-based, crime prevention basis" (38). Some of the research they reviewed suggests that imprisonment may actually *increase* an individual's likelihood of future criminal behaviour. Labelling theorists (see Chapter 13) would suggest this is because punishment may stigmatize people and reduce their opportunities for a life in the noncriminal world. Also, offenders may adjust to prison life so that the threat of prison does not deter them; they may learn criminal values and skills in prison; or imprisonment may create feelings of resentment against society that result in increased criminality when they are released.

One of the most interesting studies in their review examined whether young people reduced their offending when they reached the age of 18, when they began to be treated as adults in court. Many people believe that youth courts coddle offenders and that the more serious penalties prescribed for adults will deter criminal behaviour. However, Florida research by Lee and McCrary cited by Durlauf and Nagin showed that there was only a slight reduction in offending when youth turned eighteen. So apparently, the threat of adult penalties did not act as a deterrent.

Do Mandatory Minimum Sentences Deter Crime?

The most definitive work on the deterrent effect of imprisonment looks at the impact of mandatory minimum prison sentences for particular offences and for offenders with significant prior records. Mandatory sentences are widely used, but there has been much debate about their effectiveness.

What are mandatory minimum sentences? The Criminal Code provides a broad range of penalties for many offences. For example, breaking into someone's home can result in penalties ranging from an absolute discharge to life imprisonment. Judges have a great deal of discretion, though appeal courts set limits on that discretion. When complaints from the public follow a particularly light sentence or when a paroled offender commits a serious crime, politicians may try to limit judicial discretion by legislating mandatory minimum penalties for certain offences. Between 2006 and 2015 the Canadian government imposed or increased mandatory minimum sentences for many crimes, including cannabis-related offences.

The harshest mandatory sentencing law in any Western country is California's three strikes law. While the law is complicated, one of its components is a mandatory sentence of 25 years in prison for a third felony conviction following two earlier convictions for serious felonies (a category that includes residential burglary). This has resulted in some bizarre sentences, including cases where two men will spend much of the rest of their lives in prison, one for stealing a slice of pizza and the other for shoplifting a small package of meat. This punishment seems far too harsh, at least for minor felonies like shoplifting and other forms of petty theft. However, in 2003 the US Supreme Court ruled that it did not violate the constitutional protection against cruel and unusual punishment. This decision covered two cases, one involving a defendant who received a sentence of 25 years without parole for stealing three golf clubs, and the other a defendant who was given two consecutive 25-year sentences (50 years in all) for stealing nine videotapes in two separate incidents.

This law has been costly. According to the California State Auditor (2010), one quarter of California's prison inmates were serving time under the three strikes law. The auditor estimated that the cost of "three strikes" sentencing was $20 billion more than if the convicted had been sentenced for the actual crimes they had committed rather than for the "strikes" against them. Partly as a result of three strikes laws, California cannot afford its prison system, and in 2011, the US Supreme Court ordered the state to release 32,000 inmates because of severe overcrowding. Mandatory minimum sentences also significantly increase court costs because individuals facing long mandatory penalties are more likely to insist on a trial instead of pleading guilty. The law is also very hard on the offenders and their families.

California's three strikes sentencing laws led to massive overcrowding of prisons but had no impact on crime rates.

The high social and financial costs of mandatory minimum sentences might be worthwhile if they reduced crime rates. However, they do not. After reviewing the research on mandatory minimum sentences, Tonry concluded that "mandatory penalties are a bad idea. They often result in injustice to individual offenders. . . . And the clear weight of the evidence is, and for nearly 40 years has been, that there is insufficient credible evidence to conclude that mandatory penalties have significant deterrent effects" (2009, 100).

Tonry based this conclusion in part on several evaluations of California's three strikes laws. California's crime rate declined following the passage of three strikes in 1994, but this decline was not the result of the three strikes laws. Only one of 15 studies reviewed by Tonry concluded that the legislation reduced crime rates. Several studies, including those by Marvell and Moody (2001) and Chen (2008), found that crime rates in California did not decline faster than in other states even though the penalties in California were far more severe than in any other state. Kovandzic, Sloan, and Vieraitis (2004) arrived at similar findings, using cities rather than states as the basis of comparison. Other studies compared the California counties that used three strikes most often with the counties that used it the least and found no differences in reductions in total crime or in violent crime following the three strikes law (Legislative Analyst's Office 2005). Several of these comparative studies also found that three strikes laws produced *increases* in homicide rates, possibly because offenders facing a third strike conviction wanted to eliminate people who could identify them.

Why don't these severe penalties deter crime? One reason is that offenders may not feel they are at risk of getting caught. Potential offenders are actually correct in believing that their next crime is unlikely to lead to punishment.

Crime statistics show that most criminal offences are not reported, that most reported offences do not result in an arrest, that most arrests do not lead to a conviction, and that most convictions do not result in imprisonment. The 2014 victimization survey found that Canadians reported 6.4 million crimes (Perreault 2015) and that nearly 1.8 million crimes were reported to the police in that year (Boyce 2015). Despite this huge number of offences, only about 5,000 people were admitted to the federal penitentiary system (which includes all of those sentenced to two years or more) and 63,000 to provincial custody in the following year (which allows for the time it takes for court processing) (Reitano 2017). Thus, the likelihood of being arrested, convicted, and punished for any offence is so low that tinkering with the level of punishment makes no difference. Governments can promise to "crack down" on crime, but if the promise of a tougher response is rarely kept by the justice system, it will be ignored by potential offenders, who know from their own experience (and from that of their peers) that the odds of getting away with a crime are in their favour. This means that a harsh system like California's is really one of randomized severity in which some offenders receive very harsh sentences while many others with similar patterns of offending remain on the streets.

Deterrence is also affected by the fact that many offenders have alcohol, drug, or mental health issues that may lead them to make bad decisions (see Box 15.1). Furthermore, some offenders are unaware of the sentence they face if convicted. A study of serious firearms offenders made a striking finding: "even felons who had been *prosecuted, sentenced, and were interviewed while incarcerated* dramatically underestimated the magnitude of their *current* sentence" (Kennedy 2009, 26). An inmate who was the first person sentenced under a new US federal three strikes law said that

> I ain't never heard anything about the law until they applied it on me. I never thought anything like this would happen to me, man. . . . It is going to make a few guys think, but some other guys don't even watch TV or care; they don't know nothing about the law. (Kennedy 2009, 26)

One of the biggest failures of mandatory sentencing and other deterrence policies relates to the war on drugs. Billions of dollars have been spent combating drug trafficking and consumption without reducing the problem. More than 80,000 people were killed in Mexico's drug wars between 2006 and 2015 (CNN 2018). Even the risk to Mexican drug dealers of being murdered by other traffickers or of being killed by the police has not deterred new recruits to the drug business, which is so lucrative that when one distributor is killed or arrested, another will very quickly take his place. The failure of this costly war on drugs was demonstrated recently by a study showing that while drug seizures have increased over two decades, the price of drugs has gone *down* and their potency has gone *up* (Werb et al. 2013). Declining prices and increased quality indicate that supply has increased despite the increase in drug seizures by enforcement agencies.

Another possible reason why harsh sentences have little impact is that prosecutors and judges find ways to evade penalties such as mandatory minimum sentences that they feel are too severe. Cases may be plea-bargained to lesser charges, or prosecutors may lay related charges that do not carry a mandatory minimum penalty. A study of the use of Section 85 of Canada's Criminal Code, which imposed mandatory minimum sentences for certain firearms offences, found that many of the charges laid under this section were dealt with through plea bargaining and that about two-thirds of the charges were stayed, withdrawn, or dismissed (Roberts 2005). In 2012 the Canadian government passed legislation requiring a mandatory sentence of at least six months in prison for growing as few as six marijuana plants if the grower was involved in marijuana trafficking. Prior to cannabis legalization in 2018, it was very likely that some prosecutors and judges worked around the law in cases where they didn't feel a jail term was desirable. However, other similar offenders who faced less sympathetic prosecutors and judges went to jail.

In 2014 the Supreme Court of Canada overturned parts of the Harper government's "tough on crime" legislation on the grounds that the laws were contrary to the Charter of Rights and Freedoms. The Supreme Court struck down minimum sentences for illegal gun possession in 2015 and for a second drug trafficking offence in 2016, and lower court judges have rejected them in a number of other cases that have not yet reached the Supreme Court. The Liberal government has promised to review these laws, but had not done so at the time this chapter was written.

Finally, it is likely that the existing level of punishment is severe enough for most of us. To give just one example, there is no evidence that capital punishment is a greater deterrent to crime than a lengthy term of imprisonment. In fact, one international study found that homicide rates actually went *down after* capital punishment was abolished (Archer, Gartner, and Beitel 1983).

FOCUS   BOX 15.1

THE LIMITS OF DETERRENCE

Not all people can be deterred. Jacobs (2010) describes an incident in which

> an offender stabbed a victim after a traffic dispute in a fully lit Taco Bell drive-thru window. The . . . stabbing took place in view of at least ten potential eyewitnesses. The entire encounter was captured on surveillance video and (subsequently) broadcast worldwide on YouTube. The offender began the altercation with the victim *while the victim was on the phone with the police* (to report the traffic accident) *and under the reasonable presumption that the police were on their way*. The offender did not attempt to conceal or disguise his identity in any way. The offender attacked the victim despite the fact that he (the offender) had $6,000 worth of marihuana packaged for sale under the front seat of his car—a quantity that would trigger a charge of intent to distribute (as opposed to simple possession) if the police were to discover it (recall that the police were on their way). The offender attacked the victim despite the presence and direct intervention of two peacemakers (a cousin of the offender and an unrelated customer). Following the stabbing, the offender made no attempt to flee, despite the fact that he knew the police were coming. (428)

Questions for Critical Thinking

1. What kinds of offenders may not be deterred by the threat of legal sanctions?
2. Why is it important to know that the law will not deter some offenders?

The Impact of Increasing the Certainty of Punishment

Increasing the *severity* of punishment beyond current levels does not seem to have a deterrent effect. Even the minority of studies that have found that longer sentences help reduce crime do not show a sufficient impact to justify the enormous costs of growing prison populations. However, you will recall that Beccaria also discussed the need for *certainty* of punishment if the law was to be an effective deterrent. There is now a substantial body of research showing that efforts to increase certainty can have a strong deterrent effect (Durlauf and Nagin 2011b). Two of these measures are **hot spots policing** and **individualized deterrence**.

Hot Spots Policing

Most studies of the impact of increased certainty have focused on the police because their actions can increase or decrease the certainty of punishment. One promising strategy is "hot spots" policing. This strategy is based on the fact that a small number of addresses produce a high percentage of calls to the police. For example, half the calls to the Minneapolis police came from just 3 percent of the city's addresses (Sherman, Gartin, and Buerger 1989), and half the commercial robberies in Boston took place at 1 percent of the addresses (Braga, Hureau, and Papachristo 2011). Several studies have shown that focusing police resources on these high-crime areas can significantly reduce crime by increasing the certainty of apprehension (Braga, Papachristos, and Hureau 2014).

SEARCH FOR:
Smart Policing Initiative

hot spots policing
Most crimes occur at a small number of addresses in any community. Hot spots policing concentrates police resources on these high-crime locations.

individualized deterrence
Offenders who are heavily involved in criminal activity are individually warned that their actions are being monitored and that future violations of the law will be dealt with immediately. Extra police and/or probation resources are added to ensure that the legal system does keep its promises.

Individualized Deterrence

The most dramatic results demonstrating the importance of certainty of punishment have come from the new strategy of individualized deterrence. This involves directly informing individuals about the consequences of future misbehaviour and then ensuring that those consequences do in fact follow.

Boston's Operation Ceasefire

The best-known example of individualized deterrence is the gang violence reduction program called Operation Ceasefire. The program was developed in response to high homicide rates among young African American males in Boston.

The project involved a significant number of agencies and groups. Police, probation workers, and gang outreach workers sought to deter violence by telling gang members that violence would not be tolerated and that gangs that continued to use violence would be targeted for intensive enforcement. Operation Ceasefire was not just a police effort; it involved other law enforcement and criminal justice agencies as well as academics from Harvard University. The planning team also recruited social service agencies and local churches and community groups to work with youth in their communities. These community groups made it clear to the gang members that their violent behaviour was not going to be tolerated by the community; they also used whatever formal and informal sanctions they could to enhance the certainty of deterrence. Suppression was a major component of the project, but it also offered gang members training, counselling, mentoring, and remedial education to help them get out of the gang lifestyle. Community organizations, including faith-based agencies, were involved in providing these services.

The impact of the project was dramatic. Operation Ceasefire was responsible for a 63 percent decline in youth homicide over nearly three years (Kennedy et al. 2001). Many of the gang members said they actually welcomed the intervention because it gave them an excuse to avoid being pressured into violence by peers and because they felt safer themselves because rival gangs were also constrained. However, when the Boston Police Department dropped the program and several community groups ended their involvement, rates of youth homicide returned to previous levels and continued to climb until at least 2006 (Pollack 2006).

The US government further tested the individualized deterrence model through the Strategic Approach to Community Safety Initiative, which sponsored programs in 10 cities (Roehl et al. 2006). The results of this were also positive. For example, in Indianapolis there was a 32 percent reduction in homicide, in New Haven there was a 32 percent reduction in gun crime, and in Portland there was a 42 percent reduction in homicide and a 25 percent decrease in other violent crime. The model is now being promoted nationally in the United States through Project Safe Neighborhoods.

In Canada, the Winnipeg Auto Theft Suppression Strategy is an award-winning crime reduction program that includes an individualized deterrence component. This program, which has reduced auto theft by over 80 percent, is discussed in detail at the end of this chapter.

The evidence demonstrates that the legal system can deter crime. Even though many politicians promise us that harsher sentences will reduce crime rates, there is compelling evidence that policies that increase *certainty* of punishment are both more effective and less costly than policies that increase the *severity* of punishment.

Rational Choice Theory

Rational choice theory was developed by researchers at Britain's Home Office. While similar in some respects to deterrence theory, rational choice theory is based on research on how offenders actually make their choices about whether or not to commit crimes. Offenders told researchers they selected targets based on their perception of risks and rewards. They also described characteristics of desirable and undesirable targets and gave detailed descriptions of their criminal actions. The research showed that while criminal behaviour was goal-oriented, there was little planning involved in most crimes. That is, offenders did not carefully calculate the benefits and costs of their criminal behaviour.

This work was the basis of **rational choice theory** (Cornish and Clarke 1986), which postulates that crime is the result of deliberate choices made by offenders based on their calculation of the risks and rewards of those choices. The basic assumption of rational choice theory is that "crime is purposive behaviour designed to meet the offender's commonplace needs for such things as money, status, sex, and excitement, and that meeting these needs involves the making of (sometimes quite rudimentary) decisions and choices, constrained as these are by limits of time and ability and the availability of relevant information" (Clarke, 1995, 98).

Rational choice theory does not focus on the offender's background, but rather on the situational dynamics involved in the decision whether to commit a crime. Rational choice theorists do not believe that all crimes result from the same social processes. Thus, the analysis of particular crime problems is the key to understanding the dynamics of offences and to planning prevention programs. The factors involved in the decision to commit crime can vary even within the same crime category—the decision-making process is very different for professional thieves who steal cars to sell than for a 14-year-old who sees a car running in front of a convenience store and takes it for a joyride before deliberately crashing it. One of the most important findings of rational-choice research has been that offenders' behaviour is typically based more on short-term costs and benefits than on long-term considerations such as possible penalties (Felson and Clarke 1998). The immediate rewards of a heroin injection are more important than the eventual possibility of a jail term or the health risks, and the approval of peers for assaulting a member of a rival gang outweighs the possible costs of an assault conviction or of potential retaliation for the assault.

Environmental Criminology

The work of Patricia and Paul Brantingham on *environmental criminology* is an extension of rational choice theory. Their work examines the target search process that precedes involvement in a crime. Like everyone else, criminals have activity patterns, and the environmental opportunities they encounter in the course of these activities influence their decisions to commit particular criminal acts (Beavon, Brantingham, and Brantingham 1994). Criminals are more likely to commit their offences along the paths they travel in the course of their daily activities; it follows that criminal opportunities are shaped by road networks and other factors that shape potential criminals' daily routines. Even if these actors are not actively seeking criminal opportunities, they may take advantage of vulnerabilities they encounter in the course of their daily

rational choice theory
Rational choice theory posits that crime is the result of deliberate choices made by offenders based on their calculation of the risks and rewards of these choices.

affairs. Brantingham and Brantingham (1995) analyzed crime patterns in terms of nodes, paths, and edges. Nodes are important places to would-be offenders—the places where they live, work, and socialize—and they frequently commit crimes in the areas around these nodes. Paths are routes between nodes, and these routes are vulnerable to crime. For example, a convenience store on the route from junior high school students' homes to their school is vulnerable to shoplifting, and homes that are on the route from a large bar to the area where patrons have parked their cars may be vulnerable to vandalism and other types of minor disorder as well as to burglary (Engstad 1975). Edges are boundaries or barriers between different types land use. An example is a street that separates an industrial area from an adjoining residential neighbourhood. Crime rates are often high in these areas because neighbourhood social control may be weaker and because they may contain properties that attract or generate criminal activity. Beavon, Brantingham, and Brantingham (1994) studied the influence of street networks on patterns of property crime in Maple Ridge and Pitt Meadows, British Columbia. They found that property crimes are most likely to occur on street segments that are readily accessible, have high flows of traffic or people, and include attractive targets.

Planners can use this knowledge to help prevent crime when designing roads and accessibility routes in new communities. Also, police are now using knowledge of crime patterns as the basis for new tactics, such as hot spot policing, that have been shown to reduce crime.

Routine Activities Theory

Routine activities theory is closely linked to rational choice theory. Both theories focus on the circumstances of the criminal event. Routine activities theory was developed from research on patterns of crime, such as when and where it occurs, the immediate circumstances of crime, the relationship between victims and offenders, and the reasons why some people are more likely than others to be victimized by crime.

Hindelang, Gottfredson, and Garofalo (1978) used this approach to develop the **lifestyle/exposure theory** to account for personal victimization. This theory posits that the lifestyle and routine activities of people place them in social settings with higher or lower risks of being victimized. For example, people who spend a lot of time in public places at night have a higher risk of being robbed than people who spend their evenings at home. According to the 2014 Canadian General Social Survey, those who reported engaging in 20 or more evening activities a month had violent victimization rates four times higher than those who never went out (Perreault 2015). Those who spent 10 evenings or more in bars or pubs had violent victimization rates 7 times higher than those who never went out.

Similarly, people whose lifestyles put them in frequent contact with people who commit crimes are more likely to be victimized than those whose time is spent with law-abiding companions. For example, those who used drugs or engaged in binge drinking were much more likely to have higher violent victimization rates. Members of organized crime gangs have higher rates of homicide victimization than most other Canadians. They have chosen a lifestyle in which

lifestyle/exposure theory
A theory of crime victimization that acknowledges that not everyone has the same lifestyle and that some lifestyles expose people to more risks than others do.

violence is used as a means of settling disputes and in which factors such as the competition for the exclusive right to sell drugs in particular areas ensure that there will be many disputes to settle.

Additional confirmation of lifestyle/exposure theory comes from studies of repeat victimization. If victimization is more likely among people with risky lifestyles, then we can expect people who have been victimized once to have a higher probability of being victimized a second time than people who have not been victimized. This is, in fact, the case. Repeated victimization of the same victim (or victim's household), by both the same type of crime and by different crimes, has been observed frequently in surveys both in the United States (US Department of Justice 1974a, 1974b; Sparks 1981) and in Canada (Koenig 1977; Sacco and Johnson 1990). In the 2004 Canadian General Social Survey, of those who stated that they had been victimized by a crime during the preceding 12 months, 40 percent reported that they had been victimized more than once (Gannon and Mihorean 2005).

Cohen and Felson (1979) made the assumptions of lifestyle exposure theory more explicit when they formulated the **routine activities approach** to crime (Figure 15.1). This approach begins with the observation that three factors must be present at the same time and space for a crime to occur:

1. *A motivated offender.* Unless someone wants to commit a crime, it will not take place. Most of the theories of criminal behaviour discussed in this book try to explain why some people are motivated to commit crimes.
2. *A suitable target.* A theft will not take place unless there is property to steal, and an assault cannot happen unless there is someone to attack.
3. *A lack of guardianship of that target.* If a target is well-guarded, it will be much less likely to be victimized.

Changes in any of these factors can lead to increases or decreases in crime. While most theories of crime focus on the offender, this theory tells us that the offender is just one piece of the puzzle. We also need to consider the context of a criminal event if we are to understand it and if we are to prevent further crimes. Changing peoples' motivation can be challenging, and it may be easier to alter the target or the guardianship.

routine activities approach
An extension of the lifestyle/exposure theory, this approach assumes that crimes are the expected outcomes of routine activities and changing social patterns.

FIGURE 15.1 ■ The Routine Activities Approach

Suitable Targets

Even without additional motivated offenders, an increase in the number, the value, or the accessibility of suitable targets can result in increases in crime. For example, 30 years ago electronic equipment was bulky, heavy, and difficult to carry. Today, potential criminals have the opportunity to steal laptop computers, expensive phones, and other valuable electronics that weigh very little and that are easy to conceal. Cohen and Felson predicted that unless small, attractive items were carefully protected, theft rates would increase as these items became more common, and their data supported this view. Less suitable targets were less frequently stolen. For example, Cohen and Felson observed that not many people stole refrigerators and washing machines because these were worth far less per pound than electronic equipment and because they were much harder to carry away.

Besides providing better protection, there are other ways of making small, expensive theft targets such as smartphones less attractive. The Federal Communications Commission (2014) reported that smartphones were the targets of 30 to 40 percent of robberies in American cities. A kill switch to make the phone inoperable if it is stolen would help reduce these thefts, but the industry was reluctant to implement this solution because service providers and manufacturers make billions of dollars selling insurance on phones and providing replacements. However, several jurisdictions, most notably California, passed legislation requiring these features by July 2015, and most manufacturers now build this capacity into their phones. As a result, smartphone thefts have declined significantly in a number of jurisdictions (Claburn 2017).

Another example of the importance of suitable targets was the discovery by young people in Winnipeg and Regina that some models of Chrysler vehicles built in the 1990s were very easy to steal. This discovery helped fuel a boom in joyriding that saw rates of motor vehicle theft soar in both cities (Anderson and Linden 2014). By contrast, vehicles protected by electronic ignition immobilizers, which are almost impossible to start without a key, are very rarely stolen unless the owners leave their keys in the car.

As a final example, when the value of all types of metal rose dramatically in the middle of the last decade, thieves started stealing metal items such as manhole covers, aluminum billboards and road signs, and stainless steel tanker trailers. In Prince George, BC, thieves even tried to steal the head of a bronze statue of Terry Fox in order to recover the metal. Several people in Canada have died after cutting into live power lines in an attempt to steal the copper wire. In 2014 the city of Surrey, BC, decided to spend $9 million replacing all the copper wire in its streetlights because of the cost of repairing the lines after thefts and the inconvenience caused by power blackouts. The copper wire is being replaced with a much less valuable alloy that will be less attractive to thieves.

effective guardianship
An aspect of the routine activities approach to understanding crime victimization that argues that three key factors are required for crime to happen: a motivated offender, a suitable target, and ineffective guardianship of that target. Effective guardianship would include having locks on bikes, putting goods in the trunk of the car, or having the police regularly patrol a high-crime area.

Effective guardianship refers to actions such as having neighbours watch your home while you are on vacation, drawing a steel mesh curtain overnight across glass display windows of jewellery, and taking evening walks on busy, well-lit streets rather than walking alone in an isolated park or down a dark alley. Changes in guardianship affect crime rates. Cohen and Felson showed that as daytime occupancy of homes (guardianship) decreased because of factors such as the increased employment of women outside the home and increases in the length of vacations, there was a substantial increase in daytime residential burglaries while the proportion of commercial burglaries declined.

This perspective is consistent with the results of interviews with offenders. Bennett and Wright (1984a) concluded that risk factors were the major consideration in target selection or **target suitability**. Burglars would be deterred if they believed that someone was home or if possible entrances were visible from nearby buildings or to passers-by. When Wright and Decker (1992) asked their respondents to describe unsuitable targets, most said they would avoid targets in areas where it looked like neighbours would look out for one another. Older people were considered to be especially likely to report suspicious behaviour to the police:

> The thing is if you got a lot of elderly people on one block, that'll get you killed mostly. . . . I wanted to do [a burglary] over here by the bakery shop, but that's a retired area. Almost everybody that live on that block is retired and they constantly lookin' out windows and watchin' [out] for each other. Ain't nothin' you can do about that. (Wright and Decker, 1992, 87)

The routine activities perspective has been extended to incorporate two additional variables—*intimate handlers* and *crime facilitators*. Felson (1986) has described "the 'handled offender,' the individual susceptible to informal social control by virtue of his or her bonds to society, and the 'intimate handler,' someone with sufficient knowledge of the potential offender to [control the offender]" (119). This variable incorporates into routine activities theory social bonds such as ties to parents and other community members, which have been shown to reduce involvement in delinquency and crime (see Chapter 14). Clarke and Eck (2003) have proposed that the decision to commit a crime can also depend on the presence of physical, social, or chemical crime facilitators. *Physical* facilitators are objects such as guns to be used in an armed robbery and scanning devices that enable restaurant employees to steal debit card numbers along with their associated PINs. *Social* facilitators can be peers who teach the individual the techniques of committing crime and who provide social support during the criminal event. *Chemical* facilitators include drugs and alcohol, which reduce inhibitions and lead to acts that might not have been committed had the individual not been under their influence. These substances can also make potential victims more vulnerable.

The importance of chemical facilitators is illustrated by the results of the 2014 GSS victimization survey (Perreault 2015), which found that alcohol consumption and illicit drug use increase one's likelihood of being a victim of crime. Those who reported consuming more than five alcoholic drinks in one sitting in the past month had experienced about twice as many incidents of violent victimization during the preceding 12 months as did non-drinkers (Perreault and Brennan 2010). Those who reported using illicit drugs during the month before the survey had violent victimization rates four times higher than those who did not use illicit substances.

target suitability
Because of their vulnerability, some potential crime targets are more attractive than others. A home that is unlit, has shrubs blocking a view of the front door, and has no alarm system will be seen as a more suitable target than a well-protected home.

The Diverse Attractions of Crime

Critics of rational choice and routine activities theories suggest that they may account for financially motivated crimes but that they do not account for expressive crimes that involve strong emotions (Hayward 2007). Proponents of rational choice and routine activities theories do take the view that "opportunity causes crime" (Felson and Clarke 1998, 9). This notion is easy to understand when we think of situations such as a person leaving an expensive bike unlocked and unattended in a high-crime neighbourhood or when managers of a convenience store near a junior high school do not take precautions against shoplifting. However, these theorists also realize that the attractions of crime are very diverse and that motivations for criminal behaviour can be quite complex.

Consider the reasons armed robbers give for committing their offences in the interviews quoted below. Most of us can understand the financial motives of the first robber, but the other three quotes show that robberies are not just committed for economic reasons. These might seem like bad decisions to most of us, and few of the robberies had much advance planning. However, it is clear that for the offenders, robbery is the result of a rational choice that satisfies certain needs and desires:

> It's the fastest and most direct way to get money. There's no thrill in getting it. It's for the cash, the money that I do it. (Gabor et al. 1987, 63)

> When I have a gun in my hands, nothing can stop me. It makes me feel important and strong. With a revolver you're somebody. It's funny to see the expression of people when they have a .38 in their face. Sometimes when I went home at night I thought of it and laughed. I know that it's bad to say that. Maybe I was just fascinated. (63)

> I was mad and I had to do something to get it out of my system. I was mad at my cousins and my girlfriend. I was mad at my mom at the time. (Feeney 1986, 58)

> Just to cause some trouble. Well, we just wanted to try that, you know. Goof around, you know, have some fun—jack up somebody. . . . We thought we were really big and stuff like that. (58)

Some of the motivations for homicide are discussed in Box 15.2.

FOCUS   BOX 15.2

THE DYNAMICS OF HOMICIDE

Researchers following the interactionist approach (see Chapter 13) have interviewed violent offenders and analyzed the accounts of homicides contained in police files to better understand the dynamics of homicide events. Luckenbill (1977) examined the typical roles played by offenders, victims, and bystanders in situations that resulted in homicide. He looked at the social context in which homicides occurred and concluded that many of them were confrontations that escalated into "character contests"—that is, violence became a means of saving face for the individuals. While their choice to use violence may not make sense to most of us, from their perspective it was a rational decision.

In most cases, the individuals involved were with family, friends, or acquaintances. Often the victim and the offender had a previous history of disputes that led them to anticipate or even to seek out confrontation. In some cases, one of the parties insulted the other either intentionally or inadvertently; in others, there was a refusal to carry out some requested action. This was interpreted as being offensive, and rather than ignoring the insult or leaving the scene, the offended individual responded aggressively in order to save face. In some cases, other people at the scene either encouraged a violent response or did nothing to try to defuse the situation. These points are illustrated in one of Luckenbill's (1977) examples:

> The offender, victim, and three friends were driving in the country drinking beer and wine. At one point the victim started laughing at the offender's car which he, the victim, scratched a week earlier. The offender asked the victim why he was laughing. The victim responded that the offender's car looked like junk. The offender stopped the car and all got out. The offender asked the victim to repeat his statement. When the victim reiterated his characterization of the car, the offender struck the victim, knocking him to the ground. (181)

What is striking about this incident is just how trivial it was. A joking remark made among friends led to the death of one young man and a long prison sentence for another. This case is not like most of those you see on television or in movies or read about in the headlines, but it is more representative of the "typical" homicide than are the cases of Paul Bernardo, Clifford Olson, or Robert Pickton, which get so much of the media's attention.

Can you think of some reasons why "respect" was so important to the young men involved in this case or in the following account of a Toronto murder trial:

> When prosecutor Laura Bird began speaking yesterday, it sounded for all the world as though she had borrowed her story line from a violent video game or, in another age, a Bugs Bunny and Road Runner cartoon.
>
> Hers was a tale of characters with childish nicknames who seethed with preening masculinity, nourished ridiculous grievances over months and whose ludicrous code

of behaviour is redolent with more ritual gestures than a formal audience with royalty.

> It would have been comic, but Ms. Bird was describing the real lives of real people and the terrible and senseless death of one of them.
>
> Wayne Anthony Reid, a young black man, died in a hail of bullets on June 15 last year and, Ms. Bird said, he died because the friend he was with that night had, almost a full year earlier, either not nodded in respect, or not nodded vigorously enough, or not been seen to nod, in deference to a friend of the man now alleged to have killed him.
>
> The prosecutor was delivering her opening address, designed to give jurors an overview of her case, in the second-degree murder trial of Leon Patrick Boswell . . .
>
> The victim, the alleged killer and their two friends either lived or grew up in the notorious housing complexes of the Jamestown area of northwest Toronto, a neighbourhood where territory is so clearly marked that, Ms. Bird said, "When you walked through the turf of someone else you were expected to acknowledge the other person in order to show your respect for them. Failure to nod, or otherwise hail them up, could be considered to be extremely disrespectful."
>
> And, she said, "Disrespect was taken seriously and could be expected to result in violent retaliation" such that a code of silence envelops the whole community, "preventing citizens from coming forward to report crimes for fear that they may be next in line at the morgue."* (Blatchford 2002)

Questions for Critical Thinking

1. Why are questions of "character" and "respect" so important to people who come from impoverished backgrounds and whose paths to success are blocked by a lack of education and job opportunities?

2. How could homicides such as these be prevented?

*Adapted from Christie Blatchford, "Doesn't Take a Lot to Get You Killed," *National Post*, 27 November 2002. Material reprinted with the express permission of National Post, a division of Postmedia Network Inc.

TABLE 15.1 ■ Deterrence, Routine Activity, and Rational Choice Theories

Theory	Theorists	Key Elements
Classical/deterrence theory	Beccaria	Humans are rational thinkers. Those who contemplate breaking the law consider the positive and negative consequences of their actions.
Rational choice theory	Clarke, Cornish	Crime is the result of deliberate choices made by offenders based on their calculation of the risks and rewards of those choices.
Environmental theory	Paul and Pat Brantingham	The activity patterns of offenders and environmental opportunities influence decisions to commit particular criminal acts.
Lifestyle/exposure theory	Hindelang	Some lifestyles expose people to more risks than others do.
Routine activities theory	Cohen and Felson	Crimes are the expected outcomes of routine activities and changing social patterns.

Policy Implications—Preventing Crime

Most of the criminologists who developed rational choice and routine activities theories were looking for ways to reduce crime. Their work led to situational crime prevention, which has been very successful in reducing crime. In this section we will focus mainly on situational prevention but will also discuss the social development approach to crime reduction, which you learned about in Chapter 7. The chapter will conclude with a discussion of a successful auto theft reduction program that combines several approaches to crime prevention into one comprehensive program.

Situational Crime Prevention

Several decades ago, robberies of city bus drivers declined dramatically when transit systems installed sturdy fare boxes and implemented exact change systems so that drivers did not have to carry cash, and murders of cab drivers declined significantly when cities mandated that taxis be equipped with cameras (Chaumont Menendez et al. 2014). Most models of new cars have very low theft rates because they have electronic immobilizers that make them virtually impossible to steal without using the keys or towing them. Researchers in England found that break-in victims were often victimized again within a few weeks of the initial crime. Based on this knowledge, they worked with the victims to improve physical home security measures (such as better locks), and they established "cocoon" Neighbourhood Watch programs that enlisted the help of the victims' immediate neighbours. Subsequent break-and-enter rates declined dramatically relative to similar areas that did not have this follow-up. These are all examples of **situational crime prevention**.

situational crime prevention
Premised on the belief that most crime is opportunistic rather than the outcome of those driven to commit a crime no matter what the circumstances. This form of prevention attempts to reduce the opportunities for crime rather than just relying on the police after the crime has occurred.

Situational crime prevention assumes that much crime is opportunistic and contextual rather than that offenders are driven to commit a crime no matter what. You will recall that Cohen and Felson stated that three factors—target suitability, ineffective guardianship, and a motivated offender—must converge in space and time for a crime to occur. Efforts to reduce crime can focus on any or all of these components. Clarke (2005) has identified five categories of situational crime prevention techniques and has provided examples of strategies that have been used for each category (see Table 15.2):

1. Increasing the *effort* required to commit a crime by target hardening or by controlling access to targets or the tools required to commit a crime;
2. Increasing the *risks* by increasing levels of formal or informal surveillance or guardianship;
3. Reducing the *rewards* by identifying property in order to facilitate recovery, by removing targets, or by denying the benefits of crime;
4. Reducing *provocations* by controlling for peer pressure or by reducing frustration or conflict;
5. Removing *excuses* by setting clear rules and limits.

Hundreds of studies have shown the effectiveness of situational crime prevention programs. Some of the research cited by Clarke illustrates the potential of the approach:

1. In the UK, suicide rates declined when natural gas was detoxified, making it impossible for people to commit suicide by putting their heads in a gas oven.

TABLE 15.2 ■ Ronald Clarke's 25 Techniques of Situational Prevention

Increase the Effort	Increase the Risks	Reduce the Rewards	Reduce Provocations	Remove Excuses
1. Target harden • Steering column locks and immobilizers • Anti-robbery screens • Tamper-proof packaging	6. Extend guardianship • Take routine precautions: go out in group at night, leave signs of occupancy, carry phone • "Cocoon" neighbourhood watch	11. Conceal targets • Off-street parking • Gender-neutral phone directories • Unmarked bullion trucks	16. Reduce frustrations and stress • Efficient queues and polite service • Expanded seating • Soothing music/muted lights	21. Set rules • Rental agreements • Harassment codes • Hotel registration
2. Control access to facilities • Entry phones • Electronic card access • Baggage screening	7. Assist natural surveillance • Improved street lighting • Defensible space design • Support whistle blowers	12. Remove targets • Removable car radio • Women's refuges • Pre-paid cards for pay phones	17. Avoid disputes • Separate enclosures for rival soccer fans • Reduce crowding in pubs • Fixed cab fares	22. Post instructions • "No Parking" • "Private Property" • "Extinguish camp fires"
3. Screen exits • Ticket needed for exit • Export documents • Electronic merchandise tags	8. Reduce anonymity • Taxi driver IDs • "How's my driving?" decals • School uniforms	13. Identify property • Property marking • Vehicle licensing and parts marking • Cattle branding	18. Reduce emotional arousal • Controls on violent pornography • Enforce good behavior on soccer field • Prohibit racial slurs	23. Alert conscience • Roadside speed display boards • Signatures for customs declarations • "Shoplifting is stealing"
4. Deflect offenders • Street closures • Separate bathrooms for women • Disperse pubs	9. Utilize place managers • CCTV for double-deck buses • Two clerks for convenience stores • Reward vigilance	14. Disrupt markets • Monitor pawn shops • Controls on classified ads • License street vendors	19. Neutralize peer pressure • "Idiots drink and drive" • "It's OK to say NO" • Disperse troublemakers at school	24. Assist compliance • Easy library checkout • Public lavatories • Litter bins
5. Control tools/weapons • "Smart" guns • Disable stolen cellphones • Restrict spray paint sales to juveniles	10. Strengthen formal surveillance • Red light cameras • Burglar alarms • Security guards	15. Deny benefits • Ink merchandise tags • Graffiti cleaning • Speed humps	20. Discourage imitation • Rapid repair of vandalism • V-chips in TVs • Censor details of modus operandi	25. Control drugs and alcohol • Breathalyzers in pubs • Server intervention • Alcohol-free events

Source: "Twenty-Five Techniques of Situational Prevention," POP Center, http://www.popcenter.org/25techniques.

These photos from the Peel Regional Police Force shows how pruning trees can increase the level of surveillance for several housing units.

2. Graffiti was almost eliminated in the New York subway system when graffiti was removed from cars immediately so that the "artists" could not see their work on display.
3. Electronic tagging of library books reduced theft from libraries.

4. Better inventory control reduced employee thefts from an electronics retailer.
5. Tighter procedures for mailing credit cards helped reduce rates of credit card fraud.

Table 15.2 shows the broad variety of situational techniques that can be used to reduce crime. These and other situational techniques have been very effective in reducing crime. However, some critics have pointed out that it is also important to reduce the number of motivated offenders:

> The control of crime involves interventions on all levels: on the social causes of crime, on social control exercised by the community and the formal agencies, and on the situation of the victim. Furthermore, that social causation is given the highest priority, whereas formal agencies, such as the police, have a vital role, yet one which has in the conventional literature been greatly exaggerated. It is not the "Thin Blue Line," but the social bricks and mortar of civil society which are the major bulwark against crime. Good jobs with a discernable future, housing [projects] that tenants can be proud of, community facilities which enhance a sense of cohesion and belonging, a reduction in unfair income inequalities, all create a society which is more cohesive and less criminogenic. (Young 1997, n.p.)

Reducing Motivated Offenders
Crime Prevention through Social Development

crime prevention through social development
An approach to crime prevention that focuses on reducing the number of motivated offenders by changing the social environment.

The initiatives that Young describes are called **crime prevention through social development** programs. Stephen Schneider studied crime prevention in Vancouver's Downtown Eastside, one of Canada's most crime-ridden neighbourhoods. His experience in this community led him to a conclusion similar to Young's—that crime problems eventually must be addressed through "a comprehensive strategy that ultimately is based upon a reinvigoration of civil society, the centrality of the local community in social problem solving, and the empowerment and participation of those who are in the most need. This means that a greater share of public resources and power be allocated to the local level and to the poorest communities in particular" (2007, 306). The work of Young and Schneider has led them to conclusions that are very different from those of politicians who promise us that a bit of tinkering with the justice system will quickly end most of our crime problems. Their work helps place the solutions suggested by routine activities theory in a broader perspective. Situational measures are an important way of reducing crime, but we must also consider other methods that will help overcome the serious social problems that breed motivated offenders.

Social development programs are intended to reduce the pool of motivated offenders by altering the conditions that breed crime. These programs (several of which were described in Chapter 7) focus on factors such as family problems, peer issues, poverty, and a range of school and community factors. Some have tried to improve the parenting skills of high-risk parents; others have provided job training and employment for young people who are cut off from the labour market because they live in poor communities. Social development strategies are often targeted at young people, who appear to be the most amenable to intervention and who make up the next generation of offenders.

Stephen Romilly/Alamy Stock Photo

Transit officials in many cities have found that immediately removing graffiti from subway cars is the best way to prevent it.

FOCUS   BOX 15.3

FACTORS AFFECTING FUTURE CRIMES?

Clarke's work (Table 15.2) shows how we can make changes in our social environments that can reduce crime. In a similar fashion, we can make changes that facilitate new types of crime or alter the ways in which crimes are committed. In this box, we look at some of the social trends that will have an impact on crime in the future.

The Cashless Society

For many of us, credit cards, debit cards, Apple Pay, and gift cards have replaced cash. Sweden is leading the way to a cashless society—less than half the country's banks handle cash, and public transit as well as many stores and restaurants have gone cashless. Many Swedes never use cash unless they travel outside the country. Canada ranks near the top of countries where the use of cash has quickly declined.

This trend has had an impact on crime because cash—a very attractive target—is less available to potential thieves. The loss of this potential target is one reason for the crime decline over the past two decades. Bank robberies have declined in most countries, and robberies—once common on paydays and on days when government cheques arrived—have dropped now that governments and employers have replaced cheques with direct bank deposit. Street crimes such as robbery and pickpocketing are much less profitable in a cashless society. Offences such as tax evasion and some types of illegal transactions may also decline because electronic cash is traceable (unless digital currencies such as Bitcoin become more commonly used).

Of course the move to electronic funds has also led to criminal opportunities. You learned in Chapter 4 that credit and debit card fraud is now commonplace. To deal with this problem, credit and debit cards in Canada now use a chip and PIN system that is more difficult to counterfeit than the older magnetic stripe cards. With the older cards, criminals could attach devices to the payment terminals that would scan the customer's information from the magnetic stripe. This information could then be used on fraudulent duplicate cards. A spokesman for Interac—the network that processes debit card transactions—reported that debit card fraud in Canada dropped by 45 percent from 2011 to 2012 (Shaw 2014) because of the implementation of chip technology.

(continued)

Self-Checkout in Retail Outlets

Many stores now encourage customers to scan their own goods. Not surprisingly, some customers see this as an opportunity to reduce their food costs because self-scanning reduces the guardianship provided by the checkout cashier. While evidence is limited, one British study found that losses more than doubled following the introduction of self-checkout (Beck and Hopkins 2015). There are a number of ways of avoiding payment—customers can misrepresent items, change bar codes, or stack items to avoid scanning them separately. (One store sold more carrots than it actually had in stock because customers were taking more expensive items such as cherries while telling the scanner they had carrots; Taylor 2016). Even people who do not view themselves as shoplifters may rationalize their behaviour. For example, they may consider stealing to be a discount they deserve for doing checkout work that should be done by store employees. If someone is caught, intent may be difficult to prove, as many customers accidentally make errors while scanning their items.

Gang Life Online

Like almost everyone else, gang members use social media, and researchers are learning how this is changing their lives. In Chicago—a city with a serious gang homicide problem—police have blamed social media for encouraging shootings. According to Patton (2017), gang members use social media to insult and threaten their enemies and to brag about their own use of violence. He concludes that this *cyberbanging* actually fuels retaliation between gangs and encourages violence. One pattern he found in social media posts involved an expression of grief for a friend who had been shot, followed by threats of revenge. Once this threat has been publicly posted, it is very difficult for the person to back down. And of course the targets of the threats will make their own posts, which escalates the conflict. This makes it very difficult to interrupt the violence, and the resulting shootings keep the deadly cycle going.

Urbanik and Haggerty (2018) found a similar pattern among street-involved youth in Toronto's Regent Park development. Like Patton, they found that disputes originated and were sustained on social media, but they also explored other dimensions of online activity. These included rapping (which some hoped would lead to a career and which also built group solidarity), presenting a hyper-masculine identity, and managing the risks of giving too much information to police or other criminal groups.

Self-Driving Cars

Self-driving cars will make driving safer and allow more efficient use of roadways, but they will also provide criminal opportunities. These vehicles are actually mobile computers, and like other computers, they can be hacked. "White hat" hackers have demonstrated that they can take over a vehicle using a computer and can disable the vehicle while it is being driven on a highway. It is technically possible to take control of a car with self-driving features and drive it off the road or crash it into another vehicle. Cybersecurity is becoming a major concern of vehicle manufacturers, in order to prevent murder by remote control (Perloth 2017).

3D-Printed Guns

Many jurisdictions around the world have restrictions on who can own firearms, particularly handguns. Known terrorists, people who have lengthy criminal records for violent offences, and domestic violence offenders may be denied a licence to possess a firearm. These restrictions have always been difficult to enforce, but enforcement may soon be impossible because in 2018 the US government agreed to allow the distribution of plans for 3D-printed guns. This means that anyone with a 3D printer can manufacture a plastic gun using a piece of metal as a firing pin. These plastic weapons have limitations, but as affordable metal 3D printing technology develops, it will be possible for people to manufacture a wide range of untraceable weapons at home. Because everyone with access to the Internet will be able to download the plans, this will increase the number of weapons everywhere. However, it will have the most serious impact in countries with strict gun laws such as Australia and the United Kingdom, where even legal weapons are now hard to procure.

Questions for Critical Thinking

1. Rational choice theorists have claimed that "opportunity makes the thief" (Felson and Clarke 1998). Online shopping is growing very rapidly in Canada. What new criminal opportunities are presented by online shopping?

2. Why do you think the police are lagging behind in efforts to reduce technology-driven crimes?

One of the most promising areas involves providing preschool programs for children from deprived backgrounds. One of the few social development programs that has undergone a long-term evaluation is a Michigan program called the Perry Preschool Project. The students were 123 African American children from poor families. Children aged three and four attended a preschool with an active learning curriculum five mornings a week, and teachers visited the children's homes once a week. The program lasted 30 weeks each year. A control group did not receive these services. Like the earlier Head Start program, this project sought to remedy the impact of the children's impoverished backgrounds on their later school success.

SEARCH FOR:
Perry Preschool Program

The final follow-up of the Perry Preschool project looked at the participants at age 40 (Schweinhart et al. 2005). Far fewer of the program participants than controls had been arrested five or more times (36% versus 55%), and they had less than half the arrest rate for drug offences (14% versus 34%). The program group had higher incomes, were more likely to own their own homes, and were less likely to have been on welfare. They had greater educational achievement and lower rates of illiteracy. Program group members were more likely to have had stable marriages, and females had lower rates of out-of-wedlock births. The costs of the program had been more than recovered through reduced welfare costs and increased earnings of the graduates. Schweinhart and colleagues estimate that the saving was more than $17 for every dollar invested in the program. Those responsible for this program maintain that the intervention must be made while the children are young and must be thorough enough to overcome the range of disadvantages faced by the participants. The Canadian government has responded to this research by establishing early childhood education programs in a number of communities as well as a national Aboriginal Head Start program.

The Need for Comprehensive Crime Reduction Initiatives

Some critics have expressed fears that situational techniques may lead to a fortress society or to a "big brother" state where our actions are always subject to scrutiny through technology such as surveillance cameras. Other practitioners and academics have viewed social development as the only acceptable way of preventing crime. They have gone from the reasonable position that society needs to do something about the root causes of crime to the not so reasonable position that social development programs are the only ones that are acceptable.

In fact, the developmental and situational approaches are complementary. Rational choice theory explicitly recognizes the role of the "motivated offender" and is consistent with the view that reducing the number of potential offenders will help reduce crime. Also, we can distinguish between "criminal involvement" and "criminal events" (Clarke 1995). Criminal involvement relates to criminal careers and is appropriately addressed by social development approaches. Criminal events are short-term acts that may be more appropriately addressed by situational prevention.

The most sensible strategy to pursue is one that recognizes that all crime prevention strategies have their strengths and weaknesses. A comprehensive strategy should include prevention programs that involve cooperation among different levels of government and other agencies and groups that can contribute to solutions (see Chapter 7), that are targeted to areas where they are most needed, that use a broad range of prevention approaches tailored to the specific needs of communities, and that draw upon programs that have been shown to be effective in other places.

To illustrate the potential of this approach as a guide to preventing crime, consider a Winnipeg program that one of this chapter's authors helped plan and implement.

The Winnipeg Auto Theft Suppression Strategy (WATSS)

From 2003 to 2008, Winnipeg had North America's highest rate of auto theft. Nearly one in five Criminal Code offences in the city was an auto theft, and the 2006 rate was 67 percent higher than that of the next highest Canadian city. In addition to the property loss involved in these thefts, there was significant physical violence. In 2007, two people were killed by drivers of stolen vehicles, and an early morning jogger was seriously injured after being deliberately run down by a youth driving a stolen car. In one 16-month period in 2007–8, eight drivers deliberately tried to run down police officers with stolen vehicles. Vehicle thieves also frequently attempted to ram police cars. Some youth engaged in other dangerous behaviour, such as jamming down vehicle accelerators and launching driverless vehicles down city streets and into parking garages.

Research done by the Manitoba Auto Theft Task Force found that auto theft rates were so high because auto theft had become an important part of youth culture in parts of Winnipeg. Virtually all the stolen vehicles were used for joyriding or as temporary transportation and were eventually recovered, often with major damage. Interviews with young offenders found that they stole cars for excitement and to show off for their peers and that they were very committed to auto theft. For example, one of the respondents said he stole cars "for a joyride . . . for the rush!," and another reported that "[stealing cars] is addicting. When you find something you're good at, you want to keep doing it" (Anderson and Linden 2014, 254).

This auto theft culture developed after a few young people learned how easy it was to steal some models of cars and realized that the probability of arrest was very low. These offenders told their friends and schoolmates about this new pastime, and the number of people willing and able to steal cars grew quickly. Children in some neighbourhoods learned to steal cars at a very early age (a number of them had stolen dozens of cars before they were 12 years old), and a peer culture developed that focused on car theft. Cars were often stolen by groups of friends, and over half the respondents reported that they had taken part in contests to see who could steal the most cars in a given period of time. This culture was reinforced by the mass media as well as by peer groups. Most of the youth who were interviewed played video games such as *Grand Theft Auto*, which glamorizes stealing cars and using them to create mayhem on the streets. Several also said that movies such as *Gone in 60 Seconds* had helped teach them some of the techniques for stealing cars.

For almost a decade, the favourite targets were Chrysler products manufactured in the early 1990s, which were particularly easy to steal. Although recent models are much more difficult to steal, older model Chrysler vehicles can be entered and started in a few seconds using only an ordinary screwdriver.

The solution to this problem focused on all three components of routine activities theory:

1. *Effective guardianship.* Earlier in this chapter we discussed the notion of individualized deterrence. In the language of routine activities theory, increasing certainty is a way of making guardianship more effective. The

most serious auto theft offenders were typically in the community under conditions of release such as curfews. The WATSS program provided intensive supervision to enforce these conditions. Youth were contacted in person every day by youth probation workers or the police Stolen Auto Unit and were contacted by phone every three hours. Youth who violated their conditions of release were immediately apprehended by the police so that they did not have the opportunity to reoffend.

2. *Target suitability.* The vulnerability of certain models of vehicles was a major reason why young people were able to learn to steal vehicles. Thus a major part of the prevention strategy was a mandatory program requiring electronic vehicle immobilizers for the 100,000 most at-risk vehicles in Winnipeg. These immobilizers were immediately effective: five years after the program began, none of the immobilizers approved by the program's sponsor, Manitoba Public Insurance, had yet been defeated by vehicle thieves.

3. *Motivated offenders.* The third component of WATSS involved addressing the social causes of auto theft by working with young people and their families to try to reduce the number of young people who found auto theft an appealing form of recreation. Much of this work was done by youth probation staff. Support programs for high-risk offenders and their families were run with community partners, including the Winnipeg School Division, Big Brothers and Big Sisters, and New Directions for Children, Youth, Adults and Families. The goals were to move current offenders away from auto theft and to end the flow of new recruits to this dangerous and costly pastime.

This program was highly effective at reducing crime. As shown in Figure 15.2, rates declined dramatically after WATSS was fully implemented. Between 2006 and July 2011, auto thefts declined by 83 percent. There was no displacement to other crimes; indeed, offences such as break and enter, robbery, and theft from vehicles also declined over this period. Because of this reduction in vehicle thefts, Winnipeg drivers are paying about $40 million less each year in vehicle insurance premiums.

FIGURE 15.2 ■ **Rates of Auto Theft**

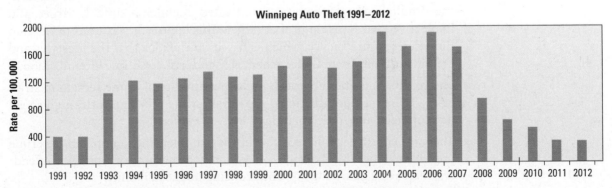

Compiled from different sources: 1991–2007 Canadian Centre for Justice Statistics, Statistics Canada. 1991–94, 2008–2009, Winnipeg Police Service, 2010–12 Canadian Centre for Justice Statistics.

The success of WATSS and other programs based on rational choice and routine activities theories of crime demonstrate the need for governments to invest in evidence-based approaches to crime reduction rather than simply building more jails. The deterrent effects of increased certainty are demonstrably more likely to reduce crime than increasing severity of punishment by legislating longer sentences. Furthermore, many situational prevention programs have been more successful than those that rely on the justice system to reduce crime, particularly when these programs are part of broad, comprehensive initiatives.

QUESTIONS FOR CRITICAL THINKING

1. What are the most significant crime problems in your community? Can you think of some strategies that might help reduce these problems?
2. The evidence presented in this chapter suggests that longer prison sentences are not an effective way of reducing crime. Despite this evidence, many Canadians strongly support these "get tough" campaigns. Why do you think people support the "get tough" approach?

Summary

- Deterrence theories focus on the factors influencing an individual's decision whether or not to commit an offence and assert that the legal system can be used to affect that decision. Research on the deterrent effects of imprisonment shows that increasing the severity of our current laws is not likely to have an impact on crime rates. However, several studies show that increasing the certainty of punishment *can* reduce crime, particularly through programs targeted at frequent offenders.

- Rational choice theory assumes that people commit crimes because they believe this will provide them with some reward. A person's decision to commit a crime may or may not appear rational to the rest of us, but it does meet a goal for the offender.

- Routine activities theory is based on the observation that crime results from the simultaneous presence of a motivated offender, a suitable target, and ineffective guardianship of that target. This approach was used to develop lifestyle/exposure theory, which is based on the idea that the lifestyles and activities of some people place them at higher risk for crime victimization.

- The routine activities approach leads to a number of crime reduction strategies. These include situational measures, crime prevention through social development, and incapacitation of high-rate offenders.

- The most effective way to reduce crime is to implement comprehensive crime prevention programs that focus on reducing the number of motivated offenders, increasing guardianship, and reducing target suitability.

NET WORK

In this chapter you have learned about the routine activities approach to crime. This approach has had an impact on crime prevention programs in North America and Europe by drawing attention to the role of the attractiveness of the target and the importance of effective guardianship. To see how these insights are used in crime prevention, look at Chapter 7 of the report *Preventing Crime: What Works, What Doesn't, What's Promising*, https://www.ncjrs.gov/works. In that chapter, by John Eck, find three projects that are intended to reduce the attractiveness of the target and three projects that increase effective guardianship. Have these projects succeeded in reducing crime?

Patterns of Criminal Behaviour

Many behaviours are illegal, but they vary widely in seriousness. Murder, for instance, is in a very different category from not putting enough change in a parking meter. In Part 3 we look at some of the kinds of misconduct that frequently occur in Canada.

When the average citizen thinks of crime, the images that most commonly come to mind are the so-called street crimes—robbery, assault, break and enter, and so on. These offences have been discussed frequently throughout this text because they occupy most of the time and attention of the criminal justice system, are the focus of the media, and have been the concern of most criminologists.

This section of the text examines three other types of crime. Chapter 16 looks at "organized" criminals, who are in the business of providing access to illegal goods and services. Chapter 17 looks at crimes committed by "respectable" people: many of our leading citizens are white-collar criminals, and many of our largest businesses are corporate offenders. This chapter makes the important point that the power we give to those in positions of authority and ownership in modern corporations may enable or encourage them to become involved in illegal activities that cause a great deal of social harm. Finally, Chapter 18 covers cybercrime, which will almost certainly become much more of a threat in the future as we live more of our lives online.

16 Organized Crime

STEPHEN SCHNEIDER
Saint Mary's University

Learning Objectives

After reading this chapter you should be able to

- Define organized crime and a criminal organization.
- Understand the characteristics, complexity, and diversity of organized crime.
- Identify the dominant types of organized crime groups operating in Canada.
- Identify the common types of organized crimes committed in Canada.
- Analyze the competing theories on the causes of organized crime and the social, economic, and political factors that give rise to organized crime in North America, and specifically in Canada.
- Compare competing theories on the organizational structures of organized criminal conspiracies.
- Understand the role Canada plays in global organized crime.

Organized crime can be distinguished from other types of crime by *how* crimes are carried out and by the ultimate *goal* of these crimes—financial profit. Broadly speaking, criminal activity is "organized" if it is perpetrated by a group of people who conspire together on a secretive basis with the goal of obtaining a financial or other material benefit. Scale is also an important factor in determining the extent to which criminal activity is organized: the broader the scope of the criminal activities, the greater the need for a high level of organization and, often, for the involvement of people in several different jurisdictions.

Defining Organized Crime

Criminal Intelligence Service Canada (CISC, 2014) defines organized crime as "a crime committed by any group of at least three people that involves the commission of a serious offence in pursuit of profit." This definition reflects how the term has simultaneously been used to denote the organization of offenders and the organization of crimes. According to von Lampe (2016, 3), "much of what is commonly associated with the term organized crime has to do with the provision of illegal goods and services." In other words, "organized crime is primarily about crime." Van Duyne (1996, 203) also emphasizes that organized crime is inherently shaped by the dynamics of criminal activities and, more specifically, illegal markets: "What is organized crime without organizing some kind of criminal trade; without selling and buying of forbidden goods and services in an organizational context? The answer is simply nothing."

Alternatively, organized crime has been conceptualized as the organization of criminal offenders. In this context, the term has been used synonymously with "criminal organization" and both are concerned with "the ways criminals are connected to other criminals" (von Lampe 2016, 5). Section 467.1 of the Criminal Code of Canada defines a criminal organization as a group, however organized, that:

(a) is composed of three or more persons in or outside Canada; and
(b) has as one of its main purposes or main activities the facilitation or commission of one or more serious offences that, if committed, would likely result in the direct or indirect receipt of a material benefit, including a financial benefit, by the group or by any of the persons who constitute the group.

The legislation goes on to state that a criminal organization "does not include a group of persons that forms randomly for the immediate commission of a single offence." While this caveat does provide some conceptual precision, the legal definition in Canada of a criminal organization remains exceptionally broad and provides little help in understanding the complexity of organized crime. Indeed, organized crime remains difficult to define or conceptualize. Vander Beken (2012, 83) notes that "organized crime is not a 'natural' crime phenomenon that can be observed, counted and classified like other crimes. More than most other types of crime, organized crime is a social construct that strongly reflects policy choices and beliefs." Put more bluntly, Beare (2003, xxi) states that "discussions related to organized crime and transnational crime—about the factors leading to the creation of illegal markets, about the size of the 'threat' and about the passing of extraordinary legislation to attack the problem—are steeped in politics."

Characteristics of Organized Crime

This section builds on the CISC definition of organized crime by elaborating on its core characteristics (summarized in Table 16.1). These characteristics can be divided into four categories: structural/organizational (traits related to the association among the criminal offenders); institutional (factors that sustain organized criminal conspiracies); commercial (the features of organized crimes and black markets); and behavioural (traits that distinguish the [subcultural] norms, values, and codes of organized criminal offenders and groups). Not all of the characteristics in the categories are present in every organized criminal conspiracy.

Structural/Organizational Characteristics

Two or More People Involved

A core trait of organized crime is that it involves multiple individuals who conspire to commit serious, revenue-generating criminal offences. The more offenders involved in such a criminal conspiracy, the greater the likelihood it will constitute organized crime.

TABLE 16.1 ■ **A Comprehensive Classification of Organized Crime**

Structural/Organizational	Institutional	Commercial	Behavioural
Two or more people involved	Continuing enterprise	Illegal activities committed for financial or other material benefit	Rationality
A systematic pattern to the relationship of the offenders	Sophistication	Serious Criminal Offences Multiple enterprises Consensual and predatory crimes	Subcultural values/Contempt for civil society
Limited or exclusive membership	Career criminals	Goods and services	Non-Ideological motivation Rules and regulations
Assigned tasks/specialization/division of labour	Insulation against law enforcement and prosecution	Illegal and legal commercial activities Monopolistic tendencies	Discipline
	Recruitment	Tactics to support commercial activities: corruption, violence, money laundering	
Multi-jurisdictional/transnational in scope			

A Systematic Pattern to the Relationship of the Offenders

To constitute an organized criminal conspiracy, there must be not only multiple offenders but also a systematic pattern to the relationship among these offenders. This systematic pattern separates organized crime from other forms of collective criminal action such as riotous mobs.

A major controversy in the study of organized crime concerns the nature of the relationships among the offenders and how these relationships are structured. There is no single pattern to such relationships, just as there is no single type of organizational structure. The pattern of relationships may be based on kinship, friendship, shared ethnicity or nationality, or business ties; also, the structure of an organized criminal conspiracy may be hierarchical (based on power relations among the offenders involved) or more symmetrical (based on the specialized tasks performed by or resources available to the conspirators).

In his seminal study of criminal groups in New York City, Ianni (1974) identified two basic forms of relationships among individuals involved in organized crime. The first are "associational networks," which are held together by close personal relationships among members. Examples of these personal relationships are kinship and shared ethnicity, as embodied by the Italian mafia "family." The second follows an "entrepreneurial model," where the bond among the offenders is less personal and determined more by business interests. The historical trend in organized crime has seen business relationships replacing associational networks as the principal binding force among the offenders involved.

Limited or Exclusive Membership

Most traditional organized crime groups place restrictions on who can become members. Group membership is based on factors such as ethnicity, race, nationality, kinship, or criminal record. Ethnicity and/or nationality has long been a major binding tie for members of organized crime groups, which explains why most of the dominant traditional organized crime groups are referred to by the ethnic backgrounds of their members (the Sicilian mafia, the Calabrian 'ndrangheta, Chinese triads, Japanese Yakuza, Russian *vor v zakone*, etc.). Many outlaw motorcycle gangs restrict membership to Caucasians (although another unique requirement is that a member must own and ride a Harley-Davidson motorcycle).

Membership in traditional organized crime groups is more than symbolic. Having been made a member of a mafia family, the "made guy," "wiseguy," or "goodfellow" can oversee his own crew and/or have jurisdiction over a neighbourhood to carry out his criminal activities. He also has greater access to criminal markets, to government, private sector, and/or union officials, and to other resources that cannot be accessed by most ordinary criminals. More importantly, criminal organizations such as the mafia and Hells Angels provide members with intimidating power, affluence, and credibility within the criminal underworld.

An important recent change in the world of organized crime has been the emergence of criminal networks that have abandoned all traditional restrictions on membership, such as ethnicity or nationality. Instead, the only criterion for an individual who wants to join the criminal network is the ability to contribute to the accumulation of profits (see Figure 16.3).

Assigned Tasks/Specialization/Division of Labour

Many organized crime conspiracies have a division of labour whereby the individuals involved are assigned certain functions (Abadinsky 2012). In a hierarchical criminal organization, this division of labour often corresponds to the member's position in the power structure. In a more symmetrical criminal network, the roles played by individual offenders are often based on their particular skills or resources. A prime example is Colombia's Medellin and Cali cocaine cartels, which established intricate divisions of labour, with different cells specializing in one specific function, such as refining the raw coca into cocaine, transportation, bribing government officials, laundering money, distributing drugs wholesale, providing security, and managing "stash" houses in destination countries (President's Commission on Organized Crime 1986; US Senate Committee on Governmental Affairs 1989).

> **SEARCH FOR:**
> **UN Transnational Organized Crime Threat Assessment**

Multi-jurisdictional/Transnational in Scope

Many of the dominant criminal groups operating in Canada are multi-jurisdictional in that they have a presence in more than one province. This is exemplified by Hells Angels, which is represented in every province by either a separate chapter or a chapter of an affiliated motorcycle club. One of the most significant trends in organized crime has been the internationalization of criminal groups and their illegal activities. Notwithstanding the historical prevalence of organized international smuggling, until the 1970s most criminal groups operated in specific local territories and usually did not attempt to function to any great extent outside their immediate sphere of influence. Organized crime is now international. The unprecedented frequency with which criminal groups and activities cross national boundaries, combined with the global structure and reach of some crime groups, has led to the emerging spectre

transnational organized crime
Criminal groups that have a presence in different countries or criminal activities that are coordinated and conducted across national borders.

of what is referred to as "**transnational organized crime**" (TOC). Hells Angels epitomize TOC in that they have chapters in more than 50 countries.[1] The transnational nature of organized crime is also reflected in the many criminal activities that now cross national borders. Indeed, the transnational nature of some crime groups is deliberate so as to facilitate international criminal activities.

[1]Hells Angels World web site, http://hells-angels.com/, accessed January 4, 2018

FOCUS   BOX 16.1

STRUCTURAL AND ORGANIZATIONAL CHARACTERISTICS OF OUTLAW MOTORCYCLE GANGS (OMGs)

To outsiders, a biker gang may represent the epitome of wild, unrestrained anarchism. Yet organizations like Hells Angels are actually highly structured, tightly knit, and quite hierarchical. There is an organizational hierarchy to each chapter, complete with management positions, a division of labour, and skills-based advancement. There is general uniformity in style of dress, colours, and motorcycles (large, modified Harley-Davidsons). Most clubs have a written constitution and bylaws. Minutes of meetings are recorded, dues and other revenues collected, and accounting records maintained.

The organizational structure of an outlaw motorcycle gang (OMG) chapter is relatively consistent. Most have a president, vice president, secretary-treasurer, enforcer, sergeant-at-arms, road captain, rank-and-file members, and prospects. The chapter president is often elected and has final say over all the business of the chapter. In addition, the president may receive all sorts of booty and monetary tribute from members. The secretary-treasurer collects dues on behalf of the chapter, acts as bookkeeper and secretary (e.g., keeps the minutes of meetings), and keeps track of who owes what and to whom. The sergeant-at-arms maintains order at meetings and on the chapter's "biker runs." This position is usually filled by the toughest member of the chapter. He may also serve as an enforcer and has the power to discipline a club member. The road captain organizes the logistics and security for the time-honoured biker run.

THE CANADIAN PRESS/Graham Hughes

Only members of the OMG are allowed to wear its "colours." Generally speaking, a chapter will have no less than six and no more than 25 members. Each chapter has prospective members ("strikers" or "prospects"), who spend from one month to one year on probation. To become a full-patch member, one must first be sponsored by an existing member, who is responsible for his prospect. During this time, the prospect must prove himself worthy of membership by following orders and committing crimes. A vote is ultimately taken by chapter members to determine whether the prospect will become a full, patch-wearing member.

The OMG and its leader are insulated from law enforcement through the chapter's organizational hierarchy and through a strict code, which strives to ensure that the ultimate loyalty of each member is to the club. Prospects, hangers-on, puppet club members, and external associates will often take the fall for particular crimes involving OMG members, especially those members who occupy management positions in the chapter.

Many of the larger OMGs have developed specialized units to carry out important functions, such as enforcement, violence, and even murder. Hells Angels enforcers used to be adorned with Nazi storm-trooper-like lightning bolts tattooed below the words "Filthy Few." The Outlaws have their "SS Death Squad," and the Pagans have the "Black T-Shirt Squad." The Hells Angels' former puppet gang in Quebec—the Rockers—had a special assassination squad called the "football team"; it also operated a "baseball team," which "was made up of members and associates who were responsible for carrying out brutal beatings of rivals" (Canadian Press 2002).

While OMG chapters exhibit a formal organizational structure, individual members often maintain networks of associates and connections through which they carry out their criminal rackets. For business purposes, each member is at the centre of a network that operates independently of the chapter. In other words, the OMG chapter's formal structure is not necessarily the same as its revenue-generating commercial structure, which is broader than the gang. But "members can call upon the muscle of the club in the event of conflict, making them formidable entrepreneurs" (Abadinsky 2000, 238). Lavigne (1996, 246) adds: "The Hells Angels are truthful when they say they are not a criminal organization. Rather, they are an organization of criminals." Indeed, "belonging to the Hells Angels guarantees to each member the possibility of running an illicit activity" (Nicaso 2001).

Questions for Critical Thinking

1. How does "organization" give these crime groups an advantage over their competition? (And by competition, consider both other criminals and law enforcement agencies).

2. While many criminals try to stay out of the public eye, groups like the Hells Angels are often very visible and easy to find. Why aren't they more likely to be arrested?

Institutional Characteristics

Continuity/Continuing Enterprise

Some organized crime groups are structured in order to last beyond the life of the current membership (Abadinsky 2012, 4). The interests of individuals are subordinate to those of the organization, and personnel can be replaced as a matter of course. There is a line of succession to leadership, and as a rule, there are no indispensable members (Salerno 1967, 7). Hells Angels has officially existed since the 1950s, with roots stretching back to the immediate postwar period (see Box 16.1). Each of the five major New York mafia families has survived for more than 75 years; so has the Montreal-based mafia. Canada's Criminal Code recognizes organized crime as a continuing enterprise by emphasizing that a criminal organization "does not include a group of persons that forms randomly for the immediate commission of a single offence."

Career Criminals

One reason why some organized crime groups persist over time is that the offenders involved are usually chronic offenders. In some crime groups, a criminal record is a prerequisite for "official" membership. Many criminal groups require their members, once initiated, to undertake a wide range of illegal activities. Members of criminal organizations often do not have legitimate jobs (though some will hide behind artificially created jobs or businesses), and even after accumulating considerable wealth or spending long periods of time in jail, many continue with their illegal activities.

Insulation against Enforcement and Prosecution

A hierarchical organizational structure helps insulate the upper echelons of a criminal group against law enforcement actions. This is done by ensuring that the hands-on execution of illegal activities is carried out by those at the lowest level of the organization or even by "associates" who are not official members of the organization. The mafia in Montreal is well-known for delegating criminal tasks to "associates," including street gang members, while outlaw motorcycle gangs often use "prospects" (probationary members of a biker club chapter), "hangers-on" (associates of a biker club), and "**puppet clubs**" to carry out their dirty work. The more buffers between those who physically carry out crimes and those in the upper echelons of the organization, the more the latter will be insulated from prosecution.

Insulation against enforcement actions is also helped by a code of silence. Central to the Sicilian mafia is a code of *omertà*. At the most practical level, *omertà* is about secrecy: members are expected to keep the operations of the family secret from outsiders and, ultimately, to protect its leaders and the organization itself from law enforcement. For decades, members of the Italian mafia in the United States and Canada escaped prosecution because of their commitment to this sacrosanct code. The once-powerful Italian mafia has been decimated in the United States, in part because members increasingly turned their backs on the code of *omertà* by becoming witnesses for the state (Reppetto 2007).

Because of the danger of electronic eavesdropping by police, those taking part in organized criminal conspiracies must often be very guarded about how they communicate and what they say to avoid providing law enforcement with evidence that can be used in court. Communication can be protected in one of two ways. First, offenders can structure their communication so that it cannot be interpreted by police; this is most often accomplished by talking in abstract codes. Second, criminal groups will undertake measures to ensure that their conversations are not intercepted by police—for example, by physically "patting down" people to guard against surreptitious recording, using electronic devices that can detect recording bugs, encrypting digital communication, and using multiple disposable cellular telephones.

Some criminal organizations are also characterized by structured channels of communication, whereby the lower echelons can only communicate with certain other group members, generally those directly above them in the hierarchy. The main purpose of these strict channels of communication is to insulate the leaders of the crime group from arrest and criminal prosecution. The Cali Cartel used an innovative network structure that was specifically designed to protect the organization and its members from law enforcement. This was accomplished by ensuring that the identities of offenders working within one "cell" of the network were unknown to those working in other cells. If one cell

puppet club
A motorcycle club that is subsidiary to a more dominant outlaw motorcycle gang and that is often expected to carry out the dirty work of the latter.

was compromised, the operations of the other cells (and the larger organization) would not be endangered (President's Commission on Organized Crime 1984, 562; Constantine 1994).

Sophistication

To maximize profits and to avoid incarceration, some organized crime groups have become quite sophisticated. The level of sophistication with which they carry out their activities separates them from unorganized criminals; it also separates the larger transnational criminal groups from smaller local gangs or networks. According to CISC (2007):

> Only a small number of organized crime groups are capable of operating elaborate criminal operations. These groups are engaged in diverse and complex activities. For the most part, they operate out of the largest urban areas but have secondary operations or criminal influence in other cities or rural areas. These groups are distinguished by sophisticated operations, often involving importation, manufacture or distribution of a wide range of illicit commodities as well as the ability to commit complex frauds, money laundering or financial schemes. In addition, many of these groups display the capability to target, coerce or employ individuals in legitimate business, professionals, such as lawyers and accountants, and other community members in order to facilitate their criminal activities. Many of these groups are difficult to target as they strategically insulate themselves from law enforcement. (CISC, 2007: 14)

Another indication of sophistication within the realm of organized crime is the expanding use of technology. Police have uncovered criminal conspiracies that have produced exact replicas of credit cards, passports, currency, and consumer goods. Some crime groups possess the computer technology to steal personal identification directly from bank cards or through the Internet. Computer hackers who are able to decode complex security systems and breach the firewalls of corporations have increasingly been linked to organized criminals whose intentions are theft for financial gain (Brown 2007; Verizon Business Risk Team 2009). "**Cybercrime** groups" even develop and market "crimeware"— malicious software specifically designed to steal confidential personal and financial information (CISC 2010, 12). Some crime groups have engineered intricate encryption codes and software to communicate surreptitiously online; others have the technology to conduct radar sweeps of drug surveillance planes to map out gaps in coverage. Some groups have even used submarines to smuggle contraband (*New York Times* 2012).

cybercrime
Illegal acts in which a computer and a network are central to committing a crime and are also the targets of the crime.

SEARCH FOR:
Criminal Intelligence Service Canada

Recruitment

Traditional organized crime groups like the Italian mafia, outlaw motorcycle gangs, and Chinese triads use "an institutionalized process for inducting new members and inculcating them with the values and ways of behaving" (Cressey 1969, 36). Recruitment is increasingly important to modern criminal organizations because of their need for specialized skills and resources.

According to the CISC (2009), "where critical skills necessary to facilitate criminal activities are absent within a criminal group, skilled outsiders are recruited or exploited to provide this service. The individual may be considered an outside contractor or part of the criminal network" (13).

Commercial Characteristics

Profit-Oriented Criminal Activities

The business of organized crime is making money. This distinguishes organized crime from crimes of passion, vandalism, and terrorism. Organized crime groups generate money through myriad activities, both illegal and legal (see Table 16.2). Drug trafficking is the biggest moneymaker for most organized crime groups. The CISC estimates that 80 percent of all identified criminal organizations in Canada are involved in the illegal drug trade (2007, 13; 2009, 9). Human trafficking comes second (according to many observers) in terms of geographic scope, the number of people victimized, and the amount of revenue generated for criminal entrepreneurs (ILO 2012; UN 2012). Many criminal groups will involve themselves in almost any activity that will make them money.

Consensual and Predatory Criminal Activities

Organized criminals are involved in both consensual and predatory crimes. A consensual crime is one where no "victim" exists; that is, two or more individuals voluntarily engage in an illegal transaction. The business of organized crime has been described as providing goods and services that are in demand by the public but that have been made illegal by the state or are tightly regulated.

TABLE 16.2 ■ Common Organized Criminal Activities

Consensual	Hybrid: Predatory/Consensual (includes both a victim and a consumer)	Predatory
Drug smuggling/trafficking	Automobile theft	Extortion ("protection rackets"); human trafficking (indentured slavery and forced prostitution)
Smuggling and marketing of legal consumer products (tobacco, liquor, fuel, digital products, clothing)	Environmental crimes (illegal dumping of waste)	Business and labour racketeering
Gambling	Counterfeiting and product piracy (bank cards, government documents, currency, consumer products)	Murder, grievous bodily injury
Migrant smuggling	Corruption (of government officials, labour racketeering)	Kidnapping
Loansharking	Illegal trade in wildlife	Consumer fraud (Ponzi schemes, telemarketing)
	Illegal trade in organs and tissue (human and animal)	Government fraud (tax, healthcare, employment insurance, social insurance and assistance)
Money laundering	Illegal trafficking in arms, ammunition, and explosives	Corporate fraud (credit card, insurance, mortgage)
	Trafficking in nuclear and radioactive substances	Stock market manipulation
	Illegal trade in stolen artifacts, art, jewellery, precious gems	Theft (including robbery, burglary, hijacking)
	Trafficking in endangered plant species	Computer crime (computer hacking)
	Prostitution/Human trafficking	

Predatory crimes are those in which a victim suffers a direct physical, emotional, or financial loss. Predatory crimes carried out by organized criminal groups include **extortion** (protection rackets), theft, **human trafficking**, currency counterfeiting, and various types of fraud.

A clear distinction between consensual and predatory crimes is often difficult to draw, given that even consensual crimes can harm the individual consuming the good or service (e.g., a drug addict or compulsive gambler) as well as society at large. Table 16.2 summarizes the wide range of illegal activities associated with organized crime and categorizes each according to whether it is a consensual crime, a predatory crime, or both.

Serious Criminal Offences

Most of the crimes on this list are serious in that they exact considerable harm on individuals and on society as a whole. This aspect distinguishes these crimes from those of individual offenders or ad hoc groups that limit their illegal activities to less serious crimes such as thefts from homes and vehicles, vandalism, and fraud under $5,000.

Multiple Enterprises

Another common characteristic of many organized crime syndicates is that they carry out more than one profit-oriented (legal or illegal) activity. It is not uncommon for members of an outlaw motorcycle gang, an Italian Canadian mafia clan, or a criminal Chinese triad to be involved in drug trafficking, gambling, telemarketing fraud, prostitution, credit card counterfeiting, and extortion, to name just a few. A notable exception to this rule is the Colombian drug trafficking cartels, which were dominant in the 1980s and 1990s and which focused almost exclusively on cocaine trafficking.

Goods and Services

Organized illegal enterprises provide both goods and services. Popular illegal goods include drugs, legal contraband (such as cigarettes or liquor), stolen goods, weapons, counterfeit currency, pirated commercial products, and even human or animal organs. Common illegal consensual services include gambling, prostitution, **loansharking**, migrant smuggling, and illegal waste dumping (which is provided to legitimate businesses seeking to avoid the high costs of obeying environmental laws).

Illegal and Legal Commercial Goods and Markets

As indicated above, most of the commercial activities undertaken by organized crime groups are illegal. But they also provide goods that are legal. For example, while cigarettes, liquor, and prescription drugs are legal products, they are also distributed through black markets. The underground markets for legal goods exist due to strict government regulations that restrict legal distribution or due to the ability of organized crime groups to provide the goods at lower prices than legal markets. These price differentials are often the result of higher taxes on consumer goods between two jurisdictions. For example, the United States has low taxes on cigarettes and liquor compared to Canada, so organized groups

extortion
An offender unlawfully obtains money, property, or services from an individual or entity through coercion and intimidation.

human trafficking
The illegal trade of people for the purposes of commercial sexual exploitation and other forms of forced labour.

SEARCH FOR:
United Nations World Drug Report 2013

loansharking
Lending money at very high interest rates, often enforced through the use of physical force.

smuggle large quantities of these products across the border, where they are sold to Canadians well below their regular retail price. Other legal products are stolen and then fenced through underground markets or through legal businesses such as bars or pawnshops. This can be done on a large scale by organized crime groups, which acquire goods through activities such as hijacking trucks.

Criminal organizations are also active in the legal business world. According to Lyman and Potter (2014, 74), "legitimate businesses offer concealment opportunities for illegal activities," such as gambling and drug trafficking; they can also help launder the proceeds of crime, provide sources of reportable and legitimate income, and help the criminal entrepreneur integrate into the local community. In some cases, the infiltration of criminal groups into legitimate companies is unaccompanied by illegal activities; they simply invest or own a business to produce another source of income. In the quest to maximize revenues, however, the entry of organized criminals into the legitimate business world is frequently accompanied by illegal acts (extortion, corruption, intimidation, violence) that are meant to help them infiltrate, control, and maximize revenue from a particular legal business venture. This is essentially what business racketeering entails: using illegal means to infiltrate a legitimate business and/or market and to subsequently maximize revenues in said business or marketplace.

Monopolistic Tendencies

Organized crime groups often seek a monopoly over the sale of a particular good or service in a particular geographic area. Typically, these monopolies are sought and maintained through violence, the threat of violence, or corrupt relationships with government, businesses, or union officials (Abadinsky 2012, 4). Competition for market share often leads to serious violence, as demonstrated by the biker war that erupted in Quebec in the 1990s. More than 160 people were killed when Hells Angels tried to monopolize the lucrative cocaine trade in that province (Sher and Marsden 2003). One goal of business racketeering is to dominate and even monopolize a particular legal commercial sector. During the 1960s the Montreal mafia gained a monopoly over the sale of pizza and Italian ice creams in the north end of Montreal through force and intimidation (Edwards 1990, 6; *Gazette* [Montreal], 29 November 1975).

Tactics to Support Commercial Activities

Many organized crimes generate revenues directly; other activities, though, are carried out to facilitate the criminal organization's profit-making enterprises. Like legitimate corporations, criminal groups must undertake certain activities to support the production, distribution, and marketing of their products and services. One factor that separates organized crime from unorganized crime is their resort to tactical illegal activities, in particular corruption, violence, intimidation, money laundering, intelligence gathering, and surveillance.

Corruption—of public officials, labour unions, political parties, and the judiciary—has long been key to organized crime tactics. In recent years, police in Canada have uncovered many conspiracies to corrupt officials working in marine ports and airports in order to facilitate the international movement of drugs, contraband, and the cash proceeds of crime (CISC 2004, 10–14; Schneider 2016, 366–67). Tobacco companies have knowingly cooperated with criminal groups to smuggle cigarettes into the country (*National Post* 2003), and Canadian financial institutions have been complicit in money-laundering schemes (Beare and Schneider 1990; Schneider 2003). Recently, a Quebec public commission investigating corruption in Montreal's public works sector uncovered evidence pointing to the Rizzuto family's influence in determining the successful bidders on public contracts; the Rizzutos, a mafia family, received a cut from the winning companies. Among those alleged to be implicated in the mafia-related graft were politicians, municipal civil servants, labour union officials, and the owners of private construction firms (Canadian Press 2012, 2013).

Gangland violence may seem indiscriminate, but it is often applied "rationally" to ensure that certain individuals—usually victims, witnesses, informants, or competing gangsters, and sometimes government officials—do not obstruct the activities of the criminal organization. Violence is also used to maintain internal discipline within crime groups and to enhance the group's reputation. As in other countries, violence is a constant in Canada's criminal underworld. According to police-reported crime statistics, in 2016 there were 141 "gang-related" homicides in Canada—roughly 25 percent of all murders in Canada that year. This number is quite variable, as there were only 96 gang-related murders in 2015 (David 2017). Outlaw motorcycle gangs have carried out some of the worst mass killings in Canadian criminal history. This includes the murder of five Quebec Hells Angels members on 24 March 1985 and the killing of eight members of the Bandidos motorcycle club in Ontario on 8 April 2006. Both mass executions were "internal cleansings"—that is, they were carried out by fellow club members. More recently, violence erupted in Quebec after Vito Rizzuto, the head of the Montreal mafia,

Wayne Leidenfrost/The Vancouver Sun. Material republished with the express permission of *Vancouver Sun*, a division of Postmedia Network Inc.

The enormous profits made by those involved in organized crime mean that these groups have significant amounts of cash that must be laundered in order to disguise the illegal sources of these funds.

was imprisoned. During his imprisonment, different factions tried to fill the void in the Montreal's criminal underworld that Rizzuto's departure had created; others manoeuvred to take over his mafia family. Many of those loyal to Rizzuto were murdered, including his son, who was shot to death in 2009; the following year, his father was murdered in his Montreal home. Vito Rizzuto himself died (of natural causes) in 2013.

One tactic for protecting the profits of organized crime is money laundering, referring to the process of legitimizing illegally earned revenue. Cash is the universally accepted mode of payment in the underground economy. Thus, organized criminals—drug traffickers, in particular—accumulate large amounts of cash, often in small denominations. This can make them targets for law enforcement and taxation officials. That is why organized criminals must devise creative methods for converting large amounts of cash into less suspicious assets while concealing the criminal source of the funds. A typical money laundering technique involves opening a cash-based business, such as a restaurant or bar, and then depositing the cash proceeds of crime in that business's bank account, thereby masking it as revenue from the legitimate business. A 2003 survey of RCMP proceeds of crime cases found that in Canada, banks are the most frequently used sector of the economy for laundering money (Schneider 2003).

A final tactic, used by more sophisticated criminals, is intelligence gathering and counter-surveillance. This includes the use of eavesdropping technology as well as placing gang associates inside enforcement agencies to gather information. In Canada, some outlaw motorcycle gangs have become well-known for their intelligence-gathering and surveillance activities, which they use against both rival gangs and law enforcement agencies. Police raids on biker clubhouses have turned up electronic surveillance equipment, confidential police radio frequency lists, and scanners. Some chapters even have a designated intelligence officer, who is responsible for compiling dossiers, including photographs, physical descriptions, home addresses, and licence plate numbers of rival gang members, police, journalists, and witnesses (Schneider 2016, 385).

Behavioural Characteristics

Rationality

Rational choice theory (see Chapter 15) posits that many offenders are self-maximizing decision makers who calculate the advantages and disadvantages associated with specific criminal acts (Clarke and Cornish 1985). Arguably, organized crime is one of the most rational forms of criminality because it responds to the laws of supply and demand in the same way as legitimate businesses. This rationality is reflected in the criminal organization itself. Criminal groups "selling illicit goods and services must, if they are to capitalize on the great demand for their wares, expand by establishing a division of labour. . . . The next rational move is consolidation and integration of separate divisions of labor into a cartel designed to minimize competition and maximize profits" (Cressey 1969, 34–35). Even violence is used rationally by criminal groups in that it is meant to support the goals of the group.

Subcultural Values/Contempt for Civil Society

Members of traditional organized crime groups, such as the Italian mafia, the Japanese Yakuza, the Russian **vory v zakone**, and outlaw motorcycle gangs, openly rebel against the social rules and values that govern civil society; instead, they organize their behaviour according to the norms of their criminal group. This particular trait of organized crime is associated with subcultural theories of criminality and violence, which argue that serious and chronic offenders adhere to values and norms that are at odds with the dominant law-abiding culture and that they learn through their immersion in a deviant subculture (Ferracuti and Wolfgang 1967). The organized crime subculture is exemplified by the term "wiseguy," which is used to refer to members of Italian American mafia groups. A wiseguy believes that anybody who follows the commonly accepted rules and laws of civil society is a sucker and deserves to be victimized. Pileggi adeptly captures the wiseguy's attitude towards society: "They lived in an environment awash in crime, and those who did not partake were simply viewed as prey. To live otherwise was foolish. Anyone who stood in line was beneath contempt" (1985, 36). Subcultural theories of crime and deviance are also epitomized by the original norms of outlaw motorcycle gangs, which initially cultivated their own anti-establishment attitudes. Revelling in their image as social outcasts, they deliberately cut themselves off from the majority culture through their label "one percenter" – the "one percent who has given up on society" (Bandidos MC Website, n.d.). Motorcycle gangs are particularly attractive to individuals who are involved in deviant behaviour because these gangs are mutually supportive of many types of deviant acts, including murder, drug dealing, and rape (RCMP 1987, 9).

Non-ideological Motivation

Organized crime groups are not motivated by political ideology, religious dogma, or a desire to change society. Their goal is to accumulate financial and other material benefits. While some criminal groups attempt to influence state actors and agencies, this is primarily restricted to corrupting government officials, a tactic used to gain protection from the state and/or immunity to continue their illegal operations. This distinguishes criminal organizations from terrorist groups, whose illegal activities have political and social change as their goal.

Rules and Regulations

Like legitimate organizations, traditional organized crime groups have established rules and regulations that members are expected to follow (Abadinsky 2012, 5). In some groups these rules are implicit; in others they are explicit and may actually be written out. The most important rules focus on secrecy and loyalty, because those are the rules that protect illegal organizations from the threats posed by law enforcement officials and by other organized crime groups.

Discipline

To ensure that the rules and regulations are obeyed, most criminal groups have strict forms of discipline based on loyalty, a code of honour, and most importantly, the fear of reprisal (death).

vory v zakone
A "thief in law." That is, a high-ranking, well-respected organized crime figure in the old Soviet underworld and the new Republic of Russia. Akin to the Italian Mafia. The code of the "Thieves World" emphasizes a rejection of government authority and traditional social norms. The "vor" pre-date the Soviet Union, but many were inmates interned in Soviet prison camps who organized themselves in an attempt to rule the criminal underworld.

Dominant Organized Crime Genres and Groups

This section provides an overview of some of the dominant organized crime groups currently active in Canada. These groups can be placed in the following categories: Italian, Chinese/Asian, Russian/Eastern European, Indigenous, and outlaw motorcycle gangs. According to the CISC, organized crime groups have different levels of capabilities. The most sophisticated groups include some Hells Angels chapters, Chinese criminal networks, the Italian mafia in Quebec, and the 'ndrangheta in Ontario. These groups, which have survived threats from the police and from competing gangs, are "distinguished by their large-scale, sophisticated operations involving the importation, manufacture or distribution of a wide variety of contraband, as well as through financial crimes such as fraud and money laundering" (CISC 2006, 6).

Italian

Italian organized crime in Canada can be traced to the early part of the 20th century, when secret Italian societies began extorting fellow immigrants. The earliest versions of secret Italian societies in Canada were loosely structured

---

FOCUS   BOX 16.2

RULES, RITES, AND RITUALS OF THE 'NDRANGHETA

In 1971, while Toronto police were searching the home of a suspected member of the Canadian cell of an Italian-organized crime network, they found 27-page document, handwritten in an antiquated Italian script, in his kitchen cupboard.

Experts from Canada and Italy would later conclude that the papers outlined the rules, rites, rituals, and structure of the *Honorata Società* (known as the 'ndrangheta). This was the first time such an authentic document had fallen into the hands of police in North America. The heading on the first page was *Come Formare una Società* ("How to Form a Society"), and the preamble read in part: "My stomach is a tomb, my mouth a bleated work of humility." Another section dictates the initiation rites of an inductee, who symbolically vows to take "a bloody dagger in my hand and a serpent in my mouth" should he betray the Honoured Society.

A 1972 *Globe and Mail* article described the remainder of the document as a "a tangle of centuries old archaic Italian, the phrases laced with flowery, mystic imagery dealing with such matters as collecting opinions from society members, punishing members who don't surrender their guns at meetings, catechism-like initiation rituals and the proper words to be used when separating a member from the group."

The papers also outlined the basic structure of an 'ndrangheta cell, which includes three levels or ranks. There were also references to the pledges and obligations of members, the most important being a vow of silence. The document uses the term *mastro di sgarru*, the obligation of members to exact vendettas against enemies of the Society. Another common term was *baciletta*, which can be defined as "extorted money" collected by Society members, which should be "given to the ones who need it, the ones who have been arrested, for the defence lawyers, to help the people the police are looking for."

The discovery of this document was a significant breakthrough in efforts by police to prove the existence of a secret criminal society in North America with roots in southern Italy.

Questions for Critical Thinking

1. Why is the code of silence so important for organized crime groups?

2. Many organized crime groups are ethnically based. What are some of the reasons for this?

Source: Based on *Globe and Mail*, "Metro Police Raid Turned Up Copy of Mafia Linked Society's Secret Rituals, Court is Told," *Globe and Mail*, 2 June 1972.

groups, influenced by the Sicilian Mafia and the Calabrian 'ndrangheta (see Box 16.2). Most of the founders, leaders, and members of Italian Canadian crime groups in Canada emigrated from Calabria or at least can trace their roots to that region. Despite this lineage, Italian Canadian criminal organizations operated for many years as wings of the Italian American mafia families: the Montreal mafia was controlled by New York's Bonanno family, while many of the Italian Canadian crime groups in Ontario were answerable to the Magaddino family in Buffalo. But in the 1950s, Italian Canadian crime groups were established in Toronto that had direct ties to 'ndrangheta clans in Calabria. Italian prosecutors allege today that in Toronto there are seven dominant Calabrian mafia groups—made up of both Italian and Canadian nationals—all of which are part of an international network of 'ndrangheta cells (*National Post* 2010b, 2010c).

Since the late 1970s, the Montreal-based mafia has been dominated by made members of Sicilian heritage. Under the command of the Rizzuto family, the Montreal group ran independently of other crime groups in either Italy or the United States. It is involved in drug trafficking, illegal gambling (bookmaking), and extortion (protection rackets), and it has been accused of rigging bids related to commercial construction and public works contracts (discussed earlier in this chapter). Once considered the most powerful mafia group in this country, in recent years it has experienced a decline because of strong law enforcement crackdowns, the jailing of its leader Vito Rizzuto in the United States (and his subsequent death in 2013), competition from rival crime groups, and the 2010 murder of the family patriarch, 86-year-old Nicolo Rizzuto (Lamothe and Humphreys 2006; Schneider 2016).

Chinese/Asian

Contemporary Asian organized crime in Canada can be broken down into six categories: (1) local street gangs made up of both youth and adults; (2) Chinese triads, which evolved from gangs in Toronto's Chinatown in the 1970s into sophisticated transnational criminal syndicates with links to Hong Kong, Taiwan, and Mainland China; (3) non-triad Chinese criminal networks, which tend to specialize in one particular criminal activity, such as drug trafficking or migrant smuggling; (4) a loose network of criminals from Mainland China (originally referred to as the Big Circle Boys), who commit a wide variety of crimes; (5) Vietnamese crime groups, which began as violent street gangs in Toronto and Vancouver and now became some of the biggest illegal marijuana producers and traffickers in Canada; and (6) Indo-Canadian crime groups, which are confined largely to BC and are involved in cocaine, and synthetic drug trafficking and smuggling (Schneider 2016, 443–44).

The most dominant and deeply entrenched Asian organized crime genre are Chinese criminal groups. During the first half of the 20th century, Chinese merchants in Vancouver were behind some of the largest opium-smuggling and trafficking rings in the country. Canada's first Chinatown in Victoria was home to illegal gambling halls, brothels, and opium dens, most of which were controlled by leading Chinese merchants. In the 1950s the RCMP uncovered illegal Chinese immigrant-smuggling operations from Hong Kong. In the 1970s, Southeast Asian heroin began to supplant the Turkish variety in North America, and before long, Chinese drug-trafficking syndicates were some of the world's biggest heroin suppliers. In the mid-1970s a plague of extortion within Toronto's Chinese community exposed the presence of Canada's first modern criminal triad, the Kung Lok. Around the same time, Chinese street gangs emerged in Vancouver. A few years later, aggressive Vietnamese gangs began to challenge the Chinese triads for supremacy in the Asian underworld in Toronto and Vancouver. By the end of the 1980s, the Big Circle Boys, former soldiers from Mainland China, were being blamed for a series of violent robberies, home invasions, and other crimes in the two cities.

Today, Chinese criminal networks constitute the most widespread, diverse, and sophisticated organized crime threats in Canada today. Their geographic strongholds are the Lower Mainland of BC and the Greater Toronto Area (GTA) in Ontario, but their reach extends into almost every province. Contemporary Chinese organized crime is characterized by a networked structure that includes triad members, youth gangs, professional criminals, and semi-legitimate businesspeople. The sources of revenue for Chinese criminal syndicates include extortion, gambling, the sex trade, illegal immigration, the counterfeiting of credit cards, digital technology, and consumer products, contraband cigarette production and trafficking, and the drug trade. Besides importing heroin from Southeast Asia, Chinese criminal networks are some of Canada's biggest producers of synthetic drugs (crystal meth and ecstasy), which are trafficked domestically and exported to the United States and other countries.

Outlaw Motorcycle Gangs

Outlaw motorcycle gangs (OMGs) emerged in the United States after the Second World War. They were originally formed for camaraderie and excitement but gradually moved into for-profit criminal activities. Initially they worked as muscle-for-hire and as street-level drug distributors. Their involvement in the production and trafficking of synthetic drugs in the early 1970s was the main impetus for their transition to a global organized crime syndicate. Canada once had many competing biker gangs; today, the Hells Angels predominates. Its first Canadian chapter was founded in Montreal in 1976, and over the next 40 years it became the first truly national criminal organization, with chapters, puppet clubs, and/or associates in every province. Indeed, Canada has become an international stronghold for the motorcycle club; at one time, there were more Hells Angels members per capita in Canada than in any other country. Drug trafficking remains a significant source of income for Hells Angels, but it is also involved in the illegal trafficking of firearms and explosives, protection rackets, automobile theft and export, fraud, and trafficking in women. To facilitate its international smuggling operations, Hells Angels relies on corruption and internal conspiracies at international ports of entry. It is believed to have infiltrated shipping lines, port corporations, and longshoremen's unions in Canada and abroad (Sher and Marsden 2004; Schneider 2016).

Russian/Eastern European

Organized crime factions from Russia, Ukraine, and other former republics of the Soviet Union are active throughout the former Communist Bloc as well as in Western Europe, North America, Israel, and Australia. Russian criminal organizations that trace their roots back for decades, like the *vory v zakone*, have been joined by younger career offenders, street criminals, businessmen, and former Soviet intelligence officers and government officials. Vladimir Putin, reputed to be the world's richest man, is said to rule over a highly criminalized state and has used criminal groups for various political and economic purposes—to extort businesses, launch cyberattacks, traffic people and goods, and even carry out assassinations on behalf of the Kremlin (Galeotti 2017).

Other Eastern European crime groups originated in Albania, Croatia, and Serbia. Most of these are involved in smuggling drugs, guns, and weapons in the Balkans and Europe. While Russian and Eastern European organized crime exploded in the chaotic atmosphere that followed the fall of the Soviet Union in the early 1990s, they had been operating on a small scale in North America since the 1970s. These loosely networked groups operated mostly in New York, Los Angeles, and Toronto.

In Toronto during the 1970s and 1980s, Eastern European criminals were involved in extortion, gambling, loansharking, and drug trafficking, much of this in conjunction with the Ontario arm of the American Cosa Nostra (Lamothe and Nicaso 1994, 45; FBI 1995; *Toronto Star* 1996; Rawlinson 1997). Today, Russian and other Eastern European crime groups are most active in large cities in Ontario, Quebec, and BC. They have varying degrees of organization and sophistication and engage in a wide array of crime, from petty theft to sophisticated fraud schemes. Financial frauds, in particular **debit card fraud** schemes, are major activities for these groups. They are also involved in human trafficking, contraband smuggling, illegal drug importation, and the theft and illegal export of vehicles to Eastern Europe (*Globe and Mail*, 1998; CISC 2002, 14–15; 2004, 7–9). In recent years, large-scale high-profile cases involving human trafficking and organized shoplifting rings have been linked to Hungarian and Romanian crime groups operating in Canada (*Globe and Mail* 2012; *Ottawa Sun* 2012; *Windsor Star* 2012).

debit card fraud
Debit card fraud entails four steps: (1) create fake debit cards, (2) steal personal identification and banking information from legitimate cards, (3) emboss the stolen information on the fake cards, and (4) use the illegal debit cards for purchases or cash advances.

Indigenous Peoples

Organized crime involving Indigenous peoples can be categorized as follows: (1) criminal groups and activities in central Canada (Ontario and Quebec) that revolve around smuggling and contraband cigarette production, and (2) criminal gangs in the Prairie provinces. The former groups play a central role in smuggling, due primarily to geopolitical factors that facilitate the movement of contraband across the Canada–US border.

The Akwesasne reserve is considered the most active smuggling corridor between the United States and Canada. Populated by the Mohawk Nation, this 5,600-hectare reserve has the unique distinction of straddling the US–Canada border, making it ideally suited for smuggling. The reserve's territory actually falls within five jurisdictions—Canada, the United States, Ontario, Quebec, and New York State—and agreements have been negotiated with federal, state, and provincial governments in both countries that uphold the right of the Mohawk people to freely cross the borders that cut through the reserve. Because of all this, and a well-honed smuggling infrastructure, organized crime groups from both on and off the reserve use Akwesasne to smuggle bulk tobacco, cigarettes, firearms, and cocaine into Canada, while marijuana and synthetic drugs produced in Canada—as well as illegal migrants from outside of Canada—are smuggled through to the American side (Canadian Press 2014; RCMP 2017).

In recent years, unregulated cigarette manufacturing plants and retail outlets have been established on several First Nations communities in Ontario and Quebec. These facilities have been blamed for a flood of contraband cigarettes on the streets of Quebec, Ontario, and other parts of Canada (National Coalition Against Contraband Tobacco 2015). Police allege that the factories and retail stores are operating illegally and have links to criminal entrepreneurs and organized crime groups from on and off the reserves. The Mohawk people contend that they are responsible for the land of Akwesasne and that because they never signed a treaty of subjugation with the Canadian, American, British, or French governments, they have the unconditional right of sovereignty over the land, its people, and all commercial activities (including cigarette production).

Indigenous criminal groups in the Prairie provinces mostly operate as street gangs. According to the CISC, they "are generally involved in opportunistic, spontaneous and disorganized street-level criminal activities, primarily low-level trafficking of marihuana, cocaine and crack cocaine and, to a lesser extent, methamphetamine. The gangs are also involved in prostitution, break-and-enters, robberies, assaults, intimidation, vehicle theft and illicit drug debt collection" (2004, 20–21). These Indigenous gangs have connections to Asian and outlaw motorcycle criminal groups, from which they purchase drugs at the wholesale level.

This chapter argued that organized criminal conspiracies—and membership in specific criminal groups—are often organized around ethnicity. This is implicit in the preceding categories of organized crime genres, which are grouped largely by ethnicity. Categorizing organized crime genres and groups by ethnicity is controversial, with some arguing it is no longer relevant. "Ethnic homogeneity" may simply be a "superficial characteristic" of criminal groups and networks that, in fact, are organized around family, friendship, shared language, or local community ties. In other words, "only rarely is the explicit claim made that shared ethnicity rather than anything else is what brings co-conspirators together" (von Lampe 2012, 193).

Also, the picture is becoming more fluid. The organized crime categories discussed above include some of the largest and most sophisticated criminal groups and networks, but they do not have a monopoly on organized criminal activities. Today, organized crime is represented by a diverse number of "genres" that have emerged from a multitude of ethno-cultural and national backgrounds. Moreover, while a defining characteristic of these dominant organized crime genres has been a shared nationality, ethnicity, and/or language, in recent years it has become apparent that these factors are no longer the most important criteria in determining who participates in a particular organized criminal conspiracy. Three BC-based gangs—the Red Scorpions, the United Nations, and the Independent Soldiers—are prominent examples of the multi-ethnic criminal groups that emerged in the 1990s (CFSEU BC 2013, 3). Thousands of individual criminal entrepreneurs work together on an ad hoc or ongoing basis in the pursuit of illegal revenues, regardless of ethnicity, nationality, or language. In this sense, modern organized crime can best be characterized as a fluid network of many autonomous buyers, brokers, financiers, middlemen, and distributors from different groups, ethnicities, nationalities, and countries, who come together to make deals by capitalizing on one another's specialties and strengths. The proliferation and increasing diversity of criminal groups in Canada began in the early 1970s and gathered speed in subsequent decades. By 2009, the CISC estimated there were 750 criminal gangs in Canada (CISC 2009, 9).

Theories of Organized Crime

Theories that help explain organized crime can be placed in two categories: those that try to identify and analyze the causes of organized crime (etiological theories), and those that attempt to understand the structure of organized criminal conspiracies.

Etiological Theories

Several theories have tried to explain the causes and existence of organized crime in North America. Some of these theories are specific to organized crime; others are based on the theories of criminality you have read about in this textbook, which have been adapted to organized crime. This chapter will focus on theories that explain the causes of organized crime. These can be grouped into the following categories: (1) alien conspiracy theory, (2) ethnic succession theory, (3) economic theories, and (4) public policy impetus.

Alien Conspiracy Theory

One of earliest theories of the origins and causes of organized crime in America is alien conspiracy theory. Originally developed to explain the origins and scope of Italian organized crime in the United States, it has also been applied to other ethnic-based organized crime genres, including Chinese triads, Colombian cocaine cartels, Jamaican posses, Nigerian crime groups, and Russian/Eastern European crime groups.

Proponents of alien conspiracy theory believe that organized crime in America is the result of the importation of secret criminal societies rooted in foreign cultures. Thus, organized crime does not emerge from American culture; rather, it has been thrust upon the United States by specific immigrant groups. When used to explain Italian American crime groups, the theory also contends that a nationwide criminal network exists, made up of two dozen or so "families" of Italian lineage (all of which are governed by a national commission) collectively known as the "mafia" or "**la cosa nostra**" (LCN).

The theory, which was not developed by scholars, was most forcefully promoted in the early 1950s by a US Senate committee chaired by Estes Kefauver (US Congress 1951). The committee alleged that a sinister secret organization originating in Sicily had made its way to the United States during the period of massive Italian immigration in the late 19th and early 20th centuries (Kelly 1987, 13). This secret society grew into a monolithic nationwide criminal conspiracy, under "centralized direction and control," that was subverting and eroding the fundamental law-abiding values of American society (Smith 1975, 138). Similar allegations were made by several subsequent

la cosa nostra
Term used to denote Italian American organized crime. It was originally applied by the FBI in an attempt to make this criminal fraternity sound ominous and threatening. Members of the so-called LCN never used this label themselves, though they have often referred to their secret society as "this thing of ours," which roughly translates into Italian as "la cosa nostra."

government inquiries, including the President's Commission on Law Enforcement and Administration of Justice (1967). Criminologist Donald Cressey lent scholarly credence to this theory in his work as a consultant to the President's Commission and in a subsequent book, *Theft of a Nation*, which overestimated the scope and power of the Italian mafia in America and implied that American values and institutions were being subverted by an invading alien force.

Like many conspiracy theories, alien conspiracy theory has some tenuous roots in reality. However, when applied to North America it has been widely criticized as xenophobic and racist. Subsequent scholarly research, and evidence gathered by criminal justice agencies, has refuted the two main pillars of this theory as an almost fictional exaggeration of the roots and scope of Italian organized crime in North America.

Regarding the first pillar: The origins and perpetuation of the Cosa Nostra in America cannot simply be blamed on the importation of a secret society from Sicily. The American LCN can trace part of its family tree to the Sicilian mafia, and the early secret societies in North America were made up of Italian immigrants, some of whom brought with them the traditions and criminal activities of the Sicilian mafia (or the Calabrian 'ndrangheta). However, the LCN—and indeed, modern organized crime—is overwhelmingly an American (and to a lesser extent Canadian) creation. It is a product of North American culture, profitably fuelled by popular vices and by the spirit of capitalism and facilitated by private and public corruption (Bell 1953).

Regarding the second pillar: There is little evidence that there was ever a truly nationwide mafia criminal conspiracy with centralized control. There were a number of Italian organized crime groups spread across North America, and these were linked through ideology, ethnicity, methods, illegal networks, and criminal activities. In addition, some influential Italian organized crime figures attempted to create a "commission" that would coordinate and regulate the competing interests of the various Italian crime groups. But a *national* commission never fully materialized, and most groups worked independently in their own cities, with sporadic cooperation (and conflict) (Albini 1971; Smith 1975). The so-called "Commission" was largely confined to New York and had only limited power over the five mafia families in that city.

In his 1975 book *The Mafia Mystique*, Dwight Smith argues that the alien conspiracy theory arose in the United States in part because self-serving government commissions, politicians, and law enforcement officials were fabricating or exaggerating stories to help secure greater enforcement and prosecutorial resources.

The notion of a national organized crime conspiracy in Canada did not resonate among Canadian scholars or government and law enforcement officials. In fact, until the early 1960s, police, politicians, and judicial inquiries typically denied that the mafia existed in Canada (*Toronto Star*, 1948; *Toronto Telegram*, 1961; Roach 1962). Thus, Canadian officials erred on the opposite direction of their American counterparts. While many of the early ethnic Italian criminal societies in this country were made up of immigrants who brought with them some basic ideologies and criminal methods from Sicily and Calabria, organized crime evolved and prospered in this country as a result of the same conditions that existed in United States. While there was never any nationwide confederation of Italian crime groups in Canada with a centralized command and control, between the 1930s and 1970s ethnic Italian crime groups in Quebec and Ontario operated as cells of American mafia families and were also linked through international criminal conspiracies that included drug trafficking, immigrant smuggling, and bookmaking. Cells of 'ndrangheta clans based in Calabria, Italy, have existed in Toronto since at least the 1950s (*National Post* 2010b, 2010c). In the early 1960s, Michele Racco, already a member of the 'ndrangheta before he immigrated to Canada in the early 1950s, established a local commission (*crimini*) that settled disputes and maintained discipline among the city's 'ndrangheta members. As the head of this ruling board, Racco became the *capo crimini* for the Toronto cells (Schneider 2016, 311–12).

Ethnic Succession Theory

Other etiological theories of organized crime in North America place greater emphasis on causes that are indigenous to American and Canadian societies. This perspective can be condensed into the adage that "societies get the crime they deserve." These theories situate the root causes of organized criminality in the broader social, political, cultural, and economic environment of North America. Several general theories of crime and criminality, detailed in previous chapters, have informed this school of thought.

Strain theory (see Chapter 10) forms the basis of the ethnic succession theory, which posits that many immigrant ethnic groups are disproportionately involved in organized crime in the United States because of the barriers they encounter in their pursuit of the American Dream (Bell 1953; Ianni 1974). Thus, the ethnic basis of many organized crime groups in North America is not tied to the importation of foreign criminal cultures or secret societies; rather, it is the result of minority groups struggling for prosperity and a place in mainstream society. Each successive immigrant group experiences strains such as discrimination, unemployment, poverty, lack of political power, and social exclusion, and some members of these groups respond by involving themselves in criminal activities. As time passes, and as legitimate and socially acceptable avenues of mobility open up to these ethnic groups, the strain subsides and members of the particular ethnic group rely less and less on crime to realize the American Dream. Ethnic succession occurs when subsequent immigrant groups fill this criminal void as they attempt to climb the ladder of success. According to this thesis, persons or entire ethnic groups that are implicated in organized crime are not committed to a deviant subculture; they are merely using available, albeit illegal, opportunities to achieve economic and social success. Thus, involvement in organized crime is a rational response to blocked opportunities (Abadinsky 2012, 46).

The history of organized crime in Canada provides some evidence supporting ethnic succession theory. In the mid- to late 19th century, Irish immigrants were disproportionately represented in violent criminal gangs in Upper and Lower Canada, in part because they were discriminated against by the English and Scots, who held most positions of power.

During the first half of the 20th century, Irish gangs were eclipsed by more sophisticated Jewish criminals, who dominated such organized rackets as gambling and drug trafficking, particularly in Montreal, where anti-Semitism was rife. Samuel Bronfman may be a good illustration of ethnic succession theory. Bronfman was born in Canada to immigrant Jewish parents, made his fortune supplying American bootleggers during Prohibition, and eventually headed Seagram's distilleries, one of the largest corporate empires in Canadian history.

During the early 20th century, Chinese merchants in BC were involved in gambling, prostitution, and selling opium. Their clientele were Chinese immigrant labourers, who found refuge in such vices in the face of constant racial hatred, violence, and legislative disenfranchisement by the white population.

The Prohibition era in the 1920s witnessed the rise of the Italian racketeers, many of whom emerged from the poverty-stricken tenements of southern Ontario and Montreal and were unable to find legitimate employment because of discrimination.

By the 1970s, Italian Canadian crime groups outside of Montreal were in decline, with the void being filled by other groups that had immigrated to Canada more recently, from China, Vietnam, the West Indies, Colombia, and Russia (Carrigan 1991; Schneider 2016).

Critics of ethnic succession theory point out that many people of Italian or Chinese heritage remained active in organized crime long after these groups were assimilated into mainstream society and found success through legitimate means (Abadinsky 2012, 94). Potter (1994) concludes that members of immigrant ethnic and racial groups may turn to organized crime but do not necessarily replace existing ethnically and racially based criminal groups. Moreover, this theory does not explain why those from the middle class become involved in organized crime, nor does it account for the organized economic crimes committed by the wealthy and powerful. Finally, this theory fails to explain how criminal organizations that are made up primarily of White Anglo-Saxon Protestants—such as outlaw motorcycle gangs—emerge in North American society.

Economic Theories

An economic analysis views organized crime not as pathological but rather as a rational system that operates according to the laws of supply and demand. In fact, basic economic concepts such as supply, demand, and price elasticity are quite applicable to underground markets. For example, research has shown that the price of illegal or contraband commodities is related to supply and demand (Caulkins and Reuter 1998; Office of National Drug Control Policy 2004; RCMP 2007). Thus, if the local cocaine supply is plentiful, the price will be low, but if the local supply is limited, the price will usually rise.

An economic approach focuses on how criminal organizations make money supplying goods and services that are in demand but that have been declared illegal by the state. Underground markets also profit by providing the public with a cheaper supply of certain legal goods (e.g., contraband tobacco and liquor), primarily by evading taxes or by supplying stolen or counterfeit goods. One significant implication of this economic analysis is that organized crime is not viewed as alien to the societies in which it operates, but as part of its commercial markets. In short, organized crime fulfills certain commercial functions, thereby creating a symbiotic relationship between criminal organizations (as suppliers) and segments of society (as consumers) (Martens and Miller-Longfellow 1982, 4; Dickie and Wilson 1993, 216).

One criticism of this economic perspective is that underground markets are highly distorted relative to legitimate markets. Naylor (2004) contends that "the facile analogy between legal and illegal firms is at best a serious oversimplification, at worst simply wrong. In illegal markets that are highly segmented, decisions are personalized, information flows constricted, capital supplies short term and unreliable, objective price data lacking, and the time horizons (indeed the very existence) of enterprises coterminous with those of the entrepreneurs" (21). Moreover, the application of traditional economic theory to organized crime only captures consensual crimes; it ignores predatory criminal activities such as theft, hijacking, kidnapping, extortion, and fraud.

The State, Public Policy, and Organized Crime

Governments decide whether particular goods or services that people desire will be made available in legal markets. A product or service only becomes illegal when the government passes laws prohibiting its sale and consumption. Generally, the state criminalizes or restricts products or services—drugs, prostitution, gambling, alcohol, cigarettes, and so on—that it views as immoral and as personally and/or socially harmful.

When a government outlaws a particular product or service that the public wants, it drives supply to the "underground market." This creates an opportunity for criminal entrepreneurs to monopolize that product or service. A fundamental reason why organized crime exists is that governments have criminalized certain vices. The best-known historical example of how government policies create illegal markets and fuel the rise of organized crime was the outlawing of liquor in the United States and Canada in the 1920s and early 1930s. Prohibition catapulted organized crime into a new level of profitability, power, and sophistication and set the stage for today's large, profitable drug-trafficking organizations and networks.

As discussed earlier, goods and services do not have to be criminalized to fuel organized crime. Taxation policies have been the impetus for the involvement of organized crime in the trafficking of legal goods such as alcohol, fuel, and tobacco. The international and domestic smuggling of legal products is usually the result of a disparity in the level of taxes that have been applied to a product by different jurisdictions (see Box 16.3).

In addition to government policies, the creation and proliferation of organized crime has also been attributed to a weak state presence in a particular country or region. Van Dijk and Spapens (2014, 215) write that mafia-type criminal syndicates "seem to have developed, and may still thrive, in countries where state authority is weak, corruption levels are high, and consequently, enforcement is lax." In these circumstances, "dominant criminal groups may even develop into an alternative for the state, by offering protection to citizens." Gambetta was one of the first to advance this idea through his protection theory, which was initially applied to explain the rise of the mafia in Sicily. Gambetta argues that the Sicilian mafia originally arose due to weak governments, which created the opportunity for private enforcers called "gambellottos" or "mafiosos" to fill the void. The mafia in Sicily is said to operate as "an industry which produces, promotes, and sells private protection" (Gambetta 1993: 1). The demand for protection, according to von Lampe (2016, 47) "typically arises in a market where there is a lack of trust between market participants and where their interests are not sufficiently safeguarded by the state."

Theories of the Structure of Organized Criminal Conspiracies

As noted earlier, a defining characteristic of organized crime is a systematic pattern to the relations among offenders; this in turn helps define the structure of a particular ongoing criminal conspiracy. In general, four theoretical models capture how the relationship among the criminal offenders is structured organizationally: (1) the bureaucratic/hierarchical model, where there is a vertical power structure with at least three permanent ranks; (2) the kinship model, structured around blood relationships; (3) the patron–client model, where influential professional criminals become "patrons" to others; and (4) the network model, characterized by a fluid association of like-minded criminal offenders connected through complementary specializations or resources.

The Bureaucratic/Hierarchical Model

The bureaucratic/hierarchical model views criminal groups as tightly structured and controlled. This model was first applied to Italian American organized crime groups, which have been viewed by some as structured hierarchically, with

FOCUS   BOX 16.3

GOVERNMENT CIGARETTE TAXATION POLICIES, SMUGGLING, AND ORGANIZED CRIME

Since the end of the American Revolution, legitimate consumer goods have been illegally smuggled into Canada from the United States due to much lower prices south of the border. This is largely because of the import duties or high taxes imposed on similar products in Canada.

Historically, tobacco products have been the most popular contraband smuggled between the two countries. In the 1890s the Canadian government imposed an import duty to protect domestic cigarette manufacturers from foreign competition. This duty raised the cost of a small package of cigarettes imported into Canada to 10 cents; in the United States they could be purchased at half that price. The result, according to an 1895 *Toronto Star* article titled "Smuggle the Vile Cigarette," was that tobacco smugglers were now "doing business on a tremendously large scale, bringing the goods both to Toronto and to Montreal." Cigarette smuggling persisted over the following century but increased dramatically in the 1990s.

In 1991 the Canadian government increased the excise tax on the domestic sale of cigarettes by almost 140 percent. However, no similar tax hikes were imposed on Canadian tobacco products destined for export. This resulted in a substantial difference between the retail price of exported Canadian cigarettes and those sold domestically. This price difference launched a wave of smuggling that involved the lawful export of tax-exempt Canadian cigarettes to the United States and the smuggling of these cigarettes back into Canada. In less than two years following the tax hike, cigarette exports to the United States rose from 1.7 billion to 15.7 billion cigarettes (Canadian Tobacco Manufacturers Council n.d.). This increase can be attributed almost exclusively to the burgeoning Canadian black market. According to a report on smuggling by the Canadian Association of Chiefs of Police (1994, 7), most of the contraband tobacco products in Canada during this period were supplied by well-organized smuggling groups and networks.

Today, legitimately produced cigarettes are being smuggled into Canada from the United States, counterfeit cigarettes are being surreptitiously imported from China, and cigarette factories are springing up on First Nations reserves in Ontario and Quebec. In 2010 the RCMP estimated the number of criminal groups involved in the illicit tobacco trade in Canada to be 175 (Canadian Press 2010; *National Post* 2010a).

Questions for Critical Thinking

1. Why do Canadian governments keep taxes high on tobacco products despite the fact this provides and incentive to smugglers?

2. What do you think Canadian governments could do to reduce the losses in tax revenue because of tobacco smuggling?

a deliberate and rational arrangement of positions and roles based on a well-defined vertical power structure and division of labour (President's Commission 1967; Cressey 1969). In Canada the ethnic Italian criminal organizations that predominated from the 1950s to the early 1980s did appear to be hierarchical, though their structure was somewhat simpler and flatter than the one detailed by Cressey in his work for the President's Commission. For example, during the late 1960s and early 1970s, Montreal's Cotroni mafia group, a wing of New York City's Bonanno family, was headed by Vic Cotroni. Below him at any one time were four or five senior lieutenants. Each lieutenant was in charge of a particular district of Montreal and had his own crew of several "soldiers," who were in charge of, or had business ties with, a number of other people outside the Cotroni group (Charbonneau 1975; Quebec Police Commission 1977; Edwards 1990).

But many experts would *not* apply the bureaucratic/hierarchical model to the Italian mafia in North America. According to Ianni and Reuss-Ianni (1972), the bureaucratic analogy arose as "honest attempts to explain syndicate organization in terms that are familiar to the public" (110). They added there was "another, more suspect motivation" behind this model, which was, that it helped buttress the government-promoted theory that the mafia was a national conspiracy, which in turn "demand[ed] the existence of a national organization." Critics of this model also contend that many aspects of a bureaucracy, such as lengthy chains of command, rigidity, and a well-defined division of labour, may not apply to Italian mafia families in the United States and Canada.

Setting aside the criticisms, this model may be applied to other criminal organizations such as the Medellin and Cali cartels. Many analysts have concluded that these cartels emulated multinational corporations and were structured to control each step required in the processing, exporting, and wholesaling of cocaine. To facilitate this vertical integration, "each of the trafficking groups in Medellin, Bogota, and Cali contain various sections, each with a separate function, such as manufacturing, transportation, distribution, finance and security" (President's Commission 1984, 562). The exact structure of a Colombian cartel varied from group to group and was quite fluid over time; Figure 16.1 provides a generic version.

Kinship Model

Ianni and Reuss-Ianni (1972) suggest that the Italian American mafia family has nothing to do with modern bureaucratic or corporate principles; instead, it is primarily a social grouping shaped by culture, patterned by tradition, and structured around kin relations. Italian American crime families are just that: families interconnected by blood or marriage (and in some cases, simply a shared ethnicity). There is no real vertical hierarchy; instead this social unit is built around a symbiotic relationship between a "patron" and a "client"—a pattern of relationships first proposed by Joseph Albini (1971).

In their study of one Italian American organized crime group, Ianni and Reuss-Ianni (1972) found that members of the Lupollo family (a pseudonym) were sustained by kinship, not criminal activities or a secret society. The Lupollo family operated as a "social unit with social organization and business functions merged. [All] leadership positions, down to 'middle management' level," were assigned on the basis of kinship (106).

FIGURE 16.1 ■ Generic Organizational Structure of the Cali Cartel

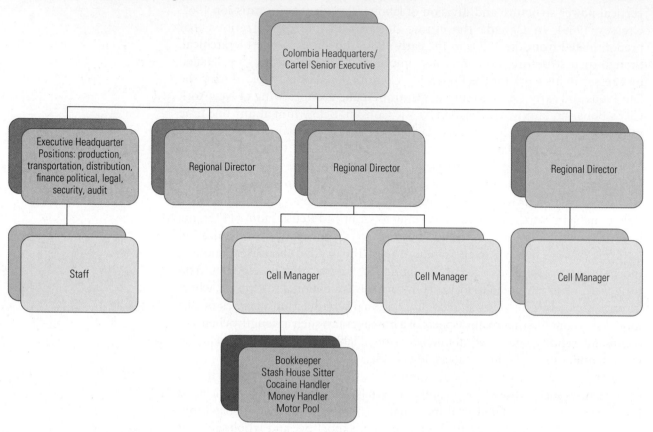

Source: US Comptroller General, Nontraditional Organized Crime: Law Enforcement Officials Perspectives on Five Criminal Groups (Washington, DC: US GPO, 1989); US Drug Enforcement Administration, Major Traffickers and Their Organizations (Washington, DC: n.d.); Thomas Constantine, "Statement before the U.S. Senate Drug Caucus," 24 February (Washington, DC: US DEA, 1994); Howard Abadinsky, Organized Crime (New York: Wadsworth, 2000), 149.

Ianni and Reuss-Ianni outlined some of the differences between mafia families and formal organizations. The latter are composed of positions, not personalities, which means that the duties and rights of a corporate executive, for instance, are clearly delineated so that the organization can swiftly replace an incumbent for whatever reason. In some mafia families, by contrast, particular members are indispensable because they possess special skills or have established highly personal contacts. The death of a member who acts as a "corrupter" may significantly disrupt the family's criminal operations because no immediate substitute has the same level of political connections. Also, formal organizations are supposed to be rationally organized, with individuals rising to leadership because of their demonstrated skill, intelligence, dedication, and expertise. Ianni and Reuss-Ianni argue that family standing and tradition are equally important— perhaps more important than merit—in determining which family members will assume leadership roles. In the Lupollo mafia family, power accrued to an individual not because he was the best qualified but because kinship or tradition demanded it.

Patron–Client Model

For Ianni and Reuss-Ianni (1972), the ongoing criminal operations of the Italian American mafia family involve a loose system of power and "business" relationships and thus require a middleman, who becomes a patron to others by providing contacts, influence, and criminal opportunities. Over time, the patron comes to dominate a network of individuals in a geographic area (Ianni and Reuss-Ianni 1983). At the centre of this patron–client model is the Capo. The Capo is less a CEO than a patron to his family and associates; he is the centre of a network of family and business relationships. In this role, he provides services, especially for those who can't or won't turn to the government—from the peasantry in southern Italy, where the government presence is weak, to the Italian immigrant unfamiliar with or suspicious of the government in the new land, all the way to the thief or murderer who cannot approach the government for help. The Capo helps ensure the welfare and security of his family, friends, and associates. For example, he puts up start-up capital to assist new enterprises, handles the flow of graft to politicians, regulates the use of violence, and resolves disputes among members (Albini 1971; Hess 1973; Gambetta 1993). A Capo is especially important as an intermediary, whether as a commercial agent bringing legitimate businessmen or criminals together to make a deal, as a political power broker helping friends get elected, or as a mediator arbitrating a conflict between two parties.

As seen in Figure 16.2, the boss is at the centre of this patron–client structure, immediately surrounded by members of the crime family, for whom he acts as a patron (and from each of whom he receives a monetary tribute). In addition, each made member of the mafia family cultivates his own network of clients, who include associates external to the family. These clients may represent a wide spectrum of society, including other criminals, politicians, law enforcement officials, judges, businessmen, and union leaders (Albini 1971). The patron–client structure has the potential to generate a wide variety of money-making connections, both by the boss and by other made members of the mafia family.

The patron–client model was developed mainly to describe Italian American crime families, although it could be applied to other organized crime groups. For example, Hells Angels and Chinese triads are known to develop extensive networks of associates, whose criminal activities revolve around specific members who act as brokers and intermediaries.

Network Model

The network model views the relationship among criminal offenders not as a monolithic, self-contained organization but as a fluid and loosely knit network of like-minded criminal entrepreneurs, none of whom has any long-term authority over the others. A network model of organized crime views the patterns of relationships not as hierarchical but as symmetrical; business partnerships are based on complementary areas of specialization that contribute to one particular deal or to a series of ongoing criminal conspiracies. In a network, relations among criminals are defined not by power but by the particular functions that individuals perform in the criminal conspiracy and/or by the financial investment that a "business partner" has made in the venture.

FIGURE 16.2 ■ **The Patron–Client Organization Model**

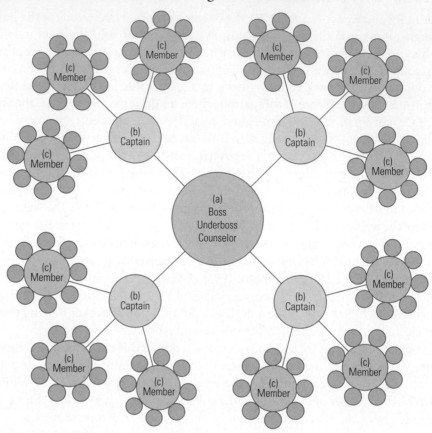

From ABADINSKY. *Organized Crime*, 8E. © 2007 South-Western, a part of Cengage Learning, Inc. Reproduced by permission. www.cengage.com/permissions.

Criminologist James Finckenauer (2005) wrote that most contemporary organized crime conspiracies are "loosely affiliated networks of criminals who coalesce around certain criminal opportunities. The structure of these groups is much more amorphous, free floating and flatter, and thus lacking in a rigid hierarchy" (65). In her analysis of Chicago crime groups, Anderson (1979) concluded that the network model may be viewed as a combination of the bureaucratic/hierarchical model and the kinship/patron–client model. She argued that well-defined criminal organizations do exist and that some entail a hierarchical structure. Traditional organized crime groups do have layers of positions, such as boss, underboss, lieutenant, and so on, but they also include various associates who are not themselves true members. These associates—who may include small-time crooks, sophisticated criminal entrepreneurs, legitimate businessmen, politicians, and even other criminal organizations—carry out many activities (both legal and illegal) necessary for the success of the group and enter into patron–client type arrangements with the members of this criminal group.

In their research into organized crime in Canada, Morselli (2005, 2009) and Morselli and Roy (2008) identified a number of "networked" aspects of contemporary organized criminal conspiracies. For example, such conspiracies arise through personal contacts and social networking among offenders. Also, criminal conspiracies have a "flexible order" that makes them resistant to law enforcement targeting and enforcement, and "brokers" play an important centralizing role within loosely structured criminal group ventures. In its 2006 annual report, the CISC elaborated on the relationships among criminal entrepreneurs that make up modern organized criminal conspiracies:

> Law enforcement is identifying crime groups that are based on temporary alliances of individual criminals who merge their particular skills to better achieve success in specific criminal enterprises. Once a specific criminal venture is completed, these individuals may continue to collaborate on further criminal activities, or the group may dissolve. Although the individuals may go their separate ways, they sometimes reform into new groups based upon the skill requirements of new criminal opportunities. The nature and success of such networks are largely determined by individual characteristics and skills among those who act as their component parts. (CISC, 2006: 6)

The network model is perhaps most applicable to large-scale drug importation and trafficking conspiracies, which rarely are carried out by a single organized group. Heroin finds its way onto the streets of Toronto through the efforts of many individuals and groups, each of which operates independently. These include the farmers who grow the opium, the chemists who turn the opium into heroin, the transportation brokers who arrange safe passage of the product, the shippers who physically transport the product, and the wholesalers who arrange for the heroin to be cut and then distributed to street dealers, who sell it at the "retail" level. A good example of the network model for large-scale international drug trafficking was the legendary "French Connection," which began in the 1940s. It brought together Turkish farmers, who cultivated the opium; Istanbul-based brokers, who trafficked the morphine; French Corsican gangsters, who processed the morphine into heroin in France and then moved the final product across the Atlantic; American and Canadian mafia groups, who coordinated its importation and wholesale distribution in North America; and diverse individuals and groups who sold the drugs at the retail level (Charbonneau 1975; Naylor 2004; Schneider 2016).

To summarize, the traditional bureaucratic/hierarchical model of organized crime emphasizes hierarchy and centralized control, while the network model envisions greater decentralization, with separate enterprises that pool resources and expertise. According to Haller (1990), such decentralization renders a business less vulnerable to law enforcement. By spreading the risks, entrepreneurs minimize their losses from police raids. Decentralization also makes sense for another important reason: "Criminal entrepreneurs generally have had neither the skills nor the personalities for the detailed, bureaucratic oversight of large organizations. They are, instead, hustlers and dealers, for whom partnership arrangements are ideally suited. They enjoy the give and take of personal negotiations, risk-taking, and moving from deal to deal" (222). To corroborate his arguments, Haller used Al Capone's criminal empire as a historical case study, arguing that Capone was at the centre of an expansive network of associates and entities (see Figure 16.3).

FIGURE 16.3 ■ **Al Capone's Crime Network**

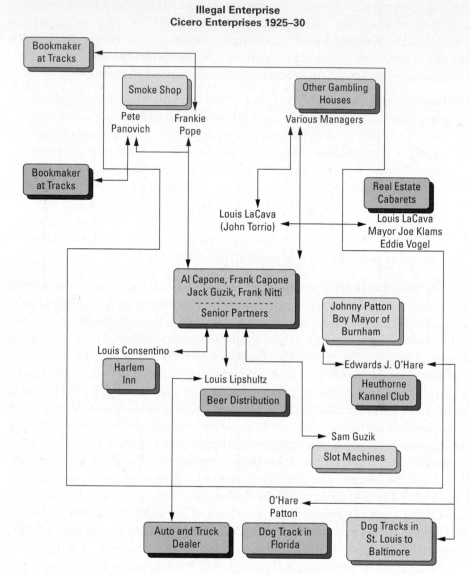

Source: Mark Haller (1990) "Illegal Enterprises: A Theoretical and Historical Interpretation," *Criminology* 28, no. 2 (1990): 207. Reprinted with permission from the American Society of Criminology.

Conclusion: Canadian Organized Crime

Organized crime in Canada spans more than 400 years, from pirates who pillaged ships and towns off the Atlantic coast during the 17th and 18th centuries, to bank robbers, smugglers, horse thieves, cattle rustlers, and currency counterfeiters in the 19th century, to opium traffickers, white slave traders, and professional gamblers of the early 20th century, to bootleggers during the era of Prohibition, to the Italian mafia, outlaw motorcycle gangs, Chinese triads, and other criminal groups that have predominated in recent times.

The past 40 years have seen a proliferation of criminal groups, networks, and organized conspiracies in Canada and worldwide. As the number of crime groups has multiplied, so have the scope, diversity, and profitability of organized criminal activities. In 2012 the UN Office on Drugs and Crime estimated that "the annual turnover of transnational organized criminal activities such as drug trafficking, counterfeiting, illegal arms trade and the smuggling of immigrants is . . . around $870 billion" (UN News Centre, 2012).

Canada continues to serve as a branch plant for transnational crime groups and as a transit point for the international movement of illegal drugs. According to the US Department of State (2002) "heroin, cocaine, and MDMA (ecstasy) are trafficked through Canada, as international drug traffickers take advantage of Canada's proximity to the United States, less stringent criminal penalties as compared to the U.S., and the constant flow of goods across the U.S.-Canada border" (V6). Canada is also a conduit for undocumented immigrants, primarily from Asia, who illegally enter the United States. Canada supplies an embarrassingly rich assortment of illegal and contraband goods, a tradition that began when BC became a major producer of smokable opium in the early part of the 20th century. This tradition continued through Prohibition, when Canada was America's main source of illegal liquor, and found new life in the 1970s, when the country surfaced as a major producer of synthetic drugs (Schneider 2016). By the start of the new millennium, Canada had established itself as the continent's pre-eminent supplier of high-grade marijuana, methamphetamines, and ecstasy: "various organized crime groups have taken great advantage of opportunities to diversify their criminal activities, enabling them to swiftly advance from domestic trafficking to global distribution" (RCMP, 2007, 1). In its 2015 report on international narcotics trafficking, the US Department of State notes that "Canada is a primary source country of both high-potency marijuana and MDMA to the United States, and Canadian synthetic drugs and amphetamine-type stimulants are exported to Asia, Europe, and Australia. . . . Methamphetamine continues to be produced in large quantities (US Department of State, 2015, 128). Police in BC have discovered fields planted with opium poppies (*Globe and Mail* 2010a, 2010b). Canada has also become a centre for telemarketing fraud and the counterfeiting of currency, bank cards, and digital entertainment products.

Why does organized crime have such an active presence in Canada? Many of the answers can be found in the theories discussed earlier in this chapter. Indeed, the etiological theories included in this chapter may be as applicable to Canada as they are to the United States.

Alien conspiracy theory explains some of Canada's organized crime problem. Many of the dominant organized crime genres active in this country—the Italian mafia and 'ndrangheta, Chinese triads, US-based outlaw motorcycle gangs, Russian and Eastern European crime groups, Colombian cartels, Jamaican posses, and so on—have their origins in other countries. Canada is an immigrant nation, and the ethnic composition of its organized crime reflects the country's multicultural makeup.

Ethnic succession theory may shed some light on historically rooted institutionalized racism, which has contributed to the "ethnic" basis of criminal gangs and organized crime groups in this country. Shut out of legitimate economic and political opportunities, members of certain minority groups have

SEARCH FOR:
Department of State International Narcotics Strategy Reports

turned to the underground economy to eke out a living. Similar social factors and structural forces have produced a growing underclass of young men, often from minority groups, and this too has contributed to the recent proliferation of gangs and criminal organizations in Canada. The postwar political economy has helped create the structural preconditions for spatial concentrations of crime in many larger urban centres by fuelling socioeconomic disparities and the amalgamation of poverty and other social problems within certain neighbourhoods and/or racial groups. The wealth of Canada and other Western nations is being held by a shrinking number of individual and corporate elites, the gap between the rich and the poor has been widening, urban centres have become segregated along socioeconomic lines, and poverty has become more concentrated in certain neighbourhoods, communities, and racial groups. These trends and developments, according to critical criminologist Jock Young (2001), are leading developed nations like Canada towards a "dystopia of exclusion," where "the poor are isolated in inner-city ghettos, in orbital estates, and in ghost towns" (20).

Another indigenous factor that is contributing to organized crime in this country is the symbiotic relationship between crime groups and the Canadian public. There is a strong demand for illegal goods and services in this country, and this has created an economic foundation for organized crime to prosper. Canada's public policies have also contributed to the proliferation of organized crime by creating contraband markets through the criminalization of heroin, cocaine, and other substances in demand by the public. In addition, high taxes have bolstered the smuggling trade and underground markets and, it follows, organized crime (in particular the contraband cigarettes and liquor trade).

Geopolitics is another factor that helps perpetuate Canadian organized crime. There is probably no country in the world that has as many factors conducive to a vibrant smuggling trade: an enormous land mass and airspace, three ocean coastlines that are impossible to adequately monitor and protect, the longest unguarded border in the world (with the United States), and a relatively small tax base for funding adequate enforcement. Most unique, perhaps, is the large concentration of Canadians living within a short distance of the US border, given that the United States is a convenient market for the contraband and offers a skilled labour pool from which to draw smugglers and distributors.

Globalization is also generating opportunities for criminal groups in Canada. Those groups now export drugs and other contraband overseas as well as to the United States. The strong demand for premium Canadian illicit products, such as highly coveted "BC Bud" marijuana, has nurtured organized crime in this country. The influx of sophisticated international criminal groups into Canada has strengthened this country's position as a global hotbed of illegal drug production, currency and credit card counterfeiting, product piracy, and telemarketing fraud.

The historical and contemporary narrative of organized crime in Canada helps shed light on the character of the country and its people. Though influenced by global forces, modernization, and the United States, organized crime in Canada reflects our own society. (See Box 16.4 for a discussion of new legislative measures implemented in Canada to combat organized crime.)

THE MOST RECENT LEGISLATIVE MEASURES TO COMBAT ORGANIZED CRIME

In the past, offenders involved in organized criminal conspiracies in Canada were charged with individual illegal offences, most of laid them out in the Criminal Code or federal drug statutes. Relevant sections of the Criminal Code included illegal gaming and betting (ss. 201 to 209), extortion (s. 346), criminal interest rate (s. 347), forgery (ss. 366 to 378), and fraud (ss. 380 to 396). There were no substantive criminal offences specifically related to organized crime.

This began to change in the mid-1990s. As Freedman notes, "Canada and a host of other countries have created new forms of individual criminal liability through targeted organized crime legislation. . . . These new laws specify culpability for individual conduct but place the act within the context of group activity, rationalizing more onerous individual punishment as deterrence of group-oriented criminality" (2006, 172). This new breed of organized crime legislation has created new offences and penalties for committing crimes in the context of an ongoing organized criminal conspiracy.

The United States was the first country to introduce such laws through the Racketeer Influenced and Corrupt Organizations (RICO) statute of 1970, which makes it unlawful to acquire, operate, or receive income from an enterprise through a pattern of racketeering activity.

For decades, Canada resisted legislation that created specific organized crime offences. It was not until 1997, when Bill C-95—officially called An Act to Amend the Criminal Code (Criminal Organizations) and to Amend Other Acts in Consequence—became law. It was enacted in the wake of the violent events associated with the turf war between outlaw biker gangs in Quebec. For the first time, the Criminal Code defined a "criminal organization," included a "criminal organization offence" and a "participation in a criminal organization offence," and prescribed specific penalties for conviction under these sections.

After further amendments that took effect in 2002, section 476 of the Criminal Code now defines "criminal organization" and designates three criminal organization offences:

467.11: knowingly participating in or contributing to any activity of a criminal organization for the purpose of enhancing the ability of said organization to facilitate or commit an indictable offence under a federal statute (with a maximum penalty of five years in prison)

467.12: committing an indictable offence under a federal statute for the benefit of, at the direction of, or in association with, a criminal organization (with a maximum penalty of 14 years in prison)

467.13: being a member of a criminal organization, and instructing another person to commit an offence under a federal statute for the benefit of, at the direction of, or in association with, a criminal organization (with a maximum penalty of life in prison).

In July 2005, Madam Justice Michele Fuerst found two members of an Ontario chapter of Hells Angels guilty of extortion and of committing that crime "in association" with a criminal organization. The ruling was viewed as a significant victory for the government, because it upheld section 467.12 and because it ruled that Hells Angels was a criminal organization. On 23 January 2002, two men wearing motorcycle club colours arrived at the home of a Barrie, Ontario, businessman who had allegedly sold them faulty equipment for stealing satellite television signals. By wearing their Hells Angels colours, the two men "presented themselves not as individuals, but as members of a group with a reputation for violence and intimidation," Justice Fuerst wrote in her decision. "They committed extortion with the intention to do so in association with a criminal organization, the HAMC (Hells Angels Motorcycle Club) to which they belonged" (*Toronto Star* 2005).

QUESTIONS FOR CRITICAL THINKING

1. How does the information presented in this chapter compare with the depictions of organized crime in the entertainment media (television, movies, games, etc.)? Are there any myths and misconceptions popularized by the entertainment industry regarding organized crime that appear to have been refuted in this chapter?

2. Compare and contrast the Criminal Code of Canada definition of a criminal organization with other definitions of organized crime. From an enforcement point of view, what are the strengths and weaknesses of this definition?

Summary

- Organized crime can be broadly defined by *how* crimes are carried out and by the ultimate *goal* of the criminal activity; it is perpetrated by a group of people who conspire together on a continuing and secretive basis with the goal of obtaining a financial or other material benefit.

- Dominant organized crime genres in Canada include Italian, Chinese/Asian, outlaw motorcycle gangs, Russian/Eastern European, and Indigenous.

- A defining characteristic of these organized crime genres has long been a shared nationality, ethnicity, and/or language. In recent years, however, these factors are no longer the most important criteria determining who participates in a particular organized criminal conspiracy. There are thousands of individual criminal entrepreneurs who work together, on an ad hoc or ongoing basis, in the pursuit of illegal revenues, regardless of the ethnicity, nationality, or language of the participants.

- Two competing and diametrically opposed theories regarding the origins of organized crime in North America are (1) alien conspiracy theory, which holds that organized crime in North America is the result of the importation of secret criminal societies rooted in foreign cultures; and (2) ethnic succession theory, which emphasizes how conditions indigenous to North America have contributed to the growth of organized criminality on this continent.

- The past 40 years have seen a proliferation of criminal groups, networks, and organized criminal conspiracies in Canada and worldwide. Canada continues to serve as a branch plant for transnational crime groups and as a transit point for the international movement of illegal drugs. The country is also a major producer of illegal drugs, including marijuana, methamphetamines, and ecstasy. Canada has also become an international centre for telemarketing fraud and for the counterfeiting of currency, bank cards, and digital entertainment products.

NET WORK

Using resources available through the Internet, examine a particular organized crime genre (e.g., outlaw motorcycle gangs) and group (e.g., the Hells Angels) by applying what you have learned in this chapter. In particular, apply the following frameworks: (1) characteristics of organized crime, (2) etiological theories of organized crime, and (3) theories of the Structure of Organized Criminal Conspiracies.

For many years, the CISC has published an annual report examining organized crime in Canada. Recent reports can be found on their website at http://www.cisc.gc.ca. Based on an analysis of recent reports, describe the impact that organized crime has on Canada.

One can play various interactive games on the Internet (or through smartphone apps) that centre on organized crime. Join one of these games and assess the extent to which the game reflects the information presented in this chapter.

Corporate and White-Collar Crime

17

JOHN HAGAN
Northwestern University

RICK LINDEN
University of Manitoba

Learning Objectives

After reading this chapter, you should be able to

- Describe the concept of white-collar crime and explain the impact the notion of white-collar crime has had on the discipline of criminology.

- Understand the occupational and organizational components of white-collar crime.

- Explain the physical and social harm caused by white-collar crime in Canada.

- Analyze how the structure of the modern corporation facilitates criminal activity.

- Understand the nature and extent of occupational crime.

- Understand the causes and consequences of our weak laws concerning corporate and white-collar crime.

We know far more about street crime and organized crime than we do about corporate and white-collar crime, as most of us are unaware of the harm done by corporate and white-collar criminals. These crimes are much more costly in dollar terms than street crime. The $6 billion lost to investors in the Bre-X fraud discussed in this chapter is far more than the money lost in all the robberies in Canadian history. Few bank robbers get away with more than a few thousand dollars, but Earl Jones, an Ontario lawyer, defrauded clients (including friends and relatives) of more than $50 million to support his lavish lifestyle. Corporate and white-collar crimes are also dangerous; many occupational deaths and injuries are the result of unsafe and illegal working conditions.

The term "white-collar crime" was introduced by Sutherland in 1940. While there is disagreement about the precise meaning of the term, the concept of white-collar crime has forced a reconsideration of some very basic criminological assumptions. No longer is it possible to take definitions of crime for granted. No longer can the official data collected on crime by agencies of crime control be accepted uncritically. No longer can we assume that the poor are necessarily more criminal than the rich. Now that the concept of white-collar crime has become central to the discipline, the criminological enterprise has taken on new form and substance.

The Extent and Nature of Corporate and White-Collar Crime

The Extent of Corporate and White-Collar Crime

The business section in your daily paper normally deals with stories involving company profits, corporate mergers, and economic forecasts. But criminal matters have become a routine part of business reporting as well. To give you some idea of the extent of corporate and white-collar crime and deviance, consider these recent stories:

- Calgary lawyer David Blott was disbarred for his handling of settlements given to residential school survivors. His firm represented 4,600 survivors, and he was accused of providing minimal service (taking an average of eight minutes per case) and of arranging cash advances for his clients at very high rates of interest. His firm stands to collect over $16 million for work done on the 1,168 cases completed up to Mr. Blott's disbarment (*Vancouver Sun* 2014).

- Montreal-based SNC-Lavalin, one of the world's largest construction companies, has been implicated in a number of scandals, particularly for bribing foreign officials to secure construction contracts. Most notably, it has been accused of paying $160 million in bribes to secure Libyan contracts from dictator Moammar Gadhafi's regime. According to the RCMP, the Montreal-based company offered one of Gadhafi's sons a job in order to help it secure further contracts in northern Africa. Several executives were criminally charged, and in 2018 the company agreed to pay $110 million to settle lawsuits related to the Libyan affair. The company is still facing criminal charges (Van Praet 2018).

- Victoria mutual fund salesman David Michaels defrauded 484 clients out of $65 million. Michaels attracted his clients through a radio infomercial and encouraged them to make very risky investments by misrepresenting the nature of those investment products (Duffy 2014). Michaels was fined $17.5 million, but by 2018 he had paid nothing.

- Hollywood producer Harvey Weinstein has been accused of offences ranging from rape to sexual harassment by dozens of women, including stars like Gwyneth Paltrow, Angelina Jolie, and Rose McGowan. In some of these cases, Weinstein threatened to harm the careers of women who rejected his advances. Weinstein now faces numerous lawsuits and in 2018 was indicted in New York on several rape charges.

- Canada's leading breadmakers and sellers (including Canada Bread, Weston Bakeries, Loblaws, Sobeys, Walmart, and Metro) are being investigated for fixing the price of bread between 2001 and 2015. The companies agreed they would not lower their prices to compete with one another and would raise their prices at about the same time. Loblaws has admitted to price-fixing and has offered customers $25 in compensation; the other companies deny the charges. Loblaws will also face class action lawsuits over its role, but because it was the first company to come forward it will not face criminal prosecution under the Competition Bureau's Immunity Program.

■ In 1998, British physician Andrew Wakefield published a paper in the medical journal *The Lancet*. In the paper, Wakefield claimed that the MMR (measles, mumps, and rubella) vaccine caused autism. Use of the vaccine, routinely given to children, declined dramatically and outbreaks of measles became common in many countries. However, Wakefield's work was both unethical and fraudulent, and the paper was partly withdrawn by *The Lancet* in 2004 and completely withdrawn in 2010, months before Wakefield's licence to practise was withdrawn by the British General Medical Council. However, Wakefield continues to campaign against vaccinations, and his work has been used as support by many anti-vaccine groups.

■ WorkSafe BC levied a fine of over $1 million against Babine Forest Products after the company's negligence led to a sawmill explosion in Burns Lake that killed two men and injured 20 more (Morton 2014).

Even the sports pages are full of stories about athletes and officials who have broken serious rules or violated the law. Some of the world's best athletes, including cyclist Lance Armstrong and baseball players Alex Rodriquez, Roger Clemens, and Barry Bonds, have been accused of using performance-enhancing drugs. Several American universities, most notably the University of North Carolina, have set up fake courses to enable student athletes to receive grades high enough to stay eligible in the sports program. In 2014, members of FIFA, the governing body of soccer, were accused of accepting millions of dollars in bribes to support Qatar's successful bid for the 2022 World Cup.

Clearly, corporate and white-collar crime is a major problem. Most stories about it remain on the business pages, but many have become front page news. The public is finally becoming aware of the harm being done by corporate and white-collar criminals.

Cyclist Lance Armstrong is one of many world-class athletes who have tried to win by using performance-enhancing drugs. Armstrong was stripped of the seven Tour de France titles he had won.

Randy Miramontez/Shutterstock.com

TABLE 17.1 ■ Types of Corporate and White-Collar Crime

Crimes against the Public
Corporate and Business Crime
Price-fixing (conspiring on contract bids or on prices for selling to the public)
Manipulation of stocks and securities
Commercial and political bribery and rebates
Patent and trademark infringements
Misrepresentation and false advertising
Fraudulent grading, packaging, and labelling
Tax fraud
Adulteration of food and drugs
Illegal pollution of the environment
Crimes by Individual and Professional Practitioners
Obtaining fees, payments, or charges through fraud and deception
Deceiving or defrauding patients, clients, customers
Immoral practices in relations with clients
Unprofessional conduct and malpractice
Falsification of statements on vital documents
Crimes within the Organization
Offences against the Organization
Theft of funds by employees
Theft of inventory by employees
Offences against Employees
Violation of workplace health and safety laws
Violation of labour laws
Discriminatory employment practices
Harassment

Source: Christopher Stone, *Where the Law Ends: The Social Control of Corporate Behavior* (New York: Harper and Row, 1975).

The Nature of Corporate and White-Collar Crime

Corporate and white-collar offenders have many ways of making money. Table 17.1 shows the range of offences committed by corporations and by individuals in the course of their legitimate occupations. In this chapter you will learn something about both types of offences.

Class, Crime, and the Corporations

Occupation, Organization, and Crime

White-collar crimes are often committed through and on behalf of corporations. While some of these activities had been illegal more than 100 years ago, it was not until 1940 that Edwin Sutherland attached a permanent name to these offences. He proposed that **white-collar crime** be defined "as a crime committed by a person of respectability and high social status in the course of his occupation."

white-collar crime
Sutherland defined white-collar crime "as a crime committed by a person of respectability and high social status in the course of his occupation."

SEARCH FOR:
Scams and Frauds RCMP Site

Since Sutherland defined the term, there has been confusion regarding the concepts of *occupation* and *organization* in the study of white-collar crime. A distinction is often drawn between "**occupational crime**—that is, white-collar crime committed by an individual or group of individuals exclusively for personal gain," and "**organizational crime**—white-collar crimes committed with the support and encouragement of a formal organization and intended at least in part to advance the goals of that organization" (Coleman 1985, 8). Organizational crime is also known as corporate crime.

Sutherland (1945) insisted that if there is a "legal description of acts as socially injurious and legal provision of a penalty for the act," criminologists should consider such acts as crimes. Despite this, many such acts go undetected and unprosecuted. For example, many stock and securities frauds can be prosecuted under provincial securities legislation *or* under the Criminal Code of Canada. Securities laws are considered "quasi-criminal" statutes. Yet the behaviours prosecuted under either body of law may be identical. Prosecutorial discretion determines whether these behaviours are officially defined as crimes. Sutherland believed that in either case, the behaviours were to be regarded as criminal. This can have a strong impact on the relationship observed between class and crime.

Consider the issue of deaths and accidents that result from workplace events. Occupational deaths outnumber deaths resulting from murder (Sharpe and Hardt 2006). It cannot be assumed that most of these deaths are the result of the illegal actions of employers; even so, there is good reason to believe that many are not simply the result of employee carelessness.

One rather dated estimate (Reasons, Ross, and Paterson 1981) holds that more than one-third of all on-the-job injuries are due to illegal working conditions and that another quarter are due to legal but unsafe conditions. At most, one-third of all such accidents are attributed to unsafe acts on the part of employees. There are many well-documented examples of employers intentionally, knowingly, or negligently creating hazards. These include failing to follow administrative orders to alter dangerous situations and covering up the creation and existence of such hazards. The penalties for these offences are very light. For example, a 2007 vehicle accident took the lives of three BC farm workers and injured 14 others. The workers had been packed into a 10-passenger van and were sitting on wooden benches without seatbelts. The RCMP recommended 33 criminal charges in this case, but none were laid. The driver was fined $2,000, but the labour contracting company that owned the van and employed the workers was not penalized (Sandborn 2010). Snider (2015) has estimated that there were just over 600 workplace deaths in Canada in 2011 that involved culpability on the part of the employer. This compares with 598 "normal" homicides.

The failure of the Johns-Manville Corporation to protect workers from asbestos poisoning is one of the best-known examples of employer liability. Asbestos has been recognized as a serious health hazard since the turn of the century, but asbestos workers were not informed and governments and the medical community ignored the hazard. At the Johns-Manville plant in Toronto, company doctors regularly diagnosed lung diseases among the asbestos workers, but they never told the workers their lung problems were related to asbestos. Many of the workers subsequently died of asbestos-related illnesses. In 2005, asbestos-related deaths accounted for nearly one-third of workplace fatalities in Canada (Sharpe and Hardt 2006).

occupational crime
Refers to violations of the law in the course of practising a legitimate occupation.

organizational or corporate crime
White-collar crime committed with the support and encouragement of a formal organization and intended, at least in part, to advance the goals of that organization.

The construction industry has high rates of death and injury resulting from failure to implement workplace health and safety regulations. For example, one Manitoba company was fined $75,000 after the death of a bridge painter who was working on a platform with no guard rails, and another was fined $27,500 for its role in the death of a young worker who was electrocuted when he was allowed to work on a high-voltage light fixture while the wires were live (McIntyre 2001). According to Swartz (1978), these deaths should be recognized as a form of murder—what is sometimes called "corporate homicide." However, as with the Westray mine disaster (see Box 17.1), corporate executives are almost never held personally responsible for their negligence. At most, their companies are ordered to pay small fines.

Social Class and Crime

There is evidence that a small number of offenders account for a large proportion of serious street crimes (see Chapter 15). The same may be true of white-collar crime. For example, crimes such as corporate homicide may be much more frequent among particular employers in particular kinds of industries. The mining, asbestos, and construction industries have already been noted.

Implicit in the discussion of street crimes and corporate homicide is the strong likelihood that different kinds of crime likely have different connections to the concept of class. Among adults, class is negatively related to street crimes of violence and is likely positively related to causing harms less directly through criminal acts involving the use of corporate resources. Similarly, among juveniles, it may be that some common acts of delinquency (e.g., forms of theft that include illegal downloading of videos and music and the unauthorized use of credit and bank cards) are related positively to class, while serious forms of violent delinquency are negatively related to class (Chapter 5). The study of white-collar crime and delinquency provides reason to believe that measures of class are connected to crime and delinquency in complicated ways.

Why do higher status people get involved in criminal behaviour? Shover and Hochstetler (2006) suggest three cultural components of middle- and upper-class life that may shape these people's criminality: a competitive spirit, arrogance, and a sense of entitlement. Many of the sports figures mentioned earlier carried out unethical acts to help them win. Athletes are told that "winning is the only thing," and some respond to this pressure by cheating. According to Shover and Hochstetler, employees at Enron (discussed later in this chapter) were continuously evaluated and 15 percent were always rated unacceptable. The resulting competitive pressure and the insecurity it generated among employees fostered a culture that encouraged misconduct. The fact that success in business is often measured by the size of one's salary helps explain why executives who are already making huge salaries will break the rules so that they can make even more money.

Shover and Hochstetler (2006) proposed that people who are used to power and authority can develop an arrogance that convinces them that the rules do not apply to them. Conrad Black explicitly contrasted his abilities with those of people who were not among the rich and powerful. Recall from Chapter 1 that Black was expelled from Upper Canada College for several offences, including

FOCUS

BOX 17.1

WESTRAY: A DISASTER OF CRIMINAL PROPORTIONS

"In the early morning of 9 May 1992 a violent explosion rocked the tiny community of Plymouth, just east of Stellarton, in Pictou County, Nova Scotia. The explosion occurred in the depths of the Westray coal mine, instantly killing the 26 miners working there at the time" (Richard 1997, vii). These words begin the report of a judicial inquiry into the Westray mine explosion that tells a shocking story of corporate and government misconduct that resulted in one of the largest occupational disasters in Canadian history.

Glasbeek and Tucker (1994) point out that the Westray explosion was not an accident; rather, it resulted from conscious decisions by those responsible for the miners' safety. This conclusion was reinforced by the title of Justice Richard's inquiry: *The Westray Story: A Predictable Path to Disaster.*

The explosion was not an accident, but nobody intended to kill the miners. Rather, their deaths were the result of "a complex mosaic of actions, omissions, mistakes, incompetence, apathy, cynicism, stupidity, and neglect" (Richard 1997, viii). The inquiry concluded that Westray managers "displayed a certain disdain for safety and appeared to regard safety-conscious workers as the wimps in the organization" (ix).

The mine was built in an area that was known to be treacherous because of geological faults and high levels of methane gas. However, only minimal safety precautions were taken. The mine owners and governments were more concerned about the economic impact of mining than about protecting the workers. The government relied on the company to meet safety standards and provided very limited compliance inspections. The company, Curragh Corporation, was having financial difficulties and put pressure on Westray to increase production levels in order to increase company revenues. Safety violations were common, and some miners quit; others stayed because of the lack of alternative employment in the province. The mine's safety conditions were summed up by Justice Richard:

> I find that the source of ignition was sparks struck by the cutting bits of the continuous miner working in the Southwest 2 section of the mine. But it became apparent as the Inquiry proceeded that conditions at Westray were of greater significance to what happened than was the source of the ignition. Had there been adequate ventilation, had there been adequate treatment of coal dust, and had there been adequate training and an appreciation by management for a safety ethic, those sparks would have faded harmlessly. (3)

Despite clear evidence of these violations, the government did not exercise its responsibility to shut down the mine until safety was improved.

Five employees of the Nova Scotia Natural Resources Department and the Department of Labour were fired for their role in the explosion, but nobody from the mining company was ever held legally responsible for the tragedy. Clifford Frame, president of Curragh Corporation, refused to testify at the inquiry and was never charged with any offence. Mine managers Gerald Philips and Roger Parry were charged with manslaughter and criminal negligence, but these charges were stayed by the Crown because a conviction was unlikely. This is but one of many cases that illustrate the inability of our laws to control corporate crime. The weakness of the law was addressed by Justice Richard:

> The government of Canada . . . should institute a study of the accountability of corporate executives and directors for the wrongful or negligent acts of the corporation and should introduce in the Parliament of Canada such amendments to legislation as are necessary to ensure that corporate executives and directors are held properly accountable for workplace safety. (57)

Six years after the inquiry, the government passed Bill C-45 (known as the Westray Act), which introduced the obligation to protect workers into the Criminal Code. However, the legislation has had little impact on worker safety; only a handful of charges have been laid, and there have been few convictions. And the only people convicted have been small business owners or supervisory personnel; major corporations have not been affected by the legislation. Bittle and Snider (2014) found that the government did not want to make the legislation so onerous that it would affect the ability of businesses to make a profit and that prosecutors did not target large corporations with this law. Many of those responsible for enforcing the new law have preferred to use provincial workplace safety legislation to deal with these issues (Giesbrecht 2012). These provincial laws do not have criminal penalties but are easier to use and offer a higher likelihood of conviction.

Questions for Critical Thinking

1. Search online for the Westray Act (Bill C-45). Most observers agree that this law has not been effective. Provide some of the reasons why it has failed.

2. Why do you think that governments are reluctant to implement laws that would hold corporate officials more responsible for their actions?

selling copies of final examinations. His arrogance is displayed in his memoirs when he discusses how he claimed that his actions were justified because he did not like the school staff:

> All those who, by their docility or obsequiousness, legitimized the excesses of the school's penal system, the several sadists and few aggressively fondling homosexuals on the faculty, and the numerous swaggering boobies who had obviously failed in the real world and retreated to Lilliput where they could maintain their exalted status by contract threat of battery: all that gradually produced in me a profound revulsion. (Olive, 2007, 1)

SEARCH FOR:
Global Profiles of the Fraudster
KPMG

A sense of entitlement may also play a role in white-collar crime. Shover and Hochstetler (2006) cite research showing that doctors who had been convicted of defrauding the US Medicare system felt they were entitled to the money they took illegally because of their status as doctors. Many executives who have been accused of criminality have long histories of using their rank in the corporation to benefit themselves in ways that would not be allowed for their subordinates. Another quote from Conrad Black illustrates this sense of entitlement. In the 1980s, Black tried to take funds that were in his employees' pension plan; he accused them of stealing from him and used this accusation to support his claim on the money (a battle Black later lost in court): "It's sometimes difficult to work myself into an absolute lachrymose [tearful] fit about a work force that steals on that scale . . . We are not running a welfare agency for corrupt union leaders and a slovenly work force" (Olive 2007, 1).

White-Collar Crime and the Social Organization of Work

Not all white-collar crimes are committed by high-status persons. Much embezzlement is committed by relatively low-status employees (Daly 1989), and blue-collar workers also commit crimes in the course of their legal occupations. However, if white-collar crime is positively related to class position, it is reasonable to ask why. The answer may lie in the power derived from ownership and authority positions in modern corporations. These positions of power carry with them a freedom from control that may be criminogenic. That is, to have power is to be free from the kinds of constraints that may normally inhibit crime. The modern corporation facilitates this kind of freedom.

Crime and the Corporation: Executive Disengagement

The organization of the corporation is crucial to understanding most corporate crime (Reiss, 1980; Ermann and Lundman, 1982; Hagan, 1982). As Wheeler and Rothman (1982) noted, the corporation "is for white-collar criminals what the gun or knife is for the common criminal—a tool to obtain money from victims."

The corporation itself is a "legal fiction," with, as H.L. Mencken aptly observed, "no pants to kick or soul to damn." The law chooses to treat corporations as **juristic persons**, thus making them formally liable to the same laws as "natural persons." Some of the obvious faults in this legal analogy become clear when we consider that it is impossible to imprison a corporation. However, there are more

juristic persons
The legal concept that corporations are liable to the same laws as natural persons. Treating corporations as individuals raises practical difficulties for legal enforcement and punishment.

subtle differences between corporate and individual actors that have equally significant consequences:

> When individuals are placed in an organizational structure, some of the ordinary internalized restraints seem to lose their hold. And if we decide to look beyond the individual employees and find an organizational "mind" to work with, a "corporate conscience" distinct from the consciences of particular individuals, it is not readily apparent where we would begin—much less what we would be talking about. (Stone 1975)*

Corporate power is relatively unchecked and thus is criminogenic. The problem is in part the absence of cultural beliefs that discourage corporate criminality (Geis 1962). There is some evidence that cultural climates vary across time and political regimes. However, even when condemnatory beliefs about corporate crime have been strong, there have been too few controlling mechanisms in place to deal effectively with white-collar crime.

Modern global corporations are huge, with hundreds of thousands of employees and many layers of bureaucracy. It is difficult for the boards of directors that are responsible for corporate governance to know the details of their corporation's daily operations. Top officers and directors can be sued by the corporation itself (through a shareholders' action) if they allow a law violation to occur through negligence. However, the courts have not imposed a duty on directors to uncover corporate wrongdoing. This provides an incentive for senior managers and directors to remain uninformed about illegal activities.

The bankruptcy of Britain's Barings Bank provides an example of **executive disengagement**. Barings, which had been controlled by the same family since 1762, was brought down by the actions of a 28-year-old trader. Nicholas Leeson lost almost $1 billion of the company's money on financial derivatives, which were essentially bets on the future performance of the Tokyo stock market. When the Tokyo market fell, Barings collapsed when it could not cover the losses. The size of this gamble was in violation of British banking laws. While bank officials were quick to blame Leeson, it is very likely that senior bank officials at least tacitly approved of Leeson's trading activities. Several financial experts have suggested that the profits Leeson had previously made for Barings led bank officials to allow him to risk their shareholders' money by making illegal trades (Drohan 1995).

executive disengagement
The custom by which lower-level employees assume that executives are best left uninformed of certain decisions and actions of employees, or the assumption that executives cannot be legally expected to have complete control over their individual staff.

The Criminogenic Market Structure

Corporate crime research suggests not only a freedom at the top of organizations from the need to accept responsibility for criminal activity below, but also a growing pressure from managers that is also criminogenic. Farberman (1975) has referred to such pressures in the automotive industry and in other highly concentrated corporate sectors as constituting a **criminogenic market structure**. The crime-generating feature of these markets is their domination by a relatively small number of manufacturers that insist that their dealers sell in high volumes at a small per-unit profit. Dealers who fail to perform risk losing their franchises. The result is strong pressure to maximize sales and minimize service. Farberman suggests that car dealers may be induced by the small profit margins on new cars

criminogenic market structure
An economic market that is structured in such a way that it tends to produce criminal behaviour.

*Christopher Stone, *Where the Law Ends: The Social Control of Corporate Behavior* (New York: Harper and Row, 1975).

to compensate through fraudulent warranty work and repair rackets. Thus, auto executives can distance themselves from the criminal consequences of the "forcing model" (high volume/low per-unit profit) they impose. The result is an absence of control over repair and warranty frauds at the dealership level.

The Large Scale of Corporations

Access to corporate resources makes it possible to commit very large-scale crimes. The organizational form has facilitated economic and technological development on a scale far beyond that achieved by individuals; it has also allowed criminal gains of a magnitude that individuals acting alone would find hard to attain.

The structure of the modern corporation has created a power imbalance in which individuals at the top experience relative freedom, while those at the bottom often experience pressure applied from the top that encourages various kinds of white-collar crime. The corporate form itself can be used to perpetrate bigger crimes than can be achieved by individuals acting alone. Access to these corporate resources is a unique advantage of class positions involving ownership and authority in business organizations. In this sense, it can be said that in the world of the modern corporation, the social organization of work itself is criminogenic.

Corporate Accounting Scandals

While corporate crime has long been a problem in North America, the new millennium saw scandals that shocked even the most avid supporters of free enterprise. Several of America's largest corporations, including the energy company Enron, went bankrupt, stock markets crashed, and the economy declined. Later, in 2008, corporate misconduct dealt the world economy another severe blow as a mortgage financing scandal in the United States and high-risk lending policies in several other countries led to another major financial crisis. Why do we keep facing these crises, which are caused by what one observer has called a "scandalous rot" (DeCloet, 2002)?

While these crises have many causes, an explanation can start with how corporate executives are paid. Many companies provide senior executives with stock options that allow them to purchase shares in the company at a later date for a price guaranteed at the time the options were issued. If the stock goes up in the future, the executive can buy it at the guaranteed price and keep the difference between the issue price and the value of the stock at the time it was purchased. If the stock goes down, the executive will not use the option and so will not lose money. The purpose of stock options is to provide executives with an incentive to work hard and raise the company's value. This will ensure that the company's shareholders benefit from the company's growth. Many companies also pay their senior employees very large bonuses if the company meets specified profit targets.

Some executives take a long-term perspective and work to build up the value of their companies; others, though, take a short-term approach that can prove disastrous for shareholders. They use a variety of short-term measures to raise both company profits and the stock price so that they can make enormous profits on their stock options and bonuses very quickly. For example, "Chainsaw Al" Dunlap (named for his willingness to reduce costs by firing employees) was the CEO of the household appliance company Sunbeam. Dunlap's aggressive methods included artificially inflating sales figures so that the company's profits appeared higher than they actually were. Sunbeam eventually went bankrupt. Dunlap was fired and fined $15 million, which was only a part of the illegal gains he had made from Sunbeam stock before its decline.

In the late 1990s, the stock market rose dramatically and CEOs became corporate superstars. Many paid themselves enormous sums of money—in large companies, as much as $50 to $100 million per year. Executives convinced themselves that they deserved this high pay even when their companies were losing money. The greed of senior executives led directly to one of the largest bankruptcies in US history.

The Collapse of Enron

How did senior managers at Enron cost their investors $63 billion? For most of its history, Enron was a pipeline company that delivered natural gas. This business was very profitable, but to CEO Kenneth Lay, it was a boring business that lacked the potential for quick profit growth. Enron developed a business model that involved trading futures contracts, which are bets on the future prices of commodities such as natural gas, electricity, and pulp and paper. This new focus proved very profitable, and the stock's price climbed. Enron became the seventh most valuable company in the United States. However, the company took greater risks, and the new business model broke down. To keep the company growing, Enron executives resorted to illegal financial measures to make it appear as if profits were still increasing. Some of these complex measures involved the company selling its own assets to itself and showing the "profits" from these sales in its revenues. The company also tried to hide its debts by transferring them to outside "partnerships" that had actually been established by Enron.

The company developed a culture of greed. Senior Enron employees acted like kids in a candy store, taking massive personal profits from the financial schemes the company had organized. Several finance department employees invested $125,000 of their own funds in one of Enron's illegal financial transactions and made $30 million in a few months (Butler 2002). As the illegal schemes began to unravel and the company began to slide into bankruptcy, Enron paid bonuses of $681 million to 140 top executives, including $67 million to CEO Kenneth Lay, who continued to encourage employees and members of the public to buy Enron stock even as he and his executives stripped the company of its remaining value (Kranhold and Pacelle 2002). Ultimately, creditors, stockholders, and other Enron employees suffered huge losses when the financial arrangements fell apart.

Enron executives must take most of the blame for the company's demise, and several have received lengthy jail terms. However, they had help from the managers of other large corporations. The Arthur Andersen accounting firm, one of the world's largest, allowed Enron's many lapses of legal and ethical standards to slip by its auditors to help it obtain lucrative consulting contracts with Enron. Many of Wall Street's largest banks and brokerage firms collaborated with Enron in order to profit from stock commissions, consulting contracts, and interest from loans. One of Canada's largest banks, CIBC, was accused of helping Enron with its fraudulent financial dealings. While not admitting any wrongdoing, in 2005 CIBC paid $2.4 billion to settle a lawsuit over its Enron dealings.

Nortel, once the most valuable company in Canada, also collapsed because of financial misdeeds. However, rather than going to prison, senior executives kept their money, and none were successfully prosecuted.

The Financial Collapse of 2008

The collapse of Enron and several other large companies led to economic crises involving stock market crashes and increased unemployment. You might have expected governments to respond to these financial disasters by strengthening regulation and making financial institutions more accountable for their activities. But they did not, at least in part because financial institutions strongly resisted increased regulation, claiming that free market forces would ensure that businesses operated properly. Thus US financial institutions were allowed to engage in extremely risky investments. These institutions collapsed in 2008, causing a financial catastrophe that cost trillions of dollars, led to the loss of hundreds of thousands of jobs in North America and Europe, and bankrupted several countries.

A major cause of this massive financial collapse was that prominent financial institutions in the United States and several other countries took on excessive risk and engaged in reckless lending practices, particularly with household mortgages. Christine Lagarde, the head of the International Monetary Fund, has described the situation as extractive capitalism, by which she means that corporations were more focused on making profits than on their social responsibilities: "We can trace the problems to the evolution of the financial sector before the crisis. Financial actors were allowed to take excessive risks, leading to a situation whereby the profits on the upside went to the industry—and the losses on the downside were picked up by the public" (2014 n.p.).

What were the risks that precipitated the crisis? Some US mortgage lenders issued mortgages that borrowers could not repay. Some issued thousands of NINJA mortgages. NINJA is the acronym for No Income, No Job or Assets. Normally, people in those circumstances are not issued mortgages because they are likely to default, thereby costing the bank its money. But in the United States, the institutions issuing these mortgages would repackage them with other mortgages and sell them to other financial institutions and to individual investors. When they turned out to be worthless, the institutions and individuals who bought them lost everything. Many banks and mortgage companies were involved in this, but few have been punished. One exception was Wells Fargo bank, which was fined $85 million for falsifying loan documents and for pushing homeowners into more costly types of mortgages during the housing boom (Rugaber and Kravitz 2011). This fine represented an insignificant amount for one of the largest mortgage lenders in the United States. J.P. Morgan, another large US bank, settled its charges for the much larger sum of $13 billion. However, even a fine that large had no impact on the bank's stock price; indeed, it may have been less than the company made selling its bad mortgages.

The greed of many of those responsible for the US banking system led to a financial catastrophe. Even those whose behaviour was at least technically legal failed to do their jobs in assessing risk, so purchasers of the toxic mortgages did not know what they were buying. When mortgage holders defaulted in large numbers, the impact spread quickly through the financial system. Yet Goldman

Sachs, one of the companies that sold the repackaged mortgages, actually profited from the defaults because in separate transactions, the company had made market bets *against* the mortgages it was selling to others. This is part of the reason why Taibbi (2010) described Goldman Sachs as "a great vampire squid wrapped around the face of humanity, relentlessly jamming its blood funnel into anything that smells like money" (n.p.).

Several senior officials of Enron and companies in similar scandals were charged and sentenced for their misconduct. However, while hundreds of charges have been laid against minor players in the mortgage industry, no high-ranking officials from the companies involved in precipitating the 2008 financial crisis were ever prosecuted (Morgenson and Story 2011). Instead, US taxpayers were forced to bail out many of these companies because letting them go bankrupt could have destroyed the economy. These companies were judged "too big to fail." And the citizens of many countries around the world have paid the price in unemployment, lost pension funds, and massive government cutbacks, while those responsible have gone unpunished.

An interesting footnote to this story is that Canadian financial institutions were relatively unaffected by the crisis, and our mortgage market remained stable. This is because Canadian politicians and regulators did a much better job of ensuring that financial institutions did not become reckless in their search for profits. In this, and in many other types of corporate and white-collar crime, aggressive regulation and enforcement can do a great deal to reduce misconduct. Unfortunately, this is often lacking, and today (2018) the US Congress is rolling back some of the protections that were put in place after the 2008 economic meltdown, bowing to lobbying by the financial industry, which is a major donor to political campaigns.

Consumer-Safety Issues

In the 1960s the consumer movement began to hold manufacturers accountable for the safety of their products. Ralph Nader's book *Unsafe at Any Speed*, which described the deaths and injuries caused by the faulty design of the GM Corvair automobile, helped focus public attention on consumer safety. Widely publicized cases, like the calculation by Ford executives that it would be cheaper to pay for lawsuits brought by the families of Ford Pinto drivers who had been burned to death in accidents than to fix the fuel tank design flaw that caused the fires, and the production of Firestone tires that came apart at high speed, led to tougher safety regulations and convinced companies that it was good business to manufacture safe products.

Over the past 40 years, governments have become more active in regulating consumer goods and products have become much safer. However, unsafe products continue to cause injury and death. In 2014, General Motors recalled about 15 million cars because of a faulty ignition switch that caused engines to shut down, leading to a loss of power steering and power brakes. General Motors had known about the problem for many years but did not warn car owners or rectify the problem—clearly, the automobile industry's culture and practices had not completely changed. As of 2015, GM had attributed 124 deaths to this problem (Korosec 2015) and had set aside more than $600 million to pay the resulting claims.

In 2007, people who took product safety for granted were surprised to learn of several incidents in which unsafe products manufactured in China were being sold in the North American market. The first was the melamine-contaminated pet food that you read about in Chapter 11. The second was the sale of counterfeit Colgate toothpaste in discount stores throughout Canada. The toothpaste contained potentially harmful chemicals. A third scandal involved children's toys, including Elmo, Big Bird, and Dora, which were recalled by manufacturers because of safety concerns. A few months later, Mattel, the maker of Fisher-Price toys, was forced to issue three recalls involving millions of toys. Some of the toys had lead paint, which can be poisonous; others had design flaws, including loose magnets that children could swallow.

Some of the blame does fall on China, where regulation is lax, corruption and bribery are common, and the government tacitly approves of a wide range of illegal practices. But Mattel is also at fault. Quality control is not nearly as effective in China as it is in North American factories. Thus, the toy companies must be responsible for doing sufficient testing of their Chinese-made products to ensure that they are safe. And what about the Canadian and US governments? There are toy safety regulations, but we know that unless regulations are actively enforced, some businesses will ignore them. Neither country does routine testing of toys, leaving that task to the toy companies.

"Drug Dealers in Lab Coats"

Canada and the United States are in the midst of an opioid crisis. In 2017, British Columbia reported 1,448 deaths attributable to drug overdoses—an increase of 46 percent from 2016 (BC Coroners Service 2018), and rates are high in several other provinces. In the United States, 64,000 people died of overdoses in 2016 (Kristof 2017), and in 2017, the government declared the opioid crisis a national health emergency.

Much of the blame for this crisis goes to the pharmaceutical industry. In the United States the majority of people who are addicted to opioids started with prescription painkillers—a change from earlier times, when most addicts began with heroin (Kristof 2017). For more than two decades the industry spent hundreds of millions of dollars promoting the increased use of opioid drugs to help control pain, claiming that these drugs were safe. This campaign was so successful that 236 million opioid prescriptions were written in the United States in 2016 (Kristof 2017).

A leading beneficiary of all these prescriptions is Purdue Pharma, the company that manufactures OxyContin. Purdue has made tens of billions of dollars from OxyContin, but is now facing many lawsuits over the way it promoted and sold the drug. OxyContin is an effective painkiller but a major reason for its huge sales is that it is highly addictive, so many users continue using the drug even after their pain issues are over. Also, it is a favourite drug of street addicts, a fact long known to Purdue executives. Purdue promoted the drug heavily and was a major force behind efforts to normalize the prescribing of opioids. Despite knowing the negative effects of the drug, sales reps falsely assured doctors that OxyContin was less addictive than its competitors (Robertson and Howlett 2016). They also provided free textbooks to medical schools that claimed OxyContin was less addictive than its competitors.

Doctors have also been complicit in the spread of opioids. Several US doctors have been convicted of taking bribes from the company Insys Therapeutics in exchange for prescribing a Fentanyl spray to patients who did not need the drug. The former CEO of Insys has been arrested and faces a number of charges in relation to bribery. A significant number of doctors in the United States and Canada established practices where they were essentially in the business of prescribing high volumes of opioids to addicts. A drug company employee described one such doctor as "extremely moody, lazy and inattentive. He basically just shows up to sign his name on the prescription pad, if he shows up at all" (Mathis-Lilley 2016). Other doctors were paid by companies to speak to other doctors about the benefits of opioids and received trips and other benefits from those companies. In many cases these speaking fees were thinly disguised bribes, as some doctors were paid a fee that was proportional to the number of prescriptions they had written for the product.

Purdue's aggressive strategy is described in a review of a book about Purdue written by Beth Macy (2018). "Particularly grotesque is the enthusiasm with which Purdue peddled its pills. In the first five years OxyContin was on the market, total bonuses for the company's sales staff grew from $1 million to $40 million. Zealous reps could earn quarterly bonuses as high as $100,000, one former salesperson told Macy, adding, "It behooved them to have the pill mills [doctors whose practice mainly consisted of prescribing opiates] writing high doses." Doctors were plied with all-expense-paid resort trips, free tanks of gas and deliveries of Christmas trees and Thanksgiving turkeys. There were even "starter coupons" offering new patients a free 30-day supply. As sales rocketed into the billions, noxious side effects began to emerge. Chief among them was the creation of a legion of addicts who, desperate to stave off withdrawal, made the leap to cheap heroin and, later, fentanyl. ("Four out of five heroin addicts come to the drugs . . . through prescribed opioids," Macy notes pointedly.) (Bruder 2018).

In 2007, Purdue's actions became known to the public when the company paid more than $600 million to settle criminal and civil cases based on the misleading claims they had made about their product. Currently the company faces lawsuits launched by hundreds of US states, counties, and cities (though as of 2018 no Canadian government had taken action against Purdue). However, even when faced with convincing evidence of illegal conduct, the US government failed to pursue felony charges against Purdue executives (Meier 2018).

As the consequences of the drug became more widely known, OxyContin sales dropped. However, Purdue is now using the same marketing techniques on a global level—a strategy that had earlier been adopted by the tobacco industry as cigarette sales declined in Europe and North America.

Environmental Fraud—The Case of Volkswagen

Volkswagen has been a trusted vehicle brand for decades. However, from 2006 to 2016 the company's executives put that brand at risk by committing fraud. All types of vehicles are subject to emissions testing, and companies must inform potential customers of the results of these tests. Volkswagen had designed what they called a "clean diesel" engine and advertised that cars with these engines were environmentally friendly. However, Volkswagen had actually cheated on the tests by installing software that was activated when the vehicles were being tested in a laboratory and that reduced emissions during the testing period. More than 10 million vehicles were sold with the engines that had gone through the phony testing process.

The fraud was exposed when the International Council on Clean Transportation contracted with university researchers to test vehicle emissions when the cars were on the road. These researchers found that nitrogen oxide emissions were as much as 35 times higher than the allowable levels in the United States (International Council on Clean Transportation 2015). These findings not only demonstrated that the vehicles were harming the environment but also reduced the value of people's cars, which were not as environmentally friendly as the manufacturer had claimed.

By 2017, Volkswagen had committed $30 billion to fix these cars, to provide compensation for owners whose cars had lost value, and to pay fines (Schwartz and Bryan 2017). Several top executives, including the former CEO, have been criminally charged in the United States, and some have already been convicted and sentenced to prison terms. While a class action lawsuit in Canada resulted in a $2.1 billion settlement for Canadian customers, no charges have been laid because the Canadian investigation is going at a much slower pace than in the United States.

However, the company may not suffer any long-term consequences of their fraud. Many felt that Volkswagen's dishonesty would have a major impact on their reputation and their sales, yet in 2016 Volkswagen became the world's largest carmaker for the first time. Apparently, its actions have not affected its public image as much as analysts had feared.

White-Collar Crime and Legal Sanctions

We can ask how effective legal sanctions are in combating white-collar crime. White-collar offences are often dealt with through the civil courts rather than as criminal matters. This may have limited impact. "We have arranged things," writes Christopher Stone (1975), "so that the people who call the shots do not have to bear the full risks." This is a consequence of the limited liabilities borne by modern corporate actors:

> Take, for example, a small corporation involved in shipping dynamite. The shareholders of such a company, who are typically also the managers, do not *want* their dynamite-laden truck to blow up. But if it does, they know that those injured cannot, except in rare cases, sue them as individuals to recover their full damages if the amount left in the corporations' bank account is inadequate to make full compensation . . . What this means is that in deciding how much money to spend on safety devices, and whether or not to allow trucks to drive through major cities, the calculations are skewed toward higher risks than suggested by the "rational economic corporation/free market" model that is dreamily put forth in textbooks. If no accident results, the shareholders will reap the profits of skimping on safety measures. If a truck blows up, the underlying human interests will be shielded from fully bearing the

harm that they have caused. And then, there is nothing to prevent the same men from setting up a new dynamite shipping corporation the next day; all it takes is the imagination to think up a new name, and some $50 in filing fees. (462–63)*

Large corporations are not quite as free as this small corporation to dissolve and reconstitute their operations. Also, the separation of shareholder and management interests creates a related problem of liability. Damage judgments against corporations are taken from the companies' revenues and rarely affect the salaries of the managers who made the decisions that led to the penalties. Thus the shareholders suffer for the misdeeds of corporate managers while the managers are shielded by the corporate structure. And the financial penalties are often much lower than the profits generated by acting illegally.

So civil remedies are not very effective. What about the impact of criminal sanctions? Earlier we discussed how the legal system has done a poor job of holding white-collar offenders to account. What about the few white-collar offenders who *have* been held criminally liable and processed through the criminal justice system? Notions of "equality before the law" are perhaps nowhere more subjective than when they are being applied to the sentencing of white-collar offenders (Hagan and Albonetti 1982). This is reflected in at least two kinds of comments made by judges about the sentences they impose for white-collar crimes: first, that white-collar offenders experience sanctions in a different way than other kinds of offenders, and second, that different kinds of sanctions are appropriate in white-collar cases.

The view, common among judges, that white-collar offenders experience sanctions differently is summarized in Mann, Wheeler, and Sarat's (1980) study of a sample of judges who tried such cases: "Most judges have a widespread belief that the suffering experienced by a white-collar person as a result of apprehension, public indictment and conviction, and the collateral disabilities incident to conviction—loss of job, professional licenses, and status in the community—completely satisfies the need to punish the individual" (479). This belief persists in the face of Benson's (1989) finding that "although they commit the most serious offences, employers and managers are least likely to lose their jobs after conviction for a white-collar crime" (474).

The use of fines in sentencing white-collar offenders is controversial. Some judges feel that fines are the only penalties that should be given to white-collar offenders. Posner (1980) argues that if fines are suitably large, they are an equally effective deterrent and cheaper to administer and thus socially preferable to imprisonment and other punishments. It has already been noted that corporate entities are liable to little else than fines. However, Mann and colleagues (1980) found judges to be skeptical of fines. The sense that emerges from this research is that judges are acutely aware of the issues of deterrence, disparity, and discrimination in the sentencing of white-collar offenders and that they try to compromise by fashioning sentences that combine sanctions. All of these findings suggest that white-collar offenders are advantaged by the specific types and combinations of legal sanctions that are imposed on them.

---

*Christopher Stone, *Where the Law Ends: The Social Control of Corporate Behavior* (New York: Harper and Row, 1975).

In both Canada and the United States, there is some evidence that the mid-1970s brought a new and somewhat harsher attitude towards white-collar crime. Katz (1980) wrote of a "social movement against white-collar crime" that began in the United States in the late 1960s, and public opinion polls from that decade found that concern about white-collar crime was increasing (Cullen, Link, and Polanzi 1982). That concern seems to have been at least in part a response to events like the Watergate Scandal in the United States and a major Canadian scandal involving dredging contracts.

So there *appeared* to be a move towards tougher legal sanctions for white-collar offences. Of course, charges must be laid before sanctions can be imposed, and the power of corporations and of persons in higher class positions made decisions to prosecute problematic (see Benson et al. 1988). Hagan and Palloni (1983) reported an increased use of imprisonment for white-collar offenders after Watergate, but they also found that the length of these prison sentences was unusually short. A study of the enforcement of securities laws in Ontario (Hagan and Parker 1985) found a similar pattern of trade-offs in the severity with which white-collar offenders were treated. Overall, the treatment of white-collar offenders seems to have been lenient in the past, and despite some examples of harsher sentences, there is no clear evidence that this situation has changed markedly. And even when white-collar offenders receive prison sentences, they typically obtain parole very early because of their backgrounds and a perception that they are at low risk to reoffend.

Major financial scandals such as Enron (see above) led to harsher treatment of corporate criminals in the United States. These crimes led to a serious loss of confidence in the stock market—why would anyone want to invest money in companies whose earnings reports could not be trusted? The scandals were so pervasive that it became obvious that major changes were needed in regulation and corporate governance. While corporate lobbying has limited regulatory changes, governments in the United States have made their laws tougher and have put more resources into investigating and prosecuting corporate crime. Many senior executives were publicly arrested and taken into custody in front of the media in "perp walks," whose intent was to show the public that politicians had acted. The jail sentences received by high-profile offenders in cases such as Enron were very harsh, but there is no evidence that enforcement has been broadly effective. A study by the Harvard Law Review (2009) concluded that new sentencing rules passed in the United States in 2002 were so harsh that judges did not follow the guidelines and imposed sentences that were lower than the legislation demanded. The study also found that the harsher sentencing rules did not lead to a reduction in corporate crime.

There is also no evidence that Canadian courts have become more punitive towards corporate criminals, and the police and securities regulators have not made much effort to clean up the business world. The fact that Conrad Black was prosecuted in the United States rather than in Canada reflects the fact that the US justice system is now tougher on corporate malfeasance than the Canadian system. Even Jim Flaherty, the one-time federal finance minister, said that Canada's securities regulations were ineffective.

Why does the justice system not deal with white-collar crimes more effectively? The public is usually more concerned about violent crime and neighbourhood safety issues, so police leaders are under pressure to invest their resources in those offences. Thus, local police typically do little white-collar crime enforcement, and federal and provincial governments have not invested sufficient resources in these investigations, which can be extremely lengthy and expensive. The Nortel investigation discussed earlier took four years and required 50 people to go through 20 million documents (*Toronto Star*, 20 June 2008), and the defendants were acquitted. The amount of information collected in these complex cases results in lengthy delays in going to trial. It is difficult to keep good investigators because they are attracted away by much higher salaries in private industry. Also, many white-collar offences involve multiple jurisdictions, which can further complicate investigations.

In response to these problems, in 2004 Canada passed legislation intended to make it easier to prosecute fraud-related offences. Maximum penalties for stock fraud were increased, new insider trading rules were introduced, protection was provided for employees who reported corporate misconduct, and new rules made it easier for investigators to gather evidence concerning fraud. Also, the federal government established interdisciplinary integrated market enforcement teams (IMETs) to investigate stock market frauds. Since then, several other pieces of white-collar crime legislation have been passed.

Despite these measures, the conviction record has been abysmal (Le Pan 2007). Bittle and Snider (2014) report that from 2003 to 2012, IMETs charged 52 individuals, of whom only 11 were convicted. They attribute this lack of success to several factors: large corporations can hire the best experts to advise them on how to get around new legislation and to defend them if charges are laid; the IMETs are limited to major cases even though it may be easier to obtain convictions in less complex ones; and corporations swamp prosecutors with huge volumes of paperwork and use other methods of delaying and obstructing investigations. Also, the RCMP has moved personnel and funds away from corporate and organized crime as the perceived threat of terrorism has increased.

Bittle and Snider also conclude that, as with workplace safety legislation, governments struggle to control corporate fraud because of their reluctance to impose tough regulations on businesses that provide jobs and that have the ear of legislators. This ensures that the interests of corporations will be reflected in any legislation that is passed and in the way in which that legislation is enforced. For example, SNC-Lavalin has been involved in several corruption scandals in Canada and abroad. If the company was convicted it could be barred from receiving federal contracts for 10 years. The government has been reluctant to move against the company because it would put many of SNC-Lavalin's 45,000 jobs at risk. It has proposed instead to implement a system of deferred prosecution agreements that would suspend criminal charges. Instead, the company would pay large fines and be required to improve its ethics and compliance systems. This dilemma suggests that instead of focusing on penalizing corporations, governments should place more of an emphasis on punishing individuals, even though the diffusion of responsibility throughout the corporation makes this option challenging.

Research does not provide grounds for optimism that governments will be able to reduce corporate crime in the future. Schell-Busey and colleagues (2016) conducted a systematic review of 106 studies and found mixed results. Regulatory policy (including inspections and educational discipline) was the only single treatment that acted as a significant deterrent, though the results were inconsistent. The authors conclude that multiple types of interventions will be needed if we are to see any reductions in corporate misconduct in the future. Paternoster has summed up the situation nicely:

> The risk of formal legal penalties for corporations or individuals within corporations is small (as are the perceived risks), with deferred and non-prosecution agreements the costs of punishment are low, corporate cultures that stress profit maximization reward noncompliance, and the rewards for corporate crime in all likelihood vastly exceed the costs. (2016, 383)

Occupational Crime

In the rest of this chapter you will learn about crimes committed by individuals who violate the law in the course of practising a legitimate occupation. As with corporate crime, at the heart of occupational crime is the violation of trust (Shapiro 1990).

Unprofessional Conduct and Malpractice

In the past, malpractice and unprofessional conduct among groups such as lawyers and doctors was dealt with privately by the governing bodies of professional associations. However, society has become less tolerant of professional deviance. Complainants have become more vocal, and more violations have come to the attention of the public. Also, governments have become more willing to prosecute in cases that involve violations of the criminal law.

In every occupation there are people who violate legal or ethical codes for their own benefit. The problem is made worse when those responsible for regulating the conduct of individual practitioners fail to do their job. Cases of sexual abuse by clergy and malpractice by doctors illustrate how the failure of governing bodies to respond to complaints against members of their professions has led to greater harm being done.

The most widely publicized cases of unprofessional conduct over the past two decades have involved sexual abuse by members of the clergy. The first major case to come to the attention of the Canadian public involved the Mount Cashel Orphanage in St. John's, Newfoundland, which was run by members of the Christian Brothers order. Abuse at the orphanage was hidden for many years. Victims complained about abuse there in the 1970s, but when the investigating officers recommended laying charges against members of the Christian Brothers, the chief of the Royal Newfoundland Constabulary refused to allow charges. No further action was taken until a Royal Commission was established in 1989 following a series of public complaints from former residents of the orphanage. The commission found that senior Catholic Church officials covered up accusations of sexual and physical abuse, as did the police chief and a provincial deputy minister. In the end, 15 members of the Christian Brothers were charged, and both the Newfoundland government and the Christian Brothers order were forced to make multimillion-dollar payments to the abused victims.

Canada's Truth and Reconciliation Commission (TRC) focused public attention on the abuse of Indigenous children living in residential schools. Those schools were in operation for more than a century and were attended by more than 150,000 Indigenous children. According to the TRC their purpose was not to educate; rather, they were established to "separate Aboriginal children from their families in order to minimize and weaken family ties and cultural linkages, and to indoctrinate children into a new culture—the culture of the legally dominant Euro-Christian Canadian society" (Truth and Reconciliation Commission 2015a, Preface). The schools were run by the Roman Catholic, Anglican, United, Methodist, and Presbyterian churches.

The impact of residential schools on Indigenous children was profoundly negative. Families were broken up and the children's cultural backgrounds were erased. Many of the children were physically and sexually abused by school staff. The TRC has documented how the experience destroyed the lives of many of the children as well as their families.

One male survivor who testified before the TRC described how he was assaulted by a staff member in a change room after the man put a bag over his head and removed his clothes:

> I remember that he had struggled with me really, really hard and I fought back and fought back and I don't know how long it was, I just fought and pretty soon he just, I don't know what he did, he had restrained me somehow. And when that happened, he had sexually abused me, he penetrated me and I was just, all I can remember was just a pain. A pain was just strong. It was really hurtful and I remember that day after that I was a very, very angry kid. (Truth and Reconciliation Commission, 2015b: 154)

This boy was far from the only victim. Neither the churches nor the law enforcement agencies did anything to end this abuse or to hold people accountable for their actions.

SEARCH FOR:
Truth and Reconciliation
Commission of Canada

Canada. Dept. Indian and Northern Affairs/Library and Archives Canada/e011080274

Many of the Indigenous children who lived in residential schools were physically and sexually abused by school staff. A report on these abuses was released by the Truth and Reconciliation Commission of Canada in 2015.

This failure of church officials to deal with abusive clergy has been endemic. In Boston, Cardinal Bernard Law resigned his post in 2002 after facing criticism that he had failed to act in many cases of sexual misconduct by priests. Not only did he fail to take action, but he covered up many instances of misconduct and reassigned several priests who had been accused of abusing children to positions where they continued to work with children. A number of these priests reoffended, including Father John Geoghan, who was accused of fondling or raping 150 children. Geoghan received a sentence of 9 to 10 years for one case, and by 2002 the Catholic Church had paid out over $10 million in settlements to 86 of his victims. Geoghan had been moved around a number of parishes in the Boston area in response to complaints, but the Church otherwise took no action until after the case had received wide publicity.

The scandal has not been limited to North America. In 2018, all 31 Chilean bishops submitted their resignations to Pope Francis because of their role in covering up sexual abuse by priests, and there have been similar scandals in Ireland and several other countries.

Medical doctors have been accused of many types of violations, ranging from false billing to ethical lapses in the treatment of patients to sexual misconduct with patients. In 2018 Larry Nassar was sentenced to life in prison for sexually molesting more than 160 young women and girls. Nassar was a member of the medical team for USA Gymnastics and at Michigan State University and used these positions to abuse gymnasts. The US Olympic Committee and the university have both been accused of failing to pursue complaints against Nassar over a period of many years.

Perhaps the most serious violations by doctors involve malpractice. Most doctors are competent professionals, but accusations of malpractice are not uncommon. In 2016, patients began 891 legal actions against physicians. Typically, only about one-third of actions against doctors are successful (CMPA 2016). Some of the cases that resulted in actions against doctors included a Manitoba doctor who was sanctioned for sewing beads into the stitches of an Indigenous woman and an American doctor who was convicted of assault for carving his initials into a patient (Henderson 2000). One tragic case of malpractice involved a Winnipeg surgeon who specialized in pediatric cardiac surgery. In 1994, 12 young children died while undergoing surgery at the Health Sciences Centre. A judicial inquiry found that at least five of the deaths were likely preventable (Sinclair 2000). The inquiry determined that the surgeon was at fault but also blamed the hospital, which failed to ensure that the surgeon was qualified, and his supervisors, who failed to take action even when there were complaints about his performance. There was a culture of secrecy surrounding the work of the doctor, and nurses who complained about the program were ignored by hospital officials.

In 2007, Toronto real estate agent Krista Stryland died of complications following liposuction surgery at the Toronto Cosmetic Clinic. Her condition deteriorated after surgery that removed more than the standard amount of fat and liquids from her body. The doctor who treated her did not respond appropriately to the resulting complications.

The surgery had been carried out by Dr. Behnaz Yazdanfar, a family physician who was not a qualified plastic surgeon. However, Dr. Yazdanfar was permitted to perform cosmetic surgery in Ontario without formal surgical training. The year before Ms. Stryland's death, another doctor had complained about Dr. Yazdanfar's lack of qualifications and about her advertising, but the College of Physicians and Surgeons of Ontario determined that she was qualified to conduct cosmetic surgery procedures and allowed her to continue doing liposuction and breast augmentations.

In 2009 the College of Physicians and Surgeons conducted hearings into a number of complaints against Dr. Yazdanfar, including the Stryland case. The Discipline Committee determined that Dr. Yazdanfar had committed professional misconduct by failing to meet the standard of practice, that she had violated advertising regulations, and that she had acted in a manner that was "disgraceful, dishonourable or unprofessional" (College of Physicians and Surgeons of Ontario 2009, 1). The committee concluded that Dr. Yazdanfar was incompetent and prohibited her from performing further surgery.

Doctors are a self-governing profession, and their governance processes are not always effective. In 2018 the *Toronto Star* published a series of articles dealing with this issue. The series began with a discussion of three doctors who had been disciplined for serious offences in the US. One had raped a pregnant patient in his Washington state office; another was a neurosurgeon who had been responsible for several serious incidents of malpractice, including cases involving quadriplegia and death; and the third who had been sent to prison for possessing sexually explicit and "sadistic" photos of young boys (*Toronto Star* 2018). What these doctors all have in common is that they were Canadian-trained and were able to return to Canada to practise medicine despite their serious misconduct. While Canadian medical authorities can usually obtain this information, they make it difficult for the public to gain access to it, so patients may not know about previous misconduct of their doctors.

Investment and Securities Fraud

Many people rely on financial advisers to help them prepare for retirement. This is usually a good idea, but unfortunately, not all advisers can be trusted. For example, Earl Jones, a Montreal investment adviser, defrauded clients of over $50 million in order to support his lavish lifestyle. Many investors had trusted Jones with their life savings and were financially destroyed by his actions (Sutherland 2009). But Jones's crimes pale by comparison with those of Bernie Madoff, who victimized thousands of people and cost them close to $20 billion. Both Jones and Madoff used **Ponzi schemes** to defraud their clients. In a Ponzi or pyramid scheme (Evola and O'Grady, 2009), investors are promised high returns on their investments. They are initially paid dividends on those investments; however, the funds paid out are not generated from actual investments. Indeed, their money has generally *not* been invested. Instead, the payouts come from the contributions of new investors. That is why the "returns" for earlier investors are often quite high—those high returns are meant to attract more investors to generate investment funds that can be spent by the organizers and/or paid out to earlier investors. Eventually the new money runs out and the scheme collapses.

Ponzi scheme
A fraud in which old investors are paid with the funds invested by new investors. When the scheme runs out of new investors, the scheme collapses.

Madoff, once a highly respected Wall Street financier, is now serving a prison term of 150 years in the United States. Jones was sentenced to 11 years in prison but was released in 2014 after serving four years.

Another type of securities fraud is insider trading, which occurs when someone—usually an owner or employee of the company—receives information about the company that is not available to the general public. It is illegal to buy or sell stock using this information because this would give the insider an advantage over other investors. In 2000, Glen Harvey, former president of Alberta-based Golden Rule Resources, was sentenced to one year in jail and fined $3.95 million for trading $4 million worth of company stock while withholding assay results showing that the company had almost no gold on one of its properties. When the news was finally released, the company shares dropped by over half. Harper was only the second person to be sentenced to jail in Canada for insider trading (Canadian Press 2000). Successful prosecutions for this offence are rare, and the penalties are usually limited to fines and restrictions on employment in the securities industry.

A third type of investment fraud is the "pump and dump." In this scam, stock promoters take a worthless company, invent a story about that company, then tell that story in order to get people to buy the stock. If they succeed, the stock price rises; the promoters can then sell their shares for a profit, leaving the other investors with worthless shares. The story of Bre-X, the most expensive stock fraud in Canadian history, is described in Box 17.2.

FOCUS   BOX 17.2

BRE-X: THE ANATOMY OF A STOCK FRAUD

The speculative segment of the Canadian stock market has had a very bad reputation. *Forbes* magazine once called Vancouver the "scam capital of the world" because of the fraudulent stocks being sold on the Vancouver Stock Exchange. Until recently, governments failed to regulate some of the more aggressive stock promoters. This neglect led to one of the world's largest stock swindles, involving Bre-X, a company that claimed to have discovered a gold mine in Indonesia.

Mines have been "salted" for hundreds of years. Owners of a worthless property can attract investors by scattering gold at the mine site or by adding it to rock samples after they have been collected. Despite this long history of fraud and deception, investors around the world fell for the story of Bre-X. Many of these investors lost their life savings, and at least one killed himself after Bre-X stock collapsed. The fraud came to light after the company's chief geologist, Michael de Guzman, jumped to his death from a helicopter. Shortly after the geologist's death, assay reports revealed that there was no gold and that the Bre-X property was worthless. Investors lost $6 billion when Bre-X stock collapsed.

Bre-X had been built on a flimsy structure of lies. However, greed led many to ignore the risks and warning signs and to believe the story spun by the Bre-X principals and by their supporters in the financial world. Jennifer Wells describes the press release by company president David Walsh, a man whose stock-promoting career had been, up until Bre-X, a disaster:

> The Walsh press release described the prospect as a "deposit," which it was not, the presumed gold resource as "reserves," which they were not, and said that drilling on the property by the previous tenant had yielded numerous intersections of more than two grams of gold per tonne, which was a lie. (1998, 122)

To raise exploration money, Walsh essentially announced that he had a producing gold mine, even though the company had not even begun to explore the property.

After initial samples showed no signs of gold, somebody—most likely de Guzman—began salting the samples. Not surprisingly, tests of these samples were more successful, and Bre-X officials used the results to regularly increase their estimates of the amount of gold. As the mythical gold reserves increased, the stock began to soar. Shares that once sold for six cents per share were soon worth hundreds of dollars.

In addition to the problems with the mine, Bre-X had to contend with the corrupt Indonesian government, which eventually took nearly half the project. When this happened, company officials simply doubled their estimates of the amount of gold. Investors were comfortable even though over half their investment had been assigned to the Indonesians and to a large mining company selected by the Indonesian government (Wells 1998).

The involvement of this company, Freeport McMoRan, spelled the beginning of the end for Bre-X and its investors. When Freeport carried out its own testing program, assay results showed there was no gold on the Bre-X property. The last nail was hammered into the Bre-X coffin by Graham Farquharson, an independent analyst, whose report concluded:

> The magnitude of the tampering with core samples that we believe has occurred and resulting falsification of assay values at Busang, is of a scale and over a period of time and with a precision that, to our knowledge, is without precedent in the history of mining anywhere in the world. (Wells 1998, 368)

Nobody will ever be punished for the Bre-X fiasco. De Guzman committed suicide, and David Walsh died of natural causes in 1998. John Felderhof, the company's chief geologist, was acquitted of fraud charges in 2007. The company is bankrupt, and nobody associated with Bre-X has the resources to pay back the billions of dollars lost by investors.

And according to Rosen and Rosen (2017) the system that allowed this to happen is still in place. In 2016 the Ontario Securities Commission dealt with the bankruptcy of Sino-Forest, a Chinese company that was listed on the Toronto Stock Exchange. Sino-Forest was a timber company that grew to a market value of $6 billion. However, just as Bre-X had no gold, Sino-Forest did not actually own any timber. When this was discovered, investors once again lost billions of dollars. And like Bre-X, nobody involved with the corporation will likely be punished for their actions (McKenna 2016).

McKenna has nicely described how our securities regulatory system has failed us:

> Life is far too comfortable for white-collar criminals in this country. Even when caught by securities regulators, they rarely pay fines or go to jail. Authorities seldom even try to recover money stolen from investors because it's deemed to be too difficult. And if things get a little hot in one province, offenders can easily move down the TransCanada Highway to exploit gaps in the country's patchwork of provincial and territorial securities regulation. (2017, n.p.)*

Questions for Critical Thinking

1. Canada is one of the few countries that do not have a national securities regulator; this task is left to each province and territory. How does this make life easier for those who choose to violate securities laws?

2. What are some of the reasons why Canada's securities regulatory system is so weak?

*From B. McKenna, 2017. "Regulators Owe it to Canadians to do Better on Fraud". *Globe and Mail*. January 1. Reprinted by permission of The Globe and Mail.

The Justice System: Wrongful Convictions

People who work in the justice system sometimes break the rules or exhibit incompetence. One consequence of this can be the imprisonment of innocent people. Besides the cases involving Dr. Smith (Box 17.3), there have been a number of wrongful convictions in Canada, including those of Guy Paul Morin, Thomas Sophonow, David Milgaard, and Donald Marshall. One factor these cases have in common is that justice system personnel had "tunnel vision"—that is, they focused on only one suspect and thus failed to properly investigate the crime or to adequately assess evidence that might have cleared the suspect during the investigation or at trial. In some of these cases, police and prosecutors deliberately withheld evidence from the defence that might have resulted in an acquittal of the accused.

Tax Fraud

Billions of dollars are lost to tax fraud. Canada's income tax system requires all taxpayers to report their income honestly. Clearly, not all do, and there is evidence that in some occupations, the rate of noncompliance is as high as 90 percent

(Gabor, 1994). The Canada Revenue Agency has conservatively estimated that the failure to pay GST/HST costs us nearly $5 billion per year (CRA 2017), and the Conference Board of Canada has estimated that the total tax gap could be as high as $47.8 billion per year (Conference Board of Canada 2017). The exact amount will never be known, but it is clear that those who do pay their taxes are being victimized by those who do not. And Canada has a relatively effective taxation system compared with many countries—on a global level, tax evasion is massive.

How do so many people avoid taxes? People who are working at jobs where all their income is paid by an employer have little opportunity to avoid tax because the employer deducts the tax and reports salary information to the government. However, a large number of Canadians work at jobs that enable them to hide income. Many of you have likely worked as servers in the restaurant industry or have friends who do. Much of servers' income is from tips, and the employer usually does not keep a record of this income if the tips are in cash. As a result, many servers do not pay tax on this portion of their earnings. Some unscrupulous contractors offer a reduced price if the customer pays in cash so that they will not have records of income that could be uncovered through an audit. These workers are part of the "underground economy," whose size in 2013 was estimated at $46 billion, half of which was attributed to residential construction, retail trade, and accommodation and food services (Statistics Canada 2016).

FOCUS   BOX 17.3

DR. CHARLES SMITH: WRONGFUL CONVICTIONS

Dr. Smith was a forensic child pathologist who gave crucial testimony in many child fatality cases. He worked at Toronto's Hospital for Sick Children and was recognized as an authority in his field despite a lack of training in forensic pathology. He was heavily involved testifying in court from 1990 to 2005, when criticism finally led to a review of his work. This review concluded that Smith had made serious errors in almost half the 45 child autopsies reviewed and that there was serious doubt about 13 cases that had resulted in a conviction. Among those convicted and later released after Smith's evidence was refuted by other experts were the following: Louise Reynolds, who served 22 months for fatally stabbing her daughter, who had actually been mauled by dogs; William Mullins-Johnson, who served 12 years after being convicted of raping and murdering his niece; and Tammy Marquardt, who was freed in 2011 after serving 14 years for murdering her son. Like many others responsible for wrongful convictions, Dr. Smith was overly zealous in trying to secure convictions. The proper role of an independent expert is to provide objective evidence to the court, not to support the Crown's case. However, Smith began his investigations with the idea that

the child had died as the result of a crime, and he saw his job as helping the Crown prosecutor prove that an accused was guilty. His technique was sloppy, he lacked knowledge of forensic pathology, and he behaved in an unprofessional manner. Smith's approach to his job led to many miscarriages of justice (Goudge 2008).

According to a judicial inquiry, Dr. Smith's competence should have been questioned much earlier, but his supervisors ignored complaints about his work. Judges, prosecutors, and his supervisors all failed to ensure that his work was competent and fair:

As this review demonstrates, for over a decade, while the danger signals about Dr. Smith kept coming, those in charge at the [Office of the Chief Coroner for Ontario] who ultimately might have done something about the mounting problem did far too little. It is a graphic demonstration of how the oversight of pediatric forensic pathology could and did fail, almost completely. In large measure, responsibility for this failure lies in three areas: the grave weaknesses that existed in the oversight and accountability mechanisms, the inadequate quality control measures, and the flawed institutional arrangements of pediatric forensic pathology in particular, and forensic pathology as a whole. (Goudge 2007, 31)

As in so many other instances of corporate and white-collar wrongdoing, much of the harm done by Dr. Smith could have been avoided if governments had provided adequate regulatory frameworks and if those responsible for supervision had actually done their jobs competently.

Questions for Critical Thinking

1. Look up one of the wrongful conviction cases mentioned in the text (Guy Paul Morin, Thomas Sophonow, David Milgaard, Donald Marshall). Why did this wrongful conviction occur?

2. How do you think the justice system can reduce the number of wrongful convictions in the future?

People often justify tax fraud by contending that taxes are too high and that governments are taking money that rightfully belongs to the taxpayer. Many Canadians were particularly upset when the GST was implemented, and there is some evidence that people in businesses such as contracting turned to the underground economy as a way of avoiding the GST.

Another type of tax fraud involves exaggerating income tax deductions. According to Alini (2018), more than 200,000 Canadians had their claims for charitable deductions rejected by the CRA because they were grossly inflated. People who donated funds to phony charities would receive tax receipts for many times the value of their donation. About $7 billion in tax claims have been rejected because of this scam, and it was unlikely that any of the donated money actually reached people in need.

Political Corruption

Canadian politicians are more honest than their counterparts in many other countries. That said, we have had our share of political scandals. In 1873, just six years after Confederation, John A. Macdonald's government was forced to resign over allegations of bribery involving the selection of a contractor to build and operate the Canadian Pacific Railway. Perhaps the most corrupt political regime in Canada was that of Maurice Duplessis, the Quebec premier for most of the period between 1936 and 1959. He created a powerful political machine that routinely violated election rules as well as many of Quebeckers' basic rights, such as the right to freedom of political expression. In addition, his supporters used inside information to make money on the stock market and accepted financial kickbacks from people who wanted to do business with the Quebec government (Corrado 1996).

Corruption has also marked more recent Quebec governments. In 2015, Justice France Charbonneau delivered the results of her inquiry into corruption in the province. The inquiry spent much of its time looking into the construction industry and found extensive links between politicians, construction companies, unions, and organized crime groups such as the mafia and Hells Angels. The inquiry heard testimony concerning the illegal financing of political parties. Gerald Tremblay, mayor of Montreal, Gilles Vaillancourt, mayor of Laval, and Michael Applebaum, interim mayor of Montreal, all resigned after testimony implicated them in various forms of corruption. Vaillancourt and Applebaum were convicted on charges of fraud, conspiracy, and breach of trust and were given jail sentences. Vaillancourt had collected about $12 million through a scheme in which construction companies gave him kickbacks when he awarded them government contracts. Also as a result of the inquiry, Quebec's former deputy premier, Nathalie Normandeau, along with her chief of staff and several employees of an engineering company, were charged over accusations they were involved in a conspiracy in which firms that did business with the government were expected to contribute financially to their political campaigns. Taxpayers were ultimately the victims in this process, as construction costs were inflated because the companies had to make payoffs to politicians and to organized crime groups.

At the federal level, a major scandal helped defeat the Liberal government in 2006. In 2002 a newspaper reported that a Montreal advertising company had received over half a million dollars for a report that was never completed. The Auditor General investigated and concluded there had been massive misspending in a government program that provided federal funding for the sponsorship of a variety of local events, most of which were in Quebec. In many cases, money was given to companies that had not actually done any work for the government. The Auditor General concluded: "I think this is such a blatant abuse of public funds that it is shocking. I am actually appalled by what we've found" (CBC 2004, n.p.).

Justice John Gomery headed an inquiry to further investigate what had by then become known as the Sponsorship Scandal. His report, released in 2005, concluded that over $150 million of taxpayers' money had been given by the Liberal government to five advertising and communications companies in Quebec with ties to the federal Liberal Party. In many cases, these companies had done nothing to earn the money. Several of the executives who received this money subsequently made large donations to the Liberal Party. Justice Gomery concluded that "whether legal or illicit, there was at least an implicit link between

Quebec Superior Court Justice France Charbonneau headed the inquiry into corruption in Quebec's construction industry. Judge Charbonneau is a former prosecutor who heard many high-profile cases, including the murder trial at which Hells Angels leader Maurice (Mom) Boucher was convicted of murder and sentenced to life in prison.

THE CANADIAN PRESS/Graham Hughes

the contributions [to the Liberal party] and the expectation that the government contracts would be awarded" (2005, 79). Thus, government money appears to have been returned to the party to use for its own purposes.

The report laid some of the blame for the scandal on prime minister Jean Chrétien, his chief of staff Jean Pelletier, and public works minister Alfonso Gagliano, all of whom had failed to ensure that government funds were spent properly. While no elected officials were charged, one government official and several marketing executives were convicted and sentenced to jail for their part in this affair.

In 2006, Stephen Harper's Conservatives were elected on a platform that included bringing greater honesty and accountability to government. However, they were also involved in a number of scandals, many of them involving election campaigns. These included violating campaign spending rules by spending more than they were allowed to, which allowed them to buy more advertising than the other parties who obeyed the limits. Conservative campaign worker Michael Sona was convicted in 2014 for arranging robo-calls to potential Liberal voters that told these voters that the locations of polling stations had been changed. This was an attempt to discourage opposition supporters from voting. Harper himself was found in contempt of Parliament for refusing to provide MPs with cost information, and his government defied court orders to release information on a number of issues—for example, documents relating to the residential school experience of Indigenous people. Several military veterans who were critical of government policies found that Veteran's Affairs had leaked their medical information in an attempt to silence them.

Despite these problems, Canada is relatively well governed. Many countries are governed by politicians who abuse their citizens by repressing dissent and denying people their basic human rights. These problems are most prevalent in dictatorial regimes such as Zimbabwe and China, but even democratic societies are not immune.

Blue-Collar Crime

The concept of white-collar crime also fits many people who wear a blue collar. Because of this, some have suggested that the term *occupational crime* may be more useful. Many tradespeople defraud the government by doing work "off the books" to avoid provincial sales tax and the GST. Some blue-collar businesses have very bad records of consumer fraud. Several investigations, most done by media organizations, have documented an appalling degree of misconduct in the auto repair business. For example, Menzies (2000) had a mechanic disable one of the spark plugs on a car that was otherwise in good working order. Menzies went to repair shops and requested and paid for an engine diagnosis that ranged in price from $69 to $103. This provided ample information available to do the repair, which should have cost about $20. Menzies visited only four Toronto repair shops, but his study reinforced the findings of a much larger earlier study (Sikorsky 1990). Only one shop, a Honda dealership, repaired the problem without recommending any further work. Of the other three, Goodyear estimated that the repair would cost $234, Speedy Auto Service estimated $300, and Canadian Tire estimated $648 would be required to return the car to working order.

Employee Fraud

Corporations are also often the *victims* of crime. In a 2001 survey sponsored by the accounting firm Ernst & Young, about 25 percent of the Canadian workforce reported either having committed fraud against their employer or witnessing someone committing fraud during the previous year. A survey of employers found that 80 percent reported having been victimized by employee fraud (CBC 2001). Examples of frauds reported to Ernst & Young included taking kickbacks from suppliers in exchange for contracts, creating phony invoices and collecting the money, stealing company property, and stealing cash from the company. Canadian retailers estimated that in 2012 they lost $1.3 billion to employee theft, almost as much as their losses from shoplifting and other types of customer theft ($1.7 billion) (PWC 2012). To put this figure in perspective, the Canadian Bankers Association reported that in 2013, losses from credit card fraud were $465 million (2013). Corporations of all sizes are victimized, but often the toll is greatest on small companies. For example, many small restaurants have been forced out of business because of theft of money and food by staff. Lisa Leduc interviewed Ottawa restaurant employees about ways of "scamming" their employers. One of the interviewees described some of these methods:

> A manager would bring in his friends, a table of, let's say, eight, and [they would have] wings and beer, and he would go into the cooler where the beer was and grab it when the bartender wouldn't even notice, and [there would be] free dinner and beer for this person's friends. . . . Also, people weren't punching in drinks and [were] pocketing the money. Cooks [were] taking food home, all staff [were] taking dishes and cutlery. (qtd. in Gabor 1994, 78–79)

In recent years, new technology and changes in financial practices have made larger corporations more vulnerable to the actions of individual employees. Earlier in this chapter you read about the illegal trades by Nicholas Leeson that drove Barings Bank into bankruptcy. Since the Leeson case, there have been several others where an individual trader has done significant harm to his company. Toronto's Stephen Duthie lost $182 million through unauthorized trading that was essentially gambling with his company's money. Duthie would have received a huge bonus if his gamble had succeeded in making large profits for his company. But the trades *lost* money, and Duthie's employer, Phoenix Trading and Research, was forced to close. These cases have become so common that the term *rogue trader* has been invented to describe the actions of people like Leeson and Duthie.

QUESTIONS FOR CRITICAL THINKING

1. In previous chapters of this text, you have studied a number of theories of criminal behaviour. Select one of these theories and assess how well it explains white-collar and corporate crime.
2. Can you think of three different actions that might be taken by governments and/or corporations to reduce the amount of white-collar and corporate crime in Canada?

Summary

- The study of white-collar crime has demonstrated that the relationship between class and crime is more complicated than early criminologists had believed. Theories of crime must account for the crimes of the privileged as well as for the crimes of the poor.

- Even when they are reported to the authorities, white-collar crimes are often not reported in official crime statistics because they are dealt with under quasi-criminal statutes.

- Corporations are instruments that enable people to commit crimes that are vast in scope. The financial and physical costs of corporate crimes are very high.

- The structure of the modern corporation provides managers with a great deal of freedom from control. This has the unintended consequence of encouraging crime. In some industries, high-level managers demand such unreasonably high levels of profit that their subordinates feel pressured to break the law.

- Corporations are subject to legal regulation, but the laws that govern them are weak. Even when punishment is administered, it is often so light that it is regarded as an accepted cost of doing business.

- There is some evidence that penalties for white-collar offenders have increased in the United States, but this does not appear to be the case in Canada.

- A major contributor to many types of occupational crime is the failure of professional organizations to adequately control the behaviour of their members. Another is the fact that many people do not strongly condemn crimes such as tax fraud.

NET WORK

There are several websites dealing with fraud. Two of the best are www.scambusters.com and www.fraud.org.

1. Go to these websites and briefly describe three different types of fraud. How can each of these frauds best be prevented?
2. How have the white-collar criminals who carry out these frauds adapted to new communications technology?

18 Cybercrime and Cyberdeviance

MICHAEL ARNTFIELD
Western University

Learning Objectives

After reading this chapter, you should be able to:

- Differentiate between cybercrime and cyberdeviance and understand why it is often difficult to separate one from the other both legally and theoretically.

- Understand how recurring or habitual computing behaviours constitute routine activities that enable offenders by placing certain users at increased risk of being victims of cybercrime.

- Discuss the connection between traditional offline physical bullying and online cyberbullying, including derivatives of cyberbullying such as Internet trolling, cybermobbing, and other forms of electronic harassment.

- Define the different forms of identified paraphilia, both criminal and noncriminal, and understand how they manifest themselves in virtual environments as predictors of offline offending.

- Understand that cybercrime is a very dynamic and changeable area of offending that requires improved training initiatives for law enforcement, as well as clarified legislation in order to hold offenders accountable and ensure the cooperation of technology providers in cybercrime prevention and investigation.

This chapter provides an overview of electronic and computer-mediated crime in Canada, including its implications for traditional criminology. Specifically, we examine the difference between crime and deviance (Chapter 1) while applying the routine activities theory of crime (Chapter 15) to offender–victim interactions in digital environments. We also address some of the determinants of victimization (Chapter 7) as they exist in virtual spaces, where contact between offender and victim tends to be asynchronous (not happening at the same time). This differentiates online offences from most other types of offending studied by criminologists.

Web 2.0, the second generation of the Internet, includes social media, wiki sites, public comment boards, and other computing environments that bring together people from disparate backgrounds. Even though Web 2.0 has existed for well over a decade, there is no consensus on how to apply existing theoretical models of crime to these spaces. Suffice it to say that the intersection of cybercrime, cyberdeviance, and criminology is a field ripe for discussion, especially in terms of how technology and legislation influence each other.

This chapter also examines how criminologists, policymakers, and law enforcement officials might develop a consensus on how to define criminality in a self-contained digital environment and how the social norms of that environment are expected to mirror the values of the conventional, offline world. Defining and legislating cyberbullying, trolling, and other forms of electronic harassment remains problematic, so this chapter straddles both established and experimental methods of inquiry while also looking to criminology's future role in helping define the different forms of online misconduct. Understanding the origins and causes of this misconduct will in turn help us better understand the very real and often very damaging effects of cybercrime and cyberdeviance beyond the digital spaces where offending begins—but does not necessarily end.

What Is Cybercrime?

The Internet continues to change how people communicate, connect with one another, and cultivate personal relationships. Digital technologies and Internet-enabled "smart" devices have changed the dynamics of work, travel, and the economy. These technologies have also changed the landscape of criminality to the extent that we might now look beyond traditional approaches to understanding offenders and their decision-making.

Because the term "**cyberactivities**" can describe any number of computing activities that rely on Internet connectivity such as email, online research, streaming media, and interactive gaming, cybercrime must be a broad concept (Miller and Morris 2012, 75). Over the past decade, police services have begun establishing specialized cybercrime units within their criminal investigation bureaux. However, no two agencies seem to have the same vision with respect to what should be investigated by these units or how cybercrime should be defined.

Despite the lack of a consistent definition of cybercrime, we can specify some activities that most people would consider to fit this category:

- *Phishing.* The use of misleading or counterfeit electronic transmissions, such as emails purportedly from credit card companies or other financial institutions, requesting sensitive personal information or password data with the intention of compromising the victim's banking or credit accounts.

- *Ripping.* The use of specially designed software or other methods of circumventing copyright protection for the purposes of downloading or copying original material from a protected media source (DVD, online video, etc.) to a hard disk, usually for the purposes of resale or redistribution.

- *Hacking.* The attempt to remotely circumvent the security or privacy measures initiated by an Internet website, server, or database, for the purposes of either stealing information or interfering with operations and compromising data through **distributed denial-of-service (DDoS) attacks**, deployment of viruses, or other malicious actions.

cyberactivities
Any number of tasks carried out through a computer and a network connection, including but not limited to Internet browsing, email correspondence, online banking, interactive gaming, media downloading or uploading, the use of file transfer protocols, and accessing social media platforms.

distributed denial-of-service (DDoS) attack
A term that describes any number of methods of varying sophistication, usually carried out by a group of hackers or by a series of bot attacks, for infiltrating and sabotaging a host server, thereby denying access to a website or online service or otherwise disrupting the operations of business, industry, or government.

- *Luring.* The act of using an Internet connection to access social media, chat rooms, or other places of electronic assembly to make contact with a child or person under 16 for the purposes of counselling them to commit a sexual act or to meet at a physical location for sexual purposes. This is typically accomplished by the offender posing online as an underage person himself in order to conceal his real identity and intentions.

- *Stalking.* The use of a computer or other network-enabled device to repeatedly make unwanted contact with a person using any number of means (emails, text messages, etc.), and doing so knowing that this behaviour is likely to cause fear or annoyance.

- *Spamming.* The use of one or more computer networks and servers to send unsolicited and unwanted bulk messages to other users, often consisting of vexatious advertisements or pornographic content delivered either by email or by pop-up windows in Internet browsers.

- *Skimming.* The use of specific software *and* hardware to intercept etransmissions containing sensitive financial data, usually related to credit card purchases. The stolen data enable the cloning or counterfeiting of specific financial instruments (credit cards, bank cards, etc.) for the purposes of theft and fraud.

- *Trafficking.* Any use of a computer network to move illicit images (or other media), controlled substances, or people. In the context of cybercrime, trafficking can include distributing child pornography; selling or distributing drugs via the portion of the "**Deep Web**" known as the "**Dark Web**"; or making contact with victims to "groom" them for human trafficking operations—essentially another version of luring but with different objectives and victims.

Most police cybercrime units are tasked mainly with investigating and interdicting criminal offences involving the exploitation of children through computers. These offences typically involve child pornography or child luring. However, a number of other offences that constitute cybercrime fall outside the relatively limited scope of typical cybercrime enforcement strategies. Moore (2005) has defined cybercrime as any criminal offence or series of offences committed through the use of a computer and a computer network, including an Internet connection. This definition would add to the previous list offences that fall under the umbrella of "cyberterrorism" (a term just as vague as cybercrime), which usually involve using a computer to orchestrate large-scale "attacks on information," including government or critical infrastructure servers or any database of interest to national security (Baranetsky 2009). While there are law enforcement units, as well as divisions of the federal government such as Communication Security Establishment Canada (CSEC) and the Canadian Security and Intelligence Service (CSIS), that address and investigate these types of offences, they are normally distinguished by the use of operational titles such as "technological crimes" or "e-crimes." Because of limited police resources, in many departments the policing of cybercrime has been restricted to those computer offences that have human victims and that

Deep Web
Sometimes called the "invisible Web," it is the parallel Internet that exists beneath the surface of conventional browsers. It features sites not indexed by search engines. It is essentially unregulated and is rife with criminal activity and illegal transactions.

Dark Web
Also known as the Darknet, it is the restricted, non-indexed portion of the Deep Web that requires a specialized Web browser and anonymous Tor software in order to gain access. The Dark Web relies on cryptocurrenices such as Bitcoin to facilitate illegal transactions, which range from drug trafficking to murder-for-hire schemes. The first Darknet market, known as Silk Road, was launched in 2011 and was successfully shut down by the FBI in 2013. The site's founder, Ross Ulbricht (who used the online alias Dread Pirate Roberts), was sentenced to life in prison with no possibility of parole after being convicted of charges that included conspiracy to traffic in narcotics and money laundering.

cause physical harm in the offline world beyond financial losses or service disruptions. Offences such as Internet child exploitation and cyberbullying are akin to cyberviolence, and like all forms of violent offending, they often involve targeted victims.

E-crime and Cybercrime

Cybercrime has come to denote online crimes that are largely analogous to offline crimes of violence and sexual offending. Computer offences committed against financial institutions or the state tend to fall under blanket terms such as electronic crime (e-crime), cyberespionage, cyberterrorism, and any number of other terms that differentiate institutional targets from human ones. These crimes are being reported more frequently in the media. In April 2014 the Canada Revenue Agency (CRA) had its website compromised at the height of the annual tax-filing season after the Heartbleed security bug was deployed by a hacker and roughly 900 social insurance numbers belonging to Canadian taxpayers were stolen. A 19-year-old university student in London, Ontario, was arrested and charged with unauthorized use of a computer and mischief (Bogart 2014). Had the incident occurred in the United States, the charges laid might have been more serious, reflecting more recently enacted laws to protect business, industry, and government from the escalating threat of complete electronic shutdown.

Despite tougher laws, these crimes continue to make news in the United States. One of the most significant cases was the December 2013 breach of Target's database at the height of the holiday shopping season. Hackers were able to access the credit card information of roughly 40 million customers of the US retail giant; this was one of the worst data security breaches ever recorded (Harris and Perlroth 2014). Several arrests were made in relation to the breach, but the full extent of the organization behind the attack may never be known. The scale of the Target breach changed the social and political climate surrounding e-crime.

SEARCH FOR:
FBI Most Wanted List

The Target case was soon followed by the revelation that five Chinese military officers had been added to the FBI's Most Wanted List in May 2014. US officials alleged that the Chinese had engaged in cyberactivities designed to infiltrate and compromise the servers of several US corporations in order to steal industrial secrets. The charges faced by this group include conspiring to commit computer fraud, damaging computers through the transmission of code commands, and theft of trade secrets, along with a host of other indictments carrying potential life sentences. All of this reflects the vulnerability of records in this digital age and points to the potentially disastrous consequences of a full cyberattack aimed at disrupting state interests (Schmidt and Sanger 2014). With each new attack becoming increasingly sophisticated and organized in its methodology, the line between e-crime, organized crime, and cyberterrorism is becoming increasing blurred.

Cyberterrorism has the potential to permanently disrupt the economic and environmental stability of entire nations or regions. Traditional, comparatively narrow definitions of cyberterrorism have included network attacks against

critical infrastructure site
Any location or asset, either physical or virtual, that is vital to the socioeconomic and physical security of a nation or region, including but not limited to water treatment facilities, telecommunications centres, hospitals and health care facilities, nuclear and other power-generating facilities, airports and railway stations, and centres of major economic activity, such as stock and security exchanges.

critical infrastructure sites (telecommunications, nuclear or water treatment facilities, etc.) through distributed denial of service (DDoS) attacks and other forms of electronic sabotage. But cyberterrorism no longer needs to be tied to geopolitical or ideological motives as in the case of offline terrorist activities. It can take the form of any attempt to damage data or cause a large-scale disruption that compromises a state's ability to carry on as usual or that affects its population's ability to obtain the necessities of life. Given our modern dependence on e-banking and other networked systems that control everything from traffic signals to aircraft controls to life support systems in hospitals, cyberterrorism is one of the most pressing issues facing government and law enforcement today. Because national security is increasingly dependent on network systems, it is difficult to know where to draw the line between e-crime and more deliberate attempts at cyberterrorism, particularly since these network systems are increasingly being contracted out to private companies. This issue also illustrates how computer crime is difficult to classify into black-and-white categories and why 20th-century laws are often inadequate when dealing with increasingly complex and constantly changing 21st-century crimes.

Lawmakers and legal analysts, including criminologists, are tasked with defining and legislating cybercrime as a more personalized and typically less organized form of cyberterrorism. Cybercrime includes attacks that are not directed against the state or institutions for the purposes of causing large-scale harm; instead, these attacks are against individuals, who may be targeted for a variety of reasons. Some new and emerging forms of cybercrime, however, such as **ransomware**, blur this line, taking on elements of both, and can see individuals and institutions targeted at the same time. Like e-crime and cyberterrorism, cybercrime, as the online version of similar types of violent, intimidating, and predatory offences that exist offline, can lead to financial and personal disruption and even threaten human life. Some well-publicized suicides in Canada have brought this issue to the forefront of public consciousness and raised its importance to legislators.

ransomware
A new term combining "ransom" and "software," it is any form of malicious software (malware) that, once deployed against a personal computer, computer server, or computer network, blocks the lawful user from accessing their own data. Much like how a ransom demand is made in cases of kidnapping crimes, the "kidnapped" files and information remain under the control of the attacker until the fee demanded is paid, usually by way of cryptocurrency such as Bitcoin. If it is not paid, the victim (either a person or an institution) loses the information or, in some cases, has it released publicly, particularly if the information is deemed valuable or embarrassing. In 2017, Canada was one of several countries affected by the ransomware known as WannaCry, with everything from home computers to hospital databases being infected.

One of the main advantages that researchers studying cybercrime have over those studying e-crime or cyberterrorism is access to data. Hacking and phishing activities tend to occur sporadically and employ any number of methods of covert delivery; cybercrime tends to be more conspicuous and is comparatively public in its methodology. Indeed, many forms of cybercrime, including cyberbullying, are harmful *because* they are carried out in the public eye. So to understand what brings victims and offenders together and what motivates cybercrime offenders is to understand how social media function as the new public sphere of the 21st century.

When Social Media Become Antisocial

Criminology has changed to reflect changes in society and culture. For example, green criminology (Chapter 1) has emerged as a subfield that studies environmental crime, even when the offences committed do not always reflect violations of criminal law. Cybercriminology has also emerged as a subfield of criminology, one that concerns itself with the study of crime in the context of computing and network technologies, even when these "crimes" are not necessarily codified or spelled out in the Criminal Code but instead amount to acts of deviance that clearly violate social norms. Cybercriminology may present a new opportunity for academics to apply the consensus model of crime in determining where the line between crime and deviance is drawn in online communities, which are interactive environments that tend to otherwise be comparatively permissive and informal. Specific operating systems (Windows, Mac OS, Linux, etc.) and social networks (Facebook, Instagram, Twitter, etc.) have their own distinct cultures and social norms, and this complicates blanket assumptions about computing habits and online behaviours as a whole. These differences underscore why determinations of which cyberactivities deserve to be criminalized need to look beyond the online environments themselves and begin with a broader understanding of computer technologies as being inherently criminogenic. Specifically, a more thorough understanding of the role of **technological determinism** in online offending is required when discussing cybercrime and cyberdeviance.

technological determinism
The theory that technological innovation is the key driving force behind changes in society and that new technologies shape culture and human behaviour, not vice versa.

The term technological determinism (Ellul 1964) helps us understand how specific technologies drive changes in culture. When the mass production of the Model T on Henry Ford's moving assembly line made cars an everyday commodity rather than a luxury, we soon saw a rise in crimes such as kidnapping and bank robbery, both of which relied on automobiles (Arntfield 2012). Today, understanding changes in computing technologies and the rise of a networked society can help us better understand cybercrime as a response to the culture surrounding those technological changes.

The architecture of a given digital environment, and the dominant culture of that environment, both play a major role in offending. Raskauskas and Stoltz (2007) initially found that the most common form of electronic victimization among adolescents was via mobile device, reflecting 32.1 percent of reported cases, with social media a distant second at 15.5 percent of documented incidents. But as technology has changed, so have mechanisms of victimization. Kowalksi and Whittaker (2015) have more recently found that as social media and smartphones have become increasingly interlinked and co-dependent, teens in particular are more likely to access their social media accounts from their phones rather than from a traditional computer. In effect, this has consolidated the ways an online user can be targeted for bullying. Earlier studies, such as one by Hinduja and Patchin (2009), also found that females were more likely to be cybervictims or at least were more likely to report an incident of cybercrime. However, newer research (Myers et al. 2017) has found that members of the LGBTQ+, in particular high school and college students aged 13 to 25, are the most prevalent victim group, regardless of gender identification. The vast majority of publicized cases of extreme cybercrime (including cyberbullying (Box 18.1), cyberstalking, and exploitation-related offences) involve the malevolent use of social media networks and digital technologies. Of course, as that technology evolves and cyberactivities change, the patterns and locations of offending also change. This means that timely and relevant research is needed to help advance effective legislation and shape public policy.

Another issue faced by criminologists studying cybercrime and also by law enforcement officials tasked with trying to enforce laws originally created for an offline, physical world is how to separate criminal behaviour that clearly violates the law from generally antisocial behaviour that is not legally prohibited. Much of the behaviour exhibited during deviant cyberactivities, including cyberbullying, has no codified definition and is more accurately defined as what Holt and Bossler (2009) broadly classify as cyberdeviance. Access to a computer and a network seems to have enabled individuals who might not otherwise show a propensity for offending to engage in behaviours that demonstrate a consistent disregard for the rights and feelings of others, as well as a general disrespect for property and the rule of law.

Social media networks are therefore prone to antisocial behaviour. In many cases this behaviour is deviant but not necessarily *criminal*. For instance, even something as harmful as cyberbullying is not necessarily illegal, and responses by authorities—if any—vary greatly by jurisdiction. Child luring, unlawfully recording and distributing copyrighted motion pictures, causing mischief to data, and electronic voyeurism are all legislated offences whose statutory wordings in the Criminal Code reflect their status as computer-mediated crimes. Cyberbullying, like cyberstalking, is more difficult to immediately link to codified offences. Similarly, in the United States the 2009 federal case of *United States v. Lori Drew* relating to offences alleged to have been committed under the Computer Fraud and Abuse Act confirmed that violating a private website's terms of use, now matter how egregious, is cyberdeviance and does not in itself constitute criminal culpability (Zetter 2009). In that case, Lori Drew created a fictitious MySpace account to infiltrate the online profile of a 13-year-old female named Megan Meier. Drew's own teenage daughter and Meier had been friends and had attended school together in St. Charles County, Missouri. By the fall of 2006, Drew was concerned that Meier was spreading rumours about her daughter. Using the screen name Josh Evans, Drew posed as a teenage boy and sent flirtatious messages to Meier's MySpace account in order to get her attention and earn her trust. When the interactions failed to turn up any real evidence that Meier was slandering Drew's daughter, a message was nonetheless sent to Meier from the Josh Evans account telling her the world would be better off without her. Other MySpace users saw this message and followed suit, engaging in what is now identified as **cybermobbing**, or the mass cyberbullying of a single victim by large numbers of users who may or may not know one another. After Meier received a flurry of these spiteful messages, she hanged herself in her bedroom closet. She was found dead by her mother. At a trial in November 2008, the prosecution was only able to secure a misdemeanour conviction against Drew for violating the Computer Fraud and Abuse Act by creating the fake MySpace account. This conviction was later vacated in August 2009. Drew was acquitted when it was ruled that violating MySpace's terms of use in creating the account did not meet the standard required to justify a criminal prosecution, regardless of how serious the eventual outcome of that violation—in this case, the counselled suicide of a young girl. Do the international implications of the *Lori Drew* case coupled with the ongoing lack of a specific statute criminalizing cyberbullying mean that cyberbullying is therefore not cybercrime by definition? Does the phenomenon of cyberbullying merit analysis by criminologists, or is it instead a social problem that is better addressed by schools and families in terms of prevention and awareness? What do you think?

cybermobbing
A group activity that in effect merges cyberdeviance with learning theories of crime and interactional models of offending. That is, many disparate users (a mob) within a virtual space follow the lead of a cyberbully and publicly gang up on a single victim by sending harassing and humiliating communications.

SEARCH FOR:
CyberSCAN

FOCUS

BOX 18.1

A SNAPSHOT OF CYBERBULLYING IN CANADA

Following a tragic incident in early 2013, the province of Nova Scotia introduced a new Cyber Safety Act in August 2013. As the first legislation of its kind in Canada, the Cyber Safety Act mandated the formation of the CyberSCAN Unit as its provincial investigative arm. The CyberSCAN Unit had no authority to lay charges but had the power and discretion to refer files to the police for criminal sanctions. The unit was staffed by civilians, but it had broad search and seizure powers relating to personal electronic information and devices. Most importantly, the unit marked the first attempt to provide a legislative definition of cyberbullying in Canada. The operating definition of cyberbullying used by CyberSCAN when initiating its investigations was as follows:

Any electronic communication through the use of technology including, without limiting the generality of the foregoing, computers, other electronic devices, social networks, text messaging, instant messaging, websites and electronic mail, typically repeated or with continuing effect, that is intended or ought reasonably [be] expected to cause fear, intimidation, humiliation, distress or other damage or harm to another person's health, emotional wellbeing, self-esteem or reputation, and includes assisting or encouraging such communication in any way. (CyberSCAN 2014)

This definition of cyberbullying did not change the law in Canada, nor did it expand the powers of police to lay charges or of judges to hand down sentences. In fact, it changed things very little except to provide a guideline for other jurisdictions in terms of establishing investigative standards and mandates. Whether a federal cyberbullying law will ultimately stem from this definition will depend in part on the perceived successes of the CyberSCAN Unit.

By 2015, it seemed an answer on that was already clear, when Nova Scotia's Cyber Safety Act and the CyberSCAN Unit were together deemed a "colossal failure" by the Supreme Court, which ruled that it was unconstitutional, and by experts, who referred to it as a "dumpster fire" that lacked coherence and who urged future versions of such an act (or investigative unit) to properly consult experts ahead of time (Sabatini 2016). There was equally some suggestion that the Cyber Safety Act was actually created in haste, in part due to intimidation tactics by hacktivist groups like Anonymous.

A unanimous Supreme Court ruling in June 2014 had previously declared that police require a search warrant under section 487 of the Criminal Code merely to obtain subscriber names from IP addresses associated with trafficking in child pornography and with other serious criminal offences online. This decision suggests that the pendulum is actually swinging towards

Thinkstock

(continued)

protecting privacy interests rather than violating privacy rights in order to make it easier to apprehend offenders. This sentiment is once again reinforced by the disbandment of the CyberSCAN Unit within two years of its creation, although the task force continues to operate with a renewed focus on education and prevention (CyberSCAN 2018).

Cyberbullying is becoming a major public concern, but at the same time, demands for increased privacy measures are impeding efforts to identify predators. Thus the coming few years are likely to see further wrangling in the courts in the search for a middle ground between safety and privacy. For now, it seems that those with the resources to hire a lawyer and file a private lawsuit forcing cyberbullies and other malicious posters of information—including specific "revenge" websites that traffic in offensive and malicious content and inevitably cater to cyberbullies (thedirty.com, reportmyex.com, et al.)—to take down or remove offensive and false statements have at least one option, while most others do not.

Apparently a two-tiered justice system now exists for victims of cyberbullying, trolling, and other forms of cyberdeviance. Recent developments suggest that old-fashioned laws may

actually be the most effective when looking to combat cyberbullying and other online predators who hide in the darkest corners of the Internet. For instance, in May 2018, two Florida men who operated the website Mugshots.com (which obtained and uploaded old police mugshots of regular citizens in order to humiliate them into paying a fee to have them removed) were arrested and charged criminally with extortion, identity theft, and other crimes (Brackett 2018). So at least for now, the future of how and when to police the Internet (if at all) is in a state of limbo in Canada, whereas in the United States, there are increasingly efforts to apply existing laws to new technology in a bid to curb a problem that is increasingly getting out of control and that is increasingly indiscriminate in its choice of victims.

Critical Thinking Questions

1. What province was the first in Canada to try launching a full-time task force specifically to address cyberbullying?

2. What are the two pieces of federal legislation that are arguably of greatest interest to both legal system and researchers who study cyberbullying, including the need to balance personal safety and with expectations of privacy?

Cyberdeviance and Digital Paraphilia

The relationship between social media and cyberdeviance suggests that a number of social networking sites taken for granted as extensions of the public sphere may actually conform to what Durkin (2009) and Roberts and Hunt (2012, 757) have called "deviant cybercommunities." Such communities are facilitated by the fact that social media can be accessed instantaneously, asynchronously, and in many cases anonymously. **Deviant cybercommunities** consist of subcultural networks made up of people who seek to circumvent the customary user experiences of these sites and who seek to exploit weaknesses and vulnerabilities, or what are sometimes called "soft targets." Deviant cybercommunities can in turn be identified by their paradoxical architecture. They serve a "social" purpose, but they also intensify deviant and antisocial impulses among some users (Durkin 2007; Quayle and Taylor 2002; Quinn and Forsyth 2005).

A traditional approach to identifying specific typologies of deviance, whether criminal or noncriminal, is through the categorization of what are known as **paraphilias**. Paraphilias are deep-seated psychological or sexual drives that are reflected in unusual or bizarre relationships to objects or circumstances. More than 500 paraphilia types and subtypes have been identified, and these have been itemized by severity, based on the threat to public safety posed by these deviant behaviours (Aggrawal 2008). While not all acts of cyberdeviance explicitly involve a sexual motivation, a review of some of the more common paraphilias suggests that cyberdeviance often encompasses one or more of the traditional offline paraphilias and that a great deal of online misconduct has an expressive sexual motivation (Arntfield and Swart 2018). We can compare offline

deviant cybercommunity
An online community whose culture and customs would be classified as deviant and delinquent if exported to the offline world, but in which socially abnormal behaviour is accepted and even endorsed in the context of the given digital environment.

paraphilia
The use of unusual objects, situations, processes, or people to obtain sexual excitement and channel obsessions or fantasies that are inherently deviant and either prohibited by law (criminal paraphilia) or deemed taboo and forbidden by conventional society.

paraphilias with similar online behaviours that range from noncriminal acts of cyberdeviance to cybercrimes:

Erotomania

Erotomania is the phenomenon of a person developing an unfounded infatuation or imagined relationship with a person unknown or barely known to them (Hickey 2010, 178).

Offline

Erotomania is commonly associated with stranger-obsessional stalking and typically involves behaviour such as sending letters, gifts, and flowers or making hang-up phone calls. Generally considered more of a nuisance and an annoyance than a genuine threat to safety, and generally noncriminal in nature.

Online

The vast majority of cyberstalking incidents involve strangers or casual or passing acquaintances (Freiberger 2008). This is because the Internet is not limited to any particular geographic location and because erotomania is stranger-obsessional in nature. It can include the compulsive viewing of social media profiles and images (known as "creeping" in the parlance of Web 2.0), creating fake social media accounts in order to gain a target's trust and initiate a dialogue, and repeatedly performing search engine queries of a target to find personal information or to view photographs. In some cases it may also include sending emails, text messages, or social media messages to a mobile device, often anonymously.

Exhibitionism

The unsolicited practice of exposing one's body in explicit or suggestive fashion to captive audiences or nonconsenting observers for attention, personal gratification, arousal, or excitement or to project power is referred to as *exhibitionism* (Hickey 2010, 178).

Offline

Exhibitionism is commonly associated with crimes such as committing an indecent act or causing a disturbance by indecent exhibition. Acts of exhibitionism can also be more subtle and noncriminal, such as undressing in front of open windows or dressing inappropriately for certain social contexts.

Online

The practice of taking digital self-portraits (selfies) is now commonplace. However, it is sexting (the sending of sexual images sent by text message) that is currently at the forefront of debates about cybercrime and cyberdeviance. Typically, sexting consists of sending inappropriate images of oneself to others, often without prompting and without consent (Rufo 2012). As in its offline version, this can be done for attention, personal gratification, arousal, and/or excitement, or to project power or to frighten. Canada's Parliament has now made nonconsensual trafficking in intimate images a criminal offence.

Scopophilia or Voyeurism

The terms *scopophilia* and *voyeurism* refer to a paraphilia that involves the sense of arousal, excitement, and power that a person obtains by secretly watching others without their consent, usually in a private or intimate setting (Hickey 2010, 179). The discreet observation of people in nonintimate, day-to-day settings is a paraphilic subtype known as cryptoscopophilia (Aggrawal 2008).

Offline

This paraphilia was made infamous through films like *Psycho* (1960) and the lesser-known *Peeping Tom* (1960) but has only recently come to be understood as extremely dangerous behaviour if left to escalate. Voyeurs of a criminal nature have historically been prosecuted under the prowling and trespass-by-night sections of the Criminal Code, but these sections were treated as minor (summary) offences until 2013, when they were changed to hybrid offences, reflecting the fact that the potential seriousness of this paraphilia was for many years not taken seriously (Kaplan and Krueger 1997).

Online

Since 2002, voyeurism—now recognized as symptomatic of one or more paraphilias and as a serious forms of offending—has become a codified offence specifically in the context of cybercrime (Department of Justice 2014b). The offence of voyeurism includes the use of electronic devices for the surreptitious and sexually motivated recording or photographing of unknown and nonconsenting individuals, whether or not there is a reasonable expectation of privacy.

Scatologia

The paraphilia referred to as *scatologia* involves an individual making obscene, threatening, or otherwise menacing (open-line heavy breathing, etc.) phone calls to either random or specific victims as means of self-gratification and to project power and dominance by causing fear and anxiety (Hickey 2010, 179). Historically known as telephone scatologia, this paraphilia is directly linked to technology and is a good example of the connection between paraphilia and technological determinism.

Offline

In the days when people had only landline telephones, Dalby (1988) and Saunders and Awad (1991) postulated that scatologia was simply a technologically mediated variant of exhibitionism. As a form of offending made possible by the instantaneity and anonymity of calls placed to unsuspecting victims, the offences of making harassing telephone calls and obscene telephone calls have long been prohibited by the Criminal Code, though they are now much less common because of the development of new technologies, including call tracing and the Internet.

Online

Few paraphilias underscore the role of technology in offending more than scatologia. Now that the telephone has been largely replaced by electronic or other preferred and virtual forms of communication—including communication between smartphones, which more closely approximates a computer interface than a traditional landline telephone—anonymous computer-mediated interactions can all be said to constitute the *new* scatologia. Regarding telephone scatologia, specific legislation has historically reflected that the telephone is an instrument for offending; however, no such laws exist with respect to analogous cyberactivities even though the underlying motives and methods are largely identical. In fact, three of the historically identified "classes" of telephone scatologists—the ingratiating seducer, the annoyance creator, and the panic creator (Aggrawal 2008, 339)—are ideally suited for online forums, where it seems that activities like trolling and cyberbullying can satisfy the offender's compulsions much more effortlessly, for they engage multiple victims at one time with essentially guaranteed anonymity.

Coprographia

Coprographia describes a disorder where a person is sexually excited and empowered by writing and delivering obscene, violent, offensive, or otherwise emotionally disturbing content (Arntfield & Danesi, 2017, 102).

Offline

Coprographia is commonly associated with letters, manifestos, and other writings created for the purposes of taunting a specific recipient or even the public at large. This paraphilia too is strongly correlated with violent criminal offending; it is often resorted to in the aftermath of murders to maximize the fear caused by those same crimes. Examples range from serial killer Albert Fish, who wrote letters to the families of his young victims in the early 20th century, to the still unidentified Zodiac Killer, to the Golden State Killer in northern California. The Golden State Killer was a highly paraphilic offender who left essays, poems, and other writings boasting of his murders near his crime scenes in the 1970s and 1980s. After more than 40 years of searching, a retired former police officer named Joseph James DeAngelo was arrested in this case in 2018 through the use of an online DNA bank (see Chapter 1).

Online

Although not all cases of coprographia involve direct acts of violence, it is important to recognize that cyberbullying, trolling, and other forms of online harassment rooted in acts of writing represent a digitally mediated form of coprographia and thus have an underlying disordered sexual component (Arntfield and Swart 2018). The person creating and delivering the offensive material may not be consciously aware of this; however, the parallels between traditional offline cases of coprographia and what might now be classified as cybercoprographia are very clear. This includes the correlation between cyberbullying and other paraphilias. One notable example is Aydin Coban, widely considered to have been one of the most prolific cyberbullies on record and the individual who harassed Canadian teen Amanda Todd to the point that she committed suicide in 2012. When he was finally arrested in the Netherlands in 2014, Coban was found to be in possession of copious files containing child pornography and to be actively involved in online child luring, charges for which he was later found guilty in 2017 and sentenced to 10 years in prison (Arntfield and Swart 2018).

New Media, New Crimes: A Changing Technological Landscape

Some cyberactivities that simultaneously qualify as both cyberdeviance and cybercrime reflect identified paraphilias more than others and also suggest more obvious correlations between offline and online offending. Pedophilia as both a paraphilia and a precipitator of child luring and child pornography is an obvious example. Another is necrophilia, or an attraction to corpses. A notorious case of the latter involved New York Police Department patrol officer Gilberto Valle, the so-called "Cannibal Cop," who in March 2013 was convicted of using chat rooms on fetish Internet sites to conspire to kidnap, torture, and commit necrophilic and cannibalistic acts against women, including his own wife and a teenaged neighbour. In 2014, Valle's conviction was overturned by a judge, who accepted the argument that Valle's actions online only represented role playing, not an actual attempt to commit a crime.

In looking at scatologia as the progenitor of what today amounts to an electronic version of anonymous telephonic harassment, we find that the connections are not as well understood. This is less a criminological or psychopathological concern than a legal one relating to how best to codify terms such as "trolling" and "bullying" as types of scatologia, especially given that these terms are highly interpretative and often mean different things to different people.

The lack of progress in combating, legislating, or even reaching a national consensus on cyberbullying is partly due the fact that most cyberbullying almost certainly goes unreported (Hinduja and Patchin 2008). Perhaps this is because of the stigma attached to being a victim of cyberbullying, in much the same way that stigma is attached to victims of offline, physical bullying. To date, the identification and classification of cyberbullying has relied by default on now-dated criminological research on the causes and consequences of physical or "corporeal" bullying as first defined by Olweus (1993). By this definition, such bullying is a frequently adolescent phenomenon that manifests itself as the causing of unprovoked and sadistic physical harm and the repeated assertion of real or perceived physical and social power differentials.

To gain a better understanding of cyberbullying and the motives of online offenders, we may need to step outside traditional criminology and draw from terminologies used in other fields such as digital media and communications, which also lay claim to the study of cybercrime and cyberdeviance (Arntfield 2014). One term often used to describe post-Web 2.0 spaces is *new media*. Note, however, that the "new" in new media is not a temporal distinction for denoting the vintage of a particular technology or media product; rather, new media describes any traditional, tactile media that now exist in newly computer-compatible forms and that rely on digitization processes for their creation, manipulation, or dissemination (Manovich 2001). The shift from the telephone to Internet or networked-mobile devices is one such example.

The relationship between new media and earlier, long-established offences is sometimes straightforward (e.g., possessing digital versions of prohibited analogue images such as child pornography). But other offences, including electronic manifestations of identified paraphilias, have no clear offline referent.

FOCUS

BOX 18.2

CORPUS LINGUISTICS AND CYBERDEVIANCE: INDEXING THE CYBERBULLY'S VOCABULARY

In the winter of 2014, the *Cyberbullying Reporter,* an open-access site created to collect samples of text appearing in cases of electronic harassment, was launched at Western University as part of a national research initiative on forensic linguistics and cyberbullying. The purpose of collecting these samples was to build a sizable list of terms (known as a corpus) and investigate the recurrence of specific keywords and word groupings with respect to cyberbullying. Unlike traditional bullying, cyberbullying requires no direct or real-time contact and is carried out largely through written content. This written content includes both words and characters, such as numerals and emoticons used to complement or aggravate those words. The study is concerned with applying **critical discourse analysis** (CDA) to aggressive or antisocial online exchanges to try to identify a bullying lexicon (word stock) common to cases of electronic harassment. Because cyberbullying relies predominantly on words to victimize, each act of cyberbullying requires that perpetrators select particular words as mechanisms of offending. These words reflect specific social symbols that have meaning beyond the digital space in which they appear (Mautner 2009, 33). The result is a written transcript of delinquent social actions that allows researchers to identify points in common among different sets of victims connected by common bullying terms online. Unlike in cases of scatologia, where victims might be bullied, harassed, or intimidated via telephone for the gratification of the offender, the fact that these statements are now in written form enables a large-scale analysis of the relationship between word distinctions and cyberdeviance using a methodology known as "**corpus linguistics**."

Corpus linguistics was first employed as a research method by Kucera (1967) at Brown University in Providence, Rhode Island. Kucera conducted a computer-based analysis of the state of everyday English as gleaned from years' worth of media articles and other field texts—an archive ultimately known as the Brown Corpus. The Brown Corpus was a compilation of millions of pieces of written text drawn from a wide array of public sources. It enabled the identification of patterns in language and of how society reserved certain words for certain situations, or paired certain words in specific contexts. Since that time, no known study has applied corpus linguistics to the study of language as it exists in purely digital environments, where nearly all forms of communication necessitate putting words into writing. This includes cases of cyberbullying, cybermobbing, trolling, and other forms of electronic harassment that rely purely on word choices to commit symbolic acts of violence.

The preliminary stages of this research are focused on collecting text samples in known or suspected cases of cyberbullying; the ultimate goal is to identify how specific digital environments shape the harmfulness of bullying content. For instance, how do personal and discrete inbox messages yield a corpus of terms that is distinct from that of more public acts of cyberbullying, which are intended to also be read by third parties (such as on a public message board) and thereby intensify victimization? The cyberbullying lexicon (the working vocabulary employed by offenders) being generated from this corpus should help develop legislation on cyberbullying prevention and enforcement.

The study is also expected to help identify a baseline vernacular to cyberbullying that reflects the "average" degree of aggression in terms of content. This will help generate a consensus on where to draw the line between deviance and criminality when it comes to harassing or scatologic cyberactivities. While the medium and the method may be new, the reality is that Canadian lawmakers and courts have long had to determine thresholds for criminality with respect to written content that falls outside the scope of freedom of expression as guaranteed by section 2(b) of the Charter of Rights and Freedoms. In fact, section 163.1(1)(b) of the Criminal Code specifies that child pornography need not consist solely of images; it can also consist of prohibited written materials (stories, poems, diaries, etc.) that contain words and phrases that sexualize children and are thus obscene. Similarly, courts have long had to weigh at what point spoken content delivered through unwanted and repetitive telephone calls crosses the line between deviant and criminal. To this point, the linguistic content of cyberbullying and its various secondary forms of cyberdeviance has not yet been closely scrutinized.

The preliminary data suggest there may be a strong paraphilic component to cyberbullying. This can include scatologia, as well as other paraphilias not yet identified but for which—at least in a digital forum—the use of the written word is integral to the commission of any offence. It is probably not coincidental that some of the best-known and most tragic cases of cyberbullying in Canada in recent years have been closely associated with pedophilic activities. These include the case of Rehtaeh Parsons (cited earlier in this chapter) as well as that of Amanda Todd, whose suicide in October 2012 touched off an international debate about the damage caused by cyberbullying. In April 2014, nearly two years after Todd's death, a 35-year-old Dutchman named Aydin Coban was arrested and charged with a number

(continued)

of crimes, including child pornography offences related to his harassment and blackmailing of the BC teen as well as other victims around the world, whom he targeted through Internet chat rooms (Hootsen and Rovers 2014). Will an examination of Coban's writings to his victims help identify a common method or pattern among cyberdeviants and help identify harmful material before more victims are targeted? Do new media and cases like those of Todd and Parsons allow us to identify the link between language and paraphilia for the first time? What do you think?

Critical Thinking Questions

1. Look at the definition of online "stalking" earlier in this chapter and ask yourself if cyberbullying might also be a version of stalking. Is there a legal difference?
2. Select two paraphilias from the list in this chapter. With the role of corpus linguistics as discussed here in mind, what two key disorders would be of greatest interest to linguists who study cyberbullying?

critical discourse analysis
A method used in linguistic analysis in which the totality of communicative exchanges (discourse) is examined in the context of the social, political, or cultural power held between sender and receiver.

corpus linguistics
The study of a language or dialect by collecting everyday samples of text, which comprise a body of keywords (a corpora), which can then be used to gauge long-term trends and patterns in communication.

SEARCH FOR:
Cyberbullying Reporter

They are therefore much more difficult to define and even more difficult to legislate. Because technology changes at a rate far faster than bills can be pushed through Parliament and laws enacted or changed, the relationship between cybercrime and new media remains poorly understood. As the technological landscape continues to evolve and as new devices and operating systems are deployed and become popularized, the law is bound to be in a perpetual state of playing catch-up.

Cybercrime and Routine Activities Theory Online

Digitization provides a permanent electronic transcript of deviant cyberactivities and allows for new insights into both online and offline offending as well as the relationship between the two. Yet while changes in technology and in the way harmful content is delivered explain *how* acts of cyberbullying are carried out, they do not explain *why*. Drawing on Cohen and Felson's (1979) routine activities theory (Chapter 15), certain correlates among victims can be identified with respect to how much time they spend engaged in cyberactivities and the nature of the virtual environments they choose to visit. For instance, an Australian study suggested that an excessive number of Facebook "likes" associated with singular profiles and other forms of oversharing is inversely related to happiness and confidence. Also, users who post excessive personal details are likely struggling to find personal connections and are trying to initiate conversations because of their social alienation (Sankin 2014). This is an important predictor of victimization using the routine activities approach, in that users already predisposed to self-esteem issues and emotional distress tend to have fewer privacy safeguards in place and may thus reveal themselves as soft targets to online predators looking to exploit the personal information being disclosed by the potential victim. Knowledge of these types of online behaviours might help us determine why certain victims are selected for cyberbullying and also why victim responses vary so widely, ranging from indifference in cases where victims are also bullied offline (Olweus 2012), to extreme responses such as self-harm, emotional despair, and even suicide.

Research on cyberbullying and cybervictimology must therefore initiate a critical reassessment of social media as a routine activity. This needs to include the assessment of risk. Victims might then be classified along a continuum of risk tolerance, ranging from infrequent users to frequent users whose communications tend to occur in or near real-time. These frequent users will have a social media and digital experience defined by negligible lapses between the delivery and the reception of aggressive or harassing communication, compared to less frequent users who only sporadically and sparingly access these same digital environments and who are less invested in what occurs in them. In this context, the duration and frequency of use—or more accurately, the inability or unwillingness to disengage from these environments—might be seen as an increased tolerance for risk among cybervictims. It therefore stands to reason that opting into a digital lifestyle where social media pervade everyday functioning, allowing all digital communications to push to a mobile device that is always present versus limiting cyberactivities to the home or workplace, creates a disproportionate risk based on frequency of routine use alone.

Digital media offer cyberbullies access to users who would normally not have direct face-to-face contact with them. As Hayward (2012) has noted, the Internet—and by extension digital culture generally—has broken down traditional barriers between life stages and led to generational and demographic confusion, thus bringing about unforeseen online collisions between groups of people with different value systems. Social media, from their earliest versions (ICQ, MSN Messenger, MySpace, etc.) to the current menu of customizable and multiplatform networks, inevitably entail a certain degree of risk-taking by all users that elevates a baseline *assumed* risk. These are risks not normally seen in offline contexts, where offenders are much less anonymous and where it would be largely impossible for a 50-year-old male pedophile, for instance, to masquerade as a teenaged girl to win over the trust of his victim. Such deceptions are, unfortunately, rather common online.

Victims are targeted by online offenders in various ways, but bullying is facilitated by digital environments that offer little in the way of suitable guardianship. These environments allow cyberbullies, trollers, and other cyberdeviants to identify victims who can predictably be found operating there, and in circumstances where they are both vulnerable and accessible. A bully will wait at the edge of an unlit and isolated footpath that serves as a customary route home from school for suitable offline targets; in much the same way, certain digital environments enable predatory violators to watch, wait, and take advantage of specific routines as they target victims online. As with the perilous but more direct or convenient route home that may bring them in contact with a predator, victims ultimately weigh the risks versus the rewards of certain routes and routines and then make decisions based on their individual tolerance for those risks. This generates the question: Who should be the guardians? As the legal and philosophical debate rages on with respect to whose responsibility it is to police and regulate these virtual spaces—and ultimately who has the authority to do so—it seems there are no clear answers.

In late 2012, Canadians generally rejected the idea that the suitable guardian in the Wild West of the Internet should be police officers or other law enforcement agents. Offline, people apparently want a police officer on every street corner to deter motivated offenders; online, it seems quite the opposite is true. Following the Council of Europe Convention on Cybercrime in 2001, the Canadian government tabled Bill C-30, which would have significantly expanded the powers of police to conduct online surveillance and ostensibly act as guardians of virtual spaces. The same bill included a requirement that technology providers relinquish Internet Protocol (IP) addresses and other personal information without a search warrant, production order, or other court order during the early stages of criminal or regulatory investigations (Press 2012). By February 2013, Bill C-30 in its original form had been scrapped, much to the delight of the federal Privacy Commissioner and many Canadians. With some aspects of the original bill being preserved in a subsequent rewriting, the future of guardianship on the Internet is now difficult to predict, and so is what that guardianship might look like and how cyberdeviance will be defined and monitored—if at all. In moving forward, criminologists may have an increasing role to play in helping moderate this socio-legal debate amid an ever-changing technological and cultural landscape rife with risks.

SEARCH FOR:
Bill C-30 Canada

QUESTIONS FOR CRITICAL THINKING

1. Many crimes are never reported to police—in Chapter 4 you learned about the dark figure of crime. Most cases of cyberbullying also go unreported, and many other cybercrimes are going undetected online. What other types of cybercrimes do you think are most likely to be unreported? Is the dark figure of crime even more prevalent in digital environments?

2. The 2009 Ontario Superior Court case *R. v. Polius* ruled that smartphones and other digital devices are more than just communication technologies, likening them to the modern equivalent of personal diaries. If this is the case, why do some users feel compelled to share so much personal information with strangers using these devices and through online forums? Is there a link between exercising common sense and informational self-restraint and avoiding being a victim of cyberbullying?

Summary

- Cybercrime is a diverse area of study that remains in its adolescence. There is a long way to go before lawmakers and criminologists reach a middle ground. As technologies change and technology providers become increasingly invested as stakeholders in the investigative and legislative process, the courts will be tasked with drawing the line between cyberdeviance and cybercrime. They will need to find ways to balance privacy interests and freedom of expression with the rights of victims and protection of the public.

- Cyberbullying as a derivative of both cybercrime and cyberdeviance is a socially and politically charged issue that has proven difficult to define and legislate, in part because it is so open to interpretation. While there is a move afoot to amend laws to prohibit trafficking in "intimate images" (sexting), little has been done to address the fact that all documented cases of cyberbullying also involve the exchange of words and written communications that are nearly impossible to police consistently.

- Beyond the linguistic elements in cyberbullying that equate it with other criminal offences encompassing obscene or offensive written content (child pornography), there appears to be a paraphilic element or etiology to cybercrime in its various forms. This suggests that offences like cyberbullying and Internet trolling may represent a new medium or electronic extension of scatologia, a paraphilia that previously relied on the anonymity and distance afforded by the landline telephone.

- Applying the routine activities model of crime to virtual environments, specifically in relation to the cyberactivities of both online predators and victims, a useful starting point might be to gain a better understanding of how specific activities and environments pose greater risks than others, and how and why certain victims are targeted in those environments.

- Despite the high-profile and tragic suicides in the wake of prolonged instances of cyberbullying, cybermobbing, and other forms of electronic harassment that blur the line between cyberdeviance and cybercrime, Canadians remain conflicted in their opinions regarding the role of the police and lawmakers in regulating online behaviour. Cyberbullying in particular is bound to be a conduit for ongoing debates about how to balance privacy with public safety in a digital world.

NET WORK

Using the Google search terms found throughout this chapter, see if you can answer the following questions:

1. How should the federal government approach redrafting Bill C-30, and how should lawmakers determine the best method for balancing privacy with pubic safety as cyberactivities continue to pervade all elements of life? Do cybercrime, cyberbullying, and Internet policing merit a national referendum?

2. Describe the advantages and disadvantages of having a cyberbullying task force comprised of civilian investigators as opposed to sworn police officers. Does this reflect the fact that because cyberbullying is not a codified cybercrime, it doesn't merit police resources?

GLOSSARY

absolute deprivation
The inability to sustain oneself physically and materially. *p. 291*

actuarial
Refers to statistical calculations of risk across time and groups. *p. 334*

actus reus
All the elements contained in the definition of a criminal offence, other than the mental elements (*mens rea*). *p. 64*

administrative record
A collection of information about individual cases. *p. 95*

adviser system
An extension of the self- or kin-based redress system of dispute settlement. It involves—albeit in a relatively passive way—a third-party decision maker (or makers). *p. 37*

anomie
A concept developed by Émile Durkheim (1858–1917) to describe an absence of clear societal norms and values. Robert Merton (1910–2003) used the term more narrowly to refer to a situation in which people would adopt deviant means to achieve goals beyond their means. *p. 281*

antisocial personality disorder
A personality disorder that involves disregard for the rights of others as well as impulsive, irresponsible, and aggressive behaviour. *p. 262*

assumption of discriminating traits
The view that offenders are distinguished from non-offenders by, for example, their high levels of impulsiveness and aggression. *p. 247*

assumption of offender deficit
The view that offenders who break the law have some psychological deficit that distinguishes them from normal, law-abiding citizens. *p. 247*

atavism
Cesare Lombroso believed that some people were born criminals. These born criminals were throwbacks to an earlier stage of evolution—atavisms—and were morally inferior to the rest of the population. Lombroso's research focused on physical differences (stigmata) that could be used to identify atavisms. *p. 234*

attachment
The degree to which an individual has affective ties to other persons. One of the social bonds in Hirschi's theory. *p. 379*

attentive gaze
A methodological requirement that researchers immerse themselves where crime occurs in the everyday world in order to better understand the ways in which crime is experienced and interpreted by individuals. *p. 338*

autonomic reactivity
A measurement of the extent to which an individual's physical organism reacts to external stimuli. *p. 258*

belief
The degree to which an individual believes in conventional values, morality, and the legitimacy of law. One of Hirschi's social bonds. *p. 380*

bourgeois class
The term *bourgeois class*, or *bourgeoisie*, was used by Marx to refer to the capitalist class in modern societies following the Industrial Revolution. *p. 44*

broken windows policing
Just as houses with broken windows indicate that nobody cares about the neighbourhood, proponents of this policing style feel that tolerating minor misbehaviour will mean that residents will be afraid to use their streets. They feel that police should quickly deal with minor incivilities such as panhandling, vandalism, and other behaviours that contribute to fear of crime. Critics feel that this policing style potentially discriminates against the poor. *p. 348*

Canadian Centre for Justice Statistics
A division of Statistics Canada, formed in 1981, with a mandate to collect national data on crime and justice. *p. 97*

capital
The primary field of activity for state or government actors, as well as those who are funded by the government, and where these actors compete to define and shape government resources and responsibilities. *p. 339*

capitalism
The mode of production based on private property and commodities owned and produced for the purpose of generating profit. *p. 44*

carceral–assistential mesh
Under neoliberalism, this is a mode of "double regulation" whereby the right (e.g., prisons) and left (e.g., social welfare) jointly function to punish and discipline the poor rather than offering rehabilitation and care. *p. 341*

career
In common use, this refers to the sequence of stages through which people in a particular occupational sector move during the course of their employment. It has also been applied to the various stages of personal involvement with criminal activity. *p. 355*

career contingency
An unintended event, process, or situation that occurs by chance, beyond the control of the person pursuing the career. *p. 363*

Charter
The Canadian *Charter* of Rights and Freedoms is part of the Canadian constitution. The *Charter* sets out those rights and Freedoms that Canadians believe are necessary in a free and democratic society. *p. 61*

class
A concept advanced by Karl Marx (1818–1883) to describe a social group's relationship to what is produced in a

given mode of production. Examples discussed below include the merchant class during the transition to capitalism, the bourgeois class during the Industrial Revolution, and the elite class in contemporary capitalism. *p. 34*

class conflict theory
Laws are passed by members of the ruling class in order to maintain their privileged position by keeping the common people under control. *p. 19*

classical conditioning
A basic form of learning whereby a neutral stimulus is paired with another stimulus that naturally elicits a certain response; the neutral stimulus comes to elicit the same response as the stimulus that automatically elicits the response. *p. 256*

Classical School
Considered to be the first formal school of criminology, Classical criminology is associated with 18th- and early-19th-century reforms to the administration of justice and the prison system. Associated with authors such as Cesare Beccaria (1738–94), Jeremy Bentham (1748–1832), Samuel Romilly (1757–1818), and others, this school brought the emerging philosophy of liberalism and utilitarianism to the justice system, advocating principles of rights, fairness, and due process in place of retribution, arbitrariness, and brutality. *p. 226*

collective solidarity
A state of social bonding or interdependency that rests on similarity of beliefs and values, shared activities, and ties of kinship and cooperation among members of a community. *p. 35*

commitment
The degree to which an individual pursues conventional goals. One of the social bonds in Hirschi's theory. *p. 379*

common law
The body of judge-made law that has evolved in areas not covered by legislation. *ALSO*: The legal tradition found in English Canada, derived from feudal England, where it became the practice for the king to resolve disputes. Decisions made by the king and courts became the basis for future dispute settlements throughout the realm. *pp. 42, 60*

community psychology
A perspective that analyzes social problems, including crime, as largely a product of organizational and institutional characteristics of society. It is closely related to sociology. *p. 247*

compensation from the state
In most provinces, victims of crimes who suffered physical or other injuries may apply to an agency to receive lump sum or monthly payments according to provincial legislation. *p. 192*

conduct norms
Specific rules or norms of appropriate behaviour generally agreed upon by members of the social group to whom the behavioural norms apply. *p. 302*

consensus theory
Laws represent the agreement of most of the people in society that certain acts should be prohibited by the criminal law. *p. 19*

conservative approach
An approach that understands "difference" between men and women as biologically based sex differences. Women are viewed as "naturally" inferior or unequal to men. *p. 157*

conspiracy
An agreement by two or more persons to commit a criminal offence. *p. 77*

continuance commitment
Adherence to a criminal or other identity arising from the unattractiveness or unavailability of alternative lifestyles. *p. 363*

core rights of victims of crime
Legislators in different countries and intergovernmental agencies such as the UN have recognized various fundamental principles of justice and rights for victims of crime, such as the right to be informed, to receive restitution, and to be present when decisions such as bail or sentencing are being decided in court. *p. 191*

corpus linguistics
The study of a language or dialect by collecting everyday samples of text, which comprise a body of keywords (a corpora), which can then be used to gauge long-term trends and patterns in communication. *p. 508*

correlate
A phenomenon that accompanies another phenomenon and is related in some way to it. *p. 121*

counselling
Procuring, soliciting, or inciting another person to commit a crime. *p. 75*

counting procedure
A consensus on how to count units and data elements. *p. 95*

crime
Conduct that is prohibited by law and that is subject to a penal sanction (such as imprisonment or a fine). *p. 56*

crime prevention through social development
An approach to crime prevention that focuses on reducing the number of motivated offenders by changing the social environment. *p. 417*

crime rate
Criminologists calculate crime rates (or rates of incarceration, conviction, or recidivism) by dividing the amount of crime by the population size and multiplying by 100,000. This produces the standard rate per 100,000; occasionally it is useful to calculate a rate per million or some other figure when looking at less frequently occurring offences. *p. 92*

criminal attempt
A criminal attempt occurs when an individual does—or omits to do—anything for the purpose of carrying out a previously formed intention to commit a crime. The conduct in question must constitute a substantial step towards the completion of the crime that is intended. *p. 76*

criminal identity
This social category, imposed by the community, correctly or incorrectly defines an individual as a particular type of criminal. The identity pervasively shapes his or her social interactions with others. This concept is similar to master status. *p. 366*

criminal law

A body of jurisprudence that includes the definition of various crimes, the specification of various penalties, a set of general principles concerning criminal responsibility, and a series of defences to a criminal charge. *p. 57*

criminal procedure

A body of legislation that specifies the procedures to be followed in the prosecution of a criminal case and that defines the nature and scope of the powers of criminal justice officials. *p. 58*

criminogenic market structure

An economic market that is structured in such a way that it tends to produce criminal behaviour. *p. 471*

criminology

The body of knowledge regarding crime as a social phenomenon. It includes the processes of making laws, breaking laws, and reacting to the breaking of laws. Its objective is the development of a body of general and verified principles and of other types of knowledge regarding this process of law, crime, and treatment. *p. 9*

crisis of legitimacy

A situation where the state no longer maintains the authority to govern. Sometimes referred to as a legitimation crisis. A number of factors can contribute to such a crisis, for which there are only two possible resolutions: (a) the state regains legitimacy, or (b) a new governing body is instated. *p. 48*

critical discourse analysis

A method used in linguistic analysis in which the totality of communicative exchanges (discourse) is examined in the context of the social, political, or cultural power held between sender and receiver. *p. 508*

critical infrastructure site

Any location or asset, either physical or virtual, that is vital to the socioeconomic and physical security of a nation or region, including but not limited to water treatment facilities, telecommunications centres, hospitals and health care facilities, nuclear and other power-generating facilities, airports and railway stations, and centres of major economic activity, such as stock and security exchanges. *p. 498*

cultural conflict

A theory that attempts to explain certain types of criminal behaviour as resulting from a conflict between the conduct norms of divergent cultural groups. *p. 303*

cultural construction

A perspective on a subject that is shaped by cultural assumptions rather than having a natural or objective basis. *p. 167*

culturally prescribed aspiration

A rejection of the notion that aspirations are entirely self-created; rather, they are defined by culture and transmitted by other members of the society. *p. 281*

cyberactivities

Any number of tasks carried out through a computer and a network connection, including but not limited to Internet browsing, email correspondence, online banking, interactive gaming, media downloading or uploading, the use of file transfer protocols, and accessing social media platforms. *p. 495*

cybercrime

Illegal acts in which a computer and a network are central to committing a crime and are also the targets of the crime. *p. 435*

cybermobbing

A group activity that in effect merges cyberdeviance with learning theories of crime and interactional models of offending. That is, many disparate users (a mob) within a virtual space follow the lead of a cyberbully and publicly gang up on a single victim by sending harassing and humiliating communications. *p. 500*

dangerous knowledge

A form of knowledge that leaves no concept, notion, or idea untouched by criticism. To achieve this relentlessly critical stance, cultural criminologists often turn to diverse sources of information (e.g., novels and street-level observation) as means to reveal alternative perspectives that might shake the foundations of our taken-for-granted assumptions about crime.

dark figure of crime

The amount of crime that is unreported or unknown. *p. 99*

Dark Web

Also known as the Darknet, it is the restricted, non-indexed portion of the Deep Web that requires a specialized Web browser and anonymous Tor software in order to gain access. The Dark Web relies on cryptocurrenices such as Bitcoin to facilitate illegal transactions, which range from drug trafficking to murder-for-hire schemes. The first Darknet market, known as Silk Road, was launched in 2011 and was successfully shut down by the FBI in 2013. The site's founder, Ross Ulbricht (who used the online alias Dread Pirate Roberts), was sentenced to life in prison with no possibility of parole after being convicted of charges that included conspiracy to traffic in narcotics and money laundering. *p. 496*

data element

Specification about what exactly is to be collected. *p. 95*

debit card fraud

Debit card fraud entails four steps: (1) create fake debit cards, (2) steal personal identification and banking information from legitimate cards, (3) emboss the stolen information on the fake cards, and (4) use the illegal debit cards for purchases or cash advances. *p. 445*

deconstruction

An opening up of seemingly closed "things." It intends to encounter the hidden and excluded elements of language, meaning, and experience. *p. 346*

Deep Web

Sometimes called the "invisible Web," it is the parallel Internet that exists beneath the surface of conventional browsers. It features sites not indexed by search engines. It is essentially unregulated and is rife with criminal activity and illegal transactions. *p. 496*

deterrence

As used in criminal justice, it refers to crime prevention achieved through the fear of punishment. *p. 230*

deviant cybercommunity
An online community whose culture and customs would be classified as deviant and delinquent if exported to the offline world, but in which socially abnormal behaviour is accepted and even endorsed in the context of the given digital environment. *p. 502*

differential association
Developed by Edwin Sutherland in the 1930s, this theory argues that crime, like any social behaviour, is learned in association with others. If individuals regularly associate with criminals in relative isolation from law-abiding citizens, they are more likely to engage in crime. They learn relevant skills for committing crime and ideas for justifying and normalizing it. *p. 366*

differential offending hypothesis
There are actual differences between racial groups in terms of the incidence, level of seriousness, and persistence of offending patterns. *p. 134*

differential treatment hypothesis
Structural inequality in the administration of justice (from police patrols to courtrooms to correctional services) is responsible for the overrepresentation of minority groups in the criminal justice process. *p. 134*

discipline
A meticulous manner or method of training. It intends to ensure constant subjection and obedience. It involves hierarchal observation, normalizing judgment, and examinations. *p. 331*

distributed denial-of-service (DDoS) attack
A term that describes any number of methods of varying sophistication, usually carried out by a group of hackers or by a series of bot attacks, for infiltrating and sabotaging a host server, thereby denying access to a website or online service or otherwise disrupting the operations of business, industry, or government. *p. 495*

drift
A psychological state of weak normative attachment to either deviant or conventional ways. *p. 355*

duress
Duress may be a defence to a criminal charge when the accused was forced to commit a crime as a consequence of threats of death or serious bodily harm made by another person. *p. 84*

ecological fallacy
An error made when information is gathered at a group level (the unemployment rate of a neighbourhood) and conclusions are drawn about individuals (unemployed persons). Areas with high unemployment may have high crime rates, but this does not tell us that those crimes are necessarily committed by unemployed persons. *p. 377*

effective guardianship
An aspect of the routine activities approach to understanding crime victimization that argues that three key factors are required for crime to happen: a motivated offender, a suitable target, and ineffective guardianship of that target. Effective guardianship would include having locks on bikes, putting goods in the trunk of the car, or having the police regularly patrol a high-crime area. *p. 412*

ego
A psychoanalytical term denoting the rational part of the personality. It mediates between the *id* and the *superego* and is responsible for dealing with reality and making decisions. *p. 250*

elite class
The social class that controls the majority of material resources and power in a modern society. *p. 39*

empirical evidence
Evidence as observed through the senses; it can be seen, touched, heard, smelled, tasted, and, to some extent, measured. This is the only form of scientifically acceptable evidence. *p. 358*

ethnic group
A group of individuals having a common, distinctive subculture. Ethnic groups differ from races; the term implies that values, norms, behaviour, and language, not necessarily physical appearance, are important distinguishing characteristics. *p. 359*

ethno-methodology
Ethno-methodological theory was pioneered by Harold Garfinkel. Roughly translated, the term means the study of people's practices or methods. The perspective does not see the social world as an objective reality, but as something people constantly build and rebuild through their thoughts and actions. Ethno-methodologists try to uncover the methods and practices people use to create their taken-for-granted world. *p. 371*

executive disengagement
The custom by which lower-level employees assume that executives are best left uninformed of certain decisions and actions of employees, or the assumption that executives cannot be legally expected to have complete control over their individual staff. *p. 471*

extortion
An offender unlawfully obtains money, property or services from an individual or entity through coercion and intimidation. *p. 437*

extroversion
A personality characteristic associated with sociability, impulsiveness, and aggression. *p. 256*

feminist approach
Understands "difference" between men and women as structurally produced by inequalities of class, race, and gender that condition and constrain women's lives. *p. 166*

feudalism
A system of economic and social organization found historically in several areas of the world based around a feudal manor, which included a central farm owned by a landlord and small landholdings for a class of bonded farm labourers called serfs. *p. 41*

field
A basic unit of social activity. The social world is divided into many fields (e.g., the "artistic" field, the "academic" field, the "economic" field). Each field of activity is defined by its own market through which

certain practices or dispositions are valued more than others. *p. 339*

free trade zone
A specially designated geographical area within a nation that is exempt from the regulations and taxation normally imposed on business. These zones are intended to facilitate cross-border production and trade. Zones like these are found along the US–Mexico border, where they are referred to as *maquilladoras*. *p. 47*

gender-ratio problem
Poses the question of why there are sex differences in rates of arrest and types of criminal activity between men and women. *p. 163*

generalizability problem
Raises the issue of whether mainstream theories of crime—which have largely been developed with men in mind—can be made to "fit" women. *p. 163*

governmentality
The art of governing. It transcends and is considerably broader than the traditional understanding of government as a state-directed activity. Government, then, encompasses a wide array of techniques, within and outside of the state, intended to (re)shape and (re)direct human actions. *p. 330*

gross counts of crime
A count of the total amount of crime in a given community, making no distinction between crime categories. *p. 102*

group conflict theory
A theory that attempts to explain certain types of criminal behaviour as resulting from a conflict between the interests of divergent groups. *pp. 20, 303*

habitus
A set of durable dispositions acquired through experience that allow one to achieve a "feel for the game" within a specific field of activity. These are internalized practices that serve as a "second nature" responsive to the immediate demands of everyday life. *p. 339*

harm to victims
The direct impact of crime on victims includes harm, such as loss, injury, pain, and emotional trauma. These can be exacerbated by the victim's experience with the police, courts, corrections, and others. *p. 188*

hot spots policing
Most crimes occur at a small number of addresses in any community. Hot spots policing concentrates police resources on these high-crime locations. *p. 407*

hegemonic masculinity
A particular idealized form of masculinity that is culturally glorified, honoured, and exalted. For example, associating "the masculine" with physical strength, aggression, independence, ambition, lack of emotion, and heterosexuality. *p. 184*

human capital
The talents and capabilities that individuals contribute to the process of production. Companies, governments, and individuals can invest in human capital, just as they can invest in technology and buildings or in finances. *p. 294*

human rights
The minimum conditions required for a person to live a dignified life. Among the rights set out by the Universal Declaration of Human Rights are the right to life, liberty, and security of the person; the right to be free of torture and other forms of cruel and degrading punishment; the right to equality before the law; and the right to the basic necessities of life. *p. 15*

human trafficking
The illegal trade in people for the purposes of commercial sexual exploitation and other forms of forced labour. *p. 437*

id
A psychoanalytical term that denotes the most inaccessible and primitive part of the mind. It is a reservoir of biological urges that strive continually for gratification. The ego mediates between the *id* and the *superego*. *p. 249*

ideal type
A theoretical construct abstracted from experience that brings together observed characteristics in different contexts to generalize for analytic purposes. Empirical observations never entirely match the conceptual ideal, which instead can only be used as a standard for making higher-order observations. *p. 35*

ideology
A linked set of ideas and beliefs that act to uphold and justify an existing or desired situation in society. *p. 94*

inchoate crime
A criminal offence that is committed when the accused person seeks to bring about the commission of a particular crime but is not successful in doing so. The three inchoate offences in the *Criminal Code* are attempt, conspiracy, and counselling. *p. 74*

independent variable
A presumed cause of a dependent variable. If unemployment is thought to cause crime to increase, unemployment is the independent variable, and crime the dependent variable. *p. 377*

indeterminate sentence
A sentence that has no fixed release date. Release is determined by a parole authority based on the individual's behaviour. *p. 235*

individualistic
A theory that focuses on explaining the behaviour of individuals and using factors or features of the individual in explaining this behaviour. *p. 387*

individualized deterrence
Offenders who are heavily involved in criminal activity are individually warned that their actions are being monitored and that future violations of the law will be dealt with immediately. Extra police and/or probation resources are added to ensure that the legal system does keep its promises. *p. 407*

Industrial Revolution
A period of social transformation from the mid-1700s until the mid-1800s, marked primarily by new manufacturing technologies and the harnessing of new forms of energy, such as coal and steam. *p. 43*

instrumental Marxism
The state is viewed as the direct instrument of the ruling or capitalist class. Instrumentalism is based on the notion that the processes of the superstructure are determined by the economic base. *p. 310*

intoxication defence
Intoxication caused by alcohol and/or other drugs may be a defence if it prevents the

G-6

GLOSSARY

accused from forming the intent required for a specific intent offence, such as murder or robbery. *p. 82*

involvement
The degree to which an individual is active in conventional activities. One of the social bonds in Hirschi's theory. *p. 380*

juristic person
The legal concept that corporations are liable to the same laws as natural persons. Treating corporations as individuals raises practical difficulties for legal enforcement and punishment. *p. 470*

justice
For Derrida, since it is perpetually deferred, justice cannot be defined adequately. It is not contained in or constrained by law. It is infinite. It is "to come." *p. 348*

kinship
Social relationships that stem from belonging to the same family, lineage, or cultural group. *p. 34*

labelling
According to labelling theory, deviance is a quality not of the act but of the label that others attach to it. This raises the question of who applies the label and who is labelled. The application of a label and the response of others to the label may result in a person becoming committed to a deviant identity. *p. 355*

la cosa nostra
Term used to denote Italian American organized crime. It was originally applied by the FBI in an attempt to make this criminal fraternity sound ominous and threatening. Members of the so-called LCN never used this label themselves, though they have often referred to their secret society as "this thing of ours," which roughly translates into Italian as "la cosa nostra." *p. 447*

legal definition of crime
A crime is an act or omission that violates the criminal law and is punishable with a jail term, a fine, and/or some other sanction. *p. 15*

levels of aggregation
Refers to how data are to be combined. Do we want city-level, provincial, or national data? *p. 95*

liberal approach
Distinguishes sex (biological) from gender (cultural) and sees differences between men and women as resulting from gender roles and socialization patterns. *p. 160*

lifestyle/exposure theory
A theory of crime victimization that acknowledges that not everyone has the same lifestyle and that some lifestyles expose people to more risks than others do. *p. 410*

loansharking
Lending money at very high interest rates, often enforced through the use of physical force. *p. 437*

master status
A status overriding all others in perceived importance. Whatever other personal or social qualities individuals possess, they are judged primarily by this one attribute. *Criminal* exemplifies a master status that influences the community's identification of an individual. *p. 361*

maturational reform
The fact that people are less likely to commit crime as they grow older. *p. 123*

mens rea
The mental elements (other than voluntariness) contained in the definition of a criminal offence. *p. 66*

methodology
Refers to the study or critique of methods. *p. 92*

micro-powers
Small and mundane relations of governance, with an appreciable effect on human behaviour. *p. 331*

mistake of fact
Mistake of fact may be a defence where the accused person acts under the influence of an honest mistake in relation to any of the elements of the *actus reus* of the offence charged. *p. 81*

mode of production
The dominant way of organizing the creation of products and services for consumption in a society. Historically, the mode of production has evolved from subsistence-based in hunting and gathering societies

to commodity-based in industrial capitalist societies. *p. 34*

modelling
A form of learning that occurs as a result of watching and imitating others. *p. 257*

moral development theory
Refers generally to theories of individual psychology that investigate how moral reasoning emerges in the individual and develops as the individual matures. *p. 252*

moral entrepreneur
Someone who defines new rules and laws or who advocates stricter enforcement of existing laws. Often such entrepreneurs have a financial or organizational interest in particular definitions or applications of law. *p. 357*

moral rhetoric
In the study of crime, this is the set of claims and assertions deviants make to justify their deviant behaviour. The moral rhetoric of a group is an important component of socialization into a deviant identity. *p. 356*

naked life
For Agamben, naked life is akin to *Homo Sacer*—an individual who is excluded from possessing human rights and can be killed by anyone but cannot be sacrificed during a religious ceremony. *p. 343*

NCRMD
The special verdict of "not criminally responsible on account of mental disorder." In order to be found NCRMD, it must be proved on the balance of probabilities that, because of mental disorder, the accused lacked the capacity to appreciate the nature and quality of the act or omission in question or to know it would be considered morally wrong by the average Canadian. *p. 78*

Neoclassical theory
Neoclassical theorists sought to allow more flexibility in the justice system—for example, by individualizing sentences to take into account offender characteristics and extenuating circumstances. *p. 229*

necessity
Necessity may be a defence to a criminal charge when the accused person commits

NEL

the lesser evil of a crime in order to avoid the occurrence of a greater evil. *p. 84*

norms
Established rules of behaviour or standards of conduct. *p. 13*

objective *mens rea*
The *mens rea* elements of a criminal offence are considered to be objective if they are based on a determination of whether a reasonable person, in the same circumstances and with the same knowledge as the accused, would have appreciated the risk involved in the accused's conduct and would have taken steps to avoid the commission of the *actus reus* elements of the crime in question. *p. 67*

occupational crime
Refers to violations of the law in the course of practising a legitimate occupation. *p. 467*

operant conditioning
The basic process by which an individual's behaviour is shaped by reinforcement or by punishment. *p. 260*

opportunity structure
Opportunity is shaped by the way the society or an institution is organized or structured. *p. 291*

organizational or corporate crime
White-collar crime committed with the support and encouragement of a formal organization and intended, at least in part, to advance the goals of that organization. *p. 467*

paraphilia
The use of unusual objects, situations, processes, or people to obtain sexual excitement and channel obsessions or fantasies that are inherently deviant and either prohibited by law (criminal paraphilia) or deemed taboo and forbidden by conventional society. *p. 502*

party to a crime
The *Criminal Code* specifies that one is a party to—and liable to conviction of—a criminal offence if one actually commits it, aids and/or abets it, becomes a party to it by virtue of having formed a common intention with others to commit a crime, or counsels the commission of an offence that is actually committed by another person. *p. 73*

patriarchy
A system of male domination that includes both a structure and an ideology that privileges men over women. *p. 167*

Ponzi scheme
A fraud in which old investors are paid with the funds invested by new investors. When the scheme runs out of new investors, the scheme collapses. *p. 485*

population
Refers to all members of a given class or set. For example, adult Canadians, teenagers, Canadian inmates, and criminal offenders can each be thought of as a population. *p. 93*

Positive School
The Italian criminologist Cesare Lombroso and his followers were among the first to study crime scientifically. They believed that crime was caused by biological factors beyond the individual's control, though social factors became more important as this school of thought changed over time. *p. 231*

power
Max Weber saw power as the ability to realize one's goals despite resistance from others. In small-scale societies, the power to make decisions and affect group life was not institutionalized in social structures, and it was shared by the members of the group. In modern societies, power has become formally encoded in law, and authority (the legitimate use of power) is bestowed by social institutions. *ALSO*: Power, for Foucault, extends beyond the state. It is not a quantity to hold or possess. It is, rather, relational, such that power is only ever evident in its exercise. *pp. 39, 331*

primary deviation
Occurs when an individual commits deviant acts but fails to adopt a primary self-identity as a deviant. *p. 355*

provocation
Provocation may be a partial defence to a charge of murder (if successful, it reduces the offence from murder to manslaughter). The required elements of provocation are (1) that the accused responded to the commission of a serious crime by the victim against the accused in circumstances that were of such a nature that an ordinary person would have been likely to lose the power of self-control, and (2) that the accused acted "on the sudden and before there was time for his (or her) passion to cool." *p. 86*

puppet club
A motorcycle club that is subsidiary to a more dominant outlaw motorcycle gang and that is often expected to carry out the dirty work of the latter. *p. 434*

racialization
A process in which categories of the population are constructed, differentiated, inferiorized, and excluded. *p. 141*

ransomware
A new term combining "ransom" and "software," it is any form of malicious software (malware) that, once deployed against a personal computer, computer server, or computer network, blocks the lawful user from accessing their own data. Much like how a ransom demand is made in cases of kidnapping crimes, the "kidnapped" files and information remain under the control of the attacker until the fee demanded is paid, usually by way of cryptocurrency such as Bitcoin. If it is not paid, the victim (either a person or an institution) loses the information or, in some cases, has it released publicly, particularly if the information is deemed valuable or embarrassing. In 2017, Canada was one of several countries affected by the ransomware known as WannaCry, with everything from home computers to hospital databases being infected. *p. 498*

rational choice theory
Rational choice theory posits that crime is the result of deliberate choices made by offenders based on their calculation of the risks and rewards of these choices. *p. 409*

regulatory offences
Regulatory offences arise under legislation (either federal, provincial, or territorial) that regulates inherently legitimate activities connected with trade, commerce, and industry or with everyday living (driving, fishing, etc.). These offences are not

considered to be serious and usually carry only a relatively minor penalty upon conviction. Indeed, many regulatory offences are sanctioned by means of a ticketing system, and the fines may often be paid online. *p. 59*

relative deprivation
Deprivation in relation to others around you, rather than judged against an absolute standard. *p. 291*

reliability
Identifies one of the standards (another being validity) against which the tools used to measure concepts are judged. Reliability refers to consistency of results over time. *p. 92*

relative autonomy
A term used in the structural Marxist perspective to indicate that the state has a certain amount of independence from the capitalist class and is therefore able to enact laws that are not in the immediate interests of the capitalist class. *p. 312*

repeat victimization
The phenomenon of a person being a victim of a crime more than once. *p. 188*

reproductive fitness variance
The range of possible offspring an organism can produce. *p. 251*

restitution from the offender
Victims of any type of crime may request that the offender pay the victim money as reparation for financial or other losses caused by the crime. *p. 192*

risk
The calculated probability of an eventuality. *p. 334*

risk society
An emerging societal form characterized by the production and increased awareness of human-made "risks," such as nuclear destruction and environmental devastation. More importantly, the risk society is organized around the management of such risks. *p. 335*

role convergence hypothesis
The hypothesis that as the work roles of women become similar to those of men, so will their involvement in crime. *p. 130*

routine activities approach
An extension of the lifestyle/exposure theory, this approach assumes that crimes are the expected outcomes of routine activities and changing social patterns. *p. 411*

sample
A group of elements (people, offenders, inmates) selected in a systematic manner from the population of interest. *p. 111*

secondary deviation
Occurs when an individual accepts the label of deviant. The result is adoption of a deviant self-identity that confirms and stabilizes the deviant lifestyle. *p. 355*

self-defence
Section 34 of the *Criminal Code* states that a person may use a reasonable amount of force in self-defence if she or he reasonably believes that they or another individual are the target of actual force or that a threat of force is being made against them. *p. 87*

self-degrading commitment
Commitment leading to a poorer opinion of oneself. *p. 364*

self-enhancing commitment
Commitment leading to a better opinion of oneself. *p. 364*

self-enhancing values
Values that emphasize social status, prestige, dominance over others, and personal success. *p. 282*

self- or kin-based redress
Self-based redress exists where the society allows the harmed party to take matters into his or her own hands in order to seek a settlement. This could be revenge or a successful negotiation of some kind of compensation. Some societies resort to *kin-based* redress, which involves a member of a kin group seeking a settlement on the harmed party's behalf. *p. 37*

self-report study
A method for measuring crime involving the distribution of a detailed questionnaire to a sample of people, asking them whether they have committed a crime in a particular period of time. This has been a good method for criminologists to determine the social characteristics of offenders. *p. 116*

self-transcending values
Values that emphasize appreciation, tolerance, protection, and the welfare of others. *p. 282*

seriousness rule
If there are several crimes committed in one incident, only the most serious crime is counted. UCR1.0 uses the seriousness rule. *p. 101*

sexism
Attributing to women socially undesirable characteristics that are assumed to be intrinsic characteristics of that sex. *p. 157*

situational crime prevention
Premised on the belief that most crime is opportunistic rather than the outcome of those driven to commit a crime no matter what the circumstances. This form of prevention attempts to reduce the opportunities for crime rather than just relying on the police after the crime has occurred. *p. 416*

social bonds
The degree to which an individual has ties to his or her society. In Hirschi's theory, social bonds include attachment, commitment, involvement, and belief. *p. 376*

social constructionist approach to crime
This approach questions the idea that there is an observable or measurable social reality, and instead proposes that a crime is whatever a particular society defines it to be. *p. 141*

social control theory
The theory proposes that people refrain from committing criminal acts because they do not want to jeopardize their bonds to conventional society. *p. 375*

socialization
The interactive process whereby individuals come to learn and internalize the culture of their society or group. *p. 250*

social structure
The patterned and relatively stable arrangement of roles and statuses found within societies and social institutions. *p. 281*

sovereign
One who holds supreme power in a territory or space. Agamben, following Carl Schmitt, claims that the sovereign is the one who is empowered to declare a state of exception. *p. 343*

state
As defined by Max Weber (1864–1920), the state is an institution that claims the exclusive right to the legitimate exercise of force in a given territory through the use of police to enforce laws or the army to maintain civil stability. While there have been stateless societies, most complex societies have state systems of formal government and administrative bureaucracies. *p. 34*

state of exception
A period of time when the sovereign declares civil liberties suspended: typically in a time of national crisis. *p. 343*

Statistical School
Associated with early social scientists such as Adolphe Quetelet (1795–1874) and André-Michel Guerry (1802–66), who began to explore the structure of emerging European societies with the assistance of statistical methods. While their early use of statistics is important, they also developed a structural explanation of crime and other social problems (crime is related to the social structure, including the social conditions in which it occurs). *p. 231*

stigma
As used by Erving Goffman (1922–82), a personal characteristic that is negatively evaluated by others and thus distorts and discredits the public identity of the individual. For example, a prison record may become a stigmatized attribute. The stigma may lead to the adoption of a self-identity that incorporates the negative social evaluation. *p. 357*

stigmata
The physical signs that a person is an atavism. *p. 234*

strain theory
The proposition that people feel strain when they are exposed to cultural goals they are unable to reach because they do not have access to culturally approved means of achieving those goals. *p. 280*

structural Marxism
The state is viewed as acting in the long-term interests of capitalism as a whole rather than in the short-term interests of the capitalist class. *p. 311*

subculture
A group of people who share a distinctive set of cultural beliefs and behaviours that differs in some significant way from that of the larger society. *p. 292*

subjective *mens rea*
The *mens rea* elements of a criminal offence are considered to be subjective if they are based on a determination of "what actually went on in the accused person's mind." The forms of subjective *mens rea* are intention and knowledge; recklessness; and wilful blindness. *p. 67*

subsistence
Production being only sufficient to meet immediate necessities. *p. 35*

superego
A psychoanalytical term denoting the ethical and moral dimensions of personality; an individual's conscience. The *ego* mediates between the *superego* and the *id*. *p. 250*

surplus
Production of goods and services beyond immediate needs. In hunting and gathering societies there was often little if any surplus since the production from hunting and gathering was used up in subsistence. In modern societies, more is produced than is needed for subsistence, so there is a surplus that takes the form of private property. *p. 35*

surveillance
The direct or indirect observation of conduct toward producing a desired outcome (i.e., conformity). *p. 331*

symbolic interactionism
A sociological perspective that focuses on the dynamics of how people interpret social situations and negotiate the meanings of these situations with others. It differs from more structurally focused perspectives in seeing individuals as actively creating the social world rather than just acting within the constraints of culture and social structure. *p. 353*

target suitability
Because of their vulnerability, some potential crime targets are more attractive than others. A home that is unlit, has shrubs blocking a view of the front door, and has no alarm system will be seen as a more suitable target than a well-protected home. *p. 413*

technological determinism
The theory that technological innovation is the key driving force behind changes in society and that new technologies shape culture and human behaviour, not vice versa. *p. 499*

terrorism
The illegitimate use of force to achieve a political objective by targeting innocent people. *p. 24*

theory
A set of concepts and their nominal definitions or assertions about the relationships between these concepts, assumptions, and knowledge claims. *p. 94*

token economy
A behaviour therapy procedure based on operant learning principles. Individuals are rewarded (reinforced) for positive or appropriate behaviour and are disciplined (punished) for negative or inappropriate behaviour. *p. 261*

trace
The mark of absence in words that is the necessary condition of thought and experience (Derrida 1976). *p. 347*

transnational corporation
A corporation that has sales and production in many different nations. Because of their multinational reach, these corporations are often thought to be beyond the political control of any individual nation-state. *p. 45*

transnational organized crime
Criminal groups that have a presence in different countries or criminal activities that are coordinated and conducted across national borders. *p. 432*

"true crime"

A "true crime" occurs when an individual engages in conduct that is not only prohibited but also constitutes a serious breach of community values; as such, it is perceived by Canadians as inherently wrong and deserving of punishment. Only the Parliament of Canada, using its criminal law power under the *Constitution Act*, 1867, may enact a "true crime." *p. 59*

Uniform Crime Reports (UCR)

Since 1962, Statistics Canada has published the Uniform Crime Reports based on a standardized set of procedures for collecting and reporting crime information. *p. 100*

validity

The extent to which a tool or instrument (questionnaire, experiment) actually measures the concept the researcher claims to be interested in and not something else. *p. 92*

value

A collective idea about what is right or wrong, good or bad, and desirable or undesirable in a particular culture. *p. 19*

victim fine surcharge

A monetary penalty similar to a fine, which can be assessed at sentence or added to a fine such as in a traffic violation, but can only be used by the government to fund services for victims. *p. 195*

victimization survey

A survey of a random sample of the population in which people are asked to recall and describe their own experience of being a victim of crime. *p. 110*

vory v zakone

A "thief in law." That is, a high-ranking, well-respected organized crime figure in the old Soviet underworld and the new Republic of Russia. Akin to the Italian Mafia. The code of the "Thieves World" emphasizes a rejection of government authority and traditional social norms. The "vor" pre-date the Soviet Union, but many were inmates interned in Soviet prison camps who organized themselves in an attempt to rule the criminal underworld. *p. 441*

white-collar crime

Crime that is committed by people in the course of their legitimate business activities. *ALSO*: Sutherland defined white-collar crime "as a crime committed by a person of respectability and high social status in the course of his occupation." *pp. 15, 466*

BIBLIOGRAPHY

CHAPTER 1

Akman, D.D., A. Normandeau, and S. Turner. 1967. "The Measurement of Delinquency in Canada." *Journal of Criminal Law, Criminology and Police Science* 58: 330–37.

Alberici, E. 2007. "What Causes People to Become Multiple Killers?" Australian Broadcasting Corporation. Web.

Beirne, Piers, and Nigel South. 2007. *Issues in Green Criminology: Confronting Harms against Environments, Humanity, and Other Animals.* Portland: Willan.

Bennett, Colin, Kevin Haggerty, David Lyon, and Valerie Steeves. 2014. *Transparent Lives: Surveillance in Canada.* Edmonton: Athabasca University Press.

Black, Conrad. 1993. *A Life in Progress.* Toronto: Key Porter.

Brayne, Sarah. 2014. "Surveillance and System Avoidance: Criminal Justice Contact and Institutional Attachment." *American Sociological Review* 79: 367–91.

Carter, Sarah. 1990. *Lost Harvests.* Montreal and Kingston: McGill–Queen's University Press.

Christakis, Dimitri, Michelle Garrison, Todd Herrenkohl, Kevin Haggerty, Frederick Rivara, Chuan Zhou, and Kimberley Liekweg. 2013. "Modifying Media Content for Preschool Children: A Randomized Control Trial." *Pediatrics* 131: 431–38.

Commission of Inquiry into the Actions of Canadian Officials in Relation to Maher Arar. 2006. *Report of the Events Relating to Maher Arar: Analysis and Recommendations.* Ottawa.

CSIA (Canadian Sportfishing Industry Association). 2007. "Federal Animal Cruelty Legislation." Web.

Doolittle, Robyn. 2017. "The Unfounded Effect." 2017. *Globe and Mail,* 8 February. Web.

Dowler, Ken, Thomas Fleming, and Stephen Muzzatti. 2006. "Constructing Crime: Media, Crime, and Popular Culture." *Canadian Journal of Criminology and Criminal Justice* 48: 837–50.

Ericson, Richard. 2007. *Crime in an Insecure World.* Cambridge: Polity Press.

Fernandez, Manny, Julie Turkewitz, and Jess Bidgood. 2018. "For 'Columbiners,' School Shootings Have a Deadly Allure." *New York Times,* 30 May. Web.

Fisher, Max, and Amanda Taub. 2017. "Manhattan Attack Is Called Terrorism. What About Vegas?" *New York Times,* 1 November. Web.

Frank, Russell. 2018. "The Media Need to Think Twice about How They Portray Mass Shooters." *The Conversation,* 16 February. Web.

Gabor, Thomas. 1994. *Everybody Does It: Crime by the Public.* Toronto: University of Toronto Press.

Ganor, Boas. 2002. "Defining Terrorism: Is One Man's Terrorist Another Man's Freedom Fighter?" *Police Practice and Research* 3: 287–304.

Gibbs, Carole, Meredith Gore, Edmund McGarrell, and Louie Rivers III. 2010. "Introducing Conservation Criminology: Towards Interdisciplinary Scholarship on Environmental Crimes and Risks." *British Journal of Criminology* 50: 124–44.

Greenland, Jacob, and Sarah Alam. 2017. *Police Resources in Canada, 2016.* Ottawa: Statistics Canada. Web.

Hagan, John. 1985. *Modern Criminology: Crime, Criminal Behaviour, and Its Control.* New York: McGraw-Hill.

Haskins, George Lee. 1969. "A Rule to Walk By." In *Crime and Justice in Society,* ed. Richard Quinney. 33–54. Boston: Little, Brown.

Henry, Stuart, and Mark Lanier. 1998. "The Prism of Crime: Arguments for an Integrated Definition of Crime." *Justice Quarterly* 15: 609–27.

Hugill, David. 2010. *Missing Women, Missing News: Covering Crisis in Vancouver's Downtown Eastside.* Halifax and Winnipeg: Fernwood.

Jouvenal, Justin. 2018. "To Find Alleged Golden State Killer, Investigators First Found His Great-Great-Great-Grandparents." *Washington Post,* 30 April. Web.

Kellett, Anthony. 2004. "Terrorism in Canada: 1960–1992." In *Violence in Canada: Sociopolitical Perspectives,* 2nd ed., ed. Jeffrey Ian Ross. 284–312. New Brunswick: Transaction Press.

Knoll, James. 2010. "The 'Pseudocommando' Mass Murderer: Part II, The Language of Revenge." *Journal of the American Academy of Psychiatry and the Law Online* 38: 263–72. Web.

LaFree, Gary, Michael Jensen, Patrick James, and Aaron Safer-Lichtenstein. 2018. "Correlates of Violent Political Extremism in the United States." *Criminology* 56: 233–68.

Leeder, Jessica. 2017. "Review of Sex-Assault Cases in New Brunswick Reveals Hundreds Were Misclassified as Unfounded." *Globe and Mail,* 21 February. Web.

Lynch, Michael J., and Paul Stretesky. "Green Criminology in the United States." In *Issues in Green Criminology: Confronting Harms Against Environments, Humanity, and Other Animals,* ed. Piers Beirne and Nigel South. 248–69. Portland: Willan.

Marin, Stephanie. 2018. "Quebec Mosque Shooter Alexandre Bissonnette Harboured Violent, Hostile Thoughts for Years: Psychologist." *Globe and Mail*, 23 April. Web.

McKeon, Lauren. 2017. "The Suicide Bomber Next Door." *Toronto Life*, 19 January. Web.

McIntyre, Mike. 2003. *Nowhere to Run: The Killing of Constable Dennis Strongquill*. Winnipeg: Great Plains.

———. 2017. "Face to Face with his Father's Killer." *Winnipeg Free Press*, 4 July. Web.

McNish, Jacquie, and Sinclair Stewart. 2004. *Wrong Way: The Fall of Conrad Black*. Toronto: Viking Canada.

Murphy, Christopher. 2007. "'Securitizing' Canadian Policing: A New Paradigm for the Post 9/11 Security State?" *Canadian Journal of Sociology* 32: 449–75.

Murray, Jane Lothian, Rick Linden, and Diana Kendall. 2011. *Sociology in Our Times*, 5th ed. Toronto: Nelson Education.

Normandeau, Andre. 1966. "The Measurement of Delinquency in Montreal." *Journal of Criminal Law, Criminology, and Police Science* 57: 172–77.

O'Connor, The Honourable Dennis R. 2002. *Report of the Walkerton Inquiry*, Part 1: *Summary*. Toronto: Queen's Printer.

Plotz, David. 2001. "Conrad Black." *Slate*, 31 August.

Rodgers, R.S. 1962. *Sex and Law in Canada: Text, Cases, and Comment*. Ottawa: Policy Press.

Schwendinger, Herman, and Julia Schwendinger. 1970. "Defenders of Order or Guardians of Human Rights." *Issues in Criminology* 5: 123–57.

Senate Committee on Legal and Constitutional Affairs. 2006. "Evidence." 4 December. Ottawa.

Shephard, Michelle. 2016. "What to Do about the Next Aaron Driver". *Toronto Star*, 21 August. Web.

Shuqin, Yang. 2010. "The Polluting Behaviour of the Multinational Corporations in China." In *Global Environmental Harm: Criminological Perspectives*, ed. Rob White. 150–58. Cullompton: Willan.

Smandych, Russell, and Rodney Kueneman. 2010. "The Canadian–Alberta Tar Sands: A Case Study of State–Corporate Environmental Crime." In *Global Environmental Harm: Criminological Perspectives*, ed. Rob White. 87–109. Cullompton: Willan.

South, Nigel. 2010. "The Ecocidal Tendencies of Late Modernity." In *Global Environmental Harm: Criminological Perspectives*, ed. Rob White. 228–47. Cullompton: Willan.

Staples, David. 2002. "Fearless, Painless, Senseless: The Sand Brothers." *Edmonton Journal*, 31 March, D1.

Statistics Canada. 2017. "Canadian Cannabis Survey—Summary." Ottawa. Web.

Sutherland, Edwin. 1940. "White-Collar Criminality." *American Sociological Review* 5: 1–12.

Sutherland, Edwin, and Donald Cressey. 1960. *Principles of Criminology*, 6th ed. Philadelphia: J.B. Lippincott.

Towers, Sherry, Andres Gomez-Lievano, Maryam Khan, Anuj Mubayi, and Carlos Castillo-Chavez. 2015. "Contagion in Mass Killings and School Shootings." *PLOS One*. https://doi.org/10.1371/journal.pone.0117259

Turk, Austin. 2004. "Sociology of Terrorism." *Annual Review of Sociology* 30: 271–86.

White, Rob. 2007. "Green Criminology and the Pursuit of Social and Ecological Justice." In *Issues in Green Criminology: Confronting Harms against Environments, Humanity, and Other Animals*, ed. Piers Beirne and Nigel South. 32–54. Portland: Willan.

———. 2011. *Transnational Environmental Crime*. Routledge: London.

Woods, Allan. 2015a. "A Canadian Supporter of Islamic State in His Own Words." *Toronto Star*, 20 February. Web.

———. 2015b. "Young Canadian's Conversion to Radical Islam Leaves Family Devastated." *Toronto Star*, 8 March. Web.

———. 2016. "I First Spoke to Aaron Driver in February, 2015." *Toronto Star*, 11 August. Web.

Wortley, Scot. 2009. "Introduction: The Immigration–Crime Connection: Competing Theoretical Perspectives." *Journal of International Migration and Integration* 10, no. 4: 349–58.

CHAPTER 2

Becker, Howard. 1963. "Moral Entrepreneurs." In *The Outsiders*, ed. Becker. New York: Free Press.

Braithwaite, John, and S. Mugford. 1994. "Conditions of Successful Reintegration Ceremonies." *British Journal of Criminology* 34, no. 2: 139–71.

Brodeur, Paul. 1985. *Outrageous Misconduct: The Asbestos Industry on Trial*. New York: Pantheon Books.

Broswimmer, Franz. 2002. *Ecocide: A Short History of the Mass Extinction of Species*. London: Pluto Press.

Brownmiller, Susan. 1975. *Against Our Will: Men, Women, and Rape*. New York: Simon and Schuster.

Carroll, Stephen J., Deborah Hensler, Allan Abrahamse, Jennifer Gross, Michelle White, Scott Ashwood, and Elizabeth Sloss. 2002. "Asbestos Litigation Costs and Compensation: An Interim Report." Santa Monica: RAND Corporation, DB-397-ICJ. Web.

Carroll, Stephen J., Deborah R. Hensler, Jennifer Gross, Elizabeth M. Sloss, Matthias Schonlau, Allan Abrahamse, and J. Scott Ashwood. 2005. "Asbestos Litigation Costs, Compensation, and Alternatives. Research Brief." Santa Monica: RAND Corporation, RB-9155-ICJ. Web.

Chambliss, William. 1969. "The Law of Vagrancy." In *Crime and the Legal Process*, ed. Chambliss. 51–63. New York: McGraw-Hill.

Clark, Lorenne, and Debra Lewis. 1977. *Rape: The Price of Coercive Sexuality*. Toronto: Women's Press.

Colson, Elizabeth. 1974. *Tradition and Contract: The Problem of Order.* Chicago: Aldine.

Comack, Elizabeth. 1985. "The Origins of Canadian Drug Legislation: Labelling versus Class Analysis." In *The New Criminologies in Canada: State, Crime and Control*, ed. Thomas Fleming. 65–86. Toronto: Oxford University Press.

Dowie, Mark. 1977. "Pinto Madness." *Mother Jones*, September–October.

Graham, James. 1976. "Amphetamine Politics on Capital Hill." In *Whose Law, What Order?*, ed. William Chambliss. 107–22.New York: Wiley.

Gray, Barbara, and Pat Lauderdale. 2007. "The Great Circle of Justice: North American Indigenous Justice and Contemporary Restoration Programs." *Contemporary Justice Review* 10, no. 2 (June): 215–25.

Grossman, Richard L., and Frank T. Adams. 1993. *Taking Care of Business: Citizenship and the Charter of Incorporation*. Web.

Gulliver, P.H. 1979. *Disputes and Negotiations: A Cross-Cultural Perspective.* New York: Academic Press.

Hall, Jerome. 1952. *Theft, Law, and Society*, 2nd ed. Indianapolis: Bobbs-Merrill.

———. 1969a. "Theft, Law, and Society: The Carrier's Case." In *Crime and the Legal Process*, ed. William Chambliss. 32–51. New York: McGraw-Hill.

———. 1969b. "Crime and the Commercial Revolution." In *Delinquency, Crime, and Social Process*, ed. Donald Cressey and David Ward.100–10. New York: Harper and Row.

Hoebel, E. Adamson. 1973. *The Law of Primitive Man*. New York: Atheneum.

Jeffery, Clarence Ray. 1969. "The Development of Crime in Early English Society." In *Crime and the Legal Process*, ed. William Chambliss.New York: McGraw-Hill.

Johnstone, Gerry. 2002. *Restorative Justice: Ideas, Values, Debates*. Oregon: Willan Publishing

Kinnon, Dianne. 1981. *Report on Sexual Assault in Canada*. Report to the Canadian Advisory Council on the Status of Women. Ottawa.

Lenski, Gerhard. 1966. *Power and Privilege: A Theory of Social Stratification*. New York: McGraw-Hill.

Marchak, Patricia. 1991. *The Integrated Circus: The New Right and the Restructuring of Global Markets*. Montreal and Kingston: McGill–Queen's. University Press.

Miliband, Ralph. 1969. *The State in Capitalist Society*. London: Quarter Books.

Newman, Katherine. 1983. *Law and Economic Organization: A Comparative Study of Preindustrial Societies*. London: Cambridge University Press.

Oxfam International. 2014."Working for the Few: Political Capture and Economic Inequality." Web.

Reasons, Charles, Lois Ross, and Craig Paterson. 1981. *Assault on the Worker*. Toronto: Butterworths.

Ross, Rupert. 1989. "Leaving Our White Eyes Behind: The Sentencing of Native Accused." 3 *Canadian Native Law Reporter* 1 at 4.

Small, Shirley. 1978. "Canadian Narcotics Legislation, 1908–1923: A Conflict Model Interpretation." In *Law and Social Control in Canada*, ed. W. Greenaway and S. Brickey. 28–42. Scarborough: Prentice Hall.

Snider, Laureen. 1999. "Relocating Law: Making Corporate Crime Disappear." In *Locating Law: Race, Class/Gender Connections*, ed. Elizabeth Comack. Halifax: Fernwood Publishing.

Snider, Laureen. 2000. "The Sociology of Corporate Crime: An Obituary." *Theoretical Criminology* 4, no. 2: 169–206.

Thompson, Edward P. 1976. *Whigs and Hunters: The Origin of the Black Act*. New York: Pantheon.

Tigar, Michael, and Madeleine Levy. 1977. *Law and the Rise of Capitalism*. New York: Monthly Review Press.

Tompa, Emile, Christina Kalcevich, Chris McLeod, Martin Lebeau, Chaojie Song, Kim McLeod, Joanne Kim, Paul Demers. 2017. "The Economic Burden of Lung Cancer and Mesothelioma Due to Occupational and Para-Occupational Asbestos Exposure." *Journal of Occupational and Environmental Medicine* 74. http://dx.doi.org/10.1136/oemed-2016-104173

Tonnies, Ferdinand. [1887]1957. *Community and Society*. Newton Abbot: Courier Dover.

Weitekamp, Elmar G.M. 2002. "Restorative Justice: Present Prospects and Future Directions." In *Restorative Justice: Theoretical Foundations*, ed. Elmar G.M. Weitekamp and Hans-Jürgen Kerner. Portland: Willan.

WHO. 2010. "Asbestos: Elimination of Asbestos-Related Diseases." Fact sheet no. 343. Web.

CHAPTER 3

Canada (Attorney General) v. Bedford, [2013] 3 SCR 1101. Online at: http://www.canlii.org/en/ca/scc/doc/2013/2013scc72/2013scc72.html

Carter v. Canada (Attorney General), [2015] 1 SCR 331. Available at: http://canlii.ca/t/gg5z4

Reference re Assisted Human Reproduction Act, [2010] 3 S.C.R. 457. Available at R. v. Beatty, [2008] 1 S.C.R. 49. Available at http://www.canlii.org/en/ca/scc/doc/2008/2008scc5/2008scc5.html

R. v. Bouchard-Lebrun, [2011] 3 S.C.R. 575. Available at http://www.canlii.org/en/ca/scc/doc/2011/2011scc58/2011scc58.html

R. v. Boudreault, [2012] 3 SCR 157. Available at: http://www.canlii.org/en/ca/scc/doc/2012/2012scc56/2012scc56.html

R. v. Briscoe, [2010] 1 S.C.R. 411. Available at http://www.canlii.org/en/ca/scc/doc/2010/2010scc13/2010scc13.html

R. v. Chaulk, [1990] 3 S.C.R. 1303. Available at http://canlii.org/en/ca/scc/doc/1990/1990canlii34/1990canlii34.html

R. v. Crangle (2010), 256 C.C.C. (3d) 254 (Ont.C.A). Available at http://www.canlii.org/en/on/onca/doc/2010/2010onca451/2010onca451.html

R. v. Creighton, [1993] 3 S.C.R. 3. Available at http://canlii.org/en/ca/scc/doc/1993/1993canlii61/1993canlii61.html

R. v. Cuerrier, [1998] 2 S.C.R. 371

R. v. Gauthie, [2013] 2 SCR 403. Available at http://www.canlii.org/en/ca/scc/doc/2013/2013scc32/2013scc32.html

R. v. Hamilton, [2005] 2 S.C.R. 432. Available at http://www.canlii.org/en/ca/scc/doc/2005/2005scc47/2005scc47.html

R. v. Hibbert, [1995] 2 S.C.R. 973. Available at http://www.canlii.org/en/ca/scc/doc/1995/1995canlii110/1995canlii110.html

R. v. Hutchinson, [2014] 1 SCR 346. Available at: http://canlii.ca/t/g62cv

R. v. Hydro-Québec, [1997] 3 S.C.R. 213. Available at http://canlii.org/en/ca/scc/doc/1997/1997canlii318/1997canlii318.html

R. v. Landry, [1991] 1 SCR 99. Available at http://www.canlii.org/en/ca/scc/doc/1991/1991canlii114/1991canlii114.html

R. v. Lavallee, [1990] 1 S.C.R. 852. Available at http://canlii.org/en/ca/scc/doc/1990/1990canlii95/1990canlii95.html

R. v. Mabior, [2012] 2 SCR 584. Available at: http://www.canlii.org/en/ca/scc/doc/2012/2012scc47/2012scc47.html

R. v. Malott, [1998] 1 S.C.R. 123. Available at http://www.canlii.org/en/ca/scc/doc/1998/1998canlii845/1998canlii845.html

R. v. Martineau, [1990] 2 S.C.R. 633. Available at http://canlii.org/en/ca/scc/doc/1990/1990canlii80/1990canlii80.html

R. v. Molodowic, [2000] 1 S.C.R. 420. Available at http://www.canlii.org/en/ca/scc/doc/2000/2000scc16/2000scc16.html

R. v. Olan, Hudson and Hartnett, [1978] 2 S.C.R. 1175. Available at http://canlii.org/en/ca/scc/doc/1978/1978canlii9/1978canlii9.html

R. v. Pappas, [2013] 3 S.C.R. 452. Available at http://canlii.ca/t/g1m5q

R. v. Perka, [1984] 2 S.C.R. 232. Available at http://canlii.org/en/ca/scc/doc/1984/1984canlii23/1984canlii23.html

R. v. Pickton, [2010] 2 S.C.R. 198. Available at http://canlii.org/en/ca/scc/doc/2010/2010scc32/2010scc32.html

R. v. Roy, [2012] 2 SCR 60. Available at: http://www.canlii.org/en/ca/scc/doc/2012/2012scc26/2012scc26.html

R. v. Ruzic, [2001] 1 S.C.R. 687. Available at http://www.canlii.org/en/ca/scc/doc/2001/2001scc24/2001scc24.html

R. v. Ryan, [2013] 1 SCR 14. Available at http://www.canlii.org/en/ca/scc/doc/2013/2013scc3/2013scc3.html

R. v. Schoenborn, 2017 BCSC 1556

R. v. Sharpe, [2001] 1 S.C.R. 45. Available at http://canlii.org/en/ca/scc/doc/2001/2001scc2/2001scc2.html

R. v. Stone, [1999] 2 S.C.R. 290. Available at http://canlii.org/en/ca/scc/doc/1999/1999canlii688/1999canlii688.html

R. v. Théroux, [1993] 2 S.C.R. 5. Available at http://canlii.org/en/ca/scc/doc/1993/1993canlii134/1993canlii134.html

R. v. Tran, [2010] 3 SCR 350. Available at http://www.canlii.org/en/ca/scc/doc/2010/2010scc58/2010scc58.html

R. v. Wholesale Travel Group Inc., [1991] 3 S.C.R. 154. Available at http://canlii.org/en/ca/scc/doc/1991/1991canlii39/1991canlii39.html

Rodriguez v. British Columbia (Attorney-General), [1993] 3 SCR 519. Available at: http://www.canlii.org/en/ca/scc/doc/1993/1993canlii75/1993canlii75.html

Winko v. British Columbia (Forensic Psychiatric Institute), [1999] 2 S.C.R. 625. Available at http://canlii.org/en/ca/scc/doc/1999/1999canlii694/1999canlii694.html

CHAPTER 4

Allen, Mary. 2018. "Police-Reported Crime Statistics, 2017." *Juristat*. Ottawa: Statistics Canada.

Bass, Gary. 2015. Presentation to International Association of Financial Crime Investigators. Burnaby: Simon Fraser University.

Boak, A., H.A. Hamilton, E.M. Adluf, and R.E. Mann. 2013. "Drug Use among Ontario Students, 1999–2013." CAMH Document Series no. 36. Toronto: Centre for Addiction and Mental Health.

Bureau of Justice Statistics. 2016. "Correctional Populations in the United States, 2015." Web.

Caneppele, Stefano, and Marcelo Aebi. 2017. "Crime Drop or Police Recording Flop? On the Relationship between the Decrease of Offline Crime and the Increase of Online and Hybrid Crimes." *Policing: A Journal of Policy and Practice*: 1–14.

Catlin, G., and S. Murray. 1979. "Report on Canadian Victimization Survey Methodological Pretests." Ottawa: Statistics Canada.

Chicago Magazine. 2014. "The Truth about Chicago's Crime Rates." May.

Dauvergne, M., and J. Turner. 2010. "Police-Reported Crime Statistics in Canada, 2009." Juristat 30, no. 2. Web.

de Silva, S., and R.A. Silverman. 1985. "New Approaches to Uniform Crime Reporting in Canada." Paper presented at the annual meeting of the American Society of Criminology, San Diego, November.

Doolittle, Robyn. 2017 "The Unfounded Effect." 2017. *Globe and Mail*, 8 February. Web.

Engstad, Peter, and John L. Evans. 1980. "Responsibility, Competence, and Police Effectiveness in Crime Control." In *Effectiveness of Policing*, ed. R.V.G. Clarke and J.M. Hough. Aldershot: Ashgate.

Evans, J., and G. Leger. 1978. "The Development of Victimization Surveys in Canada." *Public Data Use* 6 (November).

Fréchette, M., and Marc LeBlanc. 1979. "La délinquance cachée à l'adolescence." *Inadaptation juvénile* 1. Montréal: Université de Montréal.

———. 1980. "Pour une pratique de la criminologie: configurations de conduites délinquantes et portraits de délinquants." *Inadaptation juvénile* 5. Montréal: Université de Montréal.

Greenland, Jacob, and Adam Cotter. 2018. "Unfounded Criminal Incidents in Canada, 2017." *Juristat*. Ottawa: Statistics Canada.

Hindelang, M.J., T. Hirschi, and J.G. Weis. 1981. *Measuring Delinquency*. Beverly Hills: Sage.

Hirschi, Travis. 1969. *Causes of Delinquency*. Berkeley: University of California Press.

Keighley, Kathryn. 2017. "Police-Reported Crime Statistics in Canada," 2016. Ottawa: Canadian Centre for Justice Statistics.

"LAPD Misclassified Nearly 1,200 Violent Crimes as Minor Offenses." *Los Angeles Times*, 9 August 2014.

Leeder, Jessica. 2017. "Review of Sex-Assault Cases in New Brunswick Reveals Hundreds Were Misclassified as Unfounded." *Globe and Mail*, 21 February. Web.

Nettler, G. 1974. *Explaining Crime*. New York: McGraw-Hill.

Office for National Statistics. 2017. "Crime in England and Wales: Year Ending September, 2017." London: Office for National Statistics.

Perreault, Samuel, and Shannon Brennan. 2010. "Criminal Victimization in Canada, 2009." *Juristat* 30, no. 2. Web.

Piquero, Alex, Carol A. Schubert, and Robert Brame. 2014. "Comparing Official and Self-Report Records of Offending across Gender and Race/Ethnicity in a Longitudinal Study of Serious Youthful Offenders." *Journal of Research in Crime and Delinquency* 51: 526–56.

Polsky, Ned. 1967. *Hustlers, Beats, and Others*. Chicago: Aldine.

Savoie, J. 2006. "Youth Self-Reported Delinquency, Toronto, 2006." *Juristat* 27, no. 6. Web.

Shearing, Clifford D. 1984. "Dial-A-Cop: A Study of Police Mobilization." Report for the Centre of Criminology, University of Toronto.

Silverman, R.A. 1980. "Measuring Crime: More Problems." *Journal of Police Science and Administration* 8, no. 3: 265–74.

Silverman, R.A., and J. Teevan. 1975. *Crime in Canadian Society*. Toronto: Butterworths.

Skogan, W. 1978. "Review of Surveying Crime." *Journal of Criminal Law and Criminology* 69: 139–40.

———. 1981. "Issues in the Measurement of Victimization." Washington: US Department of Justice, Bureau of Justice Statistics.

Statistics Canada. 2003. "Canadian Crime Statistics." Ottawa: Canadian Centre for Justice Statistics, Chapter 6. Cat. no. 85-205-XIE.

———. 2010. *Uniform Crime Reporting Survey (UCR)*. Ottawa: Statistics Canada.

Thornberry, Terence P., and Marvin D. Krohn. 2000. "The Self-Report Method for Measuring Delinquency and Crime." *Criminal Justice 2000* 4. Washington: National Institute of Justice.

UK Statistical Authority. 2014. "Assessment of Compliance with the Code of Practice for Official Statistics, Statistics on Crime in England and Wales." London: Office for National Statistics.

US Bureau of Justice Statistics. 2012. *Prison Statistics*. Washington: Department of Justice. Web.

———. 2015. "Correctional Populations in the United States, 2015." Web.

CHAPTER 5

Aaltonen, Mikko, Janne Kivivuori, Pekka Martikainen, and Venla Salmi. 2012. "Socio-Economic Status and Criminality as Predictors of Male Violence: Does Victim's Gender or Place of Occurrence Matter?" *British Journal of Criminology* 52: 1192–211.

Aaltonen, Mikko, John MacDonald, Pekka Martikainen, and Janne Kivivuori. 2013. "Examining the Generality of the Unemployment–Crime Association." *Criminology* 51, no. 3: 561–94.

Abramsky, T., C. Watts, C. Garcia-Moreno, K. Devries, L. Kriss, M. Ellsberg, H. Jansen, and L. Heise.

2011. "What Factors Are Associated with Recent Intimate Partner Violence? Findings from the WHO Multi-Country Study on Women's Health and Domestic Violence." *BMC Public Health* 11: 1–17.

Agozino, B. 2003. *Counter-Colonial Criminology: A Critique of Imperialist Reasoning*. London: Pluto Press.

Allen, Mary K., and Superle, Tamy. 2016. "Youth Crime in Canada, 2014." *Juristat*, http://www.statcan.gc.ca/pub/85-002-x/2016001/article/14309-eng.htm#a15.

Anderson, Elijah. 1999. *Code of the Street: Decency, Violence, and the Moral Life of the Inner City*. New York: W.W. Norton.

Ansara, Donna, and Michelle Hindin. 2010. "Exploring Gender Differences in the Patterns of Intimate Partner Violence in Canada: A Latent Class Approach." *Journal of Epidemiology and Community Health* 64: 849–54.

Anthias, F. 1998. "Rethinking Social Divisions: Some Notes towards a Theoretical Framework." *Sociological Review* 46, no. 3: 505–35.

APA (American Psychological Association). 2014. "Socioeconomic Status." http://www.apa.org/topics/socioeconomic-status.

Arnavites, T., and R. Davina. 2006. "Business Cycles and Street Crime." *Criminology* 44: 139–64.

Barrett, Jessica. 2013. "Covert Racism behind Increased Numbers of Aboriginals and Other Visible Minorities in Prisons, Watchdog Says." Web.

Boritch, H., and J. Hagan. 1987. "Crime and the Changing Forms of Class Control: Policing Public Order in 'Toronto the Good,' 1859–1955." *Social Forces* 66: 307–35.

Boyce, Jillian, and Adam Cotter. 2013. "Homicide in Canada, 2012." Centre for Canadian Justice Statistics. Web.

British Columbia Vital Statistics Agency. 2005. "Selected Vital Statistics and Health Status Indicators." Annual Report 2005. Web.

British Columbia Coroners Service. 2018. "Fentanyl-Detected Illicit Drug Overdose Deaths, January 1, 2012, to December 31, 2017." Web.

Brownridge, Douglas A. 2010. "Intimate Partner Violence against Aboriginal Men in Canada." *Australian and New Zealand Journal of Criminology* 43, no. 2: 223–37.

Buxton, Jane A., Andrew W. Tu, and Tim Stockwell. 2009. "Tracking Trends in Alcohol, Illicit Drugs, and Tobacco Through Morbidity Data." *Contemporary Drug Problems* 36: 485–97.

Canadian Tobacco, Alcohol and Drugs Survey (CTADS). 2015. Table 14. https://www.canada.ca/en/health-canada/services/canadian-tobacco-alcohol-drugs-survey/2015-summary.html.

Cao, Liqun. 2011. "Visible Minorities and Confidence in the Police." *Canadian Journal of Criminology and Criminal Justice* 53, no. 1: 1–26.

Carlson, Kathryn B. 2013. "Mother 'Elated' as Ashley Smith's Jail Death Is Ruled a Homicide." *Globe and Mail.* 19 December. Web.

Charles, Grant, and Mike DeGagné. 2013. "Student-to-Student Abuse in the Indian Residential Schools in Canada: Setting the Stage for Further Understanding." *Child and Youth Services* 34, no. 4: 343–59.

Clark, Heather. 2009. "A Coordinated Approach to Student Drug Use Surveys in Canada." *Contemporary Drug Problems* 36: 409–25.

Clelland, D., and T.J. Carter. 1980. "The New Myth of Crime." *Criminology* 18, no. 3: 319–36.

Cohen, G.B., and R.J. Smith. 2010. "The Racial Geography of the Federal Death Penalty." *Washington Law Review* 85: 425–92.

Commission on Systemic Racism in the Ontario Criminal Justice System. 1995. *Report.* Toronto: Queen's Printer.

Cotter, David, Joan Hermsen, and Reeve Vaneman. 2011. "The End of Gender Revolution? Gender Role Attitudes from 1977–2008." *American Journal of Sociology* 117, no. 1: 259–89.

Daly, Kathleen. 1992. "Women's Pathway to Felony Court: Feminist Theories of Lawbreaking and Problems of Representation." *Southern California Review of Law and Women's Studies* 2: 11–52.

———. 1989. "Gender and Varieties of White Collar Crime." *Criminology* 27, no. 4: 769–94.

Dauvergne, Mia. 2009. "Trends in Police-Reported Serious Assaults." Web.

———. 2002. "Homicide in Canada, 2001." *Juristat* 22: 1–20.

David, Jean-Denis. 2017. "Homicide in Canada, 2016." Statistics Canada. Cat. no. 85-002-X ISSN 1209-6393.

Delgado, Richard, and Jean Stefancic. 2012. *Critical Race Theory: An Introduction.* New York: NYU Press.

de Souza, Elenice, and Joel Miller. 2012. "Homicide in the Brazilian Favela: Does Opportunity Make the Killer?" *British Journal of Criminology* 52, no. 4: 786–807.

Duff, Cameron, Warren Muchelow, Clifton Chow, Andrew Ivsins, and Tim Stockwell. 2009. "The Canadian Recreational Drug Use Survey: Aims, Methods and First Results." *Contemporary Drug Problems* 36: 517–39.

Dumont, J. 1993. "Justice and Aboriginal People." In *Report of the Royal Commission on Aboriginal Peoples and the Justice System*, 42–85. Ottawa: Supply and Services Canada.

Elias, Brenda, Javier Mignone, Madelyn Hall, Say P. Hong, Lyna Hart, and Jitender Sareen. 2012. "Trauma and Suicide Behaviour Histories among a Canadian Indigenous Population: An Empirical Exploration of the Potential Role of Canada's Residential School System." *Social Science and Medicine* 74, no. 10: 1560–69.

Fanon, F. 1963. *The Wretched of the Earth*, trans. Constance Farrington. New York: Grove Press.

———. 1967. *Black Skin, White Masks*, trans. C.L. Markmann. New York: Grove Press.

Fife, Robert, and Philip Ling. 2012. "Feds Studying Private Prisons as Way to Save Money." CTV News, 21 September. Web.

Fischer, Benedikt, Joseph Anthony De Leo, Christine Allard, Michelle Firestone-Cruz, Jayadeep Patra, and Jurgen Rehm. 2009. "Exploring Drug Sourcing Among Regular Prescription Opioid Users in Canada: Data from Toronto and Victoria." *Canadian Journal of Criminology and Criminal Justice* 51, no. 1: 55–72.

———. 2011. "Disproportionate Minority Contact: Police and Visible Minority Youth." *Canadian Journal of Criminology and Criminal Justice* 53: 449–86.

Francisco, Joycelyn, and Christian Chenier. 2007. "A Comparison of Large Urban, Small Urban, and Rural Crime Rates, 2005." *Juristat* 27, no. 3.

Freud, Sigmund. 1933. *New Introductory Lectures on Psychoanalysis.* New York: W.W. Norton.

Gabbidon, Shaun. 2010. *Race, Ethnicity, Crime, and Justice: An International Dilemma.* Los Angeles: Sage.

Gartner, Rosemary, Cheryl Marie Webster, and Anthony Doob. 2009. "Trends in the Imprisonment of Women in Canada." *Canadian Journal of Criminology and Criminal Justice* 51, no. 2: 169–98.

Gaylord, Mark, and John Galliher. 1988. *The Criminology of Edwin Sutherland.* New Brunswick: Transaction Books.

Goldstein, P.J. 1985. "The Drugs–Violence Nexus: A Tripartite Conceptual Framework." *Journal of Drug Issues* 15: 493–506.

Greenburg, D. 1979. "Delinquency and the Age Structure of Society." In *Criminology Review Yearbook*, ed. S.L. Messinger and E. Bittner. 586–620. Beverley Hills: Sage.

Greenberg, Hirch, Jana Grekul, and Rhonda Nelson. 2012. "Aboriginal Youth Crime in Canada." In *Youth at Risk and Youth Justice: A Canadian Overview*, ed. J. Winterdyk and R. Smandych. 228–44. Toronto: Oxford University Press.

Hagan, John. 1992. American Society of Criminology 1991 Presidential Address: "The Poverty of a Classless Criminology." *Criminology* 30, no. 1: 1–19.

Hagan, J., A.R. Gillis, and John Simpson. 1985. "The Class Structure of Gender and Delinquency: Toward a Power–Control Theory of Common Delinquent Behavior." *American Journal of Sociology* 90, no. 6: 1151–78.

———. 1987. "Class in the Household: A Power–Control Theory of Gender and Delinquency." *American Journal of Sociology* 92, no. 4: 788–816.

Hagan, John, and Fiona Kay. 1990. "Gender and Delinquency in White-Collar Families: A Power–Control Perspective. *Crime and Delinquency* 36: 391–407.

Hansen, K. 2003. "Education and the Crime-Age Profile. *British Journal of Criminology* 43: 141–68.

Hartnagel, Timothy F. 2012. "Correlates of Criminal Behaviour." In *Criminology: A Canadian Perspective*, 7th ed., ed. R. Linden. Toronto: Nelson Education.

Health Canada. 2014. "Canadian Alcohol and Drug Use Monitoring Survey: Summary of Results for 2012." Ottawa: Health Canada. Web.

Heimer, Karen, and Stacey De Coster. 1999. "The Gendering of Violent Delinquency." *Criminology* 37, no. 2: 277–318.

Henry, Frances, and Carol Tator. 2005. *The Colour of Democracy: Racism in Canadian Society*. Toronto: Nelson Education.

Henry, F., C. Tator, W. Mattis, and T. Rees. 2000. *The Colour of Democracy: Racism in Canadian Society*, 2nd ed. Toronto: Harcourt Brace Canada.

Hooghe, Marc, Bram Vanhoutte, Wim Hardyns, and Tuba Bircan. 2011. "Unemployment, Inequality, Poverty, and Crime: Spatial Distribution Patterns of Criminal Acts in Belgium, 2001–6." *British Journal of Criminology* 51, no. 1: 1–20.

Jackson, J., and B. Bradford. 2010. "What Is Trust and Confidence in the Police?" *Policing* 4, no. 3: 241–48.

Johnston, P. 1994. "Academic Approaches to Race—Race Statistics Do Not Justify Their Collection." *Canadian Journal of Criminology* 36: 166–73.

Keighley, Kathryn. 2017. "Police-Reported Crime Statistics in Canada, 2016." *Juristat*, Statistics Canada cat. no. 85-002-X.

Kelly, Nora, and William Kelly. 1973. *The Royal Canadian Mounted Police: A Century of History*, 1873–1973. Edmonton: Hurtig.

Kirk, David S. 2009. "A Natural Experiment on Residential Change and Recidivism: Lessons from Hurricane Katrina." *American Sociological Review* 74: 484–505.

———. 2012. "Residential Change as a Turning Point in the Life Course of Crime: Desistance or Temporary Cessation?" *Criminology* 50, no. 2: 329–58.

Kreager, Derek, Ross L. Matsueda, and Elena A. Erosheva. 2010. "Motherhood and Criminal Desistance in Disadvantaged Neighbourhoods." *Criminology* 48, no. 1: 221–58.

Kruttschnitt, Candace. 2013. "Gender and Crime." *Annual Review of Sociology* 39: 291–308.

Kubrin, Charis, and Eric Stewart. 2006. "Predicting Who Reoffends: The Neglected Role of Neighbourhood Context in Recidivism Studies." *Criminology* 44, no. 1: 165–97.

La Prairie, Carol. 2002. "Aboriginal Over-Representation in the Criminal Justice System: A Tale of Nine Cities." *Canadian Journal of Criminology* 44: 181–208.

Larson, Matthew, and Gary Sweeten. 2012. "Breaking Up Is Hard to Do: Romantic Dissolution, Offending, and Substance Use during the Transition to Adulthood." *Criminology* 50, no. 3: 605–36.

Laub, J., and R. Sampson. 2001. "Understanding Desistance from Crime." *Crime and Justice* 28: 1–69.

Lauritsen, Janet L., Karen Heimer, and James P. Lynch. 2009. "Trends in the Gender Gap in Violent Offending: New Evidence from the National Crime Victimization Survey." *Criminology* 47, no. 2: 361–99.

Levitt, S.D., and L. Lochner. 2000. "The Determinants of Juvenile Crime." In *Risky Behaviour by Youths*, ed. J. Gruber. Chicago: University of Chicago Press.

Li, G. 2008. "Homicide in Canada, 2007." *Juristat* 28: 1–26.

Lianping, Ti, Evan Wood, Kate Shannon, Cindy Feng, and Thomas Kerr. 2013. "Police Confrontations among Street-Involved Youth in a Canadian Setting." *International Journal of Drug Policy* 24: 46–51.

Lin, M.J. 2008. "Does Unemployment Increase Crime? Evidence from US Data 1974–2000." *Journal of Human Resources* 43: 413–36.

Lochner, L. 2004. "Education, Work, and Crime: A Human Capital Approach." *International Economic Review* 45: 811–43.

Lochner, L., and E. Moretti. 2004. "The Effects of Education on Crime: Evidence from Prison Inmates, Arrest, and Self-Reports." *American Economic Review* 94: 155–89.

Lofland, Lyn H. 1973. *A World of Strangers: Order and Action in Urban Public Space*. New York: Basic Books.

Lombroso, Caesar, and William Ferrero. 1895. *The Female Offender*. New York: D. Appleton and Company.

Ludwig, J., G.J. Duncan, and P. Hirschfield. 2001. "Urban Poverty and Juvenile Crime: Evidence from a Randomized Housing-Mobility Experiment." *Quarterly Journal of Economics* 116: 655–79.

Macdonald, Ryan, and Michelle Rotermann. 2017. "Experimental Estimates of Cannabis Consumption in Canada, 1960 to 2015." *Economic Insights*. Ottawa: Statistics Canada.

MacMillan, R., and R. Gartner. 1999. 'When She Brings Home the Bacon: Labor Force Participation and the Risk of Spousal Violence against

Women." *Journal of Marriage and Family* 61: 947–58.

MacMillan, R., and C. Kruttschnitt. 2005. *Patterns of Violence against Women: Risk Factors and Consequences.* Rockville: National Institute of Justice.

Mahony, T.H. 2011a. "Homicide in Canada, 2010." *Juristat.* Web.

———. 2011b. "Women and the Criminal Justice System." *Juristat.* Web.

Mahony, Tina H., Joanna Jacob, and Heather Hobson. "Women in Canada: A Gender-Based Statistical Report." *Women and the Criminal Justice System* (2017). http://www.statcan.gc.ca/pub/89-503-x/2015001/article/14785-eng.htm#a17.

Manzoni, Patrik, Benedikt Fischer, and Jurgen Rehm. 2007. "Local Drug-Crime Dynamics in a Canadian Multi-Site Sample of Untreated Opioid Users." *Canadian Journal of Criminology and Criminal Justice* 49: 341–73.

Mascoll, Philip, and Jim Rankin. 2005. "Racial Profiling Exists." *Toronto Star*, 31 March, A1.

Matza, D. 1964. *Delinquency and Drift.* New York: Wiley.

Maxwell, A. 2017. "Adult Criminal Court Statistics in Canada, 2014/2015." *Juristat.* Statistics Canada cat. no. 85-002-X.

Miles, R. 1989. *Racism.* London: Routledge.

Millar P., and A. Owusu-Benpah. 2011. "Whitewashing Criminal Justice in Canada: Preventing Research through Data Suppression." *Canadian Journal of Law and Society* 26, no. 3: 653–61.

Mirchandani, K., and W. Chan. 2002. "From Race and Crime to Racialization and Criminalization." In W. Chan, *Crimes of Colour: Racialization and the Criminal Justice System in Canada.* Peterborough: Broadview.

Moffitt, T., and A. Caspi. 1999. "Findings about Partner Violence from the Dunedin Multidisciplinary Health Development Study." National Institute of Justice, Research in Brief.

Washington, DC: US Department of Justice.

Munch, Christopher. 2012. "Youth Correctional Statistics in Canada, 2010–2011." *Juristat.* Ottawa: Statistics Canada. Web.

Myrdal, G. 1962. *An American Dilemma: The Negro Problem and Modern Democracy*, vol. 1. New York: Harper & Row.

———. 1963. *Challenge to Affluence.* New York: Pantheon.

National Immigration Forum. 2013. "The Math of Immigration Detention: Runaway Costs for Immigration Detention Do Not Add Up to Sensible Policy." Web.

Nivette, A. 2011. "Cross-National Predictors of Crime: A Meta-Analysis." *Homicide Studies* 15, no. 2: 103–31.

Nye, F. Ivan, and James F. Short. 1957. "Scaling Delinquent Behavior." *American Sociological Review* 22: 326–31.

Nye, F. Ivan, James F. Short, and Virgil Olson. 1958. "Socioeconomic Status and Delinquent Behavior." *American Sociological Review* 63: 381–89.

Office of the Correctional Investigator. 2012. "Spirit Matters: Aboriginal People and the Corrections and Conditional Release Act." Web.

———. 2017. *Annual Report.* Cat. no.: PS100. Web.

Owusu-Benpah, A., and P. Millar. 2010. "Revisiting the Collection of 'Justice Statistics by Race' in Canada." *Canadian Journal of Law and Society* 25, no. 1: 97–104.

Pederson, Jeanette S., Lorraine H. Malcoe, and Jane Pulkingham. 2013. "Explaining Aboriginal/Non-Aboriginal Inequalities in Postseparation Violence against Canadian Women: Application of Structural Violence Approach." *Violence Against Women* 19, no. 8: 1034–58.

Pernanen, K., M.M. Cousineau, S. Brochu, and F Sun. 2002. "Proportions of Crimes Associated with Alcohol and Other Drugs in

Canada." Ottawa: Canadian Centre on Substance Abuse.

Perreault, Samuel. 2013. "Police-Reported Crime Statistics in Canada, 2012." *Juristat.* Web.

———. 2014. "Admissions to Adult Correctional Services in Canada, 2011/2012." *Juristat.* Web.

Peterson, Ruth. 2012. "The Central Place of Race in Crime and Justice—the American Society of Criminology's 2011 Sutherland Address." *Criminology* 50, no. 2: 303–27.

Peterson, Ruth, and Lauren J. Krivo. 2010. *Divergent Social Worlds: Neighborhood Crime and the Racial–Spatial Divide.* New York: Russell Sage Foundation.

Pollak, Otto. 1950. *The Criminality of Women.* Philadelphia: University of Pennsylvania Press.

Pridemore, William Alex. 2011. "Poverty Matters: A Reassessment of the Inequality–Homicide Relationship in Cross-National Studies." *British Journal of Criminology* 51, no. 5: 739–72.

Public Safety Canada. 2014. "Substance Abuse." https://www.publicsafety.gc.ca/cnt/cntrng-crm/crrctns/sbstnc-bs-en.aspx. Accessed 15 July, 2018.

Rand, Julia. 2011. "Residential Schools: Creating and Continuing Institutionalization among Aboriginal Peoples in Canada." *First Peoples' Child and Family Review* 6, no. 1: 56–65.

Rehm, Jurgen, and Robin Room. 2009. "Monitoring of Alcohol Use and Attributable Harm from an International Perspective." *Contemporary Drug Problems* 36: 575–87.

Reitano, Julie. 2017. "Adult Correctional Statistics in Canada, 2015/2016." Ottawa: Statistics Canada. Web.

Rennison, C.M. 2009. "A New Look at the Gender Gap in Offending." *Women and Criminal Justice* 19: 171–90.

Roberts, J. 1994. "Crime and Race Statistics: Toward a Canadian Solution." *Canadian Journal of Criminology* 36: 175–85.

Sabates, Ricardo. 2007. "Education and Juvenile Crime: Understanding the Links and Measuring the Effects." In *Youths and Social Capital*, ed. J. Bynner and H. Helve. London: Tufnell.

———. 2008. "Educational Attainment and Juvenile Crime." *British Journal of Criminology* 48: 395–409.

Sacks, H. 1972. "Notes on Police Assessment of Moral Character." In *Studies in Social Interaction*, ed. D. Sudnow. New York: Free Press.

Salvatore, Christopher, and Michael W. Markowitz. 2014. "Do Life Course Transitions and Social Bonds Influence Male and Female Offending Differently? Gender Contrasts and Criminality." *Deviant Behavior* 35: 628–53.

Sampson, R.J. 2012. "Moving and the Neighborhood Glass Ceiling." *Science* 337: 1464–65.

Sampson, R.J., Stephen Raudenbush, and Felton Earls. 1997. "Neighborhoods and Violent Crime: A Multilevel Study of Collective Efficacy." *Science* 277: 918–24.

Sampson, Robert, and John Laub. 2005. "A Life Course View of the Development of Crime." *Annals of the American Academy of Political and Social Science* 602: 12–45.

Schaefer, David, Nancy Rodriguez, and Scotte H. Decker. 2014. "The Role of Neighbourhood Context in Youth Co-offending." *Criminology* 52, no. 1: 117–39.

Schneider, Stephen. 2013. "Violence, Organized Crime, and Illicit Drug Markets: A Canadian Case Study." *Sociologia* 71: 125–43.

Sharkey, Patrick, and Robert J. Sampson. 2010. "Destination Effects: Residential Mobility and Trajectories of Adolescent Violence in Stratified Metropolis." *Criminology* 48: 639–82.

Shedd, C., and J. Hagan. 2006. "Toward a Developmental and Comparative Conflict Theory of Race, Ethnicity, and Perceptions of Criminal Injustice." In *The Many Colors of Crime*, ed. R.D. Peterson, L.J. Krivo,

and J. Hagan, 313–33. New York: NYU Press.

Silver, A. 1967. "The Demand for Order in Civil Society: A Review of Some Themes in the History of Urban Crime, Police, and Riot." In *The Police: Six Sociological Essays*, ed. David J. Bordua. New York: Wiley.

Simon, Rita. 1975. *Women and Crime*. Lexington: D.C. Heath.

Skardhamar, Torbjørn, and Jukka Savolainen. 2014. "Changes in Criminal Offending around the Time of Job Entry: A Study of Employment and Desistance." *Criminology* 52, no. 2: 263–91.

Sprott J.B., and A.N. Doob. 2014. "Confidence in the Police: Variation across Groups Classified as Visible Minorities." *Canadian Journal of Criminology and Criminal Justice* 56, no. 3: 367–78.

———. 2017a. "Table 253-0003—Homicide survey, victims and persons accused of homicide, by age group and sex, Canada, annual (number)." CANSIM (database). http://www5.statcan.gc.ca/cansim/a26?lang=eng&id=2530003.

———. 2017b. "Table 051-0001—Estimates of population, by age group and sex for July 1, Canada, provinces and territories, annual (persons unless otherwise noted)." CANSIM (database). http://www5.statcan.gc.ca/cansim/a26?lang=eng&retrLang=eng&id=0510001&pattern=&csid=

Steffensmeier, Darrell, and Dana Haynie. 2000. "Gender, Structural Disadvantage, and Urban Crime: Do Macrosocial Variables Also Explain Female Offending Rates." *Criminology* 38, no. 2: 403–38.

Steffensmeier, Darrell, Jennifer Schwartz, and Michael Roche. 2013. "Gender and Twenty-First Century Corporate: Female Involvement and the Gender Gap in Enron-Era Corporate Frauds." *American Sociological Review* 78, no. 3: 448–76.

Steffensmeier, D., and C. Streifel. 1992. "Time-Series Analysis of the Female Percentage of Arrests for Property Crimes, 1960–1985." *Justice Quarterly* 9, no. 1: 77–103.

Stevens, T., M. Morash, and M. Chesney-Lind. 2011. "Are Girls Getting Tougher, or Are We Tougher on Girls? Probability of Arrest and Juvenile Court Oversight in 1980 and 2000." *Justice Quarterly* 28: 719–44.

Sutherland, Edwin. 1940. "White Collar Criminality." *American Sociological Review* 5: 1–12.

Tanovich, D.M. 2006. *The Colour of Justice: Policing Race in Canada*. Toronto: Irwin Law.

Tatum, B.L. 1994. "The Colonial Model as a Theoretical Explanation of Crime and Delinquency." In *African American Perspectives: On Crime Causation, Criminal Justice Administration, and Prevention*, ed. A.T. Sulton. 33–52. Englewood: Sulton Books.

Taylor-Butts, A., and A. Bressan. 2006. "Youth Crime in Canada, 2006." *Juristat* 28: 1–16.

The Sentencing Project. 2014. "Racial Disparity." http://www.sentencingproject.org/template/page.cfm?id=122.

Thompson, Sara K., and Rosemary Gartner. 2014. "The Spatial Distribution and Social Context of Homicide in Toronto's Neighbourhoods." *Journal of Research in Crime and Delinquency* 51, no. 1: 88–118.

Tittle, C.R., and Robert Meier. 1990. "Specifying the SES/Delinquency Relationship." *Criminology* 28, no. 2: 271–99.

Tittle, C.R., W.J. Villemez, and Douglas Smith. 1978. "The Myth of Social Class and Criminality: An Empirical Assessment of the Empirical Evidence." *American Sociological Review* 43: 643–56.

Tonry, M. 1997. "Ethnicity, Crime, and Immigration." *Crime and Justice* 21: 1–29.

Truth and Reconciliation Commission of Canada. 2014. "Residential Schools." http://www.trc.ca/websites/trcinstitution/index.php?p=4.

———. 2015. "The Survivors Speak: A Report of the Truth and

Reconciliation Commission of Canada." http://nctr.ca/assets/reports/Final%20Reports/Survivors_Speak_English_Web.pdf.

Tyler, T. 1990. *Why People Obey the Law*. New Haven: Yale University Press.

UN Office on Drugs and Crime. 2011. *2011 Global Study on Homicide: Trends, Context, Data*. Vienna.

Walklate, Sandra, ed. 2012. "Introduction." In *Gender and Crime: Critical Concepts on Criminology*, 1–5. London and New York: Routledge.

Weekes, J.R., W.A. Milson, F.J. Porporino, and D. Robinson. 1994. *The Offender Substance Abuse Pre-Release Outcomes*. Ottawa: Research and Statistics Branch, Correctional Service of Canada.

Weinrath, Michael, Janna Young, and Steven Kohn. 2012. "Attitudes Towards the Criminal Justice System in a High Crime Canadian Community." *Canadian Journal of Urban Research* 21, no. 2: 112–31.

Wesley-Esquimau, Cynthia, and Magdalena Smolewski. 2004. *Historic Trauma and Aboriginal Healing. Aboriginal Healing Foundation Research Series*. Web.

Wolfgang, Marvin E., and F. Ferracuti. 1967. *The Structure of Violence: Towards an Integrated Theory in Criminology*. London: Tavistock.

Woodworth, Michael, Ava D. Agar, and Richard B.A. Coupland. 2013. "Characteristics of Canadian Youth-Perpetrated Homicides." *Criminal Justice and Behavior* 40, no. 9: 1009–26.

Wortley, Scott. 1999. "A Northern Taboo: Research on Race, Crime, and Criminal Justice in Canada." *Canadian Journal of Criminology* 41, no. 2: 261–74.

Wortley, Scot, and Andrea McCalla. 2007. "Racial Discrimination in the Ontario Criminal Justice System: 1994–2007." In *Criminal Justice in Canada: A Reader*, 3rd ed., ed. Julian Roberts and Michelle Grossman. Toronto: Thomson Nelson.

Wortley, Scot, and Akwasi Owusu-Bempah. 2011. "The Usual Suspects: Police Stop and Search Practices in Canada." *Policing and Society* 21, no. 4: 395–407.

Wortley, S., and J. Tanner. 2003. "Data, Denials, and Confusion: The Racial Profiling Debate in Toronto." *Canadian Journal of Criminology and Criminal Justice* 45, no. 3: 367–89.

———. 2005. "Inflammatory Rhetoric? Baseless Accusations? Responding to Gabor's Critique of Racial Profiling Research in Canada." *Canadian Journal of Criminology and Criminal Justice* 47, no. 3: 581–609.

Wright, B.E. [1984]1994. *The Psychopathic Racial Personality and Other Essays*. Chicago: Third World.

Wright, Bradley, Avshalom Caspi, Richard Miech, and Phil A. Silva. 1999. "Reconsidering the Relationship between SES and Delinquency: Causation but Not Correlation." *Criminology* 37, no. 1: 175–94.

Young, Jock. 1999. *The Exclusive Society: Social Exclusion, Crime, and Difference in Late Modernity*. London: Sage.

CHAPTER 6

Adelberg, Ellen, and Claudia Currie. 1993. "In Their Own Words: Seven Women's Stories." In *In Conflict with the Law: Women and the Canadian Justice System*, ed. E. Adelberg and C. Currie. Vancouver: Press Gang.

Adler, Freda. 1975. *Sisters in Crime*. New York: McGraw-Hill.

Amir, Menachem. 1967. "Victim Precipitated Forcible Rape." *Journal of Criminal Law and Criminology* 58, no. 4: 493–502.

———. 1971. *The Patterns of Forcible Rape*. Chicago: University of Chicago Press.

Amnesty International. 2004. *Stolen Sisters: A Human Rights Response to Discrimination and Violence against Indigenous Women in Canada*. Web.

Arnold, Regina. 1995. "The Processes of Victimization and Criminalization of Black Women." In *The Criminal Justice System and Women*, ed. B.R. Price and N. Sokoloff. New York: McGraw-Hill.

Balfour, Gillian. 2008. "Falling Between the Cracks of Retributive and Restorative Justice: The Victimization and Punishment of Aboriginal Women." *Feminist Criminology* 3. 101–120.

Bertrand, Marie-Andrée. 1967. "The Myth of Sexual Equality before the Law." Fifth Research Conference on Delinquency and Criminality. Montreal, Centre de Psychologies et de Pédagogie.

Boritch, Helen. 1997. *Fallen Women: Female Crime and Criminal Justice in Canada*. Toronto: Nelson.

Boyle, Christine. 1994. "The Judicial Construction of Sexual Assault Offences." In *Confronting Sexual Assault: A Decade of Social and Legal Change*, ed. J. Roberts and R. Mohr. Toronto: University of Toronto Press.

Bronson, Diana. 1989. "A Time for Grief and Pain." *Globe and Mail*, 8 December, A7.

Browne, Angela. 1987. *When Battered Women Kill*. New York: Free Press.

Brownmiller, Susan. 1975. *Against Our Will: Men, Women, and Rape*. New York: Bantam Books.

Bruckert, Chris, and Colette Parent. 2014. "The In-Call Sex Industry: Reflections on Classed and Gendered Labour on the Margins." In *Criminalizing Women: Gender and (In)justice in Neo-liberal Times*, 2nd ed., ed. G. Balfour and E. Comack. Halifax: Fernwood.

Busby, Karen. 1997. "Discriminatory Uses of Personal Records in Sexual Violence Cases." *Canadian Journal of Women and the Law* 9, no. 1: 149–77.

———. 2014. "'Sex Was in the Air': Pernicious Myths and Other Problems with Sexual Violence Prosecutions." In *Locating Law: Race/Class/Gender/Sexuality—Connections,*

3rd ed., ed. E. Comack. Halifax and Winnipeg: Fernwood.

Canada (Attorney General) v. Bedford, [2013] 3 SCR 1101. Online at: http://www.canlii.org/en/ca/scc/doc/2013/2013scc72/2013scc72.html

Cain, Maureen. 1990. "Towards Transgression: New Directions in Feminist Criminology." *International Journal of the Sociology of Law* 18: 1–18.

Carlen, Pat, ed. 1985. *Criminal Women*. Cambridge: Polity.

———. 1988. *Women, Crime, and Poverty*. Milton Keynes: Open University Press.

Chesney-Lind, Meda, and Noelie Rodriguez. 1983. "Women under Lock and Key." *Prison Journal* 63: 47–65.

Chesney-Lind, Meda, and Randall Sheldon. 1998. *Girls, Delinquency, and Juvenile Justice*. California: Wadsworth.

Chunn, Dorothy E., and Shelley A.M. Gavigan. 2014. "From Welfare Fraud to Welfare as Fraud: The Criminalization of Poverty." In *Criminalizing Women: Gender and (In)justice in Neo-Liberal Times*, 2nd ed., ed. G. Balfour and E. Comack. Halifax: Fernwood.

Cohen, Albert. 1955. *Delinquent Boys*. Glencoe: The Free Press.

Comack, Elizabeth. 1993. "Women Offenders' Experiences with Physical and Sexual Abuse: A Preliminary Report." Criminology Research Centre, University of Manitoba.

———. 1996. *Women in Trouble: Connecting Women's Law Violations to Their Histories of Abuse*. Halifax: Fernwood.

———. 2018. *Coming Back to Jail: Women, Trauma, and Criminalization*. Halifax and Winnipeg: Fernwood.

Comack, Elizabeth, and Gillian Balfour. 2004. *The Power to Criminalize: Violence, Inequality, and the Law*. Halifax and Winnipeg: Fernwood.

Comack, Elizabeth, Vanessa Chopyk, and Linda Wood. (2000). "Mean Streets? The Social Locations, Gender Dynamics and Patterns of Violent Crime in Winnipeg." Winnipeg: Canadian Centre for Policy Alternatives (Manitoba) (www.policyalternatives.ca).

Connell, R.W. 1987. *Gender and Power*. Cambridge: Polity.

———. 1995. *Masculinities*. Cambridge: Polity.

———. 2000. *The Men and the Boys*. Berkeley: University of California Press.

Connell, R.W., and James Messerschmidt. 2005. "Hegemonic Masculinity: Rethinking the Concept." *Gender and Society* 19, no. 6: 829–59.

Cowie, John, Valerie Cowie, and Eliot Slater. 1968. *Delinquency in Girls*. London: Heinemann.

Crenshaw, Kimberlee. 1989. "Demarginalizing the Intersection of Race and Sex: A Black Feminist Critique of Antidiscrimination Doctrine, Feminist Theory, and Antiracist Politics." The University of Chicago Legal Forum, 140.

Crocker, Diane, and Val Marie Johnson. 2010. *Poverty, Regulation, and Social Justice: Readings on the Criminalization of Poverty*. Halifax and Winnipeg: Fernwood.

Daly, Kathleen. 1987. "Discrimination in the Criminal Courts: Family, Gender, and the Problem of Equal Treatment." *Social Forces* 66, no. 1: 152–75.

———. 1989. "Rethinking Judicial Paternalism: Gender, Work–Family Relations, and Sentencing." *Gender and Society* 3, no. 1: 9–36.

Daly, Kathleen, and Meda Chesney-Lind. 1988. "Feminism and Criminology." *Justice Quarterly* 5, no. 4: 101–43.

Dobash, R. Emerson, and Russell Dobash. 1979. *Violence against Wives: A Case against Patriarchy*. New York: The Free Press.

———. 1992. *Women, Violence, and Social Change*. London: Routledge.

Doolittle, Robyn. 2017. "Why Police Dismiss 1 in 5 Sexual Assault Claims as Baseless." *Globe and Mail*, 3 February. Web.

Edwards, Susan. 1985. "Gender Justice? Defending Defendants and Mitigating Sentence." In *Gender, Sex, and the Law*, ed. S. Edwards. Kent: Croom Helm.

Faith, Karlene. 1993. *Unruly Women: The Politics of Confinement and Resistance*. Vancouver: Press Gang.

Fine, Sean. 2016. "The Robin Camp Transcript: '… keep your knees together' and Other Key Passages." *Globe and Mail*, 9 September. Web.

Gavigan, Shelley. 1993. "Women's Crime: New Perspectives and Old Theories." In *In Conflict with the Law: Women and the Canadian Justice System*, 2nd ed., ed. Adelberg and C. Currie. Vancouver: Press Gang.

Gelsthorpe, Lorraine, and Allison Morris. 1988. "Feminism and Criminology in Britain." *British Journal of Criminology* 23: 93–110.

Gilfus, Mary. 1992. "From Victims to Survivors to Offenders: Women's Routes of Entry and Immersion into Street Crime." *Women and Criminal Justice* 4, no. 1: 63–89.

Glueck, Eleanor, and Sheldon Glueck. 1934. *Five Hundred Delinquent Women*. New York: A.A. Knopf.

Gotell, Lise. 2001. "Colonization through Disclosure: Confidential Records, Sexual Assault Complainants, and Canadian Law." *Social and Legal Studies* 10, no. 3: 315–46.

Hagan, John, A.R. Gillis, and John Simpson. 1985. "The Class Structure of Gender and Delinquency: Toward a Power-Control Theory of Common Delinquent Behavior." *American Journal of Sociology* 90: 1151–78.

Hagan, John, John Simpson, and A.R. Gillis. 1979. "The Sexual Stratification of Social Control: A Gender-Based Perspective on Crime and Delinquency." *British Journal of Sociology* 30: 25–38.

————. 1987. "Class in the Household: A Power-Control Theory of Gender and Delinquency." *American Journal of Sociology* 92, no. 4 (January): 788–816.

Hamilton, Alvin C., and C. Murray Sinclair. 1991. *The Justice System and Aboriginal People: Report of the Aboriginal Justice Inquiry of Manitoba*, vol. 1. Winnipeg: Queen's Printer.

Hannah-Moffat, Kelly. 2001. *Punishment in Disguise: Penal Governance and Federal Imprisonment of Women in Canada*. Toronto: University of Toronto Press.

Hannah-Moffat, Kelly, and Margaret Shaw, eds. 2000. *An Ideal Prison? Critical Essays on Women's Imprisonment in Canada*. Halifax: Fernwood.

Hayman, Stephanie. 2006. *Imprisoning Our Sisters: The New Federal Women's Prisons in Canada*. Montreal and Kingston: McGill–Queen's University Press.

Hazelwood, Roy, Janet Warren, and Park Elliot Dietz. 1993. "Compliant Victims of the Sexual Sadist." *Australian Family Physician* 22, no. 4: 474–79.

Heidensohn, Frances. 1968. "The Deviance of Women: A Critique and an Enquiry." *British Journal of Sociology* 19, no. 2: 160–75.

————. 1985. *Women and Crime*. London: Macmillan.

Heimer, Karen. 1995. "Gender, Race, and Pathways to Delinquency." In *Crime and Inequality*, ed. J. Hagan and R. Peterson. Stanford: Stanford University Press.

Hoffman-Bustamante, Dale. 1973. "The Nature of Female Criminality." *Issues in Criminology* 8: 117–36.

Hugill, David. 2010. *Missing Women, Missing News: Covering Crisis in Vancouver's Downtown Eastside*. Halifax and Winnipeg: Fernwood.

Johnson, Holly. 1996. *Dangerous Domains*. Toronto: Nelson Education.

Johnson, Holly, and Karen Rodgers. 1993. "A Statistical Overview of Women in Crime in Canada." In *In Conflict with the Law: Women and the Canadian Justice System*, ed. Ellen Adelberg and Claudia Currie. 95–116. Vancouver: Press Gang.

Jones, Anne. 1994. *Next Time She'll Be Dead: Battering and How to Stop It*. Boston: Beacon.

Kaiser-Derrick, Elspeth. 2012. "Listening to What the Criminal Justice System Hears and the Stories It Tells: Judicial Sentencing Discourses about the Victimization and Criminalization of Aboriginal Women." Master of Laws thesis, University of British Columbia.

Kelly, Liz. 1988. *Surviving Sexual Violence*. Minneapolis: University of Minnesota Press.

Kendall, Kathleen. 1991. "The Politics of Premenstrual Syndrome: Implications for Feminist Justice." *Journal of Human Justice* 2, no. 2 (Spring): 77–98.

————. 1992. "Dangerous Bodies." In *Offenders and Victims: Theory and Policy*, ed. D. Farrington and S. Walklate. London: British Society of Criminology.

————. 1993. "Program Evaluation of Therapeutic Services at the Prison for Women." Ottawa: Correctional Services Canada.

Kilty, Jennifer, and Sylvie Frigon. 2006. "From a Woman in Danger to a Dangerous Woman—the Case of Karla Homolka: Chronicling the Shifts." *Women and Criminal Justice* 17, 4.

————. 2016. *The Enigma of a Violent Woman: A Critical Examination of the Case of Karla Homolka*. London: Routledge.

Kinnon, Dianne. 1981. *Report on Sexual Assault in Canada*. Ottawa: CACSW.

Klein, Dorie 1973. "The Etiology of Female Crime: A Review of the Literature." *Issues in Criminology* 8, no. 3: 3–30.

Konopka, Gisella. 1966. *The Adolescent Girl in Conflict*. Englewood Cliffs: Prentice Hall.

Kruttschnitt, Candace. 1980–81. "Social Status and Sentences of Female Offenders." *Law and Society Review* 15, no. 2: 247–65.

————. 1982. "Women, Crime, and Dependency." *Criminology* 195: 495–513.

Laberge, Danielle. 1991. "Women's Criminality, Criminal Women, Criminalized Women? Questions in and for a Feminist Perspective." *Journal of Human Justice* 2, no. 2: 37–56.

Leonard, Eileen. 1982. *Women, Crime, and Society: A Critique of Theoretical Criminology*. New York: Longman.

Lombroso, Cesare, and William Ferrero. 1895. *The Female Offender*. London: Fischer Unwin.

Luckhaus, Linda. 1985. "A Plea for PMT in the Criminal Law." In *Gender, Sex, and the Law*, ed. S. Edwards. Kent: Croom Helm.

MacLeod, Linda. 1980. *Wife Battering in Canada: The Vicious Circle*. Ottawa: CACSW.

Mahony, Tina Hotton, Joanna Jacob, and Heather Hobson. 2017. *Women and the Criminal Justice System*. Ottawa: Statistics Canada. Web.

Martin, Dianne L. 1999. "Punishing Female Offenders and Perpetuating Gender Stereotypes." In *Making Sense of Sentencing*, ed. J. Roberts and D. Cole. Toronto: University of Toronto Press.

Martin, Dianne L., and Janet E. Mosher. 1995. "Unkept Promises: Experiences of Immigrant Women with the Neo-Criminalization of Wife Abuse." *Canadian Journal of Women and the Law* 8: 3–44.

McGillivray, Anne. 1998. "'A Moral Vacuity in Her Which Is Difficult If Not Impossible to Explain': Law, Psychiatry, and the Remaking of Karla Homolka." *International Journal of the Legal Profession* 5, no. 2–3: 255–88.

Messerschmidt, James. 1993. *Masculinities and Crime: A Critique and Reconceptualization of Theory.* Landham: Rowman and Littlefield.

———. 2004. *Flesh and Blood: Adolescent Gender Diversity and Violence.* Landham: Rowman and Littlefield.

———. 2012. *Gender, Sexuality, and Youth Violence: The Struggle for Recognition.* Landham: Rowman and Littlefield.

———. 2013. *Crime as Structured Action: Gender, Race, Class, and Crime in the Making,* 2nd ed. Thousand Oaks: Sage.

———. 2015. *Masculinities in the Making: From the Local to the Global.* Landham: Rowman and Littlfefield.

Miller, Eleanor M. 1986. *Street Woman.* Philadelphia: Temple University Press.

Morris, Allison. 1987. *Women, Crime, and Criminal Justice.* Oxford: Basil Blackwell.

Mosher, Janet E. 2014. "The Construction of 'Welfare Fraud' and the Wielding of the State's Iron Fist." In *Locating Law: Race/Class/Gender/Sexuality Connections,* 3rd ed., ed. E. Comack. Halifax and Winnipeg: Fernwood.

Moyser, Melissa. 2017. *Women and Paid Work.* Ottawa: Statistics Canada, Web.

Naffine, Ngaire. 1987. *Female Crime: The Construction of Women in Criminology.* Sydney: Allen and Unwin.

———. 1997. *Feminism and Criminology.* Sydney: Allen and Unwin.

National Inquiry into Missing and Murdered Indigenous Women and Girls. 2018. *About Us.* Web.

NWAC (Native Women's Association of Canada). 2010. *What Their Stories Tell Us: Research Findings from the Sisters in Spirit Initiative.* Ottawa. Web.

Osborne, Judith. 1989. "Perspectives on Premenstrual Syndrome: Women, Law and Medicine." *Canadian Journal of Family Law* 8: 165–84.

Pearson, Patricia. 1997. *When She Was Bad: Violent Women and the Myth of Innocence.* Toronto: Random House.

Perreault, Samuel. 2017. "Canadians' Perceptions of Personal Safety and Crime, 2014." Ottawa: Statistics Canada. Web.

Pollak, Otto. 1961. *The Criminality of Women.* New York: A.S. Barnes.

R v Ewanchuk, (1999) 1 SCR 330, reversing (1998) 57 AR 235.

R v Mills, (1998) 3 S.C.R. 688.

R v O'Connor, (1995) 4 SCR 411.

R v Seaboyer, (1991) 2 SCR 577.

Rafter, Nicole H., and Elena M. Natalizia. 1981. "Marxist Feminism: Implications for Criminal Justice." *Crime and Delinquency* 27 (January): 81–98.

RCAP (Royal Commission on Aboriginal Peoples). 1996. *Report.* Ottawa: Department of Indian and Northern Affairs.

RCMP. 2014. "Missing and Murdered Aboriginal Women: A National Operational Overview." Ottawa. Web.

Reitano, Julie. 2017. "Adult Correctional Statistics in Canada, 2015/2016." Ottawa: Statistics Canada. Web.

Ritchie, Beth. 1996. *Compelled to Crime: The Gender Entrapment of Battered Black Women.* New York: Routledge.

Scully, Diana, and Joseph Marolla. 1984. "Convicted Rapists' Vocabulary of Motive: Excuses and Justifications." *Social Problems* 31, no. 5: 530–44.

Scutt, Jocelyn. 1979. "The Myth of the 'Chivalry Factor' in Female Crime." *Australian Journal of Social Issues* 14, no. 1: 3–20.

Seshia, Maya. 2005. *The Unheard Speak Out.* Winnipeg: Canadian Centre for Policy Alternatives.

Shaw, Margaret. 1993. "Reforming Federal Women's Imprisonment." In *In Conflict with the Law: Women and the Canadian Justice System,* ed. E. Adelberg and C. Currie. Vancouver: Press Gang.

Shaw, Margaret, Karen Rogers, Johannes Blanchette, Tina Hattem, Lee Seto Thomas, and Lada Tamarack. 1991. *Survey of Federally Sentenced Women: Report on the Task Force on Federally Sentenced Women: The Prison Survey.* Ottawa: Solicitor General. User Report No. 1991–4.

Simon, Rita. 1975. *Women and Crime.* Lexington: D.C. Heath.

Smart, Carol. 1976. *Women, Crime, and Criminology: A Feminist Critique.* London: Routledge and Kegan Paul.

———. 1977. "Criminological Theory: Its Ideology and Implications Concerning Women." *British Journal of Sociology* 28, no. 1: 89–100.

———. 1989. *Feminism and the Power of Law.* London: Routledge.

Snider, Laureen. 1991. "The Potential of the Criminal Justice System to Promote Feminist Concerns." In *The Social Bias of Law: Critical Readings in the Sociology of Law,* 2nd ed., ed. E. Comack and S. Brickey. Halifax: Fernwood.

———. 1994. "Feminism, Punishment, and the Potential of Empowerment." *Canadian Journal of Law and Society* 9, no. 1: 74–104.

———. 2003. "Constituting the Punishable Woman: Atavistic Man Incarcerates Postmodern Woman." *British Journal of Criminology* 43, no. 2: 354–78.

Sommers, Evelyn. 1995. *Voices from Within: Women Who Have Broken the Law.* Toronto: University of Toronto Press.

Statistics Canada. 1993. "The Violence against Women Survey." *The Daily,* 18 November.

———. 2010. "General Social Survey: Self-Reported Victimization, by Type of Offence and Province, 2009." Web.

———. 2011a. "Cases in Adult Criminal Court, by Province and Territory, 2009/2010." Web.

———. 2011b. "Police-Reported Crime for Selected Offences, 2009 and 2010." Web.

Steffensmeier, Darrell, and John H. Kramer. 1982. "Sex-Based Differences in the Sentencing of Adult Criminal Defendants." *Sociology and Social Research* 663: 289–304.

Taylor, Ian, Paul Walton, and Jock Young. 1973. *The New Criminology*. London: Routledge and Kegan Paul.

The War Against Women. 1991 (June). Report of the Standing Committee on Health and Welfare, Social Affairs, Seniors and the Status of Women. Barbara Greene, Chair. Ottawa: House of Commons.

Thomas, William I. 1967. *The Unadjusted Girl*. New York: Harper and Row.

Truth and Reconciliation Commission of Canada. 2015. *Final Report*, vol. 1: *Summary—Honouring the Truth, Reconciling the Future*. Toronto: Lorimer.

Ursel, Jane. 1994. "The Winnipeg Family Violence Court." *Juristat* 14, no. 12.

———. 1998. "Eliminating Violence against Women: Reform or Co-Optation in State Institutions." In *Power and Resistance: Critical Thinking About Canadian Social Issues*, 2nd ed., ed. L. Samuelson and W. Antony. Halifax: Fernwood.

Walker, Lenore. 1979. *The Battered Woman*. New York: Harper and Row.

———. 1987. *Terrifying Love: Why Battered Women Kill and How Society Responds*. New York: HarperCollins.

West, Candace, and Don Zimmerman. 1987. "Doing Gender." *Gender and Society* 1, no. 2: 125–51.

Zingraff, Matthew, and Randall Thomson. 1984. "Differential Sentencing of Women and Men in the USA." *International Journal of the Sociology of Law* 12: 401–13.

CHAPTER 7

Allen, Mary. 2014. "Victim Services in Canada, 2011/2012." *Juristat*. Statistics Canada, cat. no. 85-002X.

Amernic, Jerry. 1984. *Victims: Orphans of Justice*. Toronto: McClelland and Stewart.

Canadian Victims Bill of Rights Act (2015) and numerous related amendments to the *Criminal Code, Canada Evidence Act* and *Corrections and Conditional Release Act* to recognize the interests and rights of victims of crime: Bill C-32 (*Victims Bill of Rights Act*), S.C. 2015, c. 13.

Canada, Canadian Federal–Provincial Task Force on Justice for Victims of Crime. 1983. *Final Report*. Ottawa.

Canada, Standing Committee on Justice and Human Rights. 2000. *Victims' Rights—A Voice Not a Veto*. Ottawa.

Canadian Municipal Network for Crime Prevention. www.safercities.ca.

Clarke, Lorenne, and Debra Lewis. 1977. *Rape: The Price of Coercive Sexuality*. Toronto: Women's Press.

Crooks, Claire, D. Wolfe, R. Hughes, P. Jaffe, and D. Chiodo. 2008. *Development, Evaluation, and National Implementation of a School-Based Program to Reduce Violence and Related Risk Behaviours: Lessons from the 4th R*. Ottawa: Institute for the Prevention of Crime.

European Council. 2001. *Framework Decision of 15 March 2001 on the Standing of Victims in Criminal Proceedings (2001/220/JHA)*. Brussels: Commission of the European Communities.

European Union. 2012. *Council Directive 2012/29/EU of the European Parliament and of the Council of 25 October 2012 Establishing Minimum Standards on the Rights, Support, and Protection of Victims of Crime, and Replacing Council Framework Decision 2001/220/JHA*.

Fisher, Bonnie, and John J. Sloan. 2007. *Campus Crime: Legal, Social, and Policy Perspectives*. Springfield: Charles C. Thomas.

Gannon, Maire, and Karen Mihorean. 2005. "Criminal Victimization in Canada, 2004." *Juristat* 25, no. 7.

Giffords Law Centre, PICO Network, Community Justice Reform Coalition. 2017. *Investing in Intervention: The Critical Role of State-level Support in breaking the cycle of urban gun violence*. Giffords Law Centre, PICO, CJRC. Web.

Greenland, Jacob, and Sarah Alam. 2017. "Police resources in Canada, 2016." Ottawa: Statistics Canada.

Institute for the Prevention of Crime. 2009. *Making Cities Safer: Action Briefs for Municipal Stakeholders*, no. 3 (March). Ottawa: University of Ottawa.

International Association of Chiefs of Police. 2008. *Enhancing Law Enforcement Response to Victims: A 21st Century Strategy*. Alexandria: International Association of Chiefs of Police.

International Victimology Institute Tilburg. 2006. "Towards Implementation of the UN Declaration on Basic Principles of Justice for Victims of Crime and Abuse of Power—Preparing a Draft Convention on the Rights of Victims of Crime, Abuse of Power and Terrorism." Report on Expert Group Meeting. University of Tilburg.

MADD (Mothers Against Drunk Driving) Canada. 2010. "The Magnitude of the Alcohol/Drug-Related Crash Problem in Canada." Web.

Mazowita, Benjamin, and Marta Burczycka. 2014. "Shelters for Abused Women in Canada, 2012." Web.

McMurtry, Roy. 2008. "Report on Financial Assistance for Victims of Crime in Ontario." Toronto: Attorney General. Web.

Nina's Place. 2011. http://www.jbmh.com.

Ombudsman of Ontario. 2007. *Adding Insult to Injury: Investigation into the Treatment of Victims by the Criminal Injuries Compensation Board*. Toronto.

Ontario. 1984. *Government Consultation on Victims of Violent Crime*. Toronto: Secretary for Justice.

Parliamentary Budget Officer. 2013. *Expenditure Analysis of Criminal Justice in Canada*. Ottawa.

Perreault, Samuel, 2015. "Criminal Victimization in Canada, 2014." *Juristat*. Statistics Canada, 85-002-X.

Perrin, Benjamin. 2017. *Victim Law: The Law of Victims of Crime in Canada*, Toronto: Thomson Reuters.

Reitano, Julie. 2017. "Adult correctional statistics in Canada, 2015/2016." Ottawa: Statistics Canada.

Safe Horizons. 2011. Web.

Saskatchewan. 2011. *Restitution Civil Enforcement Program*. Regina: Justice and Attorney General. Web.

Schweinhart, L.J., J. Montie, Z. Xiang, W.S. Barnett, C.R. Belfield, and M. Nores. 2005. *Lifetime Effects: The High/Scope Perry Preschool Study Through Age 40*. Ypsilanti: High/Scope.

Skogan, W., and K. Frydl. 2004. *Fairness and Effectiveness in Policing: The Evidence*. Washington, DC: National Academies Press.

Sauvé, Julie. "Victim Services in Canada: Results from the Victim Services Survey 2007/2008." *Justice Canada, Victims of Crime Research Digest*. Web.

———. 2005. "Crime Statistics in Canada, 2004." *Juristat* 25, no. 5.

Strang, Heather, and Lawrence W. Sherman. 2007. *Restorative Justice: The Evidence*. London: Smith Institute.

Thomas, Mikhail. 2004. "Adult Criminal Court Statistics, 2003/2004." *Juristat* 24, no. 12.

UN, General Assembly. 1985. *Declaration of Basic Principles of Justice for Victims of Crime and Abuse of Power* (GA/res/40/34). New York. Web.

UN, Office for Drugs and Crime. 1999a. *Guide for Policy Makers on the Implementation of the Declaration of Basic Principles of Justice for Victims of Crime and Abuse of Power*. New York.

———. 1999a. *Handbook on Justice for Victims on the Use and Application of the Declaration of Basic Principles of Justice for Victims of Crime and Abuse of Power*. New York.

———. 2005. *Guidelines on Justice for Child Victims and Witnesses*. New York.

US Department of Justice, Bureau of Justice Statistics. 2010. "Criminal Victimization in the United States, 2007 Statistical Tables." Web.

——— 2009. "Criminal Victimization, 2008." Washington, DC: Office of Justice Programs.

US Department of Justice, Office for Victims of Crime. 1999. *International Crime Victim Compensation Directory*. Washington, DC.

———. 2002. *Restitution: Making It Work*. Washington, DC.

——— 2009. "Nation-Wide Analysis—Performance Reports." Web.

US Department of Justice, Office on Violence Against Women. 2007. *2006 Biennial Report to Congress on the Effectiveness of Grant Programs Under the Violence Against Women Act*. Washington, DC.

——— 2006. *S.T.O.P. Program Services, Training, Officers, Prosecutors, Annual Report 2006*. Washington, DC.

US Government Accountability Office. 2009. *Crime Victim Rights Act: Increasing Victim Awareness and Clarifying Applicability to the District of Columbia Will Improve Implementation of the Act*. Washington, DC.

United States. 1982. *President's Task Force on Victims of Crime Final Report*. Washington, DC.

Victim Support Europe. 2010. *Victims in Europe: Implementation of the EU Framework Decision on the Standing of Victims in the Criminal Proceedings in the Member States of the European Union*. Lisbon: Associação Portuguesa de Apoio à Vítima.

Waller, Irvin. 2004. "Harnessing Criminology and Victimology Internationally." In *Lessons from International/Comparative Criminology/Criminal Justice*, ed. John Winterdyk and Liqun Cao. 233–48. Toronto: De Sitter.

———. 2008. *Less Law, More Order: The Truth about Reducing Crime*. Westport: Praeger.

———. 2010. *Rights for Victims of Crime: Rebalancing Justice*. New York: Rowman and Littlefield.

———. 2014. *Smarter Crime Control: A Guide to a Safer Future for Citizens, Communities, and Politicians*. New York: Rowman and Littlefield.

Waller, Irvin, and Norm Okihiro. 1978. *Burglary, the Victim, and the Public*. Toronto: University of Toronto Press.

World Health Organization. 2016. *INSPIRE: Seven Strategies for Ending Violence Against Children*. Geneva.

Zhang, Ting. 2011. *Costs of Crime in Canada, 2008*. Ottawa: Department of Justice Canada. Web.

CHAPTER 8

Beccaria, Cesare. [1763]1963. *On Crimes and Punishments*, trans. H. Paolucci. Indianapolis: Bobbs-Merrill.

Beirne, Piers. 1993. *Inventing Criminology*. Albany: SUNY Press.

Bunch, Adam. 2013. "Toronto's First Hanging—and How it Went Wrong." *Spacing* (Toronto). Web.

Driver, Edwin D. 1972. "Charles Buckman Goring." In *Pioneers in Criminology*, ed. Hermann Mannheim. 429–42. Montclair: Patterson Smith.

Empey, LaMar T. 1982. *American Delinquency: Its Meaning and Construction*. Homewood,: Dorsey.

Goddard, H.H. 1912. *The Kallikak Family: A Study in the Heredity of Feeble-Mindedness*. New York: Macmillan.

———. 1914. *Feeble-Mindedness: Its Causes and Consequences*. New York: Macmillan.

Goring, Charles. [1913]1972. *The English Convict*. Montclair: Patterson Smith.

Gould, Stephen Jay. 1996. *The Mismeasure of Man* (revised and expanded). New York: W.W. Norton.

Harris, Marvin. 1974. *Cows, Pigs, Wars, and Witches*. New York: Vintage.

Hobbes, Thomas. [1651]1958. *Leviathan*, pts. 1 and 2. Indianapolis: Bobbs-Merrill.

Hofstadter, Richard. 1955. *The Age of Reform*. New York: Vintage Books.

Hogan, Margaret Monahan. n.d. "Medical Ethics: The New Eugenics: Therapy—Enhancement—Screening—Testing." International Catholic University. Web.

Hooton, Ernest Albert. 1939. *The American Criminal: An Anthropological Study*. Cambridge, MA: Harvard University Press.

Langbein, John H. 1976. *Torture and the Law of Proof*. Chicago: University of Chicago Press.

Lilly, J. Robert, Frances T. Cullen, and Richard A. Ball. 2007. *Criminological Theory: Context and Consequences*, 4th ed. Thousand Oaks: Sage.

Lombroso, Cesare. 1912. *Crime: Its Causes and Remedies*. Boston: Little, Brown.

Monachesi, Elio. 1972. "Cesare Beccaria." In *Pioneers in Criminology*, ed. Hermann Mannheim. Montclair: Patterson Smith.

Newman, Graeme. 1978. *The Punishment Response*. New York: J.B. Lippincott.

Pfohl, Stephen J. 1985. *Images of Deviance and Social Control*. New York: McGraw-Hill.

Radzinowicz, Sir Leon. 1966. *Ideology and Crime*. London: Heinemann.

Radzinowicz, Sir Leon, and Joan King. 1977. *The Growth of Crime*. London: Pelican.

Rafter, Nicole Hahn. 1997. *Creating Born Criminals*. Urbana: University of Illinois Press.

Rosenhaft, Eve. "The Nazi Persecution of Deaf People." Panel presentation, US Holocaust Memorial Museum, 14 August 2001. Web.

Roshier, Bob. 1989. *Controlling Crime: The Classical Perspective in Criminology*. Philadelphia: Open University Press.

Sylvester, F. Sawyer, Jr. 1972. *The Heritage of Modern Criminology*. Cambridge: Schenkman.

Taylor, Ian, Paul Walton, and Jock Young. 1973. *The New Criminology: For a Social Theory of Deviance*. London: Routledge and Kegan Paul.

Thomas, Charles W., and John R. Hepburn. 1983. *Crime, Criminal Law, and Criminology*. Dubuque: Wm. C. Brown.

Wetzell, Richard. 2000. *Inventing the Criminal: A History of German Criminology, 1880–1945*. Chapel Hill: University of North Carolina Press.

Zilborg, Gregory. 1969. *The Medical Man and the Witch During the Renaissance*. New York: Cooper Square.

CHAPTER 9

Abrahamsen, D. 1944. *Crime and the Human Mind*. New York: Columbia University Press.

———. 1973. *The Murdering Mind*. New York: Harper and Row.

Abram, K.M., and L.A. Teplin. 1991. "Co-Occurring Disorders among Mentally Ill Jail Detainees: Implications for Public Policy." American Psychologist 46: 1036–45.

Abram, K.M., L.A. Teplin, and G.M. McClelland. 2003. "Comorbidity of Severe Psychiatric Disorders and Substance Use Disorders among Women in Jail." *American Journal of Psychiatry* 160: 1007–10.

Akers, R. 1990. "Rational Choice, Deterrence, and Social Learning Theories in Criminology: The Path Not Taken." *Journal of Criminal Law and Criminology* 81: 653–76.

Akers, R.L., and G.F. Jensen. 2006. "Empirical Status of Social Learning Theory of Crime and Deviance: The Past, Present, and Future." In *Taking Stock: The Status of Criminological Theory*, ed. K. Blevins, F. Cullen, and J. Wright. 37–76. Beverly Hills: Sage.

Alexander, F., and M. Healey. 1935. *Roots of Crime*. New York: A.A. Knopf.

Anderson, C.A., A. Shibuya, N. Ihori, E.L. Swing, B.J. Bushman, A. Sakamoto, H.R. Rothstein, and M. Saleem. 2010. "Violent Video Game Effects on Aggression, Empathy, and Prosocial Behavior in Eastern and Western Countries." *Psychological Bulletin* 136: 151–73.

APA (American Psychiatric Association). 2000. *Psychiatric Services in Jails and Prisons*, 2nd ed. Washington, DC.

———. 2013. *Diagnostic and Statistical Manual of Mental Disorders*, 5th ed. Washington, DC.

Arboleda-Florez, J., A. Crisanti, and H. Holley. 1995. "The Effects of Changes in the Law Concerning Mentally Disordered Offenders: The Alberta Experience with Bill C-30." *Canadian Journal of Psychiatry* 40: 225–33.

Babiak, Paul, and Robert Hare. 2006. *Snakes in Suits: When Psychopaths Go to Work*. New York: HarperBusiness.

Bandura, A. 1986. *Social Foundations of Thought and Action: A Social Cognitive Theory*. Englewood Cliffs: Prentice Hall.

———. 2000. "Social-Cognitive Theory." In *Encyclopedia of Psychology*, vol. 7, ed. A.E. Kazdin. 329–32. Washington, DC: American Psychological Association.

Beaudette, J.N., J. Power, and L.A. Stewart. 2015. "National Prevalence of Mental Disorders among Incoming Federally Sentenced Men Offenders" (R-357). Ottawa: Correctional Service Canada.

Birmingham, L., J. Gray, D. Mason, and D. Grubin. 2000. "Mental Illness at Reception into Prison." *Criminal Behaviour and Mental Health* 10: 77–87.

Blair, R.J.R. 2006. "Subcortical Brain Systems in Psychopathy." In *Handbook of Psychopathy*, ed. C.J. Patrick. 296–312. New York: Guilford.

Blasi, A. 1980. "Bridging Moral Cognition and Moral Action: A Critical Review of the Literature." *Psychological Bulletin* 88: 1–45.

Boduszek, D., G. Adamson, M. Shevlin, and P. Hyland. 2012. "The Role of Personality in the Relationship between Criminal Social Identity and Criminal Thinking Style within a Sample of Prisoners with Learning Difficulties." *Journal of Learning Disabilities and Offending Behaviour* 3: 12–24.

Bonta, J., and D.A. Andrews. 2017. *The Psychology of Criminal Conduct*, 6th ed. New York: Routledge.

Bonta, J., M. Law, and K. Hanson. 1998. "The Prediction of Criminal and Violent Recidivism among Mentally Disordered Offenders: A Meta-Analysis." *Psychological Bulletin* 123: 123–42.

Borum, R. 1996. "Improving the Clinical Practice of Violence Risk Assessment: Technology Guidelines and Training." *American Psychologist* 51: 945–46.

Bowlby, J. 1953. *Child Care and the Growth of Love*. New York: Penguin.

Brannigan, A. 1997. "Self Control, Social Control, and Evolutionary Psychology: Towards an Integrated Perspective on Crime." *Canadian Journal of Criminology* 39. 403–431.

Braukman, C.J., K.A. Kirigin, and M.M. Wolf. 1980. "Group Homes Treatment Research: Social Learning and Social Control Perspectives." In *Understanding Crime: Current Theory and Research*, ed. T. Hirschi and M. Gottfredson. Beverly Hills: Sage.

Braukman, C.J., and M.M. Wolf. 1987. "Behaviorally Based Group Homes for Juvenile Offenders." In *Behavioral Approaches to Crime and Delinquency*, ed. Braukman and Wolf. New York: Plenum.

Braukman, C.J., M.M. Wolf, and K.K. Ramp. 1985. "Follow-Up of Group Home Youths into Young Adulthood." Progress Report, Grant MA 20030. Achievement Place Research Project, University of Kansas, Lawrence.

Brink, J.H., J. Livingston, S. Desmarais, C. Greaves, V. Maxwell, E. Michalak, R. Parent, S. Verdun-Jones, and C. Weaver. 2011. "A Study of How People with Mental Illness Perceive and Interact with the Police." Calgary: Mental Health Commission of Canada.

Brodsky, S.L. 1977. "Crime and Dangerous Behavior." In *Abnormal Psychology*, ed. D.C. Rimm and J.W. Somervill. New York: Academic Press.

Burgess, R.L., and R.L. Akers. 1966. "A Differential Association Reinforcement Theory of Criminal Behavior." *Social Problems* 14: 128–47.

Bushman, B.J., and C.A. Anderson. 2015. "Understanding Causality in the Effects of Media Violence." *American Behavioral Scientist* 59: 1807–21.

Buttell, F.P. 2002. "Exploring Levels of Moral Development among Sex Offenders Participating in Community-Based Treatment." *Journal of Offender Rehabilitation* 34: 85–95.

Canadian Public Health Association. 2004. "A Health Care Needs Assessment of Federal Inmates in Canada." *Canadian Journal of Public Health* 95: Supplement 1.

Chaiklin, H. 2001. "Current and Prior Mental Health Treatment of Jail Inmates: The Use of the Jail as an Alternative Shelter." *Journal of Social Distress and the Homeless* 10: 255–68.

Clastner, D.S. 1967. "Comparison of Risk Perception between Delinquents and Nondelinquents." *Journal of Criminal Law, Criminology, and Police Science* 58: 80–86.

Cleckley, H. 1976. *The Mask of Sanity*. St. Louis: Mosby.

Cohen, A.K. 1966. *Deviance and Control*. Englewood Cliffs: Prentice Hall.

Coid, J., and S. Ullrich. 2010. "Antisocial Personality Disorder Is on a Continuum with Psychopathy." *Comprehensive Psychiatry: The Journal of Psychopathology* 51: 426–433.

Conger, R.D. 1976. "Social Control and Social Learning Models of Delinquent Behavior: A Synthesis." *Criminology* 14: 17–40.

Cook, T.D., D.A. Kendzierski, and S.V. Thomas. 1983. "The Implicit Assumptions of Television Research: An Analysis of the 1982 NIMH Report on Television and Behavior." *Public Opinion Quarterly* 47: 161–201.

Coolidge, F.L., P.D. Marle, S.A. van Horn, and D.L. Segal. 2011. "Clinical Syndromes, Personality Disorders, and Neurocognitive Differences in Male and Female Inmates." *Behavioral Sciences and the Law* 29: 741–751.

Corrado, R.R., I. Cohen, S.D. Hart, and R. Roesch. 2000. "Comparative Examination of the Prevalence of Mental Disorders among Jailed Inmates in Canada and the United States." *International Journal of Law and Psychiatry* 23: 633–47.

Correctional Service of Canada. 2017. "Research Results—Mental Health." Ottawa: Correctional Service of Canada. Web.

Cotton, D., and T.G. Coleman. 2010. "Canadian Police Agencies and Their Interactions with Persons with a Mental Illness: A Systems Approach." *Police Practice and Research: An International Journal* 11. 301–14.

Craddick, R. 1962. "Selection of Psychopathic from Non-Psychopathic Prisoners within a Canadian Prison." *Psychological Reports* 10: 495–99.

Daly, M. and M. Wilson. 1988. "Evolutionary Social Psychology and Family Homicide." *Science* 242: 519–524.

DeMatteo, D., and J. Edens. 2006. "The Role and Relevance of the Psychopathy Checklist-Revised in Court: A Case Law Survey of U.S. Courts." *Psychology, Public Policy, and Law* 24: 133–46.

Desmarais, S.L., R.A. Van Dorn, K.L. Johnson, K.J. Grimm, K.S. Douglas, and M.S. Swartz. 2014. "Community Violence Perpetration and Victimization among Adults with Mental Illnesses." *American Journal of Public Health* 104: 2342–49.

Drewett, A., and B. Shepperdson. 1995. *A Literature Review of Services for Mentally Disordered Offenders*. Leicester: Nuffield Community Care Studies Unit, University of Leicester.

Duntley, J.D., and D.M. Buss. 2008. "The Origins of Homicide." In *Evolutionary Forensic Psychology: Darwinian Foundations of Crime and Law*, ed. J.D. Duntley and T.K. Shackelford, 41–64. Oxford and New York: Oxford University Press.

Einstadter, W., and S. Henry. 1995. *Criminological Theory: An Analysis of Its Underlying Assumptions*. Fort Worth: Harcourt Brace.

Ewen, R.B. 1988. *An Introduction to Theories of Personality*. Hillside: Lawrence Erlbaum.

Eysenck, H.J. 1977. *Crime and Personality*. London: Routledge and Kegan Paul.

———. 1990. "Crime and Personality." In *Clinical Criminology: Theory Research and Practice*, ed. N.Z. Hilton, M.A. Jackson, and C.D. Webster, 85–99. Toronto: Canadian Scholars' Press.

Eysenck, H.J., and S.B. Eysenck. 1976. *Psychoticism as a Dimension of Personality*. London: Hodder and Stoughton.

Eysenck, H.J., and G.H. Gudjonsson. 1989. *The Causes and Cures of Criminality*. New York and London: Plenum.

Falissard, B., J. Loze, Y. Gasquet, I. Duburc, A. de Beaurepaire, C. Fagnani, and F. Rouillon. 2006. "Prevalence of Mental Disorders in French Prisons for Men." *BMC Psychiatry* 6: 33–38.

———. 2002. "Multiple Risk Factors for Multiple Problem Violent Boys." In *Multi-Problem Violent Youth: A Foundation for Comparative Research on Needs, Interventions and Outcomes*, ed. R.R. Corrado, R. Roesch, S.D. Hart, and J.K. Gierowski, 23–34. Amsterdam: IOS.

Farrington, D.P., L. Biron, and M. LeBlanc. 1982. "Personality and Delinquency in London and Montreal." In *Abnormal Offenders, Delinquency, and the Criminal Justice System*, ed. J. Gunn and D.P. Farrington. Chichester: Wiley.

Fazel, Seena, and John Danesh. 2002. "Serious Mental Disorder in 23,000 Prisoners: A Systematic Review of 62 Surveys." *The Lancet* 359: 545–50.

Friedlander, K. 1947. *The Psychoanalytic Approach to Juvenile Delinquency*. New York: International Universities Press.

Geen, R.G. 1983. "Aggression and Television Violence." In *Aggression: Theoretical and Empirical Reviews*, ed.

R.G. Geen and E.I. Donnerstein. New York: Academic Press.

Gibbs, J.C. 2010. *Moral Development and Reality: Beyond the Theories of Kohlberg and Hoffman*, 2nd ed. Boston: Pearson Allyn and Bacon.

Gilligan, C. 1982. *In a Different Voice: Psychological Theory and Women's Development*. Cambridge, MA: Harvard University Press.

Gunn, J. 1977. "Criminal Behaviour and Mental Disorder." *British Journal of Psychiatry* 130: 317–29.

Gunn, J., A Maden, and M. Swinton. 1991. "Treatment Needs of Prisoners with Psychiatric Disorders." *BMJ* 303: 338–41.

Hails, J., and R. Borum. 2006. "Police Training and Specialized Approaches to Respond to People with Mental Illnesses." *Crime and Delinquency* 49: 52–61.

Hakeem, M. 1958. "A Critique of the Psychiatric Approach to Crime and Correction." *Law and Contemporary Problems* 23: 650–82.

Haney, C. 2002. "Making Law Modern: Toward a Contextual Model of Justice." *Psychology, Public Policy, and Law* 7: 3–63.

Hare, R.D. 1970. *Psychopathy: Theory and Research*. New York: Wiley.

———. 1982. "Psychopathy and the Personality Dimensions of Psychoticism, Extraversion, and Neuroticism." *Personality and Individual Differences* 3: 35–42.

———. 1991. "The Hare Psychopathy Checklist—Revised." Toronto: Multi-Health Systems.

———. 1998a. *Without Conscience: The Disturbing World of the Psychopaths among Us*. New York: Guilford.

———. 1998b. "Psychopathy, Affect, and Behavior." In *Psychopathy: Theory, Research and Implications for Society*, ed. D.J. Cooke, A.E. Forth, and R. Hare. 105–37. Dordrecht: Kluwer.

———. 1998c. "The Hare PCL-R: Some Issues Concerning Its Use and

Misuse." *Legal and Criminological Psychology* 3: 101–19.

———. 2003. *Manual for the Revised Psychopathy Checklist,* 2nd ed. Toronto: Multi-Health Systems.

Hare, R.D., and D.N. Cox. 1978. "Clinical and Empirical Conceptions of Psychopathy, and the Selection of Subjects for Research." In *Psychopathic Behavior: Approaches to Research*, ed. R.D. Hare and D. Schalling. Chichester: Wiley.

Harris, G. and M. Rice. 1997. "Risk Appraisal and Management of Violent Behavior." *Psychiatric Services* 48: 1168–76.

Hart, S.D., D.N. Cox, and R.D. Hare. 1995. *The Hare Psychopathy Checklist: Screening Version*. Toronto: Multi-Health Systems.

Heilbrun, A.B., Jr. 1979. "Psychopathy and Violent Crime." *Journal of Consulting and Clinical Psychology* 47: 509–16.

Hodgins, S. 1995. "Assessing Mental Disorder in the Criminal Justice System: Feasibility versus Clinical Accuracy." *International Journal of Law and Psychiatry* 18: 15–28.

Hodgins, S., and G. Côté. 1990. "Prevalence of Mental Disorders among Penitentiary Inmates in Quebec." *Canada's Mental Health* (March): 1–4.

Hoge, Robert, Nancy Guerra, and Paul Boxer. 2008. *Treating the Juvenile Offender*. New York: Guilford Press.

Hollin, C. R. 1989. *Psychology and Crime: An Introduction to Criminological Psychology*. London, UK: Routledge.

Honegger, L.N. 2015. "Does the Evidence Support the Case for Mental Health Courts? A Review of the Literature." *Law and Human Behavior* 39: 478–488.

Hosser, D., M. Windzio, and W. Greve. 2008. "Guilt and Shame as Predictors of Recidivism: A Longitudinal Study with Young Prisoners." *Criminal Justice and Behavior* 35: 138–52.

Human Rights Watch. 2003. *Ill-Equipped: US Prisons and Offenders with Mental Illness*. New York.

James, D.J., and L.E. Glaze. 2006. "Mental Health Problems in Prison and Jail Inmates." *Bureau of Justice Statistics Bulletin,* NCJ 213600. Web.

Jeffery, C.R. 1965. "Criminal Behavior and Learning Theory." *Journal of Criminal Law and Criminology* 56: 294–300.

Jennings, W.S., R. Kilkenny, and L. Kohlberg. 1983. "Moral-Development Theory and Practice for Youthful and Adult Offenders." In *Personality Theory, Moral Development, and Criminal Behavior,* ed. W.S. Laufer and S.M. Day. 281–94. Lexington: Lexington.

Jones, N.J., S.L. Brown, D. Robinson, and D. Frey. 2014. "Incorporating Strengths into Quantitative Assessments of Criminal Risk for Adult Offenders: The Service Planning Instrument." *Criminal Justice and Behavior* 42: 321–38.

Kanazawa, S. 2009. "Evolutionary Psychology and Crime." In *Biosocial Criminology: New Directions in Theory and Research,* ed. A. Walsh and K.M. Beaver. 90–110. New York: Routledge.

Kelly, L., and S. Farrell MacDonald 2015a. "Comparing Lifetime Substance Use Patterns of Men and Women Offenders" (RIB 14-44). Ottawa: Correctional Service Canada.

———. 2015b. "Lifetime Substance Use Patterns of Men Offenders" (RIB 14-43). Ottawa: Correctional Service Canada.

Kerig, P.K., and S.P. Becker. 2014. "Early Abuse and Neglect as Risk Factors for the Development of Criminal and Antisocial Behavior." In *The Development of Criminal and Antisocial Behavior,* ed. J. Morizot and L. Kazemian. 181–99. New York: Springer.

Kiriakidis, S. 2008. "Moral Disengagement: Relation to Delinquency and Independence from Indices of Social Dysfunction." *International Journal of Offender Therapy and Comparative Criminology* 52: 571–83.

Kline, P. 1987. "Psychoanalysis and Crime." In *Applying Psychology to Imprisonment: Theory and Practice,* ed. B.J. McGuirk, D.M. Thorton, and M. Williams. London: HMSO.

Kohlberg, L., and R. Kramer. 1969. "Continuities and Discontinuities in Child and Adult Moral Development." *Human Development* 12: 93–120.

Kropp, P.R., D.N. Cox, R. Roesch, and D. Eaves. 1989. "The Perceptions of Correctional Officers towards Mentally Disordered Offenders." *International Journal of Law and Psychiatry* 12: 181–88.

Lamb, H.R., R. Shaner, D.M. Elliott, W.J. DeCuir, and J.T. Foltz. 1995. "Outcome for Psychiatric Emergency Patients Seen by an Outreach Police–Mental Health Team." *Psychiatric Services* 46: 1267–71.

Lamb, H.R., and L.E. Weinberger. 1998. "Persons with Severe Mental Illness in Jails and Prisons: A Review." *Psychiatric Services* 49: 483–92.

Lev, J. 1998. "Jail as a Psychiatric Emergency Room." *American Jails* 12: 72–74.

Lickliter, R., and H. Honeycutt. 2003. "Developmental Dynamics: Toward a Biologically Plausible Evolutionary Psychology." *Psychological Bulletin* 129: 819–35.

Loeber, R., and D.P. Farrington. 2012. "Advancing Knowledge about Direct Protective Factors That May Reduce Youth Violence." *American Journal of Preventive Medicine* 43: S24–S27.

Loeber, R., D.P. Farrington, and M. Stouthamer-Loeber. 2001a. "Male Mental Health Problems, Psychopathy, and Personality Traits: Key Findings from the First 14 years of the Pittsburgh Youth Study." *Clinical Child and Family Psychology Review* 4: 273–97.

Loeber, R., D.P. Farrington, M. Stouthamer-Loeber, T.E. Moffitt, and A. Caspi. 2001b. "The Development of Male Offending: Key Findings from the First Decade of the Pittsburgh Youth Study." In *Children and the Law: The Essential Readings,* ed. R. Bull. 336–78. Malden: Blackwell.

Losel, F. 1998. "Treatment and Management of Psychopaths." In *Psychopathy: Theory, Research and Implications for Society,* ed. D.J. Cooke, A.E. Forth, and R. Hare, 303–54. Dordrecht: Kluwer.

Malamuth, N.M., and J.V.P. Check. 1981. "The Effects of Mass Media Exposure on Acceptance of Violence against Women: A Field Experiment." *Journal of Research in Personality* 15: 436–46.

Markowitz, F.E. 2011. "Mental Illness, Crime, and Violence: Risk, Context, and Social Control." *Aggression and Violent Behavior* 16: 36–44.

Martin, S.E., L.E. Sechrest, and R. Redner, eds. 1981. *New Directions in the Rehabilitation of Criminal Offenders.* Washington, DC: National Press Academy.

McIntyre, Mike. 2009. "Only One Verdict Possible: Judge, Killer Ruled Not Responsible for Grisly Deed." *Winnipeg Free Press,* March 6.

Monahan, J., and S. Splane. 1980. "Psychological Approaches to Criminal Behavior." In *Criminology Review Yearbook,* ed. E. Bittner and S. Messinger. Beverly Hills: Sage.

Morash, M. 1983. "An Explanation of Juvenile Delinquency: The Integration of Moral Reasoning, Theory, and Social Knowledge." In *Personality Theory, Moral Development, and Criminal Behavior,* ed. W.S. Laufer and J.M. Day. 385–409. Lexington: Lexington.

Moretti, Marlene, Margaret Jackson, and Ingrid Obsuth. 2010. "Translating Research into Intervention: Lessons Learned and New Directions." *Court Review* 46: 58–63.

Motiuk, L.L., and F.J. Porporino. 1991. "The Prevalence, Nature, and Severity of Mental Health Problems among Federal Male Inmates in Canadian Penitentiaries" (R-24). Ottawa: Correctional Service Canada.

Nathan, P.E., and S.L. Harris. 1975. *Psychopathology and Society.* New York: McGraw-Hill.

National Commission on Correctional Health Care. 2003. "Standards for Health Services in Jails." Chicago.

Newman, J.P. 1998. "Psychopathic Behavior: An Information Processing Perspective." In *Psychopathy: Theory, Research and Implications for Society*, ed. D.J. Cooke, A.E. Forth, and R. Hare. 81–104. Dordrecht: Kluwer.

Nicholls, T.L., R. Roesch, M.C. Olley, J.R.P. Ogloff, and J.F. Hemphill. 2005. "Jail Screening Assessment Tool (JSAT): Guidelines for Mental Health Screening in Jails." *Mental Health, Law, and Policy Institute*, Simon Fraser University, Burnaby.

Nietzel, M.T. 1979. *Crime and Its Modification: A Social Learning Perspective*. New York: Pergamon.

Ogloff, J.R.P. 1996. *The Surrey Pretrial Mental Health Program: Community Component Evaluation*. Surrey: BC Forensic Psychiatric Services Commission.

——. 2002. "Identifying and Accommodating the Needs of Mentally Ill People in Gaols and Prisons." *Psychiatry, Psychology, and Law* 9: 1–33.

Ogloff, J.R.P., S. Wong, and A. Greenwood. 1990. "Treating Criminal Psychopaths in a Therapeutic Community Program." *Behavioral Sciences and the Law* 8: 181–90.

Osher, F., H.J. Steadman, and H. Barr. 2003. "A Best Practice Approach to Community Re-entry from Jails for Inmates with Co-occurring Disorders: The APIC Model." *Crime and Delinquency* 49: 79–96.

Piaget, J. 1932. *The Moral Judgment of the Child*. New York: Free Press.

Polansky, N., R. Lippitt, and F. Redl. 1950. "An Investigation of Behavioral Contagion in Groups." *Human Relations* 3: 319–48.

Porter, S., A.R. Birt, & D.P. Boer. 2001. "Investigation of the Criminal and Conditional Release Histories of Canadian Federal Offenders as a Function of Psychopathy and Age." *Law and Human Behavior* 25: 647–61.

Pritchard, Dean. 2009. "Beheading Verdict No Surprise: Family." *Winnipeg Sun*, March 5.

Province of Manitoba Review Board. 2009. "A Disposition Hearing Held in Winnipeg, Manitoba, on Monday, June 1, 2009." Winnipeg.

——. 2010. "A Disposition Review Hearing Held in Winnipeg, Manitoba on Monday, May 31, 2010." Winnipeg.

——. 2010. "A Disposition Review Hearing held in Winnipeg, Manitoba, on February 6, 2017." Winnipeg.

Queen's Bench, Winnipeg Centre. n.d.. "Between Her Majesty the Queen and Vince Weiguang Li—Agreed Statement of Facts." n.d. Winnipeg.

Quinsey, V.L. 2002. "Evolutionary Theory and Criminal Behaviour." *Legal and Criminological Psychology* 1: 1–13.

Quinsey, V.L., G.T. Harris, M.E. Rice, and C.A. Cormier. 2006. "Actuarial Prediction of Violence." In *Violent Offenders: Appraising and Managing Risk*. 155–96. Washington, DC: American Psychological Association.

Raine, A., and Y. Yang. 2006. "The Neuroanatomical Basis of Psychopathy." In *Handbook of Psychopathy*, ed. C.J. Patrick. 278–95. New York: Guilford.

Rappaport, J. 1977. *Community Psychology: Values, Research, and Action*. New York: Holt, Rinehart and Winston.

Reid, C.L. 2003. "Do Minority and Female Offenders Have Distinct 'Criminal Personalities'?: A Critique of Yochelson–Samenow's Theory of Criminality." *Criminal Justice Studies* 16: 233–44.

Redl, F., ed. 1966. *When We Deal with Children: Selected Writings*. New York: Free Press.

Reppucci, N.D., and W.G. Clingempeel. 1978. "Methodological Issues in Research with Correctional Populations." *Journal of Consulting and Clinical Psychology* 46: 727–46.

Roesch, R. 1988. "Community Psychology and the Law." *American Journal of Community Psychology* 16: 451–63.

Roesch, R. 1995. "Mental Health Interventions in Pretrial Jails." In *Psychology and Law: Advances in Research*, ed. G.M. Davies, S. Lloyd-Bostock, M. McMurran, and C. Wilson. 520–31. Berlin: De Greuter.

Roesch, R., and S.L. Golding. 1985. "The Impact of Deinstitutionalization." In *Aggression and Dangerousness*, ed. D.P. Farrington and J. Gunn. New York: Wiley.

Roesch, R., J. Ogloff, and D. Eaves. 1995. "Mental Health Research in the Criminal Justice System: The Need for Common Approaches and International Perspectives. *International Journal of Law and Psychiatry* 18: 1–14.

Ruddell, Rick. 2006. "Jail Interventions for Inmates with Mental Illnesses." *Journal of Correctional Health Care*. April

Salekin, R.T., C. Worley, and R.D. Grimes. 2010. "Treatment of Psychopathy: A Review and Brief Introduction to the Mental Model Approach for Psychopathy." *Behavioral Sciences and the Law* 28: 235–66.

Schacter, D.L., D. Wegner, and D. Gilbert. 2007. *Psychology*. Duffield: Worth.

Schoenfeld, C.G. 1971. "A Psychoanalytic Theory of Juvenile Delinquency." *Crime and Delinquency* 19: 469–80.

Scott, C., and B. McDermott. 210. "International Perspectives (I): An Overview of US Correctional Mental Health." In *Psychiatry in Prisons: A Comprehensive Handbook*, ed. S. Wilson and I. Cumming, 239–45. London: Jessica Kingsley.

Seara-Cardoso, A., and E. Viding. 2014. "Functional Neuroscience of Psychopathic Personality in Adults." *Journal of Personality* 83: 723–37.

Seidman, E., and B. Rabkin. 1983. "Economics and Psychosocial Dysfunction: Toward a Conceptual

Framework and Prevention Strategies." In *Preventive Psychology*, ed. R.D. Felner et al. 175–98. Elmsford: Pergamon.

Shenson, D., N. Dubler, and D. Michaels. 1990. "Jails and Prisons: The New Asylums?" *American Journal of Public Health* 80: 655–56.

Skeem, J., and D. Cooke. 2010. "Is Criminal Behavior a Central Component of Psychopathy? Conceptual Directions for Resolving the Debate." *Psychological Assessment* 22: 433–45.

Skilling, T.A., G.T. Harris, M.E. Rice, and V.L. Quinsey. 2002. "Identifying Persistently Antisocial Offenders Using the Hare Psychopathy Checklist and DSM Antisocial Personality Disorder Criteria." *Psychological Assessment* 14: 27–38.

Skoler, G.D., A. Bandura, and D. Ross. 1994. "Aggression." In *Readings in Social Psychology: General, Classic, and Contemporary Selections*, 2nd ed., ed. W.A. Lesko. 296–326. Boston: Allyn and Bacon.

Slinger, E., and R. Roesch. 2010. "Problem-Solving Courts in Canada: A Review and a Call for Empirically-Based Evaluation Methods." *International Journal of Law and Psychiatry* 33: 258–64.

Smith, S.L., and A.R. Boyson. 2002. "Violence in Music Videos: Examining the Prevalence and Context of Physical Aggression." *Journal of Communication* 52: 61–83.

Somers, J.M., L. Cartar, and J. Russo. 2008. *Corrections, Health and Human Services: Evidence-Based Planning and Evaluation*. Center for Applied Research in Mental Health and Addiction, Simon Fraser University, Burnaby.

Steadman, H.J., J.E. Scott, F. Osher, T.K. Agnese, and P.C. Robbins. 2005. "Validation of the Brief Jail Mental Health Screen." *Psychiatric Services* 56: 816–22.

Stewart, L.A., and G. Wilton. 2017. "Comorbid Mental Disorders: Prevalence and Impact on

Institutional Outcomes" (R-379). Ottawa: Correctional Service of Canada.

Suedfeld, P., and P.B. Landon. 1978. "Approaches to Treatment." In *Psychopathic Behaviour: Approaches to Research*, ed. R.D. Hare and D. Schalling. 347–76. Chichester: Wiley.

Swanson, J.W., E.E. McGinty, S. Fazel, and V.M. Mays. 2015. "Mental Illness and Reduction of Gun Violence and Suicide: Bringing Epidemiologic Research to Policy." *Annals of Epidemiology* 25: 366–76.

Tangney, J.P., J. Stuewig, J., and D.J. Mashek. 2007. "Moral Emotions and Moral Behavior." *Annual Review of Psychology* 58: 345–72.

Teevan, J.J., and T.F. Hartnagel. 1976. "The Effects of Television Violence on the Perceptions of Crime by Adolescents." *Sociology and Social Research* 60: 337–48.

Teplin, Linda. 1984. "Criminalizing Mental Disorder: The Comparative Arrest Rate of the Mentally Ill." *American Psychologist* 7: 794–803.

———. 1989. "Screening for Severe Mental Disorder in Jails." *Law and Human Behavior* 13: 1–18.

———. 1990a. "Detecting Disorder: The Treatment of Mental Illness among Jail Detainees." *Journal of Consulting and Clinical Psychology* 58: 233–36.

———. 1990b. "The Prevalence of Mental Disorder among Urban Jail Detainees: Comparison with the Epidemiologic Catchment Area Program." *American Journal of Public Health* 80: 663–669.

———. 1991. "The Criminalization Hypothesis: Myth, Misnomer, or Management Strategy." In *Law and Mental Health: Major Developments and Research Needs*, ed. S.A. Shah and B.D. Sales. 149–83. Rockville: US Department of Health and Human Services.

———. 1994. "Psychiatric and Substance Abuse Disorders among Male Urban Jail Detainees." *American Journal of Public Health* 84: 290–293.

Teplin, L.A., and E.S. Voit. 1996. "Criminalizing the Seriously Mentally Ill: Putting the Problem in Perspective." In *Mental Health and Law: Research, Policy, and Services*, ed. B.D. Sales and S.A. Shah. Durham: Carolina Academic.

Thomas, M.H., R.W. Horton, E.C. Lippincott, and R.S. Drabman. 1979. "Desensitization to Portrayals of Real-Life Aggression as a Function of Exposure to Television Violence." *Journal of Personality and Social Psychology* 35: 450–58.

Thompson, S. 2010. *Policing Vancouver's Mentally Ill: The Disturbing Truth*. Vancouver: Vancouver Police Department.

Thornberry, T.P., and M.D. Krohn. 2000. "The Self-Report Method for Measuring Delinquency and Crime." *Criminal Justice* 4: 33–83.

Tooby, J. and L. Cosmides. 2005. "Conceptual foundations of evolutionary psychology." In *The Handbook of Evolutionary Psychology*, ed. D.M. Buss, 5–67. Hoboken: John Wiley and Sons.

Torrey, E. Fuller. 1995. "Jails and Prisons: America's New Mental Hospitals." *American Journal of Public Health* 85: 1611–13.

Van Vugt, E., J. Gibbs, G. J. Stams, C. Bijleveld, J. Hendriks, and P. van der Laan. 2011. "Moral Development and Recidivism." *International Journal of Offender Therapy and Comparative Criminology* 55: 1234–50.

van Wormer, K. 2001. *Counseling Female Offenders and Victims: A Strengths-Restorative Approach*. Springer series on family violence. New York: Springer.

Venables, N.C., J.R. Hall, and C.J. Patrick 2014. "Differentiating Psychopathy from Antisocial Personality Disorder: A Triarchic Model Perspective." *Psychological Medicine* 44: 1005–13.

Walsh, Z., and T. Walsh. 2006. "The Evidentiary Introduction of PCL-R Assessed Psychopathy in U.S. Courts: Extent and Appropriateness." *Law and Human Behavior* 31: 209–29.

Walter, G.D. 2004. "The Trouble with Psychopathy as a General Theory of Crime." *International Journal of Offender Therapy and Comparative Criminology* 48: 133–48.

Warren, M.Q., and M.J. Hindelang. 1979. "Current Explanations of Offender Behavior." In *Psychology of Crime and Criminal Justice*, ed. H. Toch. 166–82. New York: Holt, Rinehart and Winston.

Weber, S., U. Habel, K. Amunts, and F. Schneider. 2008. "Structural Brain Abnormalities in Psychopaths." *Behavioral Sciences and the Law* 26: 7–28.

Webster, C.D., T.L. Nicholls, M.L. Martin, S.L. Desmarais, and J. Brink. 2006. "Short-Term Assessment of Risk and Treatability (START): The Case for a New Structured Professional Judgment Scheme." *Behavioral Sciences and the Law* 24: 747–66.

Wheeler, J., I.C.H. Clare, and A.J. Holland. 2013. "What Can Social and Environmental Factors Tell Us about the Risk of Offending by People with Intellectual Disabilities?" *Psychology, Crime & Law* 20: 635–658.

Widom, C. 1977. "A Methodology for Studying Non-Institutionalized Psychopaths." *Clinical Psychology* 45: 674–83.

Widom, C., and J.P. Newman. 1985. "Characteristics of Non-Institutionalized Psychopaths." In *Aggression and Dangerousness*, ed. D.P. Farrington and J. Gunn. 57–80. New York: Wiley.

Wilson, M. 2004. "The Community and Family Context in Understanding Juvenile Crime." In *Applying Psychology to Forensic Practice*, ed. A. Needs and G. Towl. 18–33. Glasgow: Malden Blackwell.

Wilson-Bates, F. 2008. "Lost in Transition: How a Lack of Capacity in the Mental Health System Is Failing Vancouver's Mentally Ill and Draining Police Resources." Vancouver: Vancouver Police Board.

Wong, S., and R.D. Hare. 2005. *Guidelines for a Psychopathy Treatment Program*. Toronto: Multi-Health Systems.

CHAPTER 10

Agnew, Robert. 2001. "Building on the Foundation of General Strain Theory: Specifying the Types of Strain Most Likely to Lead to Crime and Delinquency." *Journal of Research in Crime and Delinquency* 38: 319–61.

———. 2002. "Experienced, Vicarious, and Anticipated Strain." *Justice Quarterly* 19: 603–32.

———. 2006. *Pressured into Crime: An Overview of General Strain Theory*. New York: Oxford University Press.

———. 2009. *Juvenile Delinquency: Causes and Control*. New York: Oxford University Press.

———. 2010. "Controlling Crime: Recommendations from General Strain Theory." In *Criminology and Public Policy: Putting Theory to Work*, ed. Hugh Barlow and Scott Decker. Philadelphia: Temple University Press.

Anderson, Elijah. 1999. *Code of the Street: Decency, Violence, and the Moral Life of the Inner City*. New York: W.W. Norton.

Andrews, Donald A., and James Bonta. 1998. *The Psychology of Criminal Conduct*, 2nd ed. Cincinnati: Anderson.

Babiak, Paul, Craig Neuman, and Robert Hare. 2010. "Corporate Psychopathy: Talking the Walk." *Behavioral Sciences and the Law* 28, no. 2: 174–93.

Bernard, Thomas. 1987. "Testing Structural Strain Theories." *Journal of Research in Crime and Delinquency* 24: 262–80.

Blau, Judith, and Peter Blau. 1982. "The Cost of Inequality: Metropolitan Structure and Violent Crime." *American Sociological Review* 47: 114–29.

Braithwaite, John. 1979. *Inequality, Crime and Public Policy*. London: Routledge and Kegan Paul.

———. 1989. *Crime, Shame, and Reintegration*. Cambridge: Cambridge University Press.

Cloward, Richard, and Lloyd Ohlin. 1960. *Delinquency and Opportunity*. Glencoe: Free Press.

Comack, Elizabeth. 2016. "Feminism and Criminology." In *Criminology: A Canadian Perspective*, 8th ed., ed. Rick Linden. Toronto: Harcourt Brace.

Crutchfield, Robert D. 1995. "Ethnicity, Labor Markets, and Crime." In *Ethnicity, Race, and Crime: Perspectives Across Time and Place*, ed. Darnell F. Hawkins. Albany: SUNY Press.

Cullen, Francis. 1984. *Rethinking Crime and Deviance Theory: The Emergence of a Structuring Tradition*. Totowa: Rowman and Allanheld.

———. 1988. "Were Cloward and Ohlin Strain Theorists? Delinquency and Opportunity Revisited." *Journal of Research in Crime and Delinquency* 25: 214–41.

Desroches, Fred. 1995. "Tearoom Trade: A Law Enforcement Problem." *Canadian Journal of Criminology* 33, no. 1: 1–21.

Durkheim, Émile. 1893/1933. *The Division of Labor in Society*. New York: Free Press.

———. 1897/1951. *Suicide*. New York: Free Press.

El Akkad, Omar. 2014. "When Speed Is Greed." *Globe and Mail*, 12 April, F4.

Felte, Eric. 2001. "Finder's Keepers." *Readers' Digest*. April.

Hackler, James C. 1966. "Boys, Blisters, and Behavior." *Journal of Research in Crime and Delinquency* 3 (July): 155–64.

———. 2006. *Canadian Criminology: Strategies and Perspectives*, 4th ed. Toronto: Prentice Hall Canada.

Hackler, Jim. 2011. "Reducing Crime the Intelligent Way: Building Parenting Not Prisons." *Justice Report* 26, no. 3: 3–6.

Hackler, James C., and Eric Linden. 1970. "The Response of Adults to Delinquency Prevention Programs: The Race Factor." *Journal of Research in Crime and Delinquency* 7 (January): 31–45.

Hagan, John. 2010. *Who Are the Criminals?* Princeton: Princeton University Press.

Hagan, John, and Bill McCarthy. 1997. *Mean Streets: Youth Homelessness and Crime*. New York: Cambridge University Press.

Heinze, P., R. Allen, C. Magai, and B. Ritzler. 2010. "Let's Get Down to Business: A Validation Study of the Psychopathic Personality Inventory among a Sample of MBA students." *Journal of Personality Disorders* 24, no. 4: 487–98.

Hellenbach, Michael. 2006. *Arbeitsmotivation in Ost- und West Deutschland: Grundlagen und Vergleiche*. Saarbruecken: VDM.

Hongming Cheng. 2011. "Academic Fraud in China: Assessing the Applicability of Merton's Strain Theory." Western Society of Criminology Conference, Vancouver, 3–5 February.

Johnson, Matthew, Robert Morris, and Scott Menard. 2015. *Crime and Delinquency* 61: 1283–1310.

Konty, Mark. 2005. "Microanomie: The Cognitive Foundations of the Relationship between Anomie and Deviance." *Criminology* 43 (February): 107–31.

Leblanc, Daniel. 2011. "Bloc Takes Tories to Task on Fraudster's Release." *Globe and Mail*, 31 January.

———. 2014. "OSC Seeks Wiretap Rule Changes." *Globe and Mail*, 28 March, B4.

McGrath, John Michael. 2011. "The Son Also Stumbles: Edgar Bronfman Jr. Not Going to Jail After All." *Toronto Life*, 24 January.

Merton, Robert K. 1938. "Social Structure and Anomie." *American Sociological Review* 3 (October): 672–82.

Messner, Steven F., and Richard Rosenfeld. 2007. *Crime and the American Dream*, 4th ed. Belmont: Thomson Wadsworth.

Morris, Alison. 1987. *Women, Crime, and Criminal Justice*. Oxford: Basil Blackwell.

Naffine, Ngaire. 1987. *Female Crime: The Construction of Women in Criminology*. Sydney: Allen and Unwin.

Pinker, Stephen. 2011. *The Better Angels of Our Nature*. New York: Viking.

Quinney, Richard. 1963. "Occupational Structure and Criminal Behavior: Prescription Violation by Retail Pharmacists." *Social Problems* 11 (Fall): 179–95.

Schwartz, Robert G., and Marsha Levick. 2010. "When a 'Right' Is Not Enough: Implementation of the Right to Counsel in an Age of Ambivalence." *Criminology and Public Policy* 9, no. 20: 365–73.

Schweinhart, L.L., H.V. Barnes, and D.P. Weikart. 1993. *Significant Benefits: The High/Scope Perry Preschool Study through Age 27*. Ypsilanti: High/Scope.

Slater, Joanna. 2011. "After the Financial Crisis: A Dearth of Prosecutions." *Globe and Mail*, 19 April, B11.

Sutherland, Edwin. 1949. *White Collar Crime*. New York: Dryden.

Tremblay, Richard E., and Wendy M. Craig. 1995. "Developmental Crime Prevention." In *Building a Safer Society: Strategic Approaches to Crime Prevention*, vol. 19, ed. M. Tonry and D.P. Farrington. Chicago: University of Chicago Press.

Urbanik, Marta-Marika, and Kevin Haggerty. 2018. "'#IT'S Dangerous': The Online World of Drug Dealers, Rappers, and the Street Code. *British Journal of Criminology* doi/10.1093/bjc/azx083/4797356.

US Department of Justice. n.d. *Oil and Natural Gas Espionage: An Evolving Threat*. Web.

Zhao, Ruohui, and Liquin Cao. 2010. "Social Change and Anomie: A Cross Nation Study." *Social Forces* 89, no. 3: 1209–29.

CHAPTER 11

Althusser, L. 1969. *For Marx*. New York: Vintage.

Bartholomew, Amy, and Susan Boyd. 1989. "Towards a Political Economy of Law." In *The New Canadian Political Economy*, ed. Wallace Clement and Glen Williams, 212–39. Montreal and Kingston: McGill–Queen's University Press.

Bill C-13: Protecting Canadians from Online Crime Act. 2013. 1st Reading, 20 November 2013, 41st Parliament, 2nd Session. http://www.parl.gc.ca/HousePublications/Publication.aspx?Language=E&Mode=1&DocId=6311444.

Bohm, Robert M. 1982. "Radical Criminology: An Explication." *Criminology* 19, no. 4: 565–89.

Brickey, Stephen, and Elizabeth Comack. 1989. "The Role of Law in Social Transformation: Is a Jurisprudence of Insurgency Possible?" In *Law and Society: A Critical Perspective*, ed. Tullio Caputo, Mark Kennedy, Charles E. Reasons, and Augustine Brannigan, 316–30. Toronto: Harcourt Brace Jovanovich.

Bronskill, Jim. 2014. "Telus Tightens Info Disclosure Policy." The Canadian Press, 17 July. Web.

Cain, Maureen, and Alan Hunt. 1979. *Marx and Engels on Law*. London: Academic Press.

Canadian Press. 2013. "Canada to Get New Cyberbullying Legislation in the Fall." 26 September. Web.

Cartwright, Barry E. 2016. "Cyberbullying and Cyberlaw: A Canadian Perspective." 2016 IEEE International Conference on Cybercrime and Computer Forensics, June 2016.

CCMW (Canadian Council of Muslim Women). 2012. "CCMW Position on Femicide (not honour killing)." Web.

Chambliss, William, and Robert Siedman. 1982. *Law, Order, and Power*. Reading: Addison-Wesley.

Coburn, P.I., D.A. Connolly, and R. Roesch. 2015. "Cyberbullying: Is Federal Criminal Legislation the Solution?" *Canadian Journal of Criminology and Criminal Justice* 57, no. 4: 566–79.

Comack, Elizabeth. 1999. "Theoretical Excursions." In *Locating Law: Race, Class, Gender Connections*, ed. Elizabeth Comack, 10–68. Halifax: Fernwood.

DeKeseredy, Walter S. 1991. "Confronting Woman Abuse: A Brief Overview of the Left Realist

Approach." In *New Directions in Critical Criminology*, ed. Brian D. MacLean and Dragan Milovanovic, 27–30. Vancouver: Collective Press.

Deschamps, Ryan, and Kathleen McNutt. 2016. "Cyberbullying: What's the Problem?" *Canadian Public Administration* 59, no. 1: 45–71.

Domhoff, G. William. 1970. *The Higher Circles: The Governing Class in America*. New York: Random House.

Einstadter, Werner, and Stuart Henry. 2006. *Criminological Theory: An Analysis of Its Underlying Assumptions*. Lanham: Rowman and Littlefield.

Faucher, Chantal, Wanda Cassidy, and Margaret Jackson. 2015. "From the Sandbox to the Inbox: Comparing the Acts, Impacts, and Solutions of Bullying in K-12, Higher Education, and the Workplace." *Journal of Education and Training Studies* 3, no. 6: 111–125.

Fisk, Robert. 2010. "The Crimewave That Shames the World." *The Independent*, 7 September.

France, Anatole. 1897. *The Red Lily*. London: John Lane.

Friscolanti, Michael. 2012. "Transcripts: The Crown's Case." *The Shafia Honour Killing Trial*. Macleans e-book, 86–104.

Glasbeek, Harry. 1989. "Why Corporate Deviance Is Not Treated as a Crime: The Need to Make Profits a Dirty Word." In *Law and Society: A Critical Perspective*, ed. Tullio Caputo, Mark Kennedy, Charles E. Reasons, and Augustine Brannigan, 126–45. Toronto: Harcourt Brace Jovanovich.

Goff, Colin, and Charles Reasons. 1978. *Corporate Crime in Canada: A Critical Analysis of Anti-Combines Legislation*. Toronto: Prentice Hall Canada.

Gold, David, Clarence Y.H. Lo, and Erik O. Wright. 1975. "Recent Developments in Marxist Theories of the Capitalist State." *Monthly Review* 27 (October–November): 29–43.

Gordon, Robert, and Ian Coneybeer. 1999. "Corporate Crime." In *Law in Society: Canadian Readings*, ed. N. Larsen and B. Burtch. 101–27. Toronto: Nelson Thomson Learning.

Gossner, Céline, Jorgen Schlundt, Peter Embarek, Susan Hird, Danilo Wong, Jose Beltran, Keng Ngee Teoh, and Angelika Tritscher. 2009. "The Melamine Incident: Implications for International Food and Feed Safety." *Environmental Health Perspectives* 117, no. 12: 1803–8.

Greenberg, David F. 1993. *Crime and Capitalism: Readings in Marxist Criminology*, 2nd ed. Philadelphia: Temple University Press.

Henry, Frank. 1986. "Crime—A Profitable Approach." In *The Political Economy of Crime*, ed. Brian D. Maclean, 182–203. Toronto: Prentice Hall.

Hunt, Alan. 1993. *Explorations in Law and Society: Towards a Constitutive Theory of Law*. New York: Routledge.

Ingelfinger, Julie. 2008. "Melamine and the Global Implications of Food Contamination." *New England Journal of Medicine* 359: 2745–48.

Jiwani, Yasmin, and Homa Hoodfar. 2012. "Should We Call It 'Honour Killing'? No!" *The Gazette* (Montreal), 30 January.

Jones, Trevor, Brian D. MacLean, and Jock Young. 1986. *The Islington Crime Survey: Crime, Victimization and Policing in Inner-City London*. Aldershot: Gower.

Korteweg, Anna. 2012. "Understanding Honour Killing and Honour-Related Violence in the Immigration Context: Implications for the Legal Profession and Beyond." *Canadian Criminal Law Review* 16, no. 2: 135–60.

Kuehn, Bridget. 2009. "Melamine Scandals Highlight Hazards of Increasingly Globalized Food Chain." *JAMA* 301, no. 5: 473–75.

Lea, John, and Jock Young. 1984. *What Is to Be Done About Law and Order?* Harmondsworth: Penguin.

———. 1986. "A Realistic Approach to Law and Order." In *The Political Economy of Crime: Readings for a Critical Criminology*, ed. Brian D.

MacLean. Toronto: Prentice Hall Canada.

Lowman, John, and Brian D. MacLean. 1992. "Introduction: Left Realism, Crime Control, and Policing in the 1990s." In *Realist Criminology: Crime Control and Policing in the 1990s*, ed. Lowman and MacLean, 3–29. Toronto: University of Toronto Press.

Mackay, Peter. 2013, "Protecting Canadians from Online Crime." House of Commons. Edited Hansard 147 025, 41st Parliament, 2nd session, 27 November. Web.

MacLean, Brian D. 1991. "The Origins of Left Realism." In *New Directions in Critical Criminology*, ed. MacLean and Dragan Milovanovic, 9–14. Vancouver: Collective Press.

Marx, Karl, and Friedrich Engels. [1848]1992. *The Communist Manifesto*. Oxford: Oxford University Press.

Matthews, Roger, and Jock Young. 1992. "Reflections on Realism." In *Rethinking Criminology: The Realist Debate*, ed. Young and Matthews, 1–23. London: Sage.

McMullan, John. 1992. *Beyond the Limits of the Law: Corporate Crime and Law and Order*. Halifax: Fernwood.

Michalowski, Raymond. 1985. *Order, Law, and Crime: An Introduction to Criminology*. New York: Random House.

Miliband, Ralph. 1969. *The State in Capitalist Society*. London: Weidenfeld and Nicolson.

Mojab, Shahrzad. 2012. "The Politics of Culture, Racism, and Nationalism in Honour Killing." *Canadian Criminal Law Review* 16, no. 2: 115–34.

Mugford, Stephen, and Pat O'Malley. 1991. "Heroin Policy and Deficit Models." *Crime, Law, and Social Change* 15, no. 1: 19–36.

Nestle, Marion. 2008. *Pet Food Politics: The Chihuahua in the Coal Mine*. Berkeley: University of California Press.

O'Reilly-Fleming, Thomas. 1996. "Left-Realism as Theoretical Retreatism or Paradigm Shift: Toward Post-Critical

Criminology." In *Post-Critical Criminology*, ed. O'Reilly-Fleming, 1–25. Scarborough: Prentice-Hall.

Papp, Aruna. 2010. "Culturally Driven Violence against Women: A Growing Problem in Canada's Immigrant Communities." Frontier Centre for Public Policy. FCPP Policy Series no. 92: 1–20.

Pearce, Frank. 1976. *Crimes of the Powerful*. London: Pluto.

Poulantzas, N. 1975. *Classes in Contemporary Capitalism*. London: New Left.

Puschner, Birgit, and Renate Reimschuessel. 2011. "Toxicosis Caused by Melamine and Cyanuric Acid in Dogs and Cats: Uncovering the Mystery and Subsequent Global Implications." *Clinics in Laboratory Medicine* 31: 181–99.

Quinney, Richard. 1970. *The Social Reality of Crime*. Boston: Little, Brown.

———. 1974. *Critique of the Legal Order*. Boston: Little, Brown.

R. v. Spencer, [2014] 2 S.C.R. 212. http://scc-csc.lexum.com/scc-csc/scc-csc/en/item/14233/index.do?r=AAAAAQAHc3BlbmNlcgE.

Roth, Aleda, Andy Tsay, Madeline Pullman, and John Grey. 2008. "Unravelling the Food Supply Chain: Strategic Insights from China and the 2007 Recalls." *Journal of Supply Chain Management* 44, no. 1: 22–39.

Schembri, Jeremy. 2014. "Omnibus Bill C-13 Tackles Cyberbullying by Eroding Digital Privacy." *The McGill Daily*, 9 January. Web.

Schmit, Julie. 2007. "Pet Food Probe: Who Was Watching Suppliers?" *USA Today*, 5 July.

Schmitz, Cristin. 2013. "Privacy and Press Freedom Cites as Concerns with Cyberbully Bill." *Lawyers Weekly*, 13 December.

Sellin, Thorsten. 1938. *Culture Conflict and Crime*. New York: Social Science Research Council.

Sharma, Kirti, and Manish Paradkar. 2010. "The Melamine Adulteration Scandal." *Food Security* 2: 97–107.

Smandych, Russell. 1985. "Marxism and the Creation of Law: Re-examining the Origins of Canadian Anti-Combines Legislation, 1890–1910." In *The New Criminology in Canada: State, Crime and Control*, ed. Thomas Fleming, 87–99. Toronto: Oxford University Press.

Snider, Laureen. 1979. "Revising the Combines Investigation Act: A Study in Corporate Power." In *Structure, Law, and Power: Essays in the Sociology of Law*, ed. Paul Brantingham and Jack Kress, 105–19. Beverly Hills: Sage.

———. 1989. "Ideology and Relative Autonomy in Anglo-Canadian Criminology." *Journal of Human Justice* 1, no. 1: 27–42.

———. 2015. *Corporate Crime*. Winnipeg: Fernwood.

Spitzer, Steven. 1975. "Towards a Marxian Theory of Analysis." *Social Problems* 22, no. 5: 638–51.

Spratt, Michael. 2013. "Bill C-13: Voluntary Disclosure." *Law Blog*, 28 November. Web.

Terman, Rochelle L. 2010. "To Specify or Single Out: Should We Use the Term 'Honor Killing?'" *Muslim World Journal of Human Rights* 7, no. 1: 1–39.

Tierney, John. 1996. *Criminology: Theory and Context*. London: Prentice-Hall.

Todd, Carol. 2016. Blog: "Amanda's Snowflake Star of Hope," 4 December. Web.

Tucker, Erika. 2013. "Double Edged Sword: Who the New Cyberbullying Law Will Help and Hurt." *Global News*, 8 August. Web.

UNPA (UN Population Fund). 2000. "Ending Violence against Women and Girls." *The State of World Population 2000*. Web.

Vaillancourt, Tracy, Robert Ferris, and Faye Mishna. 2017. "Cyberbullying in Children and Youth: Implications for Health and Clinical Practice." *Canadian Journal of Psychiatry* 62, no. 6: 368–73.

Vold, George. 1958. *Theoretical Criminology*. New York: Oxford University Press.

Warrick, Catherine. 2005. "The Vanishing Victim: Criminal Law and Gender in Jordan." *Law and Society Review* 39, no. 2: 315–48.

Weiss, Rick. 2007. "Farm Raised Fish Given Tainted Food." *Washington Post*, 9 May.

West, W. Gordon, and Laureen Snider. 1985. "A Critical Perspective on Law and the Canadian State: Delinquency and Corporate Crime." In *The New Criminology in Canada: State, Crime and Control*, ed. Thomas Fleming, 138–70. Toronto: Oxford University Press.

Young, Jock. 1979. "Left Idealism, Reformism, and Beyond." In *Capitalism and the Rule of Law*, ed. Bob Fine, Richard Kinsey, John Lea, Sol Picciotto, and Jock Young, 11–28. London: Hutchinson.

———. 1992. "Ten Points of Realism." In *Rethinking Criminology: The Realist Debate*, ed. Roger Matthews and Jock Young, 24–68. London: Sage.

Young, Jock, and Roger Matthews. 1992. "Questioning Left Realism." In *Issues in Realist Criminology*, ed. Matthews and Young, 1–18. London: Sage.

CHAPTER 12

Ackerman, Spencer, and Dan Roberts. 2014. "US Government Privacy Board Says NSA Bulk Collection of Phone Data is Illegal." *The Guardian*, 23 January.

Andrews, D.A., and J. Bonta. 1998. *The Psychology of Criminal Conduct*, 2nd ed. Cincinnati: Anderson.

Balke, Friedrich. 2005. "Derrida and Foucault on Sovereignty." *German Law Journal* 6, no. 1: 71–85.

Bauman, Zymunt. 2000. *Liquid Modernity*. Cambridge: Cambridge University Press.

Beck, Ulrich. 1992. "From Industrial to Risk Society: Questions of Survival, Social Structure, and Ecological Enlightenment." *Theory, Culture, and Society* 9: 97–123.

Bosworth, Mary. 2004. "Gender, Risk, and Recidivism." *Criminology and Public Policy* 3, no. 2: 181–84.

Bourdieu, Pierre. 1984. *Distinction: A Social Critique of the Judgement of Taste*. Cambridge, MA: Harvard University Press.

———. 1986. "The Forms of Capital." In *Handbook of Theory and Research for the Sociology of Education*, ed. John Richardson, 241–58. New York: Greenwood.

———. 1990a. *The Logic of Practice*. Cambridge: Polity.

———. 1990b. *In Other Words: Essays Toward a Reflexive Sociology*. Stanford: Stanford University Press.

———. 1991. *Language and Symbolic Power*. Cambridge, MA: Harvard University Press.

———. 1992. *An Invitation to Reflexive Sociology*. Chicago: University of Chicago Press.

———. 1994. "Rethinking the State: Genesis and Structure of the Bureaucratic Field." *Sociological Theory* 12, no. 1: 1–18.

———. 1998. *The State Nobility: Elite Schools in the Field of Power*. Cambridge: Polity Press.

Brubaker, Rogers. 1985. "Rethinking Classical Theory: The Sociological Vision of Pierre Bourdieu." *Theory and Society* 14: 745–75.

Caputo, John. 1997. *Deconstruction in a Nutshell: A Conversation with Jacques Derrida*. New York: Fordham.

Chambliss, William. 1969. "The Law of Vagrancy." In *Crime and the Legal Process*, ed. Chambliss. 51–63. New York: McGraw-Hill.

Dean, Mitchell. 1999. *Governmentality: Power and Rule in Modern Society*. London: Sage.

Dekeseredy, Walter, and Brian D. MacLean. 1993. "Critical Criminological Pedagogy in Canada: Strengths, Limitations, and Recommendations for Improvements." *Journal of Criminal Justice Education* 4: 361–76.

Derrida, Jacques. 1976. *Of Grammatology*, trans. Gayatri Chakravorty Spivak. Baltimore: Johns Hopkins University Press.

———. 1981. *Positions*. Chicago: University of Chicago Press.

———. 1987. "Some Questions and Responses." In *The Linguistics of Writing: Arguments between Language and Literature*, ed. N. Fabb. Manchester: Manchester University Press.

———. 1994. *Specters of Marx: The State of the Debt, the Work of Mourning, and the New International*. London: Routledge.

———. 2005. *Rogues: Two Essays on Reason*. Stanford: Stanford University Press.

DiMaggio, Paul. 1979. "Review Essay: On Pierre Bourdieu." *American Journal of Sociology* 84: 1460–74.

Ek, Richard. 2006. "Giorgio Agamben and the Spatialities of the Camp." *Geografiska Annaler, Series B, Human Geography* 88, no. 4: 363–86.

Ericson, Richard, and Kevin Haggerty. 1997. *Policing the Risk Society*. Toronto: University of Toronto Press.

Ewald, François. 1991. "Insurance and Risk." In *The Foucault Effect: Studies in Governmentality*, ed. Graham Burchell, Colin Gordon, and Peter Miller. Chicago: University of Chicago Press.

Feeley, Malcolm, and Jonathan Simon. 1994. "Actuarial Justice: The Emerging Criminal Law." In *The Futures of Criminology*, ed. David Nelken. New York: Sage.

Ferrell, Jeff. 1998. "Criminological Verstehen." In *Ethnography at the Edge*, ed. Ferrell and Mark Hamm. Boston: Northeastern University Press.

———. 2004. "Boredom, Crime and Criminology." *Theoretical Criminology* 8, no. 3: 287–302.

Foucault, Michel. 1979. *The History of Sexuality*, vol. 1. New York: Vintage.

———. 1980. *Power/Knowledge: Selected Interviews and Other Writings*. New York: Pantheon.

———. 1982. "The Subject and Power." In *Michel Foucault: Beyond Structuralism and Hermeneutics*, ed.

Hubert Dreyfus and Paul Rabinow. Chicago: University of Chicago Press.

———. 1991. "Governmentality." In *The Foucault Effect: Studies in Governmentality*, ed. Graham Burchell, Colin Gordon, and Peter Miller. Chicago: University of Chicago Press.

———. 1997. *The Essential Works, 1954–1985*, vol. 1: *Ethics, Subjectivity, and Truth*. New York: New Press.

Garland, David. 1997. "Governmentality and the Problem of Crime: Foucault, Criminology, Sociology." *Theoretical Criminology* 1, no. 2: 173–214.

Hannah-Moffat, Kelly, and Paula Maurutto. 2003. *Youth Risk/Need Assessment: An Overview of Issues and Practices*. Ottawa: Department of Justice.

Hannah-Moffat, Kelly, and Margaret Shaw. 2001. *Taking Risks: Incorporating Gender and Culture into the Classification and Assessment of Federally Sentenced Women in Canada*. Ottawa: Status of Women.

Hayward, Keith J., and Jock Young. 2004. "Cultural Criminology: Some Notes on the Script." *Theoretical Criminology* 8, no. 3: 259–73.

Hogeveen, Bryan. 2006. "Memoir of a/ the Blind." *Punishment and Society* 8, no. 4: 469–76.

Hogeveen, Bryan, and Andrew Woolford. 2006. "Critical Criminology and Possibility in the Neoliberal Ethos." *Canadian Journal of Criminology and Criminal Justice* 48, no. 5: 681–702.

Katz, Jack. 1988. *Seductions of Crime: Moral and Sensual Attractions in Doing Crime*. New York: Basic Books.

Kohm, Steven, Sonia Bookman, and Pauline Greenhill. 2016. *Screening Justice: Canadian Crime Films, Culture and Society*. Winnipeg: Fernwood.

Lippert, Randy, and James Williams. 2006. "Governing on the Margins: Exploring the Contributions of Governmentality Studies to Critical Criminology in Canada." *Canadian*

Journal of Criminology and Criminal Justice 48, no. 5: 703–19.

Minaker, Joanne, and Bryan Hogeveen. 2009. *Youth, Crime, and Society: Critical Reflections*. Toronto: Pearson.

Minca, Claudio. 2006. "Giorgio Agamben and the New Biopolitical Nomos." *Geografiska Annaler*, Series B: Human Geography 88, no. 4: 387–403.

Morrison, Wayne. 2007. *Criminology and the New World Order*. London: Glasshouse.

O'Connor, D. 2006. *Report of the Events Relating to Maher Arar: Analysis and Recommendations of the Commission of Inquiry in the Actions of Canadian Officials in Relation to Maher Arar*. Ottawa: Queen's Printer.

Office of the Privacy Commissioner of Canada. 2014. News release: "Interim Privacy Commissioner Provides Recommendations to Parliament for the Protection of Privacy Rights in National Security Efforts." 28 January.

O'Malley Pat. 1992. "Risk, Power and Crime Prevention." *Economy and Society* 21: 252–75.

———. 1996. "Risk and Responsibility." In *Foucault and Political Reason: Liberalism, Neoliberalism, and Rationalities of Government*, ed. Andrew Barry, Thomas Osbourne, and Nikoas Rose. Chicago: University of Chicago Press.

O'Neill, Maggie. 2004. "Crime, Culture, and Visual Methodologies: Ethno-Mimesis as Performative Praxis." In *Cultural Criminology Unleashed*, ed. Jeff Ferrell, Keith Hayward, Wayne Morrison, and Mike Presdee. London: Glasshouse.

O'Reilly-Fleming, Thomas, ed. 1985. *The New Criminologies in Canada: State, Crime, and Control*. Toronto: Oxford University Press.

Pavlich, George. 1999. "Criticism and Criminology: In Search of Legitimacy." *Theoretical Criminology* 3, no. 1: 29–51.

———. 2000. *Critique and Radical Discourses on Crime*. Aldershot: Ashgate.

———. 2005. *Governing Paradoxes of Restorative Justice*. London: Glasshouse.

———. 2007. "Deconstruction." *Blackwell Encyclopedia of Sociology*. London: Blackwell.

Raban, Jonathan. 1974. *Soft City*. London: Hamilton.

Ratner, R.S. 1971. "Criminology in Canada: Conflicting Objectives." Unpublished mscript.

———. 1984. "Inside the Liberal Boot: The Criminological Enterprise in Canada." *Studies in Political Economy* 13: 145–64.

———. 1989. "Critical Criminology a Splendid Oxymoron." *Journal of Human Justice* 1: 3–8.

Schmitt, Carl. 1985. *Political Theology: Four Chapters on the Concept of Sovereignty*. Chicago: University of Chicago Press.

Simon, Jonathan. 1988. "The Ideological Effects of Actuarial Practices." *Law and Society Review* 22, no. 4: 772–800.

Taylor, Ian, Paul Walton, and Jock Young. 1973. *The New Criminology: For a Social Theory of Deviance*. London: Routledge and Kegan Paul.

van Swaaningen, Rene. 1997. *Critical Criminology: Visions from Europe*. London: Sage.

Wacquant, Loïc. 2001. "Deadly Symbiosis: When Ghetto and Prison Meet and Mesh." *Punishment and Society* 3, no. 1: 95–134.

———. 2009. *Punishing the Poor: The Neoliberal Government of Social Insecurity*. Durham: Duke University Press.

———. 2010. "Crafting the Neoliberal State: Workfare, Prisonfare, and Social Insecurity." *Sociological Forum* 25, no. 2: 197–220.

Young, Jock. 1979. "Left Idealism, Reformism, and Beyond: From New Criminology to Marxism." In *Capitalism and the Rule of Law*, ed. B. Fine, R. Kinsey, J. Lea, S. Picciotto, and J. Young. 11–28. London: Hutchinson.

———. 1998. "From Inclusive to Exclusive Society: Nightmares in the European Dream." In *The New European Criminology:Crime and Social Order in Europe*, ed. Vincent Riggiero, N. South, and Ian Taylor. London: Routledge.

CHAPTER 13

Becker, Howard S. 1963. *Outsiders: Studies in the Sociology of Deviance*. New York: Free Press.

Birkbeck, Christopher, and Gary LaFree. 1993. "The Situational Analysis of Crime and Deviance." In *Annual Review of Sociology* 19, ed. Judith Blake and John Hagan. Palo Alto: Annual Reviews.

Blumer, Herbert. 1986. *Symbolic Interactionism*. Berkeley: University of California Press.

CBC News Toronto. 2007. "Toronto Police Corruption Probe Laid a Fraction of Charges: Report." Web.

Cohen, Albert K. 1965. "The Sociology of the Deviant Act." *American Sociological Review* 30: 5–14.

CTV News. 2013. "Toronto Police to Review Violent Arrest Captured on Video." 25 September. Web.

Davis, Nanette J. 1980. *Sociological Constructions of Deviance*, 2nd ed. Dubuque: Wm. C. Brown.

Empey, Lamar T., Mark C. Stafford, and Carter H. Hay. 1999. *American Delinquency: Its Meaning and Construction*, 4th ed.. Belmont: Wadsworth.

Glassner, Barry. 1982. "Labelling Theory." In *The Sociology of Deviance*, ed. M. Michael Rosenberg, Robert A. Stebbins, and Allan Turowetz. New York: St. Martin's Press.

Goffman, Erving. 1986. *Stigma: Notes on the Management of Spoiled Identity*. Oneonta: Touchstone.

Griffiths, Curt T., and Simon N. Verdun-Jones. 1994. *Canadian Criminal Justice*, 2nd ed. Toronto: Harcourt Brace Canada.

Hewitt, John P., and Peter M. Hall. 1973. "Social Problems, Problematic Situations, and Quasi-Theories."

American Sociological Review 38: 367–74.

Hirschi, Travis. 2001. *Causes of Delinquency*. New Brunswick: Transaction.

Inciardi, James A. 1974. "Vocational Crime." In *Handbook of Criminology*, ed. Daniel Glaser. Chicago: Rand McNally.

Jankowski, Martin S. 1991. *Islands in the Street: Gangs and American Urban Society*. Berkeley: University of California Press.

Katz, Jack. 1990. *Seductions of Crime: Moral and Sensual Attractions in Doing Evil*. New York: Basic.

Keel, Robert O. 2001. "Ethnomethodological Perspective (on Crime and Deviance)." In *Encyclopedia of Criminology and Deviance*, ed. Clifton Bryant. New York: Taylor and Francis.

Lemert, Edwin. 1951. *Social Pathology*. New York: McGraw-Hill.

———. 1972. *Human Deviance, Social Problems, and Social Control*, 2nd ed. Englewood Cliffs: Prentice Hall.

Letkemann, Peter. 1973. *Crime as Work*. Englewood Cliffs: Prentice Hall.

Liberman, Akiva M., David S. Kirk, and Kim Kideuk. 2014. "Labeling Effects of First Juvenile Arrests: Secondary Deviance and Secondary Sanctioning." *Criminology* 52: 345–70.

Linden, Rick, and Cathy Fillmore. 1981. "A Comparative Study of Delinquency Involvement." *Canadian Review of Sociology and Anthropology* 18: 343–61.

Link, Bruce G., and Jo C. Phelan. 2001. "Conceptualizing Stigma." In *Annual Review of Sociology* 27, ed. Karen S. Cook and John Hagan. Palo Alto: Annual Reviews.

Matsueda, Ross L. 2001. "Differential Association Theory." In *Encyclopedia of Criminology and Deviant Behavior*, vol. 1, ed. Patricia A. Adler, Peter Adler, and Jay Corzine. Philadelphia: Brunner-Routledge.

Matza, David. 1990. *Delinquency and Drift*. New Brunswick: Transaction.

———. 2010. *Becoming Deviant*, rev. ed. New Brunswick: Transaction.

Moharib, Nadia. 2012. "Wheel and Weed Don't Mix, Says Study." *Calgary Sun*, 17 May.

Prus, Robert C., and C.R.D. Sharper. 1991. *Road Hustler: Grifting, Magic, and the Thief Subculture*, expanded ed. New York: Kaufman and Greenberg.

Sampson, Robert J., and John H. Laub. 2003. "Life-Course Desisters? Trajectories of Crime among Delinquent Boys followed to Age 70." *Criminology* 41: 301–39.

Schwendinger, Herman, and Julia S. Schwendinger. 1985. *Adolescent Subcultures and Delinquency*. New York: Praeger.

Shannon, Lyle W. 1988. *Criminal Career Continuity*. New York: Human Sciences Press.

Short, James F. 1990. *Delinquency and Society*. Englewood Cliffs: Prentice Hall.

Shover, Neal. 1983. "The Later Stages of Ordinary Property Offender Careers." *Social Problems* 31: 208–18.

Small, Peter. 2012. "Toronto Police Corruption Trial: Guilty Verdicts on Obstructing Justice Charges." Web.

Sommers, Ira B. 2001. "Criminal Careers." In *Encyclopedia of Criminology and Deviant Behavior*, vol. 2, ed. David Luckenbill and Dennis Peck. Philadelphia: Brunner-Routledge

Spector, Malcolm, and John I. Kitsuse. 2000. *Constructing Social Problems*. New Brunswick: Transaction.

Stebbins, Robert A. 1970. "On Misunderstanding the Concept of Commitment: A Theoretical Clarification." *Social Forces* 48: 526–29.

———. 1976. *Commitment to Deviance: The Nonprofessional Criminal in the Community*. Westport: Greenwood.

———. 1997. "Lifestyle as a Generic Concept in Ethnographic Research." *Quality and Quantity* 31: 347–60.

———. 2001. *Exploratory Research in the Social Sciences*. Thousand Oaks: Sage.

———. 2007. *Serious Leisure: A Perspective for Our Time*. New Brunswick: Transaction.

———. 2017. *From Humility to Hubris among Scholars and Politicians: Exploring Expressions of Self-Esteem and Achievement*. Bingley: Emerald Group.

Sutherland, Edwin H., and David R. Cressey. 1978. *Principles of Criminology*, 10th ed. Philadelphia: Lippincott.

Ulmer, Jeffery T. 1994. "Revisiting Stebbins: Labeling and Commitment to Deviance." *Sociological Quarterly* 35: 135–57.

Uscinski, Joseph E., and Joseph M. Parent. 2014. *American Conspiracy Theories*. New York: Oxford University Press.

Watson, J. Mark. 1984. "Outlaw Motorcyclists: An Outgrowth of Lower Class Cultural Concerns." In *Deviant Behavior*, 2nd ed., ed. Delos H. Kelly. New York: St. Martin's Press.

West, W. Gordon. 1980. "The Short Term Careers of Serious Thieves." In *Crime in Canadian Society*, 2nd ed., ed. Robert A. Silverman and James J. Teevan, Jr. Toronto: Butterworths.

Wolf, Daniel R. 1991. *The Rebels: A Brotherhood of Outlaw Bikers*. Toronto: University of Toronto Press.

Wolfgang, Marvin E., Terence P. Thornberry, and Robert M. Figlio. 1987. *From Boy to Man, from Delinquency to Crime*. Chicago: University of Chicago Press.

CHAPTER 14

Anderson, Elijah. 1994. "The Code of the Streets." *Atlantic Monthly* (May), 81–94.

Aronson, Elliot. 1984. *The Social Animal*. New York: W.H. Freeman.

Arum, Richard, and Irenee R. Beattie. 1999. "High School Experience and the Risk of Adult Incarceration." *Criminology* 37, no. 3: 515–36.

Bailey, Sue. 2017. "New Gas Sniffing Crisis Grips Natuashish." *CTV News*, 15 May. Web.

Biron, Louise, and Marc LeBlanc. n.d. "Family and Delinquency." Unpublished paper, Université de Montréal.

Bohm, Robert. 1987. "Comment on 'Traditional Contributions to Radical Criminology' by Groves and Sampson." *Journal of Research in Crime and Delinquency* 24 (November): 324–31.

Booth, Jeb, Amy Farrell, and Sean Varano. 2008. "Social Control, Serious Delinquency, and Risky Behaviour." *Crime and Delinquency* 54: 423–56.

Box, Steven. 1971. *Deviance, Reality and Society*. London: Holt, Rinehart and Winston.

Brody, Hugh. 1975. *The People's Land*. Markham: Penguin.

Burns, Ausra. 2006. "Moving and Moving Forward: Mushuau Innu Relocation from Davis Inlet to Natuashish." *Acadiensis* 2 (Spring): 64–84.

Caplan, Aaron. 1977. "Attachment to Parents and Delinquency." Paper presented at the annual meeting of the Canadian Sociology and Anthropology Association, Fredericton.

Caplan, Aaron, and Marc LeBlanc. 1985. "A Cross-Cultural Verification of a Social Control Theory." *International Journal of Comparative and Applied Criminal Justice* 9, no. 2: 123–38.

CBC News. 2013. "More Children Sniffing Gas, Natuashish Official Says." Web.

Chambliss, William. 1973. "The Saints and the Roughnecks." *Society* 11: 24–31.

Danko, Christina, Lauren Garbacz, and Karen Budd. 2016. "Outcomes of Parent-Child Interaction Therapy in an Urban Community Clinic: A Comparison of Treatment Completers and Dropouts." *Children and Youth Services Review* 60: 42–51.

De Boeck, Arne, Stefaan Pleysier, and Johan Put. 2017. "The Social Origins of Gender Differences in Anticipated Feelings of Guilt and Shame Following Delinquency." *Criminology and Criminal Justice*. doi.org/10.1177/1748895817721273

Denov, Myriam, and Kathryn Campbell. 2002. "Casualties of Aboriginal Displacement in Canada: Children at Risk among the Innu of Labrador." *Refuge* 20, no. 2: 21–33.

Durkheim, Émile. 1951. *Suicide*. Trans. John A. Spaulding and George Simpson. New York: Free Press.

Elifson, Kirk W., David M. Petersen, and C. Kirk Hadaway. 1983. "Religiosity and Delinquency: A Contextual Analysis." *Criminology* 21: 505–27.

Engstad, Peter A. 1975. "Environmental Opportunities and the Ecology of Crime." In *Crime in Canadian Society*, ed. Robert A. Silverman and James J. Teevan. 193–211. Toronto: Butterworths.

Fischer, Donald G. 1980. *Family Relationship Variables and Programs Influencing Juvenile Delinquency*. Ottawa: Solicitor General.

Fitzgerald, Robin, and Peter Carrington. 2008. "The Neighbourhood Context of Urban Aboriginal Crime." *Canadian Journal of Criminology and Criminal Justice* 50: 523–57.

Fréchette, M., and Marc LeBlanc. 1985. *Des délinquantes: émergence et développement*. Chicoutimi: Gaëtan Morin.

Glueck, Sheldon, and Eleanor Glueck. 1950. *Unravelling Juvenile Delinquency*. Cambridge, MA: Harvard University Press.

Gomme, Ian. 1985. "Predictors of Status and Criminal Offences among Male and Female Delinquency in an Ontario Community." *Canadian Journal of Criminology* 26: 313–23.

Gottfredson, Michael R., and Travis Hirschi. 1990. *A General Theory of Crime*. Stanford: Stanford University Press.

Hagan, John. 1985. *Modern Criminology: Crime, Criminal Behavior and Its Control*. New York: McGraw-Hill.

Hagan, John, and Bill McCarthy. 1997. *Mean Streets: Youth Crime and Homelessness*. Cambridge: Cambridge University Press.

Hamilton, A.C., and C.M. Sinclair. 1991. *Report of the Aboriginal Justice Inquiry of Manitoba*, vol. 1. Winnipeg: Queen's Printer.

Hardwick, Kelly. 2002. "Unravelling 'Crime in the Making': Re-examining the Role of Informal Social Control in the Genesis and Stability of Delinquency and Crime." Ph.D. diss., University of Calgary.

Hargreaves, David H., Stephen K. Hester, and Frank J. Mellor. 1975. *Deviance in Classrooms*. London: Routledge and Kegan Paul.

Hirschfield, Paul. 2018. "Schools and Crime." *Annual review of Criminology* 1: 8.1–8.21.

Hirschi, Travis. 1969. *Causes of Delinquency*. Berkeley: University of California Press.

———. 1983. "Crime and the Family." In *Crime and Public Policy*, ed. James Q. Wilson, 53–68. San Francisco: ICS.

Hirschi, Travis, and Rodney Stark. 1969. "Hellfire and Delinquency." *Social Problems* 17: 202–13.

Ho, Caroline, Deborah Bluestein, and Jennifer Jenkins. 2008. "Cultural Differences in the Relationship between Parenting and Children's Behavior." *Developmental Psychology* 44: 507–22.

Hutchings, Judy, Pam Martin-Forbes, David Daley, and Margiad Williams. 2013. "A Randomized Controlled Trial of the Impact of a Teacher Management Program on the Classroom Behavior of Children with Behavior Problems." *Journal of School Psychology* 51: 571–85.

Keane, Carl, Paul S. Maxim, and James J. Teevan. 1993. "Drinking and Driving, Self-Control, and Gender: Testing a General Theory of Crime." *Journal of Research in Crime and Delinquency* 30: 30–46.

Kohn, Alfie. 2014. "Dispelling the Myth of Deferred Gratification." *Education Week*, 9 September. Web.

Kornhauser, Ruth Rosner. 1978. *Social Sources of Delinquency*. Chicago: University of Chicago Press.

Kupfer, George. 1966. "Middle Class Delinquency in a Canadian City." Ph.D. diss., Department of Sociology, University of Washington.

Laub, John, and Robert Sampson. 2003. *Shared Beginnings, Divergent Lives*. Cambridge. MA: Harvard University Press.

LeBlanc, Marc. 1997. "A Generic Control Theory of the Criminal Phenomenon." In *Developmental Theories of Crime and Delinquency*, ed. Terence P. Thornberry. 215–85. New Brunswick: Transaction.

LeBlanc, Marc, Marc Ouimet, and Richard Tremblay. 1988. "An Integrative Control Theory of Delinquent Behavior: A Validation 1976–1985." *Psychiatry* 51: 164–76.

Lehrer, Jonah. 2009. "Don't: The Secret of Self-Control." *The New Yorker, 18 May*, 26–32.

Lianos, Helen, and Andrew McGrath. 2018. "Can the General Theory of Crime and General Strain Theory Explain Cyberbullying?". *Crime and Delinquency*. DOI:10.1177/0011128717714204

Linden, Eric. 1974. "Interpersonal Ties and Delinquent Behavior." Unpublished Ph.D. diss., University of Washington.

Linden, Rick, and Raymond Currie. 1977. "Religiosity and Drug Use: A Test of Social Control Theory." *Canadian Journal of Criminology and Corrections* 19: 346–55.

Linden, Rick, and Cathy Fillmore. 1981. "A Comparative Study of Delinquency Involvement." *Canadian Review of Sociology and Anthropology* 18: 343–61.

Linden, Rick, and James C. Hackler. 1973. "Affective Ties and Delinquency." *Pacific Sociological Review* 16: 27–46.

Lynch, Michael, and W. Byron Groves. 1989. *A Primer in Radical Criminology*, 2nd ed. Albany: Harrow and Heston.

Matza, David. 1964. *Delinquency and Drift*. New York: Wiley.

Mears, Daniel, and Sonja Siennick. 2016. "Young Adult Outcomes and Life-Course Penalties of Parental Incarceration." *Journal of Research in Crime and Delinquency* 53: 3–35.

Miller, Ty and Mike Vuolo. 2018. "Examining the Antiascetic Hypothesis Through Social Control Theory: Delinquency, Religion, and Reciprocation across the Early Life Course." *Crime and Delinquency*. DOI:10.1177/0011128717750393

Mischel, Walter, Ozlem Ayduk, Marc Berman, B.J. Casey, Ian Gotlib, John Jonides, Ethan Kross, Theresa Teslovich, Nicole Wilson, Vivian Zayas, and Yuichi Shoda. 2011. "'Willpower' over the Life Span: Decomposing Self-Regulation." *Social Cognitive and Affective Neuroscience* 6: 252–56.

Moore, D.R., B.P. Chamberlain, and L. Mukai. 1979. "Children at Risk for Delinquency: A Follow-up Comparison of Aggressive Children and Children Who Steal." *Journal of Abnormal Child Psychology* 7: 345–55.

Nye, F. Ivan. 1958. *Family Relationships and Delinquent Behavior*. New York: Wiley.

Olds, D., C.R. Henderson, R. Cole, J. Eckenrode, J. Kitzman, and D. Luckey. 1998. "The Long-Term Effects of Nurse Home Visitation and Children's Criminal and Antisocial Behavior: 15-Year Follow-Up of a Randomized Controlled Trial." *Journal of the American Medical Association* 280: 1238–44.

Patterson, G.R. 1980. "Children Who Steal." In *Understanding Crime: Current Theory and Research*, ed. Travis Hirschi and Michael Gottfredson. Beverly Hills: Sage.

Pearson, Ashley. 2012. "An Evaluation of Winnipeg's Electronic Monitoring Program for Youth Auto Theft Offenders." Unpublished M.A. thesis. Winnipeg: University of Manitoba.

Polk, Kenneth, and Walter E. Schafer. 1972. *Schools and Delinquency*. Englewood Cliffs: Prentice Hall.

Power, Peter. 2015. "Hunting Demons." *Globe and Mail*, 6 March. Web.

Reiss, Albert J., Jr. 1951. "Delinquency as the Failure of Personal and Social Controls." *American Sociological Review* 16: 196–207.

Rocque, Michael, Wesley Jennings, Alex Piquero, Turgut Ozkan, and David Farrington. 2017. *Crime and Delinquency* 63: 592–612.

Rothman, David J. 1971. *The Discovery of the Asylum*. Boston: Little, Brown.

Rutter, Michael, and Henri Giller. 1984. *Juvenile Delinquency: Trends and Perspectives*. New York: Guilford.

Salas-Wright, Christopher, Michael Vaughn, and Brandy Maynard. 2014. "Buffering Effects of Religiosity on Crime: Testing the Invariance Hypothesis across Gender and Developmental Period." *Criminal Justice and Behavior* 41: 673–91.

Sampson, Robert J., and John H. Laub. 1993. *Crime in the Making: Pathways and Turning Points through Life*. Cambridge, MA: Harvard University Press.

Samson, Colin. 2003. *A Way of Life That Does Not Exist: Canada and the Extinguishment of the Innu*. London: Verso.

Samson, Colin, James Wilson, and Jonathan Mazower. 1999. *Canada's Tibet: The Killing of the Innu*. London: Survival.

Savoie, Josee. 2008. "Neighbourhood Characteristics and the Distribution of Crime." Ottawa: Statistics Canada. Web.

Schafer, Walter E., and Kenneth Polk. 1967. "Delinquency and the Schools." In The President's Commission on Law Enforcement and Administration of Justice, *Task Force Report: Juvenile Delinquency and Crime*. 222–77. Washington: US GPO.

Shaw, Clifford, and Henry McKay. 1942. *Juvenile Delinquency in Urban Areas.* Chicago: University of Chicago Press.

Shoda, Yuichi, Walter Mischel, and Philip Peake. 1990. "Predicting Adolescent Cognitive and Self-Regulatory Competencies from Preschool Delay of Gratification Identifying Diagnostic Conditions." *Developmental Psychology* 26, no. 6: 978–86.

Simons, Ronald, L.Chyi-In Wu, Kuei-Hsui Lin, Leslie Gordon, and Rand D. Conger. 2000. "A Cross-Cultural Examination of the Link between Corporal Punishment and Adolescent Antisocial Behavior." *Criminology* 38: 47–80.

Short, James, Jr., and Fred Strodtbeck. 1965. *Group Process and Gang Delinquency.* Chicago: University of Chicago Press.

Sprott, Jane. 2004. "The Development of Early Delinquency: Can Classroom and School Climates Make a Difference?" *Canadian Journal of Criminology and Criminal Justice* 46: 553–72.

Sprott, Jane, and Anthony Doob. 2000. "Bad, Sad, and Rejected: The Lives of Aggressive Children." *Canadian Journal of Criminology* 42: 123–33.

Stark, Rodney, Daniel P. Doyle, and Lori Kent. 1980. "Rediscovering Moral Communities: Church Membership and Crime." In *Understanding Crime: Current Theory and Research*, ed. Travis Hirschi and Michael Gottfredson, 43–52. Beverly Hills: Sage.

——— 1982. "Religion and Delinquency: The Ecology of a 'Lost' Relationship." *Journal of Research in Crime and Delinquency* 19: 4–24.

Statistics Canada. 1998. "National Longitudinal Study of Children and Youth." *The Daily*, 28 October.

Steinmetz, Suzanne K., and Murray A. Straus. 1980. "The Family as a Cradle of Violence." In *Criminal Behavior*, ed. Delos H. Kelly. 130–42. New York: St. Martin's.

Thomas, Kyle. 2015. "Delinquent Peer Influence on Offending Versatility: Can Peers Promote Specialized

Delinquency?" *Criminology.* DOI: 10.1111/1745-9125.12069

Thrasher, Frederic M. 1963. *The Gang.* Chicago: University of Chicago Press.

Topalli, Volkan, Timothy Brezina, and Mindy Bernhardt. 2012. "With God on My Side: The Paradoxical Relationship between Religious Belief and Criminality among Hardcore Street Offenders." *Theoretical Criminology* 17: 49–69.

Tremblay, Richard E., Joan McCord, Helene Boileau, Pierre Charlebois, Claude Gagnon, Marc LeBlanc, and Serge Larivee. 1991. "Can Disruptive Boys Be Helped to Become Competent?" *Psychiatry* 54: 148–61.

Van Gelder, Jean-Louis, Margit Averdijk, Denis Ribeaud, and Manuel Eisner. 2018. "Punitive Parenting and Delinquency: The Mediating Role of Short-term Mindsets." *British Journal of Criminology* 58: 644–666.

Velarde, Albert J. 1978. "Do Delinquents Really Drift?" *British Journal of Criminology* 18, no. 1: 23–39.

Warr, Mark. 2002. *Companions in Crime.* Cambridge: Cambridge University Press

West, D.J. 1982. *Delinquency: Its Roots, Careers, and Prospects.* London: Heinemann.

West, D.J., and D.P. Farrington. 1973. *Who Becomes Delinquent?* London: Heinemann.

West, W. Gordon. 1984. *Young Offenders and the State: A Canadian Perspective on Delinquency.* Toronto: Butterworths.

Wilson, Harriet. 1980. "Parental Supervision: A Neglected Aspect of Delinquency." *British Journal of Criminology* 20: 30–39.

Wilson, James Q. 1983. "Raising Kids." *Atlantic Monthly,* (October), 45–56.

CHAPTER 15

Anderson, Jeff, and Rick Linden. 2014. "Why Steal Cars: A Study of Young Offenders Involved in Auto Theft." *Canadian Journal of Criminology and Criminal Justice* 56: 241–59.

Archer, D., R. Gartner, and M. Beitel. 1983. "Homicide and the Death Penalty: A Cross-National Test of a Deterrence Hypothesis." *Journal of Criminal Law and Criminology* 74: 991–1013.

Beck, Adrian, and Matt Hopkins. 2015. *Developments in Retail Mobile Scanning Technologies: Understanding the Potential Impact on Shrinkage and Loss Prevention.* Leicester: University of Leicester.

Bennett, Trevor, and Richard Wright. 1984. *Burglars on Burglary.* Brookfield: Gower.

Beavon, Daniel, Patricia Brantingham, and Paul Brantingham. 1994. "The Influence of Street Networks on the Patterning of Property Offenses." In *Crime Prevention Studies*, ed. Ronald V. Clarke. Monsey: Criminal Justice Press.

Blatchford, Christie. 2002. "Doesn't Take a Lot to Get You Killed." *National Post*, 27 November. Web.

Boyce, Jillian. 2015. *Police-Reported Crime Statistics in Canada.* Juristat. Ottawa: Statistics Canada.

Braga, Anthony, David Hureau, Andrew Papachristo. 2011. "The Relevance of Micro Places to Citywide Robbery Trends: A Longitudinal Analysis of Robbery Incidents at Street Corners and Block Faces in Boston." *Journal of Research in Crime and Delinquency* 48, no. 1: 7–32.

Braga, Anthony, Andrew Papachristos, and David Hureau. 2014. "The Effects of Hot Spots Policing on Crime: An Updated Systematic Review and Meta-Analysis". *Justice Quarterly* 4: 633–663.

Brantingham, Patricia, and Paul Brantingham. 1995. "Criminality of Place: Crime Generators and Crime Attractors". *European Journal of Criminal Policy and Research* 3: 5–26.

Bureau of Justice Statistics. 2009. *Sourcebook of Criminal Justice Statistics.* http://www.albany.edu/sourcebook/tost_6.html#6_a.

California State Auditor. 2010. "California Department of

Corrections and Rehabilitation: Inmates Sentenced under the Three Strikes Law and a Small Number of Inmates Receiving Specialty Health Care Represent Significant Costs." *Report 2009-107.2*, May 2010. Web.

Chaumont Menendez, Harlan Amandus, Parisa Damadi, Nan Wu, Srinivas Konda, and Scott Hendricks. 2014. "Cities with Camera-Equipped Taxicabs Experience Reduced Taxicab Driver Homicide Rates: United States 1996–2010." *Crime Science* 3.

Chen, Elsa. 2008. "Impacts of 'Three Strikes and You're Out' on Crime Trends in California and throughout the United States." *Journal of Contemporary Criminal Justice* 24: 345–70.

Claburn, Thomas. "Cellphone Kill Switches Kill Cellphone Snatchers: Mobiles No Longer Worth Stealing, San Francisco DA Declares." *The Register*. Web.

Clarke, Ronald. 1995. "Situational Crime Prevention." In *Building a Safer Society: Strategic Approaches to Crime Prevention*, ed. Michael Tonry and David Farrington. 91–150. Chicago: University of Chicago Press.

———. 2005. "Seven Misconceptions of Situational Crime Prevention." In *Handbook of Crime Prevention and Public Safety*, ed. Nick Tilley. 39–70. Portland: Willan.

Clarke, Ronald V., and John Eck. 2003. *Becoming a Problem-Solving Crime Analyst*. London: Jill Dando Institute of Crime Science.

CNN. 2018. "Mexico Drug War Fast Facts." 21 March. Web.

Cohen, Lawrence E., and Marcus Felson. 1979. "Social Change and Crime Rate Trends." *American Sociological Review* 44: 588–607.

Cornish, Derek, and Ronald Clarke. 1986. *The Reasoning Criminal: Rational Choice Perspectives on Offending*. New York: Springer.

Correctional Service of Canada. 2017. "CSC Statistics—Key Facts and Figures." Web.

Durlauf, Steven, and Daniel Nagin. 2011"Imprisonment and Crime: Can

Both Be Reduced?" *Criminology and Public Policy* 10, no. 1: 13–54.

Engstad, Peter. 1975. "Environmental Opportunities and the Ecology of Crime." In *Crime in Canadian Society*, ed. Robert Silverman and James Teevan. 193–211. Toronto: Nelson.

Federal Communications Commission . 2014. "Announcement of New Initiatives to Combat Smartphone and Data Theft." Web.

Feeney, Floyd. 1986. "Robbers and Decision-Makers." In *The Reasoning Criminal: Rational Choice Perspectives on Offending*, ed. Derek Cornish and Ronald Clarke, 53–71. New York: Springer.

Felson, Marcus. 1986. "Linking Criminal Choices, Routine Activities, Informal Control, and Criminal Outcomes." In *The Reasoning Criminal: Rational Choice Approaches on Offending*, ed. D.B. Cornish and R.V. Clarke. New York: Springer.

Felson, Marcus, and Ronald Clarke. 1998. *Opportunity Makes the Thief: Practical Theory for Crime Prevention*. Police Research Series Paper 98. London: Home Office.

Gabor, Thomas, Micheline Baril, Maurice Cusson, Daniel Elie, Marc LeBlanc, and Andre Normandeau. 1987. *Armed Robbery: Cops, Robbers, and Victims*. Springfield: Charles C. Thomas.

Gannon, Maire, and Karen Mihorean. 2005. "Criminal Victimization in Canada, 2004." *Juristat* 25, no. 7. Web.

Hayward, Keith. 2007. "Situational Crime Prevention and Its Discontents: Rational Choice Theory versus the 'Culture of Now.'" *Social Policy and Administration* 41, no. 3: 232–50.

Hindelang, Michael J., Michael R. Gottfredson, and James Garofalo. 1978. *Victims of Personal Crime: An Empirical Foundation for a Theory of Personal Victimization*. Cambridge, MA: Ballinger.

Jacobs, Bruce. 2010. "Deterrence and Deterrability." *Criminology* 48: 417–441.

Kennedy, David. 2009. *Deterrence and Crime Prevention: Reconsidering*

the Prospect of Sanction. London: Routledge.

Kennedy, David, Anthony Braga, Anne Piehl, and Elin Waring. 2001. *Reducing Gun Violence: The Boston Gun Project's Operation Ceasefire*. Washington: National Institute of Justice.

Koenig, Daniel J. 1977. "Correlates of Self-Reported Victimization and Perceptions of Neighbourhood Safety." In *Selected Papers from the Social Indicators Conference, 1975*, ed. Lynn Hewitt and David Brusegard, 77–90. Edmonton: Alberta Bureau of Statistics.

Kovandzic, Tomislav, John Sloan, and Lynne Vieraitis. 2004. "Striking Out as Crime Reduction Policy: The Impact of 'Three Strikes' on Crime Rates in U.S. Cities (1980–1999." *Justice Quarterly* 21, no. 2: 399–424.

Legislative Analyst's Office, California Legislature. 2005. *A Primer: Three Strikes: The Impact after More Than a Decade*. Sacramento.

Luckenbill, David. 1977. "Criminal Homicide as a Situated Transaction." *Social Problems* 25, no. 2: 176–86.

Marvell, Thomas, and Calisle Moody. 2001. "The Lethal Effects of Three Strikes Laws." *Journal of Legal Studies* 30, no. 1: 89–106.

Patton, Desmond. 2017. "We're Just Starting to Comprehend How Social Media Breeds Shootings." *The Trace*. Web.

Perlroth, Nicole. 2017. "Why Car Companies Are Hiring Computer Security Experts". *New York Times*, 7 June. Web.

Perreault, Samuel. 2015. "Criminal Victimization in Canada, 2014." Juristat 35, no. 1. Ottawa: Statistics Canada.

Perreault, Samuel, and Shannon Brennan. 2010. "Criminal Victimization in Canada, 2009." *Juristat* 30, no. 2. Web.

Pollack, Stanley. 2006. "Bringing Peace to Boston's Streets." *Boston Globe*, July 18.

Reitano, Julie. 2017. "Adult Correctional Statistics, 2015/2016. Juristat." Ottawa: Statistics Canada.

Roberts, Julian. 2005. *Mandatory Sentences of Imprisonment in Common Law Jurisdictions: Some Representative Models*. Ottawa: Minister of Justice.

Roehl, Jan, Dennis Rosenbaum, Sandra Costello, James Coldren, Amie Schuck, Laura Kunard, and David Forde. 2006. *Strategic Approaches to Community Safety Initiative (SACSI) in 10 U.S. Cities: The Building Blocks for Project Safe Neighborhoods*. Washington: US Department of Justice.

Sacco, Vincent F., and Holly Johnson. 1990. *Patterns of Criminal Victimization in Canada*. Ottawa: Statistics Canada.

Schneider, Stephen. 2007. *Refocusing Crime Prevention: Collective Action and the Quest for Community*. Toronto: University of Toronto Press.

Schweinhart, L.J., J. Montie, Z. Xiang, W.S. Barnett, C.R. Belfield, and M. Nores. 2005. *Lifetime Effects: The High/Scope Perry Preschool Study through Age 40*. Ypsilanti: High/Scope.

Shaw, Hollie. 2014. "Target Data Breach Could Have Been Avoided with Chip Technology Widespread in Canada." *National Post*, 21 January.

Sherman, Lawrence, Patrick Gartin, and Michael Buerger. 1989. "Hot Spots of Predatory Crime: Routine Activities and the Criminology of Place." *Criminology* 27: 27–55.

Sparks, Richard F. 1981. "Multiple Victimization: Evidence, Theory, and Future Research." In *Victims of Crime: A Review of Research Issues and Methods*. Washington: US Department of Justice.

Taylor, Emmeline. 2016. "Supermarket Self-Checkouts and Retail Theft: The Curious Case of the SWIPERS." *Criminology and Criminal Justice* 16: 552–67.

Tonry, Michael. 2009. "The Mostly Unintended Effects of Mandatory Minimum Penalties: Two Centuries of Consistent Findings." In *Crime and Justice: A Review of Research*, vol. 38, ed.

Michael Tonry, 65–114. Chicago: University of Chicago Press.

Urbanik, Marta-Marika, and Kevin Haggerty. 2018. "'#IT'S Dangerous': The Online World of Drug Dealers, Rappers, and the Street Code." *British Journal of Criminology*. doi/10.1093/bjc/azx083/4797356

US Department of Justice. 1974a. *Crime in Eight American Cities*. Advance Report. Washington.

———. 1974b. *Crimes and Victims: A Report on the Dayton–San Jose Pilot Study of Victimization*. Washington.

Werb, Dan, Thomas Kerr, Bohdan Nosyk, Steffanie Strathdee, and Julio Montaner. 2013. "The Temporal Relationship between Drug Supply Indicators: An Audit of International Government Surveillance Systems." *BMJ Open*. Web.

Wright, Richard T., and Scott H. Decker. 1992. *Burglars on the Job: Streetlife and Residential Break-Ins*. Evanston: Northeastern University Press.

Young, Jock. 1997. "The Left and Crime Control." http://www.malcolmread.co.uk/JockYoung.

CHAPTER 16

Abadinsky, Howard. 2000. *Organized Crime*. New York: Wadsworth.

———. 2012. *Organized Crime*, 10th ed. Belmont: Thomson Wadsworth.

Albini, Joseph L. 1971. *American Mafia: Genesis of a Legend*. New York: Appleton-Century-Crofts.

Anderson, Annelise G. 1979. *The Business of Organized Crime: A Cosa Nostra Family*. Stanford: Hoover Institution Press.

Bandidos MC. Web.

Beare, Margaret. 2003. *Critical Reflections on Transnational Organized Crime, Money Laundering, and Corruption*. Toronto: University of Toronto Press.

Beare, Margaret, and Stephen Schneider. 1990. *Tracing of Illicit Funds: Money Laundering in Canada*. Ottawa: Solicitor General.

Bell, Daniel. 1953. "Crime as an American Way of Life." *Antioch Review* 13 (June): 131–54.

Brown, Bob. 2007. "Cybercrime Update: Is Organized Crime Moving into Cybersphere?" *NetworkWorld*.com, 9 May.

Canadian Association of Chiefs of Police. 1994. *Organized Crime Committee Report, 1994: Smuggling Activities in Canada*. Ottawa.

Canadian Press. 2002. "Montreal Trial Told Hells Angels Videotaped Funeral of Cotroni Family Member." 9 July.

———. 2010. "Border Agents Intercept 10 million Counterfeit Cigarettes in B.C." 30 November.

———. 2012. "Mafia 'Tax' on Construction Projects Hit 30% at Height of Rizzutos' Power, Quebec Inquiry hears." 26 September.

———. 2013. "Quebec Union Had Big Ties to Organized Crime, Inquiry Hears." 2 October.

———. 2014. "Quebec tobacco ring allegedly involved Montreal Mafia and Native organized crime". http://globalnews.ca/news/1301411/quebec-tobacco-ring-allegedly-involved-italian-and-native-organized-crime/

Canadian Tobacco Manufacturers Council. n.d. "Cigarette Export Statistics." Ottawa.

Carrigan, D. Owen. 1991. *Crime and Punishment in Canada: A History*. Toronto: McClelland and Stewart.

Caulkins, J., and P. Reuter. 1998. "What Price Data Tell Us about Drug Markets." *Journal of Drug Issues* 28, no. 3: 593–612.

CFSEU (Combined Forces Special Enforcement Unit British Columbia). 2013. "B.C.'s Anti-Gang Police." Vancouver.

Charbonneau, Jean-Pierre. 1975. *The Canadian Connection*, trans. James Stewart. Ottawa: Optimum, 1975.

CISC (Criminal Intelligence Service Canada). 2002. *Annual Report on Organized Crime in Canada, 2002*. Ottawa.

———. 2004. *Annual Report on Organized Crime in Canada, 2004.* Ottawa.

———. 2006. *Criminal Intelligence Service Canada Annual Report, 2006.* Ottawa.

———. 2007. *Criminal Intelligence Service Canada Annual Report, 2007.* Ottawa.

———. 2009. *Annual Report on Organized Crime in Canada, 2009.* Ottawa.

———. 2010. *Annual Report on Organized Crime in Canada, 2010.* Ottawa.

———. 2014. *Organized Crime in Canada—Backgrounder.* Ottawa. Web.

Clarke, Ronald, and Derek Cornish. 1985. "Modelling Offender's Decisions: A Framework for Policy and Research." In *Crime and Justice: An Annual Review of Research*, vol. 6, ed. M. Tonry and N. Morris, 147–85. Chicago: University of Chicago Press.

Constantine, Thomas. 1994. "Statement before the U.S. Senate Drug Caucus." 24 February. Washington: US Drug Enforcement Administration.

Cressey, Donald. 1969. *Theft of a Nation: The Structure and Operations of Organized Crime in America.* New York: Harper and Row.

David, Jean-Davis. 2017. "Homicide in Canada, 2016." *Juristat.* Ottawa: Statistics Canada. Cat. no. 85-002-X.

Dickie, Phil, and Paul Wilson. 1993. "Defining Organized Crime: An Operational Perspective." *Current Issues in Criminology* 4 (March): 215–24.

Edwards, Peter. 1990. *Blood Brothers: How Canada's Most Powerful Mafia Family Runs Its Business.* Toronto: McClelland.

FBI (Federal Bureau of Investigation). 1995. "Eurasian Criminal Enterprises." In *Overview of International Organized Crime*, 13–37. Washington.

Ferracuti, Franco, and Marvin E. Wolfgang. 1967. *Subcultures of Violence: Towards an Integrated Theory in Criminology.* Tavistock.

Finckenauer, James. 2005. "Problems of Definition: What Is Organized Crime." *Trends in Organized Crime* 8, no. 3: 63–83.

Freedman, David. 2006. "The New Law of Criminal Organizations in Canada." *Canadian Bar Review* 85, no. 2: 172–219.

Galeotti, M. 2017. "Crimintern: How the Kremlin Uses Russia's Criminal Networks in Europe." Brussels: European Council on Foreign Relations, 18 April 18. http://www.ecfr.eu/publications/summary/crimintern_how_the_kremlin_uses_russias_criminal_networks_in_europe (accessed January 4, 2018).

Gambetta, Diego. 1993. *The Sicilian Mafia: The Business of Private Protection.* Cambridge, MA: Harvard University Press.

———. 2011. "Cops Comb Woods Behind Rizzuto Home." 10 January.

———. 2012. "Charbonneau Commission: Detective lists Construction Firms Linked to Mafia." 27 September.

Gazette. 1975. "Violi Suggested Neighbour's Burglary, Crime Probe Told". November 29.

Globe and Mail. 1972. "Metro Police Raid Turned Up Copy of Mafia Linked Society's Secret Rituals, Court Is Told." *Globe and Mail*, 2 June.

———. 1998. "Canada Braces for Eastern European Mafia Flood." 30 November.

———. 2010a. "B.C. RCMP Seize 60,000 Poppy Plants in Record Haul." 26 August.

———. 2010b. "Delta Police Seize Opium Poppy Pods Worth $760,000." 15 September.

———. 2012. "More Arrests Made in Massive Human-Trafficking Ring." 13 July.

Haller, Mark. 1990. "Illegal Enterprise: A Theoretical and Historical Interpretation." *Criminology* 28, no. 2: 207–234.

Hess, Henner. 1973. *Mafia and Mafiosi: The Structure of Power.* Lexington: Heath Lexington.

Ianni, Francis. 1974. *Black Mafia: Ethnic Succession in Organized Crime.* New York: Simon and Schuster.

Ianni, Francis, and Elizabeth Reuss-Ianni. 1972. *A Family Business: Kinship and Social Control in Organized Crime.* New York: Russell Sage Foundation.

———. 1983. "Organized Crime." In *Encyclopedia of Crime and Social Justice*, ed. Sanford Kadish, 1094–106. New York: Free Press.

International Labour Organization. 2012. "ILO Global Estimate of Forced Labour: Results and Methodology." Geneva.

Kelly, Robert. 1987. "The Nature of Organized Crime." In *Major Issues in Organized Crime Control*, ed. Herbert Edelhertz. 5–43. Washington: National Institute of Justice.

Lamothe, Lee, and Adrian Humphreys. 2006. *The Sixth Family: The Collapse of the New York Mafia and the Rise of Vito Rizzuto.* Toronto: Wiley.

Lamothe, Lee, and Antonio Nicaso. 1994. *Global Mafia.* Toronto: Macmillan Canada.

Lavigne, Yves. 1996. Hells Angels: Into the Abyss. New York: HarperCollins.

Lyman, Michael, and Gary Potter. *Organized Crime*, 4th ed. Toronto: Pearson.

Martens, Frederick, and Colleen Miller-Longfellow. 1982. "Shadows of Substance: Organized Crime Reconsidered." *Federal Probation* 46 (December): 3–9.

Morselli, Carlo. 2005. *Contacts, Opportunities, and Criminal Enterprise.* Toronto: University of Toronto Press.

———. 2009. *Inside Criminal Networks.* New York: Springer.

Morselli, Carlo, and Julie Roy. 2008. "Brokerage Qualifications in Ringing

Operations." *Criminology* 46, no. 1: 71–98.

National Coalition Against Contraband Tobacco. 2015. "Taking the Oxygen Out of Organized Crime: Three-quarters of Ontarians Want Tougher Penalties for Illegal Tobacco Traffickers." Press Release, 19 November.

National Post. 2003. "Tobacco Company Accused of Smuggling." 28 February.

———. 2010a. "'There's Nothing We've Done That's Illegal': Mohawk Leaders Deny That Organized Crime Is Involved in the Industry." 21 September.

———. 2010b. "A New Mafia: Crime Families Ruling Toronto, Italy Alleges." 24 September.

———. 2010c. "Mafia 'Ndrangheta in Canada." 25 September.

Naylor, Tom. 2002. *Wages of Crime: Black Markets, Illegal Finance, and the Underworld Economy.* Ithaca: Cornell University Press.

New York Times. 2012. "Smugglers Go under the Sea to Move Drugs." 10 September.

Nicaso, Antonio. 2001. "Angels with Dirty Faces: Part 15—How the World's Richest and Most Ferocious Motorcycle Gang Is Expanding Its Wings in Canada." *Tandem News,* June 24.

Office of National Drug Control Policy. 2004. "Technical Report for the Price and Purity of Illicit Drugs: 1981 through the Second Quarter of 2003." Washington: Executive Office of the President. Pub. no. NCJ 207769.

Ottawa Sun. 2012. "Police Are Warning Ottawans to Be on the Alert for a Gang of Thieves That Distract." 29 September.

Pileggi, Nicholas. 1985. *Wise Guy: Life in a Mafia Family.* New York, NY: Pocket Books.

Potter, Gary. 1994. *Criminal Organizations: Vice, Racketeering, and Politics in an American City.* Prospect Heights: Waveland Press.

President's Commission on Law Enforcement and Administration of Justice. 1967. *Task Force Report: Organized Crime.* Washington, DC: United States Government Printing Office.

President's Commission on Organized Crime. 1984. *Organized Crime and Cocaine Trafficking. Record of Hearing IV, November 27–29, 1984.* Washington: US GPO.

———. 1986. *America's Habit: Drug Abuse, Drug Trafficking, and Organized Crime.* Washington, DC: US GPO.

Quebec Police Commission. 1977. *The Fight Against Organized Crime in Quebec: Report of the Commission on Organized Crime and Recommendations.* Québec: Editeur officiel du Québec.

Rawlinson, Patricia. 1997. "Russian Organized Crime: A Brief History." In *Russian Organized Crime: The New Threat?,* ed. Phil Williams, 28–52. London: Frank Cass.

Reppetto, T. 2007. *Bring Down the Mob: The War against the American Mafia.* New York: Holt Paperbacks.

RCMP (Royal Canadian Mounted Police). 1987. "Outlaw Motorcycle Gangs: Modern profiles." *RCMP Gazette* 49, no. 5: 9–10.

———. 2007. "Drug Situation Report, 2007." Ottawa: RCMP, Criminal Intelligence Directorate.

———. 2017. "Investigation Cendrier: Several Arrests for Trafficking Illegal Tobacco." News Release, 17 December. http://www.rcmp-grc .gc.ca/en/news/2017/investigation-cendrier-arrests-trafficking-illegal-tobacco.

Roach, Wilfrid. 1962. *Report of The Honourable Mr. Justice Wilfrid D. Roach as a Commissioner Appointed under the Public Inquiries Act by Letters Patent Dated December 11, 1961.* Toronto: Commission of Inquiry.

Salerno, Ralph. 1967. "Syndicate Personnel Structure." *Canadian Police Chief* 55, no. 3.

Schneider, S. 2003. *Money Laundering in Canada: An Analysis of RCMP Cases.* Toronto: Nathanson Centre for the Study of Organized Crime and Corruption, York University.

———. 2016. *Iced: The Story of Organized Crime in Canada,* 2nd ed. Toronto: HarperColllins

Sher, Julian, and William Marsden. 2004. *The Road to Hell: How the Biker Gangs Conquered Canada.* Toronto: Knopf Canada.

Smith, Dwight. 1975. *The Mafia Mystique.* New York: Basic Books.

———. 1948. "Windsor Grills Detroit's Chief on Race Data." 27 February.

———. 1996. "Russian Crime Hits Metro Area." 1 June.

———. 2005. "Being Hells Angel Is Now a Crime: Court Case a Test of Antigang Law." 1 July.

Toronto Telegram. 1961. "RCMP, FBI Suspect Mafia of Ruling Metro Gangland." 14 April.

UN. 2012. *Global Report on Trafficking in Persons, 2012.* Vienna: UN Office on Drugs and Crime.

———. 2013. *World Drug Report, 2013.* Vienna: UN Office on Drugs and Crime.

UN News Centre. 2012. "New UN Campaign Highlights Financial and Social Costs of Transnational Organized Crime." 16 July. Web.

US Congress. Senate. 1951. Special Committee to Investigate Organized Crime in Interstate Commerce. Final Report of the Special Committee to Investigate Organized Crime in Interstate Commerce. Pursuant to S. Res. 202 (81st Cong.) As amended by S. Res. 60 and S. Res. 129 (82d Cong. Washington, DC: US GPO.

US Senate Committee on Governmental Affairs. Permanent Subcommittee on Investigations. 1989. Structure of International Drug Trafficking Organizations Hearings. Washington, DC: US GPO.

United States Department of State. 2002. *International Narcotics*

Control Strategy Report. Washington, DC: Department of State, www.state .gov/p/inl/rls/nrcrpt/2001/rpt/8478 .htm.

———. 2015. *International Narcotics Control Strategy Report, 2015.* Washington. Web.

US Drug Enforcement Administration. 2001. "Drug Trafficking in the United States." September. Washington.

van Dijk, J., and T. Spapens. 2014. "Transnational Organized Crime Networks." In *Handbook of Transnational Crime and Justice,* ed. P.L. Reichel and J. Albanese, 2nd ed., 213–226. Los Angeles: SAGE Publications.

Van Duyne, Petrus. 1996. "Organized Crime, Corruption, and Power." *Crime, Law and Social Change.* 26: 201–238.

Verizon Business Risk Team. 2009. "2009 Data Breach Investigation Report." New York: Verizon Business. Web.

von Lampe, K. 2012. "The Practice of Transnational Organized Crime." In *Routledge Handbook of Transnational Organized Crime,* ed. F. Allum and S. Gilmour, 186–200). London and New York: Routledge.

Windsor Star. 2012. "Windsor Police Foil Plans for Human Smuggling, Fraud, Escape to Mexico." 9 August.

Young, J. 2001. "Identity, Community, and Social Exclusion." In *Crime, Disorder, and Community Safety: A New Agenda?,* ed. M. Roger and J. Pitts, 26–53. London: Routledge.

CHAPTER 17

Akers, Ronald. 1973. *Deviant Behavior: A Social Learning Approach.* Belmont: Wadsworth.

Alini, Erica. 2018. "The CRA has Denied over $7 Billion in Tax Claims Due to This One Scam". *Global News,* 9 April. Web.

BC Coroners Service. 2018. "Illicit Drug Overdose Deaths in BC, January 1, 2008–March 31, 2018". Web.

Benson, M.L. 1989. "The Influence of Class Position on the Formal and Informal Sanctioning of White-Collar Offenders." *Sociological Quarterly* 30: 465–79.

Benson, M.L., W.J. Maakestad, F.T. Cullen, and G. Geis. 1988. "District Attorneys and Corporate Crime: Surveying the Prosecutorial Gatekeepers." *Criminology* 26: 505–18.

Bittle, Steven, and Laureen Snider. 2014. "The Breakdown of Canada's Corporate Crime Laws." In *Locating Law,* ed. Elizabeth Comack, 178–97. Halifax: Fernwood.

Bruder, Jessica. 2018. "The Worst Drug Crisis in American History." *New York Times.* 31 July. Web.

Butler, Steve. 2002. "Colossal Enron Collapse a Good Thing for the Rest of Us." *Winnipeg Free Press,* 22 February, A15.

Canadian Bankers Association. 2013. "Credit Card Fraud and Interac Debit Card Statistics—Canadian Issued Cards." Web.

Canadian Press. 2000. "CEO Jailed for Insider Trading." *Winnipeg. Free Press,* 19 September, B8.

CBC. 2001. "Study Shows Employee Fraud Prevalent in Workplace." Web.

———. 2004. "Auditor-General's Report 2004." Web.

CMPA (Canadian Medical Protective Association). 2017. *2016 Annual Report.* Ottawa.

Coleman, James. 1974. *Power and the Structure of Society.* New York: W.W. Norton.

———. 1985. *The Criminal Elite.* New York: St. Martin's.

College of Physicians and Surgeons of Ontario. 2011. Yazdanfar, Behnaz CPSO #: 67947. http:// www.cpso.on.ca/docsearch/details. aspx?view=4&id=%2067947.

Conference Board of Canada. 2017. "Canadian Tax Avoidance and Examining the Potential Tax Gap." Ottawa: Conference Board of Canada. Web.

Corrado, Raymond. 1996. "Political Crime in Canada." In *Criminology: A Canadian Perspective,* 3rd ed., ed. Rick Linden. 459–93. Toronto: Harcourt Brace.

CRA. 2017. "Estimating and Analyzing the Tax Gap Related to the Goods and Services Tax/Harmonized Sales Tax." Ottawa: Canada Revenue Agency. Web.

Cullen, Francis, Bruce Link, and Craig Polanzi. 1982. "The Seriousness of Crime Revisited: Have Attitudes toward White Collar Crime Changed?" *Criminology* 20: 83–102.

Daly, Kathleen. 1989. "Gender and Varieties of White-Collar Crime." *Criminology* 27: 769–93.

DeCloet, Derek. 2002. "Deceit Began This Scandalous Rot." *National Post,* 11 July.

Drohan, Madelaine. 1995. "Barings Was Warned of Risk." *Globe and Mail,* 6 March, A1.

Duffy, Andrew. 2014. "B.C. Securities Commission Rules Victoria Man Committed $65 Million Fraud." *Victoria Times Colonist,* 13 August.

Ermann, M. David, and Richard Lundman. 1982. *Corporate Deviance.* New York: Holt, Rinehart and Winston.

Evola, K., and N. O'Grady. 2009. "As Fraud Schemes Proliferate—Are You the Next Investor to Crash and Burn?" *Journal of Investment Compliance* 10: 14–17.

Farberman, Harvey. 1975. "A Criminogenic Market Structure: The Automobile Industry." *Sociological Quarterly* 16: 438–57.

Gabor, Thomas. 1994. *Everybody Does It.* Toronto: University of Toronto Press.

Geis, Gilbert. 1962. "Toward a Delineation of White-Collar Offenses." *Sociological Inquiry* 32: 160–71.

Giesbrecht, Matthew. 2012. "Canadian Corporate Criminal Liability in Workplace Fatalities Evaluating Bill C-45." MA thesis, University of Manitoba.

Glasbeek, Harry, and Eric Tucker. 1994. "Corporate Crime and the Westray Tragedy." *Canadian Dimension,* January–February, 11–14.

Gomery, Mr. Justice John. 2005. *Who Is Responsible? Fact Finding Report*. Montreal: Commission of Inquiry into the Sponsorship Program and Advertising Activities.

Goudge, Mr. Justice Stephen. 2008. *Inquiry in Pediatric Forensic Pathology in Ontario*, vol. 1: *Executive Summary*. Web.

Hagan, John. 1982. "The Corporate Advantage: The Involvement of Individual and Organizational Victims in the Criminal Justice Process." *Social Forces* 60, no. 4: 993–1022.

Hagan, John, and Celesta Albonetti. 1982. "Race, Class, and the Perception of Criminal Injustice in America." *American Journal of Sociology* 88: 329–55.

Hagan, John, and Alberto Palloni. 1983. "The Sentencing of White-Collar Offenders Before and After Watergate." *Paper presented at the American Sociological Association Meetings, Detroit*.

Hagan, John, and Patricia Parker. 1985. "White Collar Crime and Punishment: The Class Structure and Legal Sanctioning of Securities Violations." *American Sociological Review* 50, no. 3: 302–16.

Harvard Law Review. 2009. "Go Directly to Jail: White Collar Sentencing after the Sarbanes-Oxley Act. *Harvard Law Review*, 122: 1728–816.

Henderson, Tanya. 2000. "Delivered and Signed." http://abcnews.go.com/onair/2020/2020_000428_zorro_feature.html.

Inernational Council on Clean Transportation. 2015. "EPA's Notice of Violation of the Clean Air Act to Volkswagen." Web.

Katz, Jack. 1980. "The Movement against White-Collar Crime." In *Criminology Review Yearbook*, vol. 2., ed. Egon Bittner and Sheldon Messinger. Beverly Hills: Sage.

Korosec, Kirsten. 2015. "Ten Times More Deaths Linked to Faulty Switch Than GM First Reported." *Fortune*, 24 August. Web.

Kranhold, Kathryn, and Mitchell Pacelle. 2002. "Enron Paid Top Managers $681 Million, Even as Stock Slid." *Wall Street Journal*, 17 June, B1, B4.

Kristof, Nicholas. 2017. "Drug Dealers in Lab Coats." *New York Times*. Web.

Lagarde, Christine. 2014. "Economic Inclusion and Financial Integrity." *An Address to the Conference on Inclusive Capitalism*. London, 27 May.

Le Pan, Nick. 2007. "Enhancing Integrated Market Enforcement Teams, Achieving Results in Fighting Capital Markets Crime." Report submitted to the Commissioner of the RCMP.

Macy, Beth. 2018. *Dopesick: Dealers, Doctors, and the Drug Company That Addicted America*. New York: Little, Brown.

Mann, Kenneth, Stanton Wheeler, and Austin Sarat. 1980. "Sentencing the White Collar Offender." *American Criminal Law Review* 17, no. 4: 479.

Mathis-Lilley, Ben. "Pharma Execs Arrested in Shockingly Organized Scheme to Overprescribe Notorious Opioid 2016." *Slate*, 9 December. Web.

McIntyre, Mike. 2001. "Deaths Cost Firms Dearly." *Winnipeg. Free Press*, 3 March, A1, A4.

McKenna, Barrie. 2016. "Nobody Will go to Jail for Canada's Biggest Stock Scandal." *Globe and Mail*, 22 April. Web.

———. 2017. "Regulators Owe It to Canadians to Do Better on Fraud." *Globe and Mail*, 1 January. Web.

Menzies, David. 2000. "Looking for Mr. Goodwrench." *National Post*, 23 September.

Meier, Barry. 2018. "Why Drug Executives Haven't Really Seen Justice for Their Role in the Opioid Crisis". *Time*. 15 June. Web.

Morgenson, Gretchen, and Louise Story. 2011. "In Financial Crisis, No Prosecutions of Top Figures." *New York Times*, 14 April.

Morton, Brian. 2014. "Sawmill Owner to Appeal Record $1.01 Million Fine for Fatal Explosion." *Vancouver Sun*, 3 April.

Olive, David. 2007. "The World According to Conrad Black." *Toronto Star*, 11 March. http://www.thestar.com/News/article/190677.

Paternoster, Raymond. 2016. "Deterring Corporate Crime: Evidence and Outlook." *Crime and Public Policy* 15: 383–86.

Posner, Richard A. 1980. "Optimal Sentences for White Collar Criminals." *American Criminal Law Review* 17, no. 4: 409–18.

PWC. 2012. "Canadian Retail Security Survey, 2012." Web.

Reasons, C., L. Ross, and C. Paterson. 1981. *Assault on the Worker: Occupational Health and Safety in Canada*. Toronto: Butterworths.

Reiss, Albert. 1980. *Data Sources on White Collar Law Breaking*. Washington: National Institute of Justice.

Richard, Justice K. Peter. 1997. *The Westray Story: A Predictable Path to Disaster, Executive Summary*. Halifax: Government of Nova Scotia.

Robertson, Grant, and Karen Howlett. 2016. "How Little-Known Patent Sparked Canada's Opioid Crisis." *Globe and Mail*, 30 December. Web.

Rosen, Al, and Mark Rosen. *Easy Prey Investors*. 2017. Montreal: McGill–Queen's University Press.

Rugaber, Christopher, and Derek Kravitz. 2011. "Wells Fargo Fined in Mortgage Case." *Globe and Mail*, 21 July, B7.

Sandborn, Tom. 2010. "Hard Thanksgiving for Injured Farm Workers." *The Tyee*, 11 October. Web.

Schell-Busey, Natalie, Sally Simpson, Melissa Rorie, Mariel Alper. 2016. "What Works? A Systematic Review of Corporate Crime Deterrence." *Crime and Public Policy* 15: 87–416.

Schwartz, Jan, and Victoria Bryan. 2017. "VW's Dieselgate Bill Hits $30 billion after Another Charge." *Globe and Mail*, 29 October. Web.

Shapiro, Susan P. 1990. "Collaring the Crime, Not the Criminal:

Reconsidering the Concept of White-Collar Crime." *American Sociological Review* 55: 346–65.

Sharpe, Andrew, and Jill Hardt. 2006. "Five Deaths a Day: Workplace Fatalities in Canada, 1993–2005." CSLS Research Paper 2006–04. Ottawa: Centre for the Study of Living Standards.

Shover, Neal, and Andy Hochstetler. 2006. Choosing White-Collar Crime. New York: Cambridge University Press.

Sikorsky, Robert. 1990. "Highway Robbery: Canada's Auto Repair Scandal." *Reader's Digest* (February): 55–63.

Sinclair, Judge Murray. 2000. The Report of the Manitoba Pediatric Surgery Inquest. Winnipeg: Provincial Court of Manitoba. Web.

Snider, Laureen. 2015. *Corporate Crime*. Winnipeg: Fernwood Publishing.

Statistics Canada. 2016. "The Underground Economy in Canada, 2013." *The Daily*, 20 June. Ottawa.

Stone, Christopher. 1975. *Where the Law Ends: The Social Control of Corporate Behavior*. New York: Harper and Row.

Sutherland, Anne. 2009. "Montreal Man's $50M Disappearance 'Shatters' Friends." *The Gazette* (Montreal), 13 July.

Sutherland, Edwin. 1940. "White Collar Criminality." *American Sociological Review* 5: 1–12.

———. 1945. "Is 'White Collar Crime' Crime?" *American Sociological Review* 10: 132–39.

Swartz, Joel. 1978. "Silent Killers at Work." In *Corporate and Governmental Deviance*, ed. M. David Ermann and Richard Lundman. 114–28. New York: Oxford University Press.

Taibbi, Matt. 2009. "The Great American Bubble Machine." *Rolling Stone*, 0–23 July. Web.

Toronto Star. 2018. "Medical Disorder, Part 1. Bad Doctors Who Cross the Border Can Hide Their Dirty Secrets. We Dug Them Up." 1 May. Web.

Truth and Reconciliation Commission of Canada. 2015a. *Honouring the Truth, Reconciling for the Future*. Ottawa.

———. 2015b. *The Survivors Speak*. Ottawa.

Vancouver Sun. 2014. "Calgary Law Firm under Investigation Stands to Earn $16.6 million." 14 June.

Van Praet. Nicolas. 2018. "SNC Strikes $110-Million Deal to Settle Lawsuits." *Globe and Mail*, 23 May, B1, B6.

Wells, Jennifer. 1998. *Fever: The Dark Mystery of the Bre-X Gold Rush*. Toronto: Viking.

Wheeler, Stanton, and Mitchell Rothman. 1982. "The Organization as Weapon in White-Collar Crime." *Michigan Law Review* 80: 1403–26.

CHAPTER 18

Arntfield, Michael. 2012. "1921–1940." In *The Social History of Crime and Punishment in America*, ed. Wilbur R. Miller, 2201–19. Thousand Oaks: Sage.

———. 2014. "Towards a Cyber-victimology: Cyberbullying, Routine Activities Theory, and the Anti-Sociality of Social Media." *Canadian Journal of Communication* (in press).

Arntfield, Michael, and Marcel Danesi. 2017. *Murder in Plain English: From Manifestoes to Memes—Looking at Murder through the Words of Killers*. Amherst: Prometheus Books.

Arntfield, Michael, and Joan Swart. 2018. *Depression, Predators, and Personality Disorders: Social Media and Mental Health*. San Diego: Cognella Press. In press.

Aggrawal, Anil. 2008. *Forensic and Medico-Legal Aspects of Sexual Crimes and Unusual Sexual Practices*. Boca Raton: CRC.

Baranetsky, Victoria. 2009. "What Is Cyberterrorism? Even Experts Can't Agree." *Harvard Law Review*. Web.

Bogart, Nicole. 2014. "Hacker Charged in CRA Heartbleed Breach 'Straight-A' Engineering Student." *Global News*. Web.

Brackett, Eric. 2018. "Owners of Mugshots.com Charged with Extortion and Other Crimes." *Digital Trends*. Web.

Cohen, Lawrence E., and Marcus Felson. 1979. "Social Change and Crime Rate Trends: A Routine Activity Approach." *American Sociological Review* 44: 588–608.

CyberSCAN. 2014. "Nova Scotia Cyber Safety." http://cyberscan.novascotia.ca.

———. 2018. "Nova Scotia Cyber Safety." https://novascotia.ca/cyberscan.

Dalby, J. Thomas. 1988. "Is Telephone Scatologia a Variant of Exhibitionism?" *International Journal of Offender Therapy and Comparative Criminology* 32: 45–48.

Department of Justice. 2014a. "Backgrounder: Cyberbullying and the Non-Consensual Distribution of Intimate Images." Government of Canada. Web.

———. 2014b. "Voyeurism as a Criminal Offence: A Consultation Paper." Government of Canada. Web.

Durkin, Keith F. 2007. "Show Me the Money: Cybershrews and On-Line Money Masochists." *Deviant Behavior* 2: 355–78.

———. 2009. "There Must Be Some Type of Misunderstanding, There Must be Some Kind of Mistake: The Deviance Disavowal Strategies of Men Arrested in Internet Sex Stings." *Sociological Spectrum* 29: 661–76.

Ellul, Jacques. 1964. *The Technological Society*. New York: A.A. Knopf.

Freiberger, Kimberley L. 2008. "Examining Incidents of Cyberstalking: An Exploration of an Emerging Crime." Ph.D. diss., Virginia Commonwealth University, Richmond.

Harris, Elizabeth A., and Nicole Perlroth. 2014. "Target Missed Signs of a Data Breach." *New York Times*. Web.

Hayward, K. 2012. "Pantomime Justice: A Cultural Criminological Analysis of 'Life Stage Devolution.'" *Crime, Media, Culture* 8, no.. 2: 213–29.

Hickey, E.W. 2010. *Serial Murderers and Their Victims*, 6th ed. Belmont: Wadsworth.

Hinduja, Sarneer, and Justin W. Patchin. 2008. "Cyberbullying: An Exploratory Analysis of Factors Related to Offending and Victimization." *Deviant Behavior* 29: 129–56.

———. 2009. *Bullying Beyond the Schoolyard: Preventing and Responding to Cyberbullying*. Thousand Oaks: Sage.

Holt, Thomas J., and Adam M. Bossler. 2009. "Exploring the Applicability of Lifestyle-Routine Activities Theory for Cybercrime Victimization." *Deviant Behavior* 30: 1–25.

Hootsen, Jan-Albert, and Roeland Roovers. 2014. "Man Accused in Amanda Todd Case Vows to Fight Extradition to Canada." *Globe and Mail*. Web.

Kaplan, Meg S., and Richard B. Krueger. 1997. "Voyeurism: Psychopathology and Theory." In *Sexual Deviance: Theory, Assessment, and Treatment*, ed. D. Richard Laws and William T. O'Donohue. 297–310. New York: Guilford.

Kowalski, Robin M., and Elizabeth Whittaker. 2015. "Cyberbullying: Prevalence, Causes, and Consequences." In *The Wiley Handbook of Psychology, Technology & Society*, ed. Larry D. Rosen, Nancy A. Cheever, and L. Mark Carrier, 152–57. Malden: John Wiley and Sons.

Kucera, H. 1967. *Computational Analysis of Present-Day American English*. Providence: Brown University Press.

Manovich, L. 2001. *The Language of New Media*. Cambridge: MIT Press.

Mautner, Gerlinde. 2009. "Corpora and Critical Discourse Analysis." In *Contemporary Corpus Linguistics*, ed. Paul Baker. 32–46. London: Continuum.

Miller, Brooke N., and Robert G. Morris. 2012. "Cyber-Related Violence." In *Violent Offenders: Theories, Research, Police, and Practice*, 2nd ed., ed. Matt DeLisi and Peter J. Conis. 75–94. Burlington: Jones and Bartlett.

Moore, Robert. 2005. *Cybercrime: Investigating High-Technology Computer Crime*. Burlington: Anderson.

Myers, Zachary R., Susan M. Swearer, Meredith J. Martin, and Raul Palacios. 2017. "Cyberbullying and Traditional Bullying: The Experiences of Poly-Victimization Among Diverse Youth." *International Journal of Technoethics* 8, no. 2: 42–60.

Olweus, Dan. 1993. *Bullying at School: What We Know and What We Can Do*. Cambridge: Blackwell.

———. 2012. "Cyberbullying: An Overrated Phenomenon?" *European Journal of Developmental Psychology* 9, no. 5: 520–38.

Press, Jordan. 2012. "Canadian Government under International Pressure to Pass Controversial Internet Surveillance Bill." *National Post*. Web.

Quayle, Ethel, and Max Taylor. 2002. "Child Pornography and the Internet: Perpetuating a Cycle of Abuse." *Deviant Behavior* 8: 47–63.

Quinn, James F., and Craig J. Forsyth. 200. "Describing Sexual Behavior in the Era of the Internet: A Typology for Empirical Research." *Deviant Behavior* 26: 191–207.

Raskauskas, Juliana, and Ann D. Stoltz. 2007. "Involvement in Electronic and Traditional Bullying Among Adolescents." *Developmental Psychology* 7: 22–43.

Roberts, Joshua W., and Scott A. Hunt. 2012. "Social Control in a Sexually Deviant Cybercommunity: A Cappers' Code of Conduct." *Deviant Behavior* 33, no. 10: 757–73.

Rufo, Ronald A. 2012. *Sexual Predators amongst Us*. Boca Raton: CRC.

Sabatini, Cara. 2016. "Cyber Safety Laws Bullied into Submission." *NOW Magazine*. Web.

Sankin, Aaron. 2014. "Lonely People Share More on Facebook." *Salon.com*. Web.

Saunders, Elisabeth B., and George A. Awad. 1991. "Male Adolescent Sexual Offenders: Exhibitionism and Obscene Phone Calls." *Child Psychiatry and Human Development* 21: 169–78.

Schmidt, Michael, and David E. Sanger. 2014 "8 in China Army Face U.S. Charges of Cyberattacks." *New York Times*. Web.

Zetter, Kim. 2009. "Prosecutors Drop Plan to Appeal Lori Drew Case." *Wired*. Web.

INDEX